# SIMPLE MINDS

# HEART
## OF THE
# CROWD

## A FAN HISTORY

*RICHARD HOUGHTON*

**THIS DAY** IN MUSIC BOOKS
www.thisdayinmusicbooks.com

# SIMPLE MINDS

The publisher makes no representation, express or implied, with regard to the accuracy of the information contained in this publication and cannot accept any responsibility in law for any errors or omissions.

The right of Richard Houghton to be identified as the author of this work has been asserted by him in accordance with sections 77 and 78 of the Copyright, Designs and Patents Act 1988. No part of this book may be reproduced in any form without permission from the publisher except for the quotation of brief passages in reviews.

A catalogue record for this book is available from the British Library.

This edition © This Day In Music Books 2020. Text ©This Day In Music Books 2020

ISBN: 978-1838078300

The author and publisher gratefully acknowledge the permission granted to reproduce the copyright material in this book. Every effort has been made to trace the copyright holders of the photographs in this book but one or two were unreachable. We would be grateful if the photographers concerned would contact us.

Production Liz Sánchez and Neil Cossar
Design and layout by Gary Bishop
Front cover design by Stuart Crouch
Album and singles images & additional artwork/photography by Ian T. Cossar
Thanks to Dave Evely and all at Sound Performance. Printed in Italy

This Day In Music Books Bishopswood Road, Prestatyn, LL199PL

# THIS DAY IN MUSIC BOOKS

www.thisdayinmusicbooks.com

Email: editor@thisdayinmusic.com

Exclusive Distributors: Music Sales Limited 14/15 Berners St London W1T 3JL

*Friends since school: Joe Donnelly (right) and Jim Kerr*

# JIM KERR

*September 2020*

There were no fans in the beginning.

Like everyone else, when you start out you must begin from a position of being completely unknown. No option.

Yet somehow, after a couple of gigs only, we started to recognise a few new faces amid the gang of regular friends who we depended on to flesh out the damp pub cellars that we'd started to play in.

Strangers initially, with more and more turning up repeatedly at each subsequent gig. Some even began to look like they had started dressing a little bit like us.

Eventually a couple approached one night in a gig car park, timidly knocking on the door of an old school bus that we occasionally used as our mobile dressing room.

'Um. This is our tenth Minds gig. Would it be OK for us to record the gig on our cassette player? It's just that ... we love the band. And uh, we'd really like our pals at work to hear the music also. Keep telling them how great you are, but they don't believe us.'

As soon as they'd wandered off to make sure they were stood at the front of the stage - the exchange had us wondering aloud.

'Ten times? Wow! Are they our first fans?'

It may well have begun with them. But 40 years later the relationship between Simple Minds and our fans continues worldwide. This book, if anything, is a testament to that and so much more.

Thanks to all who have inserted themselves into the heart of the crowd.

---

# JOE DONNELLY

*Roman Catholic Church of St Brigid*
*1975, Toryglen, Glasgow, Scotland*

Before we had Simple Minds, even before Johnny and the Self Abusers, there was Biba-Rom, the greatest glam rock band ever to come out of Glasgow. Or so we thought. Biba-Rom consisted of Jim Kerr (vocals), Charlie Burchill (lead guitar), Tony Donald (bass guitar), Brian McGee (drums), and yours truly on rhythm guitar. We were all just 15 years old and in our last year at Holyrood Secondary School when we formed the band.

We were big fans of Lou Reed, David Bowie, Roxy Music, Cockney Rebel and Genesis with Peter Gabriel, who were all a massive influence on us and our music. We had seen them all play live at the famous Glasgow Apollo and, during a few 'unofficial' school absences; we even got to help the roadies load the gear into the venue. We were eager apprentices to the world of rock 'n' roll.

Biba-Rom's first rehearsal studios were in the cramped basement of Brian McGee's parents' house. Realising we needed more space and with our heads full of dreams, we approached the priest of St Brigid's in Toryglen and asked if we could use the school hall to rehearse in. The priest didn't share our artistic vision and almost chased us down the road with shouts of, 'Be away with your devil music!' Or words to that effect.

What happened next? Well, the priest was to get the full blast of Jim's Mum, Irene. Once we told her of our plight, she had her coat on and marched down to confront the priest. No competition! Irene took the situation in hand and we were booked in for our first rehearsal at St Brigid's the following week.

Sadly Biba-Rom only ever played one gig, a five-year old's birthday party. We kicked off with 'Heroin' by The Velvet Underground which led to all the parents covering their kids' ears, dragging them screaming from the hall. Were we on to something here? I am sure some of those kids are still in therapy. Jim and I joke about putting Biba-Rom back together for a one-off show.

Fast-forward a good few years and I had joined The Silencers. We were blessed to go on tour with Simple Minds and we had an absolute ball. I'm now part of a new band, Caezar, and am delighted that we will be supporting Jim and Simple Minds once more, at Blenheim Palace next year.

My friendship with the guys goes back many years. Jim and I have been friends – brothers - since we were three years old. And I've known Charlie since we were about eight years old. Looking back, I've got some great memories and I wouldn't change a thing. I'm thrilled for Jim and Charlie and the success they've enjoyed as one of the world's greatest bands.

# SCOTT CLARK

*Prospecthill Circus*
*Toryglen, Glasgow, Scotland*

It was a Sunday night. I lived at home with both my brothers and my mum and dad on the twentieth floor of a tower block in the south side of Glasgow. Prospecthill Circus, Toryglen to be exact. I was still at school.

Sunday night was always the night I got the TV to myself, it being bingo night for my parents who were out the door at 7pm, regular as clockwork. However, this particular night was going to be different as, earlier that afternoon, a drum kit had been dropped off and then set up in the bedroom I shared with my older brother. It wasn't long before I realised that no amount of TV volume would drown out the noise level of said drum kit, and before I knew it, I was out in the rain with my mates. I hasten to add, it wasn't a lack of interest in music as at that time I was learning guitar, albeit in music classes in school. But being the younger brother, I knew the drill. I was 'surplus to requirements' so off I toddled.

Sometime later that night I recall standing at the ice cream van and hearing the cacophony coming from upon high, my bedroom window wide open and people asking what was going on. I guess there was an element of pride in telling them a band were rehearsing in my room, although at the same time I was slightly miffed at being out in the drizzling rain.

Looking back, who would have thought that two of the people present that very night would go on to form one of the biggest and best live rock bands in the world? Those two people were Jim Kerr and Charlie Burchill - and the band was Simple Minds!

Well the tower block has long been pulled down and I'm still trying to learn the guitar. However, my claim of best live band is borne out of personal experiences over the years in my career as a producer. Not a musical one but as a film, video and TV producer who has over the years attended countless gigs and produced hundreds of music videos and live shows. A great live sound was something that Jim and Charlie always strived for and I think we can all agree they have achieved.

From those early gigs in the Mars Bar and City Halls in Glasgow and at the Norbreck Castle Hotel in Blackpool, to feeling proud as punch sitting in the Royal Box at Wembley Stadium, it's been some trip. Not so much 'kiss and fly', more a case that time really does fly. 40 years still going strong. Long may it continue.

## SHEILA FORBES

*Doune Castle*
*11 April 1977, Glasgow, Scotland*

John Milarky and myself were introduced to Jim and Charlie by Martin Hanlin (of Silencers fame) at the Doune Castle. My brother's band were playing that night. I remember thinking to myself that Jim was a bit different as he was wearing his jacket over his shoulders a la Bowie. Little did I know that night that they would soon be playing their first ever gig here within a few weeks as Johnny and the Self Abusers.

They rehearsed at John's dad's house with Tony Donald, Brian McGhee, Alan Cairnduff and Allan McNeill. I used to listen from upstairs. Some of us used to meet up at the Moll's Myre in Toryglen just to chat about music and what the buzz was. That's where I first met Shirley, who went on to become Mrs Brian McGhee.

Glasgow had never seen anything like it when Johnny and the Self Abusers took to the stage. Charlie with his flying V guitar and Jim on keyboards and vocals. Punk had arrived in Glasgow. They even had Shirley and her mates in stylish black bin liners dancing behind. The place was buzzing and packed to the hilt. It wasn't just a gig, it was more a performance bursting with innovation and energy. It was the beginning of something new and encouraging. It also attracted some Hell's Angels who decided to wreck the joint. I remember hiding in the loo with Shirley!

It didn't stop the next gig there, in May '77. I remember it well as it was my 22nd birthday that night. I knew during that summer of '77 that there was a vision developing within Jim and Charlie.

## JAINE HENDERSON

*Zhivago's*
*21 July 1977, Glasgow, Scotland*

It was July 1977 and my brother David was doing the sound for Johnny and the Self Abusers who were playing at Zhivago's, an occasional punk club in St Enoch Square in Glasgow. David was working during the day in Graffiti, a record shop in Queen Street managed by Scott McArthur, who also 'managed' Johnny and the Self Abusers and who recruited David to operate the desk. I saw the band play first with him and my friend Muriel at the Saints and Sinners pub and they seemed to consist of around eight people. There were three vocalists, keyboards, sax, various guitars and possibly some backing singers or 'stage invaders' as I recall… a bit of a rammy but an entertaining night!

I went along to the club in the afternoon to receive my surprise birthday present from David. It was a beautiful white bass guitar made by the talented young artisan guitarist Charlie Burchill! A gift full of promise and possibilities. I still have it.

I remember in the club there was a guy from the band standing on a seating bank in the foyer looking cool so I decided to try and disarm him by showing him my present. That's the first time I remember meeting Jim Kerr.

That was a good day.

*Johnny and the Self Abusers*

## RONNIE GURR

*The Pantile Hotel*
*19 August 1977, West Linton, Peeblesshire, Scotland*

I saw Johnny and the Self Abusers a couple of times. I found some photos of a gig they did supporting Generation X back in '77. It was at the time when Edinburgh City Council had ruled that punk gigs were illegal. They withdrew the licence on the day of the Generation X gig, so what the promoters did was get three buses and get the entire audience to a place called West Linton which is just outside the city limits and there's a hotel there and they just did the gig at the hotel. So that was the first time I saw the Self Abusers.

## LYNNE CULLEN

I was around in the early days, when Jim Kerr and Charlie Burchill were in Johnny and the Self Abusers, a tongue-in-cheek band in the punk genre. I can't recall many gigs around Scotland but remember being rerouted to the Pantiles Hotel, West Linton when Edinburgh venue Clouds became unavailable due to licensing laws. The headliners were Generation X, fronted by trademark bleached blond, Billy Idol.

As with all bands, there are always artistic conflicts, Jim Kerr and Charlie Burchill breaking away to form Simple Minds, one or two remaining Self Abusers turning into the Cuban Heels. The first gig in this new format was a very punky, loud outing at one of the buildings at Glasgow School of Art, with a lot of destruction in the hall at the end of the night. Simple Minds were born!

---

## MARTIN HANLIN

*August 1977*
*Dunfermline, Scotland*

My first ever gig, thanks to an invite from Jim - the first of many in my career - was opening for Johnny and the Self Abusers in Dunfermline, probably in mid to late '77. The Suck was the apt moniker we played under. I was on drums, my good friend Joe Donnelly was on guitar and my other good friend Marco Guarino on vocals.

Our night started with an argument with The Abusers about who would play the Sex Pistols' version of 'No Fun' by The Stooges. The argument did not end amicably. But that didn't matter. Since we went on first, we went ahead and played the song anyway.

It was a wild night and although I can't remember much of our set, I do remember the fight that stopped the gig. A number of biker dudes/heavy rockers were in the crowd and they really didn't care much for punk music at all.

Our set was largely ignored, and rightly so, but when The Abusers hit the stage, the tension was quite palpable. Around halfway into their set, Johnny Milarky stepped up to the mic and the band broke into 'Pablo Picasso' – 'All the girls think you're an asshole.' Most of his venom was directed at the leather-clad bikers. As you might expect, they did not take it well and stormed the stage. It was all over in a few minutes.

Fortunately, The Abusers and us and a couple of punk fans managed to emerge mostly unscathed and victorious. As we were about to leave, the two punk fans that helped us out during the fight stepped up and handed me a homemade badge with their band's name on it - Skids. Hello there, Richard Jobson and Stuart Adamson.

That was my only ever punk gig. The Suck, appropriately enough, sucked off and later became The Silencers. After a couple of great records, in 1982, the Skids split up and became Big Country. The Abusers became Simple Minds. The rest is history.

---

# RICHARD JOBSON

*Skids*
*August 1977, Scotland*

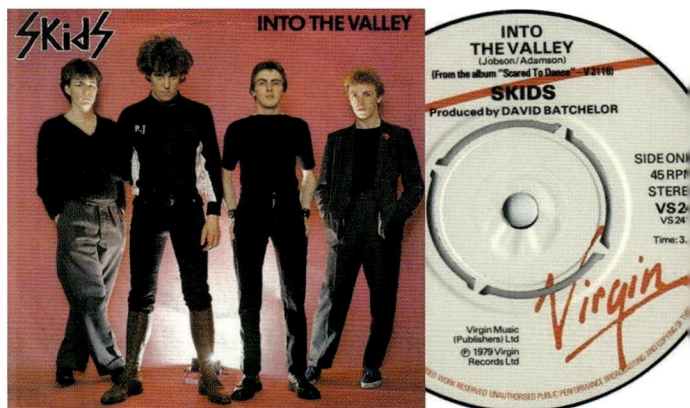

They played with us when they were called Johnny and the Self Abusers, the band that they were before they became Simple Minds. They were a Glasgow art school sub-underground kind of thing. Most of the Glasgow art school bands were a bit like that; a very Lou Reed/Bowie-orientated version of punk rock.

I think Johnny and the Self Abusers did their first ever gig in the east of Scotland, supporting us. They tried to steal all our equipment. I caught them in the van and offered them all out for a fight on my own. That was the beginning of a beautiful friendship!

---

# MARTIN HANLIN

*Doune Castle, Glasgow, Scotland*
*November 1977*

I remember well where I was when Jim said five memorable words, 'I'm starting a new band.'

It was a Saturday night in Glasgow's south side. I was hanging with the usual crowd in the Doune Castle pub. As was my want, I was not drinking, but everyone else was way past sensible as they staggered across the road to Minsky's discotheque, Shawlands' idea of late night fun and dance.

The music was disco: 'Black is Black' by Belle Epoque, 'Magic Fly' by Space, 'Yes Sir, I Can Boogie' by Baccara. I'm sure there was 'I Feel Love,' a Donna Summer hit that was a favourite of Brian McGee's and myself. Jim was enjoying it, too.

I was standing by the bar with a soft drink in my hand, tapping my toes to the groove of 'I Feel Love' when Jim approached. We said our hellos. When I asked him what he was up to, his reply took me aback.

'I'm quitting the Abusers and starting a new band,' he said.

'Who's in it?' I asked. 'I don't know yet,' he replied. 'But I have a name.' Of course, I had to ask what it was. 'Simple Minds,' he said. And he walked away. Sometimes you've just got to follow the leader.

---

# PROINSÉAS O'DOHARTAIGH

As a young boy growing up in a council scheme in Port Glasgow, Simple Minds' music transported me to another world. I would often look out my bedroom window, especially in winter time, and see my friends playing in the car park at night; our parents would not let us out as school work and early bed was the order of the day.

My older brother would listen to Radio Clyde and Luxembourg and it was here that I first came across Simple Minds. The music seemed to stand out as different almost from another world. Songs like 'I Travel', 'Love Song' and 'The American' transported us to a different place, and I often drifted off to sleep with the music in my ears.

We had a particular ear for Scottish bands, with Simple Minds and The Associates seeming to blend in with our older brother's influence of Bowie, Springsteen and Pink Floyd. Simple Minds instilled in me a love of not just music, but of sitting down and truly listening to music that has stayed with me to this day!

---

# YVAN RUEL

Born and raised in Montréal, Canada in the Seventies, everybody around me was listening to the same music, either disco or progressive rock. Like everything I touch, I knew there was something different, I was different! Came in my world at the time was Joy Division, Kraftwerk and… Simple Minds. You made me what I am today, as simple as that!

---

## MICK MACNEIL

*Simple Minds keyboard player, 1978 - 1990*

Being the only guy Simple Minds knew in Glasgow that had a synthesizer, I got the job as a keyboard player based on that. They weren't looking for somebody who could play the organ really well, or the accordion. They were looking for a synthesizer, whether I was the guy behind it or not. It just so happens there was no other guy behind it and I got the job.

---

## THIERRY RAVET

Aged 9, I received a radio receiver as a gift for my communion. I was listening to RTL France and Max Meynier's show, Les Routiers Sont Sympas, when one evening he said something that will stay with me all my life, 'Here is now a very young Scottish band and they make good music. I'm sure they will go far.' That's the first time in my life that I heard Simple Minds, when I listened to 'Chelsea Girl'.

---

## ELISABETH BRADON

John Peel introduced me to the band back in 1979, when I first heard that amazing intro and those thrashing keyboards. I was 14 years old and mad about David Bowie and all things electronic. 'Chelsea Girl' represented all things important to me at the time - wonderful, exciting, glamorous, new, different. I remember saving my pocket money for weeks so I could buy the single and I finally found it, complete with picture sleeve, from some random record shop in Liverpool. I couldn't wait to get home to play it. I played it non-stop for months and drove my dad mad!

---

## DAVY MALCOLM

Living on an Edinburgh council estate aged 14, I was stopped in my tracks by a song by a band I had never heard of being played on some long-forgotten radio show. At the first opportunity it was onto a bus into town, my entire pocket money scraped together to buy this single with its interesting artwork. After buying the single I didn't have enough change to pay for the bus back so had to walk the several miles back to my house. Insult was added to injury by my bus-driving dad going past and mistaking my frantic waving as a friendly greeting rather than a desperate cry for a free lift.

---

# BILLY SLOAN

*Satellite City*
*17 January 1978, Glasgow, Scotland*

I wasn't really aware of Johnny and the Self Abusers because there was so much punk rock stuff going around at that particular time. You were getting swamped by releases coming out on a weekly basis. My first encounter with Simple Minds was in January of 1978. There was a gig on in a place called Satellite City in Glasgow, which was a disco up above the old legendary Glasgow Apollo. It was a rundown disco up on the top floor of the Apollo. It was primarily a dance hall but occasionally they would stage gigs there. A local promoter promoted a gig with the reggae band Steel Pulse, who had just released a single called 'Ku Klux Klan', which was their one and only hit single. I think it entered the Top 40. It wasn't a big hit but they were the band of the moment. And he put three sort of punk bands on with them.

We were just desperate because the problem we had in Glasgow was that we were geographically 450 miles away from the epicentre of punk rock in London. So you'd go and see anything that had any kind of even loose punk rock tag or label simply because you wanted to be involved.

I went along to the gig. I was 22. I think I was covering it for a magazine called *Clyde Guide*. It was fairly well attended. First on the bill was a group called The Nu-Sonics, all floppy fringes and staring at their feet and jangly guitars. A few months later they changed their name to Orange Juice. Third on the bill was a band called Rev Volting and the Backstabbers. Brilliant name! And sandwiched in between them was this group called Simple Minds. I had never heard of them. I didn't even know the name.

It turned out that this was their debut gig. They walked on stage and you could see right away that they were a little bit different. For a start, they didn't look very punk rockish. They were more art rock than punk rock to be perfectly honest, even in the way they dressed. And the instruments they had - Charlie Burchill with a Flying V guitar and a violin. What was punk rock about somebody playing a violin? Sham 69 didn't have a violin and neither did The Clash and neither did The Sex Pistols.

I think they played about six songs. They played 'Wasteland' and 'Act of Love' and they played a song called 'Pablo Picasso', with the lyric 'Pablo Picasso, all the girls think you're an asshole', so that went down well with the punks. And the last song they played was a song called 'Pleasantly Disturbed' which became the big epic closing track of what turned out to be the first album the following year.

I just thought, 'This band are amazing.' The punks weren't really that interested in them because it was a bit more art-rocky. You couldn't pogo to it, put it like that. The other thing that really struck me was the singer who was this guy who it turned out was Jim Kerr. He didn't look like any Glasgow or Scottish guy I'd ever seen before. He didn't know anybody I knew from school or anybody that I'd walked alongside or anything like that. He was really nervous and he looked like he would rather be anywhere than standing under the centre spotlight as the singer of the band. He was just so ill at ease. That just endeared them to me even more. He had this pretty striking pudding-bowl haircut and he wore a black priest's frock coat that was buttoned up to the neck. He was very striking, he looked pretty otherworldly, he was nervous and his singing was pretty staccato. But I couldn't take my eyes off him. I just thought, 'This guy's fucking amazing. Who is this kid?'

After the show finished, I went round to the dressing room and the door was opened by Charlie Burchill. I said, 'Excuse me, mate, but I'm reviewing the gig and could you tell me the name of your singer?' And he said, 'Yeah, Jim Kerr' and I wrote it in my little notepad and off I went. The next day I wrote my review of the gig and that was how I got to know them.

Simple Minds were striking. I thought, 'I'm going to watch out for this lot because there's something a bit special here.' There were probably another 10 or 15 people in the audience who thought that as well. The rest of the audience was probably waiting for Rev Volting and the Backstabbers to come on so they could start spitting and pogo-dancing.

*Charlie and Jim, Mars Bar, Glasgow, 1978 - Photo Laurie Evans*

# JIM DUNLEAVY

*Mars Bar*
*1978, Glasgow, Scotland*

I was playing the Mars Bar at the same time as the Minds. Our band were called Lawdy Mama and we were lucky enough to play there on a Saturday afternoon and at that time the Minds had the Saturday night residency. That was where I saw them for the first time and I think everyone knew there was something special. While we were playing covers they were playing their own material. Later I was lucky enough to meet Jim and Charlie at a record signing in Glasgow where I said to Jim that we played the Mars Bar at the same time and how we played Saturday afternoons and used to kick their gear out the way. Jim came back at me and asked what the name of the band was and I said Lawdy Mama. He pondered for a moment and then said, 'Eh yeah, and if I remember right you were a hard act to follow!' Put me in my place.

---

# SHIRLEY MCGEE

Whenever I meet Jim and Charlie, they greet me by saying, 'You're one of us, Shirley!' And I really feel I am, for I met Jim and Charlie 50 years ago. All of us were kids, all hanging around the Toryglen high rise flats where we all lived. But they two were different from the rest, they had vision and a commitment to go places. And I wanted to be part of that!

At the age of 14 I was dating Brian McGee, the drummer of Johnny and the Self Abusers. Brian was the only guy that could drive, so up and down the country the band and I went in old clapped-out vans, in a very overcrowded space with equipment squeezed on top of us. It was fun but gruelling. On returning back to Glasgow after long drives throughout the country, Brian and I had to drop all the band members off at their homes first, which meant we got in about 6am. Then, with three or four hours sleep, it was off again to another part of the country and another gig! But I loved every minute.

I recall the Glasgow pub and club venues such as The Saints and Sinners and also the Mars Bar. Early days, but the gigs were explosive and always jam-packed with the initial fans. My friend Cathy Harkins and I danced on stage in black bin liners till we dropped. Sheila Forbes, who was a dancer, gave us such encouragement for our efforts each night. It was mad!

*Shirley McGee first met Jim and Charlie 50 years ago*

As time passed, the dynamics changed and Simple Minds arrived with new sounds. Life was amazing for me. With Brian, who I eventually married, I got to travel VIP-style to see gigs all over Europe. I got to hang backstage, meeting other great bands, sitting endlessly in studios like Rockfield and many more, listening to their music ideas translate into a new single or a new album track. I even found myself sitting with Grace Jones at a gig in New York. Seeing Johnny Rotten was fab. Seeing Peter Gabriel in concert plus meeting David Bowie - truly it was mind blowing for me.

Even now, all these years later, Jim sends a car to take me and others to gigs in Glasgow when Simple Minds play. I'm so spoiled. Brian and I married in 1981 for 35 years with three children. He decided to leave the band in '81, and who knows why? But it never stopped my friendship with Charlie and Jim. My kids are fans also and come along to the gigs! My grandsons also are always excited, waiting to attend the Glasgow soundchecks. I cherish all my memories with the band and the people I met along the way. For me it's like being in one large family with Simple Minds.

---

## SHEILA FORBES

Sunday nights at the Mars Bar in Glasgow belonged to Simple Minds. People queued up to get in as it was quite a small venue. The atmosphere was cranked up by the innovative sound and light from Jaine and David, leading to a crescendo of excitement. If I could have bottled it, I would have. To this day 'Pleasantly Disturbed' still sits with me. From watching them at the Alva Glen Hotel in front of about 30 people to supporting Steel Pulse at Satellite City to Barrowlands, the SECC (the 30th anniversary show was fantastic and emotional) to the Hydro and everything else in between, and those still to come, it has been a musical journey of pleasure and pride. A friend, but also a fan.

---

## RICHARD JOBSON

They changed their name to Simple Minds and started to get a bit of a vibe about them. I'd become a friend of Jim and Charlie's by that time, and of the people that worked for them. There was a girl called Jaine who did the lights and her brother David did the sound. We were a little gang. I'm from the east of Scotland, so I started going to Glasgow more often to hang out with those guys and to see their early gigs. I knew immediately that they were going to be a bit special. The stand out song at the time was 'Chelsea Girl'. It was one of the first songs outside of a Skids song that I learnt to play. Charlie taught me to play it.

I started to go to lots of their gigs, so much so that when the Skids had finished touring or recording and weren't doing anything, I actually used to go and hang out with them on tour. I just used to hang out because they were my friends.

They were in that zone between being post-punk Goth and the whole new elaborate electronica that was about to happen. Nobody was quite sure what they were at the beginning. The audiences that they were playing in front of weren't particularly enormous but they were obviously people that were very interested. They also attracted idiots who didn't know what to expect and didn't like it very much. So for a strange period I actually became their security guy. I never had to do much. I was pretty crazy when I was a kid. I'm slightly embarrassed about it now but I really got stuck in, as they say, and they appreciated that. They were interviewed by Steve Jones (of the Sex Pistols) on his radio show recently and Steve said, 'Have you seen Jobbo?' (Jobbo is the nickname Jonesy gave me when I was a kid. Jim calls me Jobson). Jim said, 'Jobson used to just come on tour with us, in the bus all the time. And if there was any trouble he was out there sorting it out at the gates. It was hilarious.'

Me being their minder is very funny, because the Skids at the time were pretty big. We'd had big, big hits and were playing massive gigs and Simple Minds weren't. Their first album was just about to come out. They became very close to my heart in those early days.

## RONNIE GURR

I did one of the first articles on Simple Minds back in '78 or '79. They hadn't put a record out. They were still demoing. I was still at university in Edinburgh and I was doing freelance stuff and I got a call to say, 'There's a band called Simple Minds and great things are expected of them. Why don't you go over to Glasgow - they're in the studios - and do a feature?' I'd done a couple of features and I'd been aware of Johnny and the Self Abusers. I didn't know them. But I was told, 'Go through to Glasgow and we'll give you expenses,' and I said, 'What are expenses?' It was the first time I'd ever got expenses for anything. He said, 'Take the singer to lunch and interview them.' So we arranged to go to an Italian restaurant and I still josh Jim about this because I said, 'Right, dig in, it's on expenses so you can have the most expensive things' and Jim had a bowl of minestrone soup. It was still when he had the bowl haircut and looked quite psychotic, like Anthony Perkins (in *Psycho*) or something. That was the first time I met them.

*Ronnie Gurr treated Jim to a bowl of minestrone soup*

# BRUCE FINDLAY

*Astoria*
*5 October 1978, Abbeymount, Edinburgh, Scotland*

Simple Minds formed out of the ashes of a previous band, Johnny and the Self Abusers. That band split and two or three of the original band formed The Cuban Heels. And the other three - Jim, Charlie and Brian McGee - formed Simple Minds and immediately went into the studio and recorded a demo of about five tracks. They then did their first gig at Satellite City with The Nu Sonics, an early incarnation of Orange Juice. I didn't see them then. I knew Johnny and the Self Abusers; in fact, I think I'd seen them supporting someone in Edinburgh at some point in 1977. But midway through 1978, Simple Minds developed quite a reputation in Glasgow over a period of two or three months and managed to get themselves a residency at the Mars Bar in Glasgow, which was a pub gig in quite a big back room, where they built up a little bit of a head of steam.

They got in touch with me in Edinburgh. I'd already started an independent record label two years earlier called Zoom, and I had several artists on it. And I was nervous with my own label that it would get swallowed up even though we were the only independent in Scotland apart from The Rezillos' Sensible Records. I'd released four or five different records from four or five different acts, all doing really well.

Because I had a chain of record shops, I was very well known in the music scene in Scotland. Bands often came to see me – Billy McKenzie before he got the deal as The Associates, the Skids - just because I sold records and sold tickets for gigs. Jim got in touch and said, 'Look, can we come and see you? It's been suggested you might give us some advice.' They weren't looking for a deal or anything. They came to Edinburgh because they were playing a gig supporting The Only Ones. I couldn't go and see them that night. But Jim and David Henderson, who was the soundman/mentor/van driver, came to see me during the day and played me the demo and I was really impressed.

I liked them. Jim looked and sounded unusual. He was very fierce, and he was very passionate about his band and what they were doing. He spent about an hour in the office with me and the demo was sensational. I absolutely loved it and said, 'Oh, this is fantastic, I'd love to be able to help you. I can't come to the gig tonight.'

They said, 'We've got a residency at the Mars Bar and we play every Sunday. So why don't you come on Sunday?' My assistant in Zoom Records, Brian Hawk, went to see them (in Edinburgh) and he phoned me first thing in the morning before he even came into the office and said, 'Bruce, that band Simple Minds are sensational live and their songs are completely unique and not like any other band. They're a mixture of Roxy Music and a little bit of Velvet Underground and this that and the other.' He waxed lyrical about them. I was completely convinced that I had to go and see them on the Sunday, so I did.

And I went backstage afterwards and hung out with them. I thought every song was brilliant and Jim was very charismatic, but they all were. Derek Forbes looked amazing on bass, they all looked great. Charlie was playing a Flying V guitar. And the sound of the band was extremely contemporary and unique. And like all great pop music it's what I call 'bastard music' - a mixture of so many different things. They wore all these different influences on their sleeves and yet there was something unique about them. So I fell in love with them and for the next couple of months I hung out with them and went to just about every gig they did and became their pal and mentor.

And that's how we started and how I became involved with them. They'd never played England at this point. But record companies began to show a real interest in the band. All the majors began to show interest, as word got out that Simple Minds was happening. They were sniffing around. Jim used to say, even though I wasn't their manager, 'Speak to Bruce.' I was like a wise old man. I was in my mid-thirties. They were teenagers, Jim was 19. Jim said he wasn't going to London and I said, 'No, you shouldn't go to London to play.'

I knew from having been in the business a few years and managing a band called Café Jacques, major record labels would call from London and it was always, 'When are you playing London?' or 'we can get you a gig, we can get you a support slot', but it would be some stupid little gig in London so they could go along and see it. My favourite line at that time, when one of the record companies phoned up and said, 'When are they coming to London?' was, 'They're not coming to London.' 'Oh, I thought they were happening?' and I said, 'They are happening up here, in Scotland.' 'Well, tell us when they're coming to London and we'll definitely get one of our guys to come along and see them.' And I said, 'Well, you'll wait forever because we're not coming to London, not until we've got a deal and done the deal. Then we'll play London'. And the guy seriously said to me, 'Well, how am I meant to see them?' and I said, 'Well we've got loads of gigs lined up, a couple in Glasgow, a few in Edinburgh, Dundee. Different places in Scotland…' The band were beginning to gig prolifically at this point. I helped them get gigs by becoming their pal, not their manager, but just helping out.

I'd have loved to have signed them to Zoom but Zoom was a singles label. My idea was to release a couple of singles from a band and let them use me as a stepping-stone to get a major deal. I didn't see myself as a major player.

Simple Minds had three or four standout songs at the time. People went nuts every time they did 'Chelsea Girl'. To me it was just a smash hit record and I could have perhaps persuaded them to release the single but they needed to get a major record deal.

This guy said, 'It's a long way to come to Glasgow just to see a band.' I said, 'It's a hell of a long way for five guys and maybe a couple of others, a roadie and me, to come to London.' He said, 'Yeah, I get your point.' I said, 'We're not doing this. We're not playing that game.'

The attitude was, you wanted to get on in the music business? You couldn't do it from Scotland. We began to accept that like little puppy dogs. But I'm fiercely independent. I fought for them to be here in Scotland, and gradually the record companies did begin to come to Scotland to see the band. Jim and I had talked. Jim said, 'Look, of course I want a record deal. I want a proper long-term deal that will give us some security. I want the clout.' Even he understood the importance of having distribution with the media, partly because of the funding they could never get from a little label like Zoom. At the same time, they would have loved the kudos that came with an independent like Stiff. He'd already been with Chiswick with Johnny and the Self Abusers and had just a tiny little taste of what it was like.

I already had a distribution deal with Arista for my label, Zoom. So Arista said, 'What about us giving you the money for you to sign them to Zoom? We can fund you, we'll have a licence deal and you'll be in charge.' So I did a deal with Arista in order to sign Simple Minds. It was quite a big advance, enough money to put them all on wages, make the first album and - if I wanted - to make a second album, and enough to buy some equipment. In those days very few venues had their own PA system. Even small bands had to hire a PA to do gigs and it was expensive. We bought our own PA and lighting and were able to put David and his sister, Jaine, who did the lighting, on a retainer. Several producers were talked about and John Leckie came up and saw the band, either in St Andrews or Dundee, with Charles Levison and the A&R man at the time, Ben Edmonds. The band liked John and John liked them and they were in the studio within weeks of signing the deal and making the first album very, very quickly. It was finished before the end of the year and released early in 1979.

Virtually all the gigs they did at that point were when I became their mentor. I'd split from my wife at the time, so I was almost a bachelor. Jim lived on the 14th floor of a high rise flat in Toryglen and I used to go there, sit up all night with Jim discussing the revolution and then crash out on his mum's couch. Sometimes we'd crash out at Brian McGee's parent's house because they had a bigger house. I virtually lived with the band for the first six months I was involved with them.

We didn't do *Top of the Pops* for years. *Top of the Pops* was never an ambition. The television exposure that bands were getting those days was mostly the *Old Grey Whistle Test*, which you had to be a really well known or hip or American band to get on.

The exposure from John Peel was brilliant. John would play all the stuff I was releasing. and I did a newsletter, so it was a British record shop newsletter, but it was a bit like a fanzine. So I was well known and well established. I knew I was well known through Rough Trade and the little hip independent shops in the country because they'd been buying my records and I'd been buying theirs.

New records began to spring up a little bit. There was a revolution going on at the time. It wasn't just bands, this great new wave of music was exciting but also a whole bunch of record labels were starting up and we were one of the very first. A couple years later, for example, Postcard Records started up. But I was way ahead of the game, so I knew these people and had a lot of contacts.

We didn't want to do Saturday morning television shows. 'That's for kids.' Simple Minds saw themselves as serious contenders. They wanted to earn the respect of the audience, the crowd, the public and the media. But they wanted to be seen in the same light as Peter Gabriel or Roxy Music. They didn't see themselves like the Bay City Rollers or the pop groups of the day. Maybe it was a kind of musical snobbery but they certainly saw themselves as an alternative kind of act. Although I thought the first album was commercial, the record company couldn't get us daytime play. The music just wasn't conducive for daytime airplay and to have a hit record, you needed daytime radio.

## MARK HALDANE

### *Town Hall*
### *9 October 1978, Grangemouth, Scotland*

When asked about my favourite gigs over the years - and I've been to a fair few - this one tops it. Ultravox then were mesmerising and way ahead of the game. But so too were Simple Minds. 'Chelsea Girl' is part of my genes. The song was ingrained in my memory at that time. They were support on 8 October 1978 and went down well and were back on their own on 28 December 1978. I was in the Town Hall when Jim Kerr and the guys came in for the sound check. I remember Jim wearing very stylish red Chelsea boots.

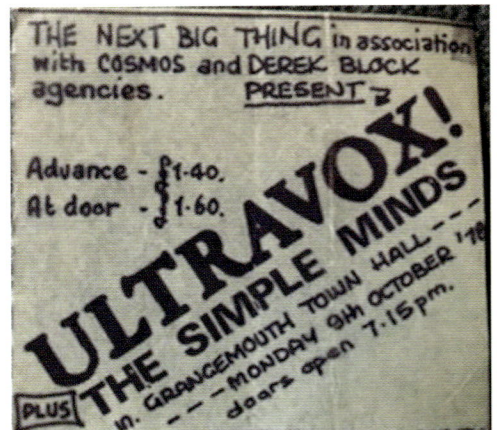

*Photo Paul Chatham*

## STEPHEN WYPER

I was just shy of 14 when I first saw Simple Minds, on a Monday night away back in 1978. Me and a group of friends all got tickets for a gig in Grangemouth Town Hall to see Ultravox, who were being supported by 'The Simple Minds'. My hair was all spiked up with Vaseline, ready for a night of punk. When Simple Minds were on stage there was a lot of spitting going on, directed at the band, and I am sad to say that I was part of this, fancying myself as a wee punk rocker, something I am deeply embarrassed about now - the spitting, not the punk rock!

Getting up the following morning for school was hard work but not as hard as getting the Vaseline out of my hair! After attempting to wash it first with water followed by shampoo I can't even begin to describe the state it was in when I went to school that morning. Electrocuted punk comes to mind. Anyway, despite my protestations, while the band were on stage I did actually enjoy the music although I'd never have said so to my mates, I bought the 'Chelsea Girl' single shortly thereafter.

## JOHN McKENZIE

*Bungalow Bar*
*13 October 1978, Paisley, Scotland*

I was a student at Reid Kerr College in Paisley. The Bungalow Bar was almost next door to the college. I had been a bit of a punk and the Bungalow Bar was great at supporting and introducing new bands like Siouxsie and the Banshees and the Skids so was a regular haunt. One night this band from Glasgow were introduced that I hadn't heard of - Simple Minds. They were enthusiastic, loud and a bit raw but very engaging, and I told my mate I was impressed, but he wasn't as keen and told me they'd never be heard of again!

I did lose track for a short while but was in a record store called Listen in Paisley when 'Love Song' was playing. I asked the guy behind the counter (who, bizarrely, went on to be Kurt Cobain's guitar tech) who it was we were listening to as I had to buy it. 'Simple Minds,' he told me. I was back on board and they have been my favourite band ever since. They're amazing live and, being a Rangers fan, I can even forgive their allegiance to Celtic. I mean, nobody's perfect, right?

## EDDIE CAIRNS

*Simple Minds road crew*
*Tiffany's*
*22 October 1978, Edinburgh, Scotland*

I was working with semi pro bands in and around Glasgow when I first met the two Dougies, Wee Dougie (Wragg) and Big Dougie (Cowan). They both gave me a lot of advice and help what with buying PA's for some bands, how to set up a desk, etc. and general information on gear. I had been working with semi pro bands for years, since I was 16. I was just another frustrated drummer! At that time (1978-ish) I had heard of Simple Minds and had been to see them several times at the Mars Bar where they had a residency.

23

I started working as a pro roadie with Rosetta Stone, an offshoot of The Bay City Rollers, and at that time moved to Edinburgh and started to share a flat with Wee Dougie. He was doing various things around town and I managed to fit in a few of the gigs with him, usually non-paying. One was in October 1978 in Tiffany's in Edinburgh for Simple Minds and I also did a few other gigs helping out that year (Astoria, Edinburgh, Robert Gordon Aberdeen, University of Edinburgh, etc). The crew at that time was David and Jaine Henderson, Paul Kerr, Billy Wharton and Wee Dougie, if memory serves.

---

# BILLY SLOAN

## *Glasgow Apollo & Edinburgh University*
## *27 October 1978, Glasgow & Edinburgh, Scotland*

I wasn't reacquainted with them for another 12 months. I didn't go to any of the Mars Bar gigs when they did this weekly residency. I think the next time I saw them play might have been when they played Glasgow School of Art with a band called Berlin Blondes. They then opened for Siouxsie and the Banshees at the Apollo. As soon as they finished, they had to jump in the van because they were opening for a group called The Pleasers, a Jam-style power pop punk band. They played two gigs in the one night.

In '79, I was working at a magazine called *Clyde Guide*, a Radio Clyde magazine and I was approached by a guy called Brian Hawk who was the PR guy at Zoom Records, run by Bruce Findlay. He said, 'Simple Minds have just finished their album. I'll send you a cassette. I'd like to bring the band through and do an interview to get a piece in the paper.' And that was the first time I sat down with them. It wasn't the whole band. It was Jim, Mike MacNeil and Bryan McGee. We photographed them in Glasgow and interviewed them in a pub around the corner. That was the first time I really spoke to them face to face and really got to know them.

I don't think there's any Scottish band that's sold as many records, sold as many concert tickets globally and had the impact that they've had globally.

'79 was a good year for them, but also a good year for me. I got a show on Radio Clyde and then began doing the music column for the *Sunday Mail*. I started writing about them in my music column. So suddenly they had a kindred spirit working in the biggest newspaper and the biggest local radio station. I was playing the records and flying the flag for them. When the first album came out, I played tracks from it and plugged their gigs and mentioned them. I used to do a programme on Radio Clyde from midnight till two o'clock in the morning on a Thursday night. Everybody says it was like the Scottish version of the John Peel show, which is very flattering, but all I used to do was just sit and play my favourite records. I figured that if I liked them then somebody else might quite like them as well. I would be playing Simple Minds,

U2, Orange Juice, Aztec Camera, Josef K, Siouxsie and the Banshees, Altered Images - that kind of stuff - and because it was the only show of its kind in Scotland, we used to get a huge audience.

And then there would be times, and it used to happen quite a lot, where Simple Minds would be in the Town House studio in London recording for Virgin and Jim would come up on the last shuttle flight from London and get into Glasgow at half nine. He would get a taxi from the airport to Radio Clyde in the centre of Glasgow and leave a package for me. When I came in at 11 o'clock, there would be this package with a note saying, 'We're in the Town House and we've just finished mixing the single' and 'here's the first copy. If you like it, give us a play on the programme.' He would come and leave me a copy of the new single even before he went home to see his mother. It was just a relationship that went hand-in-hand because a lot of the papers weren't covering alternative music.

Jim and Charlie were like a couple of nomads. When they were 15 or 16, they hitchhiked around India with just a carrier bag and three clean t-shirts and two pairs of pants and two pairs of socks. I don't think they were even organised enough to have a rucksack. That was pretty adventurous for two young guys.

They opened for Magazine in Europe and they opened for Peter Gabriel in Europe. When you think of the third album, *Empires and Dance*, it's almost like a picture postcard. Instead of sending a postcard back to your mother saying 'here I am in Prague and this is what's happening' or 'here I am in Paris and we've been to this great museum', they put it all in songs. The song 'I Travel' was almost like a picture postcard musically, from all these lands that they were discovering and traveling to.

I still have postcards from Jim, 'We are in San Francisco' or 'here we are in Rome' and 'tomorrow night we're playing at the Kabuki Theater in San Francisco' or 'the tour has been going great.' They went into the world and soaked it up and that manifested itself in the music. The fact that they were prepared to go away from home for long periods and play anywhere means they've got fans from everywhere. They were discovering the world and it was all being soaked up into their lyrics and into their music. And that's what made it so potent.

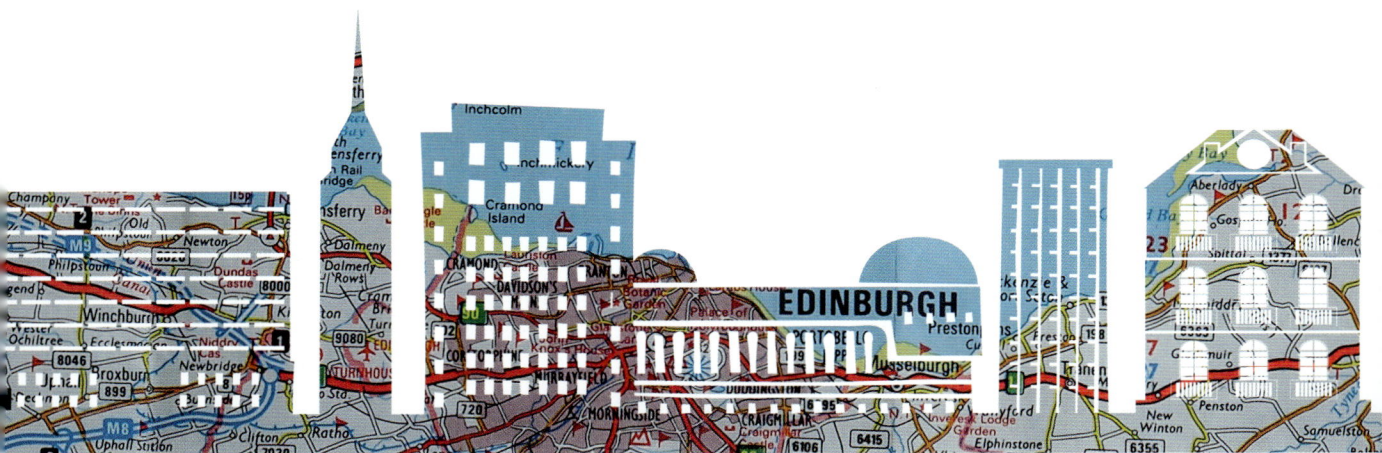

# LIFE IN A DAY

## MICK MACNEIL

Our first producer was John Leckie. He built his apprenticeship up through EMI and Abbey Road. I hadn't met him until the first day of recording our first album. It was pretty scary. This was the first of three albums we would do with him. The idea was to keep the band as a band and set up in a kind of barn arrangement and work like we would in a rehearsal room. We headed to London to a farm in Chalfont. I will never forget the first day. We headed straight from Glasgow to London and had eaten a lump of hash on the way to the plane from Glasgow. We were all wrecked. We hadn't really flown before. Charlie looked out the window and said, 'Look! The people are tiny!' We hadn't even left yet. He was looking at the rivets on the wing....

Once we arrived in London at the baggage reclaim, we were waiting for the bags and they had sent somebody from the record company to come and meet us with a chauffeur. And the girl that came was Julie Hooker and I used to fancy her. And I'm still 'flying' at this point but I was waiting for my bag to come round. I forgot that my mother had packed mine - a really bright, green, flowery one. It was on the conveyor belt but I just couldn't get the nerve to pick it up. I was too embarrassed. And the boys were asking if it was my bag but I said, 'No, they must have lost my bag.'

And because we were the new kids on the block as far as Arista Records were concerned, they kept on getting limos for us at the airport so we're driving this limo to Chalfont, totally stoned. By the time we got there, it was about two in the afternoon and we had all fallen asleep so we went to bed. And I woke up around seven or eight o'clock at night and nobody else was about. But I knew John Leckie was in the studio setting up the equipment. I was really

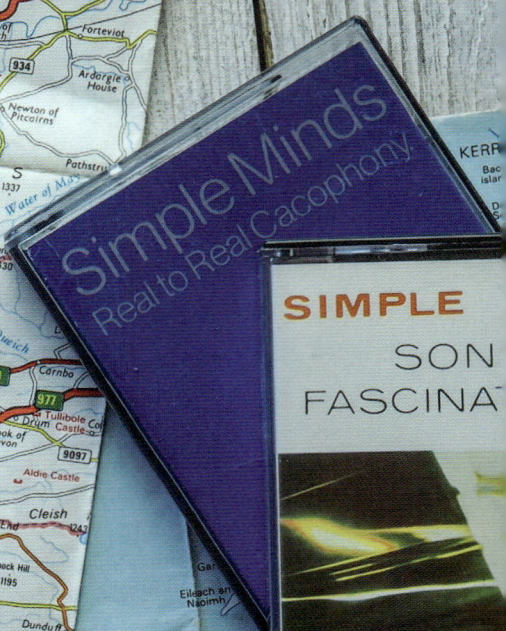

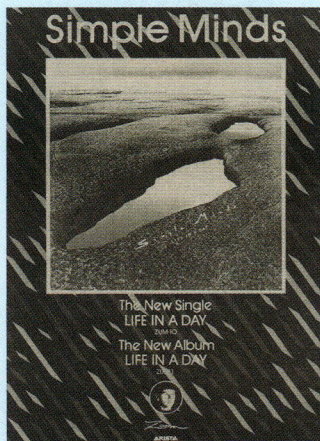

frightened. I was waiting for Charlie or somebody to suggest going to meet him together. I was scared he was going to ask me to play something and then realise how rubbish I was and then leave. Then the band might ask where he went and I'd have to tell them that he realised how rubbish I was and that he'd split. But he was a great producer.

I guess that's why we went back again and again. And, as well as having a really good time with the guy, it turned out to be pretty creative most of the time, especially on the second album when we went in without a single idea. We kind of kept the same format as starting a record on a remote farm. One of the places we used was down in Wales, at Rockfield. It bonded everyone together. We did everything together as one group for a few months. Iggy Pop was doing an album in a studio next to ours. We were sat in the living room, and he walked right in and we just went totally silent. We were genuine fans. He was making *The Soldier* album. James Williamson, the producer, asked if I could track some keyboards on Iggy's album. I said 'aye' and my mind was racing thinking about what to say. James said, 'Come in and listen to the track.' I listened for a couple of days and I wondered what to say to him. I eventually said, 'Maybe a harpsichord would be good.' James turned with a look of confusion and said, 'Maybe....' I was still really excited but petrified, wondering what I was going to do. The next thing I know, David Bowie shows up and there's a big fight. James legs it and gets on a plane to New York. I didn't want to then go tell David and Iggy that I was supposed to play for them, but it all turned out well anyway because David Bowie asked us all to join in and sing on a song. So it ended happily.

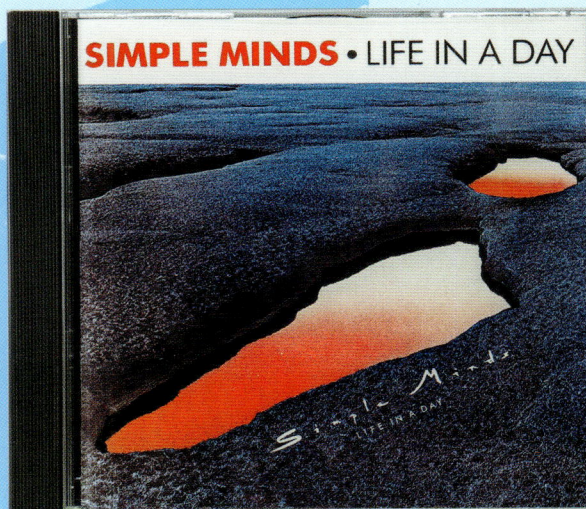

## JULIE TILLEY

Times were tough in Plymouth in 1979 but we scrimped and saved to buy the latest records. Having bought *Life in a Day* with his very first wage packet, my brother Trev put it on my bed. 'Bloody waste of money, that was.' I put it on the turntable and listened and magic filled my ears. I drove Mum and Dad to despair by playing it so much. I learned every word, every beat and chord, and danced and sang my heart out in the confines of my bedroom. I adorned my walls with posters of Simple Minds, much to my parents' horror. I kissed the band all good night, every night. I used to dream of meeting Jim. 40 years on, I still do.

I still have all the albums and CDs, but not my cassettes. I came home from work one day to find that Charlie, our Macaw, escaped from his cage and stiff as a board, covered in dried emulsion paint and surrounded by reels and reels of cassette tape. Very much alive but not so kicking! I spent the next five hours carefully scraping every bit of dried paint from his feathers. My beloved tapes were not so lucky.

We tried to start a family and had five attempts at IVF. Sadly, no babies have come for us but Simple Minds was blaring out at the hospital during the IVF procedures. Not having a family left a void which we've filled with the opportunity to go to lots of concerts. The first one I booked was to see Simple Minds at Birmingham. From the moment they came on stage, I danced and sang and there I was - back in my bedroom in 1979.

## EDWARD BALDWIN

In 1978 we formed a band called Photon Madness. Joe, the two Marks and me. One of the Marks was my best friend. He believed so much that he was a drummer that he made me believe I was a bass player. We lived in a factory town outside Philadelphia. We wanted to be like the Minds, and Ultravox, and Roxy. We covered *Life in a Day* when only a handful of people on this side of the pond had ever heard of Simple Minds.

By *Real to Real Cacophony* I had learned the bass line to 'Changeling'. Then 'I Travel', which really stretched me. They all did. In my jump from Dylan-style guitar strummer to new wave bassist, the Minds were everything to me. All my bass lines were bad copies of Derek's that eventually grew into their own.

In the Eighties, our band played the local clubs, recorded a demo, and broke up. We were two sets of best friends. Everything we did was intense. Mark and I journeyed to Scotland in August of '87. Jim was on the cover of *Melody Maker* that week. It was like a sign from heaven.

In the Nineties I left the Minds. But I came roaring back in the 2000s and bought everything. I started playing bass again. Started reconnecting my own journey to all the wild stuff we did when we were looking ahead at our lives and dreaming of a world bigger than our little town.

A lot has changed since Photon Madness practiced in Mark's basement. The cancer took him a few years back. The other guys and I got straight jobs. I work in a cube. But I still keep my big 1980s bass amp. I never did get as good as Derek. But when the mood takes me, I can thunder up a swirl of dreams and passion that I learned practising to the Simple Minds.

SOMEONE · LIFE IN A DAY · SAD AFFAIR · ALL FOR YOU
PLEASANTLY DISTURBED · NO CURE · CHELSEA GIRL
WASTELAND · DESTINY · MURDER STORY

® 1982 VIRGIN RECORDS LTD. © 1986 VIRGIN RECORDS LTD.

# BRUCE FINDLAY

*April 1979*

They did get on John Peel and some of the late afternoon, early evening shows, so that was our foray into the commercial market. They did Scottish television as well, but the only major television show was the *Old Grey Whistle Test*. And they were good on it but a bit stiff. They did 'Chelsea Girl' and 'Life in a Day', the two most commercial songs from the first album. The album stiffed. 'Life in a Day' charted but very low. The same week, 'Are Friends Electric?' by Tubeway Army charted about two or three positions above Simple Minds, like 40 or something, and we were 47 or something. He got *Top of the Pops*, we didn't. He got in as the new entry, and about two weeks later he was number one and our record had dropped out of the charts.

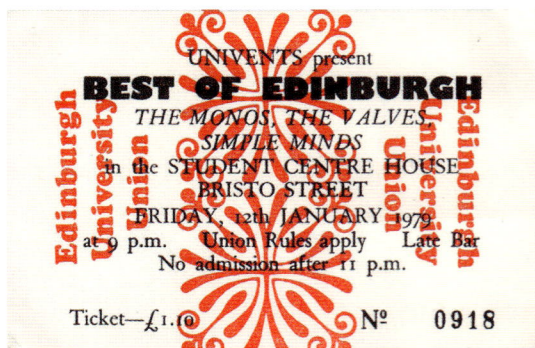

---

# MARK FOGGETT

*King George's Hall*
*17 April 1979, Blackburn, England*

I saw this tour at King George's Hall, Blackburn and it was one of the first gigs I ever went to – my first being The Clash at the same venue. I was, and still am, a huge Magazine fan. It was the first band I had ever seen with prominent keyboards and that night I got two for one with Simple Minds supporting. I am still a fan of bands that have keyboard players even though I actually play bass. I am not sure whether I had heard of Simple Minds before that night or not but I remember watching their whole set, as I always watched the support bands in those days as they often went on to be famous themselves. Both bands were amazing that night.

After the gig we came out and we saw Simple Minds getting into a van outside. I seem to recall them loading equipment into a Transit-type van. We then asked them if they could give us a lift home as we explained that we lived a 30-minute bus journey away in Clitheroe. They said they were going straight on the M6 north so it was the wrong direction and so not possible. I then asked Jim Kerr for his autograph and he signed it on a torn open Players No 6 cigarette packet that I picked up of the floor. And they went on their way.

Meeting Jim that night was the start of me meeting three of Patsy Kensit's ex-husbands. I later met Dan Donovan in a kebab shop in Nottingham and Liam Gallagher at a back stage party after Kasabian played the V Festival.

---

## PETER HULMES

Magazine were on their *Secondhand Daylight* tour. I was a huge fan but, on the night, Simple Minds blew them away. It could have just been a bad night for the headliners, but I honestly think they were struggling to follow these magnificent young upstarts! I had no idea who Simple Minds were at the time, but as soon as I had enough money saved from my paper round I bought *Life in a Day*, loved it and have never looked back.

## GRAY LIGHTFOOT

My memory is of not being arsed to come out of the bar in the King George's Hall to listen to the support band – Simple Minds - who turned out to be one of the biggest groups of the time.

## NIGEL PROKTOR

I was a kid in Blackburn bitten by the punk rock bug and forged in its white heat. The guy who booked gigs at the local municipal King George's Hall was a far-reaching fella called Geoff Peake who also ran a heavy rock disco called 'Peepers'. But that's another tale...

Geoff was all feathered haircut, moustache and brushed denim and no doubt had a penchant for The Allman Brothers if truth be told. That said, he was 'down with the kids' and duly did his duty with gusto and booked 'the now' to come and rock our town. The Clash, The Jam, The Adverts, Blondie, The Police, etc. Power pop with steel toe-caps on. You get the picture?

Now a gig was a gig back then in the Blackburn backwater. We were all under 17 so no-one had a driving licence and travelling by hired coach to Manchester or Liverpool was a rare but expensive treat. 17th of April 1979 came Magazine with Simple Minds in tow.

At that time I wasn't a huge Howard fan.

*Nigel Proktor was at St George's Hall for the Magazine tour*

Knew of his part in Buzzcocks and 'Spiral Scratch', although the chance of getting hold of a copy came around about as often as a Preston Guild. Magazine's first album, *Real Life*, had thrown the cat amongst the pigeons with the punk purists. Mainly due to Dave Formula's keyboards methinks. Heaven forefend. Hadn't we just gone through the punk wars only to be returned to a progressive past?

Fair to say it was the toppermost rock show I'd witnessed to date. And Simple Minds were no mere bystanders neither. They rolled their sleeves up - well, the singer did - and played their part with aplomb. Sprinkling the trifle with hundreds and thousands as they went about their shift.

A fair hearing was granted and fair verdict pronounced by the gap-toothed crowd. They were good. Better than good. 'Life In A Day', 'Someone' and 'Chelsea Girl' being the most memorable moments. The highest compliment was given by purchasing their long-player the next weekend with the old pocket money spends. 'Life In A Day'. Zoom Records. ZULP1.

Cut to 1984. In the interim, I'd journeyed through mandatory 'O' and 'A' level examinations and pitched up in London Town to attend art school. My intentions were honourable. To design record sleeves. No stopping a confident man despite all the piss and vinegar. In June 1984 I was suddenly now 'a professional' having completed the course with honours to boot. They didn't know it yet but it was now a choice between Bruno Tilley at his Island Records Art Department, or Peter Saville and his Associates or Malcolm Garrett's Assorted iMaGes. Someone was going to get lucky!

Bruno liked the stuff but quite rightly and quite quickly appraised that, with me having no actual real-time studio experience, he couldn't take time out to get me up to actual professional speed.

Peter was a turn. Wore a black polo neck jumper, white Levi's and had his pens neatly arranged 'just so' on his desk. He also chain-smoked. Alternatively Gitanes from the left back pocket. Gauloise Disque Bleu from the right back pocket. Or was that Left Bank / Right Bank pockets? You decide. Anyway the future Commander Saville waltzed me off to The Groucho Club and promptly ordered an egg-white omelette and an exceedingly dry sherry from Iberia. I had a Guinness. A fine old time was had but I decided I couldn't work for him. In a million years…

Malcolm came up next and came in like the 7th Cavalry. 'Have you got a passport?' 'Er, yes…' 'OK. You're hired. Can you turn up on Monday? You're off to Dublin to meet up with the Eurythmics. They're on a tax year so that's the closest to the UK they can be. They've got a new album. A soundtrack to the film *1984*. You want in?' 'Where do I sign?'

A week or so later, a fella walks into the Assorted iMaGes studio from the recording studio next door. I swear it was Billy Currie. And he kept on popping in and out regular as a clockwork mouse. Back then Shoreditch had two pubs. One for the suits, The Barley Mow, and one for non-suits, The Bricklayers, we didn't go to the Barley Mow. One night 'Billy' was at the bar. I joined him introducing myself, along with, 'Billy Currie, isn't it? You recording in the studio?' No. My name's Dave. Dave Formula, and I own the studio'.

'Oh. Nice to meet you...'

Six months later, Barry Adamson pitches up and he's telling me tales of running with Tapper Zukie in Moss Side and school days Shaft-lite sideburns. In 1972 the NY set Shaft film as cool as. It's lead, 'John Shaft' was equally cool. Supercool even. And the younger, still at school, Barry decided that since Shaft was cool he could have a shot at raising his playground game if he took to looking like the private dick that's a sex machine to all the chicks. Can you dig it?

To that end he twisted his locks, pulled them down in front of his ears and taped them to his jowls and slept on them overnight. Carefully, in the morning, Barry removed the tape, and hair pesto! Instant diggers! Mutton chops for playground chops. No longer just Barry, but now big, bad Barry! The strut was in. This ruse lasted until lunchtime, when unbeknownst to Barry, gravity took a hold of the game and returned the teezy-weezy structure back to nature. Slowly. Cantilevering his instant sideboards back to base. Afro Central. The strut was out.

A couple of months later Howard pitches up and joins the gang at assorted iMaGes as, nominally, 'book editor'. 'Well, he can string a few words together. Why not give him a go' went the logic…

Meanwhile, Simple Minds set to work and went off to become stadium fillers.

Jump to 2008 and I'm running the show and taking care of business in a flash for Howard, Barry, Dave and John, along with Noko on guitar, for Magazine's highly anticipated return to the boards in 2009. The shows are being prompted by Mike 'call me Pod' Raven of The Gig Cartel, who it turns out he was in the crowd at King George's Hall on 17th April too. Small world, huh?

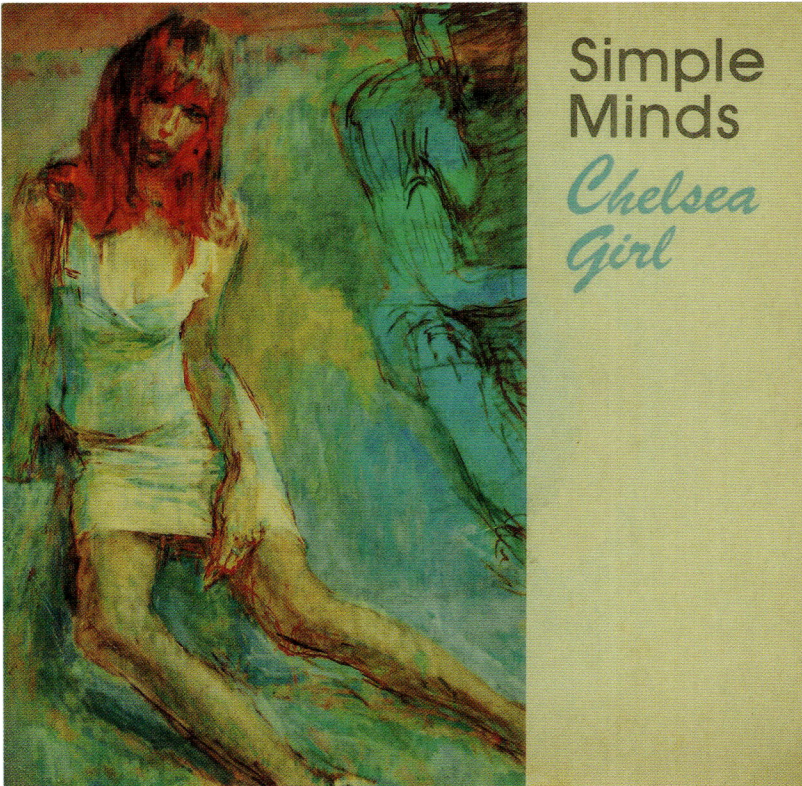

Originally it was just to be two shows. Manchester and London. But demand for the shows was so strong that more were added to the itinerary. Glasgow, another in Manchester and another London night are announced. Guest list ligs flew in left and right. One such was from a certain Jim Kerr. 'Could I please be added to the Glasgow list. I cannae wait…'

## PHIL MILLER

I travelled to the Manchester Apollo to buy tickets with my big brother. We were mad punks back then - believe it or not we used to sniff petrol! Whenever we went to gigs (Buzzcocks, Swell Maps, Magazine, Jam, Hawkwind, Motorhead, 4-Skins, etc) we'd get there early to see the support bands and the Apollo gig didn't disappoint! Skids were up first and they sounded excellent loud. Amps were stacked on the left and right of the stage and up to the ceiling. Me and our kid remember how mint 'Life in a Day' was and the crowd at the front shouting for 'Chelsea Girl'. Our night was topped off by Magazine playing an excellent set. All that greatness for £3.60!

## STEPHEN FLETCHER

*De Montfort Hall*
*19 April 1979, Leicester, England*

Me and a few mates saw Magazine's *Secondhand Daylight* tour at De Montfort Hall, Leicester in '79. I remember Jim's pudding basin haircut. Simple Minds were good enough for me to buy 'Life in a Day' and 'Chelsea Girl' not long after.

## BILLY BARNES

*Clouds*
*20 April 1979, Edinburgh, Scotland*

I went to see Magazine. I always wondered what happened to Simple Minds! Actually, their set was okay. They had their own wee crowd with them so got a decent reception.

# JOHN GREER

*University of St Andrews
22 April 1979, St Andrews,
Scotland*

In February 1978, at the age of 18, I went to work at St Andrews University. I got to live the life of a student, playing football and going to see gigs at the University union. Over the years I saw early outings for bands such as the Police, Dexy's Midnight Runners, Squeeze, Undertones and New Order but the band that stood out were Simple Minds. I had seen them on the *Old Grey Whistle Test* about a month before they came to play as support for Magazine. I was very excited to see them, as I loved the single 'Life in a Day'. The gig was great and seven months later they came back to support the *Real to Real Cacophony* album. That night I met Bruce Findlay who was there with Richard Jobson of the Skids. Bruce gave me two Zoom/Simple Minds badges and we got to meet the band. Charlie Burchill signed the back of a band photo with a message saying that if they ever come back to St Andrews he promised to play 'No Cure'! I gave it away years later hoping to get into a girl's knickers... without success!

Simple Minds were my band. I travelled one night to see them play at Edinburgh's Nite Club and had to sleep rough as I'd missed the last train home. I went back to Edinburgh to Bruce's Records to buy an *Empires and Dance* red and black t-shirt. Over the years I saw them in various venues from Dundee's Caird Hall and Coasters in Edinburgh to Meadowbank Stadium, where the gig was rescheduled from Murrayfield.

In recent times, I saw a great intimate gig at King Tuts where they showcased their new album *Black & White*. I won the tickets through a *Sunday Mail* competition run by Billy Sloan. Two of the last gigs I saw were one Saturday evening in July 2009 in a monsoon rainstorm at Edinburgh Castle Esplanade and then the wonderful homecoming *Celebrate* gig at Glasgow's Hydro that was recorded for a DVD release.

*Photo Stuart Holland*

## PAUL BUCKLEY, AGE 15

*Apollo Theatre*
*23 April 1979, Manchester, England*

I was (and still am) a big fan of Magazine and went with my best friend and my brother. We hadn't heard anything by Simple Minds but I remember seeing a display in the Lewis's record shop window in Manchester city centre for the *Life in a Day* album and feeling excited as I thought it looked cool. It was a lovely sunny evening. At the concert, we were in the stalls fairly close to the stage and, as was quite usual with support bands, there were quite a few empty seats. What you could sense though was that the crowd were slowly being won over after an initial tepid response, myself included. We Mancunians aren't easy to impress at the best of times. You could see lots of people, mostly lads, looking at each other and nodding in approval. I think 'Chelsea Girl' was the main turning point, which well and truly grabbed our attention. Not long after the concert, I eagerly bought the first two singles. I had become a fan.

## TERRY CLARKE

Four or five of us from Blackley in Manchester excitedly made our way to the Apollo to see Magazine; we'd followed Howard Devoto from Buzzcocks. Magazine were amazing, as expected. But the thing I remember most clearly is us five, and then most of the top deck of the bus, singing 'Chelsea Girl' all the way back to Piccadilly bus station, something that's never happened before or since. A brilliant night! The next morning I went to Virgin Records in town and bought *Life in a Day*.

## PHIL HARTLEY

I'm pretty sure that my only experience of them at that point was from a couple of tracks they'd performed on *The Old Grey Whistle Test* a few days before. It's fair to say that the auditorium was pretty full when Simple Minds strode on to the

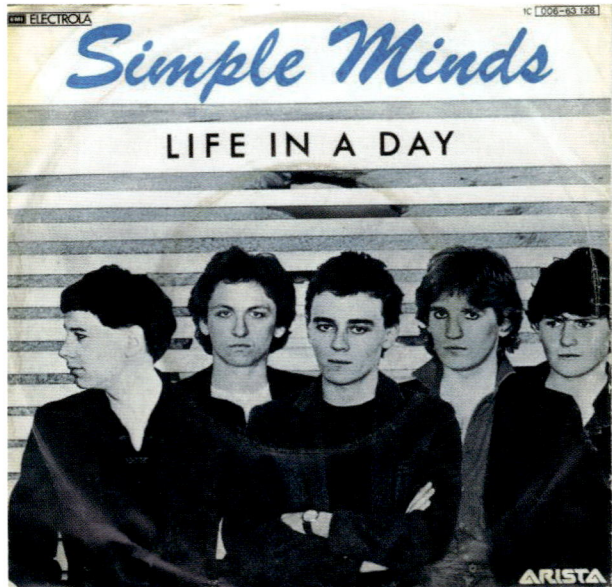

stage. They got a great reaction from a very appreciative crowd and their guitar and keyboard-driven new wave/ post punk tunes made them a perfect complement to Magazine. That night remains one of my favourite complete shows in terms of the support and the headliner. They captured many new fans that night and I saw them many times over the next three or four years.

## SEAN HALLIGAN

*City Hall*
*25 April 1979, Newcastle,*
*England*

I met Jim Kerr on the steps outside and we talked for a while. He gave me a badge that moved depending on which way you looked at it. I had it pinned to my speakers on my record player for years but sadly it is now lost. Jim also signed my ticket on the front. Howard Devoto signed it on the back!

*Sean Halligan got his ticket signed by Jim*

## ROB WILD

*Victoria Hall*
*26 April 1979, Hanley, England*

I couldn't take my eyes off Jim's pudding basin hair cut. They were good enough for me to buy a few of their records, a big decision for a skint schoolboy.

## PHIL SADLER

I saw them at Victoria Hall, Hanley but really can't remember much about it apart from the fact the crowd was tiny for both Simple Minds and Magazine.

## ADRIAN MAY

*Colston Hall*
*30 April 1979, Bristol, England*

I remember I was quite struck with them and became a fan after that gig. I don't know why but I bought a badge at the gig, which in itself is odd as I wasn't an avid badge collector. But there were Simple Minds badges for sale and I remember the badge quite vividly. It was a square badge probably just over an inch in size, and one of those badges which changes with the angle you look at it. It was Jim looking slightly sideways and in one direction his eyes turned red. I don't know why it sticks in my mind but there you are!

## ALASDAIR MEADOWS

I hadn't heard much about Simple Minds before but they were brilliant even then. The memory is a bit dimmer now but I seem to recall them playing most of *Life in a Day*, Jim's funny haircut and a lot of eyeliner. We went backstage after Magazine had performed and they were happy to chat and sign autographs with everyone. I think Simple Minds had left by then though!

## TIM PICKFORD

As an excited 16-year-old from sleepy Somerset I went to see my favourite band Magazine at the now infamous Colston Hall in Bristol. If my memory serves the concert only cost two or three pounds to get in. How's that for value for money? I was naturally focussed on Howard Devoto, McGeoch, Adamson, Formula and Doyle but I distinctly remember being extremely impressed by Simple Minds and more specifically can see in my mind's eye a violin being played and remembering a song called 'Chelsea Girl' hitting home.

Magazine remain my favourite band of all time but like many fans I have been introduced to Simple Minds via them. I have every record Simple Minds have ever made and have seen them perform numerous times, most recently at Burgos in Spain on the *Acoustic* tour with my son. He and my two daughters have been to quite a few SM concerts in Spain over the last few years. I have remained loyal for the simple reason that they are what they are - a class act that produce excellent music both in the studio and live.

## MARTIN SLADE

I first heard the name Simple Minds on a lads' summer holiday in Torquay, Devon. Some lads from Glasgow in the apartment above ours used to dress - oddly at the time - in white boiler suits to go out clubbing. One of them told us they were emulating their heroes in an amazing new band calling themselves Simple Minds. Back in Bristol a friend was going to a gig by a punk band called Magazine and asked me if I wanted to come along. To my surprise the support act that night were Simple Minds! I didn't go much on the main act but I really enjoyed the SM set that night - dark, atmospheric and with bundles of attitude. I saw them again as soon as they came back, this time headlining their own tour with a little-known Liverpool duo supporting them called China Crisis. I've seen the guys many times since, with many different line-ups but always with the

*Martin Slade saw Simple Minds supporting Magazine*

omnipresent Burchill and Kerr. I own all of their albums and was fortunate to have my face appear on their album *Cry*, along with those of hundreds of other fans. Simple Minds have always been 'my' band.

## DARYL COLES

### *Great Hall, University of Exeter 1 May 1979, Exeter, England*

I guess I wasn't really there for Simple Minds but it was a great night. Magazine were epic. Maybe others can remember more. I still have this flyer as it is autographed by Magazine on the reverse. 'Howie is God' had been written on the dressing room door backstage, not sure whether that was on the rider.

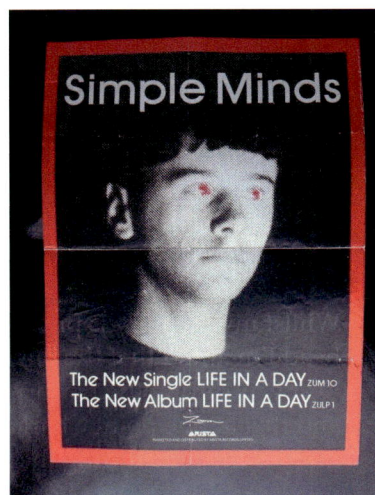

*Daryl Coles has Magazine's autographs on a Simple Minds flyer*

## TONY STOKES

It was my first gig and was amazing. I went with a school friend, primarily for Magazine because 'Shot By Both Sides' had been on *Top of the Pops*. Simple Minds were brilliant. On the basis of their set I went out and bought the *Life in a Day* album.

---

## BRUCE FINDLAY

*Theatre Royal Drury Lane*
*2 May 1979, London, England*

The first time we did London, we had to buy onto a Magazine tour. Magazine were touring their new album and then our album came out and we had to pay to be on their tour. And that was the first time the band played England. Simple Minds went down a storm just about every night - we were getting encores. Except when we went to London. Halfway through the band's set, the plug got pulled on them. Somebody tripped over the main cord and the sound went off, which was really anticlimactic. It took about five minutes to get it back on again. There were always rumours it was sabotage. It spoilt the gig because at that point we were going down an absolute storm and it was a good mixture, because Jim loved Magazine and liked Howard Devoto. We saw ourselves as being like the early - John Fox - Ultravox and Magazine. Magazine were the same age, the same time as Simple Minds. So we identified with them, but we were very much our own act.

   After the first album came out we got a record, we got an agency and began to tour prolifically. Edinburgh had more clubs than Glasgow. And we used to do all the different London venues – the Nashville, the Marquee, the Hope and Anchor. There were about ten or twelve. You could spend two weeks in London alone.

---

## CARLOS NEEDHAM

*Corn Exchange*
*4 May 1979, Cambridge, England*

Whilst my memory is pretty good and I'm still able to see the band playing in my head I'm afraid that the only thing I can really recall was how dreadfully nervous Jim Kerr was during the performance, that he sported a terrible 'pudding basin' haircut and that at one point Charlie Burchill played violin. I'm a synth aficionado and spent most of my time during the set looking at Mick's manipulations in real time of his

Korg MS20. Still, they were good enough for me to go and buy the album.

That particular night was also John McGeoch of Magazine's 21st birthday. He and Richard Jobson of the Skids were getting plastered backstage, so having struck up a conversation with them I joined in!

---

## SIMON WHITAKER

*Refectory, University of Leeds*
*5 May 1979, Leeds, England*

I reference this gig amongst my friends and peers as being one of the best value for money gigs I've ever attended and - to date - one of the loudest. It was a Saturday. Vice Versa (who later changed their name to ABC) were first on followed by the Simple Minds, with Magazine headlining – all for about £3.50. It was a great Saturday night.

*Simon Whitaker was at the Leeds Uni gig*

---

## STEPHEN CROOKS

*Empire Theatre*
*6 May 1979, Liverpool, England*

My older sister's boyfriend took me to Liverpool Empire. My first ever gig. I fanatically followed Simple Minds afterwards and have told the story a thousand times of seeing them as support to Magazine.

---

## RONNIE GURR

I remember everyone at the weekly meetings saying how the single didn't go higher because Arista had basically fucked up. They had obviously made the decision that they weren't going to carry on. It was tradition, on the last night of the tour, that you take the band out for dinner. Except there was a memo going round at the end of the Magazine tour that it was beer and wine only and nobody was to order cocktails.

So even then they were clamping down on the budget just as they were going out the door. Of course, I told Bruce Findlay who had had a couple of drinks prior to dinner and, sat at the end of the table, Bruce banged his glass, smashed it and said, 'Everybody I've got an announcement to make. If anybody wants a cocktail, the pina coladas are on me'. Then everybody ordered a cocktail and at the other end of the table the head of the company was just going nuts. That evening ended up costing them a lot more than they budgeted for.

## BRUCE FINDLAY

We began to build up a live fan base very quickly, although we weren't selling vast amounts of records, and were beginning to build up a real head of steam. The band almost rejected the first album after it came out. Jim particularly was kind of dismissive of it. They were writing new stuff and the record company said, 'Look, you should make your second album now.' They had a fixed two album deal. What bands did in those days was sign a five album deal with the record company. So you made one album and the record company had options for four more. But they could drop you. Jim was very astute. Jim said to me, 'Look, I don't want one of these so-called five album deals which is really only a one album deal. So if our first album is piss we get dropped. I don't want that.' I negotiated at least two albums with an option for three further albums, still a five album deal.

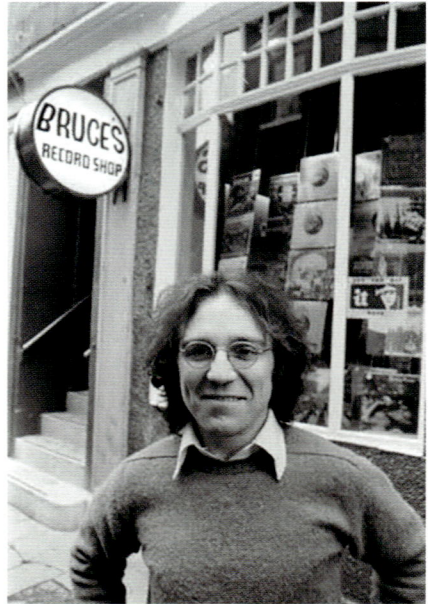

*Bruce Findlay - photo The Scotsman*

## ALAN GEBBIE

*Ayr Pavilion*
*23 May 1979, Ayr, Scotland*

My introduction to Simple Minds was at Ayr Pavilion. Living in Troon was so handy. After the Ayr gig I convinced my fellow course mates at the University of Glasgow to attend the gig at the Queen Margaret Union in November 1979, where they were delighted to be introduced to this up and coming Glasgow band.

A few years later myself and a few of my pals together with our then current 'wives' had the great idea of going to Shepton Mallet. 'Shepton where?' was the cry. 'Look, get the tickets and worry about that later.' Two cars set off from Ayrshire to start the long journey to Shepton Where? Having just started a new job, money wasn't exactly liberal so the idea was to camp and use any spare funds for petrol and, more importantly, beer. However, no one had told my 17-year-old Ford Escort we were not just going 'doon the road'. Having a few days to take off, we decided to take our time getting there at a speed considerably less than warp factor 0.5, which is just as well as we broke down three times on the way down on a three day trip. Remember, this was before sat nav and working off a well-thumbed AA road atlas. We even had the embarrassment of being overtaken by a caravan on the M5. However, it was well worth the trip for the gig and the various escapades on what was supposed to be a two-day trip, which turned into a week-long continual laugh, with frustration that 'Thor' would only get up to about 45 mph and that was downhill. Having been to several gigs since, and enjoying the band more and more as I grow older, I can honestly say these have been in more comfort than it was back then. But it's never been the same experience, travel-wise.

## STUART HOLLAND

My best friend's bigger brother knew a guy who worked at the door of the Pavilion, so with both of us only being 14 it was easier to get in. I was desperate to see this new band after hearing 'Life in a Day' on some guy's ghetto blaster at school. At the concert our friend waited on us outside just to make sure we got in okay and he also gave us some posters. 90 per cent of the crowd were there to watch Magazine as 'Simple Minds' were only a support band. But by the end of the gig you would have thought it was the other way around. This concert set off a 40-year love and obsession with a few guys from the streets of Glasgow.

## PAULINE MILNE

As I gaze at the battered Mel Gaynor drumstick deftly caught at a spectacular concert at the Roundhouse, I reflect on how Simple Minds have influenced my life and shaped the person I am today.

The adventure began in 1979 when I was 14 and a friend innocently placed his new album on the record player. I was instantly hooked and as I sat there that afternoon, time would freeze for me. It was the beginning of what would be my life in a day. As luck would have it, a few weeks later I won tickets to see them at Ayr Pavilion, and the journey continued from there.

After a phenomenal concert 'down the front' at Tiffany's in 1982, an 18-year-old me was sorely disappointed not to get to meet the band so opted for a bag of chips as consolation. However, fate played a hand again when a chance meeting with a bouncer in the queue (and chip butty bribe) meant my best mate and I were soon backstage with Jim, Charlie and the boys. My crumpled autographs and photos of that night are amongst my most treasured possessions.

Over the past 41 years Simple Minds have enabled me to escape my busy life as a nurse in the NHS. My memories include two Nelson Mandela concerts, rubbing shoulders with Donald Dewer at the Kosovo relief concert, being on the guestlist a few times (no need for chip butty bribes now), home turf concerts at the legendary Glasgow Apollo and Barrowland, stadium events at Ibrox (yes, really!), Wembley and Hyde Park to London's Borderline for Jim's intimate Lostboy venture; a negroni or two at Villa Angela, a chance meeting with Charlie in Covent Garden, and even holding my hen party at a Thetford Forest concert.

Since that day in 1979 there have been countless iconic venues and experiences - the band, the music, and the fellow fans I've met at the 40-plus gigs I've enjoyed have all helped carry me through this topsy-turvy thing we call life, and as I reflect, my life really did start on that day back in 1979.

---

# PHIL HARTLEY

*The Factory, The Russell Club*
*1 June 1979, Manchester, England*

On the back of the Magazine tour, Simple Minds played some headline dates of their own, including a show at the Factory/Russell Club in Hulme, Manchester. It was within just a few weeks of the Manchester Apollo gig. We got there quite early and to say the crowd was sparse is probably overstating it. I reckon there were about 20 people there. We were near the door as Jim and Derek Forbes entered and their look of disappointment was obvious. On the back of such a great reception at the Apollo, they clearly hoped for a bigger crowd. Still, they put on a great show, playing much of *Life in a Day*, but also (I think) one or two new songs that would go on to make up *Real to Real Cacophony*.

---

# RICHARD JOBSON

*Summer 1979*

When the Skids were recording *Days of Europa* they were down the road preparing their first album in Rockfield Studios. They used to come up and raid us at night with air guns. And I used to go, 'But you are the wimpiest band in the history of Scottish music. Fuck off!' It was good fun.

They weren't so close to Stuart Adamson or any of the other guys in the Skids. Rusty Egan was our drummer by then. He ran a club called Blitz in London, which was the heart of the new romantic movement, so really took to Simple Minds and started to play them a lot in that environment, in amongst all the Kraftwerk, Bowie and his own group, Visage. But it was as the drummer in the Skids that he first encountered them, and it grew from there.

# SHELLEY GUILD, AGE 17

*Barbarella's*
*30 June 1979, Birmingham, England*

I'd heard the band played by John Peel. I quite liked them but wasn't a huge fan and used to go to the club a lot around that time. I remember it was quite crowded and thought Jim Kerr had similar mannerisms or movements on stage to Howard Devoto, who'd I'd seen at the same club in December '78. I hadn't gone to see Simple Minds and Magazine at the Odeon earlier that year because the venue was seated. Quite ironic, really, because seats are now appreciated at gigs. It's funny that they should come back to Brum so soon after and to a smaller club, but then they were headlining.

# ANDREW MCKERNAN

*Eric's Club*
*27 July 1979, Liverpool, England*

Pete Wylie of The Mighty Wah! and Ian McCulloch of Echo & the Bunnymen were probably present at this gig, in an audience of about 100.

## SIMON WHITAKER

*Fforde Green Hotel*
*29 July 1979, Leeds, England*

Leeds University as the support to Magazine was the first time I'd seen Simple Minds. They must have impressed me as I went to see them again in the Fforde Green - long gone but legendary at the time - in Roundhay, Leeds. That pub had one hell of a reputation at the time (for the wrong reasons) and a small music room in the back. I sat three feet away from the stage and Steve Singleton from Vice Versa joined us at our table and signed my leather jacket. I remember showing him my JJ Burnel signature and jokingly saying, 'You can sign it too. Who knows - you may be famous one day!' Little did I know that Vice Versa would later become ABC.

Both the 1979 Simple Minds gigs I saw in Leeds were superb and full of energy. I'm biased, as I've always liked their first two albums the best, even if they were less commercially successful than the later stuff.

## BRUCE FINDLAY

*Hurrah's*
*24 October 1979, New York, New York*

Having released the first album, they were back in the studio again two months later making second album *Real to Real Cacophony*, which is sensational. It was experimental sounding and quirky, unusual, just very different from the first. They shook off all their early influences and discovered themselves, finding their unique sound, the sound of Simple Minds. The record company's head of marketing, a commercially-minded guy, really didn't like it. You could just tell from their faces they didn't know how to promote it.

We had allies in the music papers with *Melody Maker*, *Sounds* and

*Photo Ian Cossar*

*NME* in particular, with Paul Morley. They had picked up on the band live and began to like them. The more hip, more aware journalists liked it. John Peel, who quite liked the first album but wasn't raving about it, fell in love with it. He started to play it a lot.

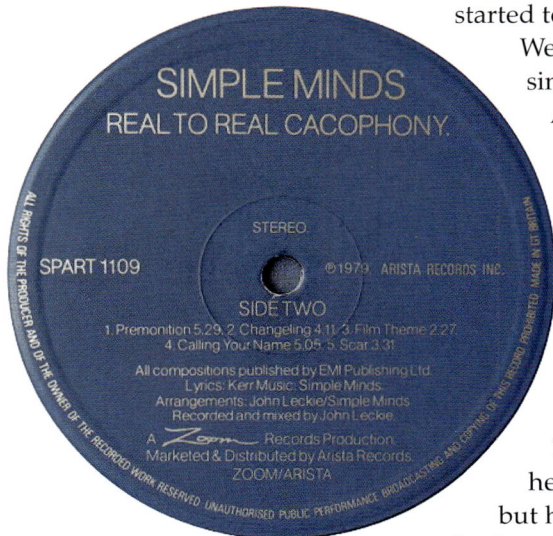

We couldn't get British television and didn't have a hit single so no *Top of the Pops*. I got in touch with Mike Appleton, who said, 'Unfortunately Bruce, I'm in America filming the Average White Band for a month when it comes out. If the band were in America in New York on such-and-such a weekend I'd take some time off, because I'd love to film them.'

There was a girl called Ruth Polski, an American New Yorker who loved English new wave music artists. Ruth said she could get them a gig at Hurrah's, New York. I said to Charles Levison at Arista, 'Look, if we were in New York, we should get *The Old Grey Whistle Test*'. I should give Arista credit here. I thought they were awful at marketing the band, but he said, 'I'll give you the money to go,' we worked a budget out and I flew over with the band.

They filmed three songs: 'Premonition', 'Changeling' and 'Factory'. I tried to get Clive Davis to come along and see them. He wouldn't even meet with me. Bastard. He sneaked in and out again without making his presence felt to the band. They did nothing for the band in America. But *The Old Grey Whistle Test* filmed us, it went out in the UK and we really began to take off. The record completely stiffed and didn't sell in quantities enough to get it into the top 20. And it was quite frustrating because it was obvious the band were building a real following. We were beginning to play to 500 - 1,000 people a night and getting biggish tours.

---

## BILLY SLOAN

It was filmed for *The Old Grey Whistle Test* and you suddenly see guys from Toryglen in Glasgow in the hippest club in Manhattan on *Whistle Test*. It was fucking mind-blowing. Again, Jim looked the nervous kinda guy who looked like he'd been beamed down from outer space. But it remains one of the best *Whistle Test* performances I've ever seen.

---

## MICK MACNEIL

We were doing the first ever gig in New York for *The Old Grey Whistle Test*. We just went over there with a couple of shows booked. It was difficult to haul all the equipment so we decided it would be cheaper and easier to rent what we needed. We gave them this spec of requirements and I was quite fussy in what equipment I wanted to play. We turned up and there was none of the stuff I requested. All I had was a CS-80. I didn't know how to work it. We had one day's rehearsal with it until the live TV show and I did the best I could. On that particular recording, I sang backing vocals, which I dreaded; I managed to convince our manager Bruce to give me the tape back to Glasgow from New York so I could fix the keyboards in the studio. I can't believe they trusted me. There were no tracks left so I had to wipe my backing vocals to put down keyboards. I think I wiped the CS-80 too and put down my silly keyboards.

## THOMAS 'BUBBA' LÖVKVIST

*Errol's*
*27 October 1979, Gothenburg, Sweden*

There was a radio programme in Sweden in 1979 called *The Record Mirror* that played popular music, when only state radio existed and having a radio programme that only dealt with popular music was always controversial. They played 'I Travel' and it hit me like a cannonball. That autumn I saw them play live at a small nightclub in Gothenburg. I have followed them ever since and this great band are like a family member to me, always in my heart and soul.

## EDDIE CAIRNS

*University of Stirling*
*15 November 1979, Stirling, Scotland*

In 1979 I finished with Rosetta Stone and was working as resident sound engineer in a bar in Edinburgh – Eric Brown's – when Dougie asked me to help out at a rehearsal for Simple Minds at the Odeon in Edinburgh and, after that, I joined the crew, starting in University of Stirling doing the monitor mix, which Big Dougie later made his speciality. The crew at that time consisted of the two Dougies, Billy Wharton (road/tour manager and sound), Jaine Henderson and myself.

From Stirling I did the next few gigs up to Keele University. If I remember rightly, once we finished that gig we got back to the hotel, which was right next to the motorway, and the band decided they all wanted to go home, there and then. So I had to drive them! God knows how I made it and whom I stayed with when we arrived but I was completely knackered. I got them home safe though, and then it was back to the day job at Eric's. I was then basically on call as one of their roadies.

## ANDREW BALL

I saw them support Magazine at the Theatre Royal in London and bought 'Chelsea Girl' and 'Life in a Day' but never really followed them further. I was glad to see their success. Bruce Foxton of The Jam was there and we got the same train home.

## GARETH EVANS

I saw them play K Block at Horsham (University of East Anglia) in late 1979. The tickets were free, as were the tickets for two U2 performances that took place a year or so later. Simple Minds were unbearably loud.

## RICHARD JOBSON

*Theatre de Palace*
*12 January 1980, Paris, France*

I went to see them in Paris. It was their first Paris gig. I got on stage and sang with them that night. They did 'Street Hassle' by Lou Reed as an encore and I shared the mic with Jim. We sang it together. It was great. Jim was very focused on where the band was going. I always knew that about him. I remember going out for some big grand dinner with the record label after that Paris gig. We were sitting having dinner and Jim got stuck next to me. He didn't want to be next to me. He wanted to be next to the Parisian record executives because he wanted to talk to them about what the band was. So there was a business thing going on with him that was pretty sharp.

At the time I was living in Berlin. And I speak German. Jim, for some unknown reason, started calling me Herman the German. I missed them when they came to Berlin but I went to see them in Brussels when they played there. Then, by the nature of things and living in a different country, we just started to go in different directions.

I didn't see them very much after that. My whole life was very transient at the time. I just wanted to go and explore different things. My girlfriend died in Berlin so I came back via Brussels for a while and then back to the UK.

By that time, they had happened. They were off to America and playing bigger venues. It was going to be big. I wasn't sure about the stadium part of Simple Minds. I've such fond memories of the early days and them playing smaller venues. The music to me was a little more interesting lyrically and had a different kind of dynamic. They went down that U2 route without being U2. U2 were a very specific band to that era that could very easily adjust to stadia. I wasn't quite sure about Simple Minds doing that. I think the last time I saw them was when they played Milton Keynes. It wasn't for me. It was pouring with rain. It just felt wrong. I was never a big fan of stadium rock.

Simple Minds had much better-looking women at their shows than the Skids, who were much more a boys' band. We never really attract women. We played Newcastle recently. It was an amazing gig and the promoter came backstage. He hadn't seen us since we were kids. He was really blown away and said, 'You must feel like David Cassidy. There's about 600 people at the stage door waiting to meet you.' I went, 'Really?' He said, 'Yeah, they won't go unless you come out.' I went, 'Wow! How many of them are women?' He went: 'None!' It was 600 fat bald blokes from Newcastle! Simple Minds always attracted quite attractive girls.

---

# EDDIE CAIRNS

## *YMCA*
## *23 February 1980, London, England*

I think the next gig was Stirling Uni in February 1980 and, after that, my job was backline, drums and driver for the band. I remember I got the train through to Glasgow and was met by Brian and we set off to pick up the band and go to London for the YMCA gig, then on to Europe.

The band had very kindly got together between the last gig and my picking them up to make a nice little welcome tape for me. As we were heading down the A74, Jim asked me to put on a tape. They were all in the back of the minibus and were having a chat. The tape had some Beatles tracks on it and, all of a sudden, there was this conversation over the music which started off along the lines of, 'Who is that baldy bastard that's driving anyway?' with a reply of 'I don't know but if he doesn't watch out he'll be getting a clip round the ear' (or words to that effect) and so it continued for at least a good few minutes, with many insults and threats. Although I knew them I honestly didn't know where to put my face that day until I got up the courage to look in the rear view mirror to find the lot of them almost pissing themselves with laughter at the look on my face. Bastards one and all – but it certainly broke the ice!

When we got to London we checked into the hotel and some of us went out for a bite to eat – Jim, Charlie, Mick and I think Big D was there. On the way back we were walking towards the hotel and a couple of lads were coming the other way, all dressed up for a good night out, when all of a sudden two buckets of water hit them right between the eyes – an absolute bull's eye. I had seen something out of the corner of my eye and looked up and – guess who? Brian and Derek. The poor guys were soaking wet and mad as hell and wanted to kill. Of course, muggins here had to say it couldn't have been our crowd as the window they thought the water had come from was mine and I couldn't have done it because I was watching it happen, it must have been some other rotters. Anyway, they left and, needless to say, we found Brian and Dan almost pissing themselves with laughter.

---

## ROSS STAPLETON

*Simple Minds' original Virgin publicist*
*Lyceum Ballroom*
*24 February 1980, London, England*

It might be a cliché: 'I remember it like it was only yesterday.' You want time and place? Easy! Fashionable West Berlin nightclub, around 1am, Saturday, 2 February 1980. Two days before I had been in the surreal Iron Curtain world of East Berlin to see Tangerine Dream, the first western rock band officially invited to play a concert 'over there'.

Now more agreeably ensconced on the other side of the wall and lubricated by doubles of some of Scotland's finest, it was another export that was about to rock my world. The club is wall-to-wall leather and über-chic. It's also vampire dark and the house music is in synch with all this. With me is Richard Jobson (Skids) and Dave McCullough (*Sounds* journalist), who accompanied me to see history made at the Palast der Republik, East Berlin.

As I'm drowning in Scotch along with Jobson's thick brogue, suddenly I'm breaking away from conversation, instead responding to some incandescent super-fresh sound of illumination. Listening to this big rumbling bass, the clever clicks of drumsticks, fiendishly ghostlike keyboard squiggles. But best of all are the beguiling, stabbing guitar flourishes. Then it relaxes a notch as the song seeks space for the vocal as it sings of 'original sin'. I am mesmerised by all these elements. What is this brilliantly controlled intensity? Who are these dudes? I'm massively impressed.

Jobson immediately puts me right. 'Yeah, Simple Minds... they're brilliant... and they're Scots,' he says with a typically extravagant Celtic pride. 'Premonition'... how apt. No other song could so perfectly encapsulate for me all that would follow. While not a Blues Brother Jake-like mission from God, I was entranced in my mission! First thing Monday morning I legged it less than two blocks from Virgin Records' label HQ off Portobello Road to Rough Trade to get my hands on *Real to Real Cacophony*. A brooding beast of a record, it was everything and more that I had been anticipating.

Three weeks later I was at the Lyceum bursting to see them live and kicking. Less than a week later at the same venue, I saw Joy Division and Killing Joke (contenders as next big thing) swell the ranks of the hugely-overrated... to me at least.

Conversely, Simple Minds didn't just play a blinder and give me an updated definition of live greatness, until then defined for me by Television with Tom Verlaine at Hammersmith Odeon in 1977, Talking Heads in '79, or Australia's The Angels. But to this day, without a second thought, when Jim Kerr and band unleashed and cranked up 'Celebrate' that night, it remains one of the transcendent moments of my life.

Thereafter our paths were destined to cross because nothing could shake me from the realisation that I had just seen the greatest live band in the UK, if not the world. Before the year was out, by hook or by crook, I would be plotting how to get them signed to Virgin. And despite the many obstacles and lots of serendipity, it came to pass as if preordained.

Well into the recording of what would become *Sons and Fascination/Sisters Feeling Call*, Jim popped his head into my office one morning and said he had a great idea for the as yet untitled album's name. 'Let's call it... are you ready for this? 'Fucking Brilliant'!'

That was Jim, the effervescent cheeky, irreverent Glaswegian, not the egoist. But it sure as shit captured the essence of what was to come. From Berlin to the Strand, Glasgow to Hammersmith Odeon, Futurama '81, first WOMAD '82 and all the way to venues around Australia, for almost four decades they've never been anything to me other than fucking brilliant.

## EDDIE CAIRNS

*March Musikhalle*
*24 March 1980, Hamburg, West Germany*

Europe went well, even though we had to get another minibus as our first one broke down in Paris, and continued with a left-hand drive unit. That was weird and a first for me. They put us into a holiday camp in Holland for the duration of the Dutch leg of the tour, which was an education. We had two houses and it was chaos all the time!

We played some very strange places that leg. In Groningen we were told to help ourselves to some new beer (to us) and filled the sleeper cab of the truck with Grolsch.

I think we were meant to be coming home after the Dutch jaunt but were told to go and support Gary Numan on his European tour – that was different but there was one really funny part right at the start. When we were in Amsterdam, Dan had met this young lady and they had become good friends. When we got to Hamburg for the first Numan gig, the first person Dan sees is this young lady so he goes over to her, thinking she had come to see him. No chance! She met Numan in Amsterdam after we left and had brought her along as his friend for the rest of the tour. Poor Dan didn't know where to look, so got pissed!

## CRAIG BUCHAN, AGE 14

*Ruffles*
*1 May 1980, Aberdeen, Scotland*

In 1980, Simple Minds were playing Ruffles Nightclub. One of my mates and I skived off school. We were only 14 and headed into Aberdeen from Dyce. We managed to get into Ruffles in the afternoon, just as the soundcheck was finishing. After a quick intro from a manager we got to meet Jim, Charlie, Derek, Brian and Mick, ending up with a swag of goodies, plectrums from Charlie and Derek and drumsticks from Brian. I also remember a button badge from Zoom, like a ying/yang or china face mask-type thing, then an autographed poster of the band standing on a beach by those wooden breakers. I remember Charlie sported a snazzy paisley-pattern scarf in that poster. The band then played some pool in the area upstairs.

They tried to get us on to the guestlist but Ruffles was having none of it as it was over-18s. We didn't even look close to it. I had to wait until 1982 and the New Gold Tour at the Capitol in Aberdeen, where I think China Crisis were the support, and then 1985 down at Barrowland.

I moved to New Zealand. All going to plan, I will see Simple Minds again in Wellington. I'm so looking forward to it.

# BRUCE FINDLAY

## 'I Travel' released 1 September 1980

The record company were aware we were becoming talked about and were hot, particularly as a live act, but weren't selling the numbers of records required. New artists were beginning to get picked up and break through, like Spandau Ballet and Duran Duran, and others were beginning to happen. Simple Minds still weren't selling records in the numbers required. We were in debt to the record company to the tune of £150,000 but they were reluctant to drop us, so they said, 'Make a third album.'

Within two years, the band made three albums and recorded the third album for Zoom, *Empires and Dance*. To me, it was more like a mixture of the first album with one or two great, catchier tunes but all of the new elements of *Real to Real Cacophony*, with the sound of Simple Minds. Driving, rhythmic, dance sounds. This was the beginning of a new dance scene where people were doing 12-inch remix singles, extended six and seven-minute-long tracks which were great in clubs.

'I Travel' was the first choice from the album and it was a classic. DJs Peter Powell, Kid Jensen and John Peel all played it, al the good record papers picking up on the band as one of the most exciting of the time. Yet we were still not making the charts. Arista screwed up on the 12-inch remix, which was selling prolifically. They only pressed 1,000 or 2,000 copies, which sold out in the first week, and couldn't get more done. I believe they had to get them pressed in France and were slow on the uptake. Our record company were not prepared for Simple Minds taking off. I really fell out with them big time. The record did not do the business again.

To me, it should have been a smash. It should have been a top-five album and we should have had two or three hits off it. We weren't looking for No.1-type hits. They weren't making that kind of music. But a single was a way to get an album sold, for a band to be heard by the mainstream and the main body of the population. A Top-20 hit would have been more than perfect.

At the end of that period, we were really falling out with the record company. Their marketing was crap. They didn't understand the band, giving away free Showaddywaddy t-shirts with the album and thinking it was a great ploy. I was like, 'Why don't you make Simple Minds fucking t-shirts, you arseholes? What are you trying to do to ma boys? It's terrible.'

---

## BRUCE FINDLAY

*Peter Gabriel Tour*
*September/October 1980*

I met the band in mid-'78 and by 1980 they'd released three albums, been to America, toured Britain four or five times and toured Europe. On the last album of the Zoom/Arista deal, we were struggling. We'd been into Europe a couple of times and the distribution company for Arista in Europe was Ariola, who picked up on the band and quite liked them.

Peter Gabriel had also picked up on the band and fell in love with them. Peter was famous for hearing new acts and getting them out as his support act, giving bands a break. He got in touch with the record company and said, 'I'd love to have Simple Minds on my big European tour.' He was doing arenas, or residencies like five nights at Paris Olympia. Now Peter Gabriel is God-like. We love Peter Gabriel. The record company were on the verge of dropping us and were really confused because we were one of the hottest bands in the world now, but still not selling records. They said they'd give us some money, but we had to find the rest ourselves. I got in touch with Ariola and they in turn put up more of the shortfall. I got in touch with Peter as well, because you got 50 quid a night as the support act. He said, 'I'll persuade our promoters to give you 500 quid a night', which was a big boost in terms of costings. So, we got a really good support act fee and Ariola put up the rest of the cash we needed.

What a tour that was. It was sensational. Peter was a joy to work with. He watched the band every single night and came in and talked to them afterwards. You know, he really encouraged them. He was just terrific. That *Empires and Dance* tour of Europe gave us the confidence that we were happening. It still didn't break us through as a commercial act and we managed to persuade Arista to let us go. We guaranteed that our royalty stream from the first few albums with whoever we went to would be redirected to them to pay off the debt. That was the only way to get out of the deal.

---

*Simple Minds in Berlin, September 1980. Photos Ronnie Gurr*

# RONNIE GURR

*Berlin*
*3 September 1980, West Germany*

We remained friends and I wrote about them, then after I left *Record Mirror*, I got a job at Arista Records and they were on the third album by that time. The last job I did for *Record Mirror* was when I did the photos from Berlin, when they were on the Peter Gabriel tour. Bizarrely, the photo that isn't included in that is a portrait I did of Jim. The way music newspapers were laid out, before computers, was very Dickensian. We used to get a slide and a projector and project it onto a piece of paper taped to a wall and you'd move the projector to the size of the paper then sketch what was going on the front cover. I'd done a shot of Jim in the dressing room on that trip, my favourite photo, I'm not a photographer, I hasten to add. Those photos were taken on a cheap Nikon I was given on my 21st birthday and I was just trying it out. I found those photos three years ago and there's just an atmosphere. Jim actually ordered two huge prints for himself and Charlie last year for his 60th birthday.

It was a great day, taking those photos in Berlin, because we'd had the day off on the Peter Gabriel tour. We'd driven from Düsseldorf or maybe Hamburg to Berlin, so we'd driven through East Germany and that was just a revelation. Jim said he looks at those photos and it's like a dream, you know. 'Was that real? Were we really there?' Then the photos just bring it back. That shot in the wasteland is actually… I mean Wim Wenders' *Wings of Desire* was shot there. It was part of their discovering Europe, you know, young Scottish boys discovering the world. John Leckie, the producer, was there and had a car that we went through east Berlin, which was bizarre, because they timed you as you entered this bit and if you got to Berlin too soon, they fined you for speeding. And if you got there too late you were questioned: 'Why did you get there so late?' The exits to the motorways had tanks on them, it was a really intimidating time. So we went to a bar and quickly realised we could sit in that bar for about three months and not spend all the money we'd changed. Again, they pitched it so you had West German money and you couldn't take East German money back, so they made money both ways. I think there's a photo of Charlie playing a kid's toy saxophone - about

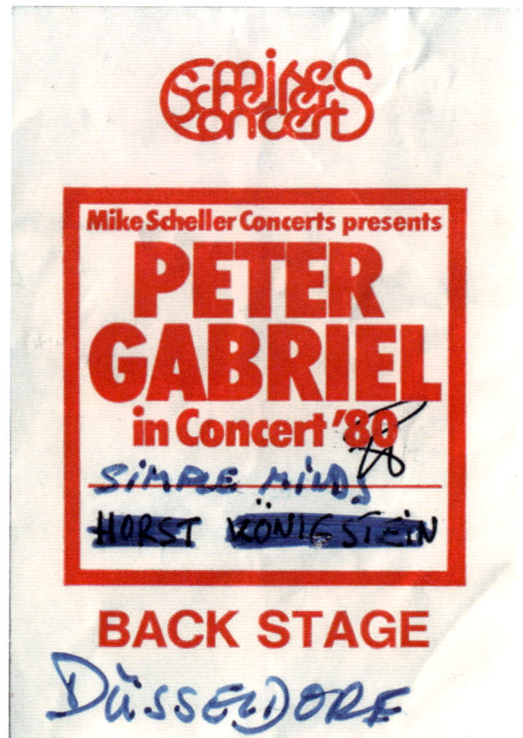

the only thing we could buy at the big department store. The window display had catering-sized jars of pickles in a pyramid.

I remember it was a scorching hot day, and we came back and got pulled up by the East German-Russian troops at the checkpoint. They asked us to open the boot and it stuck - we literally couldn't get it open. We'd had a few drinks and it got laughable. They just left us to swelter for over an hour. It was like we weren't going anywhere until we opened the boot of that car, kicking the shit out of this rental car trying to get it open.

---

## EDDIE CAIRNS

*Olympia*
*9 – 13 September 1980, Paris, France*

On the Peter Gabriel tour we were in a hotel in Paris when some of the band (guess who?) went on the hunt for me and, again, got the wrong room. In fact they got the wrong floor. They found that the doors were open, with nobody in there. Seemingly the whole floor had been set aside for a delegation or something, and they decided to help themselves to the contents of the mini-bars of most of the rooms. They found a cleaner's cupboard and filled plastic bags with their treasure then came and found me to open the minibus so they could put their ill-gotten booty in the storage space under the front seats. When we handed the minibus back, it went back still with some miniatures in the storage trays. We did drink well on that tour!

There's also the night we were coming away from a gig somewhere in Europe. It might have been Holland. Wee D was driving the truck, we were following him. He took a tight corner and clipped a car mirror, managing to damage it. He probably didn't even know he'd done it but this guy on roller-skates saw and started shouting at the truck and, when it didn't stop, set off in hot pursuit. We were in the minibus at the back of him, killing ourselves laughing. He followed us all the way to the hotel and was serious about calling the police. He was doubled over, out of breath, trying to tell the hotel management what had happened. He must have chased the truck for about five miles.

'The Offenbach Arabs' were a surly pair who appeared a few times on tour and consisted of two pissed band members (I will let you guess who) carrying buckets of water and dressed with towels over their heads, their underpants keeping the towels on. Water and pissed band members make a terrible combination! Offenbach was the first time they appeared and how they got the name. They decided they were going to drench me and came to knock on my door, then threw the buckets of water over me when I opened the door. But the stupid buggers got the wrong room and soaked some poor German hotel guest. All he could report was that two naked Arabs had knocked on his door and soaked him when he answered. He could tell they were Arabs because of the head-dress they were wearing. This of course was a total mystery to the hotel - there were no Arabs staying in the hotel that night!

The second time was during the Peter Gabriel tour when the band and crew were taken out by the record company. I stayed behind to keep the fan club secretary company. We were in my room and they didn't need to knock on the door that time. Big D let them in and they soaked her, and my bed. Bastards!

We then set off on the last tour I did with the band throughout Britain, starting in Kidderminster – the only time I saw Charlie lose it, completely and utterly. Some guys were doing the spitting thing and I asked the security to stop them. They did nothing about it and I just climbed back up onto the side of the stage when I turned and saw Charlie ripping his guitar off and leaping into the crowd. Guess who had to sort it out and take the punches from the idiots and the security. I managed to drag Charlie to the dressing room before being told the security wanted a part of me for pushing one of them over. It certainly was a different start to the tour.

I finished the *Empires and Dance* tour and took them and their gear to some rehearsal studios but, sadly, Brian left and the replacement had their own roadie, who he wanted to come along, so I moved to London and started work with a PA hire company, got some record company work and was on tour in Europe with another band when, as far as I was told after, a call for me to join Simple Minds again came through – too late for me to do so, but Big D carried on with them until his death.

Wee Dougie moved on and Billy was getting beyond control at the end. I was pleased he'd been removed - he was becoming a threat to himself and the band. When we were on the Peter Gabriel tour it wasn't just a few occasions that he took a full bottle of brandy with him to the mixing desk for the show and it didn't come back. He was losing it big time. Last time I saw him he had got himself together somewhat and was either married or living with a lady. I assume it was drink, drugs or both that contributed to his death. Johnny Ramsay took over after that and did a great job.

I am so proud to have been there at the beginning and seen them through some difficult times, and times where they were learning about their music and themselves. Pity it couldn't carry on but there are some wonderful memories that nobody can take away of some really great guys that were so inspirational to me and others around them.

# GEORGE DE BONO

I got my first taste via the *Empires and Dance* album on frequent play in the La Trobe University Record Store in Melbourne, Victoria. Having almost worn the grooves out, I did the same with *Life in a Day* and *Real to Real Cacophony*.

## RONNIE GURR

*Hammersmith Odeon*
*21 October 1980, London, England*

I took Jim and Charlie to see the Skids at Hammersmith Odeon because they were the first of the Scottish bands to get to that level. Hammersmith Odeon used to have the hot dogs and the sweet counter as you went in, and there was Stuart Adamson in the queue to buy sweets. I said, 'What are you doing?' and he said he wanted to buy a Mars Bar and a Twix. I said, 'But you're headlining', and he said, 'Yeah but I'm not gonna go and ask someone to buy me sweets for me.' When Stuart passed, Jim remembered that as a mark of his humbleness.

## IAN MACCONNACHIE

*Odeon Theatre*
*31 October 1980, Edinburgh,*
*Scotland*

16 years old on a school night. I had to get the number 12 bus, which seemed to take forever. Once there I never forgot what I saw. The band were incredible. 40 years later the hairs on my arms still stand on end when I hear their music.

## ALISON COLLINS

*City Halls*
*5 November 1980, Glasgow, Scotland*

As a 16-year-old in Glasgow, Billy Sloan's show on Radio Clyde was essential listening. I remember hearing 'Changeling' many times but didn't pick up on who the band was. I was fortunate to have a schoolfriend regularly introducing me to new music. He said I had to come with him to see this really cool band. Not only was I then introduced to much of the

*Alison Collins saw the Minds at Glasgow's City Halls*

*Empires and Dance* album, but they played 'Changeling'. That was the start of being a lifetime fan and I was at every Glasgow show until the mid-'80s when I moved away, including the legendary Tiffany's residency and their first show at the Apollo. I've gone on to see the band many times over the years and was especially delighted to attend the *5x5* show at London's Roundhouse.

I also remember being gobsmacked one evening on the train home from Glasgow Central to see JK get on our carriage. As a giddy teen fan, my friends encouraged me to go and say hello. He was of course charming and gave us a little wave as he got off at his stop! I also met Jim and Charlie in the mid-'90s at Madrid airport. I was with my husband and parents. My dear Mum, being a typical chatty Glaswegian, proceeded to tell them stories about all the nights I'd kept her up late while I was out seeing the band. I remember Jim and Charlie both laughing hysterically and me feeling rather embarrassed rather than the cool fan I wanted to appear.

I dragged my daughter along to a concert at Wembley about 10 years ago when she was a young teen. Afterwards I asked her if she enjoyed the show, which she seemed to at the time. 'Oh yes,' she said, 'it was great and I particularly like the Mary song.' 'Mary song?' I thought. Then a few moments later it came to me – 'The American'!

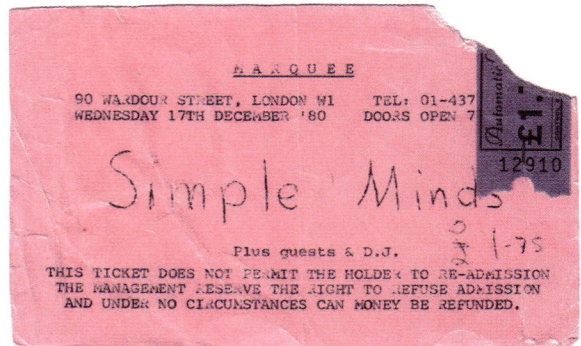

## STEVE ROSEN

In 1981 I met a witty, and already infamous young soundman named Frank Gallagher, while working in a NYC recording studio. Not long afterwards, he asked if I'd be interested in doing backline for a band that was coming in from Glasgow for a tour across Canada, and then down the west coast to LA. He said they'd be heading to Australia from there, but he just needed someone for the North American dates. I had some studio experience, and knew my way around guitars, but I'd never been on the road, so I told him I'd like to go, but had no experience, and I recall him saying something like, "aye wee man, they're a great band, but they don't have the budget for someone more experienced, and besides any fucking idiot can do this gig, so you'll be perfect". Ironically he turned out to be right.

So, we gathered up some worn out rental gear, and found a vacant auto repair shop in the village to set up and rehearse, and that's where I met the Simple Minds for the first time. They were young, and looked a little trendy, but they weren't bothered at all by the smell of stale oil, or the scruffy gear. They just seemed happy to be there, and once we fired up the gear, I was happy to be there too, although it took some time before I could understand a word they said.

Part of my job was to drive the gear to the next venue after each show, and Canada is just a few specs of civilization, separated by vast expanses of wasteland, so it was a relief when Jim decided to drive in the truck, instead of travelling with the band for some gigs. I guess he wanted to see what Canada was like. I could have told him, but I was afraid he wouldn't have gone.

When we got to LA, Gallagher announced that he had an emergency back in NY, and he couldn't go to Australia, so it was off to Sydney, with a crew of one, and three whole weeks of experience under my belt. Turns out Simple Minds were huge stars in Oz, and we were supporting Icehouse, one of the biggest bands in the country at that time. So it was quite a ride for my first tour, but we had a very tight budget, and Scotsmen aren't know for their lavish spending to begin with, so Jim, Bruce Findlay, the band's manager, and I all shared one small room in a Bondi Beach flea bag hotel, with three beds across and barely any space between. Looked a little like a hospital ward in a developing country. But, the truth is, I probably never had a better time, and if I could, I'd do it all over again.

Working with Jim and Charlie never felt much like a job. They were as great offstage as on, and when the band wasn't playing, we spent most of our time taking the piss out of each other and laughing like a pack of unruly kids. So it came as no surprise that when Gallagher and I went to see them play in New Orleans recently, not much had really changed. The band was near perfect, Jim and Charlie sounded better than ever, and they just tore it up for hours.

Later that night I recall Jim jokingly saying that he "might still have some growing up to do", and I remember thinking to myself; yeah man, I sure as hell hope so because whatever you've been doing is working just fine.

---

# GEORGE PORTER

*Edinburgh Nite Club*
*31 December 1980 & 1 January 1981, Edinburgh, Scotland*

1980 saw Scotland's modern industrial history being systematically dismantled by Thatcherism. No jobs and what seemed like a bleak future for a 16-year-old George Porter. That was the backdrop to my introduction to Simple Minds. The arpeggiated intro to 'I Travel' hypnotised me like a moth to a flame. I was a boy about to enter a man's world.

Simple Minds became my escapism, my own private swimming pool that resided in my mind and on the turntable in my bedroom. I dived straight into the deep end with *Empires and Dance*. 'This Fear of Gods' was sublime. However, *New Gold Dream* will always be my most treasured album. It's just so complete and is the music on which I test every new car, home and hi-fi equipment I've ever had since. I've had many brilliant experiences from being a Simple Minds fan and met so many great friends along the way.

My first live gig was Edinburgh Niteclub in 1981. I've seen every tour since, but one gig sticks out more than others; the *Acoustic* show at Hackney Empire. Maria and I were a bit skint and could only afford seats in the gods of this beautiful venue. Once seated, we could see the stage. That was going to be good enough for us both. However, this woman appeared with a torch and invited a few of us down to the front row to watch the show. We couldn't believe our luck... was it luck, or Jim and Charlie's plan all along? To this day I don't know. I've been travelling with the band since 1980. Everything is possible.

---

# BRUCE FINDLAY

## *Signing to Virgin Records*
## *February 1981*

By this time, I had become their manager, officially. We managed to persuade Arista to let us go. I already had several other record companies chasing for the band - EMI, Polydor and Virgin. So I negotiated a new deal with Simon Draper and Virgin Records.

The first two years were remarkable. The band made three albums and toured Britain and Europe prolifically, building up a massive head of steam. We signed to Virgin and recorded two albums at once. Right off, we never wanted to call it a double-album. Double-albums were for progressive rock bands of the mid-'70s. We didn't want to be seen as dinosaurs. We called it a twin-album and released it as a package, which was unusual in those days. Then we split the album and sold them independently of each other. Well, that was the other thing, they'd made the first three albums with John Leckie.

When we went to Virgin, Simon Draper said, 'John Leckie's wonderful and you've done really well, but you've not had a hit yet. Maybe you should think about working with a different producer.' A few people were suggested, including Steve Hillage, of all people. The band called him Cabbage Head.

I'd worked with him ten years earlier with Gong, who were nothing like Simple Minds, except they were different from the other artists around at the time. It was a marriage in heaven. I thought he was a great choice, although very unusual because he was 'old but new' school. He was a hippy.

I think *Sons and Fascination* is my favourite Simple Minds album. *Sons and Fascination/Sister Feelings Call* finally broke through. They didn't have a hit single on the album. Although there were some great tracks they were still struggling to get daytime airplay, but the album charted reasonably high. If we'd released it as a single album rather than the twin-pack, which cost more money, I think we would have had a top-10 album. As it happened, we made the top 20, it broke the band through and again we became the darlings of the media.

---

## MICHELE GAROFALO

I discovered the Minds thanks to my father, a Genesis lover and devoted Peter Gabriel fan. He bought *Empires and Dance*, probably because he was fascinated by some article in which Gabriel promoted their music. Then Jim and his partners opened for Gabriel in Europe.

The first sound literally tattooed in my DNA was the MacNeil synth line in 'I Travel'. I was seven, it was an autumn evening and the notes came out of the speakers of a Grundig stereo from the early Seventies. I was paralysed. Those sounds terrified me and at the same time had a powerful evocative charge. I found everything very sexy, dark and mysterious. It all started like this.

---

## RONNIE GURR

*February 1981*

I found myself doing the press at Arista, when they were on the third album, and it was great because I was doing the PR. But it became fairly obvious that Arista were about to drop them. The hippest label when I was a journalist was Virgin and I was really good pals with the people there, because we'd go and have a drink with them on a Friday night.

There's photos of me at the Simple Minds signing at Virgin in Simon Draper's office, as I kind of gave Virgin the tip-off that they were about to be dropped. I think there were other discussions going on - obviously Bruce was talking to people - but I know I told Keith and Ross in the Virgin press office. That was the first heads-up they knew that Simple Minds were gonna be out of contract fairly soon. I think they signed August/September and I went and joined the press office in Virgin the following March. So, we kinda moved alongside each other and I've just been friends with them since.

There's the band, Simon Draper and Bruce and I in Simon's office in Virgin. Not what you expect from the office, but that's why they signed to Virgin, because we were a very different company. It was great to see them develop. Arista did quite well from the three albums but not well enough to pick up the fourth, it was too expensive. Virgin took them to new heights.

There are photos of me and Jim mucking about at the signing. For some reason we've got paper cups in our mouths, like fake noses. I think we were pretending to be Jimmy Durante.

---

# SIMON DRAPER

*Signed Simple Minds to Virgin Records*
*February 1981*

Recently I was reminded that Bruce Findlay came to see me in 1980 and wanted to license Zoom to Virgin. At the time, he had quite a good relationship with The Waterboys and Mike Scott, who we were trying to sign anyway, and he came and spoke to me about Simple Minds. I was very involved in Magazine and I'd seen Simple Minds supporting Magazine and thought they were competing with each other. We were already committed to Magazine, who I have the greatest admiration for, so I wasn't that keen to sign Simple Minds. But in the following years there was a huge increase in support of Simple Minds as a result of all their touring. Also, the records were getting better, and they were lucky enough to have a hit with 'I Travel'. We started getting retail shops approach us, saying, 'You know, this band is about to happen,' so it forced me to go back and re-evaluate really. I can't remember who else wanted to sign them. But I put a lot of effort into securing a deal and took a bit of a risk because Steve Hillage had been with Gong, who I signed in '73. Steve Lewis was my deputy-managing director at the time and was managing Steve Hillage. I'd used him to produce a guy called Ken Lockie who'd been involved with Public Image Ltd and was in a band called Cowboys International.

I know they heard the stuff Steve Hillage was producing, because he was working with Ken Lockie. That was my kinda trump card, I thought Steve Hillage would be perfect for them. Luckily, they thought it was a good idea. I think the album they made with him was one of the best they ever made.

The big thing was to try and break them in the States, because they were happening everywhere else. So when they got to Jimmy Iovine and Bob Clearmountain for *Once Upon a Time*, they were starting to play big venues. That was the start of the music becoming more bombastic, and they played an inordinate amount of times on stage. I started to be bored with it. They played endless encores, playing for hours, and it was stadium rock. They were still making great records, 'Belfast Child' and all that, but personally the first two albums for Virgin – *Sons and Fascination* and *New Gold Dream* - were the best.

Jim has a lot of charisma as a vocalist and performer. That coupled with everything else about them, they had the recipe for big success. I don't know how big they ever were in America. I read in the newspaper recently that they still feel a bit funny about doing that song from *The Breakfast Club* ('Don't You (Forget About Me)'). We had to really twist their arms to get them to do it, but I could see why they didn't wanna do it. If they'd have been told, which I don't think they were at the time, Bryan Ferry had turned it down they might have dug their heels in, but that broke them in the States. I think it was a No.1 there.

---

## SEAN EGAN

*The Venue*
*3 March 1981, Victoria, England*

I recall hearing 'I Travel' in a club in 1980 in London. I asked the DJ who it was. He said the name and my life changed. I went out over the next few weeks and bought all the albums and singles. I saw them live on my birthday at the now-defunct Venue in Victoria, London. What an 18th birthday present!

I saw every tour I could, even going to Germany in 1984 and Belgium in 1985. I even met the group in 1986 at a record store signing in the Virgin Megastore, London - what a nice group of people, so charming. I look forward to every release. They're always new and full of energy.

---

## MALCOLM GARRETT

*Simple Minds designer, 1981 to 1989*
*September 1981*

I went to university in Reading for a year then transferred to Manchester Poly from 1975 to '78, the glory years of punk. My life changed forever. A student in the year above me, Linda, was an illustrator. She started to do some handbills and things for Buzzcocks but realised she didn't want to be a designer. She suggested they work with me and we did the first sleeve, 'Orgasm Addict', together. I did four single sleeves and an album sleeve for them. Then Howard (Devoto) left Buzzcocks and formed Magazine and I introduced my flatmate, John McGurk, to Howard. Then I did record sleeves for Magazine, so I had quite a healthy portfolio by the time I graduated in 1978.

I'd seen Simple Minds at the Lyceum when they supported Magazine on tour. Virgin signed them just as they were beginning to be become really interesting. Third album *Empires and Dance* had great tracks on it. They were really beginning to make a make a name for themselves but were notoriously camera-shy. I think they'd been in the studio with Steve Hillage and recordings were ready but they'd been keeping quiet about it. I got this call, 'We need a sleeve record by Monday.' The first sleeve was for 'The American'. There were no photographs of the band - they didn't like having their pictures taken and I was at a loss knowing what to do because I hadn't met the band and hadn't really heard the music. I don't recall them even sending me a cassette. I sat in front of a television screen with my 35mm camera and shot some images off the TV screen then used those as transparencies. If you look at the sleeve for 'The American', they've got this grainy TV screen-like feel. One of the images was of Elizabeth Taylor from *Suddenly Last Summer*. We basically used what was copyright material, but because it was off a TV screen nobody knew what it was. I did this recklessly for 'The American' and everybody liked it.

Pretty soon after we were doing 'Love Song', 'Sweat in Bullet' and the album recordings were going really well, they'd done a fantastic number of songs. It was almost enough for a double album. So they made a selection of tracks for *Sons and Fascination*, then decided they'd put the remainder of the tracks on a companion album, which Jim called *Sister Feelings Call*. But for some reason in the marketing department, they got cold feet about releasing this as a double album, deciding to release *Sister Feelings Call* as a budget album. That meant they could shrink wrap it with the 'main' album. That's why the sleeve is blue and black, because they didn't allow me for a full colour printing. This is a budget album so I can only have two colours and it had a different catalogue number. It was only later, when they realised, 'Actually, this is a great album in its own right', that they reassigned a new catalogue number for later release and made it a full price album. It was too late. The sleeve to me already looked like a budget sleeve. I had a conversation with various people who don't know that story about the quality of the sleeves, and they just thought it was a deliberate choice by me to make it that way. Had I been given full colour, I'm sure it would have been a white album sleeve and all the rest. So, my introduction to Simple Minds was very short and we just got on with one another straight away.

I went to see them wherever they were recording. I was a young, naïve, quite shy person so didn't introduce myself to Steve Hillage, even though I'd been a huge fan from when he was in Gong. I regret that to this day. But I met the band, well mainly Jim, and to a lesser extent, Charlie, because, you know, they came as a package. But Jim did most of the planning - Charlie was more interested in making the music. It's quite remarkable and something you don't really think about. Jim wasn't a musician, he didn't play anything. He just wrote words and, working with Charlie, created music.

I met Jim in the lead-up to producing artwork for *Sons and Fascination*. Virgin really wanted me to make them visible and so there was pressure from Virgin to get them on the sleeve. I'd worked quite a lot with the photographer Shelia Rock, who I met when I was at Radar. We decided we would set up, taking photographs of buildings which, incidentally, would have the band in the photos, so they were more architectural or structural, almost like the band were extras in a film scene. We were looking for some modernist, futuristic but sort of evocative and not exactly menacing but moody architecture, then to plant our five Simple-Minded protagonists in the shot. We went to the Isle of Sheppey to look at the power station and were chased by security guards.

Eventually, we got permission to film at New Covent Garden, near Vauxhall, but the only time we could shoot was at night because it was in use during the day and we wanted it dark. I think we started shooting around midnight. Sheila had this fantastic Polaroid camera which shot ten by eight Polaroid's and we saw exactly the pictures we were going to get. They've got that kind of fluid quality to them and are slower exposure. So we were able to use the lighting and long exposures to put even less emphasis than we planned on to the figures in the images. So the image on the front of *Sons and Fascination* was an eight by ten Polaroid. Some of the images on the back are just out of the building itself and were conventional kind of SX-70 type Polaroid.

Jim and Charlie are two of the most gentle, loveable people you could ever hope to meet. In 40 years of knowing Charlie, I don't think I ever saw him without a huge grin on his face. But when we were setting up for this photo-shoot at New Covent Garden, the five of them were hanging out and we were saying 'get the lights ready' and doing whatever and a couple of ne'er-do-wells showed up looking like, you know, there was going to be trouble. 'What the fuck are you guys up to?' And immediately, the whole of Simple Minds locked into gang from Glasgow mode. It was just such a surprise that somebody easy-going and mild-mannered and polite and soft-spoken as Jim could turn into that if he needed to. It was like a switch went on.

I worked with Simple Minds continuously for longer than any other band, for eight years from being introduced to them early in 1981 through to 1989, with one break where I missed this one album. Out of all of the bands I worked with between 1981 and '83, the band that got most airplay in the studio and the band I felt emotionally closest to was Simple Minds. They were important to me and to the studio. And I think we were important to Simple Minds because we managed to get them onto the album sleeve with their faces for the first time. Also, as art director for a magazine called *New Sounds, New Styles*, working with the photographer Jamie Morgan, I think we were the first to put Jim Kerr on a magazine front cover. In that short period between the middle of 1981 into the middle of 1982, we managed to get them from hiding in the shadows to the cover in a kind of easygoing manner. Back then, you wouldn't have thought he was shy and reticent. He didn't feel comfortable standing in front of cameras. It was like being a photographic model wasn't in his psyche.

# CRAIG JOHNSON

*Futurama 3, Bingley Hall*
*6 September 1981, Stafford, England*

I was there in 1978 for David Bowie's triumphant *Stage* tour. Now I was back at Stafford's Bingley Hall, a short drive from Birmingham, a Sunday in September, with Vicky H, and *this* is Futurama. Jim's perched on his microphone stand. I think there might be rungs on it, like a ladder. Whatever, he's hovering and I'm floating.

1984. I couldn't sleep a wink last night. Of course I couldn't, I was falling in love for the first time. Her name's also Vicki H (I know, incredible but true - a coincidence that's stayed with me for over 35 years). Notting Hill, London (the second great city). I'm in a flat-share on Ladbroke Square and she's just round the corner. We're both studying design and photography at Central School of Art. She has the top floor and a record player. And I have the *Sparkle in the Rain* LP.

2012. What I need on a very hot Saturday in April in a very sweaty Sister Ray Records. Is that your name on the vinyl that shaped that romance? I ask and, although you weren't meant to, you give (the instruction was you'd only be signing the new 'Theme for Great Cities' remix). It had been signed by Malcolm Garrett earlier that year, someone who played an integral part in my life and yours.

And so to *5x5* at the Roundhouse. That opening intro/montage has me grinning like a Cheshire cat. This is going to be a special night. I'm filming 'Love Song' (seems appropriate) and Jim gestures to me. And I'm floating again.

## ALLY SCOTT

*City Hall*
*21 September 1981, Newcastle,*
*England*

In 1980 I met my husband. I'm from Australia and Steve was in the Merchant Navy, working on the P&O liners sailing from Sydney. Steve is from Newcastle-upon-Tyne. By mid '81 we were married and living in Newcastle. It was a totally different experience for me but I loved it. I loved the nightlife but hated the cold,

*Ally Scott with Jim. She first saw the band in 1981*

and certainly did not want to go out on a freezing cold night to see a band I'd never heard of. But I'm so glad I did. It changed my life.

I found myself squashed, almost at the front. I had no idea where Steve was when the band came on. I was mesmerised from the first second. Here was this incredibly bendy man, with the most unreal presence, then he started to sing. Seriously, from then on I was lost! I've never to this day seen another band like them. Ever since that night I've seen them every time I could, in the UK and back in Australia. I remember the *Street Fighting Years* tour. I can honestly say in that year I played no other music in our house. I just love them. They really are the theme music to my life – the best band, my happiness music.

---

## JEAN-PIERRE LECOZ

*Hammersmith Odeon*
*25 September 1981, London, England*

When I got on the train in summer 1980 in Marseille to travel to Paris then cross the channel to England, I didn't know how my life would change. I heard 'Changeling'/'Premonition' on Radio 1, asked my older English roommate, 'Who is it? Where are they from?' and from that moment wanted to know everything I'd missed about the band.

My first concert in London in autumn 1981. I've crossed the years with the music of Simple Minds. I've succeeded against some hard moments in life by listening to their music. Listening in cars, trains, in the air, over the seas....

Then came my sons, now 26 and 25. They came with me to three concerts in 2012 and 2018 - Arles, Belfast and Carcassonne. One of my sons is a fan of 'Dolphins'. The other one is in love with 'Up on the Catwalk'.

I'm proud to have introduced friends to their music – the same age, older and younger. I've even introduced my mum and grandmother to their music. They love 'Somebody up There Likes You' and 'Rivers of Ice'!

I attended 27 gigs between 1981 and 2018 and was due to attend two more in 2020, both cancelled because of the pandemic. Every time I hear their sound it's always like the first time. A kind of 'new sunshine morning'.

---

# MIKE WILLE

*Fryfogle's*
*23 October 1981, London, Canada*

I live in Stratford, Ontario, a small city and a dead zone for music back in my youth. All you got was top-40 radio. I'd just purchased my first real stereo system and needed to pick it up from London, Ontario. I asked a friend who played bass in a band if I could score a ride and he agreed on condition that we took in a show at a club called Fryfogle's as a band called Simple Minds were playing.

That night totally changed my musical world. I just loved the show. I even got up on the dancefloor and moved to the sound, something my shy self didn't normally do. The next day I set up the new stereo system and went to the local record shops and picked up *Life in a Day* and *Sons and Fascination*. One or other of those was on the turntable for a long time.

CFNY FM out of Brampton had a *Thursday Night Live* programme featuring bands playing live in the Toronto area. I taped a Simple Minds concert. I can't count the number of times that tape was played. My favourite time to listen was on my Walkman at work while I was welding away, off in my own little world.

In September 1983, a buddy and I borrowed a car to go see Simple Minds at Massey Hall, then 45 minutes into the trip, the car shook and banged and I watched in my rear view mirror as the drive shaft bounced down the road. I pulled over and recovered it. Then along came a police car. 'Could you use a hand? Could you get a buddy to come and get you?'. We got my bass-playing buddy, who lived nearby, and at his place I called another buddy in Stratford. We made it safe and sound, just as Simple Minds took the stage.

In 2019 Simple Minds came closer to home in London, Ontario. We got VIP tickets and we were the first in line that day. I was so nervous but could not shut up. I said, 'It's come full circle. The first time I saw you was at Fryfogle's in 1981 and here we are in London in 2019.' This started a conversation with Jim and Charlie about the name of the club.

During the Q & A session that followed, Jim was talking about coming to Canada in the early days and the name of the club slipped his mind. He looked my way and I yelled out 'Fryfogle's!' Later on, Jim mentioned 1981 and said 'Fryfogle's' and we exchanged a thumbs-up. When Jim was talking with the crowd about playing in London back in 1981, he gave me a shout-out for reminding them of the name of the club. At the end, Ged Grimes came over and handed my wife one of Cherisse's drumsticks. An awesome night.

## DOUG MACLEAN

*Caribbean Sands*
*1 November 1981, Calgary, Canada*

I have an incredible memory of seeing Simple Minds live, in a small bar basement situation, in Calgary, Alberta back in the mid-1980s. It was incredible. The music was absolutely stunning for the times, and being of Scottish heritage (way back) a band from Scotland in Calgary... who'd have thought? Then to have the band so absolutely mindblowing was stunning. Since then, Simple Minds have been on my 'to see again' list. I hope it can happen in the future.

## ELLE HAYTER

*Capitol Theatre*
*13 November 1981, Sydney, Australia*

Sydney in 1980/81 were heady days for a teenage music lover. My friends and I had been listening to radio Double J (later Triple J) since 1975, discovering amazing music by independent Aussie artists and overseas imports. We were huge new wave fans; Simple Minds were our favourite along with OMD, New Order and China Crisis. Red Eye Records opened in 1981 and we'd travel into the city to buy our vinyl then make mixed reel-to-reel tapes to dance to at parties. Every weekend we watched live gigs at pub venues and locally we'd been following the Flowers (later Icehouse) and couldn't believe our luck when Simple Minds announced to tour with them in late 1981. That hooked us as lifelong fans!

Some 20 years later in New South Wales, I met Craig Evans while singing for a local theatre production. On our first date, after dinner, he asked if I'd like to listen to his favourite band and put on Simple Minds' *Live in the City of Light*. We danced all night to his collection of Simple Minds albums and watched the sunrise together. He told me 'Alive and Kicking' got him through some of the darkest times in his life. Since then we have not parted.

Together we've travelled to Sydney to see Simple Minds in 2012 and in 2017 and for many years it has been our dream to see them perform in the Teatro Antico ruins in Sicily. Scrolling through the 2020 tour dates, looking for Sydney, I randomly landed on the Taormina gig. On a whim I purchased ticket numbers 2 and 3 and we booked to stay at Villa Angela. We were thrilled to be able to spend our 15-year anniversary (and July birthdays) overseas and looking forward to adding more Simple Minds melody to the soundtrack of our love and life.

## DAVID WHITING

*Festival Hall*
*17 November 1981, Melbourne, Australia*

'First time in Melbourne,' says the bassist from a little known Scottish band. I'm here to see my favourite band, Icehouse. It's my first major concert. Icehouse had toured Europe as support for Simple Minds and now the favour was being reversed. Simple Minds were like aliens. Stylish outfits. The lead singer prowling the stage and seeking inspiration from the crowd. The guitarist hunched over his over-sized guitar, swaying along with the beat. The bassist pounding his bass as if he was looking for attention. The drummer appearing to have four arms as he kept the beat constant and fast. And at the keyboards, a stern stare from the creator of a thousand sounds. It was fast, colourful, energetic, mysterious, new - and it was a start.

The effect lasted for a number of days. The new concept 12-inch singles and twin-albums were released locally and I played them to death. It was like travelling into another world.

Simple Minds records were hard to obtain in Australia. It was a while until I discovered the heavily European-influenced *Empires and Dance*, the derivative *Life in a Day* and the experimental yet intriguing *Real to Real Cacophony*. *New Gold Dream* came at a time where I was starting my first job, leaving home, living in a shared house. Everything had led to that.

I do miss the band from Festival Hall. The band has changed many times and sometimes the albums would miss the mark, although there was often a gem found. They disappeared from Australia for a little while, which was not totally unexpected. To justify the long trip there must be interest and a sponsor.

Recently, a return to form. The fans from those early days start to reappear from domestic life and new fans pay attention. The newer songs show strength, showing the roots from the past. The tours return and we are back on course to travel to magical and different new gold dreams.

# TRACEY HIGGINS

*Cloudlands Ballroom*
*28 November 1981, Brisbane, Australia*

Dear Jim,

I feel like I'm writing to an old friend, a kindred spirit. Born in Liverpool, England, I came to live in Brisbane, Australia with my family in 1965. Brisbane, a sleepy city, was going through an interestingly creative, underground musical change... and it changed my life.

Simple Minds influenced my life in so many ways, like a spiritual calling. Discovering your treasured band in 1981, listening to 'Love Song' on an underground radio station, this musical experience transcended into many parts of my life. It transformed my fashion sense, my art, my poetry, make-up and hair. I danced just like you, Jim, and loved it. My heart and soul were captured by the beauty and magic of this New Gold Dream called Simple Minds.

I learnt to play 'Themes for Great Cities' by ear on my friend's Moog with its 8-track memory so I could layer it. Hours of fun.

Musically, '79 to '85 has a special place in my heart. Everything was new and exciting and all yet to be discovered. My friends and I would dance at the alternative nightclubs, filling the floor when Simple Minds came on, with our lopsided haircuts and black Egyptian-like make-up. We floated along to the beautiful waves of your music.

I bought all your music, books and magazines, all of which I still possess. I've included photos of my books, artwork and photos of when I saw you play at The Refectory, St Lucia University in 1982, and from Boondall in 1986. I saw you play there again in 1989. Thank you for all the beautiful memories.

---

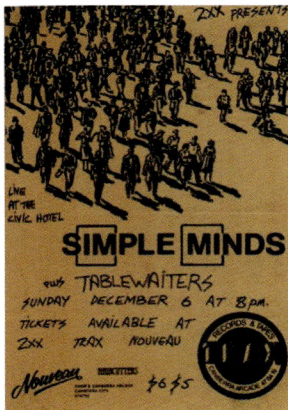

*The flyer for the Civic Hotel gig in Canberra*

# CRAIG TIGWELL

*Cock 'n' Bull Bar, Civic Hotel*
*6 December 1981, Canberra, Australia*

The band was brought to Australia initially by Flowers/Icehouse. For those that didn't want to attend the Icehouse show, Simple Minds came back to us and played the tiny 'Cock 'n' Bull' bar in the Civic Hotel, Canberra. About 300 of us got to see a very early version of Simple Minds and Jim was kind enough to write the setlist out for me afterwards.

---

## GILLIAN SPENCER

My best friend and I used to travel around the Sydney pubs seeing awesome Aussie bands, one of which was called Flowers/Icehouse. I'd been reading in *Juke*, *NME* and *RAM* magazines about a Scottish band who were about to take on the world and grace our shores. Wow oh wow! There had never been anything like it. Cameras were a no-no but we risked it anyway and I managed to get one picture of Jim before nearly being tossed out. I was captivated and totally mesmerised. Who was this super cool guy with smouldering good looks? This was the day Simple Minds became my number one.

On the *Walk Between Worlds* tour in Manchester I actually met Jim. It made that 24 hour flight from Australia to the UK well worth it. I saw them at the Roundhouse in London and in Paris on that same trip. My daughter came along and has become a Simple Minds fan too. I've made some incredible friends because of the love we all share for this band.

## TONI KASCH

FM104 radio was hosting an Australia-wide phone in with Jim. I was lucky enough to get through. I was so nervous my heart was pounding. I was prompted by the announcer to ask their question, 'How do you go about preparing for an album?' which I dutifully asked. Then, to the radio announcer's angst, I cheekily asked when Jim and the band were going to tour Australia again. He laughed and said how much he loved Australian audiences and how the band were keen to get back there. I still have the cassette I recorded the conversation on – but nothing to play it on!

## DEREK FORBES

*Simple Minds bass guitarist, 1978 – 1985 and 1995-1998*
*Manly Vale Hotel*
*4 December 1981, Sydney, Australia*

We were booked for a TV show in Melbourne, the world famous *Countdown* - no, not that one, the music show hosted by the flamboyant Molly Meldrum. We had been booked to play a show at Manly Hall in Sydney that evening, and the show in Melbourne was an early start and it would go 'live' at five o clock. We were on last, and would be finished just before six o clock.

Previously....

We got up from our lack of sleep and quickly dressed. I was sharing with Kenny Hyslop as usual. Kenny was my alarm. Every morning he would scream at the very top of his voice, 'No no no!!!' What a fright I would get. We both went downstairs and got into a waiting Land Rover with the rest of the band. We were rushed to Sydney airport, and it wasn't long before we boarded the 600 mile trip to Melbourne. We had a bit of a rock and roll breakfast, then a sleep. We were approaching Melbourne airport in no time. Soon we were in a couple of limousines and making our way to the TV studios. When we arrived, we went through some camera checks and then we were set free for a few hours. I went with Mick to the hairdressers and then we all milled about the stores and shops, eventually ending up in a café for food and refreshment. We got back to the studio and met up with Molly, who was outrageous as ever with his double entendres around Jim, who he would call 'Jimmy boy'. Life around Molly was tantamount to playing a part in a *Carry On* film. Next, make up, and another camera check and then it was our time to go onstage to perform 'Love Song'. The studio supplied the instruments for us. Jim went onstage with a little bag strapped around him, which has for years confused everyone. It was because we were leaving straight away! As soon as we had finished we jumped straight offstage, moved through the rather large crowd and headed for the exit. There were the limos waiting for us. We jumped in and off we zoomed to an empty Australian field. Within a minute or so, we heard the rotors of two helicopters coming out of the sky towards us. They landed, we got in and they flew us right to the stairs of the jet at Melbourne Airport and on we went. Up went the jet, and in an hour and a half we landed in Sydney. We were met again by the Land Rovers and sped to Manly Hall with no time to spare. We were ready for the show and went straight onstage to an amazing Australian crowd. They went berserk as we entered the stage. We played for two hours, and we were sweating in the baking heat of the venue, so much so that our road crew would come on and drench us with buckets of cold water to keep us hydrated and cool. Eventually, after a few encores, we came offstage and collapsed in the dressing room. We partied on for the rest of the night and into the wee small hours, before falling into our rooms at the hotel. What a day that was.

*Kenny Hyslop in Australia December 1981 - photo Stuart Holland*

## JOE VIZVARY

I'm a member of a Vancouver-based band called Images In Vogue. In 1981 one of our synth players, Glen Nelson, opened for Simple Minds on the *Sons and Fascination* tour in 1981 Edmonton and Vancouver. In Vancouver there was some problem with drummer Kenny Hyslop's drum synth. When Canada's largest music store chain were unable to supply a replacement our bass player, Gary Smith, drove to our rehearsal space in the suburbs to get ours and Kenny used it that night.

Simple Minds were in Vancouver for a few weeks after the *New Gold Dream* tour before leaving for their next destination and we ran into each other several times, particularly Charlie and Mick, at places like the nightclub Luvafair, a speakeasy called Club Soda and at downtown restaurants. When we ran into the guys at the restaurant Kamei Sushi, we gave them a copy of our newly released EP.

## FABRICE GUILHAUMON

*Once Upon a Time* was the most listened to album of my youth. It sounds heroic, with a feeling nothing can happen to you. I listened to that tape so much I broke it. Two months later, I came across 'Promised You a Miracle' and 'New Gold Dream' on the radio. The melody and the lyrics sounded mystic and I ran to buy *New Gold Dream* with its very kitsch sleeve. I love the whole album!

## JANE DICKSON

I was working away from home, living in a hotel, when I saw Simple Minds on *The Tube*. 'New Gold Dream' stood out for me and still does. My best friend and I, also an avid fan, have seen them all over and it was great to see them live in Glasgow!

## MARK HAWLING

I was too young to see them in the Eighties in Australia, too cool to like them in the Nineties and never managed to see them live on later tours. The nearest I got is the tape my sister made of the 1982 Manly Vale show from Sydney, broadcast by 2JJJ Radio. I played it until the tape become mud. I still have the TDK D-90, and finally got a copy of the show off the internet. I still think it's amazing.

# KOH CHI KIAN

In 1982, a geeky teenager was so taken with *Empires and Dance* and *Sons and Fascination* he decided to uproot himself from his tropical island home in Singapore to experience first hand 'decadence and pleasure towns' in continental Europe. He travelled around on his student card, looking at cities and buildings falling down, proclaiming himself as Asia's stolen new born son. He read the *NME* and Paul Morley. As he grappled with the French language in the Basque city of Pau, a soon-to-be prized copy of *New Gold Dream* (courtesy of a *Smash Hits* contest) took his breath away. 'How do you do it?' he asked Jim Kerr in a gushing note to the fan club in Basildon, shamelessly name-dropping Bowie, with bits of Proust and talk of how everything is possible in the game of life. Some time in 1983, a postcard came calling back from San Francisco.

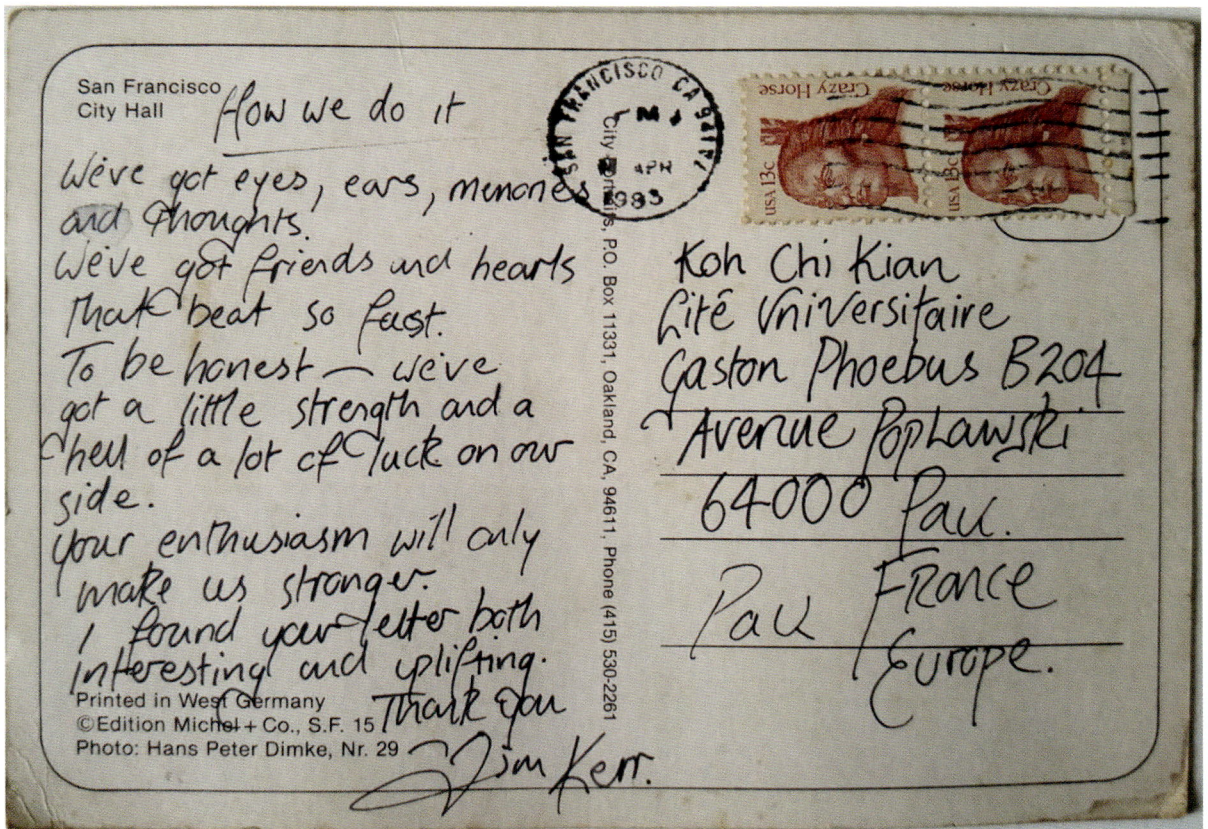

*Koh Chi Kian got a postcard from Jim*

# HÅKAN

*Underground*
*20 February 1982, Stockholm, Sweden*

I became a fan when I heard 'Love Song' the first time. I bought both *Sons and Fascination* and *Sister Feelings Call*. I was 14 at the time. I had a fever but cried my way out so my mom couldn't stop me from seeing my first concert in Stockholm in 1982. I've been to eight shows now. As my life changes, it seems that the band write just the music I need!

# FINN ERIK SOLDAN JACOBSEN

*Odd Fellow Palaeet*
*22 February 1982, Copenhagen, Denmark*

It is 38 years since I went to my first and only Simple Minds concert. Seeing Jim on stage with these very tense eyes, I thought, 'This guy has a problem!' It was a great concert. I loved it, and I still have the t-shirt. You can see right through it. I've had a lot comments about the cross on the chest: 'Are you religious?' 'Yes - in some ways!'

I'm a great fan of OMD too, so when Simple Minds toured with them some years ago my friend from '82 and I planned to go to the UK to see them both, buying tickets for the flight and the concert only for my friend to cancel the day before.

Simple Minds still blast my ears. I see some of the concerts on YouTube but also buy the CDs. After all, no one can make a living on a 'thumbs-up'!

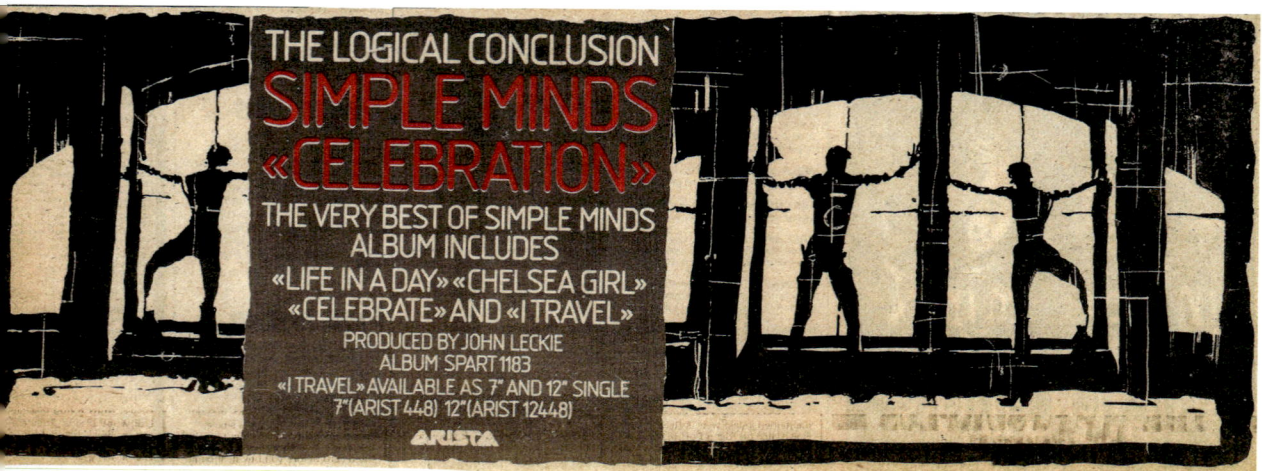

# TONY BLACK

## *Rotation*
## *2 March 1982, Hannover, West Germany*

Searching the back streets of Hannover, looking for where a band from home (relentlessly touring the continent yet again) were performing, I eventually found the gig, an old factory come club. Squeezed inside, like a foot in a shoe several sizes too small, a very excitable crowd roared the arrival onstage of Simple Minds. Already well known to me and many others before I left Scotland a couple of years earlier, the band were now a well-honed group who knew their craft. Kenny Hyslop was driving the beat along with the four original band members. It was the first time for me seeing the band in the flesh, up close and personal.

*Tony Black's autographed copy of Sons and Fascination*

The band kicked off and that hypnotic noise filled the room. Incessant beats, riffs and vintage Simple Minds, cruising through 'I Travel', 'Celebrate', 'The American', 'Love Song', 'Changeling', 'Pleasantly Disturbed', 'Sweat in Bullet', playing on and on...

After a burst bass drum and numerous encores, I was lucky to be invited into the dressing room (boy, it was rough) to meet a very sweaty band. They were so generous with their welcome and brandy. Curious to know how a Paisley boy came to be there, Jim and Charlie were more than happy to chat and pose for a picture, the band signing my album sleeve and offering me a lift back into the city. An all-night bar was sounded out where Charlie, Mick and I laughed and drank, planning our sequels.

Kenny was already settled in when we arrived, and eventually a great night had to conclude as I boarded a night train, in time for a bleary but happy-eyed attendance straight into work.

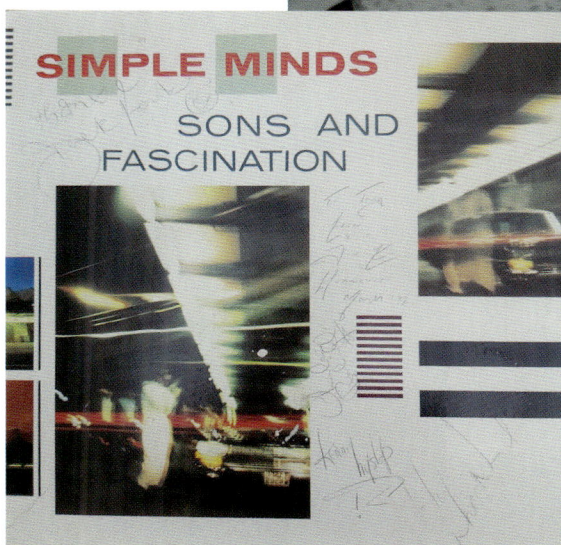

## ULRICH STEENKEN

*Schüttorf Festival*
*5 June 1982, Münster, West Germany*

Me and some friends went to the Schüttorf Festival, where Frank Zappa was headlining a line-up including The Stray Cats and a band called Simple Minds. As long-haired hippies, we looked like we seemed to have missed punk, new wave and electronic music completely, and were eagerly waiting for our icon Frank to enter the stage. Temperatures were unusually high for that time of year so we took a bath in the River Vechte, near the stage. Apart from us, most people were naked and when I got out of the water my shirt dried within minutes. Suddenly there was this bass and keyboard sound that got my attention completely. I slowly moved forward to the stage in order to get a closer look. There were naked women and men dancing around me, but I was stunned by these young boys and got carried away by music I've never heard before. Some fragments of the songs seemed familiar but, wow, it sounded so unique and innovative.

The following Monday I went to the local record shop in Oldenburg to buy *Sons and Fascination* and the compilation *Celebration* and identified tracks like 'Premonition', 'Changeling', 'Love Song' and 'Sweat in Bullet' from the setlist. A few months later *New Gold Dream* came out and I got a new haircut. A life-changing experience almost 40 years ago.

I've never missed a tour since. In 2006 I took my daughters to an open-air festival in Hamburg and all of us, including the band, seemed to have a special time a few weeks before the World Cup in Germany. Another hot summer to remember. Then, 12 years later my granddaughter enjoyed standing in the front row on her very first Simple Minds gig on the lovely island of Norderney. Dolphins at sundown. Can you ask for more?

---

## PARDEEP SEKAND

*Massey Hall*
*7 September 1982, Toronto, Canada*

I was 17 when I first heard 'Life in a Day' on our local radio station, CFNY. It immediately caught my attention with the instrumentation and urgency in the vocals. Simple Minds songs were so different from anything I'd heard before; their range was so wide – from subtle to intense to psychedelic. The music was cerebral, trippy and cathartic. Atmospheric synths, swirling guitars, pulsating rhythms, and the beautiful, chanting vocals that not only carried a message but felt like an instrument in itself. When you're scraping together money to buy albums, you tend to choose carefully. Many bands typically had more fillers than good songs on an album. Simple Minds was the best return on investment I could get, because most songs on the albums were so good.

Similarly, I had to pick and choose the concerts I went to carefully, because I couldn't afford to go to many. In 1982, Simple Minds announced the *New Gold* tour. That Massey Hall show forever changed the way I would view concerts. Tons of energy from both the band and the crowd, sonically perfect. But it was the lights - oh my God, the lights in syncopation with the music - that sent my spirit and imagination soaring! I had never seen anything like it. It was a feast for all my senses that set the benchmark for every band since. Thank you for showing me that when a band cares for its audience, it can make all the hearts beat as one for a few special hours.

## STUART FERGUSON

*Coasters*
*8 – 10 September 1982, Edinburgh, Scotland*

I heard 'I Travel' for the first time through the PA at a Teardrop Explodes gig at Tiffany's in Glasgow, went to Virgin Records on Union Street next day and bought the 12-inch single, double-sided with 'Changeling'. My first gig was Coasters in Edinburgh in '82 and I've been a fan ever since.

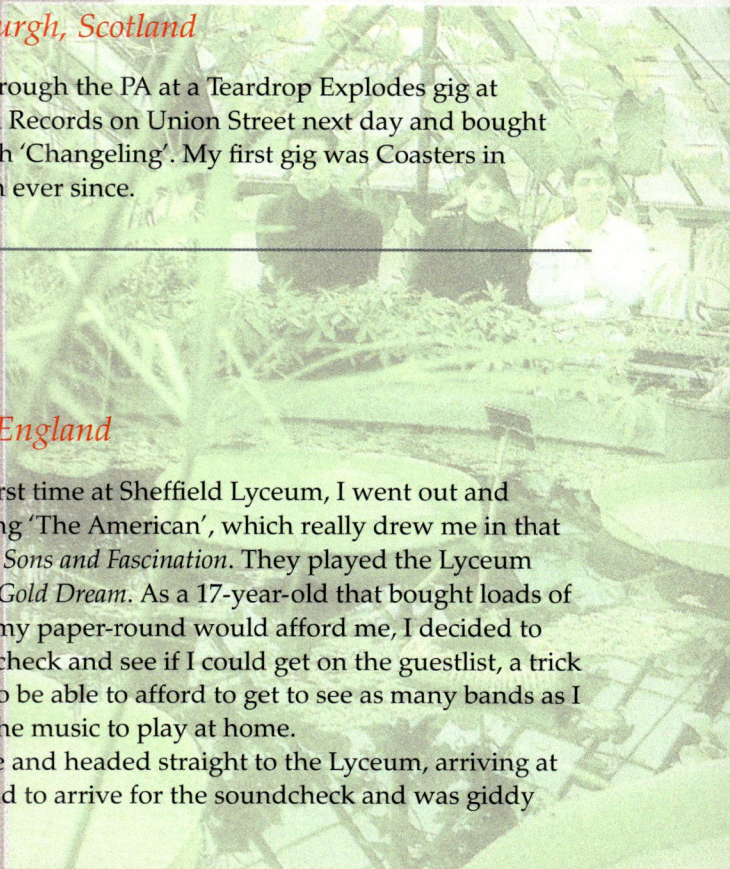

## CHRIS JOHNSON

*Lyceum*
*11 September 1982, Sheffield, England*

After seeing Simple Minds for the first time at Sheffield Lyceum, I went out and bought *Sister Feelings Call* for the song 'The American', which really drew me in that night. I also bought its sister album, *Sons and Fascination*. They played the Lyceum again shortly after, to promote *New Gold Dream*. As a 17-year-old that bought loads of music and went to as many gigs as my paper-round would afford me, I decided to try and meet the band at the soundcheck and see if I could get on the guestlist, a trick my cousin had taught me in order to be able to afford to get to see as many bands as I could whilst still being able to buy the music to play at home.

I took the bus into Sheffield centre and headed straight to the Lyceum, arriving at around 3.30pm. I waited for the band to arrive for the soundcheck and was giddy

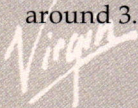

and nervous as Jim and Duncan arrived. They both signed my albums and were quite friendly. I asked Jim if I could get on the guestlist as I didn't have a ticket. He point-blank refused and made his way inside the building. Being shy and not one to ask for things, I felt awkward and thought I'd been too rude. I stayed at the stage door waiting for the other members to arrive, deriding myself for being insolent. Suddenly the stage door burst open. Jim stood there and asked, 'What's your name?' I told him. He nodded and closed the door. I was beside myself. I ran to the phone box in Pond Street and rang my cousin. 'We're in... Jim has put us on the guest list.'

It was a dream come true. After seeing the first gig at the Lyceum and being blown away, the second gig was equally mindblowing. I will never forget the kindness of Jim. Simple Minds' music and the kindness of the lead singer towards an eager young fan was paramount in making them such an important part of my musical life.

# GARY HOLMES

*Lyceum*
*12 September 1982, London,*
*England*

My older brother Martin introduced me to the band when I was just 15 years old. I recall him giving me money and me then cycling up to the local record shop to buy the recently-released *New Gold Dream*. For me the record is a pure masterpiece and on that day I was instantly hooked. It's still my favourite and gets better with each and every listen.

When I saw them play live at the Lyceum in London, a bargain at a mere £3.75, I remember dancing close to the stage and being totally captivated. They led with '70 Cities

*Gary Holmes was at the Lyceum in 1982*

as Love Brings the Fall' and then weaved through many *New Gold Dream* classics, finally wrapping up the evening with a fantastic encore of 'Love Song'.

I've had the pleasure of seeing the band play on six different occasions, in the UK and USA. Each and every time I'm impressed by their energy and the love they show for their loyal fans. Even my teenage children are fans, as they hear the band's music constantly played at home.

In October 2018, I was able to take my wife Rebecca to her first Simple Minds concert at Boston's Orpheum Theatre as an anniversary surprise. We were able to attend the soundcheck too. From 'The Signal and the Noise' through to 'Sanctify Yourself' we didn't stand still throughout a two-set show. It was a memorable and exciting experience, made even better when Jim high-fived my wife and asked her, 'Are you having a good time?' We both nodded yes, and have been for the last 38 years, thanks to the music of Simple Minds.

## BRUCE FINDLAY

*New Gold Dream released 13 September 1982*

We knew we were on the verge of breaking through properly. The next album gave them their first hit. That was *New Gold Dream*. The band, having changed producers, changed again, which I didn't agree with. I thought Steve Hillage did such a fabulous job, we should stick with him, but Jim said, 'We've made the break now. We've learnt a lot from Steve Hillage like we learnt a lot from John Leckie, I want to learn more.'

So we got a new producer for the next album and, lo and behold, he did give us our first UK hit single, 'Promised You a Miracle'. As it happens, 'Love Song' was a hit in Canada and Australia and we'd toured these places by this time. We were beginning to get a reputation in America, Canada, Australia and, obviously, a big reputation in Europe. So *New Gold Dream* was a smash hit but never quite made No.1. It really did cement Simple Minds as a major act though, and they began headlining festivals to huge crowds. Those were the breakthrough years.

At that point it was downhill all the way, in as much as the band became a major act and we hired a lot more people and I expanded my office. I had several book-keepers working on Simple Minds. They were a hard-working band, touring prolifically and recording. *New Gold Dream* came out in 1982, their fifth album. And the first came out in 1979. That's up there with The Beatles in terms of being prolific and touring, doing 100/150 gigs a year.

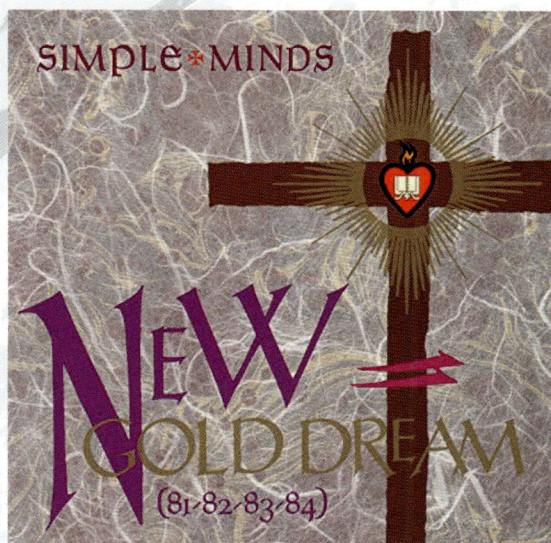

# NEW GOLD DREAM

## DAVE FAGAN

My journey with Simple Minds began in 1982 when a friend invited me around to listen to a new tune. It was the 12inch version of 'I Travel'. Then I watched *Late Night in Concert* with Annie Nightingale and Simple Minds live at Newcastle City Hall and I was blown away, especially by 'New Gold Dream'. From then on, I championed this band with friends and family, believing there was nobody better live. I have seen Simple Minds live over 300 times. No other band on earth is as good and their music has lifted me through good times and bad.

## PAUL ECCLESTON

It was October 1983. The country was in the grip of recession but I had got a job as a stock control clerk for a local furniture manufacturer. I was paid the princely sum of £40 a week. To save money I'd walk the four miles to and from work. One Saturday morning, I had been to work to earn some overtime. Walking home I saw a ten pound note at the bus stop. There was no one around who might have dropped it so I decided to spend my windfall on a copy of *New Gold Dream*. I turned around, walked back into Kingswinford and into Gould's record shop. I played that album so often on my old record player that the stylus wore grooves into the album. I am so grateful that I found that ten pound note. I can't remember what I spent the change on - but it was probably beer!

## BRIAN PATERSON

The first time I saw Simple Minds, they were the support band for The Stranglers in a club in Aberdeen called Ruffles. Five years later I heard and bought *New Gold Dream* and really started to get into them. 'Someone Somewhere (in Summertime)' became and remains my all time favourite song.

## ERMANNO FARINELLI

It started with the cover of the album. The cross is the most powerful symbol the world has ever known and will ever know. And the music was heavenly. The keyboards made my mind and heart drift to happy deep places. The guitar and drums were magical. But it was the bass riffs at the core that tugged at my centre. And then Jim's voice brought it all together, passionate and honest. I used that album as therapy. I would play it as I went to bed at night to aid me in sleep. I'd play it in the car and at home, all day every day for years. I'm still playing it to this day.

## GRAEME BRAGMAN

Growing up in the Eighties in South Africa we were never really exposed to what was happening outside of our borders, music-wise. Our go to was either *Smash Hits* or *No.1* where, if you heard a song on the radio, you would read up on the band and, if and when you saw the cassette, album or 7 inch single, you bought it. Taping music from the radio was also an experience that today's kids would never understand. It's how we made our mix tapes.

My lifelong devotion to Simple Minds began in 1983 living in Hillbrow in Johannesburg. Up to that point I had never heard of Simple Minds or any of the music. I was in a store one day when *New Gold Dream* caught my eye. The two things that struck me was the name of the band and the album cover design. The medieval-type design grabbed my attention. Without even first listening to the record I bought the album, went home to listen and have been hooked ever since.

## FABRICE FINCK

September 1986. New school, new friends. I heard that a girl called Nadine was an SM fan so I asked her if she could lend me *Sparkle in the Rain*. She lent me a tape of *New Gold Dream* instead. The next day she asked me what I had thought of the title song (her favourite tune) but I hadn't listened to it. When I heard the first song on the album, I couldn't go any further. I just played it again and again and again the whole evening. I couldn't believe what came into my ears. 'Someone Somewhere (in Summertime)' was the song that made me become a true Simple Minds fan.

## CATHERINE DURAN

In 1982, the beginning of free radio in France, I was doing a show every day at a brand new station, Radio Harlequin in Rouen. A few days earlier, I came back from England with the single 'Promised You a Miracle'. That's the song I choose as the theme song for my show and since then I've never stopped listening to and loving Simple Minds

## IAIN CAMPBELL

I was introduced to Simple Minds in 1985 on holiday in Flamborough Head. After what seemed like a week's drive from Fife to North Yorkshire (it would have been six hours), we arrived at the holiday cottage we had rented for the week. My mother, father, sister and best friend Steven were busy unpacking when I heard a click. Steven had brought his cassette tape recorder with him, the one he used to load games on his ZX Spectrum. Out from the tiny crackling speaker came the first beats of 'Someone Somewhere (in Summertime)'. I had never heard anything like it before. I wasn't really into music in a big way at that time. I was always down the park with a ball and big sis belted out Duran Duran and Nik Kershaw all day.

How the rewind button on the deck never gave in I will never know. That cassette was played over and over and over for the full week and, as a 14-year-old in the height of a beautiful summer, I could not have been happier. Nearly 35 years later, those same songs are on the playlist today and are always heard about the house or in the car.

## JONATHAN GOLDMAN

Growing up in Phoenix, Arizona it was hard to find music on the radio beyond country or rock and roll, but every now and then something new would break and capture my imagination. I was a young teenager longing for romance when I heard my first Simple Minds song, a dreamy combination of melodic, driving guitar, deep, yearning lyrics and heavenly synth all surrounding the subject of something Phoenicians knew all too well — summertime.

I rode my dirt bike to the mall in 100-degree heat and hit The Record Shop where I found *New Gold Dream*. Normally I'd stick around the mall to play video games or grab a slice of pizza but this time I went straight home. I'll never forget opening that album. I was blown away before I even heard the first song. I was expecting standard black vinyl, so when I pulled out a transparent gold record with purple marbling I thought I found some kind of Willy Wonka secret treasure. It was the first time I'd ever seen coloured vinyl. I must've played the entire album side-to-side a dozen times straight while reading the lyrics on the sleeve and pouring over the credits on the backside of the cover. It all felt so new and personal, right down to the bottom of the record, 'Made in Summer '82'.

## NATHALIE POUNETTE

I live in France and discovered Simple Minds when I was 14, with the album *New Gold Dream*. Simple Minds stood out from other fashionable bands in the Eighties for me because of Jim's elegance and charisma. My friends and I were in love with him, like many girls around the world. And then this voice! This music! Just the first time you listened to a song, you let yourself get into the world of Simple Minds.

When I was 17, an age when you live your adolescence - have fun, go out, dance - I couldn't. I became very ill, with a disease that destroyed my body and left scars and which still handicaps me a lot today. I listened to music and Simple Minds in particular. I did not understand everything - my English is far from perfect - but the music carried me away and relieved my ailments. Despite my health issues, nothing and nobody will prevent me from being able to realise my dream, to finally see my favourite band on stage. I have waited almost all my life for this moment and I can't wait to finally see them live in Lille.

## RONNIE MACKINTOSH

In late 1982 I was a young detective constable in the West End CID office in Edinburgh. In the middle of the night a uniformed patrol car stopped a van and found it was stuffed full of stolen gear, mainly taken from parked cars. We had the job of sorting it all out. Amongst it all was a cassette, *New Gold Dream* by Simple Minds. I popped it on to help pass the time and from the first notes was completely hooked. I played it over and over during that night and the following day went out and got myself a copy.

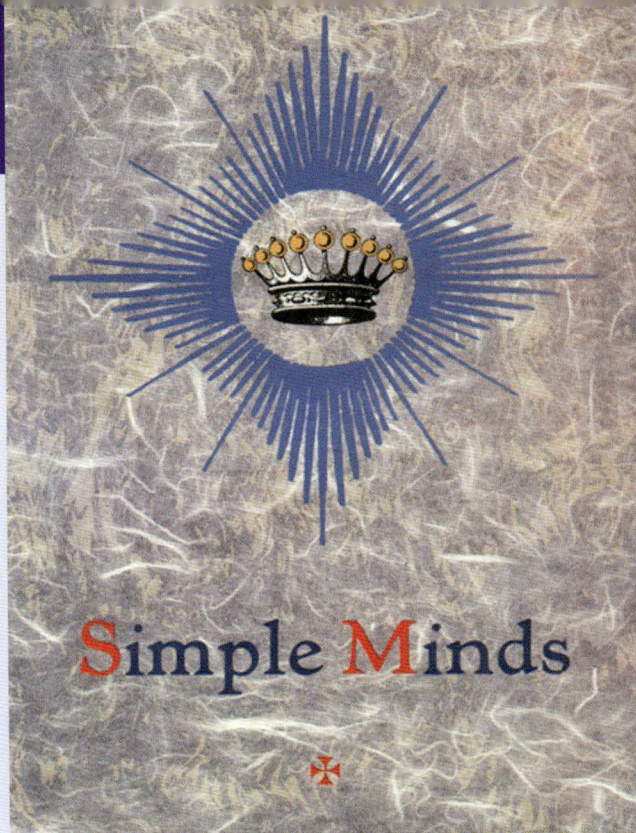

Simple Minds

## STEVE MARGGRAF

When I was just 20 in 1980, I bought myself a little block of land in the rainforest, high in the mountains of South East Queensland in Springbrook, Australia. There I built a small cabin with no electricity. These were wonderful years. I had a good, small battery-operated stereo and, as I loved music, I used to turn it up loud as there was no one else living close by. I used to listen to radio station 4ZZZ and one night in 1981, I heard 'New Gold Dream'. OMG, this changed my life for ever!

## HECTOR DYLLA

I was 15 when I heard 'I Travel' for the first time. It was 1980 and I regularly heard the British Forces Broadcasting Service. John Peel was a mandatory event for us post-punks in Germany. The next day I ran into a record store and bought *Empires and Dance*. And the day after that I ordered *Life in a Day* and *Real to Real*. That was the beginning of an everlasting love... Later I even tried to put 'Simple Minds' as my religion on my ID!

I have seen countless Simple Minds concerts all over Europe and Jim and Charlie accompany me musically through my life... they are immortalised on my skin, their music is the soundtrack of my life. If I was only allowed to take one album to a desert island it would be *New Gold Dream*.

## ALEX MÜLLER

I was born in 1965 in West Berlin. I grew up with the music of The Beatles. Punk, blues and rock music accompanied me through my life. I was absolutely thrilled with the first synthesizer sounds from Depeche Mode. Then a friend gave me *New Gold Dream* and it all made sense. I've been a fan and have attended every Simple Minds concert in Berlin since.

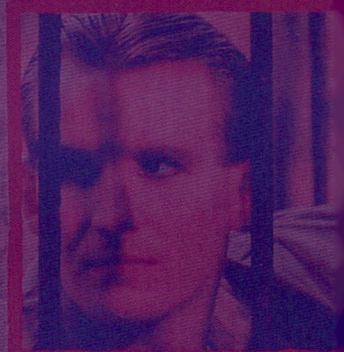

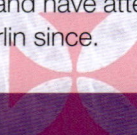

## DANIEL DI FEBO

I was roller skating with my cousin Miguel Rodriguez on a boardwalk by the sea in the south of Spain, near Malaga. Under a very hot sun, we were gliding on wheels listening with our Walkmans to the *New Gold Dream* album. We felt like we were flying out of this world. One year later my cousin and I went to see them in concert in Lausanne, Switzerland for the *Sparkle in the Rain* tour. It was so awesome.

## JOHN HAMMOND

*New Gold Dream* was released and I thought, 'I'll give this a go' as I got fed up with all and sundry banging on about how brilliant U2 were. Don't get me wrong, they're a great group, but once you start listening to *New Gold Dream*, you find you have to keep playing the album.

## PETER WALSH

*Producer,* New Gold Dream *(81-82-83-84)*

I will never forget the first time I saw Simple Minds in concert. They were performing in a small club in Liege on the European leg of the *Sons and Fascination* tour. Watching the reaction of the audience I could see that this was the beginning of something huge. I wanted to be a part of it. I recorded the show on my Walkman, using it later as a reference in the studio. I wanted to make sure that this unique energy and excitement translated into everything I produced in the studio with the band.

As a producer and sound engineer, you're always searching for the soul of the music, digging deep to reach the place where it is at its most powerful and pure. You need to have a very special bond with the artist to do this. Trust and belief from all sides in what you are doing. With Simple Minds the chemistry existed from our very first meeting and it has lasted till

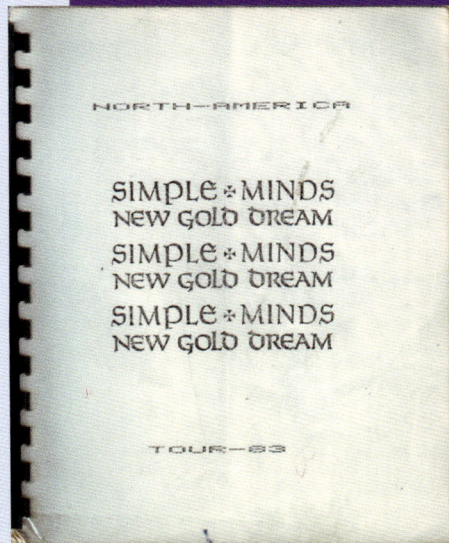

NORTH—AMERICA

SIMPLE ⬩ MINDS
NEW GOLD DREAM
SIMPLE ⬩ MINDS
NEW GOLD DREAM
SIMPLE ⬩ MINDS
NEW GOLD DREAM

TOUR—83

this day. Only when you have this combination is it possible to unlock the potential that is waiting to be tapped.

I have followed the band closely over the years and the success they have achieved is a pleasure to see. The last time I met Jim we had a lovely lunch up at his place in the Highlands, and we talked about the good ol' days. Memories of our time together making *New Gold Dream*.

The preproduction in Fife, huddled around an open fire in the barn, working on song arrangements and experimenting with instrumentation. Recording rhythm tracks at the Townhouse, Mel and Mike playing drums together in the Stone Room for the title song, 'New Gold Dream'. They both played the main beat, but I asked Mel to play the tom fills and Mike to play the cymbals. Watching Jim perform his characteristic twist while recording lead vocals. Only when the twist was at its most pronounced did I feel we had achieved the best take!

Small details spring to mind too, like asking Jim to pronounce the word 'earth' in 'Hunter and the Hunted' in a slightly less Glaswegian accent. You can imagine the response! I think that's when my nickname of Arthur of the Britons first came up. Never mind the haircut, I sometimes had to be careful with what I suggested.

Seeing Charlie catapulted across the studio floor of the Manor after receiving an electric shock while attempting to reconfigure his guitar effects late one night. I'm happy and relieved to see that he finally got the pedal board of his dreams later on in life!

'Do you remember the night you stepped on a hedgehog while recording the piano with Mick on 'Summertime'?' Jim asked. That's another thing I'll never forget! What a surreal night that was, turning up barefoot at Oxford Hospital A&E at 4am.

We've all got such special memories of those days when we were just starting to find our way in the music business. I'm sure Jim will remember writing the lyrics for the song 'New Gold Dream' in the bath somewhere in Sweden too. It was the last chance to get a vocal on the song, otherwise it could have been an instrumental. Can you imagine that?

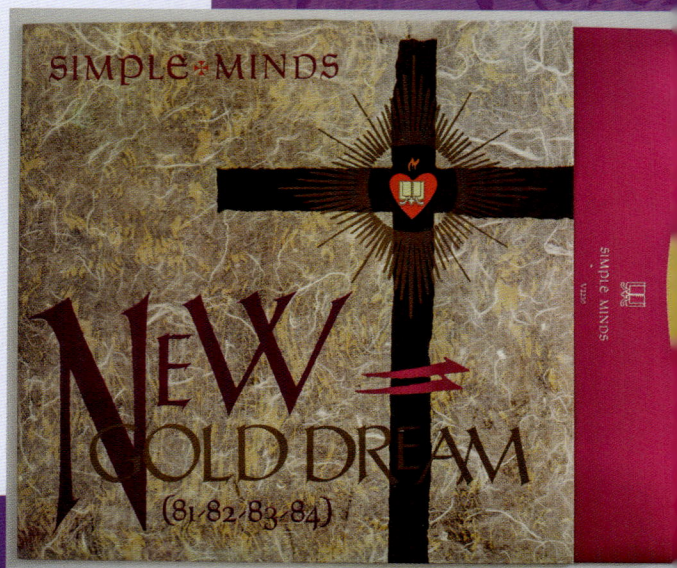

## JANE FREDERICK

I began my creative life as a fine art student at Lincolnshire College of Art and Design in the mid-1980s, my head brimming full of electronica and new wave sounds that blended into one glorious mash of melodious dream pop. Simple Minds, The Associates, Cocteau Twins, Prefab Sprout… I have absolutely no doubt that the records that sounded like the inside of my head became a fundamental influence on the artist that I am today. My very favourite album was then and still is *New Gold Dream*.

I knew it was important and also understood that it had a crucial role to play in my own creative process. It accompanied me on a gap year sketching trip around the world, during which I wore the original tape cassette version out on my Walkman but managed to find a bootleg version in Bali.

It began working on my imagination from the first mind-bending listen. I have always enjoyed visiting and drawing historical stately homes and gardens, their immensity and ability to provoke wonder and delight is for me, mirrored in the huge shimmering sounds of each track. The multi-dimensional soundscape flicked some kind of switch in my head and somehow manages to unlock my imagination, opening up space for new connections and ideas to evolve.

Synaesthesia could go some way to explaining how audio sensation can be experienced and reinterpreted through visual-spatial senses. When those sensations are drawn or painted then they can be projected outwardly for others to share. To sum up, I could say that if my work were to succeed then it might look something like the sound of *New Gold Dream*. Perhaps.

# AGLIA SAMARAS

*La Trobe University*
*30 September 1982, Victoria,*
*Australia*

Upon hearing 'Love Song' on weekly pop show *Countdown* back in 1981 I became an instant fan. Simple Minds had such a fresh and unique sound. I saw them live the following year when they played La Trobe University, where I was attending. Who'd have imagined my band would come and play my uni? Back then, many artists - local and international - would do the pub and university circuit in a vibrant music scene in Australia.

I saw them again in early 1984 on the *Tour du Monde*, attending the concert on my own because I didn't know any other fans. Progressively the venues they played grew in capacity. I also managed to see them in Melbourne in October 1986 and November 1989. I was so grateful to have seen them perform their biggest four albums.

Then there was a long hiatus in Australia. When they returned in 2006, I thought all my dreams had come true. By this stage I was married and dragged along my 10-year-old daughter Elizabeth. I was waxing lyrical about their energy and amazing live performances. Once she saw them live, she too was a fan – hook, line and sinker. So much so that when they announced the *30 Years Live* tour in the UK, we had to be there. The main draw card was to hear *New Gold Dream* in its entirety. We attended six dates in the UK, starting in London and ending at the *Cash for Kids* gig in Glasgow.

Over the last few years we've seen them live in three different states across Australia. We flew up to Sydney in 2010 and then to the Gold Coast in 2011 as well as numerous hometown gigs here in Melbourne. Now there's an extremely long wait to see them again in Australia. I eagerly await their return.

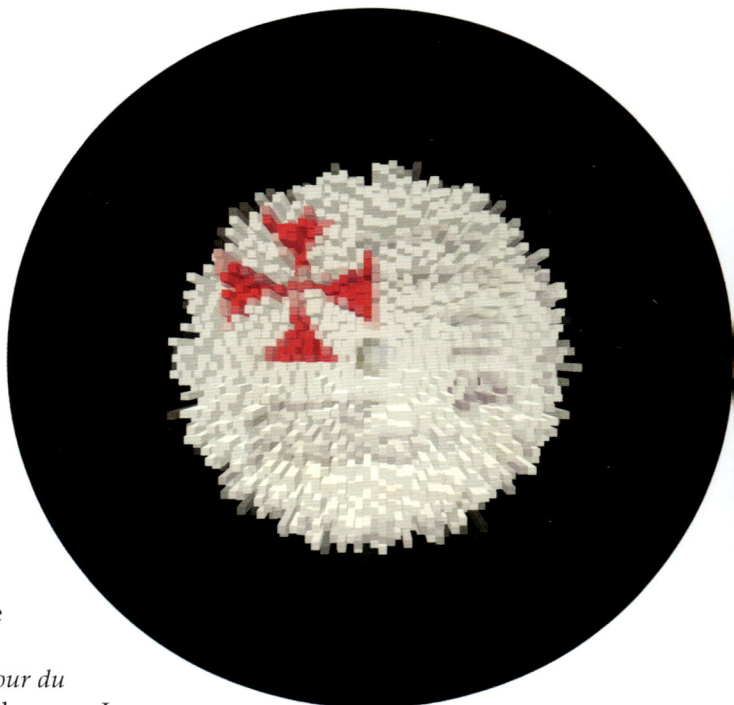

# GRANT ROBINSON

*Collendina Hotel*
*3 October 1982, Ocean Grove, Australia*

I can distinctly remember hearing Simple Minds for the first time. It was the early '80s and I was 16. The place was my home in Victoria, Australia. 'Promised You a Miracle' came on the radio and I was simply amazed. It was one of those moments where a song hits you in a deeper way than merely liking a tune. I rushed to the radio cassette player and hit 'record', only to get little over half the song. Which was then rewound and played, rewound and played and rewound and played in all its truncated glory. I needed - like actually needed - to hear the whole song again. It was raining and miserable yet I mounted my trusty pushbike, pockets rattling with enough hastily-scavenged change for a vinyl single (around $1.25) and headed to town where the record store was, 45 minutes later heading home in the rain again, where that single ended up being flogged for weeks on repeat. From there a wonderful world of incredible music opened to me, not just Simple Minds, but a whole genre of post-punk '80s epicenes.

   The next year they toured and played a large pub isolated in the beachside bush, an half-hour's drive from my home. I was completely blown away, finding one of the greatest bands to have ever created music. Going backwards in time through their catalogue, *Sons and Fascination*, *Empires and Dance*, *Real to Real Cacophony* and *Life in a Day* were no less than mesmerising. Then *New Gold Dream* and *Sparkle in the Rain*, still on heavy rotation to this day, over 30 years of musical joy.

# RICHARD OWEN

My first memories of Simple Minds were when my father played the early albums on holiday in the car on tape. 'Promised You a Miracle', 'Waterfront' and 'Don't You (Forget About Me)' are all early music memories to me. Since then I've become a big fan, seeing them four times, three times with my father.

# RACHEL MORRIS

*Mac Hall, University of Calgary*
*29 October 1982, Calgary, Canada*

Anyone living in Calgary, Canada in the early '80s is likely to have learned of Simple Minds by watching local cable TV show, *FM Moving Pictures*. That's how I came to be at the University of Calgary's Mac Hall to see them perform. There were around 500 people there. Shriekback were the opening band.

The music and atmosphere were incredible, and I was right up front, where I've liked to be ever since. My high school friends and I talked our way backstage after. Jim Kerr had more eyeliner on than we did, and a swooping fringe over one eye, as did I. I swear I still have a lazy right eye now. He wore a leotard, and moved like a cat. He said he saw me, which annoyed my jealous friends. Too bad I was too shy to talk much to anyone, though I remember Mike Ogletree telling me off for being homesick for Britain, saying Thatcher had made it a shitehole and I should be happy where I was. Then Liz's dad came to pick us up so we had to go. 16, going on 17.

I made the mall record store I worked at order mountains of *New Gold Dream* LPs and cassettes, every unit of which we shifted as I refused to ever take it off the 'now playing'.

I saw them perform in Vancouver a few years later; in my Dad's birthplace of Llandudno in 2013; in Dubai with friends and family for my 50th birthday in 2016. Fantastic shows, wonderful music, but nothing can beat the intimacy and discovery of that first show, at an age when the world contains new marvels, new glamour, new gold dreams, when you find your tastes and tribe and feel you might be kind of cool for the first time ever.

Mike Bezzeg was the host of *FM Moving Pictures*, and is thought to have been Canada's first VJ, with an encyclopaedic knowledge of music, introducing our redneck town to so much. I admired him from afar for years, then got to know him through social media decades later. He became one of my

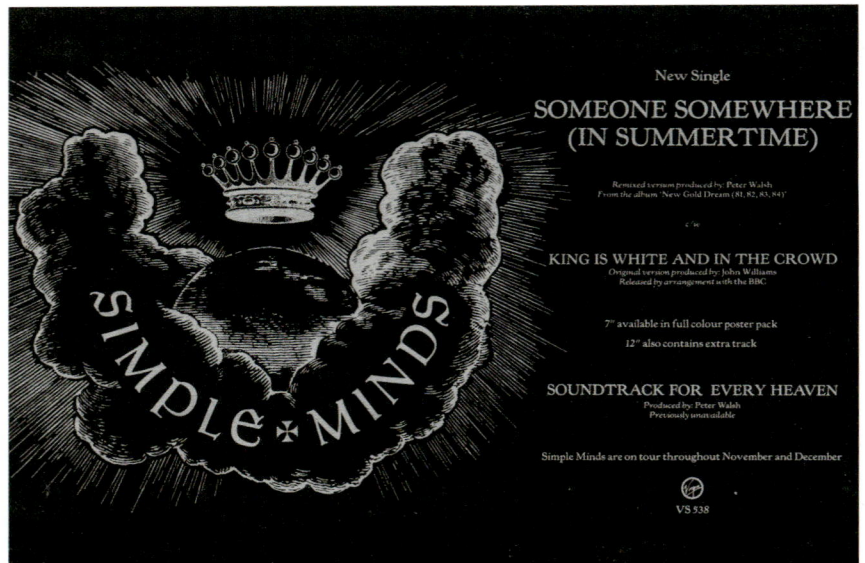

New Single

**SOMEONE SOMEWHERE
(IN SUMMERTIME)**

Remixed version produced by: Peter Walsh
From the album 'New Gold Dream (81, 82, 83, 84)'

c/w

**KING IS WHITE AND IN THE CROWD**

Original version produced by: John Williams
Released by arrangement with the BBC

7" available in full colour poster pack
12" also contains extra track

**SOUNDTRACK FOR EVERY HEAVEN**

Produced by: Peter Walsh
Previously unavailable

Simple Minds are on tour throughout November and December

VS 538

most supportive friends. I had to pinch myself when I became Facebook friends with Mike Ogletree, while living back in Britain after all, and both Mikes had a discussion about Donald Trump on my page one day, using the term 'dickweed' a great deal. It felt like the chapters of my life were sticking together.

Mike Bezzeg died after a terrible car crash in early 2020. Both my parents died in early 2020. Live music is a virtual thing, like my digital 'scrapbook' of scanned memories. The music of life is muted. But there's still friendship, connection, and memories of a British music heaven on the Canadian prairies. The glory days, you know, they come and go. Or so I've been told.

---

## ANNE MCGLASHAN

*Tiffany's*
*18 November 1982, Glasgow, Scotland*

I first saw Simple Minds on *Top of the Pops*. I think it was the video for 'Glittering Prize'. I then saw them at Glasgow Tiffany's and the following year at Glasgow Barrowland. I'm not sure how many times I've seen them there.

---

## GRAEME WEST

*Ulster Hall*
*22 November 1982,*
*Belfast, Northern Ireland*

I've followed Simple Minds since the age of 15, first introduced to the band by my older brother, who left Belfast in 1978 to go to Southampton University, where he saw

*Graeme West first saw the band at Belfast's Ulster Hall*

a lot of bands doing the uni circuit, including Simple Minds. When he came home to Northern Ireland at the end of term, I'd be exposed to all the early releases. My brother still teases me today that I've been a steadfast fan all these years yet he was the one who originally introduced me to the band.

I've been fortunate to see Simple Minds in concert many times. The most memorable was my first, in the Ulster Hall in late '82. I attended with my brother, home from university especially to attend with me. We did our customary revision of the *New Gold Dream* album, released only a couple of months before. Around the time, the band were making an impact on the UK music scene with the release of 'Promised You a Miracle' and 'Glittering Prize'. It was a time in Belfast when few bands ventured over the Irish Sea due to the Troubles, the crowd very enthusiastic and appreciative. When selecting our standing position we were careful not to be caught up in a sea of people being squashed and shunted around – we were there to enjoy the music!

The concert lived up to our high expectations. Jim Kerr was probably at his most ebullient self then, at his most hypnotic and mesmerising in his stage movements. The highlight was the performance of 'Hunter and the Hunted', when Jim repeatedly performed his swooping lunges to the floor in full 1980s regalia with green make-up. It was like a male version of a Kate Bush video – very theatrical and totally original as far as I was concerned, accompanied by Jim's vocal overlay, Charlie's guitar, Derek's keyboard and Mel's pulsating drumbeats. It was the stand-out performance of any I've seen at any concert, and I've seen many bands, including U2. The good acoustics of the Ulster Hall was central to the high level of performance. I didn't quite catch Mel Gaynor's drumsticks that night but came darn close.

In 1990 I was working in London after University but unhappy being away from Northern Ireland. It was the release of 'Belfast Child' that made my mind up to hand in my notice in at work and head back to my homeland. I tend to see it as an intervention by Simple Minds music that diverted my life in a different direction for the better, resulting in new family connections – a wife and fatherhood in my native Northern Ireland which itself has left behind the negative press coverage.

Recently on holiday in Taormina, Sicily accompanied by one of my childhood friends, we did the long hike from the town centre up to Villa Angela, Jim's hotel. At 54 years of age and in warm May weather, it was a bit of a struggle, creaking knees ascending all the steps then following a winding road to the hotel. I'll make sure I take a taxi next time. But when you've followed a band for 40 or so years, you'll risk the odd heart attack along the way. We were rewarded with a memorable lunch of pasta and red wine, and were looked after by Jim's engaging Glaswegian nephew, who was happy to talk about the band and show me some memorabilia on the hotel walls.

My continuing connection through the years is all down to the ability of the band to bond with its fans through music and performance in the context of changing musical styles and line-ups over five decades. Jim Kerr and Charlie Burchill have been the glue that held it all together. What an achievement! Thanks for the memories.

## MIKE REYNOLDS

*Apollo Theatre*
*28 November 1982, Manchester,*
*England*

In the summer of 1982 my brother Christopher took me to the Hacienda in Manchester, where Simple Minds were playing. Unfortunately, we couldn't get in as the place was packed out. But the name stuck and after seeing them on *Top of the Pops* I went and bought two tickets for Manchester Apollo that November.

*Mike Reynolds' Simple Minds journey started in Manchester and took him to Denmark*

From then on, I was hooked, mesmerised by Jim Kerr's moves and charisma and of course the lyrics and sound, which was and still is different from other bands.

In 1986 I met a Danish girl in London. We immediately connected, sharing the same taste in music. That summer Simple Minds played the Tourhout Rock Festival in Belgium so I invited 'the Danish girl' to this concert. This turned out to be the first of many Simple Minds concerts we've been to together. I followed her back to Denmark, where we've lived together since 1987.

# CULLUM BRENTON

*Royal Court*
*29 November 1982,*
*Liverpool,*
*England*

In 1981 I was 15 and, having just finished with my love of the new wave music revolution and especially The Jam, I found myself drifting towards the new romantic music scene. I bought an album called *Modern Dance*, a compilation of the latest bands like Japan, The Associates and Simple Minds. I heard 'Sweat in Bullet' for the first time and was immediately entranced. It sounded so different to the all-electronic bands, encapsulating the fresh sound of new romanticism whilst holding on to the new wave guitar. I went out and bought their back-catalogue and another Simple Minds fan was created.

*Cullum Brenton has seen Simple Minds 42 times*

I've seen them 42 times. My first concert was in 1982 in Liverpool for the *New Gold Dream* tour. To this day it is my favourite album, probably due to nostalgia more than anything, with *Walk Between Worlds* and *Real Life* just as musically good in my opinion. 'New Gold Dream' and 'Hunter and the Hunted' are my 'go to' songs. I introduced my wife, 10 years younger, to Simple Minds. When she heard songs like 'Glittering Prize' in her childhood she thought she was listening to INXS. She is now more educated!

## PAUL BROWN STONE

It was August or September 1981. Being 18 and unemployed, I spent nearly all day in my local record shop talking to Pete, the owner, listening to whatever was new. Thumbing my way through older records, I remember like it was yesterday the first crackles through the speakers as the needle hit the vinyl. It was one of those hallelujah moments and stopped me dead in my tracks. I rushed to the counter, asking, 'Who is that? It's amazing.' 'Not sure, think it's a band from Scotland' was his reply. It was the opening to 'In Trance as Mission'. We both sat there and listened to the whole *Sons and Fascination* album. Then I begged him to play it again, which he did. I rushed home, raided my piggy bank and went back to buy it, then rushed home again to play it to death.

I became obsessed with Simple Minds, even painting my wall in later years with the *Sparkle in the Rain* artwork. I joined the fan club and still have my membership card, No.124. Next was the wait to see them live, which I finally did for the first time at the Royal Court, Liverpool in 1982. It was beyond amazing.

---

## NICK GIBSON, AGE 16

*Top Rank*
*30 November 1982, Cardiff,*
*Wales*

It was a Tuesday, cold and dry, and I was in my first year of college studying Electrical Engineering. My mate had bought tickets for £3.50 to see Simple Minds and China Crisis, who were supporting. We queued outside the Top Rank. We got in and I bought a programme, badge and a drink. Well I didn't - I was only 16. We got down by the stage and the first thing I noticed was a real big drumkit. China Crisis came on and I enjoyed the show. I'd only seen Simple Minds live on *The Tube* and loved *New Gold*

*Nick Gibson saw Simple Minds at Cardiff's Top Rank*

*Dream* and *Sons and Fascination*, but was in two minds about seeing them live.

The house lights went off and I could smell the dry ice. The band appeared, picked up their instruments, and bang – they're off! 'New Gold Dream' screams out of the PA. Jim Kerr appears between the drum and keyboard riser, off moving around the stage like a man possessed. By 'Hunter and the Hunted' I was mesmerised. I couldn't believe how good this band were live - and so powerful. The sound, the lights - everything was amazing. I was also struck by the level of musicianship. Burchill's guitar unleashed and unrestrained, Forbes playing like a demon, MacNeil just adding layers and layers of sound. The drummer - I had no idea who he was – was propelling the band along, not missing a beat. Mr Kerr was outstanding as a frontman, with a really strong voice and great stage presence. My mates and I were dumbstruck, lost for words. A bunch of blokes were pissed and I think one of them threw a glass on stage so unfortunately the band didn't do an encore. Some 38 years later my mates and I still agree that was the best concert we've ever been too. If I could get hold of a time machine, after going back in time to meet family, Simple Minds' Cardiff Top Rank would be the next port of call.

---

# GARY SHINNER

I became aware of Simple Minds back in the late '70s when John Peel played bands just bubbling under the radar. He played a track I didn't discover the identity of until a few years later; it was 'Changeling'. Where I live, a small town in West Wales, we only had a small record shop that did indie type releases. I recall seeing the *Empires and Dance* LP. I was intrigued by the stark cover but didn't know 'I Travel' was on it. When I heard 'Love Song' in the late summer of 1981, I just had to get it. I travelled to my nearest city, Swansea, where WHSmith had the double-album *Sons and Fascination /Sister Feelings Call*. It felt like my birthday. It's an album I treasure to this day.

Once home and listened to, I soon went to local store, Falcon Music, to get *Empires and Dance*, another joyous album. I saw them live at the Top Rank. I was 18 that summer, my older sister at Cardiff Uni, so I was able to see a number of concerts. I was mesmerised by Jim Kerr leaping about the stage.

Since then I've managed to see them five times, including Cardiff Arms Park in 1989. If asked, I can't pick a favourite song but 'Waterfront' is brilliant live and I love to hear 'I Travel', 'Love Song' and 'The American.'

# MARK HAGLEY

*University of Exeter*
*1 December 1982, Exeter, England*

I used to buy loads of rubbish pop compilation albums of the hits of the day. This one included 'Japanese Boy' by Aneka among other gems, but one track made me go, 'Wait a minute, what is this?' as it was so different from anything else on there. The track was 'Love Song' and I remember playing it over and over again. I had to find more Simple Minds stuff! Before YouTube, etc. the only real way to discover more about a band was to buy more of their music. I went to my local store to find the album with 'Love Song' on it, *Sons and Fascination*. I was amazed when they gave me *Sister Feelings Call* as well!

*Mark Hagley first saw Simple Minds at Exeter University*

Simple Minds were on tour promoting the album *New Gold Dream* and coming to Exeter Uni, so I got some mates together and off we went. I remember the stage setup, the keyboards and drums on raised platforms either side, with a gap in the middle. The band opened with 'Theme for Great Cities' and then Jim walked on between the raised areas and I thought, 'Wow, this guy is so cool!'

I bought the back-catalogue and everything since. I've completely lost count of the number of gigs I've been to but it's fair to say Simple Minds have been the soundtrack to my life and given me so much pleasure and so many memories and I can't thank them enough for lighting up my life!

# TONY BIONDI

In 1979 I was 13 and into post-punk and John Peel. My first memory of Simple Minds was discovering the 'Life in a Day' single in the Rumbelows' bargain bin. I was drawn to the cover and, on taking it home, to that almost theatrical Bowiesque/ Roxy Music style. It was through Peel that I heard 'Changeling', 'Celebrate' and 'I Travel'. The latter's electrifying fusion of Euro-disco sequencer and post-punk resonated with me, alongside bands like Joy Division and Bauhaus. As an Italian born in the UK, I loved the European connection. My first Simple Minds album was the double *Sons and Fascination/Sister Feelings Call*. These songs were marvellous cinematic landscapes. 'Themes for Great Cities', 'The American' and 'Love Song' are songs I still revisit.

*New Gold Dream (81–82–83–84)*, the next Simple Minds transition, was reflected in my own life – experimenting with makeup at one level, and exploring spirituality at another. I finally got to see the band live on the *New Gold* tour at Exeter University in December 1982, an amazing gig with a collection of their most ethereal and majestic songs. The support was the excellent China Crisis.

I must have been subconsciously attracted to Steve Lillywhite's production by 1983, because by the time I heard 'Waterfront' I was already enjoying U2's *War* album. My musical tastes were following my spiritual journey in those days, and I was listening to both pretty much in tandem. Both were moving towards that bigger sound with *Sparkle in the Rain*, *The Unforgettable Fire*, *Once Upon a Time* and *The Joshua Tree*.

I lost track and it wasn't until my kids bought me the *Acoustic* album for Christmas that I reconnected. My 17-year-old son became a fan many years ago, and especially enjoys *Sons and Fascination/Sister Feelings Call*. Inevitably, I'm tied to the originals, but the reworking of these classics demonstrates what timeless compositions they really are.

---

# ARUN KENDALL

## *Lyceum*
## *8 December 1982, London, England*

Born in the UK in 1953, I grew up in Australia in the late '70s but always had a keen interest in music from the UK. Back then, all we had in Australia was the *NME*, delivered months late. However, at this time, a youth radio station was set up by the Government, Double J (later Triple J when it moved to FM) and this became the singular source for new music.

I didn't know Simple Minds when they first toured Australia in 1981 and I was finishing high school at the time so didn't get to see them. However, Double J had a series called *Live at the Wireless* and recorded a Simple Minds gig in Sydney. I recorded this off the radio and was absolutely blown away. I've been obsessed ever since, but that *Sons and Fascination* era just blew my mind, the Euro-disco sound mixed with punk brashness. I still have the cassette I recorded from this session, with songs like 'Chelsea Girl', 'Changeling' and 'Life in a Day'. I sought out and was obsessed with *Sister Feelings Call* and *Sons and Fascination*.

The next year I took a gap year before starting university and travelled around

Europe, mostly by bicycle. I heard 'Promised You a Miracle' and in Paris bought a cassette of the newly-released *New Gold Dream*. I cycled through France, Switzerland and Germany, listening to it endlessly on my Walkman. I still do. During this trip I stayed with my aunt and uncle in Yorkshire and managed to get tickets to both Lyceum shows in London in late '82, supported by another favourite band, China Crisis. The first night I was up front, the second I sat at the back. The best two gigs I ever attended.

For various reasons, I never managed to see Simple Minds play live again - they rarely visited Australia and weren't playing whenever I travelled to Europe. But I loved that period and still listen to *New Gold Dream*, *Sons and Fascination* and *Sister Feelings Call* incessantly. Simple Minds represent a musical awakening for me and hold a very special place in my heart.

## MARTIN LANE

My older brother threw me an album and said, 'Here, you might like this.' It was *Sons and Fascination*. That focused my musical attention for the summer of '81 and, to give more depth to my budding obsession, the accompanying *Sister Feelings Cool*. I was 15, eating up as much of Simple Minds as I could. On my 16th birthday, me and my two big brothers travelled to London to the Lyceum Ballroom for the *New Gold Dream* tour, showcasing the earlier-released album. I couldn't have been any readier to see my first indoor gig (living in Milton Keynes I'd gone to the first gig at the Bowl, featuring The Police).

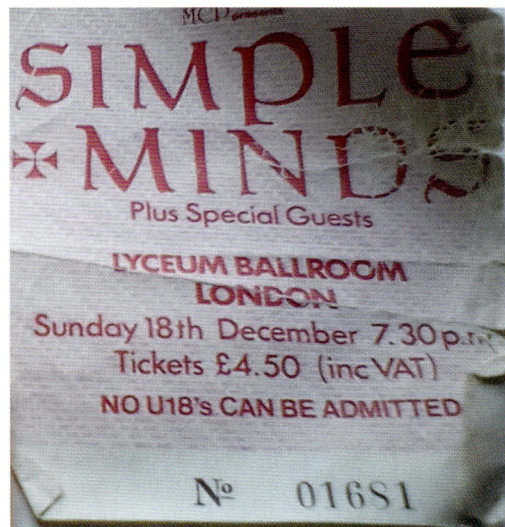

*Martin Lane first saw Simple Minds at the Lyceum in London*

Seeing the band up close with the live sound blew my mind and made all the albums seem sedate in comparison to the energy I witnessed that December night. I wanted the thundering drums and vocal strength, especially on closing number, 'New Gold Dream'. I came out of there dizzy and excited for more. I bought the tour t-shirt and my first job when I got home was to make the playlist on a spare cassette! I returned to the Lyceum and then the Hammersmith Odeon for the *Waterfront* tour. That first night was timed just right, with me turning 16. I came out of there older and wiser. Now 53, people from school still remember I was the guy who knew. I still do.

## NIGEL HENSHAW

I saw Simple Minds at the Lyceum. It was a great show and the band were really on top of their game. We were on the second floor, in the balcony area. To our right was the sound guy at the mixing desk. A few songs in, I glanced across and saw a young Bono run up to the mixing desk, followed by Adam Clayton. They started asking the sound guy a bunch of questions. They liked how good the sound was and Bono was determined to have U2 sound equally as good as one of their peers.

## CAROL LOUDON

*De Montfort Hall*
*12 December 1982,*
*Leicester, England*

Later in the year a tour was announced, so the day the tickets went on sale I hoofed it down early to the box office at the Town Hall Square and was the only one there, getting tickets one to four for De Montfort Hall!

On the day of the gig it was snowing, but I dragged my brother, sister and niece down early. We got there at half past four to queue – and there was no queue. A little later we saw Jim Kerr inside and he waved to us. I thought I was going to pass

**DE MONTFORT HALL, LEICESTER**

MCP presents

**SIMPLE MINDS**

plus GUESTS

Sunday 12th December

at 7.30 p.m.

**STANDING £3.75** INC. V.A.T.

Tickets not transferable or money refunded

**01**

To be retained

*Carol Loudon was at the head of the ticket queue at De Montfort Hall. There was no one else*

out. The doors opened and we got right to the front. The gig passed in a blur of tears and fab music. I got a setlist off the stage, still one of my most treasured possessions. A friend said she was going to wait at the stage door but having my young niece with me and also having that fear of meeting your heroes, I didn't. She told Jim about me and how much I was into them and he wrote me a note - unbelievable!

## SANDRA LONGMUIR

*Caird Hall*
*17 December 1982, Dundee, Scotland*

I went to see Simple Minds in the Caird Hall in 1982 as a naïve 17-year-old. China Crisis were the support. I will never forget the atmosphere, the music pounding through my body. It's my very first and still my favourite concert, despite seeing Michael Jackson in 1988 at Roundhay Park, Leeds and attending *Live 8* in London in 2005.

## ANDY PULLAR

I first saw the Minds live at the Caird Hall in 1982. I always loved their music, but this gig cemented my absolute love of the band. I worked as a waiter in the Angus Hotel, just along from the venue. I was always meeting celebrities, giving Paula Yates her breakfast then meeting the Boomtown Rats later that day. Superb. Other frequent visitors were the Glasgow Celtic team - many a good story can be told about their antics! The absolute highlight was getting back to the hotel after the '82 gig, where I sat with Charlie and Jim and chatted away. I asked them to name the next supergroup. Jim replied, 'There's a band coming out of Ireland, they will be huge. Watch out for Bono and U2.' The guys went on to sign my programme.

## JAMES HARRISON

*Playhouse Theatre*
*19 December 1982,*
*Edinburgh, Scotland*

Starting my apprenticeship in 1981 meant leaving Peterhead as a 17-year-old and heading to Edinburgh to attend a full-time college course. This brought together a group of young lads from all over the

PLAYHOUSE THEATRE
Greenside Place
Edinburgh

Sunday
19 December 1982
at 8.00 pm
Doors Open 7.00 pm

REGULAR MUSIC PRESENTS

SIMPLE MINDS

IN CONCERT   Plus Guest

V 28

STALLS £4.00

NO Cameras or Tape Recorders Allowed   NO RE-ADMISSION

No ticket exchanged or money refunded—Retain this portion

UK, so pubs, nights out and music was what it was all about! The cheapest spots and best music venues were student unions, where the Minds really gripped me. Their music was so different. Passing the Playhouse Theatre one day I was delighted to see them highlighted on the billboards.

I couldn't wait to hear all the tracks we had listened to on many nights in the student unions – 'Love Song', 'Sweat in Bullet' and 'The American'. The Playhouse was a great venue and although our seats were on the upper balcony it felt brilliant to be there. My nervous anticipation on the night was new to me. The buzz when the lights went out and the crowd began anticipating the band's arrival was awesome. Then 'Theme for Great Cities' started and the hairs on the back of my neck stood on end. After what seems like ages the group appeared on stage to a tremendous reception.

First impressions did not disappoint. They were dressed in black suits with knee-length black boots. Jim loved the frontman role and the way he held the mic was typical of a guy oozing confidence. Charlie played amazingly, mouthing every word as Jim sang. Throughout, all the lights would go and just one brilliant white light would come from the centre of the stage to illuminate the crowd. The music was awesome. Looking back to those early albums and hearing them live was superb.

I've followed the band since, in stadia, small venues, outdoor forest gigs and arenas. But you never forget your first!

## DAVID GALLAGHER

*Tiffany's
20 & 21 December 1982,
Glasgow, Scotland*

I introduced my wee sister Elaine to Simple Minds when she was 13 or 14 with the *New Gold Dream* album, although she'll probably say I didnae! I took her to her first concert at Tiffany's in Sauchiehall Street, Glasgow. She was underage as it was a licensed venue, but with a bit of lippy and 'in you go'

REGULAR MUSIC Presents
**THE SIMPLE MINDS**
PLUS GUESTS
at TIFFANY'S GLASGOW
Tuesday, 21st December 1982
Doors open at 7.30 pm
Ticket £3.75 (in advance)

The management reserve the right to refuse admission

Nº 0846

back then. It was a magical night for both of us, especially when 'Hunter and The Hunted' came on. It was a great honour to take her to her first concert and to see the delight on her face. She was madly in love with Jim and his white face look and 'Hitler haircut', as I called it.

The band were so ahead of their time and I couldn't believe their sound came from my hometown of Glasgow. Charlie's guitar was magical and I loved his guitar solo add-ons before each song. Mick, Mel and Derek are all heroes of the city.

I live in Perth, Western Australia now and many days I stick on 'Love Song' or 'I Travel' to get me in the mood on the way to work. My sister still lives in Glasgow.

Simple Minds are legends and should have a street or statue in Glasgow named after them. Can we have a smaller or indoor gig next time in Perth?

## ROY MCALLISTER

Whilst I was in Chicago in 1982 or '83, Jim was interviewed on TV, an interview he ended abruptly. It was something to do with being asked, 'Whereabouts in England do you stay?' Jim replied, 'Glasgow'. The interviewer said, 'Whereabouts in England is that?' Jim got up and walked off the set. Hilarious.

## JAAP ALBERTS

*Koninklijk La Carre*
*1 March 1983, Amsterdam, The Netherlands*

In the spring of 1982, I had just lost my promotion job in the music industry. With nothing else available and bills to pay, I took on a job as a swimming pool lifeguard. At night, I played records at a disco in Bombarde, Hilversum. Here I received regular requests to play 'Promise You a Miracle' by Simple Minds, I liked it, but had never heard of them.

A phonecall woke me one afternoon. 'Come for a coffee, I am starting Virgin Records in Holland, I am looking for a press officer.' The deal was done. I started 1 August. My first activity that Monday morning was to file the press archive. Reading through I learned – oops! - Simple Minds had made many more records than what I'd heard. There was no time to read up on them now, or listen to their back-catalogue. My first album promotion was already pressing, *New Gold Dream (81,82,83,84)*. I had been playing it 24/7 and it literally became a life-changing experience.

The first time I met the band was in March 1983. I was 26 and it was the European *New Gold Dream* tour. They stayed in the Sonesta Hotel, Amsterdam, an industry hotspot, in preparation for their gigs in the local Carre and at de Doelen, Rotterdam. Then there was a week's tour in Belgium, returning to play de Vereniging in Nijmegen.

The concert in Carre was mesmerising. Although not a real dance theatre, with seating only, the experience was electrifying. De Doelen was my second concert and the band thought the evening was below par, but I did not share their opinion. Nijmegen, to all involved, felt it was first class.

Simple Minds came back to Holland one more time that year, in May, to headline Pinkpop. A massive concert and a grand finale to their *New Gold Dream* tour. Their coach, sadly, left for Glasgow that same evening.

---

# FABRICE TUCH

*Cirque Royal*
*2 March 1983, Brussels, Belgium*

I remember going to this show with my childhood friend, Aldo. I was 15. I didn't know them at all and immediately became a fan. In 1986 I decided to organise a bus for the Paris-Bercy concert. 100 people wanted to go! My grandfather drove me to Paris to buy the tickets.

In 1989 I took my nine-year-old sister Geraldine to Brussels, Dortmund and Amiens, where Jim pulled everyone aside to give her a hug after the concert. She then became 'The Baby Simple Minds'. Since then, at every concert Jim throws her a little 'hello Geraldine'.

My whole family are fans. In July 1991 in Brussels we celebrated Jim's and my birthday with champagne in front of the hotel. In 2012 I took my eight-year-old daughter Jade to her first concert at Brussel for the *5x5* tour. In 2015, my son and I went to the first concert of the *Big Music* tour in Lisbon, which allowed me to befriend Marc Lichtenstein, whose wedding I witnessed in 2019. In 2017, for my 50th birthday, my family arranged a stay at the Villa Angela hotel for me and my wife, Mylène. It was a wonderful surprise.

During our trip to Glasgow in 2018, we listened to the soundcheck at the

Barrowland and attended the photo-shoot. We were able to chat with the band and that remains an extraordinary memory. The same year, with Geraldine and Marc, we went to the Arena in Nîmes, where we were dazzled by the performance and the beautiful location.

During the 2020 tour, my wife and I were supposed to celebrate our 100th concert. Life decided otherwise.

## MARC FALLA

In 1983, a friend said, 'You want to come to see Simple Minds at the Royal Circus of Brussels?' Jim enchanted me the whole concert. I felt he was addressing each of us personally. I haven't missed a tour since. In 1986, myself and four friends got to meet Jim after the soundcheck at Paris-Bercy. We got his autograph, but I was too overwhelmed to speak!

## LIESBETH BAKKER

*De Doelen*
*6 March 1983, Rotterdam, The Netherlands*

It started with the album *New Gold Dream* for me. My first time seeing them was at the Doelen, sat on the second or third row. It was fantastic to see the band and Jim so close up and we had a great evening with friends. The second time was at the Werchter Festival, 3 July 1983. My two favourite bands, U2 and Simple Minds, sharing a stage. The highlight was Bono and Jim together on the stage, singing 'New Gold Dream'. Amazing!

The concert at the Ahoy in Rotterdam in March 1984 was also special. It was all seated, standing not allowed, but Jim was waving at the crowd, saying 'Come on, come to the stage.' He kept asking. Myself and the rest of the crowd ran up to the stage. The stewards couldn't stop us. I saw the rest of the concert singing and dancing in front of the stage. I think they took the seats out of the Ahoy after that.

## ALAIN CANNOOT

Simple Minds are part of my music life. They became bigger and they changed but they're still the best and still bring me happiness after all these years.

# FAT EDGARDO

*Palazzo dello Sport*
*14 March 1983, Bologna, Italy*

I started to get to know the music of Simple Minds at the beginning of the '80s by attending discos, hearing songs like 'I Travel', 'Love Song' and 'The American'. With the release of *New Gold Dream* I started following the band, buying the back-catalogue and discovering goodies I didn't know. I saw them for the first time in Bologna in 1983 and it was fantastic. And then Milano '86, Modena and Verona '89, Bologna, Modena and Verona '91…. I'm not going to list them all. There are many.

I was lucky enough to meet Messrs. Kerr, Burchill, Forbes and Gaynor. I've also met other fans I stayed in contact with over the years. My desire to follow the band never ceased. Theirs has practically been the soundtrack of my life, one in which I have taken refuge and fantasised more than once.

---

# INGA HAAS

*Philipshalle*
*21 March 1983,*
*Düsseldorf, West Germany*

My school friend gave me a ticket to see them at the Philipshalle for my 14th birthday. I had never heard their music before, but the next day I bought every record I could get my hands on. Then I saw them in Dortmund. That was even more amazing. In 1986, my friend and I met them at their hotel in Düsseldorf, just before going

to see them again at the Philipshalle. That night I went up on stage to give Jim a hug while he was singing 'Someone Somewhere (in Summertime)' and probably gave him a big fright.

I've been to Simple Minds all over the world. I left Germany in 1989, moved to London for 16 years and then Japan. I now live in Perth,

Australia. The last concert I saw was in Perth's Kings Park in 2017 and it was fantastic to see them again. Their music still gives me so much love and pleasure and the best memories of my teens. It has helped me, given me strength in not so good times and made it possible for me to achieve the best I could. I am forever grateful.

## MARK COATES

I was serving in Germany and Simple Minds were on a European tour. Normally we would buy tickets at a little record shop in Menden,or you could combine the purchase with a train ticket at the nearby station. This time a mate had purchased a new diesel Mercedes and was going to take the four of us to the Philipshalle gig. Get tickets before? No, we were told. It won't be a problem. Buy on the door.

Big mistake. We got to the car park and the queue went around the building. Forlorn, we gave up and went to the adjoining restaurant. The gig started and we listened for 40 minutes or so before being asked to give up the table. To cap a miserable night, it was pouring with rain and the Mercedes ran out of diesel on the autobahn heading home. Not the best of nights.

## ÖJJE HOLT

*Konserthuset*
*27 March 1983, Stockholm, Sweden*

Their music has been a dear friend and stable companion in my life ever since I heard 'I Travel' on the radio in 1980. From my first live experience in Stockholm in March 1983 to my recent one in Stockholm in March 2020 - 37 years and over 50 concerts attended. All the times I've stood in rain and cold outside arenas in Europe, waiting to say 'hi' and perhaps get an autograph. The joy when another Simple Minds fanzine landed in my mailbox. The music that soothed my teenage heartaches, the music that held my hand through misery and most of all happiness. My email address (aliveandkicking@) is a Simple Minds song, with that song also the theme song at my wedding. I can't write a story that reflects all that in the right way. All I can say is thank you.

# LENNY LOVE

*Simple Minds Tour Manager 1980s*
*Agora Ballroom*
*5 May 1983, Cleveland, Ohio*

I first met Simple Minds whilst visiting my friend Bruce Findlay in his office, above one of his shops (Bruce's Record Shops) in Shandwick Place, Edinburgh. They were young and shy. Bruce had signed them to his Zoom label and played me their song 'Chelsea Girl', which I thought was great. However, after being asked to become their tour manager, I was off to Canada with them, where I first met their amazing lighting man, Steve Pollard – a total poser, with a wickedly acid-sharp line in comebacks. Brilliant – what's not to like?

I remember when I shared a room with Jim at the old dingy hotel in London we used in the early days (whose name I can't recall) and I took a phone call while Jim was in the bath. It was an Australian journalist wanting to interview him before a tour there. I knocked on the bathroom door and told Jim, and he said to hand the phone to him, so he could do the interview while he was lying in the bath.

I also remember the band were booked on a European tour - taking in Sweden, Denmark, Belgium, Holland, Germany and France – I think it was something like 28 dates in 32 days, and I was driving the band in an American-style, left-hand drive, luxury minibus. Due to the lack of sat-nav in those day, bass player Derek Forbes says I had to make dozens and dozens of U-turns. Probably true. However, it soon appeared that the agent responsible for scheduling the tour did so by throwing darts at a map of Europe, because there were hotel rooms booked for the band on a few nights that had to be cancelled, and I had to drive overnight to get the band to the next venue in the next country in time for them to do a soundcheck. I think Sweden to Germany was one, and Germany to France another.

However, right from the very start of that Euro tour, it was obvious that the band's reputation for delivering the goods was filling every club or venue they were booked into. After we'd reached Sweden and done two or three dates there, I was told by the Swedish promoter's road manager there had been a problem with the next venue, and the gig had been moved to another. OK, but when we got to the replacement venue and the band had finished their soundcheck, they went into their dressing room, and the audience were allowed in. I collared the promoter's man and asked

what they were playing at - the venue was easily twice the size of the one originally scheduled, so I said I wanted to renegotiate the deal – or the band wouldn't play. I was told the promoter couldn't be contacted (no mobile phones then), but he said 'it would all be OK'. I was adamant – no performance until I had double the money in my hand.

Around this point, Charlie came into the room and asked when they were going on stage. I turned to him and said something along the lines of, 'Not until we've been paid, so please just wait in the dressing room, as we might be leaving early.' Charlie raised his eyebrows, and ducked back out. The promoter's man then 'excused himself' and was back in less than 15 minutes – with the cash!

I also recall a night on a tour in America. We were in Cleveland, and by that time the band and I all had individual rooms. I was in my room – at least a couple of floors up - talking to a nice lady who one of the record company promotion people, and there was a knock. On the window. I pulled back the curtain, and there was Derek Forbes, standing on the two-foot wide ledge, stark naked, laughing his head off. Nutter!

There are many, many other stories that could be told, but my lips are sealed!

---

## JULIE BYRNE

*Pinkpop, Burgemeester Damen Sportpark*
*23 May 1983, Geleen, The Netherlands*

I remember trying to get to the front of the crowd with two trays of six beers (those were the days). I didn't take a camera as I would only lose them after a few too many, which happened far too often.

Another time there was an anti-apartheid rally in Hyde Park. I'd been on nightshift so went straight there, stood at the front until 6pm and fell asleep. Then I ran round the back to see them. I was so busy looking for Jim, I missed Mel coming out and the chance to talk to him.

---

## MARY LEITH

'They can remember quiet side of midnight.' I used to think they were saying 'the bright side of midnight'. Well, whatever, I remember both. They were such an edgy band and we Scots in Europe loved them. We used to laugh at to how to translate the name into Dutch. I think it would be 'eenvoudige zielen-simple', as in a clear straightforward sense.

Their music could be the soundtrack of my life. I've been at their concerts in the Netherlands and in Scotland with my three loves. One in the past, one dead and one still with me, who used to be able to leap high like Jim Kerr on stage. But as you get older, the leaping stops.

The one who died? We had tickets for Edinburgh Castle. I thought the phone call was to arrange the travel but, no, it was his brother dealing the awful blow. I still went to the gig. The rain was unnatural. Get in, get out of the rain. But at least the gig went on, though nobody had anywhere to get out of the rain. It's like the heavens protested his death as torrents flowed down the Royal Mile. Then driving North through the monsoon conditions in an old Merc with a cassette player. I had a charity shop cassette playing 'This Earth You Walk Upon'. I was in my own movie, Simple Minds supplied the soundtrack, aquaplaning up the A90 as the sky and earth merged into unnatural darkness and always the pain of loss in me.

Live they are magnificent, but it's how their music and lyrics encapsulate times and feelings. Not all sad. 'Speed Your Love to Me' will always be the soundtrack of an illicit affair on a thundery night in Amsterdam and yeah - more misinterpreted lyrics – 'The American'. 'Ameri, ameri, ameri…' We thought you were singing our wee daughter's Dutch name, 'Ameri, ameri, maria, Marijke.' That's ok. Just know the glittering associations those words and music have for ordinary beings in the crowd.

---

## MATT DOZIZO

I was 18 and spend most of my weekends in a club called Dolhuis in Dordrecht in the Netherlands. It was there in November 1981 that I heard 'Love Song' for the first time. I ran to the DJ and screamed, 'Who are they? Who are they? Who are they?' He answered, 'Simple Minds.' At first, I thought he was telling me I had a simple mind because of the way I reacted to the music. I asked him again. He replied again, 'Simple Minds.'

The first time I saw them live was at Pinkpop in 1983. After that I saw them every time they played the Netherlands. The 1989 show at De Kuip (Feyenoord Stadium) was phenomenal. Then I discovered the website Simpleminds.com and the fan forum and found a lot of like-minded people, and then Facebook came along….

Over the years I've seen Simple Minds lots and met fans that have become friends, which has taken me to Ireland, Germany, Scotland, Belgium… and who knows where else this journey will take me.

---

# PETER MINNEBO

*Rock Torhout/Rock Werchter*
*Festivalpark*
*2 & 3 July 1983, Belgium*

It was in 1984 that I started searching for the Simple Minds music treasure after a pupil gave a lecture about the song 'Big Sleep' in a religious lesson at secondary school. And when I heard 'Up on the Catwalk' coming out of the speakers at teenage parties I knew my mission was to follow these Minds! And we were lucky in Belgium, them playing the Torhout-Werchter festivals in 1983, '84 and '86.

In 1997, I had the opportunity, together with 10 other dedicated fans, to interview Jim Kerr live on Radio Donna in the Antwerp Sportpaleis venue. Now we know he has no special preferences backstage - no fresh sea water in his bath like Michael Jackson asked for - but just wants to eat delicious Japanese miso soup.

Jim wrote, 'I know a special place, been going there for nearly 30 years. For me there is no better place to sit a few minutes and watch the day begin.' I knew where he meant. On 25 July 2014, at exactly 10.49 am, I found him, alone on the terrace of a restaurant, enjoying the Sicilian morning sun. I got to talk to him. It was very agreeable, but my legs were shaking!

---

# NANCY MARSELOO

It was my first ever festival ever, with Simple Minds, U2 and others. It was a case of 'wow! I liked new wave music. I also remember a beach festival in Zeebrugge with sun, a good vibe and great music, and remember them as the opening act on a Rolling Stones tour. I'm convinced the Stones pulled the plug after an hour because the concert was that great!

I've seen them loads of times since. In 2009, I got the hotel, flight and ticket for a Simple Minds concert in Taormina and then couldn't be there. But a friend called me up so I could listen to the concert over the phone!

---

# JO MARTENS

I saw Simple Minds for the first time at the Torhout-Werchter Festival in the '80s. I've also seen them a few times at Deinze Brielpoort. That's when I took a step into the unknown, ending up on the tour bus with a friend. But Mel, the drummer, advised us to leave the bus because we were so young. Wisely we listened to him - I just heard

my dad - and we got back on our feet and the bus driver stopped the tour bus and let us back out. My dad, who came to pick me up, had been in the car for a while and was very angry. He'd been waiting more than half an hour. I couldn't sleep that night. That accidental meeting with my favourite band was a highlight of my youth!

---

# MERCK MERCURIADIS

Simple Minds in 1982 were all about faith and love. They were a band you could genuinely believe in and the love that they had for their audience, their team, their family, anyone who wanted to help - as well as each other - was given back ten times over. They're proof of concept for the law of attraction, and the original Golden Rule - Do Unto Others As You Would Do Unto Yourself - come to life. They knew 'the secret' decades before it became a book. The love we all had for each other, the belief and the faith could not be corrupted by anyone or anything between 1982 and 1986.

The cast of characters, including Mick, Derek (New Gold Dan!) and Mel as well as Lenny Love, Big John Ramsey, Matt Dunn, Stephen Pollard (the heartthrob of our gang, you had to be Simon Le Bon to steal his girl!), Pete Hendrie, Paul Kerr, Matt Dunn, Andy Battye, Leslie Ann Milthorpe and - later on - Jimmy Devlin, Deb Caponetta, Robin Clark, Sue Hadjopolous et al was led from the top by Jim, Charlie (Piranha!) and the incomparable Bruce Findlay.

It meant everything to me to be part of that inner circle (still in my teens!) and play a small role in their success, and still does. I had a barely high school education but everything that allowed me to become who I am today was learned in those days at the University Of Simple Minds, and in turn the PhD level education we all received from our obsession with everyone from The Doors, Lou Reed, Iggy Pop and Bowie to Faust, Neu, Can and Kraftwerk through to Genesis/Peter Gabriel, Roxy, Doctors of Madness, Television, Patti Smith, Chic - and Bach. Listen to the Brandenberg Concertos as a starting point!

Jim and Bruce were the teachers and I learned everything from the importance of integrity to knowing, as I do at this moment, as I write these words, that the only thing that really matters besides music are your friends and family. The people that you believed in and that believed in you before anyone else did. This was my job, to make people believe … in the majesty of *New Gold Dream*, *Sparkle in the Rain* and *Once Upon a Time*. We lived in buses, the Columbia Hotel (full of ghosts!) was the centre of the universe and we were each other's entertainment.

I'm pretty sure I was annoying as fuck as my enthusiasm and obsession with music, and Simple Minds in particular, was relentless but somehow they were all gracious enough to put up with me. This extended to their families and Jim's dad and mum were special people who loved Jim Reeves ('He'll Have To Go'!) and grew up hard in the Gorbals, where you were 'a faggot' because you read books.

Helping the band get their first gold records for *New Gold Dream* and in the process dragging *Sons and Fascination* to the success it deserved is one of the most special things I have ever been a part of. There were plenty more to come, but those are incredibly memorable because the 'New Gold Dream' was now becoming a reality.

In those days Jim would black out the windows of every hotel/motel we would encounter and I remember trying to show the glittering prize of these shiny gold awards to Jim in the darkness while the sun was blazing outside. He was excited, but his only real concerns were to make sure the people that really helped the band 'get here' would be acknowledged, and the concert that was to take place that night.

Live, the band had very few peers and the highlights are so numerous, from the Concert Hall and Massey Hall in Toronto to the Barrowland, Madison Square Garden, the first arena shows in Glasgow at the old SECC and the Zenith in Paris (and the world gets hot!).

I'd have to single out Torhout and Werchter (Belgium) in the summer of '83 as the most important weekend in the future of the band. Imagine Warren Zevon, John Cale, Eurythmics, U2, Simple Minds, Peter Gabriel and Van Morrison all on one day, two days in a row either side of Brussels (I Travel!). Simple Minds and U2 were the most important 'new' bands in the world that summer, and it was agreed that on the first day U2 would be on before Simple Minds, then vice versa the second day. The respect, rivalry and friendships born that weekend are still with us today. The Edge and Dave Stewart telling us about working with Holger Czukay was eye-watering. I remember Larry Mullen and I watching Simple Minds in awe from the side of the stage while reminiscing about Mission Of Burma. Eurythmics and Peter Gabriel were sensational. All of us were shaking in the presence of Van Morrison… but it was clear that weekend the world would belong to U2 and Simple Minds!

Another thing I remember about that weekend and summer is that the airwaves belonged to David Bowie and the *Let's Dance* album and single he made with Nile Rodgers. That album was a massive influence on the crossover of Eurythmics, U2 and Simple Minds, demonstrating what was possible.

It's important to mention that I fell in love over Simple Minds. I lost that love in this same period and the only thing I know about that person more than 35 years later is that Jim and Charlie are still in touch with her, as they are with everyone that helped them 'get here'. We lost our love for each other but our love for Simple Minds, and theirs for us, still remains.

We all became vegetarians in this period, when Jim met Chrissie, and 35 years later I'm still vegan and have children aged 18 to 32 that have never had animal products pass through their mouths. Such was the influence.

My job is still to make people believe in what I believe in and I have built a billion pound company on the back of those lessons, learned from Bruce Findlay and Jim Kerr while we were running around the world at 30 frames a second.

I also remember we were all speechless when listening to Herbie Hancock's solo on 'Hunter and the Hunted', including Mick. The combination of Mick and Charlie rivals that of Pink Floyd's Richard Wright and David Gilmour in my book.

Then there was Jim and I discussing The Clash. We both loved them but Jim saw their view as very London-centric, whereas he was excited about the possibilities of the world … travel round, travel round decadence and pleasure towns, tragedies, luxuries, statues, parks and galleries… I Travel!

Also, Jim and I driving around a frozen Woodstock, New York listening to the demo of 'Sanctify Yourself', written that night. Our car broke down and we had to walk about seven miles back to the studio through the dead of night, guided by what to us appeared to be a magical stray cat. Love is all you need!

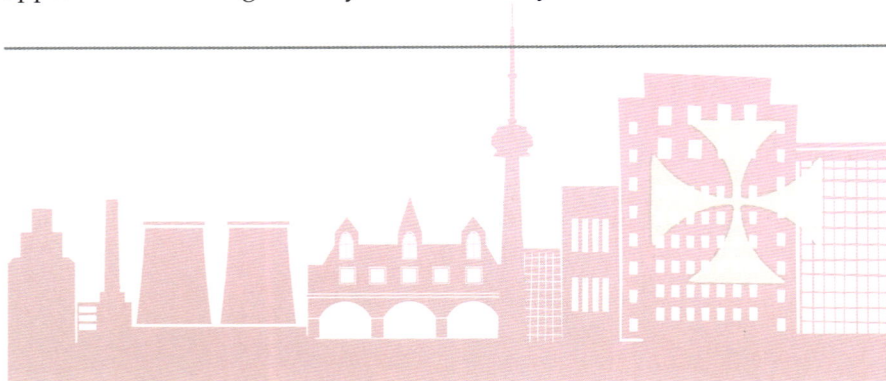

# LUIGI ABENA

*Tursport Arena*
*7 July 1983, Taranto, Italy*

I was in the early months of my long military career. During evening guard service, a few metres from the training base where I served, on a starry, summer night I'll never forget, echoed Jim's voice, Charlie's guitar and the splendid notes of 'New Gold Dream'. That night the soundtrack of my life was written.

# MIREILLE, AGE 20

*Elixir Festival*
*15 July 1983, Toulouse, France*

I went with my two best friends and all three of us were totally possessed by the band's performance. I think it brought us together in a weird way, creating a bond between us. We already spoke a common language; the music of the '80s and Simple Minds were definitely a big part of it.

  It's hard to pinpoint what made Simple Minds' music so exceptional for us. We saw The Police and Alice Cooper a couple of days before, but it didn't have the same impact (and Alice, I definitely don't think wearing a boa constrictor around your neck is an incentive for your audience to bond with your music). There was a chemistry in the group. The combination of Mick MacNeil's keyboard riffs, Charlie's magical guitar and Jim's soothing vocals and tip-toeing across the stage. God knows why we were into the group's music, and God sure works in mysterious ways, but I assure you it was and remains a true musical revelation for me.

It was probably the reason I moved to London in 1985 with my two friends, to be at the heart of this inspiring musical scene. We also hitchhiked our way in Scotland that year to get acquainted with the mysterious Scottish moors. Eerie, isn't it? To imagine that a couple of Scottish lads with weird '80s hairdos and eyeliner could move us with their music.

During three years in London, we spent most of our time going to concerts - Simple Minds and U2, but also bands like Lords of the New Church, The Jesus and Mary Chain, The Damned, The Alarm, The Waterboys. I always had a soft spot for music and still do, despite working in the music industry for a few years (that sure as hell can put you off!), but I'd be at loss to try and explain why Simple Mind's music resonated with me.

When I came back to Paris in 1988, I was working for French radio (Skyrock) and they sent me to interview Jim in 1991 for the release of *Real Life*. It was a sort of reality check, we had a nice chat about music and this and that, but it didn't enlighten me in any way as to why Simple Minds felt so special to me.

I don't work in the business anymore. I stopped going to concerts too. I've grown up but in 2018 was invited by a friend working at OUI FM to a Simple Minds private concert in Paris at the Réservoir and am not afraid to admit I totally enjoyed it. It felt cozy, like I had reunited with some old Scottish friends for the evening and, despite all these years, the spirit of the band is there and still resonating with me. So, hands up to you guys – it's definitely nothing to do with the hairdos. Your magic touch is still there, and I'm still smitten.

# FRANK MCALEVEY

*Phoenix Park Racecourse*
*14 August 1983, Dublin, Ireland*

The lineup was Perfect Crime, Steel Pulse, Big Country, Eurythmics, Simple Minds and U2. I loved them all but Simple Minds were my band. It was my first 'daytime date' with my then girlfriend, now wife of 28 years, a scorching hot August day in a field of young beautiful people, optimistic for the future and full of the energy and vitality of youth. My favourite moment was Jim hunkered down, arm outstretched, beckoning the setting sun while singing 'Someone Somewhere (in Summertime)'. Absolutely perfect.

# DEREK HAYDEN

I heard 'The American' on a Dublin pirate radio station and a few days later purchased the 12-inch single from a record store on O'Connell Street. Little did

*Derek Hayden first saw Simple Minds at Dublin's Phoenix Park*

I know that this was the start of something very special that four decades later would still be a part of my life. My first gig, at Phoenix Park Racecourse, was the debut for 'Waterfront'. All my mates that day were big U2 fans but blown away by Kerr and co, while I declared it an away day win for the Glasgow boys in my hometown.

Six months later those same mates came along to see Simple Minds at the SfX centre and another memorable night was had. I was so chuffed in 1986 to see the band I was so into being on top of the world, playing to over 70,000 people in Croke Park. The day before I left my house on the north side of Dublin and pen and paper in hand headed to the airport, getting soaked on the way. It was all worthwhile as I got to meet my idols and I remember sticking my head in the back of the black limo and reminding Jim not to forget his 'beret' for the gig.

Now, 34 years later, living just outside Glasgow, I'm still getting to hear this amazing band produce amazing new music and seeing them tour regularly. I'm 51 and can't believe this journey started when I was a 12-year-old boy. I remember Jim being interviewed many years ago and saying if you've got endless energy and if you're mad enough and brave enough you will succeed. Well, succeed they certainly have.

# JANET DOWLING

It was a hot summer's day and my brother and I queued to see my very first live gig, the best gig I ever had the pleasure of going to in Dublin. I relive that gig over and over and tell everyone how great it was. Simple Minds were as brilliant live as they are recorded. And we missed our bus home.

In town years later on Grafton Street, on another lovely sunny day, I realised Jim Kerr had walked past. I nearly fell out of my shoes and couldn't wait to ring my brother to tell him. I love to wind him up about my meeting and seeing great artists.

# ELAINE FERGUSON

*Barrowland Ballroom*
*20 November 1983, Glasgow, Scotland*

*Elaine Ferguson's ticket for the Barrowland shoot*

Occasionally we'd travel into Glasgow for a night out. On a Saturday in November 1983 we were so glad we did. We headed for Nightmoves, Sauchiehall Street, a disco full of posers and Gary Numan/Pete Burns/Boy George etc lookalikes. It was fantastic. The DJ projected stills of the latest Simple Minds video, 'Waterfront', onto a big screen, saying filming would resume the next day at the Barrowland Ballroom, ticket entry only. We raced to the DJ to find out how to get tickets, only to be told they had been issued free via a Radio Clyde phone-in. How did we miss that?

The next morning, we got glammed up and caught an early train into Glasgow, heading straight for the Ballroom – with no tickets. We were among the first to arrive, which would have been great had we been able to get in. We tried pleading with Billy Sloan for tickets. That fell on deaf ears. A policeman who saw how desperate we were also tried to get us tickets, with no luck. Then, out of the blue, a guy came over and offered us his. He said we would appreciate the experience more than he would and said we could stand with his friends near the front of the queue – result!

The atmosphere when the doors opened was electric. The band came on and Jim said he didn't know how to thank us all for coming (him thank us?!) so the best way to do that was to perform a concert. The only downside was that I've never seen myself in the video, despite wearing a neon green bow in my hair). But I was definitely there. I have the ticket to prove it.

# IRENE KANE

My big sister Karen would play their records in our shared bedroom. My first concert was them at Glasgow Barrowland at the end of 1983. My sister bought the tickets since I was only 14 and she was 18. I attended Charlotte Street Secondary School and would proudly walk back and forth to school

*Irene Kane's first gig was to see Simple Minds at the Barras*

*Fans queue for a Simple Minds concert outside the Barrowland Ballroom, Glasgow, Nov 83. - photo Trinity Mirror / Mirrorpix / Alamy Stock Photo*

with my homemade artwork of Simple Minds on my ring binder, showing it off to everyone. We lived across from St Mungo's Boys School on the Gallowgate, a short walk to the Barrowland. Every time SM played there in the '80s we'd go. I remember everyone going crazy the night Bono came on stage.

On the nights we couldn't afford a ticket we'd walk down and listen at the front doors. It might sound sad but they were good times. We always stood just to the side, in front of Charlie. One time I ventured into the middle at the front of the stage and thought I was gonna die, so I quickly retreated to my favourite spot. I can't really remember too much from my teenage years, but the Barrowland has a very special place in my heart.

## KAY MELROSE

Of all my memories, from jumping into a minibus complete with holes in the floor on the way to the Columbia Hotel in London, to dancing wildly on the lawn of The Manor at dawn when *New Gold Dream* had just been completed through the night, one of the most magical times was the day Simple Minds brought the now-legendary Barrowland back to life. The band chose to film the video for 'Waterfront' in the disused Glasgow ballroom in 1983. The audience, who all got their tickets via a phone-in to Radio Clyde, lined the streets outside. As the doors opened there was a mighty stampede as fans charged to the front of the stage. I remember the palpable feeling of hysteria and exhilaration from the crowd as a ghostly abandoned hall was resurrected. As I dashed to the ladies during the show I was shocked (and bemused) by the deafening sound coming from the empty room; the fans jumping up and down on the sprung dancefloor upstairs caused every single cubicle door to slam back and forth to the beat of the music. The building itself was alive and kicking.

## AGNES BURNS

*Barrowland Ballroom
21 – 23 December 1983,
Glasgow, Scotland*

I was 16 and quite small for my age. I lived in a place called Nitshill and this was my first big concert, venturing into town. When

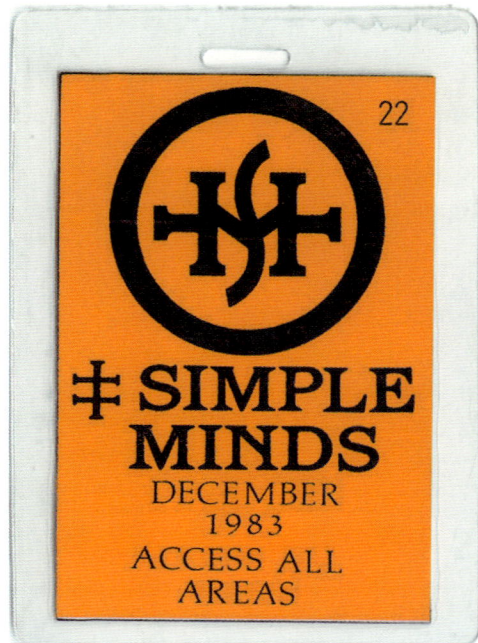

there, I tried to push my way to as near the front as I could. The concert was amazing. When Jim wiped his face and threw his sweaty towel into the crowd, I somehow managed to leap up and grab it, but only for a split-second. Then I suddenly became more of a focus than the band. I sadly had to give up that towel and went home buzzing and beeling I never got it!

My cousin lived near Jim's mum so a few days later I called her. She asked how I managed at the concert, being only wee, and that she couldn't imagine herself in a crowd like that. She chatted to me for ages and that conversation more than made up for the loss of the sweaty towel.

---

## JIM KERR

My name is Jim Kerr (*no, not the Jim Kerr!*) and I've been devoted to the band since first hearing 'Promised you a Miracle' in April 1982. Over the past 38 years I've played Simple Minds every week. My wife would say I play their music every day!

With the release of *New Gold Dream* I was pretty much obsessed with the band and it was tough to hear my parents tell me I was too young to hitchhike to see them play Phoenix Park or the European festivals in 1983. I remember getting on the train from Dumfries to Glasgow just to see the *New Gold Dream* displays in the Virgin and HMV windows.

But with the band announcing three concerts at the Barrowland that December I was beside myself with excitement. I caught the train to Edinburgh and spent the entire (freezing) night outside Ripping Records to get tickets. Once I had them in my hand it was like a winning lottery ticket. I couldn't stop looking at them, wishing the days away till December.

Those two concerts were incredible. I caught an early morning train from Dumfries to Glasgow, arrived at Central Station around 9.30am and literally ran to the Barrowland. It was another freezing day and I stood outside from about 10am until the doors opened at 7pm. But was worth it when Mick, Charlie and Derek came walking by. Charlie was besieged and ran into a shop where the shop-owner locked the door to keep other fans out - I was in there with him! Eventually he got out - a Beatles moment!

I was first in line to get in the door, a large crowd now behind me, and as soon as those doors opened I bolted up the stairs and was right against the stage both nights. The band were incredible and every bit worth the 18-month wait.

Jim's shoe was stolen that night by an eager fan and he had to go off and get another, mid-concert. The following night his shoe came off again - right into my face – and mid-song he shook his head at me as if to say 'please do not steal that shoe'. I happily slipped it on him, Cinderella-like. To reward me, he gave me his scarf, which I had to battle to keep from all the other grabbing hands.

I remember leaving the venue, lifting my shirt. I was freezing and soaked with sweat and after 2,500 fans pushing me into that stage I was covered in bruising. But I had that scarf! Next morning, when I woke up and looked at it, it seemed a lot less impressive than it had, which I put down to my excitement from the previous night. And 20 years later, the mate that was with me confessed to getting up in the middle of the night and cutting the scarf in half so he could have it as well!

I've seen them around 40 times in multiple countries. It would have been double that had I not lived 20 years in the USA where they were not touring. But I'd fly back whenever possible to catch them. I remember being in Brighton and driving to Aschaffenburg to see them one Sunday, a journey that took the entire day. Another time I was in Sacramento, California, thinking, 'If I leave now I could just make the show in New York tonight.' Two flights, a train, three taxis and nine hours later, I walked into the Roseland Ballroom as they walked on stage – I made it almost to the minute.

The most bizarre time I saw them was in Kelseyville in 2002. I got there early in the day and you had to choose steak or chicken with your ticket as a meal was part of the deal. The venue was like a wedding reception. It was likely a low point for the band. I met them all that day and even got some one-to-one time with JK. All those years of waiting. All those questions I had about the band and their incredible journey. Facing him, my mind went completely blank and the first thing I asked was, 'How's the sushi restaurant doing?' Dear me. I'm still embarrassed about that.

# LESLEY MCMURTRIE

*Barrowland Ballroom*
*21 – 23 December 1983, Glasgow, Scotland*

It was a long way from logging onto the internet back in 1983 and concerts were a lot smaller, so you had to make the effort to get off your backside if you wanted a ticket to see your favourite band. My parents had gone away for the weekend, trusting I would behave responsibly at the age of 18. So what did I decide to do? With my friends, I jumped on a train and arrived to queue for tickets the day before they went on sale. We turned out to be first in one

THOUSANDS of fans queued for hours yesterday for a ticket to see Glasgow super-group Simple Minds, led by singer Jim Kerr.

Some had even camped out overnight at the Locarno in the city's Sauchiehall Street.

A staggering 8000 fans had spent hours waiting for tickets to go on sale for the group's only Scottish appearances this year—on December 21 and 22.

But half of them went away empty handed, for only 4000 tickets were available.

One of the fans who camped out — John Docherty, 18, of Chapelhall,

## Just the ticket for loyal rock fans

Airdrie — said: "We listened to cassettes of the band's music and took turns at snatching a snooze."

But there was good news for the youngsters who failed to get tickets.

Simple Minds are to tour Scotland again in February.

*Lesley McMurtrie was first in the queue for Barrowland tickets - photo Daily Record*

of the very first overnight queues for tickets. The atmosphere was great and the queue just got longer and longer. When the *Daily Record* showed up to do a story, I never thought I'd be caught out by my parents. We were over the moon to get our precious tickets and proudly waved them at the queue that went on and on. But thank you, *Daily Record*, because of your story I got away with sleeping on the street in Glasgow. Although there wasn't much sleep!

---

## MATT DALKIN

*Entertainment Centre*
*28 & 29 January 1984, Melbourne, Australia*

I was 13 in 1981 when I heard the chorus of 'Love Song' on the radio and thought 'who sings this?' My brother came home with a tape, I played the intro and the rest is history. Still to this day that's my all-time favourite song.

I first saw them in January 1984 with Pseudo Echo and The Eurythmics at what is now the Glasshouse in Melbourne. They started with the throbbing, extended intro of 'Waterfront' and then – boom! - Jim launched onto the stage: 'Hello Melbourne!' When 'Love Song' was played as the final song of the encore, the crowd went berserk. I have a vivid memory of Mel throwing his sticks into the crowd at the end.

During senior year of high school in 1985, 'Don't You (Forget About Me)' and 'Alive and Kicking' were our theme songs. For the Australian tour in 1986, I bought 20 tickets - I had a lot of friends who wanted to experience them. After Melbourne in 1989 there was a significant gap until 2006 and the Palais Theatre, St Kilda. That was an epic concert, Jim stating 'there is a lot of energy here'. I got to shake Eddy Duffy's hand before, as he was mingling with the crowd.

I also went to Scotland in August 1992, my brother playing cricket in the Midlands. I toured up to Lochearnhead and drove up to the gate of Bonny Wee Studios. No one was home.

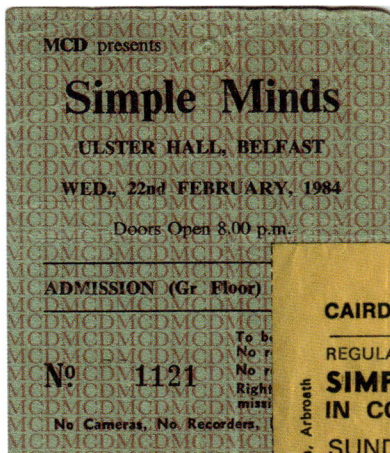

MCD presents

**Simple Minds**

ULSTER HALL, BELFAST

WED., 22nd FEBRUARY, 1984

Doors Open 8.00 p.m.

ADMISSION (Gr Floor)

Nº 1121

No Cameras, No. Recorders,

CAIRD HALL, DUNDEE

REGULAR MUSIC presents

**SIMPLE MINDS**
**IN CONCERT**

SUNDAY, FEB. 26, 1984

Doors open 7.30 p.m.

GALLERY
£4.00

217

Playhouse Theatre
Greenside Place
Edinburgh

SATURDAY
25 February 1984
at 7.30 pm
Doors open 6-30 pm

REGULAR MUSIC Presents

**Simple Minds** 2
PLUS SUPPORT

E 37

STALLS £4.50

NO Cameras or Tape Recorders Allowed   NO RE-ADMISSION
No ticket exchange or money refunded—Retain this portion

# BRUCE BUTLER

*Waterfront Restaurant*
*January 1984 (Burns Night), Sydney, Australia*

I first discovered Simple Minds whilst living in London in 1979, buying their first two albums and even a copy of Johnny and the Self Abusers' single. But it was on hearing the *Empires and Dance* album that I became a full-blown fan.

*Burns Night January 1984 - photo Lisa Watt*

On returning to Australia I started working for CBS Records just as they picked up the rights for Virgin Records. I became Promotions Manager for the Epic and Virgin labels and in 1981 Simple Minds released their debut Virgin album, *Sons and Fascination*, and toured Australia for the first time. That tour was the start of a long relationship with the band with many highlights, such as presenting Simple Minds with their first ever gold album on their return to Australia in 1982.

In 1982 the relationship between the band and those of us working for Virgin was one of friendship, mutual respect and fun. On that tour we took the band out to the

NSW State Forest for a true Aussie BBQ and scared the hell out of them with stories of the ferocious drop bears!

But it was the next tour in 1984 that cemented the friendship. Virgin Records Australia had now been set up independently of CBS and we were having great success with our new Simple Minds releases of 'Waterfront' and 'Speed Your Love to Me' when the band arrived in Australia for their biggest tour to date.

The band arrived in Australia in time for Robert Burns Day, 25th January, so we had decided to put on a traditional Rabbie Burns Supper for the band. We had already decided to have a big dinner for the band at the Waterfront Restaurant at The Rocks in Sydney so we thought changing a few menu requirements wouldn't be too difficult.

But what we didn't know was that haggis was at that time illegal in New South Wales. However, we found a couple of butchers had special license to make them exclusively for Burns Day celebrations. Even though our order was very last minute, we managed to secure a haggis. We also wanted a full-dress bagpipe player to pipe the haggis into the restaurant and to the table, also a hard call at the last minute on Burns Day.

On the night we were all gathered in a private room upstairs at the Waterfront when the sound of bagpipes could be heard entering the restaurant. Simple Minds, who had no idea of what was planned, became very excited, and as the piper appeared at the top of the stairs followed by the silver tray containing the haggis, there were shouts of approval and laughter. The Haggis was placed on the table in front of Jim and Charlie who quickly decided that Charlie should be the one to stand and recite some Robert Burns prose, which may have included the 'Selkirk Grace' and bits he could remember of 'Address to a Haggis' before he took a carving knife and plunged it into the Haggis. Derek was given carving duties and the Haggis was shared around as we drank whisky and other beverages until we Aussies could no longer understand a word the Scots were saying.

*Virgin presented the band with their first gold disc in Australia in 1982 - photo Lisa Watt*

# SPARKLE IN THE RAIN

## JASON BEARDSALL

'Just buy it!' I had been looking through the new releases section in one of Barnsley's few independent record stores for a while. A few pounds had been burning a hole in my pocket since leaving college that day and I wanted something new to listen to when I got home.

My best friend was becoming irritated. I had picked up a 10-inch single with a great cover and adorned with a sticker proudly stating, 'limited edition 10 inch includes free poster'. My only real recollection of the band was from a music video I had seen on Saturday morning TV. The video had stuck in my head due to the technology used to multiply the band members as they disappeared into the distance. That and the lead singer's wild kicks and flailing arms!

I took the single to the counter, paid for my purchase and we made our ways home. I played 'Promised You a Miracle' and was happy with my purchase. But then, I played the B side. 'Book of Brilliant Things' took me completely by surprise. The immense majesty of the sound, the emotion and energy of the lyrics, the pure brilliance of the arrangement. I listened and listened and fell deeper and deeper in love with this song. Within days I was buying back catalogue releases, posters, t-shirts and badges. My love affair with this band started in that little, long gone, record store 33 ago, when my friend insisted: 'Just buy it!'

## BENJAMIN STURTEVANT

In the summer of 1984, I was 19 with one year of college under my belt. I waited tables at a restaurant in Ogunquit, a beach resort in Maine, and sharing a room above an art gallery with two friends. One of them had just purchased *Sparkle in the Rain*. I distinctly remember looking at the album artwork and thinking, 'What an odd record cover' and 'funny name for a band'. But as soon as I heard 'Up on the Catwalk' for the first time, I was hooked. We must've listened to *Sparkle* nearly every night after working the dinner shift. We'd return to our room, strip out of our foul-smelling restaurant uniforms, crack open a few beers, pass a joint round and listen to it over and over, mixed in with some New Order, Violent Femmes and Talking Heads. *Sparkle in the Rain* was a huge part of my prime-of-life soundtrack. That's why I love to listen to it to this day.

### SOPHIE DELATTRE

Simple Minds have almost always had a part of my life and were the first band I saw live, in December 1985. I was 13. I had a revelation that day and decided I would learn to play the drums like Mel Gaynor. Some months later, I was breaking my piggy bank and bought the drums, but I've never taken lessons. I taught myself!

My life has been as tumultuous as that of a rock star but there has always been a light that has put me back on my feet, a light called Simple Minds and two songs in particular, 'Speed Your Love to Me' (the extended version) and 'Seeing Out the Angel'. The energy they send out - the Derek Forbes bass lines, the Michael MacNeil keyboards, the constant evolution and innovation - still helps me today.

### PHILIP ADAMS

It was a Friday afternoon drive along the old Roman road (A50) towards the Staffordshire Market town of Uttoxeter. Radio 1's Peter Powell show was on in the background and he was wittering on about his record of the week. 'Bugger that, I'll put a cassette in.' As I reached over to insert the tape, Powell mentioned Simple Minds. 'Hold on, that's the band me and a mate were going to see the night I broke my ankle playing 5-a-side football and didn't go!' I turned the volume up just as the intro to 'Waterfront' flooded the car.

What a sound; it reached through the cheap stereo in my Mk3 Ford Escort and right into my stomach. It was rattling the windscreen. I thought, 'I've got to get this,' and I did - the 12-inch single with the sleeve artwork to match the outer worldliness of the sound of the track.

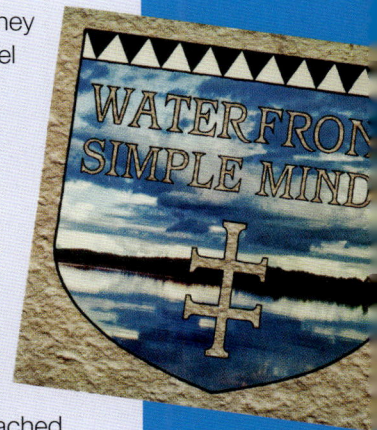

## MAGALI BOURGEOIS

I discovered Simple Minds by borrowing *Sparkle in the Rain* from my brother's tapes. The music helped me through tough times and made good times special. As a teenager in the Eighties I was inspired by the band members and their political involvement. There's always a song or an album you can listen to that will correspond exactly to the mood you're in.

My first concert was in Frejus, my 18th birthday too. It was far too hot, and I nearly passed out because of the heat. But some great people in the audience helped me out and it was an unbelievable experience in the old Roman arena, a very special memory.

In my early twenties I suddenly felt very ill. The doctor's prognosis was rather poor, and they gave me only a few hours. I decided the only thing I wanted to do was to spend those hours listening to the music that had carried me so far. I found something precious in the music - a wakeup call that allowed me to hang on to and to pursue my dreams.

For 20 odd years I have been part of the Simple Minds fan community, sharing a passion for the music and travelling the length of Britain and Europe, going to places I would have never thought to holiday in, meeting friends everywhere with a guarantee I'd have a great time with like-minded people. The most remarkable time was the week spent in Taormina. It was surreal, with the backdrop of the Roman columns, Mount Etna smoking in the background and the Mediterranean Sea further below. The music lifted us and took us on a musical trip through the years and left us in a surreal state afterwards. It was magical and we did well to stay in the village for a few days as it felt somehow that the magic was still hanging around.

I have become addicted to that irreplaceable feeling you get when you attend a concert and are with a fantastic crowd. What mattered is the music, what it wakes up inside you when you hear the first notes from the stage before the lights come on.

As a student from Nice in the south of France, I spent a lot of my holidays in Scotland. From my first visit I knew I wanted to live there. Walking down the streets of Glasgow, listening to the Minds, brought the music to a new level for me. It makes me smile now as I live in front of the Clyde. I haven't chosen this place because of it, but would you guess that my favourite song has always been 'Waterfront'.

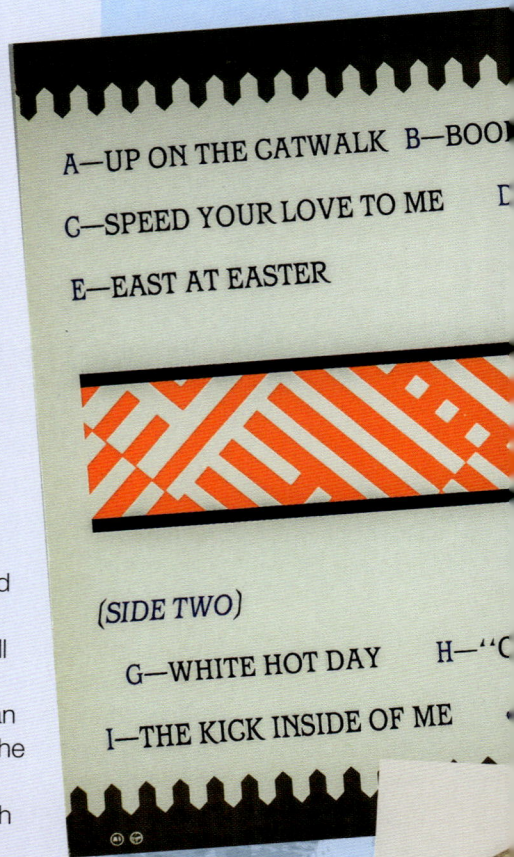

A—UP ON THE CATWALK  B—BOO
C—SPEED YOUR LOVE TO ME  D
E—EAST AT EASTER

(SIDE TWO)
G—WHITE HOT DAY   H—"C
I—THE KICK INSIDE OF ME

## IAN COSSAR

I think the band made one of the decade's most extraordinary albums when they entered the studio with Steve Lillywhite. There are few other albums by British artists from the Eighties that still defy that decade's usual 'sound'. Back then, I played my copy to some rock musician friends – they were captivated by Charlie's massive guitar sound, especially on 'Waterfront' and 'The Kick Inside of Me'. I still think he is one of the most versatile guitarists these islands have produced and his song-writing partnership with Jim is the reason they are still making great music almost four decades after *Sparkle in the Rain*.

## STEPHANIE LANGLAIS

I am in Aurilla, France. I am 12 years old, I unwrap my new CD, *Glittering Prize 81/92*. One hour before, I had heard 'Don't You (Forget About Me)' on the radio and immediately asked my mum to drive me to the record shop. I lie down on my duvet, topped with flamingos flying above the clouds, and close my eyes. I press play and wait for the first track to begin. It's a brand new sound, a kind of music I have never listened to before. It's a revolution in my head, in my heart, and I can feel my interior world starting to change. The purity of this piece of music touches me deeply. It's more than a beautiful moment, it's a founding moment. Thanks to 'Waterfront', I truly entered the adult world.

## PAULA GREENE

*Barrowland Ballroom*
*28 February 1984, Glasgow, Scotland*

I am a Glasgow girl. I loved the Minds from
the first time I sneaked out to a Glasgow
Barrowland concert aged 14. My dad was
so strict he grounded me for a month when
he found out. My big sis grassed me in, the
wee tosser, but it was the best grounding
ever! Then I went to Ibrox in 1986, aged
16. I remember Lloyd Cole throwing a
hissy fit. I did my Higher English essay
on the experience and got an A. Andy, my
childhood friend from Crookie, got me
tickets to Barrowland. I met Charlie. He
shouted, 'Andy, she looks your kinda girl -
no history here!' Ha ha ha. It wasn't brilliant.

*Paula Greene met Charlie*

## ROBERT MCGREGOR

*Gaumont Theatre*
*10 March 1984, Southampton, England*

A Glasgow boy. A graduate from the University of Strathclyde. A schoolboy footballer
from Claremont High School (I understand Derek attended that school but don't
remember him as he was four years older). Introduced to Simple Minds by my
Celtic-loving brother-in-law around the *Empires and Dance* period. Bought the back-
catalogue. Bought everything since. I finally got to see Simple Minds at the Gaumont,
having moved to Southampton to work. The concert combined *New Gold Dream* and
*Sparkle in the Rain*. It was everything I hoped. What a performance and what an aural
spectacle. I somehow found out where the band were staying and, at the end of the
gig, headed straight to the hotel. As a Glasgow boy in a similar age group, I managed
to hang around for a short while, but was way too shy to approach any of the band.
I was rumbled when I tried to buy a beer – 'Residents only, sir'. Time to leave, but I
ended the night with wonderful memories of a bunch of young guys from Glasgow
making me feel proud and giving me anthems for the ages.

# SIMON WARBURTON

There used to be heavy curtains at the front of the stage. 'Open up,' said Jim, somewhat desperately as the drapes refused to budge, until eventually they moved. I remember the lighting effect of what felt to me like Scottish tartan colours and every single person on their feet as 'New Gold Dream' pounded out.

I've spent the following 36 years trying to see the band where possible, including Frankfurt, where the brilliant Silencers were first on, and Manchester City's old Maine Road football ground, with The Stranglers, who opened with,

*Simon Warburton (right) with his mate Kev at Leeds in 2018*

'We're the support act'. Perhaps most memorable was at Edinburgh Castle in the wettest conditions I've experienced at a concert, where they fittingly opened with 'Waterfront'. I was due to be at Glasgow Hydro in 2020, but that's been rearranged. I'm also due to be in Taormina. Who knows when that's going ahead? When it does, I'll be there.

---

# AJAY MISTRY

## *De Montfort Hall*
## *12 March 1984, Leicester, England*

I remember the crowd being really, really boisterous to the point where Jim, when he used to introduce and preface some of the songs, demanded that the crowd should 'be quiet!' and 'shut up!' on a number of occasions. 'Waterfront' even contained lyrics from Norman Greenbaum's 'Spirit in the Sky', particularly relevant for me since it was the UK No.1 when I was born. Selfishly, I think of it as a dedication of sorts!

*Photo Stuart Holland*

And whilst I love the slow version of 'New Gold Dream' from *Live in the City of Light* I will never, ever forget the turbo-charged version they played at the De Mont, laced with lyrics from Talking Heads' version of Al Green's 'Take Me to the River' and The

Doors' 'Light My Fire'. Indeed, when Jim was singing, 'C'mon baby light my fire!' and repeated 'Fire! Fire!', jabbing the air with his hand, I remember it sounding more like a celebration of fire, rather than something to fear!

Whilst the Minds have never let me down when I've seen them live, I'm convinced the band were spurred on to new heights by the crowd that night. There were times when Jim was just absorbed in the songs, prowling around the stage and looking like he was taking numerous run-ups and threatening to make that final glorious leap into the crowd. Perhaps thankfully for himself, he never did.

Forbes particularly, was in a world of his own, bouncing up and down and, not content with staying to the left of Jim, one second he'd be next to Mel, the next having a joke with Charlie by his shoulder. I walked out of the venue that night absolutely buzzing, 10 feet tall.

---

# RICHARD ELLITHORNE

## *Odeon Theatre*
## *13 March 1984, Birmingham, England*

Odeon Theatre, Birmingham

M.C.P. presents—

**SIMPLE MINDS plus Guests**

Tuesday, 13th March 1984
Evening 7.30

**FRONT STALLS**
£4.50

19

No Ticket Exchanged nor
This portion to be retain

A. B. Cooper (Printers) Ltd., Manchester

*Richard Ellithorne's iPhone wallpaper*

KEEP CALM & Listen to SIMPLE MINDS

I bought 'Promised You a Miracle' when it broke into the Top 20 in 1981. 'Themes for Great Cities' was on the B-side, and what a B-side! I was an aspiring bass player in a couple of school bands and loved Derek's superb basslines and riffs. My first gig was Birmingham Odeon. They opened with 'East at Easter', Jim perched on a huge mic stand. Apparently, he had the flu (no one would have guessed) and was too ill to do an encore.

I went off them when John Giblin wasn't doing Derek's basslines live, although I played *Live in the City of Light* to death. Malcolm Foster was in the band when I went to Paris for the *Street Fighting Years* tour. That was a coach journey and a half! And I was at Milton Keynes Bowl in 1991 for the *Real Life* tour. Broadcast live on Radio 1, the DJ was serenaded with 'Gary Davies - what a wanker, what a wanker' as he introduced them. There was a huge surge when they started 'Love Song'.

After a seven-year hiatus I saw them at the NEC on the *Floating World* tour, when they started playing live again. I saw them seven times with Eddie Duffy on bass. A highlight was when they played the whole of *New Gold Dream*.

I've seen them 14 times with Ged on bass. My first was at Cannock Chase in 2011. My gig buddy Paul Redman was travelling up the M40 to meet me and was involved in a car accident when a driver fell asleep at the wheel and collided with him. Paul was okay but missed the gig. It peed it down. Jim said, 'Moisture is good for the skin!'

Because they treat each gig as the last, they always put on a good show and do their best for the fans and audience. They are and will always be the best band in the world.

---

# CLAES FREDRIKSSON

*Johanneshov Isstadion*
*24 March 1984,*
*Stockholm, Sweden*

I was at high school in the early '80s. Vinyl records, John Peel show and local live music dominated life in my circle of friends and I played guitar in a Swedish punk band, Pogo Production. Some of my friends were heavily into new rock music like U2, Big Country or bands like the Undertones. MTV and music videos were a new phenomenon and one music video that caught my attention was 'Love Song', with its hypnotic rhythm and a ground-breaking new synthesizer soundscape mixed with a unique and appealing style. Later, I would discover and enjoy 'The American' and 'Sweat in Bullet' from the same trance-inspired era. These came in the form of 7-inch vinyl singles and EPs from my local import record shop.

I moved to university with a substantial record collection and soon made friends with Magnus, a blond, stylish, like-minded student. Together, we colonised the student station Radio Ryd and were entrusted with a weekly half-hour show featuring our own flavour of new wave and post-punk, such as Echo & the Bunnymen and Talking Heads. In the winter of 1983, the powerful bassline of 'Waterfront' hit the ether and in my mind, this was their majestic impact peak.

Magnus and I managed to get tickets to see them in Stockholm, a couple of hours away from our university. I don't remember much of the trip or what we did in Stockholm but the concert was memorable and I liked the support band, China Crisis, too. Although I've seen Simple Minds a couple of times in more recent years, these were the days! Grumpy old man living in the past? Nah, these really were the days!

---

# CHRISTIANE DEKONING

## Ancienne Belgique
## 28 March 1984, Brussels, Belgium

'East at Easter' gave me the most goosebumps. It was absolutely awesome. Watching my hero sing so close was like a dream. Jim was so cute, and above all mysterious, with such a great aura. And wow, I liked his dance moves - so charming. I'd never seen such an intriguing singer, and never heard such overwhelming music sounds.

The gig in Brussels after the terrorist attack in Paris is also one to remember, with the minute's silence before the start of the concert. It was a very emotional evening but despite the sad and uncertain conditions, they gave a great performance.

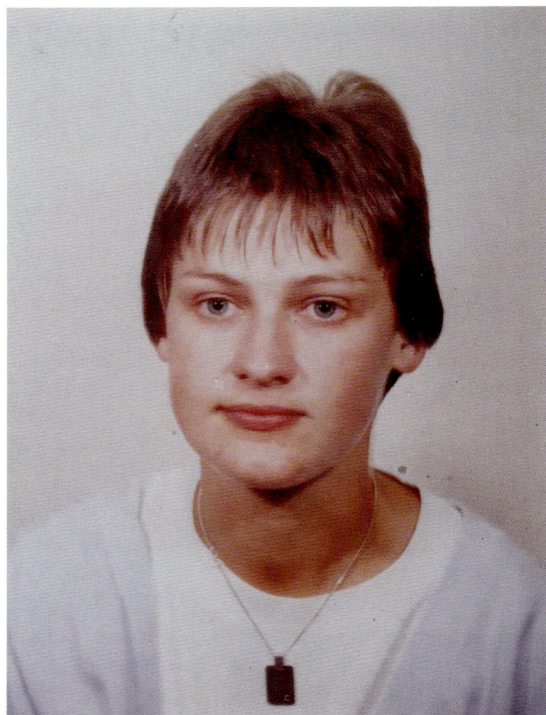

*Christiane Dekoning was at the 1984 Brussels show*

# MARTINE DEHEYDER

I saw them in concert in Brussels. China Crisis were support. I was determined to stand on the front row and got a handshake from China Crisis's singer. But it got really heavy in front of the stage and only a few moments before Simple Minds started, I was getting crushed and was pulled out to be taken backstage. After a few moments I was able to return and enjoy the concert, but missed Jim sitting in the middle of the stage when the curtains opened.

Years later, my husband and I were returning home from a city break in Porto. Waiting to check in at the airport, I saw a man who looked very familiar. It was Charlie Burchill. We were with a little group in business class and had to wait for a special taxi to come and collect us. Charlie was very modest and didn't want special treatment but got it anyway. On the plane I spoke briefly to him and he was so kind. We talked a bit. You can't imagine how excited I was, meeting a member of my most favourite band in person!

# DIRK REXER

*Musikhalle*
*5 April 1984, Hamburg, West Germany*

I really loved *New Gold Dream*. It had so many wonderful and meaningful songs
and became my most loved and played album of the summer of 1983. It sounded
so elegant and tasteful, a piece of pop-wave-art. The perfect arrangements, the
sophisticated overdubs, the screaming cutting sounds of Charlie Burchill's guitar. It
was like a bunch of flowers, every song a surprising new blossom! Then came *Sparkle
in the Rain*. Less golden shimmery pop and more intense. Faster and heavier, I found it
more concrete. I loved it, and one thing I knew: I want to see this band live as soon as
possible!

    The show in my hometown of Hamburg was sold out. They opened with
'Waterfront', which had the power of a hymn. Beautiful sounds, brilliant moments,
wonderful feelings - the show was awesome in every way. This evening became a
sparkling night to me! But the best thing came at the end. Me and a few other guys
were hanging around the back door of the Musikhalle, hoping to catch a glance of one
of the musicians, and there they were - Mick MacNeil, Charlie Burchill and Jim Kerr.
They talked to us. And they talked to me. But
it was hard to understand a word because of
their Scottish accents... Very different from the
English language I learned at school!

---

# IGOR POPOVIC

*Circus Krone Bau*
*8 April 1984, Munich, West Germany*

It's the start of the *Sparkle in the Rain* tour.
I'm 22, I'm in the music business and inform
the editor of the bestselling rock magazine in
the country about my trip. Immediately he
provides a pass for me from Virgin and tells me,
'Don't come back without an interview!' I must
say, I was not a journalist, just a big fan of the
band.

    I'm off to Munich with my friends. On the
day of the concert, at the soundcheck, I meet
the band members and talk to Charlie Burchill

EUROPEAN TOUR '84
SIMPLE MINDS

*Sparkle in the Rain*

ACCESS ALL AREAS

and Mick MacNeil on the bus, and Jim's brother, who managed the band. I tell them their previous album, *New Gold Dream*, was the bestselling published foreign album in Yugoslavia last year. They are delighted. No sign of Jim.

We arrive at their hotel and I wait, to no avail. The kind lady from the Virgin office tells me to come back after the concert and not to lose hope. I can't see Jim anywhere.

After the fantastic concert, I go backstage, meet Mel Gaynor and regretfully refuse an invitation to the party. I return to the hotel. And wait. And lose hope slowly. Around midnight, the same kind lady from the Virgin office tells me Jim's waiting for me in his room. Still unable to believe I'll be one-on-one with my idol, I knock on the door and enter. 'Hi, I'm Jim. Would you like some tea?'

I don't know how long we talked, two to three hours at least. At one point, the telephone rings and it's obvious Jim is talking to a lady friend, so I feel a bit awkward - it's a bit like I'm intruding. 'I'm in love,' Jim says, smiling. Soon after that, that lady friend will become his wife. Her name is Chrissie Hynde.

At the very end, Jim invites me to be their guest for a week in the part of the tour in northern Italy. That was the hardest 'no' in my life. I tell him I must return to Belgrade - I have scheduled studio hours for the remix of my band Jakarta's first album. He says he can totally understand.

That was the first, last and only interview I conducted with anyone in my life. And it was great, as if a real journalist made it, not a fan. There are still two audio cassettes with it in my drawer to prove it wasn't just a dream.

Life goes on. At one point, both Igor and Jim live in Italy - Igor in Milan and Jim in Taormina.

Igor returns to Serbia, forms the band again and after a 30-year hiatus, prepares a new CD for release, opening with a cover of the song 'Someone Somewhere (in Summertime)' under the Serbian title 'Letim'. Approvals for the cover are duly acquired.

So the story with Igor and Simple Minds goes on.

---

# MARIE GRENET

*Stadion De Vitrolles*
*17 April 1984, Marseilles, France*

I remember my first Simple Minds show. It was in Marseille. There weren't many people there. The stage was under a marquee like in a circus, on a car park by the Parc Chanot. The place was more than half-empty, but suddenly the band arrived, Jim started to sing, and it was hypnotic. He had such charisma, and the place suddenly felt crowded as we danced and sang. It's one of the best shows I have attended out of hundreds, and the first of many Simple Minds shows for me.

## ALAN BRITTAIN

*Odeon*
*5 May 1984, Birmingham, England*

I discovered Simple Minds in 1983 through 'Promised You a Miracle' on the radio and, later that year, coming home from the pub and watching *Late Night in Concert*, which featured the Newcastle City Hall gig for *New Gold Dream*. I remember thinking, 'These are not bad'!

Sue (my girlfriend then, now my wife) and I first saw them at the tender ages of 18 and 20. The first live track we heard? 'East at Easter'. We were blown away by the sound, the lights, the crowd.

In 1986 we saw them at the NEC in Birmingham and Milton Keynes Bowl. We went in a clapped-out Austin Allegro and experienced the whole outdoor SM gig – the human pyramids and bottles of undrinkable fluid being hurled across the Bowl, before a ceasefire when the band took the stage in glorious evening sunshine.

I remember, too, the Nelson Mandela 70th Birthday Concert at Wembley Stadium, losing my best mate after two hours and only bumping into him at the encore, when he had been only stood about 15 yards away all day. That was a stunning set which took the roof off Wembley, metaphorically speaking, Charlie jamming with Johnny Marr!

I can't not mention the Edinburgh Castle gig and that biblical rain cascading down the street and through the stands. I think we'd have been drier if we'd cut the middle man out and jumped straight into the Firth of Forth. But despite the deluge it was a great night that could not dampen our spirits. In the words of the song, 'and the band played on'.

---

## RACHEL MURRAY

*Hammersmith Odeon*
*15 May 1984, London, England*

I was 13 and David was 16 when he took me to see Simple Minds live at Hammersmith Odeon. It was my first concert, far more exciting than I ever imagined a concert could be. After, we waited outside hoping to get some autographs. I was thrilled to meet Jim and Charlie. Soon after David and I broke up and despite living only a street from each other, only crossed paths a couple more times in the following years. My younger brother later 'borrowed' and lost my treasured signed programme.

By 2012 I'd moved to British Columbia, Canada. David and I were Facebook friends but never did more than exchange birthday greetings. On a visit back to England, I arranged a get-together with friends and was surprised to see him. That meeting of less than an hour was enough. It was love at first sight for both of us and seemed like the years in between had never happened! Both married (unhappily) to others at the time, we met a year later and got back together during another trip I made to London. I arranged a surprise night out to see Simple Minds in Southend, just like all those years before. Then we spent a week in Toronto, including another concert and, just like old times, we waited around after and I got a photo with Jim. We've since seen our favourite band once more together in Vancouver. David moved to join me in Canada in July 2017. Our happy ever after includes our concert tickets from 15 May 1984, which I had framed for David's 50th birthday and which I found in an old school diary.

*Dawn Volans had a younger sister who couldn't wait to see the band*

## DAWN VOLANS

I worked after school at a chip shop so I could afford to go to gigs. My younger sister Julie wasn't allowed to travel to London with me. I bought her a tour t-shirt. As soon as she was allowed she came with me to their gigs and still does to this day.

## GRAHAM KEOGHOE

I was mainly into heavy rock and heavy metal. I was at work when a friend, Dave Webber, said he had a spare ticket for a Simple Minds concert at Hammersmith Odeon and did I want to go? I declined - it was not my type of music. But 10 minutes later I rang him back. Any chance of seeing live music is a must. I loved the concert and was a fan from then on.

# LEIGH CHAPMAN

*Hammersmith Odeon*
*12 – 19 May 1984, London, England*

I was beside myself with excitement. The first of eight nights at the best venue in London, watching the best band in the world – Simple Minds. I'd already seen them on the *Tour de Monde* at the Southampton Gaumont and several times before. At Southampton I met up with Colleen, a bubbly young woman from Canada who travelled over to the UK to follow the tour. We got on so well that we decided to meet up at Hammersmith. That evening I got my gig clothes on, checked I had my ticket and was about to leave when the phone rang. It was Colleen, from a phone box in Hammersmith saying, 'Don't bother, they've cancelled.'

*Derek Forbes at Hammersmith Odeon (photo Leigh Chapman)*

They cancelled due to Jim's throat infection. The gigs were rescheduled for May. But poor Colleen had to go home at the end of the week. However, we spent those days together, two girls giggling stupidly at Simple Minds references, listening to *Sparkle in the Rain* on repeat until she caught her flight home.

May arrived. As a die-hard fan, I made sure I got front-row seats. Every night I was there at the front, every single night at Hammersmith Odeon, an experience that will stay with me forever. Not just the music but also the camaraderie at the stage door where we waited for the band to emerge. Some nights I was lucky and got an autograph and a smile. No selfies in those days. But I did manage to

*Charlie in 1984 (photo Leigh Chapman)*

smuggle my camera in for some photos of the performance.

Colleen never saw the Minds again. She died the following year of cancer, aged 21. I was devastated. We'd kept in touch and I had no idea she was ill until her mum wrote to me. I wrote back, saying the time we'd had together was precious and Simple Minds would always remind me of her. And they still do.

*Jim at Hammersmith Odeon (photo Leigh Chapman)*

# ROY LAPORTE

*Massey Hall*
*6 June 1984, Toronto, Canada*

I was 15. My brother Kurt, seven years my senior and guitarist/singer in the local Toronto new wave/post-punk scene, came to visit my parents for the weekend and brought me *Sons and Fascination*. Having followed their career to date, he called it 'their dance album'. I loved it and became obsessed.

When *New Gold Dream* came out and I saw the slicked back hair and shaved sides, I had to get that look too. Needless to say, I didn't quite achieve it. The album (and the title - wtf?) was magical, mysterious, romantic, ethereal and utterly intoxicating, unlike anything I'd ever heard. I wrote a review for a high school English assignment; thank you for being so cool, Mr. Moyle! I read the rave reviews of *Sparkle in the Rain* over the winter prior to its release in Canada in 1984. My friends joked about my imitation of Jim's dancing à la 'Up on the Catwalk' when we were at a club, saying it looked like I was 'shooting craps in an alley', me swooping down on bended knee and touching the ground with one hand.

I finally got to see Simple Minds live at Toronto's grand old dame, Massey Hall. I went downtown, having heard rumours that you could purchase or rent a ticket stub at intermission to get you in, which I did for $10. I think full price was $15 or perhaps $20. I didn't really have a seat so stood in the aisle and soaked it all in. After the stage slowly emptied to the sequencer melody of 'Big Sleep', I left in a daze. It was good to be alone right then. I liked being alone with my thoughts that warm summer night.

---

# SUZANNE BIEHL

*Queen Elizabeth Theatre*
*14 June 1984, Vancouver, Canada*

It must have been 'Waterfront' that I first heard on the radio in early 1984, prompting me to purchase the album. Up until that time, I had the good fortune to have older brothers with a sizeable record collection. *Sparkle in the Rain* was the first one I picked up for myself. Not too long after, I was excited to find out Simple Minds were going to be in Vancouver in June. It was my first concert and I remember two things clearly about Jim. Firstly, he was wearing a shiny blue suit – dashing, but not exactly what I expected from a rock band. Secondly, he looked out to the crowd with an expression of wonderment and joy that has stuck with me ever since. I thought, 'Now, here's a guy who loves being up there,' an intriguing and somewhat foreign concept to my shy 14-year-old self.

In 2018 I took my husband to see them when they came through Vancouver again. It was a similar-sized venue to 1984, which afforded me a close enough view to see and feel the same sentiment I felt years before. I almost had this sensation of being back in the '80s.

---

## JAMES B KOHLER

*Hollywood Palladium*
*15 June 1984, Los Angeles, California*

My father was working for CBS Records in LA and had crafted me into a music aficionado. I was a junior in high school when a neighbour turned me on to *New Gold Dream*. This was something special and I've never looked back since seeing them the night after my high school graduation on the *Sparkle in the Rain* tour. They opened with 'Waterfront'.

---

## KEITH SANDUCCI

I was 15 years old in 1982 when I first heard Simple Minds on KROQ, the soundtrack of my youth. They stood out from the influx of new wave bands in that momentous year. When I graduated high school in 1984, I worked part-time for a record store chain and remember purchasing *Sparkle in the Rain* and listening to it on my turntable the first time in my headphones. It was a masterpiece of sound like no other. Mel Gaynor's powerful drumming, Charlie Burchill's soaring guitar, Derek Forbes pulsing basslines (especially on 'Waterfront') and Mick MacNeil's wonderful command of the synths. But it was Jim Kerr's voice singing to those lyrics, painting images and moods throughout those songs, that made it a magical, indescribable combination. I had the pleasure of seeing Simple Minds supporting *Sparkle in the Rain* and was not disappointed.

---

## MATT WOOLERY

As a big Pretenders fan I started to take Simple Minds seriously when I learned Chrissie Hynde and Jim Kerr had married.

---

## JURGEN LAETHEM

*Rock Torhout
7 July 1984, Torhout,
Belgium*

I was 16 when I saw them for the first time at Rock Torhout in Belgium on the *Sparkle in the Rain* tour. Since then I've followed them to Germany, Italy, the UK and France and seen them lots in Belgium. I will be a fan until the end!

## KRISTEL VANMUYSEN

My slightly older neighbour plays the *New Gold Dream* record very loud and, hearing it through his bedroom window while playing badminton outside, I think, 'Wow, what a sound!'. I'm 14 and immediately crazy about Simple Minds. I go to the Rock Werchter concert. Heaven on earth, with U2 and Simple Minds. I'll never experience such extreme concert feelings again.

## LEO

Simple Minds are, together with my other favourite Scottish bands Ultravox and The Blue Nile, always in my heart and head. I have so much respect that Jim and Charlie Burchill are friends forever and the beating heart of the band. A live performance by them is always exciting, because they love their fans. The first time I saw Simple Minds was at Torhout-Werchter in the summer of 1984. I'll always remember the way the performance started. A black curtain was pulled up and Jim jumped on the stage in a nice suit. The energy and ecstasy that he radiated was huge.

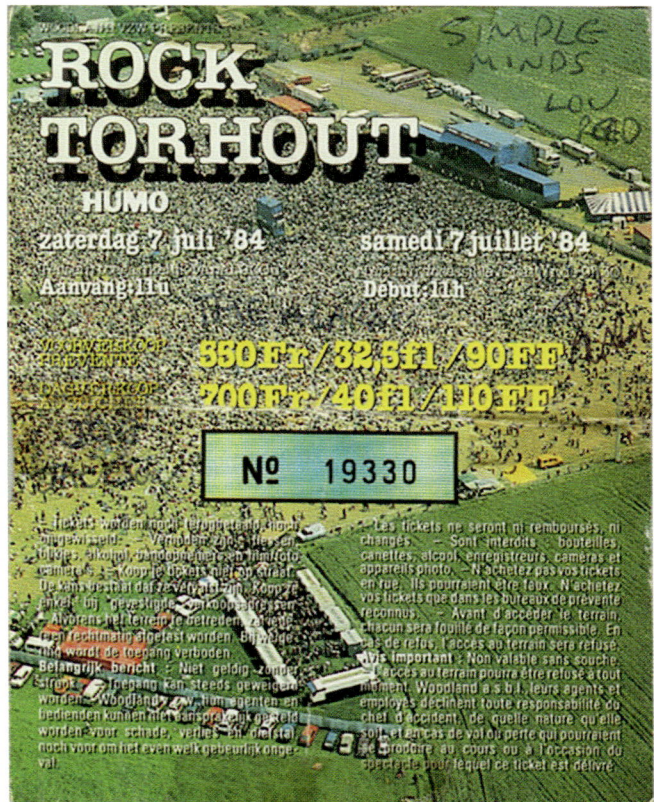

# DON'T YOU FORGET ABOUT ME

## JANET CRITCHLEY

On New Year's Eve night in 1985, Simple Minds were on TV in concert. I was on my own and really loved every minute. That's when I really got into the band and Jim's amazing voice, so much so that a few years later they were on in concert in Manchester. I really wanted to go but had no one to go with. I'd been let down. I had all the CDs and DVDs, but it doesn't compare to seeing a live band. My eldest son asked me what bands I was into, so I told him, thinking nothing of it. Then I saw the *40 Years of Hits* tour advertised and thought, 'I must get tickets for that…'

At Christmas 2019, my son got tickets for him, me and my other son to see Simple Minds in Leeds. I couldn't contain my excitement as I thought that, after 35 years, I was finally going to see them. Then, alas, coronavirus intervened, and we couldn't go. Roll on February 2021 when hopefully I will get my chance to see them at long last. This could be my last chance! Don't you forget about me.

(Strangely enough, my friend Carolann Gemmell used to live next door to Jim's parents. It's a small world, isn't it?)

## SANDRA MCNULTY

I got into Simple Minds through my now husband Hugh chatting me up and asking me if I'd dance to a Simple Minds song if one came on, not realising he'd already requested 'Don't You (Forget About Me)'. Our girls met the band when we queued to meet them at HMV. My youngest was in her buggy so we got to meet Jim's parents that day and I can honestly say I have never seen my husband so starstruck in my life. We even played 'Don't You' as our second dance at our wedding. Every time we are out our friends always make sure the song is played. Even when I was in hospital having my youngest daughter, my eldest got her dad up to dance when the song came on at a party.

## DANIELE BERNARDEN

I was 16. I used to go to a riverside spot close to my home, in Northern Tuscany, together with some friends. One day a new guy arrives with a ghetto blaster on his shoulders. He puts it down and starts playing 'Don't You'. One time, two times, three times… He didn't need to rewind the tape: the whole cassette was recorded with that song, just that song. Eventually, I approached him and asked, 'Who the fuck are you? And who the fuck are they?' 'Hi,' he replied, 'I am Steven and they are Simple Minds. They are amazing, aren't they?'

### STEPHANIE FARINELLI

From the first time I heard 'Don't You (Forget About Me)' on the radio in 1985 I adored it. It was my senior year in high school, such an important year, but so hard for me because my dad passed away suddenly. I was devastated but Simple Minds helped me through all of it. Every time I heard 'Don't You (Forget About Me)' I thought of my dad, and still do. He is no longer here with us, but the song brings great feelings of happiness, thinking about our life together.

### SVEN LÜCKEL

I discovered Simple Minds from a song on the radio, 'Don't You (Forget About Me)'. Then I saw the movie, *The Breakfast Club*. The music is a perfect addition to the movie. It is and will always stay in my head. Thinking back, it reminds me of friends and parties, feelings that will never disappear.

### RAMIRO ARIÑO GALVE

The first song I enjoyed was 'Don't You (Forget About Me)' at a foam party at a disco in La Pineda in Tarragona. After that I discovered the album *Live in the City of Light*. The first time I saw them was in 1989 in Barcelona with The Silencers. I was also lucky to see them live in Zaragoza in 1995 on Saint George's Day - for free! I am a great fan of pop music and Simple Minds is one of the groups that are responsible for this great hobby and, of course, always Vivos y Coleando ('Alive and Kicking'.)

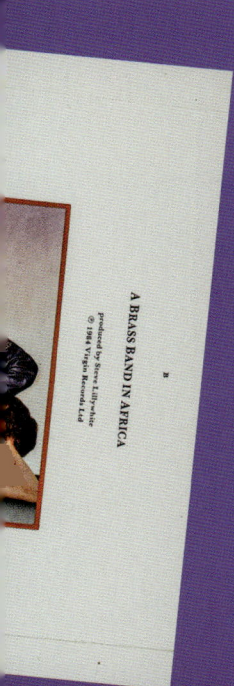

## WIN-HONG HO

Being half Chinese and eating with chop sticks was my introduction to Simple Minds. I was hitting every bowl and pot on the table and my mother thought it was enough and time to get some proper drum lessons.
'Notes! Do you need to read notes with playing the drums?' That was my thought when my teacher sent me home with a cassette to write out the notes of a track. First lesson, first homework track: 'Don't You'. This was such an amazing track. I played it over and over.

A couple of years later my grandmother gave me 50 guilders to buy one of my first CDs. CD players had just come out at reasonable prices. I had enough money to buy *Street Fighting Years* but, damn, not enough to buy *Street Fighting Years* and *Once Upon a Time*. *Real to Real* was a bit cheaper and I had enough to buy that instead. Holy Buddha, I am so happy that I bought that album! This is such a rhythmic album – 'Premonition', 'Changeling'. I was hooked! Very soon I bought all their earlier work, realising this band created so much great music and still do. Guys, keep up the awesome music and thank you.

## JR ZIMMER

I first discovered Simple Minds via *The Breakfast Club* and 'Don't You (Forget About Me)'. Such a classic song which fits perfectly in this equally classic cinema treasure. I immediately went out and purchased the back catalogue and have been a fan ever since. I have always been saddened by what I feel is a lack of notoriety and respect within America for a group which has clearly stood the test of time. No simple feat in the music industry.

## SIBYLLA FROM GERMANY

When I heard the voice of Jim Kerr for the first time, it was 'Don't You (Forget About Me)' and my ears felt like they were getting bigger and bigger. They were simply hypnotised, the skin tingled and my mind turned round and headed up just for this music and the magic voice. This voice and music went right into all my nerves, surrounding my heart and capturing my soul. It's what I would describe as the 'rat catcher of Hamelin' effect, if you know the story about the man who made not only rats and mice but also every child to follow him just by whistling his flute. You simply can't resist Jim! Does anyone in the world sings a simple 'la lalala lalala lalalalalalalah...' as Jim does? Like this 'lalala' was a whole lovesong?

So if I close my eyes and Jim sings, I would follow everywhere....

## OSCAR MAURICIO SERRANO LÓPEZ

Being a Salvadoran living in Guatemala City, I had managed to find a great place to buy music. It was March 1985 when I acquired the 45rpm of 'Don't You (Forget About Me)'. A rookie in New Wave and Alternative Rock, I was pleasantly surprised to see it located at number one on the Billboard Hot 100 on May 18, 1985 and thus become an anthem of the Eighties.

## JOSEPH WEBER

*Pine Knob Theater*
*12 August 1984, Detroit, Michigan*

I was given a copy of *Sparkle in the Rain* to listen to in 1982 and it changed the way I listened to music. From 'Up on the Catwalk' to the closing 'Shake Off the Ghost', I was hooked and the journey had begun. I sought out all the albums and listened to them over and over. My favourite memory is a show in Detroit, pressed up against the stage. Right in front was Charlie, to my left Jim, with Mel on the drums and Michael on keyboards. I sang along to all the songs played that night and by the end my voice was shot. I held Jim's hand as he sang 'Biko', shook Charlie's hand at the end and got a high five from Mel to end the evening. I was floating. I even named my son Charlie for my favourite guitar player from my favourite band.

## FRANK DEVOY

*Barrowland Ballroom*
*3 - 5 January 1985, Glasgow,*
*Scotland*

It began with the Glittering Prize that she was. She shone her light on the teenage me but, sadly, our lives were out of sync. I had a girlfriend when we met, then she hooked up with my best mate. When our school group dispersed into adulthood, I never saw her again but the song stayed with me.

REGULAR MUSIC

*presents*

**SIMPLE MINDS**

at GLASGOW BARROWLAND
on FRIDAY, 4th JANUARY, 1985

Doors open at 7.30 p.m
Ticket £6.00    Nº   1350

Management reserve the right of admission — strictly over 18.
No Cameras or Tape Recorders.  No exchanges or refunds.

When I first saw Simple Minds at the Barrowland gig in early January 1985, they opened with 'Glittering Prize'. It was only my second big concert after Thin Lizzy, a tough act to follow. One track in - that track - and the Irish boys were beaten. Together the band and the crowd sang songs from earlier albums that would become the sound track to my future life: 'Ameri, am-eri, ameri, amereee - American!'

I've lost track of the number of gigs I've been to. From the incredible day with The Cult at Ibrox to the pissing down Edinburgh Castle gig, where we splashed to the so apt 'Waterfront' and worried about getting hit by lightning. 'Get in, get out of the rain!' Aye, fat chance up there on the ramparts. The steamy train from Waverley hummed of wet Weegie and Tennent's lager as we sang and hawneee-hooed the bits we didn't know all the way back to Queen Street.

The only point where I worried was Portsmouth about five years ago. The crowd fidgeted through the early numbers while daftie here tried to help the band out. I almost got thrown out for enjoying myself too much. The next gig was the *Acoustic* Hackney Empire set, songs adjusted to fit with veteran vocal ranges. I cried more or less the whole way through.

At Pompey, I thought our days were numbered but, hopefully, there are many more gigs ahead. I'd bought tickets for 2020. Simple Minds, Glasgow, Saturday night, with a bunch of mates, staying in a hotel right next door. What could possibly go wrong, right?

---

# GORDON MACHRAY

My first Simple Minds gig was January 1985 at the band's spiritual home, the Barrowland, Glasgow. I was still at school, so myself and a group of friends told our parents we were staying over at each other's houses to cover for the fact we were heading through to Glasgow for a concert. I'm not sure how we got in as the venue was licensed. But we were only there for the show and a lemonade.

As the music from the mixing desk faded our heroes took to the stage. 'Tonight's a party and this is called 'I Travel'!' proclaimed Jim. What we didn't realise at the time was that in only six short months this version

*Jim signed Gordon Machray's t-shirt*

would morph into 'Ghostdancing' and would be played in front of thousands in Philadelphia, millions in the UK and billions around the world at *Live Aid*.

Barrowland wasn't my first gig. I saw The Stranglers at Edinburgh's Playhouse, a Victorian theatre. The Barrowland was completely different, even more intimidating than a bunch of punks in the capital. I was soaked in sweat before the band even came on stage and by the end of the show had to be peeled off the stage at the front, where I had managed to guide myself, in line with Derek, over the course of the evening.

In today's terms it was a short set of a dozen songs. However, each song was stretched out from the original version as we went higher, higher and higher through the set. It was a triumphant experience, fans lapping up every song. 'Book', 'Catwalk' and 'Speed' were played back to back. How I would love to hear that again. For the encore of 'New Gold Dream', Jim paused five minutes in or so to josh with the fervent crowd that they had a new singer trying to join their band.

The monologue of him introducing that peculiar fellow from Dublin is captured in the *Silver Box* set. However, it doesn't begin to replicate what it was like to be there when U2's Bono stepped on the stage to sing with the band a medley of 'New Gold Dream', Al Green's 'Take Me to the River' and The Doors' 'Light My Fire'. I still have the bootleg cassettes from these three iconic shows and must play them again one day. At the end I managed to grab one of Mel's sticks and with my pocket money bought a Simple Minds t-shirt I think was only sold at the Barrowland. In later years I was lucky enough to meet Jim and ask him to sign that t-shirt, which I subsequently auctioned along with Mel's drumstick for two deserving causes.

I've been to every Simple Minds Barrowland gig since 1985 and actually met my wife Angelique at the 2012 *5x5* gig. That night may well trump my first gig there, but I have to say that, in case the missus reads this.

---

# HUGH TEES

The phone rings in my mum's house. It was my pal Billy ringing, 8pm on a Saturday night. 'Simple Minds tickets go on sale tomorrow morning at 9am.' 'We need to go now and queue up,' I said, 'to have any chance of a ticket.' So off we went. We got there at nine. The tickets were going on sale at Virgin Records on Union Street in Glasgow. We joined the ever-growing queue at Fraser's department store around the corner. By midnight that night, it had snaked right round the block. It was a cold night, some taking shelter in one of those old red-and-white striped BT workmen's tents.

By eight the next morning, the amount of people was staggering, taking everyone by surprise - especially the police. I remember the sheer weight of the crowd leaning against the Boot's window and – bang! – the window shattered!

Anyway, happy days... me and Billy got tickets for two nights, one of them the night Bono came on to sing 'New Gold Dream'.

---

# SHARON LOVE, AGE 16

I got the chance to see Simple Minds at Barrowland with my pal. I hadn't been to many gigs before. We lived in Clydebank and were just about to leave to get the train home when Jim Kerr announced to the crowd, 'I would like to introduce you to a friend of mine…' and on walks Bono. The place went mental.

---

# NEIL STEWART

I've attended over 150 live shows with a special group of friends - Robbo, Andrew, Bob, Drew and Clynt – in multiple cities across Europe, North America, Australia and Africa. I smile when I think how easy it is to organise tickets, flights and hotels. To get a ticket for my first show I had to join an orderly queue weaving its way around the Barrowland on a cold Glasgow evening. I was there from 7pm to await tickets going on sale the following morning. I was one of the

*Jim reaches out to Neil Stewart on stage in Blackpool - photo Vince Barker*

*Neil Stewart's big birthday cake - photo Neil Stewart*

lucky ones to witness Bono on stage that night, and my obsession with Simple Minds started. As tickets became easier to purchase I had to be there every night they were in town and as travel became easier it was France, Holland, Belgium, Germany, Taormina and Barcelona. Friends, family and work colleagues thought I was mad going to the same show night after night. After years of explaining, they now get it. The standout trip was the 2018 North America tour. It got off to a poor start as a bad accident on the M8 motorway in Glasgow caused me to miss my flight to London. A bundle of cash was exchanged for a new flight direct to New York, the rest of the trip a memory I'll never forget, seeing shows in New York, Boston, Pennsylvania and Washington before going on to Atlanta and St Petersburg on my own, meeting new friends along the way.

# RITA MCINTOSH

My love for Simple Minds began when I saw a picture in my older sister's music magazine in my bedroom in Port Glasgow. I was 13. By offering to do chores, including a lot of ironing of my older brother's brown flared cord trousers, I earned enough money to buy *Real to Real Cacophony*. My brother took me to a record store in Glasgow for me to look for it while he went off to buy Status Quo records. I only discovered last year the record shop was Bruce Findlay's. I didn't want to look at any other stuff. I just wanted the train home from Glasgow Central to play my new album. I was actually shaking taking the album out of the bag. Nothing has ever made me feel this way.

Skip a few years and 'Glittering Prize' was on *Top of the Pops*. I was mesmerised - the outfits, the dance moves, the image and that haircut of Jim's. I remember seeing adverts for them in Glasgow and being frustrated I wasn't 18, wishing I was older so I could go to clubs to see them.

My first gig was the Barrowland. I slept out to buy tickets, my mum sat in the car all night as she was concerned about my safety. I remember the stewards shouting out how many tickets were left and worrying I wouldn't get one. I still worry today, but now it's sitting on the presale and having palpitations at not getting the best there is, being able to get tickets for my friends.

Over the years I've attended as many gigs as I could commit to. In 2015, I missed the Edinburgh gig as my husband was having a cancerous tumour removed in Edinburgh Royal. I was sat in an Edinburgh hotel that night, totally distraught at both events taking place that evening. I still have my unused tickets. To make up for it my husband bought myself and my daughter VIP tickets to London.

I had friends who said never meet your hero. I met Jim when I was 19 at a record signing in Glasgow. I think at that point he was as nervous as I was but my feet were stuck to the floor and I couldn't speak, but 30 years later he was confident. But he did say this was the first meet and greet he'd done and he wasn't sure what the fuck to do! This made everyone relax. Meeting the band was fab and Jim signed photos of himself taken by Harry Goodwin that I'd bought in a *Top of the Pops* auction. It was an amazing day.

I lost my hubby to cancer aged 53. Dave wanted me to build memories, which I have. It was his wish that I continued following -

*Mason getting ready to meet Jim and Charlie at HMV*

or stalking, as he called it - Jim. He left me a Simple Minds tour fund and said my fellow fans would look after me, which they have. This fund has taken me to Rome, Hamburg and most recently New York, where I did the meet and greet, and Boston – a trip with other fans I've met through the fan site.

I've made lifelong friends through Simple Minds, as has my daughter. We went to a HMV signing with her newborn son, Mason. He was wearing a Simple Minds t-shirt and we arrived to find a huge queue outside. But as we had the baby we were taken to the front and Mason got to meet Jim and Charlie.

---

# BRUCE FINDLAY

When *New Gold Dream* broke through, we were a major band. On the next album, again another producer, Steve Lillywhite and the new drummer Mel Gaynor. We became an arena act at that point. *Sparkle in the Rain* went straight in at No.1 in the charts. It sold millions of copies but didn't crack America. However, we were touring America, not massive tours but we had a good cult following. The alternative scene there - the dance clubs - liked Simple Minds. Our remixed records were doing well in the clubs and we had a big following in student land. Some of the hipper producers and promoters liked us.

We were big in the big cities, the big urban areas - New York, Chicago, Philadelphia, San Francisco, LA. We were big in Canada. America likes the vulgarity of top-20 records. I was happy to be part of an underground scene. However, the pressure was on to have an American hit and the record company persuaded us to record 'Don't You (Forget About Me)' for *The Breakfast Club*. John Hughes was one of the hottest directors in the film business at the time, making essentially teen movies. This being an A&M-sponsored movie, they were delighted to record what became the film's song. Essentially *The Breakfast Club* is a six million dollar video for the song.

The band were very, very reluctant to record it. They took a lot of persuading to record it and were furious when it became the lead single. They thought it was just going to be an album track.

A&M distributed Virgin in America at the time, so we needed them on our side. Success for them is a vulgar thing, very black and white. Success to them is selling a million records plus, simple as that. But when they get behind a record in America, nothing else matters. They can make a hit by virtually buying hit records in America. Otherwise, you remain an underground cult. Personally speaking, I'd have been happy at that.

However, we went for it and I equally got caught up in the 'Don't You' thing and helped persuade the band to do it. We went from being a headline arena/stadium band in the UK and Europe to a headline arena act in America.

The next album we half made in America, with Bob Clearmountain and Jimmy Iovine. It became our biggest-selling album because it went to No.1 in the UK and all over Europe, all over the world, but also top-10 in America. 'Don't You (Forget About Me)' is not on the album. The record company were furious that we wouldn't put 'Don't You' on the album. We said, 'We never wrote it, it was just in a movie.' We played it live. We didn't play the game in America. We compromised. We half played the game. That was the problem.

But we wanted to please and again, with a new producer, the album came out and it was a monster album. It was a very different sounding album from just two or three years earlier, the *Sons and Fascination* period, and even *New Gold Dream*. *New Gold Dream* was a change from being a dark, mysterious, rhythmic, robotic, European-sounding band to becoming a more mainstream kind of album, with great songs but lighter sounds. It was a crossover album between the old and the new.

## ADAM CURTIS

Once upon a time, one man on a lonely platform, North London. My journey begins. Waiting on a train, a green signal signifies the line is clear, I listen to the steel rails hum, spirited away, see my glittering prize, the Clansman leaves a wake of swirling dust and dirt as it gallops through to Charlie's solo on its way to journeys end.

In the early '80s, passing through Edge Hill just before the tunnels to Liverpool Lime Stree, 'Someone Somewhere (in Summertime)' shimmers as we pass under the city, the beat crashing along the way. She is your only friend, until the bitter end.

Still in the '80s, on the London Underground, it's time to go to Brixton and look around, see what's missing. I'll tell you everything I need, belief is a beauty thing.

One million years from today, I'm on a trip to Jungleland to see the Highrise Land. Over the River Clyde I see the waterfront, I'm gonna get out of the rain, move on up and sanctify myself. While the river's in front of me, that's where I'm goin' to be. I see the lights and a kid called Hope. You make me feel so sad to be here all alone.

During the street fighting years I take a walk on the wild side, it's the way it was planned. Money can't buy me, I've got time, time is on my side. Now there's good news from the next world, and all I've got now in my defence is my innocence, I'm hypnotised. The band played on in a criminal world.

I'm on the Moscow Underground now, descended from a world that's lost control. I don't know where else I can go. Rain keeps falling down. Won't you call my name?

The Big Music led me to a sense of discovery. You put your hands on me, thank you.

## STEPHANIE BATES & MELISSA BEECH

Sisters in our 40s, we've followed Simple Minds for years. It's where we both make time for each other and everything else goes out the window. It's escapism and the band hit all the right notes for us! We love it when they come to our hometown, Stoke-on-Trent, but we travel far and wide. Our party starts in the car, on a train or even a plane. At every concert, we couldn't ask for a more magical night, something we've shared since childhood. Thank you for the entertainment.

## JEAN-PAUL COHEN-SOLAL

*Live Aid* was a slap in the face for a 13-year-old kid. I was immediately captivated by Jim's charisma and the energy released by the band on stage.

## OONAGH O'NEILL

### *Live Aid*
### *13 July 1985, Philadelphia, Pennsylvania*

The *Live Aid* concert had been announced for London and early in the summer, rumour had it that a second show was happening in the USA and Philly was the frontrunner. At that stage it was all speculative, no one knew if it would happen, who was playing or where it would be for sure, but the buzz was enough for me and I decided I was going. It was the 1980s and I would be there or be square!

Schedule for the big event confirmed, news channels swooped in, MTV went into overdrive on announcements, tickets went on sale - it was all taking place in July on the same day as *Live Aid* in London. I took my savings and headed for the ticket office; I purchased six seats

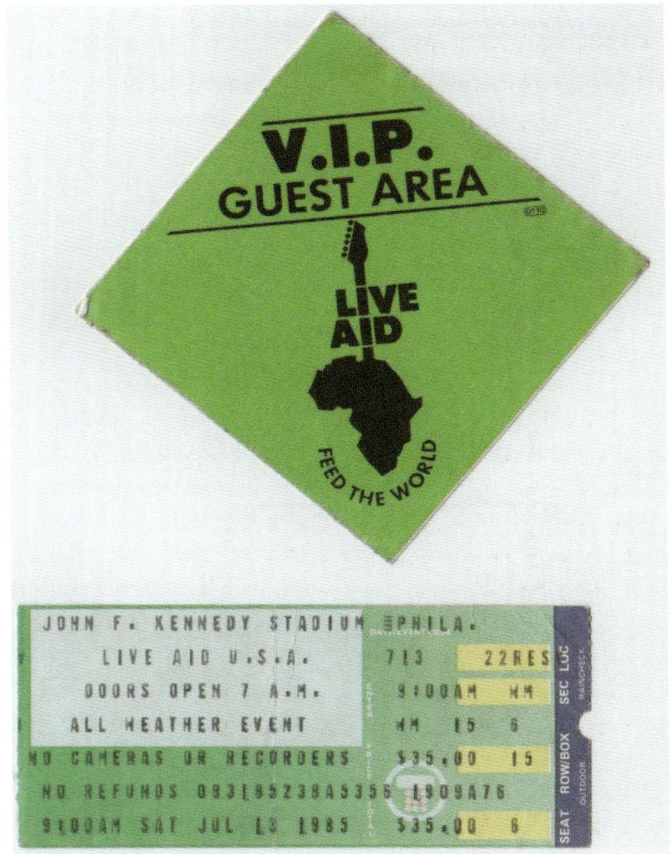

*Oonagh O'Neill's ticket and VIP pass for Live Aid*

and handed over those hard-earned dollars. I'm sure I wasn't the only music devotee who put their money up before a single band was even positively booked, and perhaps that's how it all actually happened. Years later, I read that Bruce Springsteen had been asked why he hadn't performed considering he lived just across the bridge in New Jersey. His reply was, 'I didn't know it was going to be so good.'

Saturday 13 July 1985 dawned and at 6.30am I was behind reception at the Palace Hotel, Philadelphia telling anyone who would listen that after work I was going to the concert. On the preceding days, teenage 'Durannies' had perched on the sidewalk at the front of the building. That morning no fans turned up. They had all decamped to join the thousands who swarmed down Broad Street from all over the States, bringing South Philly to a standstill.

However, in front of my desk all was cool as a roundup of pop icons, actors and musicians surfaced from their suites ready to participate in the concert that would contribute to 'Feed the World'. All the way through the morning they congregated in the lobby, awaiting transport to the stadium. As Simple Minds headed for the door I offered an affectionate good luck send off. Eventually Stuart, my manager, could listen to my whinging no more and off I went too. I had a guest VIP pass so caught a ride in the next minivan leaving the front door of the hotel to convey bands to and from the JFK Arena across town.

Arriving at the offstage area at the back of the stadium, I perplexed a security guard as I tried to point out that even though I did have a backstage pass I also had a ticket and wanted to meet my friends out front. He told me the only way to do that was to actually go under the stage, explaining that when I came out the other side, I would never make it past the encroaching crowds to find my seat. He opened the gate and let me out into a scary no-man's land, a parking lot filled with huge 40 foot rigs, tour buses and delivery trucks.

I had no idea which direction to go, and as I tried to navigate a way through the maze was accosted by two of the city's finest police officers. They demanded to know how I'd got in there. Imagine the bewilderment when I displayed my VIP pass and explained I was not trying to get in - I wanted to find a way out!

From within, the roar of the crowd reverberated around the arena. Simple Minds were on stage, and as Jim Kerr belted out 'Don't You (Forget About Me)' I circumnavigated the exterior of JFK stadium, trying to find my gate to get back inside. I should have gone to the VIP guest area and heard the band play.

It was one of the most momentous shows of the 20th century; Joan Baez introduced it as the Woodstock of our generation. On that day Simple Minds played in front of 110,000 people, it was televised live across America to an audience of millions plus the one forlorn fan outside on the verge of tears. I was missing the greatest gig of that era.

During that afternoon the throng of music revellers melted in the sweltering temperatures, the concert sound system was poor and link-ups from London were problematic, but nobody cared. We all cheered in unison, stomped our feet and exploded with every anthem, a deafening sound lifting up across the City of Brotherly Love. It was the hottest day of that east coast summer but eventually the sun lowered in the sky, and temperatures finally dropped to a bearable 90 degrees.

I Mexican-waved and added out of tune vocals to every song until the very end. I should have gone early to return to the hotel to work my second shift of the day, serving refreshments to the returning celebs who now stood on stage for a culmination of the day's performances. But I stayed for the memorable finale and got to see my teenage music idols from Glasgow standing alongside legends from an earlier decade.

I had been Someone, Somewhere in Summertime. I had lived that Life in a Day.

## PAUL MCCUNNELL

We were involved in the Falklands War. I was 17 and in the Royal Navy when introduced to Simple Minds. I started to listen over the next couple of years. Then I saw the *Live Aid* performance and was well and truly hooked. Simple Minds tapes went with me on every posting during my naval career. I loved every concert I've been to. I now like to sit in the garden with a beer and listen and sing along. My grandson listens too.

## MARLENE B. COLANGELO

*Radio City Music Hall*
*2 November 1985, New York, New York*

My relationship with Simple Minds began with *The Breakfast Club*, 'Don't You (Forget About Me), the MTV age and all that, but developed into something more when *Once Upon a Time* came out. It was then that I experienced Simple Minds live in concert at Radio City Music Hall. I took my younger sister and we had excellent seats, row 15 centre. That show - the energy, the camaraderie between audience and band – sealed it for me. The fact that Jim, Charlie, Mel, everyone, gave such a great performance and had such a great time doing it. It was one of the best concerts I've ever been to. Next day I went out and purchased any CD I could find.

As a home furnishings designer for over 25 years, styling bedding, accessories and window treatments, etc., I took the patterns and trims to put together to sketch into what would become the next Spring or Fall collection to be shown at Market Week, and always had music playing, helping me create. Many times Simple Minds were the Muse. They never disappointed.

I work in a nuclear plant now and my schedule meant I couldn't see their last US tour. I'll see the next one though.

# ONCE UPON A TIME

## DAVID WILKES

I first recall Simple Minds on the Australian weekly music programme *Countdown* in 1981, watching them perform 'Love Song'. I could not remember their name, just the singer dancing with his large 'hip carry bag' around his neck and the drummer with his futuristic drums. I thought how cool the ever-moving lead singer with sunglasses looked and I loved hearing this repetitive foreign beat, especially as I was brought up listening to Beatles records by my mum.

In 1984, I came across the 'Up on the Catwalk' video on television. The shape-throwing majestic singer was continually moving, singing lyrics about currencies that etched into my mind. I immediately was entranced and quickly discovered their back catalogue, including the beloved *New Gold Dream* album.

In 1985 during my final year of high school, I eagerly awaited the release of *Once Upon a Time*. It got me through the cramming study hours, and I wore out the cassette tape on my extravagant Sony Walkman. A year later compact discs arrived, and I could relive all their albums with portable discs that could skip songs and shuffle!

Whether waiting all hours of the night in the Southern Hemisphere to watch them perform at *Live Aid* or hearing the first beats of 'Waterfront' at the emotive Mandela 70th birthday concert, I recall shivers running through me. Tears fell when Jim first sang 'Mandela Day'.

Simple Minds brought me to Amnesty International and instilled in me a passion for human rights. And they have passion too. It shows through when they play and shows it's not just about how well you play or sing. My father told me they would be a fad I'd grow out of. But I want 'Alive and Kicking' to be played at my funeral.

## DARYA PAKHOTINSKIKH

I am 17 years old fan from Russia. I discovered Simple Minds when I came across the film *Dare to Be Different* and saw Jim Kerr talking about one of my favourite actors, Jack Nicholson, announcing Simple Minds at *Live Aid*.

The first Simple Minds song I heard was 'All the Things She Said'. It seemed very unusual in the sound and development of the melody, and I immediately fell in love with it. I feel something really magical about it. This song makes me leave the real world and plunge into the universe of beautiful music. I love the unique voice of Jim Kerr, who is able to transmit light and incredibly kind energy through music.

## TODD FIDUCCI

Every summer for nearly 50 years, my family has vacationed in Boulder Junction in northern Wisconsin, a very pretty area with forests and lakes. They sold cassettes at this small town's grocery store and I thought I'd give *Once Upon a Time* a try. From the first note, I knew that I was going to like this band's music. It was a great cassette all the way through and I gave that cassette a workout that week. I've bought other albums since, and their music has stuck with me for 30 plus years. I still have that cassette, sitting not more than five feet from me.

## ALEXANDRA LEUPOLD

One evening I saw a live recording of Simple Minds on the TV show *Rockpalast* and fell in love with the band. I didn't have much pocket money each month so had to sell all my old childhood toys on Stuttgart flea market every Saturday. With this money I bought my first records. Every new record in my collection was like Christmas to me. One of my first albums was *Once Upon a Time* and I loved it. I must have listened to it over 100 times. Aged 15, I found my real friends in the punk scene. They were interested in the same things as me. I felt like I was coming home. A short time later, I was kicked out of home but found a new place in a shared flat with other young people. It was the best thing that could have happened to me, always with my music in my ear and in my heart. And Simple Minds were always a part of it. Their music helped me through very bad times and gave me the strength and power to never give up and it also accompanied me in very happy and sweet moments. It's music from the heart and it hits into mine.

## JULIE HARRINGTON

After listening to several SM songs on YouTube, I decided to buy the greatest hits album and listened to it on a several hours long road trip to visit a friend. I realised I had been missing out on all these great songs. I slowly began accumulating more Simple Minds music. I gave *Walk Between Worlds* to my dad as a gift and he had it on repeat in his car for weeks because he loved it so much. It's now a bucket list item for me to see a Simple Minds concert at least once. My favourite Simple Minds song is 'Sanctify Yourself'. I love the energy and the message, and Jim's outfit and hat in the music video. I think berets were in fashion then!

# ALIVE AND
# KIC
—(84

# SI
# M

● 18 Oct. Perth Ent. Centre ● 20 Oct. Ad
○ Sydney Ent. Centre ● 25 Oct. Canberra

## LETICIA DE ANDA AGUILAR

I am Mexican. My history with Simple Minds began with *The Breakfast Club* movie and 'Don't You (Forget About Me)'. I was captivated. I researched Simple Minds in music magazines and I remember raising money to buy my first cassette. I don't remember how many times I listened to it.

The magic of Simple Minds arrived on January 1, 1986 with my crazy and very personal tradition of making 'the song of the year' the first song I was listening on the radio during the first minutes of the New Year. That song would be my lucky song and in 1986, 'Alive and Kicking' was my song and it marvellously accomplished its mission. If I was studying for a school exam and listened to it, I closed the book because I knew that I would get an excellent mark. If I listened to it casually, I knew that something nice would happen. Even today that magic happens when I listen to that song. The extraordinary thing is that in 1988, my song was 'Don't You (Forget About Me)' and, in 1990, 'Waterfront'. So the magic grew.

Simple Minds songs accompanied me when I studied medicine and gynaecology/obstetrics. Over the years and decades, as an adult with greater responsibilities, I know that if I casually listen to any Simple Minds song on the radio, no matter how complex the moment, the song will improve things. All that incredible and marvellous magic motivated me to travel to LA to meet the group. I still remember being close to Jim, Charlie, Greg and - well everyone! But I was so paralysed I couldn't even speak. It was one of the most important moments in my life. Thank you Simple Minds for the magic you have brought into my life.

## SUE HOLLAR

The song 'Alive and Kicking' came to me out of nowhere, buried in my subconscious memory for over 30 years. Googling the song and then the band took me on a ride down the Simple Minds rabbit hole for the next 10 months. I asked a friend, an extremely intelligent friend, why a song would come to me after 30+ years. She said that psychologically speaking, it's usually because something happened years ago that the brain couldn't process at the time and saves it for later when it is 'safe'. She recommended therapy. Therapy did not work. I thought about hypnosis. I read self-help books. Then I wrote a timeline of the early Eighties, where I lived, what car I drove, what job I had, who I dated. And there it was, the memory of a young man for whom I had very deep feelings, a best friend that had been my confidante for a dozen years and a betrayal. You can fill in the blanks.

After learning the 'truth' (in 1985) I sat in front of the TV and stared at MTV and VH1 for a good 10 to 12 hours, trance-like. The memory went back to when 'Alive and Kicking' debuted on the music channels. After a few tears and some choice words that I wish I had said back then, I got on with my life. Feeling 10 years younger and lighter I'm happy that I finally reclaimed my memory.

*You turn me on*

## JEANETTE HEPWORTH

I would record *Top of the Pops* on our video recorder and learnt the lyrics by using the pause button to stop the tape so I could write the lyrics down. I learnt them all singing along in my mum and dad's living room, much to their annoyance.

I absolutely fell in love with Simple Minds when I heard 'Alive and Kicking'. I was 14 and they were a massive part of my teenage years. When I married Kristian last summer, we chose 'Alive and Kicking' as our 'walk down the aisle' song. The last time the band played Hull, Kristian was on crutches after a knee operation. We were stood at the side of the hall during 'our song', leaning against a post. Jim looked at Kristian, pointed to him and put his thumbs up. It made Kristian's night!

## PABLO IANNINO

I am from Buenos Aires in Argentina and I have been a follower of the band since 1985, when 'Don't You (Forget About Me)' was played every day on the radio. From that moment I began to investigate the band. I bought the cassette *Once Upon a Time* and first heard 'Alive and Kicking', my favourite song to this day.

## GUILLERMO GARCÍA-FERNÁNDEZ

My parents met and fell in love in the Eighties, dancing and listening to the songs of the moment, in English or Spanish. We had cassettes with songs of rock and new wave songs, including 'Don't You (Forget About Me)' and 'Alive and Kicking'. This helped me to love English music rather than Spanish!

I started a major in English Literature in college thanks to my interests in translating SM songs into Spanish. My listening skills were poor but improved thanks to listening to Simple Minds. I was able to introduce their ideas and quotes to different cultures because I have been singing with some pals since 2009 and employed some Simple Minds songs. It's not plagiarism – it's a homage to the band I love the most.

## IAN WILSON

My wife was pregnant with our child. The doctor told us from an ultra sound scan that the baby could be Downs Syndrome and asked did we want to terminate the pregnancy? We said no. Our baby was a boy and it turned out nothing was wrong with him. Patrick is now 22 studying civil engineering and plays bass guitar. My song for my son is 'Alive and Kicking'.

*What's it gonna take to make a dream survive*
*Who's got the touch to calm the storm inside*
*Don't say Goodbye*
*Don't say Goodbye*

## LUKE VAN DEN BERG

Me and a friend were playing *Grand Theft Auto V*, in which players have different radio stations. It's there I heard 'All the Things She Said'. It's my favourite song of all time.

## STEPHEN MOORE

In 1986, a mate of mine put a song on and I'd never heard anything so magical. 'Who the fuck is this?' I demanded. 'Simple Minds - you've never heard of these?' The song was called 'All the Things She Said' and, as (Radio 1 DJ) Steve Wright, said, 'What a video.' I was determined to hunt down the back catalogue of this classic band and got *Life in a Day* for £3.29 of my pocket money. I must say I was a bit underwhelmed. I asked my mate, 'Are there two Simple Minds?' I got a similar shock with *Sons and Fascination* - especially '70 Cities as Love Brings the Fall', although you get used to the cow horns! 'Theme for Great Cities' is cathedral music fused with classic funk – superb!

## BEN BARCLAY

'All the Things She Said' mesmerised me. It was melodic, ballsy and joyous. At the time I presumed Simple Minds were American, such was my youthful naivety. Fast forward three and half years. I made up for lost time and had scoured record fairs, scrolled my fingers down miles of *Record Collector* columns hunting down all previous UK releases.

I lost an auction bid on their first '77 single, 'Saints and Sinners' by Johnny and the Self Abusers and I was gutted. But six months later it turned up again and I wasn't missing out this time. I telephoned the bloke immediately and got first dibs on it as soon as my cheque arrived. A week later it popped through the door. He'd posted it in a seven inch record sleeve but had turned it inside out, perhaps already thinking about our planet. Inside the card sleeve was the return address and date of the previous sender. It turned out he was the bloke who had beat my bid in the previous auction on the very same single.

Having completed my collection, I wrote to *Record Collector* magazine, outraged that Simple Minds hadn't featured for three years. At the time I was working as a trainee graphic designer. I used both the dark room and printer to produce my own letterhead. I also thought it would be highly amusing to give myself a title to appear official, and incorporated the Claddagh design as used on their live album and created a logo for myself, 'The Official Simple Minds Disciple'. Despite my stationery they did write back, agreeing it had been a while and would I like to write the article and compile the discography? I neglected to mention I failed my O level English resit a year or two before. Now I'm not going to suggest that the article was a literary masterpiece, far from it, but it did give me an opportunity to fabricate some future CD box set releases featuring B-sides and unreleased material.

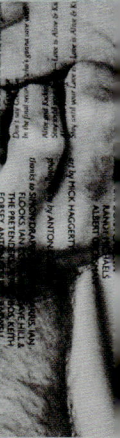

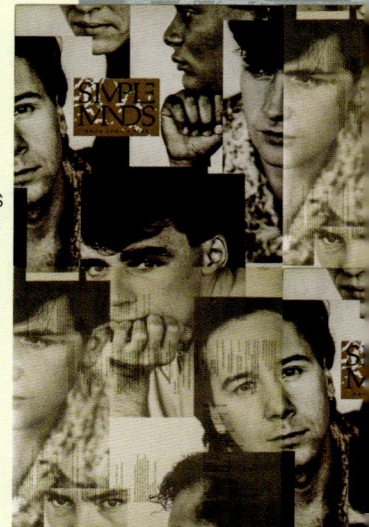

Essentially, I saw this as a subtle way of asking for what I actually wanted, should anyone of note read the article. When I compiled the complete UK discography, having painstakingly acquired it, who wouldn't forgive me for increasing the prices by a healthy 10 to 25%? I even got paid £100, which seemed fair at the time although I would have done it for free.

Shortly after the article was published in April 1990, and as fate would have it, I was contacted by Steve Pritchard of Virgin Records. He said that Virgin were actually working on a series of box sets that later came out as the *Themes Volumes 1-5*. He must have thought I had good connections and knowledge of the band and asked me if I wouldn't mind proofing the sets. How could I refuse? I was sent drafts of text and details of the track lists, etc. in a document that also included a Glasgow fax number. I did correct some errors here and there in the text. He was keen for me to hear the collection before it went to press and suggested sending some DAT tapes to me? Yeah, like a cheeky 18-year-old is going to own a DAT deck in 1990! When I received my complimentary *Themes* box sets, I did notice some errors in the tracks. The B-side of 'Love Song' was supposed to include the instrumental version (not vocal) of 'This Earth That You Walk Upon' and 'Someone Somewhere (in Summertime)' missed off Charlie's guitar intro as featured on the 12 inch. These errors were rectified when they released the CD singles individually. Perhaps it would have been cost effective to have sent me DAT player after all.

I also helped out with the CD issue of *Celebration*. That DAT deck would've perhaps come in handy again as Virgin included the instrumental of 'Kant Kino' which immediately follows the CD album version of '30 Frames a Second'. The instrumental didn't feature on Arista's original compilation. After this, Omnibus Press contacted me then to help with artefacts for their visual documentary book. My singles collection and other bits were included in that.

My geeky journey was almost over, although it very nearly turned a different direction altogether, one which could have fused my musical heroes with my self-proclaimed graphical talents. Steve Pritchard of Virgin told me that he'd passed on my contact details to Jim Kerr, as he'd said that he was looking for somebody like myself to be involved in the fan club. Several weeks later I was out one evening. It was probably on one of those extremely rare occasions that my brother was home from university to get his clothes washed and bug the crap out of me. On my return, Guy shot down the stairs. 'You'll never believe who rang for you tonight!' excitedly at the top of his voice, and still in shock. 'JIM KERR!' My heart sank as my brother gave him the full 'oh my god, you're a celebrity' treatment. The last thing I wanted to do, as I felt he was hardly a celebrity type yearning for limelight. I'd figured out he was much more down to earth. Guy said, 'Come to think of it he was starting to get pissed off when I kept saying, 'Really, really!'.' Game over, man.

A follow up call didn't materialise. It was not meant to be.

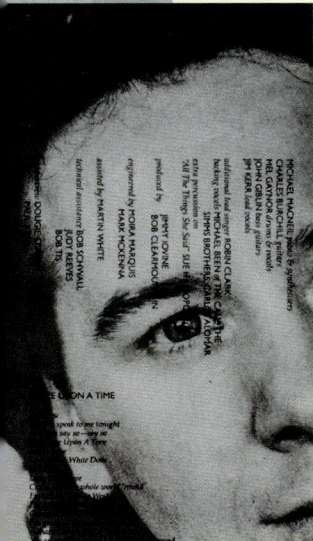

# JOE SCOTT

*Constitution Hall*
*4 November 1985, Washington DC*

I thought they were The Smiths. It was early 1985, and I knew who they were, due mostly to ubiquitous US hit 'Don't You...' but that and maybe 'Theme for Great Cities' were the extent of my exposure to Simple Minds at the time. I also vaguely knew who The Smiths were.

Some DJs on legendary Maryland radio station WHFS were fond of playing long sets without interruption and then running down the artists and songs played at the end. The DJ played such a set one day in early '85, and I caught the last minute or two of The Smiths' 'How Soon is Now?' which intrigued me. However, by the time the set of songs ended and he started listing the bands, skipping song titles, I had lost count. I thought Simple Minds had recorded 'How Soon is Now?'

Not knowing the song's title - or correct band - I started buying Simple Minds records searching for a Smiths song. *New Gold Dream*? Nope, but damn, what a record! *Sparkle in the Rain*? No, but for me an even stronger connection than *New Gold Dream*. I kept going. Eventually I had all their albums and was wearing them out. By November I was a committed fan and sat in awe of their performance at DAR Constitution Hall. It was pouring rain outside. I'm pretty sure they opened with 'Waterfront'. I knew then that they weren't The Smiths.

---

# ALEX KIRBY

*Maple Leaf Gardens*
*8 November 1985, Toronto, Canada*

I first heard 'Someone Somewhere (in Summertime)' around June 1983 on Toronto's CFNY - The Spirit of Radio indeed. Like an instant injection of inspiration, the blend of Charlie's guitar, Mick's keyboards and Jim's voice and words transported me to a world filled with hypnotic grooves, cascading keyboards and driving, dramatic drumbeats.

Maple Leaf Gardens was my first Minds gig, and when the opening chords for 'Waterfront' hit it was spine-tingling. I couldn't believe I was there. I had to pinch myself.

Other concert highlights include: Usher Hall in Edinburgh in 1995, where Jim introduced 'Waterfront'

*Alex Kirby first saw the Minds at Maple Leaf Gardens*

as 'here it is - the 39th best song' after *The Scotsman* published some ludicrous top Scottish songs of all time (for me it's The Stadium Song of All Time); Glasgow Carling Academy with a James fan who knows a bit about fandom and devotion and says he's never witnessed anything like that night; and the Hydro in Glasgow in 2015 with my 10 year-old-son, who played air guitar all night.

Most bands become karaoke versions of themselves but Simple Minds have managed to keep it fresh by putting in the effort and experimenting, including several reinterpretations of classics. I love the acoustic take on 'Chelsea Girl' and the 'electro' version of 'Speed Your Love to Me'. Both cut to the essence of what makes each brilliant.

---

# MARLEEN KORT

*Ahoy*
*2 December*
*1985,*
*Rotterdam,*
*The Netherlands*

My first concert was at Rotterdam Ahoy in December 1985. It was magic. I didn't have a camera at that time, but made a portrait drawing of Jim. They were magic again in Oslo in March 2020.

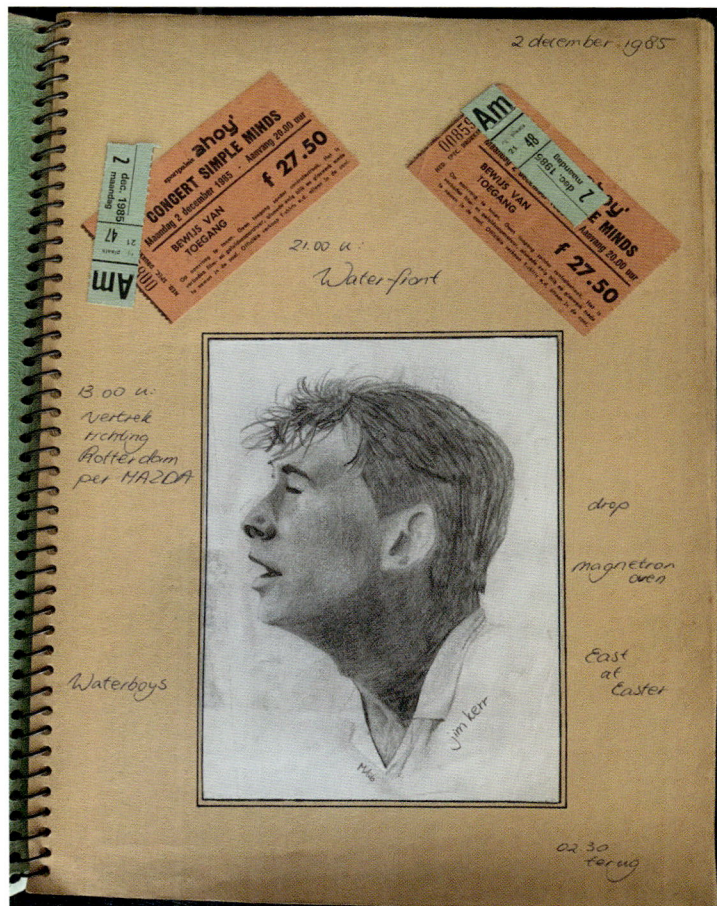

Marleen Kort's portrait of Jim

## JONATHAN ROWE

*Palais des Sports*
*5 December 1985, Lyon, France*

I would phone Dial-a-Disc every night to listen to the singles from *New Gold Dream*. I've seen the band several times. In December 1985 I was spending a year as an English assistant in a lycée as part of my French degree. For my 21st birthday I took a dozen kids to Lyon to see Simple Minds at the Palais des Sports, only a couple of years older than most of them.

   Some friends in Lyon had bought me the tickets (90 francs, about £9). Being a student, I had no money or credit card so after meeting them and collecting the tickets we went to the show. It was fantastic. Afterwards we missed the last train home and had to spend the night in the train station waiting for the first train back. The parents were not happy but the kids thought it was great. It wouldn't be allowed nowadays!

## ELISABETH GROUILLER

My three children were raised on their songs and now are fans with happy childhood memories. When cassettes disappeared, I bought CDs, sometimes twice, one for the car and one for the house. I bought a ticket for a concert in Orleans, but my husband wouldn't let me go alone. I still have the ticket.

## FELICE MINERVINO

I heard a cassette of *Sparkle in the Rain* at a friend's and was struck by the beauty of the songs. I asked my friend to make me a copy but later bought the original cassette and discovered my friend had forgotten to copy 'East at Easter'! My daughter Rebecca was eight years old when I took her to Taormina. Jim and Charlie were really kind to her. Jim shook her hand and said, 'How are you princess?'

## PAUL WISSE

A friend and I were walking across a snow-laden field in Yorkshire. As the sun was setting, he passed me his Walkman and said, 'You have to listen to this....' It was the first time I ever heard 'A Brass Band in African Chimes'. It was a spiritual moment and without doubt the exact moment I fell in love with music and the band, my band.

## RODOLPHE HUGUET

The first time was 1985. I've never missed a Lyon show. Simple Minds are part of my life and not a day goes by without me listening to a song by the band. I'm looking forward to seeing them again at the Halle Tony Garnier in 2021.

## FRÉDÉRIC NOTE

*Patinoire de Mériadeck*
*9 December 1985, Bordeaux, France*

'Someone Somewhere (in Summertime)' and 'Hunter and the Hunted' were looped on my cassette radio during college years. Their music has never left me since. I saw them for the first time in 1985 in Bordeaux for the *Once Upon a Time* tour and still have those images and the sound in my mind.

## BÉNÉDICTE ALIÉ, AGE 17

*Forest National*
*11 December 1985, Brussels, Belgium*

I was in my room listening to the radio when my attention was caught by 'Glittering Prize'. It was a real musical love at first sight. In 1985 the walls of my room were lined with posters and pictures of Simple Minds and Jim Kerr.

I will never forget my very first concert. I went with my best

*Bénédicte Alié discovered Simple Minds around the time of New Gold Dream*

friend, Jean-Luc. He is no longer here to talk about it, which makes it all the more moving. My father drove us to Brussels from Liège, 100km away. We were so excited! I had written a letter to Jim and made 20 copies of it. My idea was to throw them on stage so at least one made it to him. My friend and I were in the pit. We were not the only ones who were very excited! With the crowd movements, we were moving

173

away more and more from each other. After support from The Waterboys, the tension increased more and more. I'm not very tall. I couldn't see much and I began to feel oppressed.

Finally, Simple Minds arrived on stage. The crowd was wild! I started taking the letters out of my coat pocket and tried to throw them on the stage but was too far away. Suddenly, a big guy next to me who I didn't know took the letters and started throwing them too. Some of them landed on the stage.

I felt crushed, I couldn't breathe. Then I felt lifted up from the ground. Dozens and dozens of arms took me behind the security fences, where I stayed for the rest of the concert. Jim was so close to me. When the concert was over, I found my friend back in the crowd as it was dispersing. We fell into each other's arms, crying. We were both happy and deeply moved. And 35 years later, I haven't forgotten anything about this first concert. I kept the ticket... like all the others.

Has my letter been read? I don't think so. But who knows? I haven't kept a copy. How did I not think to do so? What did I write? As far as I can remember, it was something like, 'I'm not in love with you, Jim, but I love you and your music makes me feel so good.' The words of a teenage fan, overwhelmed by her emotions. Naively, I had left my address.

Jim, if you wanted to answer, I don't have the same address any more.

---

## OLGA VALBUENA

I heard my older brother playing *New Gold Dream* day after day and somehow ended up in the Brussels Forest National Concert Hall with him, 10 minutes from home and first in line. We were so close and there was such strong empathy between the band and audience. I've flashes in my head of Jim looking straight into the eyes of the crowd, Charlie – with his lovely smile - scratching the guitar, and Mel's impressive percussion. In 1997, I moved to Madrid, where me and my younger sister were too busy with real life, trying to build our future in another country. But in recent years, I rediscovered the magic power of SM music: many songs still make me shiver all along the body. I'm looking forward to the *40 Years of Hits* tour in Madrid.

---

## SERGE CHOQUET

Everything began at school in Brussels, aged 15. *Sparkle in the Rain* was a new record and a friend proudly let me listen to it. The record stayed in my head day after day, the one that made me become another boy. It gave me more confidence, more optimism, more reasons to believe in the future.

*Serge Choquet with Jim*

As a teenager I idolised the band members and saw them as divinities. When I got older, I understood they were 'just' humans, and you don't have to be a god to write good songs and touch the soul of mankind. And 35 years after that first moment, everything is still clear in my head. I remember the first concert in Forest National, the Werchter Festival, watching *Live Aid* on TV, meeting the band on a small boat in the Port of Antwerp, talking to Charlie, awkwardly asking Jim a question.

So many memories, coming back to the surface like pieces of my life. Studying, working, loving, raising kids, buying a house, divorcing… Every moment of my life is tied to a song.

Today I feel this wonderful relationship with Simple Minds music is stronger than ever. Whatever happens, Simple Minds will be the only thing in my life that's unchanging. When it rains, my horizon always looks like an old, unforgettable melody: 'Get in, get out of the rain…'

## WALTER WUYTEN

I've been a Simple Minds fan since the release of *New Gold Dream*. In 1982, I was 15 and rode my bicycle 30km to a warehouse selling the album here in Belgium. Back home, the first thing I did was put the disc on my Technics record player, turn on the amplifier and listen in a trance. My neighbours were tolerant in those days and didn't complain, even though the amplifier was set to the higher levels!

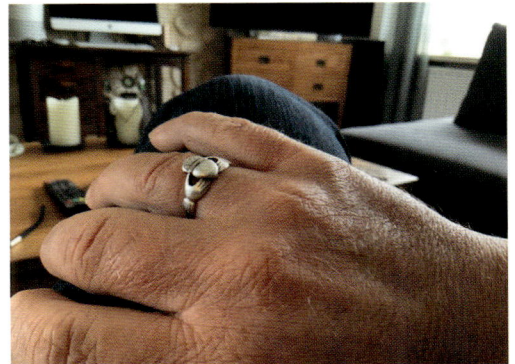
*Walter Wuyten became a fan on hearing New Gold Dream*

I first saw Simple Minds perform in Brussels, in Vorst Nationaal Concert Hall. The show began late because Jim had a broken leg or foot. I still recall his coming on to the stage and starting off the show by saying, 'Didn't I promise you a miracle?'

Even after almost 40 years of being a fan, I still get shivers when I hear 'New Gold Dream' or almost every song on *Sparkle in the Rain*. I'd love one day to get a picture of me with Jim and Charlie. That picture would stay forever in my book, my book of brilliant things.

## ALISON EVANS

It was a Friday night in December 1985 in Glasgow and the queue grew longer as the hours passed. Cold was an understatement and the rain was battering down. Everyone came well prepared – sleeping bags, hats, scarves and two pairs of everything. The guy with the ghetto blaster even brought extra batteries as he knew it was gonna be a long night. But none of that mattered. The important thing was getting the tickets going on sale at 10am. We huddled together, shared the contents of our flasks and pieces wrapped in tinfoil. We sang our hearts out, and laughed and made new friendships due to a shared love of the music. No-one slept and no-one cared. We were soaked through, freezing and tired, but the feeling of holding those tickets the next morning was the best feeling ever. Everyone waved their tickets in the air and waved goodbye to new friends. 'See you at the gig' was the parting cry.

The night of the gig arrived and – oh, what a night. I was 15 years old and had never experienced anything like it. The lights. The music. The band were right in front of me and that was the first of many, many nights in the company of Simple Minds. Over the years I've been to countless gigs at the best venue in the world (yeah, Barrowlands), several other venues in and around Glasgow and Scotland and the Bataclan in Paris too. A stand out is Edinburgh Castle in the pissing rain with Jim kicking off with, 'As they say in Glasgow . . . ah fuck it.' There was a party to be had and boy did we dance, sing and have the time of our lives.

## JANIE MCFARLANE

It was Barrowlands in the Eighties. On they came, the crowd went wild and I thought, 'Hang on, I've only had one drink - why am I swaying?' The floor was heaving up and down with the crowd. I felt like I was on a boat in a stormy sea.

## RONAN MORRIS

My older brother came home from a Simple Minds gig in Dublin in the Eighties. His ticket was blue with 'Simple Minds' in gold writing. I was hooked on the ticket alone, and then the stories from my brother and the music - everything seemed to fit. I've lost count as to how many times I've seen the band, but remember them all - different crowds from gig to gig, from country to country. They seem to just get better and better.

## JOSHUA RADU

Living in Montreal it's hard to see them live so I always tried to catch a show when travelling in the UK but the timing was off. Now I've seen them twice in Montreal. It's great to actually feel the music of one of the best live bands you'll ever see.

## JEAN-MARC PRADINES

My first Simple Minds experience was *New Gold Dream* followed by *Sparkle in the Rain*. I have never stopped listening to their music and have seen concerts in Paris, Toulouse and Nîmes. Their music has been a real joy in my life. Please don't stop.

## ANDREW BRUCE

I first heard 'Promised You a Miracle' and loved 'Glittering Prize'. After hearing sessions on Kid Jensen and album tracks on his and Peel's Radio 1 shows, their album was a must buy. I've attended 17 different venues to get my fill, mostly with my younger brother (somehow, he has been to more shows than me!) but also with various friends. I can't wait for the rescheduled tour and right now I need to listen to *Live in the City of Angels*.

## CHRISTOPHE HAYOZ

I was 16 when I discovered the band whose music has been present in all the greatest moments of my life. I have been fortunate enough to stay at Villa Angela and am looking forward to one day seeing them play in their hometown of Glasgow

*Christophe Hayoz at Villa Angela*

## GIORGIO SFERRA

Sometimes I've slowed down the turntable to make the instrumental parts sound even more intense. My memories are permeated with their sounds.

## BEATE BRAHM

*Westfalenhalle*
*13 January 1986, Dortmund, West Germany*

In 1986 the Westfalenhalle trembled so much, thanks to an enthusiastically singing and dancing crowd, that the wooden cycle racetrack broke down and the show had to be interrupted. The day I found a bootleg of this special concert on a flea market in Dortmund made me a very happy girl.

## KLAUS DE PILLECYN

At school we had a really progressive religion teacher who often put on records during class. When he put on *New Gold Dream* I went straight to The Kitchen, our local record store, after school and got the album. It was the beginning of a collection that continues to grow. I saw the band for the first time in Vorst Nationaal, then travelled to Le Zenith in Paris for one of the gigs that became *Live in the City of Light*. I have seen the band more than 60 times in Belgium, UK, France, Germany and the Netherlands and am still going strong.

But it's about more than just the gigs with Simple Minds. It's also about meeting like-minded fans from all over the world. Some of them have become close friends. That's what Simple Minds and music in general is all about, bringing people together and sharing their love for a band and their music. My most memorable gigs? That's a bit difficult. There are so many, but let's say *5X5* at Barrowland, Köln and Brussels are up there. Who knows what the band will do next? We still travel…

## MICHAEL SIEFEN

*Philipshalle*
*14 January 1986, Düsseldorf, West Germany*

I went with my friends Alex and Andreas. I'd already listened to a number of Simple Minds songs, such as 'Waterfront' and 'New Gold Dream'. I'd also seen artists such as Kim Wilde, Talk Talk and Frankie Goes to Hollywood live. But that evening, Simple Minds, their energy and wall of sound just blew my mind. I've lost count as to how many live concerts I've seen since. The *30 Years Live* gig in London was smashing. The atmosphere was so good, the party continuing on our way back to the city. Fans were singing out loud and jumping in sync. It almost caused the overcrowded Tube train to derail!

## MARCUS SATTLER

*Kongresshaus Stadthalle*
*16 January 1986, Heidelberg, West Germany*

I first saw Simple Minds on the *Once Upon a Time* tour in Heidelberg, Germany. Highlights include travelling to London with a friend in 1989 to see them at Wembley Stadium. Getting tickets for an English concert in Germany wasn't easy in the days before the internet. But I was back in Britain two years later at Milton Keynes Bowl on the *Real Life* tour. Next stop? Offenbach 2021.

---

## CHRISTINE DROSS, AGE 17

*Olympic Hall*
*17 January 1986, Munich, West Germany*

It was my first concert in a big venue. Due to huge demand they changed the venue to the biggest indoor hall available, with a capacity of about 8,000, and it was absolutely packed. I went with a couple of friends from school and we could hardly move. People were pushing and shoving but somehow we managed to get pretty near the stage.

I didn't know much about Simple Minds, only owning the *Once Upon a Time* album, but was absolutely thrilled from the moment the gig began. I loved everything - the stage setting, the outfits (even though they were very 80s), the atmosphere between band and audience, the pathos and of course the music. What a wall of sound! I could sing along without knowing the songs. Admittedly, the la la la's aren't that difficult. Looking back, with the experience of many different bands in many very different venues, there's a special connection between Simple Minds and their fans that goes beyond the norm. The longer they play, the more fun they seem to have.

Of course, I had a crush on Jim Kerr afterwards, like so many others. He seemed so nice and friendly and somehow close. He knows how to interact with the audience like no other. I left the concert thrilled and with a good feeling that lasted a couple of days. Since then Simple Minds have been part of my life.

I've always invited family and friends to share my passion. My son, now 21, recently told me he sometimes had the feeling of growing up in a musical dictatorship. It could have been worse – I could have been a Duran Duran fan! Anyway both he and my daughter have been to see the band and enjoyed it. Even my mother, who sadly passed away last year, got involved in my Simple Minds hysteria. I asked her to go to a 'meet and greet' at WOM (record store) and get an autograph for me as I was on holiday. It was a bit awkward for her amongst all the youngsters, but she got me the autograph, telling me later there was absolutely nothing special about it.

# CHRIS THOMPSON

*Phillipshalle*
*19 January 1986, Dusseldorf, West Germany*

I was working as a civilian attached to the British Forces in Germany and one of our main links to home was seeing concerts. In 1986 Simple Minds were due to play the Phillipshalle, Dusseldorf. It sold out almost instantly but somehow they managed to squeeze in a second performance on the Sunday that same week.

German audiences were notorious for not standing until the encore at the earliest, so having heard and been hooked by 'Waterfront' (the greatest rock anthem of all time) I didn't know what to expect. The stage set-up was pretty basic and there seemed to be a series of what appeared to be old gymnasium-type wooden block steps. The curtains opened and Jim was on top of these steps. To a man and woman, the audience not only stood as the first chords belted out but stood on the chairs for the whole concert. I'd never heard music like it, was permanently hooked and immediately bought everything I could. I can't remember what the first song was, but who cares? It changed everything. I've been lucky enough to see them around 15 times, but that first night in 1986 in Dusseldorf will stay with me forever.

Jim, Charlie and the band have never forgotten fans have been with them for 40 years and want to hear the music of that lifetime. They never fail to play the classic tracks we love and want to hear. Even though they must have played some a million times, they play them again for us like it's the very first.

---

# MARC MAYER

*Eissporthalle*
*20 January 1986, Berlin, West Germany*

I was a rebellious 15-year-old when I went to my first rock concert with best friend Alessandro and some schoolmates. A magic night. The only letdown was that I was picked up by my dad outside the hall afterwards, as I had an exam at school the next morning.

They set standards for the emerging indie rock scene of the 2000s, giving birth to bands like Interpol, Editors, Franz Ferdinand and many more, their guitar riffs inspired by Charlie Burchill! One day, Charlie popped up in the Italian restaurant Bocca di Bacco that Alessandro runs in Berlin. Since then, we've become friends and I've realised it's not only the music of Simple Minds that fascinates me – it's the people too.

---

# ANN-CHRISTINE HOLST

## *Arena Scandinavium*
## *24 January 1986, Gothenburg, Sweden*

I was just about to turn 15. My friend Elisabeth Thörnblom and I saw an advertisement in the newspaper - Simple Minds had a concert in Gothenburg on my birthday. We lived an hour and a half away and our parents didn't usually let us go to the big city all by ourselves, but since it was my birthday they did not want to spoil it, with two hysterical teenagers accusing them of ruining their lives. My older sister bought *Once Upon a Time* and we listened to the songs a few times before so we at least knew know some of the lyrics.

*Anki Holst and Elisabeth Thörnblom saw Simple Minds in 1986*

On the day we caught the bus to Gothenburg. We didn't know what to expect, having never been to a rock concert. We figured it would be a great idea to stand in the front row, but our tickets said we had seats - one of the conditions our parents had placed on us before agreeing to let us go, thinking it was very dangerous for two young girls to go to a rock concert. We went to collect our tickets and, when we were standing in line, the man supposed to give us our tickets said, 'There is something wrong. I have two standing tickets.' Me and my friend looked at each other and simultaneously said, 'We will take them!' so we accidentally ended up in the front row!

The strong lights in the Arena Scandinavium turned off and the red lights on the stage were turned on, accompanied by the music. Everybody on the floor of the arena started to jump up and down. The band came on and when Jim Kerr started to sing, both my friend and I were totally in love with Simple Minds. It was a magical experience. We loved every minute!

---

# JOAKIM AFZELIUS

## *Johanneshov Isstadion*
## *25 January 1986, Stockholm, Sweden*

My life was changed forever when I heard 'I Travel' on Swedish Radio in 1980. Then I saw them live for the first time in Stockholm. I still remember when the band walked on, opening with 'Waterfront'. I was on a cloud for months after my first gig.

---

# THOMAS LARSEN

*Valbyhallen*
*27 & 28 January 1986,*
*Copenhagen, Denmark*

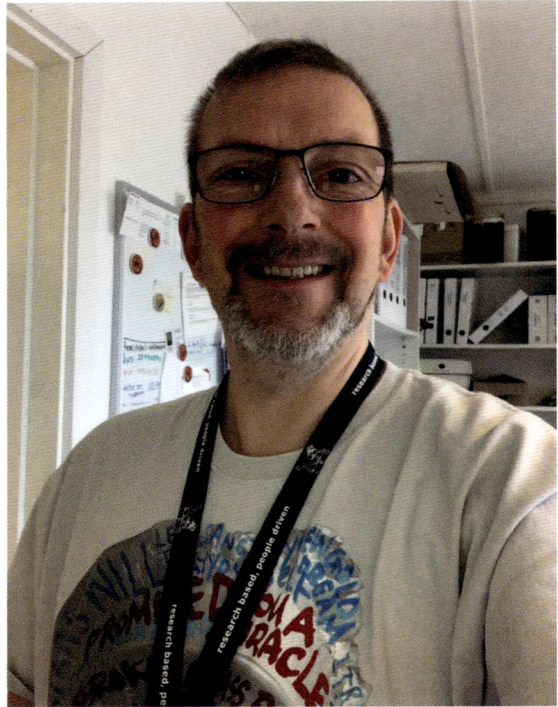

*Thomas Larsen fell in love with the band after hearing a bootleg*

I heard Simple Minds for the first time in 1981. A classmate made a mixtape and on it was 'Careful in Career'. At the time it sounded a bit on the noisy side to my taste, but there was something intriguing about it. I don't remember what else was on that tape, probably Depeche Mode, OMD and Visage as we were into the electronic scene. Money was short as we were merely school kids with no jobs - buying records was not an everyday thing. Home-taping was, though.

At some point in the mid-80s I came across a bootleg recording called *Selfluminous*, recorded at the Falconer Theatre in Copenhagen on the *Sparkle in the Rain* tour. That blew my socks off. What energy. Of course I had to go and see Simple Minds next time they were in my hometown.

Since then Simple Minds has been my band, a big part of my life, although not in a bonkers way. Well, maybe some would say I'm a bit bonkers. I see it more like supporting a football team. You stick with your band through thick and thin and support them a bit more passionately when they're on a downward streak. I collect the records and go to the shows. I've seen Simple Minds live on every tour since 1987, whether they play festivals, big or small venues. Sometimes I see them several times on the same tour. Me and the missus have made a habit of going abroad to see Simple Minds, just the two of us or with friends. It's a great way to travel the world.

# OLIVER LINDNER

*Eilenriede Halle*
*29 January 1986, Hannover, West Germany*

I heard 'Up on the Catwalk' at a school party in April 1984. Dancing in the clubs of Hannover that summer, I heard songs like 'I Travel', 'Someone Somewhere (in

Summertime)', 'Theme for Great Cities' and 'Love Song'. I started to acquire the back-catalogue. *New Gold Dream* sounded fantastic through headphones on my father's hi-fi system.

Then it was finally time. I'd been looking forward to the concert for weeks. It totally overwhelmed me, somehow carried from the second row to the fourth during the concert - like a wave.

In 2001 I was again live with the Minds in Bielefeld and have been regularly at their German concerts since. A highlight was in Hannover in 2006 where I organised the official after show party in the club Acanto, with the help of Sanctuary Records. I also DJ'd.

## RICH POWELL

*Sporthalle Böblingen*
*30 January 1986, Stuttgart,*
*West Germany*

As a young officer in the US Army in the early 80s, being stationed in Germany was a pretty heady assignment. The Berlin Wall was still standing. So was the Soviet Union. The one thing that made everything seem OK was the music coming out of the free world, with bands like Simple Minds, Depeche Mode and U2 the ones I latched onto for my own sense of identity. Whether it was driving down a country lane in Germany or basking in the sun in Gibraltar, as long as tunes like '81,82,83, 84', 'Up on the Catwalk' or 'Don't You (Forget About Me)' were keeping me company, all was good with life.

Seeing them in 1986 cemented my everlasting opinion of them: It doesn't matter if it's vinyl, tape, disc, online or live; Simple Minds is Simply Good!

## NORBERT PRINS

They played in 1986 in the Amsterdam Forest and I was able to follow the whole concert from the backyard of my parents' home. Directly afterwards I saw *The Breakfast Club*. 'Don't You (Forget About Me)' was always on my mind. During my high school years, I bought several singles and especially liked the extended version of 'Alive and Kicking', 'Belfast Child' and 'Sanctify Yourself'. I was hoping to see them in April 2020 in Amsterdam. Unfortunately, Covid-19 put paid to that!

## FLAVIA SIRCI MORETTI

*Palasport*
*6 February 1986,*
*Padua, Italy*

I discovered Simple Minds through a DJ playing 'Don't You (Forget About Me)' at an outdoor club outside Tolentino in Italy, surrounded by lavish vegetation and under a starry sky. He'd play it at least twice in a row.

It snowed at Rome when I went to see them play, so it was a gig to remember - it snows very rarely in Rome. I went with my best friend Livia and I drove, very

*Flavia Moretti is a huge fan of Simple Minds*

challenging in the conditions. We were down in the stalls in the crowds fighting for our space toward the stage. The place was full as an egg, thousands and thousands of fans jumping, dancing and singing along. It was so stunning! I still remember the moment JK threw a handful of glittering dust on us, during 'East at Easter' or 'Book of Brilliant Things' - a really magic moment to cherish, with Jim in black beret, white shirt and black leggings.

---

## FRANCESCA DE FAZI

*Palaeur*
*9 February 1986, Rome, Italy*

First time I saw Simple Minds live it was, unusually, snowing in Rome. That was a sign! I was a photographer so before the show I went to the Sheraton Hotel to collect my concert pass and casually met Jim Kerr. I was wearing a long blond, fascinating ponytail. I could not go unnoticed! Later I was at the Palaeur, under the stage taking pictures, when Jim announced ''Don't You (Forget About Me)'… to Francesca', I had a shock! He was only joking about the fact I disliked the song. I changed my mind after that!

My sister Bianka was with me. She'd just started her singing career with her first single and first name, Lilith. We wanted to work in the music business and our friendship with the band through the years truly encouraged us to not forget about our dream. That summertime we attended the Zenith concerts in Paris, when *Live in the City of Light* was recorded. We totally fell in love with their music!

This love was an occasion to rebel against our destiny. We were brave enough to prove to ourselves we weren't crazy, so with the savings of a lifetime inherited from our sweet granny… we bought flights to Japan to follow the last leg of the 1986 tour of Tokyo, Osaka and Nagoya! It was quite an adventure, going round the ultra-modern non-English speaking metropolis and asking for directions. Lilith (Bianka) met Simple Minds promoter Mister Udo, who liked her and wanted to give her a record deal, but actually she wasn't ready for it. I guess she needed my help with the guitar!

Simple Minds inspired our choice to become serious musicians. Japan was the greatest trip we made, even if it wasn't the last. I attended around 30 concerts until the last one in Rome in 2018. We haven't lost touch with Simple Minds after all this time. Their music keeps evolving and it's always on my playlist. *Street Fighting Years* frames my golden age dreams.

---

# ANTONIO CHEMI

It was a summer's day in Taormina, Sicily. I was 14 years old, and my older brother Giuseppe brought home *New Gold Dream*. The music was unknown to me but from the first listen - as if by magic - it got right under my skin. I listened to it loudly and repeatedly, day after day. God knows how many times I listened to it. Eventually I got into trouble from the old lady who lived above our apartment.

By 1985, on the release of *Once Upon a Time*, I began thinking how I'd like to see my favourite group live. Finally, the '86 tour was announced. Simple Minds would play in Rome. The problem was that, although that was the nearest show, it was over 500 miles away. My father wasn't keen on letting his teenage son go alone all that way to see a rock group. Nevertheless I begged and finally my father, seeing how much it meant, agreed to let me go on the condition he accompanied me. Great!

Unfortunately my father, who is afraid of crowds and quite a timid man, insisted we sit all the way at the very back of the arena, so far from the stage and right near the exit door! I just wanted to be in the heart of the crowd - dancing and singing. But at least I was there.

By 1989, much older, I travelled to Lausanne, Switzerland as my friend who had moved there informed me Simple Minds would be coming to perform. What a difference - I had a seat in the second row of the arena!

Then once again I travelled to the same Rome venue to see them. Originally a group of friends had planned on taking the train but for some reason they dropped out, leaving me to go alone. There was no way I was going to miss out! Since then I have travelled to so many gigs to see them.

I was really keen on getting a photo taken with the band. I've had many pics taken with famous people who have visited my family's restaurant. You can see them hang on the walls of the dining room. But I really wanted a pic of me and Simple Minds. I became obsessed with that desire. I wanted my idols on the walls with me. That finally happened in 1995 after I travelled to the north of Italy to see them in Treviso. Wandering around the city pre-concert with my girlfriend Elvira, I noticed some Simple Minds road crew people dressed in t-shirts and tour jackets, etc. hanging around outside a fancy hotel. That made me think that maybe the band was staying there, so I decided to wait around and see if any of them would appear.

About 45 minutes later, out walked Jim with one of the crew and I asked if I could take a picture. 'Sure. Come over here and we can do it together,' he says. Well, you can imagine how I felt. Jim asked where we were from and smiled when I told him I was from Taormina, telling me he'd already been to my town, where he stayed and how much he liked Sicily. All the time I was thinking, 'What? You came to my little town and didn't come to my restaurant, La Botte, one of the most famous and well-known restaurants? How could you, Jim?'

Anyway, that was the first of hundreds of pics together. Because the next time Jim came to Taormina he did indeed visit my restaurant. And my house. In doing so, we became family friends. His parents visited when they came to Sicily. His kids too. Then eventually I and my brother and cousin visited both Jim and Charlie in their countryside studio/house in Scotland, staying with them for a few days.

From this a much bigger story evolved, but it is a story I know Jim wants to tell in his own book someday. And through it all, I still listen to the music of Simple Minds and look forward immensely to seeing them play my hometown again next year!

# ANNE CLINCHARD

## *Palais Omnisports de Paris-Bercy 16 February 1986, Paris, France*

Thanks to my youngest brother Bertrand, I saw the band for the first time at Paris-Bercy in 1986. The show was brilliant, with great music, songs and rhythm, full of positive energy.

*Anne Clinchard first saw Simple Minds at Paris Bercy*

# JONATHAN SWEENEY

*National Exhibition Centre
23 February 1986,
Birmingham, England*

My relationship with Simple Minds has survived a series of relationships and marriages. In recent years my wife struggled to get it. I've tried to explain that at a concert it's like meeting great friends you've known for ages and you're picking up where you left off. We've had arguments, me getting angry with the sit-down brigade (call yourselves fans?) but also when I've stood on her foot as I leap

*Jonathan Sweeney's first show was at Birmingham NEC*

deliriously to any number of classics.

I had a ticket to see them at Leeds Uni in March 1984 but was sick. So Birmingham NEC was when the journey really started. I went with an operator called Event Travel, where you got the coach and a ticket. Seeing them at the NEC was like watching the Rotterdam Ahoy show from *The Tube* in real life.

Income and access to travel was when things started to change and the notion of going to multiple dates in different venues became an option. I've now seen them 40 times. A highlight? Grabbing the mic during 'Don't You (Forget About Me)' on the *Black and White* tour in Auckland in 2006 and singing to the crowd. Jim duly retrieved the mic and said, 'You wanna listen to him - or me?'

---

# SIMON CORNWELL

The Top 40 show on BBC Radio One was a prerequisite for any music fan in the 1980s. It was broadcast in crystal-clear FM, allowing you to rip singles straight off the air onto your trusty Ferguson cassette player. I was in possession of a motley collection of dog-eared cassettes, rewound and replayed to destruction.

But it was Annie Nightingale's *Sunday Request Show*, which followed, that the cool kids listened to. She was a true devotee, dipping into the alternative scene and playing The Cure, The Cult, The Psychedelic Furs, often finding obscure 12-inch remixes. The trusty Ferguson, set up to record known and anticipated top-40 singles, remained poised. Conscious of saving valuable tape and dreading end-of-reel syndrome, I often clipped out any preamble which could identify the song and soon become the curator of a library of disembodied and anonymous songs.

Several were so diverse in their sound and style that I simply didn't realise they were by the same band. The penny dropped the day I realised that the propulsive nu-disco of 'I Travel', the guitar-driven anthem 'Speed Your Love to Me' and Krautrock-inspired 'New Gold Dream' were all by the same band. I had now become a fan.

Among my Christmas gifts that year were a Sony Walkman and a cassette of *New Gold Dream (81,82,83,84)*, my first official Simple Minds release. I curled up on the sofa and listened to it obsessively. It was the start of the collection. 34 years later that same cassette, much played, battered and worn, would appear on the sleeve of a Simple Minds record.

Terry, whom I sat next to in maths and was destined to become my best mate, was also a fan. He already had a small collection of their albums on cassette. It was a no-brainer to book tickets to see them and so my first gig was at the soulless NEC, a large purpose-built conference hall on the outskirts of the UK's second largest city. The whole process was relatively painless, thanks to the local coach companies who ran excursions to such events. My father gave me a fiver; I didn't know what I was going to spend it on. After all, we were just going to see the band, right?

My vague memory of pre and post gig is of overriding, barely contained chaos. There were streams of fans, various merchandising stalls, copious fast food joints and expensive beer outlets everywhere. Our seats were stage right, on an elevated section with a fair view of the stage and a better view of security throwing the drunks and troublemakers out. Security earlier wanted to confiscate my ever-present Walkman, until it was pointed out that it couldn't record anything. Terry couldn't understand why I'd even brought it.

Three aspects of the performance stood out: Jim's sheer athleticism as he prowled, pranced, jumped and leapt from the various staircases dotted around the stage, contrasting with the static persona of their earlier videos; his combo of black leggings, white flowing shirt, patterned flowered jacket and beret; the music.

They seemed to fly away from their recorded output, songs evolving beyond and above their studio versions and stretched into new, extended forms. The hall erupted with 'Waterfront', now an eight-minute epic, 'Up on the Catwalk' had a spine-tingling 'You Spin Me Round' middle-eight, 'Once Upon a Time' was extended and allowed Robin Clark to shine, and the now-unrecognisable 'Book of Brilliant Things' was elevated to a majestic theme rather than the choppy bounce of its *Sparkle in the Rain* predecessor.

On the way out, I purchased a legit tour programme and a bootleg poster. The fiver from my dad had come in useful.

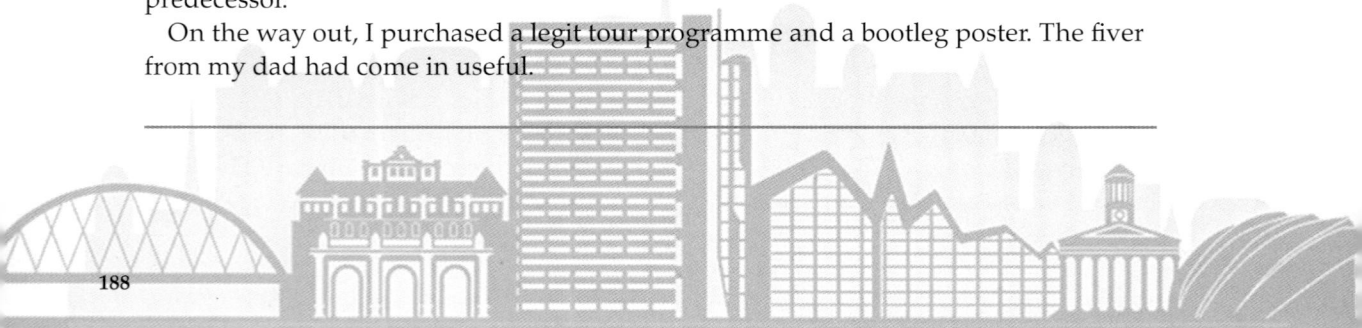

# GILLIAN BURRELL

## *Scottish Exhibition and Conference Centre*
## *28 February 1986, Glasgow, Scotland*

I grew up in Livingston. I was quiet at school and not one of the popular ones. You know them, the ones everyone wants to be like. I longed to be understood with a love of music, art and science. Not many people were on my wavelength. I felt lonely and different. Simple Minds from early on were one of my favourite bands but along came *New Gold Dream* and I finally felt that at last someone got me. Or should I say got into my soul. The music elated me, comforted me. I could lose myself sitting in my bedroom and just feel overwhelmed with joy. When I listen to the album now, I go back into my own world and smile at how happy it made me. I was at the SECC 1986 and seeing my favourite songs played live for the first time was amazing.

---

# RICKY GILLESPIE

My wife was six months pregnant at the time. Dancing on the chairs, she got her foot stuck between the seat and the back of the chair.

---

# SEAN GRAHAM

I remember going to sleep outside the SECC queuing for tickets with my friends, John and Jamie. When I first told my mum about the idea, she thought we were off our heads. But she knew nothing would stop us heading over to try and get tickets to see them, so made sure we were wrapped up and had our sleeping bags to keep us warm. She need not have worried.

On arrival at the SECC, we saw many fans had already started to gather. Songs could be heard. Everyone seemed to be in great spirits as they either sang or settled down to wait for the venue to open. Although settling down was not really an option as a football appeared from somewhere

*Sean Graham and Charlie*

and sleeping bags were used as goalposts as the biggest sidey we'd ever seen got underway. It certainly passed a few hours!

Getting the tickets in the morning and eventually getting to see the band for the first time on the *Once Upon a Time* tour, was special. This was the start of a love affair with the band. I've seen them on various tours with great support acts like OMD and The Stranglers. Seeing them and Ultravox - another favourite - play the Hydro, a place I watched being built over the years on the walk to work, was a dream come true. My girlfriend Tracey, now my wife, also loves the Minds. Or the lead singer at least!

I've so many great memories of the band over the years, even being able to meet them briefly and chat with Jim, Charlie and Andy. The *Acoustic* live gig one was memorable for three reasons. I'd been going through a battle with cancer (which has returned) and we attended the gig with our friends Viv and Cammy. Tracey climbed over seats to grab Jim Kerr's arm as he walked round the hall and she was so stunned that she just said, 'oh my God, oh my God!'. Also, Steve Harley coming out to sing 'Come Up and See Me (Make Me Smile)' was a surprise, and we all sang along.

## TONE ELLEN JØNDAL

The LP *New Gold Dream* was my introduction to Simple Minds and I loved it so much and still listen to it almost every day. My boyfriend in the 80s was studying in Glasgow and I was so lucky to see them at the Exhibition Centre then and in my hometown of Oslo in 2015. It would be wonderful to meet them one day, give them all a big hug from this huge Norwegian fan!

*Tone Ellen Jøndal travelled from Norway to the SECC*

## GIANLUCA GENOVESE

*Wembley Arena*
*2 & 3 March 1986, London, England*

In the spring of 1983, I was 15 and walking down the main street in my hometown and came to this small strange shop which sold lots of things, including records. My attention was

*Gianluca Genovese with Jim in Zagreb*

captured by that brown cross with a red heart and a book on it and that waterfront picture on the other side. That was the day it started. My first time seeing Simple Minds live was 2 March 1986 at Wembley Arena for the *Once Upon a Time* tour. And now I share my love of Simple Minds with my son Alessio, who is 15. It's like a rewind of my life.

# GARY CHARMAN

I was lucky enough to see Simple Minds in concert on the *Once Upon a Time* tour at Wembley Arena. To this day I still feel the buzz of the Tube journey and the walk to the venue. The guitar, drums and vocals inspired me to collect further albums and find out more about the band.

I was working at a well-known bank in London when a fellow worker advised me Simple Minds were doing an album signing at the Virgin Megastore. I was working a night shift the night before, so on the day of the event left work bleary-eyed at 7am and caught the Tube to Oxford Street.

I was desperate to get an album cover and poster signed. I was among the first five people in the queue and the sun was out. There was only two hours to wait before the band's arrival at 10am. We watched through the main window as long tables and seats were set up for the autograph session.

At 10am the door for the lengthy crowd opened and we were herded into the signing area. A door within the shop opened and two security staff walked out and positioned themselves behind the tables. The band followed behind.

The line started to move and I shuffled forward, the crowd in the queue behind me buzzing and the album playing in the background as we waited our turn. As I placed the cover in front of Mel he began to sign in gold pen, but at the point of me passing him the poster the bulky security person shouted, 'Only one item allowed!'

I looked at Mel and pleaded that I'd come off night-shift and stood for two hours in the sun for this moment. Mel winked at me, signed the poster and promptly passed it down the line to the rest of the band, advising them all of my story. I slowly passed each member, saying thank you in a sheepish manner as they gave me two signatures each. Charlie was the last to sign. I gave my final thank you and walked out of the shop, knowing this was five minutes of my life I would never forget.

I never have.

191

# Wembley Arena

## CHRIS TAMS

I was a young teenager growing up in West Yorkshire. I'd been into very early synth music like Vangelis and Kraftwerk and searching for something I could relate to as a young working-class kid. *New Gold Dream* was it! I bought the vinyl album from EGS Records in Wakefield in September 1982. I was far too young to get into gigs – open-age gigs didn't exist and music festivals were 'for long-haired hippies', so my dad said. Luckily for me Simple Minds often released live tracks on their singles, so that kept me in love with the band.

I was amazed how they could take studio versions of tracks and weave them into masterpieces – slowing down certain songs, speeding up others, introducing epic guitar and piano solos and generally just rocking the bloody crowd with amazing energy.

There wasn't the internet then, so fans had to either be in fan clubs or read music press to get snippets of info. My first glimpse of them playing live was watching a friend's dog-eared VHS recording of *Live Aid* on a portable TV and video at school.

I first got to them live at Wembley Arena. It was a Sunday and I'd travelled down on a coach organised by the same record shop I bought *New Gold Dream* from. At 14, I was probably the youngest on the coach by about six years.

*Chris Tams saw the Minds at Wembley*

I loved the gig. It was almost like a religious experience. I couldn't believe the sound that came from half a dozen people on stage, and Jim had the crowd eating out of his hand from the start of the first track all the way through to the end.

The band then released *Live in the City of Light*, which took my enjoyment to an all-time high and back to that Wembley Arena gig. The track-listing was almost identical to the gig I'd been at and the piano on 'Book of Brilliant Things' still makes me shiver with its haunting brilliance.

My next gig was Wembley Stadium in August 1989, the band at their stadium rock peak. Again, it was a day coach trip from Wakefield. I didn't even bring a coat or jumper, just the Simple Minds t-shirt I wore. It got soaked through with sweat during the gig, making the five-hour coach journey home slightly uncomfortable. I travelled alone but instantly seemed to make friends in the section at the front. Again, I had an almost religious experience and was putty in Jim's outstretched hands. Every time he said 'let me see your hands' I knew he was talking directly to me.

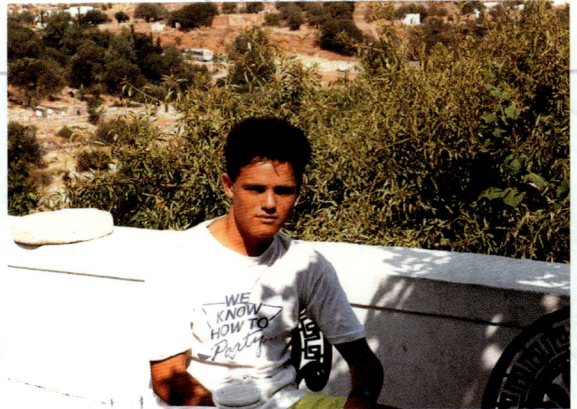

I've had a 20-plus year career in the music industry, meeting them many times but sadly never working with the band. After 50-plus shows I still get the same feeling seeing them live as I did that first time. I hope it will continue for a long time to come.

---

## PAUL ALVAREZ

*Mesa Amphitheatre*
*13 April 1986, Phoenix, Arizona*

'Someone Somewhere (in Summertime)' was floating through the cold desert air west of the great city of Phoenix. It turned out it wasn't a Roxy Music B-side from *Avalon* but the Scottish band Simple Minds. My copy of *New Gold Dream* was followed up with *Sparkle in the Rain* when employed at Tower Records, the import section providing me with a Simple Minds release a week tied to my weekly pay check. I needed that beat, that fix. Purchases of *Life in a Day*, *Empires* and *Dance and Real to Real Cacophony* followed. 1984 was the year of *Sparkle in the Rain,* an explosion of youth and energy and my favourite party album. Then '*Don't You (Forget About Me)*' catapulted to No.1 in the States and I realised Simple Minds wasn't my secret anymore - the whole world now knew. I finally got to see them for the first time in 1986, hundreds of members of *The Breakfast Club* streaming between the runways and the moat in the heat of the amphitheatre.

---

## KEITH BACON

*Open Air Theatre*
*19 April 1986, San Diego,*
*California*

I was nearing the end of my senior year in high school when Simple Minds came to town, playing my favourite venue in San Diego. I'd been a fan since *New Gold Dream*, but like a lot of people my age, it was 'Don't You (Forget About Me)' that became a monumentally personal anthem for me and my closest friends. We even ran a photo in the yearbook of us posed like *The Breakfast Club*. It was that important to us.

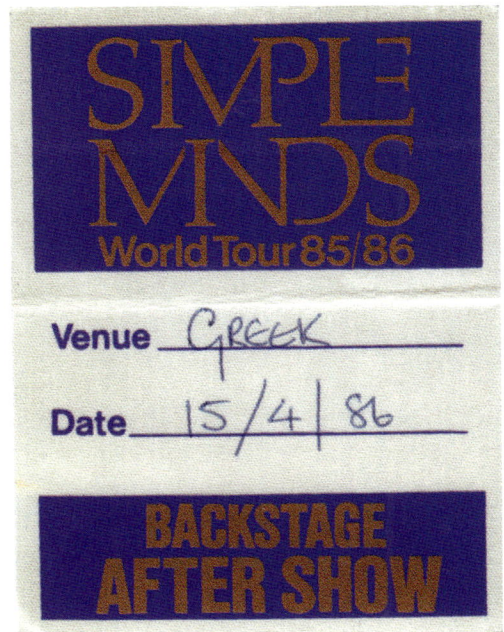

Two months after that concert under the stars, we graduated, and after the summer, went our separate ways. But that night we were living only in the moment together, dancing and singing and losing our collective minds. During the concert, when Jim raised both his arms to us in the audience, we did the same back to him. Afterwards we got the tour shirt with the image of Jim holding that iconic pose. It really summed up the joyous, massive, near-religious experience of that epic show. It became our not-so-secret handshake. We'd flash that pose to each other in the school hallways and locker bays, in our last days together.

For years I associated Simple Minds with the past, with saying goodbye to those times and those friendships, gone but not forgotten. That finally changed in 2013, when I learned the band would be playing in Amsterdam on the last night of my honeymoon there. My husband is ten years younger than me and was really only familiar with one song: that anthem for everyone. But he wanted to know more, because the music and experience of seeing Simple Minds was such a meaningful part of my history. It was an incredible show. And since that night, I have a new fan in my life to see the lights with.

---

# PAUL BULLOCK

## *Greek Theater*
## *26 April 1986, Berkeley, California*

On seeing Simple Minds for the first time I had not one of their records. All I knew was what I'd heard on radio and TV: the hits mostly. But that July night in Berkeley, California won me over. Sometimes it is the live experience that pushes the heart farther than the needle on the record, and that night was no exception. Friends and the radio had been playing tracks off *New Gold Dream* and *Sparkle in the Rain* for a while. *Once Upon a Time* was the album that led me to becoming a fan.

From the 1986 tour at the Berkeley Greek Theater to 1995 at The Edge nightclub, where I met Jim and Charlie and had Charlie do some improvisational poster signing for

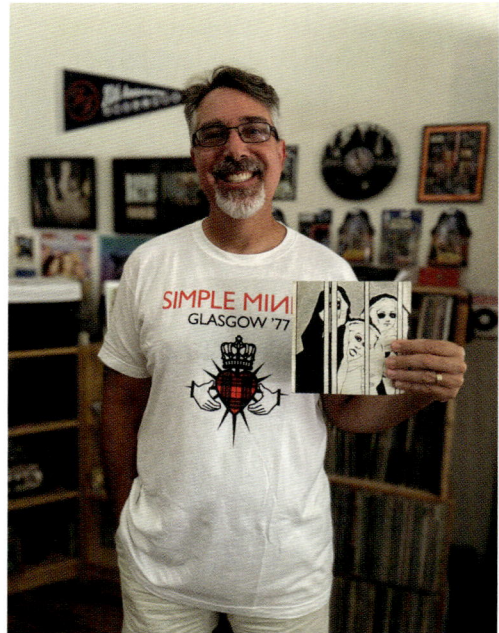

*Paul Bullock first saw the Minds at Berkeley's Greek Theater*

me, in which he wrote I 'have a nice onion' (when you ask your favourite band to make something up on the spot, autograph-wise, you just take what you get, so thank you Charlie) to October 2018 and the *Walk Between Worlds* tour in San Diego, Simple Minds have always been a soundtrack to my life. Whether walking around London listening to *Empires and Dance*, strolling through a field listening to *Street Fighting Years* or driving around beach communities listening to the *Acoustic* album, Simple Minds know how to set the mood. It is the main reason they are relevant to me and why I still buy the records and see them live.

# PHILIPPE LABELLE
*Forum De Montréal*
*17 May 1986, Montreal, Canada*

It wasn't exactly love at first sight. It started slowly, progressively, hearing songs played on local FM radio along with those other great bands that were part of the new wave of the early 80s. The first Simple Minds song I remember hearing and taking notice of was 'Love Song'. I guess it was in a bar. Was I in love at the time? Maybe, but it didn't really trigger anything special. A year later, at a friend's place for dinner, he played *New Gold Dream* on his turntable. This time I paid more attention. The songs on that record were so nicely chiselled with vocals, guitars, keyboards and drums all blending well together. It was simply irresistible! I bought the audio cassette version and started listening on a regular basis. But I wasn't really a fan and had yet to see the band live on stage.

In the summer of 1983, opportunity knocked when a quadruple-header event was scheduled at the Olympic Stadium, featuring The Police, Talking Heads, Peter Tosh and Simple Minds. But just a few weeks before, Simple Minds cancelled, to be replaced by Stevie Ray Vaughan. That whole night was terrific but I felt sorry not to catch the Minds live.

In late 1985, I was at home, listening to a music programme on TV when the video for 'Sanctify Yourself' came on. I said to myself, 'I have to see this band next time they're in town!' In the spring of '86, the *Once Upon a Time* tour stops at the Montreal Forum and it's time to discover their stage magic. I was going out with a little red-haired girl and we were both ecstatic at their performance. From the first notes of 'Waterfront' to the last encore, the Minds conquered many hearts that night!

The beginning of a love story that carries on to this day.

## HIEDI WOODS

*Radio City Music Hall*
*26 – 28 May 1986, New York, New York*

Back in 1983 I was desperate to listen to British new wave music and found a university station which specialised in the genre. 'Promised You a Miracle' instantly drew me in. I loved the lyrics and music of that entire album. It was so different from everything else. The imagery of light in the lyrics appealed to my love of poetry. Before heading out for a night, my friends and I took turns playing our favourite songs on the turntable. 'Glittering Prize' was always my choice. Going to school in rural Connecticut, we didn't have the new wave bands coming to us. In May 1986, I drove two friends into New York City. We were in the last row and the only people dancing our hearts out in the section – it was a weird crowd - but we didn't care. Simple Minds were on stage and I swear to this day Jim waved to us!

   Sitting in my Southern California dining room on a quiet Saturday years later, I was scrolling through Facebook. A 'suggested for you' post appeared and it was a Simple Minds entry. I thought to myself, 'Wow, they are still around?' Through the years of moving across the country, finding a career and starting a family, I simply forgot about my favourite band. I found my CDs, asked Alexa to play newer Simple Minds, followed them on social media and the joy of the music was back. I watched with jealousy for a couple years as Europe was treated to concerts. I had to wait 32 years but October 2018 brought another live show, in San Diego with a meet and greet and soundcheck.

---

## IRENE KANE

*Ibrox Park*
*6 & 7 June 1986, Glasgow, Scotland*

My sister queued all night outside Ibrox Stadium for tickets. She said it was a great night. Everyone was in good humour, peaceful and singing through the night. Unfortunately, when the police officers changed in the morning more people turned up for tickets and the police ignored the original queue and started a new one with the newcomers and it was chaos. My sister couldn't get a ticket but was given a voucher to apply. Thankfully, she got them.

   I worked in Edmiston Drive at the time, right next to Ibrox. I remember running out of work early (I was a very outnumbered Celtic fan in an office filled with Rangers supporters) on the Friday. The queue for the toilets in the stadium was ridiculous so my sister's boyfriend got us to use the gents while he stood guard at the door, not letting anyone in.

Growing older and getting on with life we both drifted from going to gigs. I didn't realise Simple Minds were still going until my sister saw they were playing the Hydro in 2015. She suggested we go for her 50th birthday. I travelled over from Ireland to see the concert but wasn't really expecting too much. Boy, was I wrong! What a brilliant night we had. I felt like I was 14 again, the best night I'd had in a long time.

## ANDREW MOWATT

Simple Minds changed my insular view of the world and revealed what it was like on the 'other side'. They were the first band I was allowed to openly listen to and enjoy. Growing up in Dundee during the early 80s, my father was a vicar and did not care for the sinful music coming on the radio via the BBC. I was allowed to listen to the Edinburgh Tattoo on record player and not much else. Then one day I heard Simple Minds' *Sparkle in the Rain* at a friend's birthday party. It changed everything! With such titles as 'Book of Brilliant Things' and 'East at Easter', I managed to bring up the idea to my dad that these young lads from Glasgae were modern-day Christian missionaries

*Charlie in action - photo Andrew Mowatt*

spreading God's Word to the Scots who should be in church. The auld man bought it!

I was given a few quid to go to the record shop and buy the vinyl. I was allowed to listen once a day, never on Sunday. I burned the shite out of that record. I think Dad even sneaked a few lines from 'East at Easter' into a sermon once. It was the most life-altering event until it came to shagging years later.

I managed to see Simple Minds at Ibrox, home of the mighty Glasgow Rangers. It was quite a show. I snuck away from home to see it and my dad gave me a good hiding when I returned. It was worth it.

I saw Simple Minds again in October 2018 at New York City's Beacon Theater, where I live now. I got to finally meet Jim, Charlie and crew before the show. Don't tell my hen but it was the greatest day of my life. Simple Minds gave me courage to be myself and stop living under a rock. Life is better because they exist!

---

# JIM GILLIES

I'm a lifelong fan. I first saw the band at Ibrox in 1986. Like many, we got married and family and career took our lives in a new direction, leaving us our memories to hold onto. My next Minds gig was when my wife Carolanne and I travelled down to London Wembley for the *40th Anniversary* tour. We found ourselves sat in front of Patsy Kensit, just up to the left side of the stage. We actually thought Jim was waving to us!

---

# KIT CUMMINGS

I was 16. Although I was quite clearly the world's greatest expert on music, I hadn't quite found my fashion 'tribe' yet. The hit TV show of the moment was *Miami Vice*, cop Don Johnson chasing drug dealers in sports cars and speedboats. Don's dress code was rather distinctive; all pastel shades, suit jackets (sleeves rolled up) and slip-on shoes - no socks.

Almost exactly what I was wearing as I made my way, not to Miami Beach in a Lamborghini, but to Govan on a No.23 bus to see Simple Minds at Ibrox football stadium. Ignoring the inclement weather and creatively cruel taunts of the locals, I thought I looked superb. I went with a friend from school who I didn't know very well. He was similarly dressed and we both found out many things that day. For example - the newly-imported Turkish Kebab craze was indeed tasty but messy, not everything in a pint glass is lager, and slip-on shoes are absolutely not suitable for down the front of a Minds concert.

Needless to say the show was electric, the band in perfect sync with the crowd and, as I walked home that night with one shoe missing and chili sauce down my pastel t-shirt, my friend and I talked animatedly about what it must be like being in Simple Minds, touring and playing stadia.

A few years later, that same friend and I formed a band, signing to a major label and managed by none other than Simple Minds' legend Bruce Findlay. We had a pretty magical adventure for a time and, although our band was distinctly unsuccessful, we made many great friends on the journey, a journey that culminated among other things, in working directly for Jim and Charlie these last 15 years.

A journey that started decades ago at a Simple Minds show, dressed as a pound-shop Don Johnson, trying to find a slip-on shoe during 'Ghost Dancing'. To this day, when Charlie plays the opening few bars, I always glance downwards, relieved to see both shoes exactly where they should be.

---

## ANGELA MORRIS, AGE 15

I've been following Simple Minds since 1979. I was eight, my dad the captain of the Boys' Brigade that met in Castleton Primary School in Castlemilk. The janitor of the school was Mr Forbes, whose son was Minds' bassist Derek Forbes. He gave me some badges and a cassette of the album *Life in a Day* after he saw me listening to music on my Walkman one night. As soon as I heard 'Life in a Day' I was hooked - and I've been hooked ever since. When I saw them at Ibrox in 1986, I thought I was going to die with excitement. My friends thought I was daft as I didn't like Duran Duran, but where are they now, girls?

---

## NEIL NOCETE

I grew up in the Philippines listening to new wave music during the Eighties. The experience and excitement of witnessing Simple Minds perform live in a concert twice in the USA were both unbelievable and a dream come true as I never expected to hear 'Don't You (Forget About Me)' and 'Alive and Kicking' performed live in front of me.

---

## BRIAN RODDEN

The first time I saw the band was 1986 on the *Once Upon a Time* tour at Ibrox. It was my first concert and amazing it was too. I was brought up on their music. My favourite song will always be 'Waterfront', its intro second to none. When they started with this at the SECC another time the place was bouncing.

---

## ALAN JARVIE

I've been a fan of Simple Minds since their Johnny and the Self Abusers days. I remember seeing them in the late 70s in the Mars Bar in Glasgow, buying their 'Saints and Sinners' single. I've followed them since and have seen them, in various incarnations, several times. Their concert at Ibrox Stadium (close to the boyhood homes of Jim and Charlie) remains one of my all-time favourite gigs.

I was lucky enough to meet Jim and Charlie at a football DVD launch at the SECC in Glasgow a few years ago. I was also lucky enough to meet Jim again in 2016, when I had the pleasure of interviewing him for my radio show. Although I was only allocated 20 minutes, we ended up chatting for nearly an hour and he told me many stories (some not for broadcast on air unfortunately!) about his life and career. I remain a big fan to this day and always will be.

---

## JOHN GRAFFEN

I was in a nightclub in Hamilton in 1982 when I suddenly heard this incredible sound beaming out of the speakers, stopping me in my tracks. 'Ameri-Ameri-Ameri-Ameri-Amer-American.' I never heard a sound like it and needed to know instantly, 'Who is this band and what's the name of this song?' I went straight over to the DJ and he informed me it was Simple Minds and the song was 'The American.' I wrote this down on a piece of paper in case I forgot it in the morning.

When I went to college in Glasgow that Monday, the song was still in my head and I mentioned it to a friend on the same course. By coincidence, he recognised the song and the band instantly. Turned out he was a massive fan and had many versions of this song at home. He kindly gifted me the 12-inch version and my love affair with the band sprang from there. I quickly introduced my two brothers to the band and they got hooked, just like me.

My favourite Simple Minds concert was at Ibrox. Tickets were red hot and we queued overnight as you had to in those days for one of the best bands in the world. My brothers and I excitedly entered the stadium, onto the Ibrox turf, a surreal experience for three Celtic supporters. Before the concert started, we pretended we were in an Old Firm game with an imaginary ball and, waiting for a cross from my eldest brother, I positioned myself in the penalty box. Unexpectedly, the crowd in the Broomloan Stand picked up on our madness and began cheering. My brother delivered a perfect cross with his imaginary ball and I of course finished with a clinical header into the corner of the goal, to loud cheers. As always, Simple Minds delivered a brilliant gig, and wonderful memories for my brothers and I.

---

## DEBORAH MCCAMLEY

I first heard them on the radio in the 80s and loved them. My first gig was at Ibrox Stadium. I ended up going alone, aged 13, to the big bad Castle Grayskull. It was amazing and that was it – a drug. I saw them at every Glasgow show after that, and all over the UK.

My son was born in 1994 and what else could I name him but Kerr? As I grew older, my musical tastes were firmly set in the heavy metal genre except for my loyalty to the Minds. My partner's been dragged all over to see gigs, meet them, etc. At Edinburgh Castle it rained like I've never seen before. Because of that, if the rain gets heavy, everyone I know now refers to it as 'Simple Minds rain'.

My partner goes to the odd record fair and is always on the lookout for *Sparkle in the Rain* on white vinyl, but no luck. Or so I thought until I got it a few Christmases ago. I burst into tears - it's been a lifelong want.

A few years ago I saw AC/DC at Hampden Park but spent the night in shock as Derek Forbes was sat in front of me. I never did pluck up the courage to speak to him.

---

## NIELS VAN DER SLUIJS, AGE 15

*Amsterdamse Bos*
*10 June 1986, Amsterdam,*
*The Netherlands*

I went alone to my first Simple Minds gig as none of my friends were allowed to go. My mother bought me the ticket as I was at school when they went on sale. My obsession had started. I didn't miss

*Niels van der Sluijs interviewing Jim for the Endless River magazine*

a show in the Netherlands from 1986, and in 1995 I did my first 'tour' through Europe, visiting Germany, France, Belgium and Holland. I even got on the guestlist for some shows, and met Jim and Charlie at the aftershow of the last gig.

Meeting a lot of Dutch Minds fans at every concert, and with the Dutch fan club folding, I helped set up and run the magazine *Endless River* for a couple of years until the internet overtook. We got in touch with the record company, Chrysalis, and met tour manager Stan Tippens, who arranged for us to talk to Jim and Charlie and got my parents backstage at the *Night of the Proms*, where I got a picture with Jim and my parents. Later, I interviewed Jim at the American Hotel in Amsterdam and he referred to meeting my parents and asked how they were doing, a sign of what a normal guy Jim is.

I've been to more than 80 concerts. One highlight was Glasgow with my daughter. We were front row and Jim talked to her and another young kid next to us. 'I hope you enjoy it. And if not, remember it could be much worse - Spandau Ballet!' Another highlight was the Paradiso concert for the *Walk Between Worlds* tour. I was front row and during the first song Jim walked towards me and touched my head!

an evening with
**SIMPLE MINDS**
and very special guests
**SIMPLY RED**
and introducing
**TEN TEN**

dinsdag 10 juni 1986, aanvang 5.00 uur,
Paardesportcentrum Amsterdamse Bos

**P R E S S**

**dit is geen toegangskaart**

---

# DAVE GREEN

*Milton Keynes Bowl*
*June 1986, Milton Keynes, England*

The first time live was something special. I travelled down from Hull in an old mini, then back again. It was a long but awesome day. The last time live was Hull City Hall about three years ago. It was great to see them in my own backyard. I took my youngest son, singing all the hits at the top of my voice.

---

## LARELLE READ

I only recently became a big SM fan. I was fairly fair weather prior to the summer of 2014. I've not been a long term fan. I haven't been following the band since 1979. I've not gone to any big stadium gigs, Roundhay Park or Milton Keynes Bowl.

I created an image from a superimposed blend of images I mashed together, a lovely painting of a Kyoto snow scene just randomly found via a Google search that I thought evoked the image the lyrics to 'Hunter and the Hunted' along with a photo of Jim on the cover of *Melody Maker* magazine in front of a Canadian flag. I posted it to the SM Facebook visitor wall. Jim noticed it and did a lovely post about it. My heart pounded in my chest for hours! Then another friend suggested I ask if he would sign a copy of it for me. And so I asked via Messenger. 'Someone will be in touch,' came the reply. 'Oh, that's nice,' I thought. 'Well at least I wasn't ignored'. But I believed it was just a fob off. I don't know who actually replied. Perhaps it really was Jim?

Anyway, I sent a copy of it to be signed and – it was! It has been on my bedroom wall ever since. Sometimes I can gaze upon it and it just brings me to tears.

## CHRISTOPHE AVRIL

Simple Minds made me become a musician when I was young. I started a band to cover their songs and then make my own. I didn't make a career in music, but became a regular man working in an office. But now I have created a tribute band called City of Light!

## SUSAN BULLOCK

I travelled to Paris to see Simple Minds. I was gobsmacked at how good they were – not just Jim but Charlie too. And Mel Gaynor is a far better drummer than Phil Collins!

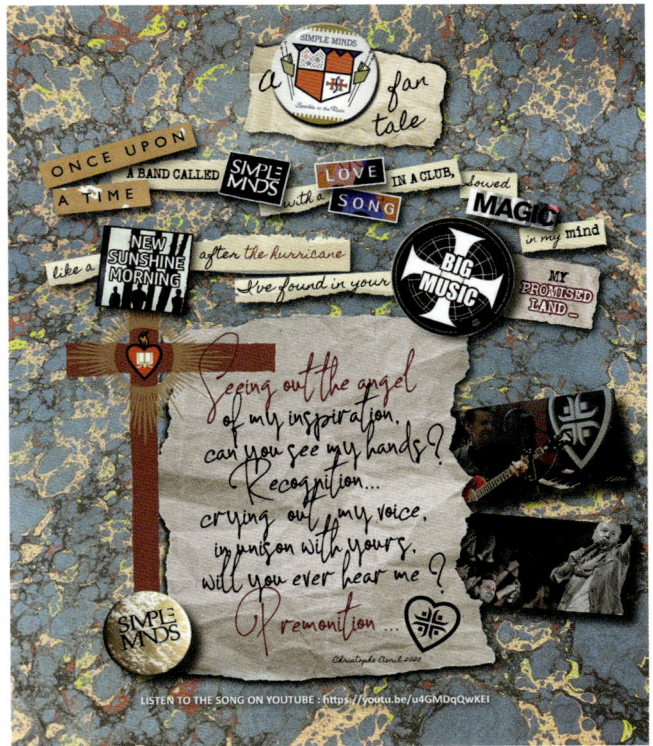

*Christophe Avril's artwork creation*

## ADAM GRAY, AGE 15

A group of us got one of our older brothers to drive us to the concert as we were all under age. It was the most amazing concert I've ever attended. The pure excitement of seeing my favourite band on stage just a few feet away blew my mind. It was truly a life-changing event. I've followed Simple Minds' evolving musical journey ever since and seen them in concert over a dozen times in the UK. They set the bar for live performances.

## JIM JOHNSON

Simple Minds were a huge band for many of our peer group and when two mates, Dan and Russ – loyal followers of the band since the *Sons and Fascination* era - got tickets for the Milton Keynes Bowl on 21 June 1986, myself and my best mate Al chose to join them. So much of our childhoods were crystallised that day. Four 15-year-olds with our lives in front of us, our first out of town gig, and sunshine. Opening with 'Waterfront', the bassline hit you in the chest, JK calling it 'the best night of my life'.

Sadly, the following year, Al was killed in a road accident and I remember feeling uneasy about going to see the band again when they toured in 1989, just as we all came of age. But I went to Roundhay Park, they opened with 'Street Fighting Years' and the line 'my thoughts return to you my dear young friend' resonated hugely. It continues to resonate to this day.

## LAWRENCE LOWE

One Easter holiday, my sister and her boyfriend Mark came into my parents' lounge with a large selection of albums, including titles from Spear of Destiny, The Chameleons and Simple Minds. They were going out so I asked if I could have a listen whilst nobody else was in the house. After a couple of worried looks and a slight grumble, I was given permission. This is where it all changed for me. It was 1984 and I was 15. Mark had purchased *Sparkle in the Rain*....

Only the biggest and most popular bands could fill certain venues, so two dates at Milton Keynes Bowl was certainly a statement. The band had appeared on TV a number of times and my bootleg collection proved their energy and live ability.

My memories of Milton Keynes are not so much about the

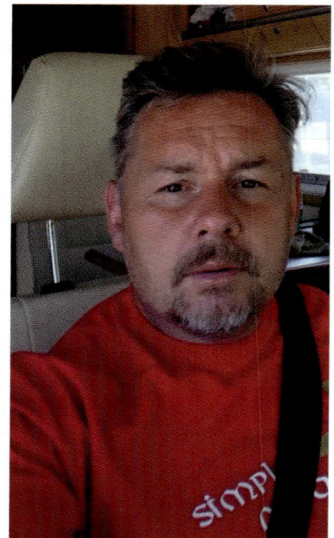

*Lawrence Lowe first saw Simple Minds at Milton Keynes*

songs as the atmosphere: the journey by train; the football match before; the support bands; the sky of plastic bottles and waves and waves of energy produced by the crowd that swept so many people off their feet; holding on for dear life and struggling to stay above the dusty hot ground churning up with the heat; and the excitement of the crowd. The t-shirts were, in my opinion, the best ever and that summer it seemed every town, city and holiday destination around the world endured at least one fan with a Simple Minds t-shirt on their back.

## CHARLES MUSSARD

The first time I started noticing the band was 1982, when they were on the pages of *Smash Hits*. My first concert was Milton Keynes Bowl in 1986. Scotland were playing in Mexico at the World Cup and Jim kept updating us with the score. I recall Charlie fell over at one point! I also saw them at Wembley Arena, when Mel hit his snare drum so hard it had to be replaced mid-song. My last gig at Cambridge Corn Exchange was the loudest I've ever been to. It was made

*Charles Mussard remembers Jim updating the Milton Keynes crowd on Scotland's World Cup match*

more special as Jim seemed to notice I was the only one who knew all the words to 'Broken Glass Park'. Great songs, great live, great band.

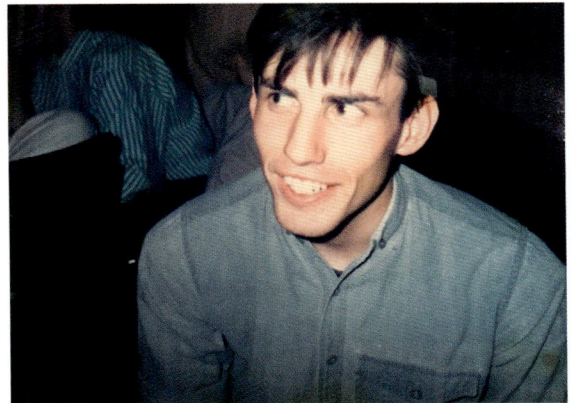

## PETER SHIELD

I was 12 years old in the school holidays of 1983. I lay on my mate's sofa listening to his brother's record collection, some random compilation album. Song after song played when all of a sudden I heard this new sound that made the hairs on the back of my neck stand up. I leapt up and counted the tracks on the vinyl. It was 'Promised you a Miracle'. As soon as it had finished it went on again. As it played for the second time I looked through the collection for another song by this band Simple Minds and found another compilation album with 'Love Song' on. I played that. I was smitten.

My first gig was in 1986 at Milton Keynes Bowl. What a show, although in all honesty it felt too big for me at 15. The gigs continued on a regular basis, Charlecote Park in 2004 and Rock City in 2006 favourites due to the intimate nature of the shows and my front-row position at both.

Why Simple Minds? Easy. They were first to make the hairs on my neck stand up and 35 years later, when I met the band on a VIP experience in San Francisco, I got that exact same feeling. I was like a babbling school kid.

# ROSARIO MASTROPIERRO

I tagged along with a mate who had a spare ticket after someone dropped out. At this point I could recollect liking 'Up on the Catwalk', 'Waterfront' and 'Don't You (Forget About Me)'. I was pretty underwhelmed with the whole concert as I thought the sound was terrible from where I was sat on the bank of this open-air venue, what seemed like miles away from the stage. Not the band's fault, I'm sure, so I blame the sound engineers on the mixing desk. Back in the 80s there probably just wasn't the technology there is now to ensure a crisp sound whatever weather was thrown at an open-air festival. It was also boiling hot in the daytime, with quite a strong crosswind, then absolutely freezing cold in the evening and during the concert. Again, hardly the band's fault.

It was after Milton Keynes that a friend lent me a VHS tape of *The Tube* performance at the Ahoy

*Rosario Mastropierro was at Milton Keynes Bowl*

in Rotterdam. Despite Jim Kerr's questionable stage outfit, I couldn't stop listening or watching this tape. It only featured five songs, but absolutely blew me away, particularly Charlie's shimmering guitar and the huge epic sound the band were producing. I wore that tape out. My thoughts were that this could not possibly be the same band I saw in Milton Keynes during the summer of 1986.

When *Live in the City of Light* came out, the penny dropped. This live album captured everything from that televised concert footage I had seen on that VHS tape. I kicked myself for not paying closer attention to the band. And 23 shows later, I now consider myself an avid fan.

# JAMIE SINCLAIR

In May 1986 my Mum unexpectedly offered me a gift - to see a live concert. My choices were Queen at Wembley or Simple Minds at Milton Keynes Bowl. After much deliberation I went for the Minds, although my older brother Nick was a huge Queen fan and I loved them too.

My pals and I were getting excited as the gig approached, hopelessly trying to make our own t-shirts and wearing eyeliner - but when it started to get hot, didn't that stuff itch? We all looked like Gary Numan, especially me as I had jet black hair. Our tickets, from the Concert Travel Club, were guarded like the crown jewels!

On the morning of the show we had to get the coach from the local train station at 5.30am to get to the gig by mid-afternoon. It was one hell of a journey but, with the help of some music and the tins of lager we sneaked on, all was well.

Arriving at Milton Keynes Bowl was like entering a small city, with trucks and coaches as far as the eye could see. We got as near to the front as possible, which took ages. It was then that everything started to gather momentum. Only at that point did I realise how much Simple Minds meant to so many people.

After a brief stage turnaround everything was set. Stage smoke bellowed from either side and stage left was a simple, single clock on the black backdrop. At 9.15pm, 'Waterfront' started. The emotion was indescribable. There wasn't a dry eye in the house. The atmosphere and being only seconds away from what became the best live act in the world was something to behold. I've never fully experienced that again, hundreds of Minds gigs later.

The gig was pure magic. The sound was huge and at the front the sheer noise coming from the stage side fills was just as powerful as the PA. The band were literally sparkling, note-perfect. Mick was on fire, as was Mel. Robin Clarke from New York was amazing in songs such as 'Once Upon a Time'. Gigs were more intense then - no one was holding a phone and filming it. I've always been too busy singing, dancing and fighting back the odd tear. The whole thing to a boy was so overwhelming. When we left, the silence was painfully deafening, the majority of the people utterly dumbstruck by what we'd just experienced. If only I could have bottled that atmosphere!

My life changed that day. I realised I wanted to be a part of this grand artistic circus, with a career in the music industry - a life and a living! A year later I started at Virgin Records. Still going strong 28 years later, I'm in the music publishing business now, inspired by that show. Whenever I'm asked, 'Why are Simple Minds so special to you?' the answer is always, 'How long have you got?'

## NIGEL THOMAS

The first time I saw Simple Minds was at Milton Keynes Bowl. They were absolutely brilliant that day and 'Oh Jungleland' and 'Someone Somewhere (in Summertime)' were highlights, but the whole day still holds fantastic memories.

---

## JONATHAN THOMAS

At school there was a boy in my year called Shaun. He had a mass of curly hair and always wore a Manchester United scarf. We weren't friends but in 1985 sat together in art class. We talked about music, discovered we both liked Simple Minds and both had *Once Upon a Time* on our Christmas lists. Next day he brought *Sparkle in the Rain* into school for me to borrow. I let him copy my maths homework. We have been best friends ever since.

I loved *Sparkle* and wanted to hear more, so the following weekend caught the train to Hereford and purchased *Real to Real Cacophony* and *New Gold Dream*. Christmas came - as did *Once Upon a Time*.

The first Simple Minds gig Shaun and I attended was

*Charlie with Shaun, Jonathan White's best pal, brought together by the band's music*

at Milton Keynes Bowl on 21 August, a date I've often used as a PIN code over the years (perhaps not now!). It was a beautiful summer's day and the World Cup football was on. Shaun's dad drove us the three hours there in his brown Austin Allegro, then went to a pub to watch the football.

On arrival we were overwhelmed by the sight of thousands of people, many in Simple Minds t-shirts or Celtic t-shirts. I didn't experience this with Cliff Richard in

MCP presents

015576

MCP presents

SIMPL
MND

Plus Special Guests

MILTON KEYNES
AT JUNE 21st 3.0

*Jim at Milton Keynes (photos by Jonathan Thomas)*

**BOWL**

**SAT JUNE 21st 3.00 p.m.**

**GATES OPEN AT 12.00**

Tickets: £12.50 Advance
(Subject to booking fee)

**NO CAMPING IS ALLOWED**

209

Do not arrive with the intention of camping as there are no facilities available
licensed bar applied for.

COMPLIMENTARY

COMPLIMENT A

Rhyl! I remember thinking, 'Oh, maybe I'm not the biggest Simple Minds fan ever after all.' We bought t-shirts and programmes and I also purchased a set of tour badges, now part of my collection of 155. We managed to position ourselves in the centre, quite near the front. We both enjoyed the supports, with pubescent tingles at In Tua Nua's Lesley Dowdall and Susanna Hoffs of The Bangles. Then amazing performances by The Waterboys with Mike Scott and The Cult with Ian Astbury. Great frontmen but no more tingles.

Some fans were throwing bottles at The Bangles during their performance. Shaun got very protective towards Susannah Hoffs and was so annoyed he wanted to confront the bottle throwers. For his own safety I had to pull him back by his Manchester United scarf!

After the support bands I remember the atmosphere became more intense and the crowd denser in anticipation of Simple Minds coming on. Then suddenly the bassline to 'Waterfront' erupted. Jim walked on stage in black leggings, a lilac silk shirt - and no socks! The crowd were sent into a mad frenzy – by the music, not the lack of socks. Young and easily influenced, l chose not to wear any socks myself for months thereafter.

We just couldn't believe we were there, watching our favourite band. The setlist was incredible and included 'Come a Long Way'. I've only ever heard this song live once and the bootleg cassette I have of the gig is a great souvenir.

Mid-gig, Jim changed his lilac silk shirt for an orange one. The clothes may have changed but the music didn't. It continued to blow us away, and we were so in awe throughout. Any disappointment felt at being forced to the back was very soon forgotten.

I'd brought my dad's binoculars. A rather pretty girl behind us asked if she could borrow them. Obviously, I said 'yes' but she then disappeared. I remember thinking, 'Well, I won't be seeing those bins again. Sorry, Dad.'

'Brazil and France have drawn one all – 'Once Upon a Time',' said Jim as the band launched into the album's title track.

As it got darker, fires were lit around the perimeter of the Bowl. It was a great atmosphere.

Our only disappointment of the gig was having to leave early, during 'East at Easter' so we could meet Shaun's dad on time. As we left Jim was sat on the drum-riser wearing a red tartan jacket. I remember feeling sad that the gig for us had come to an end. But not as sad as Shaun. A girl spilt coffee over his newly-purchased t-shirt and the stains never came out in the wash, something he still hasn't got over.

For weeks after I felt so low and deflated from the comedown. I cut out the words 'Milton Keynes how I missed you' from an unrelated newspaper article, omitted the letters 'e' and 'd' and stuck the phrase 'Milton Keynes how I miss you' on my huge black and white *Live Aid* poster. I still have it but my girlfriend doesn't get very excited about the thought of it pinned to our bedroom ceiling.

To this day Shaun and I are thankful to his dad for taking us to our first gig at Milton

Keynes Bowl, and thankful to my dad for taking us to our second Simple Minds gig, the Nelson Mandela 70th tribute concert two years later.

Oh, and I got the binoculars back.

---

# MARK WILLIAMS

I saw them at Birmingham Odeon and at the Milton Keynes Bowl in 1986 the night Diego Maradona scored his Hand of God goal. Jim had to sympathise with tens of thousands of England fans.

---

# MIKE WILLIAMS

The first opportunity I had to see the band live was the summer of 1986. At the tender age of 14 years and 11 months I joined 60,000 fans at the Milton Keynes Bowl. I still can't believe my mum and dad allowed me to part with the money for the ticket, let alone take the long bus trip from Hereford with school chum Lee Collins. I bought the ticket from Our Price and stuck it on the ceiling of my bedroom above my bed for safe keeping.

The day of the concert was a warm one. The support acts were In Tua Nua, The Waterboys, The Bangles and The Cult. I invested in a t-shirt and wore it with pride. This was before the days of big screens so Lee and I made our way to the front as the time for Simple Minds to appear approached. I recall the noise and energy of the crowd as the band took to the stage.

*Mike Williams travelled from Hereford to Milton Keynes to see Simple MInds*

As the sun set, I remember a moment where Jim was silhouetted against a red summer sky, his baggy purple shirt blowing in the breeze. It's an image that's stayed with me. Charlie was a regular visitor to our side of the stage and I remember he took a tumble as he walked down the ramp, stage right. Ever the professional he kept playing whilst he regained his footing.

As the show neared its end, I realised my pal had deserted me to get a better view of the light show from up on the grass bank. I was on my own but recall not caring. I was in my element, up at the front with the band I loved.

At the end of the show I got lost in the crowd and nearly missed the bus home. It didn't detract from what remains one of the most memorable days of my life.

---

## LARRY BLISS

My favourite bands were U2, The Who, Yes and ELP. One night I had dinner with a cool couple. As I perused his record collection, I pulled out an album with a cover full of strange emblems and the intriguing title *Sparkle in the Rain*. 'I don't like that one,' he said, 'it's too noisy. You can have it.' I placed the LP on my turntable and out banged Mel Gaynor, playing like a man possessed, accompanied by ecstatic keyboards and this Glaswegian cat with a soulful voice. It was an epiphany akin to hearing 'I Will Follow' for the first time. By the time 'Waterfront' tracked in with That Bass I knew Simple Minds had made it into the rotation.

## SEBASTIEN JEANPAUL

I was working for a very well known and prestigious antiquarian fair in Paris called La Biennale des Antiquaires. Its location was the prestigious Grand-Palais, next to the Champs-Elysees. The place is majestic with a canopy engineered by Gustave Eiffel. During the exhibition, the musical background was classical music, sticking to the style and concept of the event. Shortly before the opening of the fair, Simple Minds released the *Theme Volumes Collection Box 2* and I have to say that the extended mix of 'Speed Your Love to Me' was one of my favourite songs. It was talking to my head, my heart… and my feet.
As a junior member of the administrative staff, I had access to the guy in charge of the music programming and play list, and guess what? We did it! For maybe 20 minutes - before the General Secretary of the Exhibition realised what was going on - 'Speed Your Love to Me' had a few plays in this wonderful, historical building. I had a big smile on my face, listening to the music of my favourite band, as thousands of mostly elderly people came to visit the fair. It was an unforgettable moment.

## FIONA PETCH

I went to buy *New Gold Dream* as soon as I could with the small amount I earned as a Saturday girl in a pet shop. I fell in love with 'Book of Brilliant Things' based on the lyrics, 'I thank you for the lightning that shoots up and sparkles in the rain.'

# LINDA COX

Linda Cox with Jim

My brother Jaime offered to take me to KROQ where Jim was being interviewed. He had arrived in the company of a US rep before quickly slipping inside the studio. As I was a bit shy about asking to take his photo, Jaime asked on my behalf. When Jim stopped on the staircase to pose for me, Jaime told him, 'No, she wants a photo of the singer' and pointed to the rep. Of course, I was embarrassed but everyone else chuckled. But I got my photo and the faux pas actually worked out okay, as we were put on the list for their TV taping of *Rock of the 80s* the following day in Hollywood.

Before the taping, I was determined to overcome my nerves and actually speak to Jim and get a photo with him. He came out and was chilling out in the parking lot when I asked a friend to take our photo while I was chatting with him.

Years passed and I found myself settled in Margate, England. Simple Minds had added Margate to their 2003 tour itinerary and I was looking forward to seeing them live after all these years, but I also wanted give Jim reprints of my live shots. Before soundcheck, Jim stopped to sign autographs and when he got to me, I presented him with the photo of us from 1984. He looked at it and then me and said, 'Is that you? You haven't changed at all.' I was so flabbergasted that I completely forgot how to respond, finally blurting out, 'Neither have you!' I also forgot to hand him the packet of live photos I had for him, so asked one of the road crew to pass them on for me.

In 2010, I learned that Jim had his own Facebook profile and that he was quite interactive with his fans. After adding him as a friend, I messaged him and attached digital files of the photos I had sent backstage seven years prior, in case he never received them. Within days, he not only used several of my live photos as his profile pic, but actually featured the photo of him and me on his page, which led to a flood of friend requests from other fans from around the world. With all the wonderous images I have been able to get of the band, none have had more significance than that blurry little photo set in a parking lot in Hollywood that sunny June day.

---

# EDWIGE CAMP

I'm French but became fluent in English in order to understand the lyrics as well as the books on Simple Minds I had bought. I became interested in Scotland and visited on several occasions, including for my honeymoon. But I also developed an interest in Scottish politics through songs like 'Waterfront' and 'Soul Crying Out' and I prepared a PhD in this field as well as additional diplomas to become a full university professor.

---

## ALEX HALLIDAY, AGE 20

My favourite band were pretty much on top of the world at this point in their career. Whilst queuing at the entrance to the Bowl and being amazed at the amount of stacked-up, confiscated alcohol, I could hear In Tua Nua playing as the wind teasingly swept the sound from the stage to the main entrance. I remember thinking, 'I can't believe I'm here.' The Bowl was filling fast and the atmosphere was electric. There was a lot of sunbathing going on and big queues for the beer tent.

The support bands were all excellent, especially The Waterboys and The Cult. As the day went on, the heightened anticipation for the main men spread through the crowd, and by the time the Minds were due on, the place was fully adrenalised and ready. When they came on, each member was the epitome of cool, then Jim bounded on - larger than life and completely in the moment. His charisma and enthusiasm were like a magnetic field. Within seconds we were eating out of his hands, he introduced 'Waterfront' and the place went nuts! The bassline pulsed through the whole crowd, turning it into a single ecstatic throbbing mass. This moment was just immeasurable as an experience. I was laughing with sheer joy as I was jumping up and down as part of this single body of frenzied people.

Jim admitted to suffering from a head cold, but you wouldn't have thought there was an issue. His voice was as soaring and powerful, as on the records, every note crystal clear! Jim even updated us on the France v Brazil World Cup quarter-final and teased the crowd about the big England game the next day. The set was just blistering, with hit after hit of sonic bliss, and by the encore, I was physically but happily drained. Simple Minds had painted each song into the sunset, as a memory to savour on the journey home - and forever more. What a day!

## ASHLEY AGER

I wasn't into the band during the early years. It was more mainstream rock 'n' roll that rocked my boat. But a friend persuaded me to go to Milton Keynes Bowl in 1986. It's probably the best gig I've been to, dancing around campfires listening to 'Once Upon a Time'. I've been to various places around the UK ever since to see the boys. Thank you, Jim and Charlie, and thank you Mel, the guv'nor of the skins! Legends!

## LYN-ANNE SEDLMEYR

I love the instrumental work. It is so complex. It is like listening to a classical work. The instrumental arrangements have an almost eerie sense about them that make the hairs on your body stand up.

## JANINE RANDS, AGE 23

My first Simple Minds gig opened with the song where it all started for me – 'Waterfront'. It was just turning to dusk as they arrived on stage. I remember Jim Kerr in his purple flowing shirt doing his jump-kick. Brilliant!

My best memory has to be Manchester Arena, 2013. I was singing and dancing to 'Love Song' when I caught Jim's attention. He came over, started dancing and asked, 'How are you?'

---

## MARK EVANS

I went with a friend to my first big outdoor gig at Milton Keynes Bowl, to see Simple Minds headline. The main support was The Cult, who we both loved too, but on the day they just did not impress. The funniest bit was Ian Astbury shouting, 'If one more bottle hits me, I'm walking' just as another plastic bottle filled with some dubious liquid hit him right on the forehead. The crowd roared but in fairness he carried on. My friend was only there for The Cult, but he was actually blown away by Simple Minds. It taught me you don't necessarily have to like their music to end up being moved by their live performance. They're just great live entertainers.

---

## STEVE MEREDITH

In the late spring of 1982, a young lad of 15 just coming out of the Mod scene as I'd heard on the grapevine The Jam were going to call it a day, I'd already started to enjoy some of the new romantic bands coming through – ABC, Soft Cell, Ultravox, Visage and Heaven 17. I used to go to the house of a girl, two years older, and she'd be getting ready to go out to local pubs and clubs, doing her make-up like Blondie and Adam Ant. She'd have a drink and put her music on while she did. This time she was playing a song on repeat, singing away, dancing and getting in the party mood as I sat on the end of the bed. The song was 'Promised You a Miracle'. It really got to me. By the third time hearing it I was singing it too.

I went down to the record shop in town, purchased *New Gold Dream*, raced home and played it. I was blown away. I went back to the shop and bought everything they had in stock by Simple Minds.

1985 was the best year of my life. I turned 18 and started working in London, at the best restaurants and hotels as a chef. I made some amazing friends - and *Once Upon a Time* was released. That album was completely out of this world and remains by far the best Simple Minds ever produced. Even the merchandise was a cut above the rest. I remember seeing an advert for *The Tube* about a one-off special featuring Simple Minds live in Rotterdam. That night, me and my room-mates sat around the telly with beer and fags, not knowing what to expect. Boy, did they deliver! There was not a dry eye in the house, especially when they performed 'Book of Brilliant Things'. I still watch that concert - my favourite live performance by anyone.

So what's the next best thing? 'Let's go and see the boys live.' I couldn't believe my luck. They were performing at Milton Keynes Bowl, near my hometown. It was the hottest day. I got blisters on my face from the sun, watching the acts and waiting in anticipation. The Waterboys were excellent and got everyone on their feet. And before you knew it - bang – the Minds were on stage, delivering an amazing performance. There was one moment I will never forget. When they did 'Book of Brilliant Things', Jim was crying and said, 'You are a fucking amazing crowd' and thanked us all. I walked away feeling drained and emotional, and as we got out of the crowd the sweat on our shirts made us cold. But there was so much excitement flying around, we didn't care.

For my birthday in 2018, my new partner took me to see Simple Minds at Swindon's Lydiard Park. She sang along and enjoyed herself. In a way, I've now introduced them to her.

## STEVE CLARKE

*Simple Minds road crew*

When we played two sell-out shows at Milton Keynes, the t-shirts all sold out on the first day. Me and a few more crew members went down to London that evening to a printing works and worked all night, printing t-shirts for the next day.

As Simple Minds and myself are big football fans, it was great to be able to arrange VIP passes for them to meet the players at a Juventus match before a show that night in Torino. They also played two sell-outs at the San Siro Stadium, Milan, where we were allowed to play on the pitch and visit the players' dressing rooms. Simple Minds also had their own football team and we would play local teams.

One of the saddest times was when Simple Minds played Sarajevo just after the Bosnian War. I remember thousands of white crosses all over the hillsides marking the dead as we drove into the city.

I've been in the rock 'n' roll industry over 40 years now, working with the biggest bands and artists in the world, but my best times have always been with Simple Minds.

## AMANDA PICKETT

I went with my best friend Julie Richardson. We travelled from Nottingham by coach on a 'rock trip' organised by Way Ahead Records. We had a fantastic day, arriving back in Nottingham about 3am. We both purchased white t-shirts with the gold and black Simple Minds logo. I was thrilled when I heard they were performing at Newark Castle in August 2018. My husband managed to acquire two tickets for a small open-air concert, supported by KT Tunstall and The Pretenders. As we stood on the banks of the River Trent by Newark Castle, I anxiously waited for the support acts to perform. There was a short interval before Simple Minds came on. On a balmy summer evening, everybody was dancing, singing and waving their arms. The majority of the audience were middle-aged, having – like we - grown up loving Simple Minds for the last 38 years. I was hoping they'd play 'Sanctify Yourself', my favourite. And they did. It was the last song.

## DAVE MCGOWAN

I was 15 in 1982 and, like many kids of that age, eagerly watched *Top of the Pops* on a Thursday night. On came a new band called Simple Minds with new single, 'Promised You a Miracle'. New to me, anyway. Truth is, I didn't like it that much and wondered about the fashion on display by Jim and the band. Then in 1984, I heard 'Waterfront' and that was it - I bought *New Gold Dream*, my first CD, and *Sparkle in the Rain* and played them both to death.

My first concert was Milton Keynes Bowl in 1986, and what a day it was. Big Audio Dynamite and The Waterboys were amazing! It gives me goosebumps just thinking about it and the album at that time, *Once Upon a Time* - my favourite Simple Minds album. I still love the cover design and it reminds me of a great time in my life.

## PAUL THACKER

My first gig was Milton Keynes Bowl. Supporting were Dr and the Medics, No.1 at the time with 'Spirit in the Sky'. Brilliant. I'd just a few weeks before started dating my first girlfriend, so taking her all the way to Milton Keynes from Newport, South Wales was a big step, especially for our first real date. But my desire to see the band and get her on a date was not the best planning I've ever done. We couldn't get a train home after and somehow ended up in the waiting room at Wolverhampton train station. When we eventually got home, she had to explain to her parents what had happened.

I guess it couldn't have been too bad as we've been married 29 years now, with four grown-up children and two grandkids! Keep touring, Jim and Charlie - and I'll keep coming!

---

## JIM McCAFFERTY

Several of us Cestrians made a nightmare coach journey through the sticks of North Wales to Milton Keynes Bowl. I met my wife shortly before the gig but she didn't know me well enough to travel. I went with two friends, my sister and two of her friends. Dr and the Medics were accused by the crowd of not playing live and showered with objects. I think the drummer's hand was hurt and they wrapped up sharpish.

Simple Minds were late coming on for their set and the weather turned darker. As rain fell 'Waterfront' opened the set. The whole Bowl rising up at the back was bouncing. I remember Jim giving a teaser a couple of times of how the England – Argentina game was going, ribbing the crowd about Maradona's infamous 'hand of God' incident. My mate, who has MS nowadays, drank and smoked so much that day it would still be a world record. Ah, the halcyon crazy days of youth!

---

## DAVID PINNER

I was peeved to learn I would miss England's quarter-final showdown with Argentina by accompanying my mate Mark to Milton Keynes to see Simple Minds. He assured me it would be a great gig, even though I wasn't really a fan.

Having passed my driving test a few months before we clambered into my 'fridge white' Morris Ital on the morning of the gig for the journey from Burton-upon-Trent. It's amazing how technology has moved on since 1986. We now have start-stop technology in modern vehicles. I used to say a prayer of thanks if my car started twice in a row!

Having negotiated the mythical islands of Milton Keynes and spotting a concrete cow, we arrived at the Bowl to be greeted by a sea of probably more people than I'd ever seen in one place before. There was a horseshoe of burger vans and beer vendors around the upper level. At the far end was the stage.

Down in the Bowl it was a carnival atmosphere, with plastic beer containers being traded by my fellow revellers; cool liquid good, warm liquid dubious. A raft of support acts came and went and I was yearning for a TV to watch the football on.

The day started to warm up properly with the arrival of Celtic rockers The Waterboys at around teatime, followed by a lull and growing sense of anticipation for the main event. It seemed an eternity staring at an empty stage; and I joked to Mark that the band were probably watching the England game.

Eventually, we were greeted by the throbbing opening bassline of 'Waterfront' and the whole field started to bounce. At the time the band were showcasing their American-style rock phase, but highlights for me were 'Speed Your Love', 'Book of Brilliant Things' and a couple of songs I hadn't heard before, 'The American' and final song of the day, 'Love Song'.

Jim even announced the score: England 1 (cheers and flying beers), Argentina 2 (boos and flying beers).

And my car did start for the journey home.

---

## JOHN HAMMOND

My earliest memories of recognising the brilliance that is Simple Minds was on my school geology field trip to Wales in 1982. I was doing my O-levels and the tutor for my course was a real cool character. His room was right next door to our dorm. Every night he blasted 'Promised You a Miracle' on a high-end stereo system. From then on, it's been a fantastic journey of albums played endlessly and record sleeves read front to back and watching live performances around the country.

June 1986 particularly sticks in the mind. The Minds were playing Milton Keynes Bowl on the same day England clashed with Argentina in the World Cup quarter-finals, in the days before mobile phones - us desperate to find out the score. Jim had only just finished the opening number – 'Waterfront' - and succumbed to the crowd's chant of, 'What's the score, what's the score?' You could tell, him being a Scotsman, he loved every minute of telling the whole crowd England had been beaten. But our disappointment soon went as they ripped through another brilliant set of live music.

---

## MATTHEW RACKLEY

The most amazing band ever. I saw them in 1986 supported by Big Audio Dynamite and Lloyd Cole. Michael MacNeil stole the show. They went downhill when Derek Forbes and then Michael left. They cracked America and changed forever.

---

# JAMES SWINDLES

As a teenager, I heard many Minds tracks emanating from my older sister's bedroom, including the irresistible propulsion of 'I Travel', followed by the more ethereal sounds of 'Glittering Prize' a few years later. However, it wasn't until 'Don't You (Forget About Me)', swiftly followed by the album *Once Upon a Time*, that Simple Minds hit me front and centre. I excitedly entered a local radio phone-in competition and, much to my disbelief, won two tickets to see them at Milton Keynes Bowl. I'd been to a couple of gigs at small indoor venues but no band before or since has created such an impression on me.

By early evening, the anticipation was rising to fever pitch and when the bassline of 'Waterfront' began, masses of fans frantically pushing forwards, the Bowl became a jumping frenzy as the band finally took centre-stage. Gleefully singing along to songs I knew so well, it was also ecstatic to hear tracks I was unfamiliar with, such as 'New Gold Dream' and 'The American'.

After that, Jim Kerr became an icon and I bought everything I could by them. *Sons and Fascination* would blare out from my bedroom window day in, day out, much to my neighbour's exasperation. My sister said I was becoming known as 'the kid who loves Simple Minds'.

# JUSTIN BALL

In December 1985 I discovered 'Alive and Kicking' on the *Now That's What I Call Music!* Compilation. Thus began my turn from heavy rock to this unreal new sound. Six months later, at the tender age of 15, myself and two other schoolfriends ventured to our first gig, Simple Minds at Milton Keynes Bowl, with a bus full of concert-going grown-ups for company.

We arrived, awaiting the moment when 'Waterfront' belted out. The huge crowd came alive, hairs on my neck stood on end. It was an amazing experience and made me a lifelong lover of the band. I can still smell the air and feel the atmosphere. Possibly the single most defining moment of my life.

# MARK JONES

It was 1984. I'd gone out with my friend to a local town and we entered a music shop. He picked up a record and I said, 'What's that?' He said, 'I've heard this album is brilliant! Will you buy it?' I said, 'I've never heard it.'

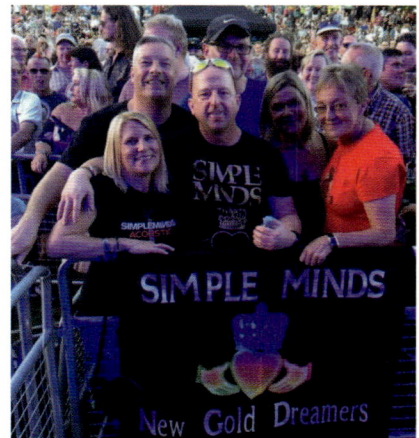

*Mark Jones was at Milton Keynes back in 1986*

I remember him saying, 'If you buy it and don't like it, I'll buy it off you' as he didn't have enough money. So I bought it. I was awestruck. Shortly after, *Once Upon a Time* was released and I was even more in love with this band that I'd only heard of a year ago. My friend said, 'Do you want to go to see Simple Minds in Milton Keynes?' To be honest, I'd never really left Wales up to that point, so I thought, 'Why not?' So Milton Keynes it was!

## DAVE BEANEY, AGE 17

I was very apprehensive about attending such a large gig, my first major concert. Nonetheless, I just had to see the band live so a coach trip was booked from Folkestone. I couldn't wait for the support acts to finish so I could finally see Simple Minds.

Seemingly out of nowhere, the bass intro to 'Waterfront' started and I had shivers all over. This was it. Except for one thing. I couldn't see anything. I was only five foot six and everyone in front of me was way taller. Suddenly I had a tap on the shoulder from someone wearing an 'All Access' pass.

*Dave Beaney was at the Bowl*

My initial thought was, 'Oh, what have I done?' I vividly remember him saying 'You can't see, can you? Come with me.' He took me to the steps of the sound and lighting rig, handed me his pass and said, 'Go up and watch from there - on one condition; I need the pass back afterwards.' I took the pass, put it on and climbed up the rig, stood with the engineers, and had the most fantastic view. I felt so privileged and looked out on the crowd as if to say 'look at me!'

After the show, I found the stage crew at the bottom of the rig and handed his pass back and thanked him a million times. He simply smiled. He knew he'd made my day complete.

Fast forward to September 2014 and Simple Minds playing Margate Winter Gardens. I had no problem seeing this time. I was right at the front, and they were just as good – if not better – than I remembered them 20 years before.

## STEPHEN HYNES

Myself and my girlfriend (now my wife) travelled over from Ireland. It was the day of the England vs Argentina World Cup quarter-final. The crowd didn't know the score and when Jim and the guys came on stage, there was a resounding cry of, 'What's the score? What's the score...?' Jim said, 'You don't want me to tell you...' and as the crowd pushed him to tell them he said, 'England 1… (won?)' – the crowd began cheering and going wild – 'Argentina 2! Don't you forget about me!' The band launched into the song and the crowd went crazy, plastic water bottles and plastic glasses flying everywhere.

## JON RICHARDSON

England vs Argentina, Azteca Stadium, Mexico City. Me at Milton Keynes Bowl along with 85,000 fans and Simple Minds. Jim is running up and down ramps, singing his heart out. Suddenly he stops and shouts, 'Youse English, youse lost!' Maradona had just scored his second goal. That's what I will always remember from that concert. Thanks Jim.

## PATRICK REILLY

*Croke Park*
*28 June 1986, Dublin, Ireland*

I missed their support slot at Dublin's Phoenix Park in 1983 due to being too young, not having enough money or being plain stupid - or a combination of all three! I've since read that Phoenix Park was one of Jim's fondest memories.

   At Croke Park, nobody could have asked for a more beautiful summer's day. Over the pond in Wembley, Wham! bowed out in front of 72,000. In Dublin an estimated 80,000 went wild to 'Waterfront' when Jim, Charlie and company hit the stage. With such a rich back-catalogue, the band honed to perfection, there wasn't a dull moment. 'God is watching the show tonight', said Jim. Indeed it was. Local lad done good Bono joined for the encore of 'Love Song'/'Dance to the Music'/'Sun City'. The crowd left drained but elated. Mobile electronic devices didn't exist so people were left to their own recollections of a memorable evening. I replayed that gig for months after in my head and even to this day it remains a special memory of a band at the top of their game.

## DAMIEN BUGGY, AGE 14

I'd been listening to the band for a couple of years and this was my first chance to see them. I was so glad it was in a huge place. The show did not disappoint and I still love to watch the bootleg video clips on *YouTube* from that show. The excitement of the crowd is amazing to see. I moved from Ireland to London during their next tour, summer 1989, just before I turned 18. I really wanted to do something that would get me involved with the band, so kept writing to Virgin Records in Harrow Road. I eventually got a job in the finance team and found myself dealing with all the creative team that worked on the band. They were really lovely people, especially Ellie and Catherine. It was a brilliant time, all around the *Real Life* project.

Everyone knew I was a huge fan and I was asked to Jon Webster's office to hear some of the new album, including 'Let There be Love' and 'Real Life'. I loved hearing them and said what I really liked about the feel of the songs. I felt very privileged to be one of the first people that would hear these songs. They would also give me previews of new artwork and packaging, which was so exciting. Then the tour for the album happened. I got to travel to see them in Paris and a pass and ticket were left for me at a hotel on Rue Kleber. I saw the show at the Bercy, which was mind-blowing. I got to see a ton of arena and stadium shows on that tour. I was backstage at many of the shows and Jim and Charlie would walk past, say hello, and I was always too shy to speak, which I regret now of course. I've seen them so many times since, and get just as excited now as I did back in 1986.

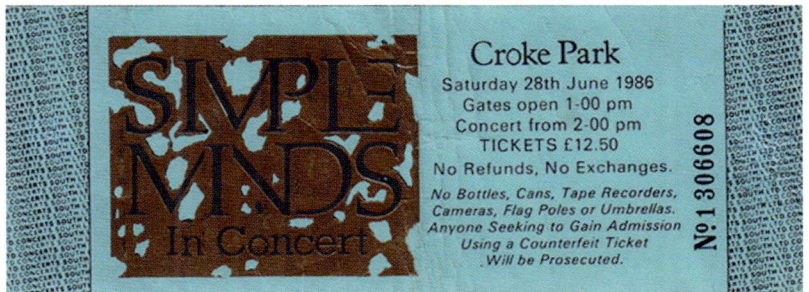

## MARK FINNEGAN

It's early 1986 and on Dublin's Northside life's tough, unemployment is high and making ends meet is a hard slog for many, my parents included. Lots of families were in the same boat, but no one complained - we just did the best we could and got on with it. Hindsight could trick you into believing life was really hard but I remember my teen years fondly. It was hard to be miserable growing up in the early 80s, especially with all that great music. New wave, new romantics, synth-pop, electronica, goths - it was a very eclectic time but such an incredibly creative and exciting time to be a teenager.

I'd only been to one concert but was hungry for more. Big stadium gigs looked so fantastic, I couldn't wait to go to one, but who would it be? As winter became spring the big summer gigs in Ireland were being announced and one stood out from all others – Simple Minds at Croke Park. The excitement was off the charts. Everyone I knew - friends, schoolmates, cousins, absolutely everyone - wanted to be there. My brothers and I were no different.

That's when reality struck home. I'm the oldest of four brothers. Tickets for three of us (the baby of the family was a bit younger) was an expensive outlay for our parents. Chances of attending weren't good. In fact, they were non-existent. One brother used his birthday money to get a ticket but my other brother and I were going to miss out. It was tough but we made our peace with it. We had to because in my experience miracles didn't happen regularly.

The week of the concert came around and absolutely everyone we knew was going to the show. It's all they were talking about. I put on a brave face but it sucked. Sitting at the dinner table the night before, family talk turned to the next day's event. There was some sadness about missing out and maybe even a bit of resentment. And then it happened - The Miracle! My parents had somehow found a way to buy two tickets. My brother and I were in. It was like all my Christmases and birthdays had come together. I couldn't believe it but it was real.

The next day dawned bright and sunny. The entire neighbourhood was alive and kicking because everyone seemed to be going to this concert. The next 12 hours are still among the most treasured memories of my life. The weather was great, the excitement was at fever pitch and - the show? The show was outstanding. Great support sets from In Tua Nua, The Waterboys and Lloyd Cole and The Commotions. Then Simple Minds at their stadium-rocking best, with a cameo from Bono and even an amazing lightning storm for the finale.

It was the most magnificent day, and a concert that's now legendary in Ireland. The number of people I've met over the years who were there and no one has a bad word to say about it. It was epic. My first stadium gig is still the one by which I judge all others. Thanks to Simple Minds for a truly unforgettable day. And thanks to my parents for a gift and memories that will last a lifetime.

---

## EAMONN QUINN

I first heard 'Don't You (Forget About Me)' on MTV in 1985, I was 15. More than anything it was Mel's drums that grabbed me. I kept seeing the video. I bought the baggy suit, the slip-on shoes. I was hooked. I waited patiently for the new album and in October that year I raced down and got a copy the day it was released. I looked at the back cover. No 'Don't You?' Must be a mistake. Disheartened I went home, played *Once Upon a Time* and loved every bar. Thankfully 'Don't You' was released as a 12-inch and the extended drum intro was heaven on vinyl.

In early 1986 tickets went on sale for a gig in Croke Park on 28 June. The longest wait ever. The day dawned and it was a sunny day in Dublin, perfect for my first concert. Jim's first words are still with me as the bassline of 'Waterfront' quite literally went through my body, 'It's great to be back in Dublin's fair city….1-2, 1-2-3-4.' The euphoria of seeing the world's biggest band. In my backyard. Playing songs I knew every word to. I recall an orange being thrown at John Giblin by some clown. John used his bass like a machine gun and pointed at the general area where it had come from – with a smile on his face.

It goes without saying the electrical storm that played out for the last 30 minutes or so will stay with me and the 60,000 people there forever. Mother Nature was a fan of the Minds that day. Bono joined Jim on stage for 'Sun City' and the crowd went wild. A year later U2 would come back to Croke Park having conquered the world with *The Joshua Tree*. But that day, they were in the shadow of Simple Minds. Best concert ever….

---

# TERRY ROWLEY

I am a Philly native. In 1985 we hosted the world's best concert, *Live Aid*. I was not there but like many watched it on TV. Homes with access to cable were few and far between. My friend Mike's older sister, Cathy, had cable. I'm not sure Cathy realised she was going to be hosting a bunch of 16 and 17-year-old boys for nearly 16 hours. I still remember preparations for

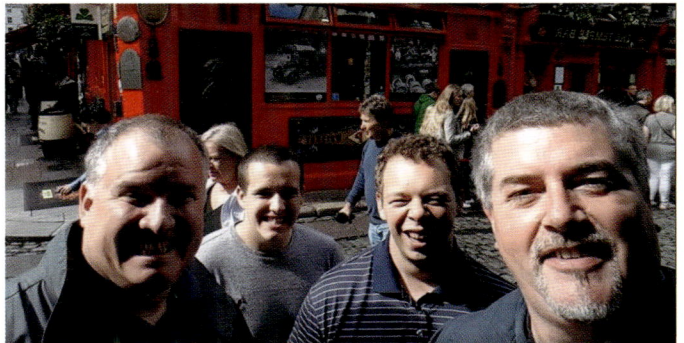

*Terry Rowley was at Croke Park in 1986 and returned to Dublin with his son and his friends in 2017*

the day - snacks, soda and a lot of VHS tapes. We thought we were going to record 16 hours of music that day. I'm not sure how many hours we managed. I do recall that the video recorder had a remote control, tethered to the VCR by a 15 to 20-foot-long cord. No wireless anything back then.

I had a list of 'must see' groups that day. Simple Minds weren't on it. If anyone in the USA was claiming to be tuning into Simple Minds at the time for anything other than 'Don't You (Forget About Me)', I'd say they were truly forward-thinking. What also came from the band that day in JFK Stadium were 'Ghost Dancing' and 'Promised You a Miracle'. 'Ghost Dancing' really got me. It was the first time I heard this song and the band delivered a performance packed with unbridled energy.

Next summer I graduated from Frankford High School. My graduation gift to myself was a trip to Ireland and England for the summer. My plans included drink, dancing and music. But I had to decide between a Queen concert at Wembley or Simple Minds at Dublin's Croke Park. A buddy, Paul Johnson, sold me on the trip to Dublin from Dundalk, County Louth. Croke Park it was.

My memories from the day are almost as vivid as they would be documented through the lenses of a mobile phone. Claps of thunder and lightning added special effects to the event. U2's Bono added flavour to 'Love Song' and a couple of covers, 'Dance to the Music' and 'Sun City'. This was a group of musicians educating us about South Africa and apartheid while striving to bring about change in the world. The audience on this day sang along to 'I ain't gonna play Sun City!'

I appreciate having the Queen *Live at Wembley Stadium* DVD to look back at now. I am truly thankful to have the memories of Simple Minds live at Croke Park.

## TERRY WHELAN

Whilst going to Croke Park in Dublin in 1986 I met Jim, Charlie and Derek. I have their autographs on the back of my birth certificate to prove it. Fast forward to 2017 and the morning after the Inverness gig, I bumped into Jim in a place called the House of Bruar and managed to have a lengthy conversation with him along with getting photos outside the shop. Thanks, Jim, for taking the time to talk to me and my wife that morning.

## MICHAEL CARROLL

I first saw Simple Minds in the City Hall in Cork in 1984 and was blown away by them. When they announced a headline gig at Croke Park in Dublin I just had to go. This was my first big stadium gig, and what a line-up! An absolutely brilliant day and I've been a fan ever since. It was great also to see the band return to Cork a few years ago at the Marquee.

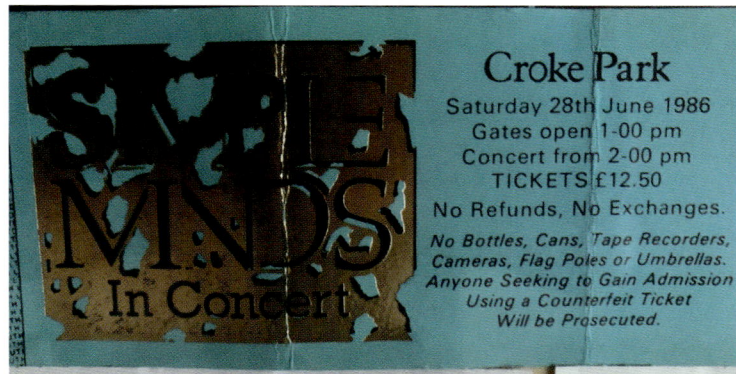

*Michael Carroll's ticket for the Croke Park show*

# BART WILLEMS

*Rock Torhout*
*5 July 1986, Torhout, Belgium*

In the early 80s at high school, Simple Minds was our preferred band. My good friend Johan and I enjoyed our first parties, dancing like mad when their music was playing. We liked the initial albums, but *New Gold Dream* triggered something special. Even now, when I play 'Someone Somewhere (in Summertime)', I get goosebumps. It made us happy, joyful, emotional, inspired, strong.

In 1986 I went to my first big festival, Rock Torhout in Belgium. As heavy rain poured down, Simple Minds were singing 'rain keeps falling, rain keeps falling', the crowd happily singing and dancing in the rain.

Over the years, Johan and me went our separate ways, living in different places. But when Simple Minds have a concert nearby we call each other to arrange to see them, reliving these good old days. I'm amazed how the band plays each concert with the same energy and enthusiasm. It's like time stood still.

# FILIP BOLLAERT

My first concert, as a 16-year old, was at the Torhout/Werchter festival in Belgium. I still remember incredible live versions of 'The American' and 'New Gold Dream'. In the three years I waited to see them again I saw a small advert in a local magazine from someone looking to swap live tapes. I got in touch and made friends with Piet Hillewaert. He, Tony Weytens, John Provyn (aka JohnnyBGood) and I stayed in touch, meeting between tours, travelling to concerts together. Piet introduced me to the secret tricks for meeting the band before or after concerts, at artist entrances or in hotel lobbies, resulting in unforgettable moments close to the band.

A couple of my personal highlights are Brussels in June 1989, the day after the Tiananmen Square massacre in Beijing. Jim

*Filip Bollaert with Jim and Charlie*

made a speech about it. It truly was street fighting years at that time. Another is Dalhalla, an abandoned limestone quarry in Rättvik, Sweden in July 2012. The best acoustics I ever experienced at a concert.

Being part of the Simple Minds fan community is about friendship, sharing, meeting, experiencing life and music together. It's about travelling to people and places you probably never would meet or visit otherwise. It's about identifying yourself with the core values of Simple Minds, such as the fight for human rights and respect for all people.

---

# VERONIQUE WATTIAUX

## Rock Werchter
## 6 July 1986, Werchter, Belgium

I started to adore the band when the song 'Promised You a Miracle' was first broadcast, followed by 'Theme for Great Cities'. Then I heard 'Waterfront' and was mad about the song. Only then did I realise all three songs came from the same bunch of guys: Simple Minds. Aged 13, I waited for the store to open so I could grab my copy of new album *Once Upon a Time*. When I learned they were to play Torhout/Werchter, I wasn't going to let it

*Veronique Wattiaux met Jim*

happen without me. I collected money from empty bottles. My sister agreed to buy my ticket and told my mum we were going to the park (I was only 14), and off I went, taking the bus to Werchter.

My mum could not understand why we were not back home by 8pm. She phoned the police to report me missing because she was worried. Then she turned on the TV in case they'd mention the killing of a teenager and saw a live broadcast of Simple Minds. She then phoned the police back to tell them she thought she knew where I was!

When I came home she was so mad, but also realised how determined I was to see them. When we heard about the *Live in the City of Light* event in Paris, she got on the bus with me and waited outside. Even then she panicked and thought she'd lost me. She told me later that she saw the band backstage because she told the staff she had lost her daughter!

I did all the European tours from that point until 1998. I worked in a shop after school to save money to buy an Interrail card to follow them. I told my mum I'd stayed with people I met in various concerts when, in fact, I was touring the whole of Europe with almost no money. I had to sleep on trains during the night, catching night trains from Italy to Switzerland and back and so on. Twice I was nearly raped, but somehow got saved by people jumping on the train each time at the right time! I bought many Interrail tickets over the years. I have to thank some of Simple Minds managers big time, because they put me on the guestlist each time. If not for them, I'd have never seen the band so many times.

Of course, like many foreigners I wanted to live in Scotland because of Simple Minds. As I was studying engineering, I learned that if I chose a diploma that had no equivalence in Belgium, my fees would be paid for. I found a double engineering diploma in physics and electronics, jumped at the opportunity and landed in Dundee. My mum died about four months after I arrived and I had to work full-time to pay for my living expenses, but it was the best time of my life. I loved the country, the food, the mentality, the booze, the boys... yep, heaven!

It took me six months to become fluent in English but I managed to acquire a Dundonian accent. I once had to go to the bank on the English border and as soon as I started talking, I got insulted by an English bloke, telling me to go back home to my sheep. Believe me, to be insulted for sounding Scottish is one of the most memorable moments of my life and not an insult! (unfortunately, I now juggle three languages on a daily basis and have no accent anymore).

With my diploma, I got a job in the Netherlands and now have the money - but not the time - to follow Simple Minds anywhere. I've flown across the world to Singapore, Australia and the USA to see them. I've seen them live at least 150 times. Over the years I've met so many nice people.

---

# SJOERD DE ROOS

The first Simple Minds song I heard was 'Promised You a Miracle'. I liked it but wasn't immediately a fan. As a lover of classic 60s and 70s rock, it was too much like 80s synthesiser pop for me. Then 'Don't You (Forget About Me)' was released. That's what I wanted to hear: rock 'n' roll. After that I heard the album *Once Upon a Time* with a long row of huge hits – 'Alive and Kicking', 'Sanctify Yourself', 'All the Things She Said' and 'Ghostdancing'. All great songs. Then I discovered *New Gold Dream* and *Sparkle in the Rain*, the best Simple Minds albums ever made.

In 1983, Simple Minds played the Rock Torhout Festival in Belgium, half of the Torhout/Werchter Festival. U2 were also there in 1983. Jim Kerr and Bono gave Belgian TV an hilarious interview, announcing they were to marry each other, with Annie Lennox of The Eurthymics as best man. In Werchter, Jim joined U2 on stage to sing '11 O'Clock Tick Tock'.

They played Torhout/Werchter again in 1984 and returned once more in 1986, the first time I saw them. They had become too big for the festival by then. The rest of the line-up in 1986 were support acts for Simple Minds. While watching and listening to the show in Torhout, in the pouring rain, I bought the bootleg album of their show from Rock Werchter 1984. The festival was very important for bands like Simple Minds and U2 in both Europe and the rest of the world, but these bands were also important for the festival. They grew up together.

## CORINNE MARION-GALLOIS

*Arènes De Frejus*
*15 July 1986, Frejus, France*

I had the chance to see the band in the Arena in Frejus, the town where I lived. The support was The Waterboys, who I also loved. What an incredible show! I was really impressed by Jim's energy. I think I was secretly a little in love with him. I had another opportunity to see them in Morzine for a summer festival a few years ago. I even convinced my husband to spend two nights at the Angela Villa, Taormina, in beautiful Sicily. And as a manager and producer, I've founded my own music label, and had to name it New Gold Dream Records, after my favourite song. With such a name, I'm sure I cannot fail to succeed!

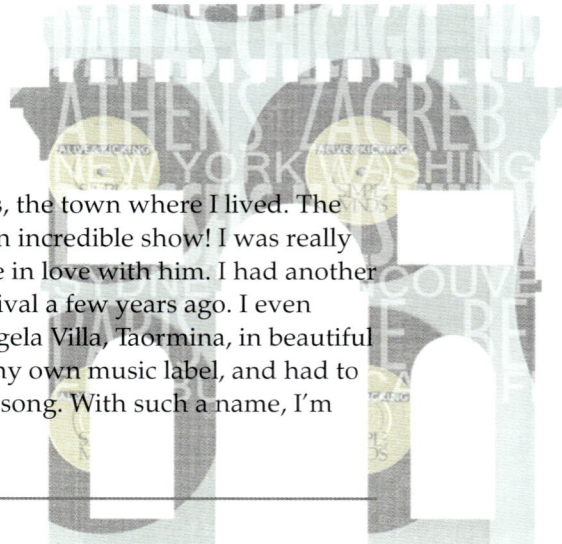

## MATT FORBES

*Le Zénith*
*13 August 1986, Paris, France*

The definitive album was *Once Upon a Time*. I bought it on cassette at WH Smith's at Paddington Station, aged 12, and then went home via Reading. 'Sanctify Yourself' will always remind me of what I now know to be Reading West Junction East - I drive past it daily. What sealed it for me was Le Zenith in 1986. I was in the crowd with my cousin. 'Someone Somewhere (in Summertime)' was and remains my all-time No.1 favourite. It evokes so many fond memories, and when I hear it I'm taken back to that night.

Simple Minds have been part of my life forever. You lot have seen me through the best and worst bits of my life. Thank you so much.

---

## FRANCISCO VILLANUEVA JORGE, AGE 13

*Estadio Ud Levante*
*17 August 1986, Valencia, Spain*

My story with Simple Minds began in the summer of 1985 with the song 'Don't You (Forget About Me)', although I'd seen a video clip of 'Speed Your Love to Me' broadcast on a television programme before. I was 12 and started to get interested in their music and gradually discovered their discography. In 1986, I collected money in a piggy bank for my concert ticket to see them in Valencia, my first concert of theirs and a night I will never forget. I went with my brother, who also liked the band.

In 1989, in my first job, I had to invent I had a wedding to go to on a Saturday to be able to see them at the Vicente Calderón Stadium in Madrid on the *Street Fighting Years* tour. Since then I've seen them perform on every occasion I've been able to, and their music has accompanied me in the good and not so good moments of my life. In 1997, I was going to see them in Los Alcázares. Due to a problem at work I missed the bus, so convinced my parents to drive me 150 miles to Murcia to see the show. We planned to stay over, but there were no hotel rooms left!

---

## VICENTE ANDREU LLOPEZ

I discovered their music in the 80s through songs like 'Alive and Kicking', 'Love Song' and 'Don't You (Forget About Me).' There isn't a bad song. I've seen them twice. I couldn't buy many records but listened to them on the radio, in pubs and at the disco. If I was a DJ I'd never be bored. I'd play Simple Minds all the time.

---

## KEVIN EGAN

I remember as a young teenager looking through my cousin's record collection. How, after a decade knowing my mother's taste in music off by heart - from ABBA to dance and groove - was I now discovering this music? From a New Gold Dream book, a heart burning love on a cross drew me in for good. It captured my heart that day, leading me on a journey to follow and worship Simple Minds.

---

## YOKO UCHISHIMA

*Tokyo Kousei Nenkin Kaikan*
*12 October 1986, Tokyo, Japan*

The first time I saw Simple Minds live was in Tokyo in 1986. I couldn't even see their faces from our distant seats. But my friends and I were very excited and bought tickets for an additional performance after seeing them for the first time. We talked about Simple Minds every day and loved buying their old records and CDs.

We were so crazy about Simple Minds that we decided to go to a UK concert in 1989. It took about 30 hours one way, flying the cheapest route with Pakistan International Airlines. We were so ignorant. On the day of the concert, when we tried to buy a ticket from the tout, it was very expensive – a £16.50 ticket was £100!

Jim and Simple Minds have given me a lifetime of happiness. After going to see them live, I was waiting behind the stage to see them up close. Many other fans were waiting too. Everyone talked to them when they came out and slowly moved to the bus. It was like people flocking to the Messiah. I was embarrassed, just watching from afar. Then Jim turned around and beckoned. I looked right and left. Jim smiled and said, 'You, come on!' Oh my God! I was sure I was going to die the next day!

I've been to several Simple Minds concerts in England, Scotland and Germany, the last time in the UK in 2008. They no longer come to Japan and it's difficult for me to go to concerts anymore, but I'm supporting them from the Far East.

---

## RANJIT DUTTA

*Sydney Entertainment Centre*
*24 October 1986, Sydney, Australia*

I was 18 when I heard Simple Minds' 'Love Song' playing on the radio one night, whilst swotting for a particularly difficult subject in first year engineering at Sydney University. Just that opening phrase of sequencer dropping a couple of tones, the distorted phased guitar and that crashing beat was enough to hook me in.

I went back into their catalogue and grew forward along with them, hearing the evolution of their sound and maturity in their songwriting. I loved what I heard and felt. I first saw them perform live at Sydney Entertainment Centre supporting the *Once Upon a Time* album. I was so jealous of my little sister. Her school friend's dad, Dr Webb, was the tour doctor for the Australian leg. He had tickets and backstage passes for his daughter and my little sister and they got to meet my heroes. And they weren't even fans!

December 2012 and I'm there at the front of the crowd in Sydney, brand new camera in hand, rocking out and taking photos like crazy. Then I do it again in 2017 at Bimbadgen Winery on the hottest February day in 40 years, 43 degrees Celsius, and again in 2018 at the Newcastle Supercars concert.

The older tracks have matured with age, and the new material shows the band's creativity is still fresh and very much alive. The brilliant music has been a friend through the many twists and unexpected turns of my life – student, young husband, family man, older man, and back to a single man again.

Many years ago, I saw a photo of Jim and his beautiful Boxer dog, Bella. I was completely blown away, being both a lifelong Boxer fan as well as a Simple Minds fan. Keep doing what you do!

## JUDY OWEN

*Bruce Indoor Stadium*
*25 October 1986, Canberra, Australia*

My favourite band… Simple Minds. I've always referred to Jim Kerr as my boyfriend - not in a stalkerish way, but in jest. I always said to my husband how lucky the band's partners are to have such talent in their homes around the house and at the ready, to be able to sing and play guitar, etc. Those songs, the instrumentation, lyrics and vocals – it's a collaboration that just works wonders.

My first Simple Minds concert was in Canberra. To this day, it's one of the best concerts I've ever seen - loud, passionate, vibrant and with that unmistakable guitar sound resonating throughout Bruce Stadium! We fans are so grateful that they keep making the long trip to visit us in Australia.

## COLETTE GILLARD

Living in Christchurch, New Zealand with my sister, Michelle, 'Sanctify Yourself' came on the music channel and she said 'turn it up!' so I did. I've always loved their music. My neighbour doesn't like it, but I don't care what they think.

## PHIL BAKER

*Entertainment Centre*
*27 October 1986, Brisbane, Australia*

I was first captivated by Simple Minds at the age of 15, during the *Once Upon a Time* era. I bought the album then proceeded to purchase the back-catalogue, one by one at six-week intervals due to my limited income. By the time I got *Real to Real* almost 12 months later I was beginning to wonder if I'd stumbled upon another band with the same name! But that's what Simple Minds do - they constantly evolve.

I remember buying the *Life in a Day* LP the same day Simple Minds played in Brisbane. It was my first stadium concert and, on my way to catch the train, Mick MacNeil walked right past me! Being a shy 16-year-old, I was too starstruck to stop him and say hello.

## MARIANO MAZZEO

*Sports & Entertainment Centre*
*31 October 1986, Melbourne, Australia*

My earliest memory of Simple Minds was hearing 'Love Song' in 1981 and thinking, 'What a catchy drum beat and synth sound!' I instantly loved this song and started following the band in whatever media news I could read, see or hear about them. I finally got to see them live in 1986 for their *Once Upon a Time* tour in Melbourne, then again in 2006 on the *Black and White* tour. Then my two favourites united in 2010, Simple Minds and the Australian Formula 1. I made sure to head for the front of the stage as soon as that last lap was ending and enjoyed every minute. The piercing sounds of the V8 F1 engines slowly disappeared out of my head, which was then filled with the glorious sounds of Simple Minds.

## MARIA POMEROY

*Christchurch Town Hall*
*4 November 1986, Christchurch, New Zealand*

At 23 years old with hopeful, shitty boyfriend, tickets purchased for the *Once Upon a Time* tour. Boyfriend called out of town at the last minute, girlfriend accompanied instead – bonus, no angst! Dressing up for the show, looking pretty, young, full of vibrancy. Sitting awaiting the show, the lights hit - bam! Simple Minds take stage. My world lights up! The music, the light show, the energy, the venue, dancing in the aisles. Perfection on a plate. A night I will never forget and cannot be replaced. Star-struck and forever a fan.

2010, Christchurch flattened - earthquake city. Most is lost but the Town Hall locks down for 10 years while repairs are agreed and made, my heart yearns for the memories held dear.

2019, mosque shootings. Christchurch hit again.

2019, *40 Years of Hits* tour announced. Against all odds, tickets booked for Paris in April 2020, trusting to scrape the money together to make it happen.

2020, life happens on this planet. Jobs lost and lives lost. Still dreaming of Simple Minds, listening to the lyrics week after week, hoping against hope to see you again live with someone, somewhere, in the summertime. It will happen. As long as you tour, I have the chance.

And Christchurch Town Hall has just reopened, waiting and ready for Simple Minds to liven the fans hearts again in a new gold dream.

---

## MARK ROGERS

My first Simple Minds concert at the Town Hall was photographed in the local paper. And I was there, down in front (where I like to be) of Robin Clark. It was an amazing concert.

---

## RACHEL BURKE

*Michael Fowler Center*
*6 & 7 November 1986, Wellington,*
*New Zealand*

I was ecstatic when I found out they were coming to New Zealand as part of the *Once Upon a Time* tour. Back then, there weren't barriers and stuff in front of the stage so you could get right up close to a band. My friend Wendy and I queued for about six hours to get to the front row. The gig was amazing but for me the most incredible moment came when

*Mark Rogers in the Christchurch Press in New Zealand*

235

Jim was within touching distance. In typical teenage girl crazed fan fashion, I grabbed the material of his tights and hung on.

His reaction was swift. 'Fuck off!'

I just about passed out. Jim had spoken to me. To me! I let go, my fingers imprinted on the sweaty material. I don't blame him for swearing at me. I would have done the same.

Still a superfan.

## SUSAN CONN

### Golden Discs Record Shop
### May 1987, Belfast, Northern Ireland

I was unwell and off work one day. From my sick bed I was listening to local radio and entered a competition for a Simple Minds meet and greet. Jim, Charlie and Mick were coming to Belfast to do some promo for the release of *Live in the City of Light*, signing copies of the newly-released album. The question wasn't too difficult given I was a fan. However, you had to be caller number seven, but seven was my lucky number, and needless to say it was my lucky day!

I was 25. Imagine my excitement. On the day of the meet and greet, I and the other

*Susan Conn met Jim at a record store signing in Belfast*

winners met the DJ John and we were brought into the record shop. This was great because there was a massive queue outside. We were even inside before the guys turned up and got about half an hour with them before the doors opened. I still have the photos I took that day. And of course my signed copy of the album.

## JIM MACDONALD

### Barrowland Ballroom
### 14 – 16 December 1987, Glasgow, Scotland

One day my best friend George said, 'Jim, would you like to go to the Barrowland to see Simple Minds at the *Cash for Kids* concert?' He was a fan and his cousin got us both guest tickets. He was a commis chef on tour and was kindly given an opportunity by the band through the Easterhouse project, a fantastic local charity Jim and the boys supported.

Unbeknown to George I was earlier a fan of Johnny and the Self Abusers, the young punk band who were now Simple Minds. We went to the gig straight from my office, had a few too many beers and plucked up the courage to get to the front of the stage, where I lost my jacket and keys to my office. The next day I had to face the music with my boss and remember the response, 'You lost my keys at the gig but nothing matters but the Minds!' That's youth for you.

George is no longer with us, having passed away with Motor Neurone Disease in his early 40s. But no one can take away our youth and fantastic memories. Our favourite song was 'Don't You (Forget About Me)'. Seems quite apt now.

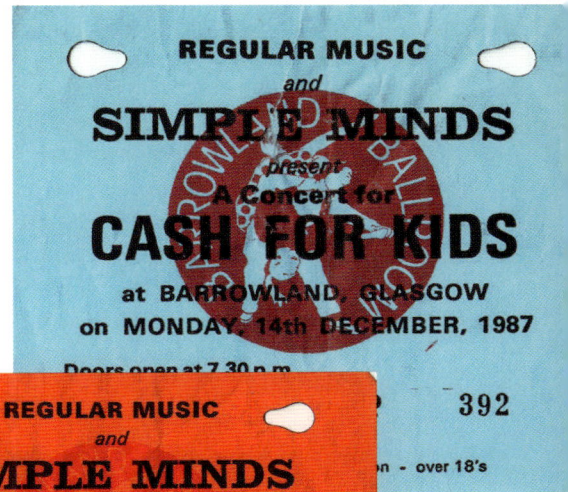

REGULAR MUSIC
and
SIMPLE MINDS
present
A Concert for
CASH FOR KIDS
at BARROWLAND, GLASGOW
on MONDAY, 14th DECEMBER, 1987
Doors open at 7.30 p.m.
392
on - over 18's

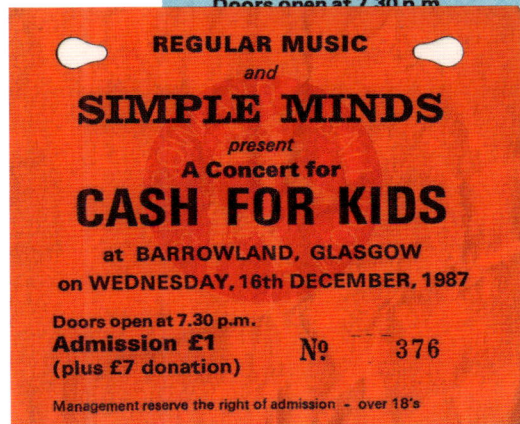

REGULAR MUSIC
and
SIMPLE MINDS
present
A Concert for
CASH FOR KIDS
at BARROWLAND, GLASGOW
on WEDNESDAY, 16th DECEMBER, 1987
Doors open at 7.30 p.m.
Admission £1
(plus £7 donation)
Nº 376
Management reserve the right of admission - over 18's

*Carlos Loureiro saw the Minds in Rio*

# CARLOS LOUREIRO

*Praca Da Apoteose
7 January 1988,
Rio De Janeiro, Brazil*

In 1983 I lived in the UK, an awesome experience for a Brazilian boy, and it is there that I heard Simple Minds for the first time. I encountered their music again back in Brazil in 1985 with the sound of 'Don't You (Forget About Me)'. I liked the sound and the voice so much I bought a maxi-single, a rare thing in Brazilian stores, with an extended 'Up on the Catwalk' as a B-side. Which I immediately liked better than 'Don't You' and which was the trigger to get to know more of their music.

Some months later I bought *Once Upon a Time*. I had my first real girlfriend and she lived in an apartment with a huge balcony over Guanabara Bay in Rio de Janeiro. We put the record on the stereo and the wall of sound whilst looking out over the bay gave me a fantastic, electric feeling!

In 1986 I was travelling through America with my family, looking for Simple Minds in record stores, and found both *Sparkle in the Rain* and *New Gold Dream* in San Francisco. As it was close to my birthday my father told me I could pick one and I chose *Sparkle* because I recognised 'Up on the Catwalk' from the single. A couple of days later, on my birthday, my father gave me the copy of *New Gold Dream* he'd also secretly bought. Once I heard those records - those perfect records - I became what I am, a Simple Minds fan forever. In 1988 I went to my first concert, a huge one in Rio. I don't miss those. I prefer the smaller venues.

## MARK DIXON

*Wembley Stadium*
*11 June 1988, London, England*

It was March 1987, the day of our Grandad's funeral. I was 15 and after the wake my cousin Karl suggested we go into town. After a drink and bite to eat in the café upstairs at Martin's Newsagents on Chelmsford High Street, we found ourselves in the music department at the back of the shop on the ground floor. Karl, already a big Simple Minds fan, picked up a copy of *Once Upon a Time* and handed it to me, telling me how great it was. Being a whole year older and that much wiser than me, I took his recommendation and bought it. I was blown away by the album and in the following months spent many hours browsing through the back-catalogue in record stores, buying whatever I could get my hands on. It wasn't just vinyl either; t-shirts, posters, even gold Claddagh rings fuelled what was to become an obsession for us both.

I was desperate to see the band live and was so excited when I managed to get tickets for the Mandela tribute concert. My mates and I made the short trip from Essex to the old Wembley Stadium with its iconic twin towers. We awaited eagerly for the bands set before Emily Lloyd and Denzel Washington finally announced their appearance and, as the mighty bassline of 'Waterfront' hammered throughout the famous old stadium, I climbed onto my friend Clarky's shoulders. All around me a sea of people rocked in waves to a terrific wall of sound coming from the stage – Simple Minds were incredible that day!

# TONY FERRIS

It was 1985 and I was 18. I went to a friend's house with U2's *War* album under my arm, excitedly instructing him, 'You've got to listen to this.' He said, 'You've got to listen to this!' and played me a cassette of 'Don't You (Forget About Me)'. I sought out my own Simple Minds cassette to play in the car and came across *Sparkle in the Rain*. I and my friends played it constantly, never getting tired of it. I marvelled how the words 'see moon, cry like a baby' could be incorporated into a song.

I spent the next several months acquiring their back-catalogue, dreaming of seeing Simple Minds live. I joined the fan club, got some stickers and typed correspondence and felt part of something special. One of my friends even wrote to Jim Kerr on my behalf. He never told me what he put in the letter or if he got a reply.

I was in a pub when I heard a song played on Radio 1. I missed the start but when I heard the slide guitar kick in, I instantly knew it was Charlie Burchill playing. What a song! I think it was Simon Mayo who went on to explain it was written for the upcoming 70th birthday Mandela tribute concert.

I got a ticket and got to Wembley Stadium before dawn to guarantee getting down the front. Simple Minds were everything I hoped they'd be live - engaging, atmospheric and a true live representation of their music.

Highlights of the last 30 years? Wembley 1989, the *Acoustic* show at Birmingham in 2017 (my daughter's first show), the Roundhouse in Camden for the *Walk Between Worlds* tour, and the whole crowd singing 'Don't You (Forget About Me)' in its entirety at Roundhay Park, Leeds.

# STEVE COLIN

The late Eighties – too much television on a white-hot day in Southern France, a different world during holidays made me watch *The Breakfast Club*. Someone, somewhere in summertime discovered his soundtrack for every heaven.

Back home, I had to come a long way to find 'Love Song', not appearing on any album I checked out in a local record store. And when 'Alive and Kicking' played on radio I was hypnotised. Around then, *Live in the City of Light* was out, a masterpiece making me go one step closer to collect the entire cacophony of the mighty Minds.

Soon after, *Street Fighting Years*. I was 13, caught in a dream to celebrate this band live, with a New Gold Dream for me in Amnéville, France during the *Real Life* tour.

I feel like swimming towards the sun every new sunshine morning when I listen to any theme for great cities created by the best rock band in the world. Each song makes me feel I travel in every heaven, focused on this big music.

Happy is the man to see the lights of an ongoing band that played on with different line-ups. A life shot in black and white would not be the same without each song for the tribes and sound in 70 cities. Thank you for the voice, eyes and memories!

# LIVE IN THE CITY OF LIGHT

## ALBERTO SCORZINO

I discovered Simple Minds via *Live in the City of Light*, on my first study trip to Birmingham, which I was visiting to try and improve my English. In the early Nineties, I was studying at Milan University. One day I switched on my favourite radio station, Radio 105, to hear that Jim and Charlie were guests in the studio. I said to myself, 'The radio station is not too far and I can reach the studios before the end of the interview!' I didn't think twice, jumping on my little motorbike and riding into the centre of Milan. I arrived at the studios and waited for hours, not knowing if they were still there. But I managed to get their autographs in my diary, which I still have.

## JASON HODGSON

It was in a battered old mini bus taking an under 18 football team to a match when the larger-than-life goalkeeper began to sing. There was no music, just him belting out the lyrics to a song that I had not heard before, 'Cities, buildings falling down.' Soon he was joined by a couple of the other players and the bus was bouncing. All I could do was watch open mouthed and wide-eyed. 'Do you not know Simple Minds, Jase?' he asked. Fast forward two weeks, and at just 16 I am moving to London to start my first job, which for a boy brought up in the North East is a big move. The company is based just off Piccadilly Circus, which in 1987 was home to the massive Tower Records store. Five days later, armed with the contents of my first ever pay packet, I head in to Tower Records. As I enter, there is a poster with a male dressed all in black next to the Forth Rail Bridge. Whilst I do not recognise the man, I recognise the bridge and I am sure that the words Simple Minds ring a bell. Wasn't that the name of that the band the goalkeeper was singing? I left the store that day with a shiny new double cassette - Simple Minds *Live in the City of Light*!

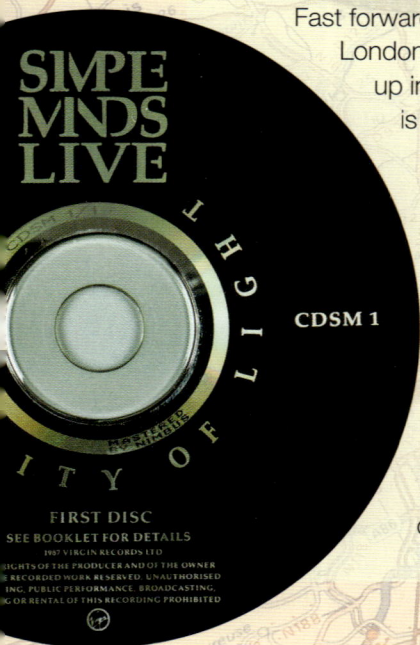

### ALLISON KING

I started babysitting for my baby cousin and discovered my uncle was a big Simple Minds fan. His first dance at his wedding to my mum's youngest sister was 'Don't You (Forget About Me)'. The cassette he played regularly and often let me borrow was *Live in the City of Light*. Their music opened up a new avenue of storytelling through music.

### VITO AZZOLLINI

The record that made me fall in love with their music was the double live album *Live in the City of Light*. I have indelible memories of 'East at Easter', 'Someone Somewhere (in Summertime)', 'Big Sleep' and 'Waterfront'. I grew up with their music. It was my soundtrack of my adolescence. They will always remain an indelible memory.

### ASHLEY DEAN

I bought *Live in the City of Light* on cassette soon after it was released. I had heard 'Don't You' so put on side three first. From the emergent cheering of the crowd then Charlie's reverberating chords I was hooked.

## DAVID ANDERSON

I was 17 when I met Jim. It was February 1987 and I was in fifth year at Queensferry High School. Rumours had been going around for a few weeks that he was living locally so it shouldn't have been such a shock to see him wandering around the small Coop at the bottom of the Loan. But I still found myself initially starstruck and slightly in awe as I double checked the figure strolling up and down the aisles. Even with a basket in arm, Jim was unmistakable; a magnetic, majestic figure and bona fide rock star. I waited anxiously until he was outside and had organised himself safely onto his bike (I hadn't expected that) before approaching him. Despite being somewhat nervous, starting a conversation was quite straightforward simply because I'd recently seen Simple Minds live in Glasgow. Before we parted company that day, I suggested that he should shop at Drysdale's, the local grocery shop that I worked in each weekend. Fast forward to the next weekend and I found myself handing over a box of messages to him at his beautiful, penthouse flat at Bridge House.

Over the next few weeks and months, I would take several deliveries along. I'd also continue to bump into him in the shop and even spent time at the local park with him and his children. We talked mostly about music and books. I also wrote music then (still do). He offered to 'nip up and have a listen'. But I remembered that I hadn't tidied my room that day and was too embarrassed to take up the offer!

My favourite memory from this time, however, was when he invited me up to the flat to listen to the new album, *Live in the City of Light*. He'd just received the advanced promo and I would be the first person outside the band's immediate circle to hear it. I will never forget standing in his living room, staring over the River Forth at the Bridge, listening to 'Waterfront'.

A few weeks later, I would bump into Jim again for the last time. I was out with one of my friends and had walked into the Hawes Inn. There was Jim at the bar, 'David, hi there. Can I buy you and your friend a drink? Sorry, I can't come and sit with you but the band are round in the garden. Tell them I've sent you and you can drink with them.' It was a beautiful summer's evening and the band had been signing copies of the *Light* album at HMV in Princes Street earlier in the day. They were all at a table, along with Bruce Findlay. Rather sheepishly I told them that Jim had sent us round to join them. I was his message boy. Immediately they asked us to join them and Bruce informed me that Jim had enjoyed telling the story of my chance listening to the promo copy. I'd be lying if I said I didn't feel, well, kind of special. As did getting to listen to the stories told that evening and being bought several pints of Tennents lager by the members of one of the world's biggest bands at that time.

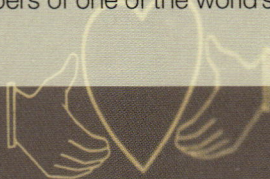

I would never go back to see Jim at Bridge House again. But I would see Simple Minds more times. I always wanted to get in touch, to remind him, that age old cliché of, 'Remember me, one of thousands?' But it never really seemed like a good idea. Kind of pointless. Until now, when I can add it to the other voices of those who have had some small, insignificant part in the story of Simple Minds.

### ALAN SANDERSON

As a 22-year-old, I decided to join the British Army. To help me get some personal time I bought a portable CD player and one of the first CDs I bought was a double CD of *Live in the City of Light*. Whilst I had heard many of the songs before, I had not been a fan and yet it soon became a daily ritual to finish training and then lie on my bed and listen to the whole album. It soon became obvious just what I had been missing.

### TONI SERRA

After reading good reviews about their music, I decided to buy Live in the City of Light and I have not stopped following them since. They're the band I've seen live, and the band I've seen the most times. They've never let me down.

### CARL PHILLIPS

My dad was an early fan of the Minds after seeing them support The Skids. When he got *Live in the City of Light* as a birthday present, I started to take notice too. The raw energy on that album hit my 14-year-old self square on the jaw. I listened to the album over and over on a headset, volume cranked up high and eyes closed, imagining I was in the crowd. It still gets the hairs on the back of the neck up.

### JEAN-SÉBASTIEN CHABANNES

*Live in the City of Light* is the album I have listened to most. 'Promised You a Miracle' with that final guitar solo? I still love to listen to it. And the version of 'New Gold Dream' that ends the show? Completely magic!

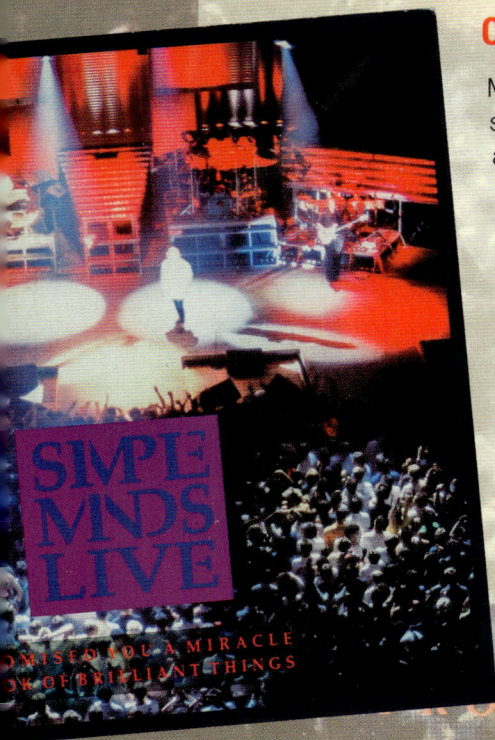

PROMISED YOU A MIRACLE
BOOK OF BRILLIANT THINGS

# VINCENT BARKER

## *Simple Minds road crew*

I'm a roadie. I've been doing this as a full-time job since 1980. I grew up in Australia, so was doing sound for bands out of school and then local top-40 bands, a very healthy circuit in Australia in the late 70s. You could earn a living in these small towns all over Australia as a house band playing top-40 tunes.

I was born in England but hadn't been there since we emigrated. I was 22 and didn't know anybody when I arrived in '83, but started going to pubs in London whenever there was a band playing and would strike up conversation with the sound guys, who I felt I had something in common with. Gradually I got a list of names of sound companies in London. This is well before the internet. We only really had Yellow Pages. I would ring them up every Wednesday and Friday and say, 'Have you got a job for me?' After a few weeks Dick Hayes, head of ML Executives, based at Shepperton Film Studios, invited me down to meet them. I ended up doing a lot of work for them and for Entec, also based at Shepperton. They also had a lot of rehearsal stages down there. The Who, Genesis and all these people would always be rehearsing down there. It was quite rock 'n' roll, a fun time to be a kid in London.

I did three main tours that year - Kim Wilde, Whitesnake and Supertramp - as part of the sound crew. I started with Simple Minds when they used ML Executives for 1983 Christmas shows in London and Glasgow. Then in Spring '84 they asked me to work for them, looking after Nick's keyboards, so I worked for them until 1991 then started with them again in 2011, just looking after keyboards and any music technology that centres around that. We've pretty much known each other since we were all about 23.

The first Mandela show wasn't that unusual for us at the time. It was just another big show with the added chaos of lots of different bands on. At some point somebody stole a bunch of keyboard equipment that belonged to Stevie Wonder and there was this panic going on after. During the show, somebody came up to me to see if they could borrow one of our keyboards for Dire Straits, because they'd been nicked as well. I think they managed to get all this gear back. They found out it was another band's crew. It was a memorable day, because of all the different bands that were on. There's no doubting that. The guest artists on stage with Simple Minds that night were quite special - Peter Gabriel, Jackson Browne, Daryl Hannah, Little Stephen and Richard Gere jumped up and sang backing vocals on 'Sun City'.

It's funny what you forget. For me, the Verona concert is more memorable in a lot of ways. I think it was filmed very well. They did an amazing job. It wasn't without its calamities on the night. All the barriers collapsed at one point.

At Milton Keynes Bowl, I remember one of Mick's keyboards having a technical fault as the music was playing for the band to go on stage. Our boss at the time, Dougie Cowan, had to get that fixed very, very quickly - the band were literally walking on stage. I remember doing *Saturday Night Live* in New York and our truck didn't make it through the border with all the equipment on, so there we all were for rehearsals and no equipment - people having to rapidly try and bring some in, ringing around various New York hire companies who could get equipment to us within the hour. I remember some weird glitch we had on a tour. All 60 of us on the crew had to go in early in the morning, open up every speaker box in the PA system and replace every high frequency drive in the PA because Charlie's guitar was acting as an aerial, putting this high frequency through the whole PA and blowing all the drivers at one gig.

I also remember a concert in Brazil where lots of fans organised between themselves to have cards with 'la la la la' written on them. They all held them up during the chorus for 'Don't You (Forget About Me)'. There were so many of them. Probably 80 people holding these cards up.

## ANNE HOOPER

In June 1988, finishing the end of my first year at secondary school, with Bros particularly popular among my peers, my older sister was watching the *Mandela 70th Birthday Tribute Concert* from Wembley. Hearing it, I wandered into the living room and sat with her to watch Simple Minds and remember being fixated with the song 'Mandela Day'. Being a rather geekish 12-year-old, I set about finding out lots about Mandela and Biko, which led to me taking history at GCSE, A-Level and degree level, eventually going on to become a history teacher. I really do think it can be traced back to that concert. When I teach apartheid in South Africa to Year 9 pupils each year, I always cite this story!

*Anne Hooper attributes her love of history to the song 'Mandela Day'*

# NIGEL LILL

When the Mandela concert at Wembley was announced I was 18, old enough to see Simple Minds for the first time. I hotfooted it to the ticket office with such excitement and came away ticket in hand. I had sleepless nights in the run-up, such was my excitement at the prospect. Hearing the opening chords of 'Waterfront' belting out across Wembley is one of the most euphoric feelings I've ever had. What a set and what a feeling. I've watched that gig on *YouTube* so many times. Oh, the memories.

I saw them a few more times and carried on following the band. *Good News from the Next World* got a lot of play. But then I seemed to lose interest. Something was no longer causing the same buzz. Maybe I was just getting old. Then out of the blue I saw the Minds were playing Sherwood Pines. Tickets were promptly purchased and I took my wife and eight-year-old son. It's a massively different venue to the stadia but that made no difference. I'd forgotten how much I love this band. As soon as the boys hit the stage, I was 18 again.

# LAWRIE LOWE

There are times in your life that something changes inside you, when you think for one moment you were put on this earth to live a certain feeling. For all these years it had only been a fun experiment. That moment came in 1988 for me.

I was already totally living the Simple Minds dream, listening to them at every spare moment and buying any memorabilia I could get my hands on. I was already a veteran of a few gigs and very proud to share my love for this band and what they represented in my life. But Mandela Day was about to take place and I was determined to be at the front of the stage to see my band play their part on this special day.

I had no idea who else were going to be playing - rumours were flying about U2, etc. But I just wanted to see Jim Kerr and the boys. The day started slow and there was a lull in the air. Something needed to pick up the momentum, but

*Jim at Wembley (photo by Laurie Lowe)*

nobody knew who was coming on. Then Denzel Washington and Emily Lloyd came on stage and they had an electric feeling about them. Denzel had such a powerful voice and his enthusiasm for the next act was huge. He started introducing the band that 'was totally committed to the cause that day' and both Denzel and Emily screamed, 'SIMPLE MINDS! SIMPLE MINDS!'

From that second, the crowd erupted. I was in the first few rows and, sad bugger that I am, started to jump to 'Waterfront' completely out of synch, just so Jim could see me. But I was within a huge group of Simple Minds fans from across the UK and the floor was falling away underneath me with the power of the surge around me. It was totally terrifying but also incredible! It was as if everyone in the stadium was there to prove Simple Minds ruled the live stage.

There were so many special moments, with 'Mandela Day' (the only song written by a band for the day, even though that was the task for all bands), 'East at Easter', 'Summertime Blues' with Johnny Marr, 'Sanctify Yourself' (which the TV tuned off for), and of course 'Sun City', which just had the most incredible musicians coming on stage to celebrate Little Steven's fantastic song. Who can forget Steven hugging Jim and shouting 'Simple Minds, Simple Minds', with the crowd chanting their name?

But the highlight of all highlights was 'Alive and Kicking'. It was just magical, Jim's voice was perfect, the band were brilliant and just a few little tweaks in Jim's singing drew the crowd in. The man of the people had made his true mark on the world stage. It was the Queen *Live Aid* moment of the day.

I was shattered, but on Cloud 9. I was oblivious to the crowd, but knew I was part of a huge energy and memory for thousands of fans. Simple Minds were truly alive and kicking.

## Belfast Child + Mandela Day + Biko

### AJAY MISTRY

I was rushing back from my Saturday job at Woolworth's in Leicester. I'd already missed quite a bit of the gig. I desperately wanted to ensure I was back home in time to see the Minds. Not only had there been huge media interest debating the rights, wrongs, lefts and rights of the concert, but I was proud to say my favourite band were right at the heart of it. Then there was the music... always the music. The playing of 'Mandela Day' on the radio in the weeks up to the gig was a thrill... remember, this is pre-internet, kids! And we hadn't caught sight of the band since the live album came out the previous year.

Cometh the evening, cometh the band. I recall the sheer thrill and excitement of Denzel Washington and Emily Lloyd's announcement and the pulse of 'Waterfront' kicking in. A band in peak form, the centrepoint being a towering, masterful version of 'Mandela Day'. Charlie's guitar solo - oh wow! Mesmerising stuff.

Whilst I will never forgive the BBC for interrupting their set for the news, it was by far the best performance of the day. And they probably didn't realise how many teenagers they educated back then!

3" CD (SMX CD3) – CASSETTE (SMXC3) – 12" (SMXT3)

# STREET FIGHTING YEARS

## BRENDAN QUINN

Simple Minds were the first band I could really identify with. The defining moment was 'Belfast Child'. Writing about my home city added another dimension to the song. It transcended the divide and hoped for better days to come. The Celtic feel to the song and the video really was a masterpiece.

## DANIELA SCHÄFER

A friend said to me, 'Let's go to a club tonight to dance'. She told me about a new band whose music she really wanted to hear. At some point they played 'Someone Somewhere (in Summertime)' and we went straight to the dance floor and then it was done for me. Their music still carries me through the day. I sometimes have days when I can't really get off to a good start, but if I listen to 'Belfast Child' I am amazed. These wonderful lyrics combined with this energetic and partly traditional music is a fantastic mix.

## MICK MACNEIL

When we did 'Belfast Child', I remember how tangled up we got with midi time code. We'd recorded the song, the acoustic guitar and Jim singing, and me playing the accordion in the living room in our house. And then we started building on the arrangement of that, which drifted quite a lot at times. We'd go up and down, and we got the dynamics. It was a fantastic way to play a song because it was just 'play the thing'. So that worked really well as far as arrangement and the dynamics would go. We set about recording 'Let It All Come Down' with a drum machine and programming tempo changes.

'BALLAD OF
SIMPLEMINDS
THE STREETS'

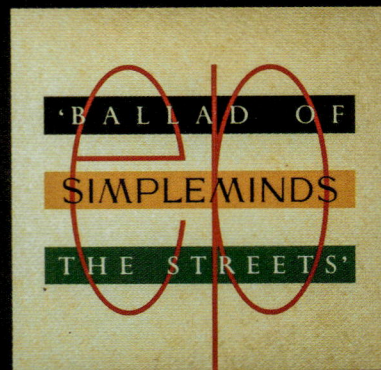

1. Belfast Child (Edit)
2. Belfast Child (Full length version)

Excerpt from 'BALLAD OF THE STREETS' EP

## NIK MARCY

One day I heard 'Mandela Day' on the radio. I immediately ran to a record store and bought my first Simple Minds tape. I was in love. Soon everyone who got in my red Renault 4 car knew I only listened to Minds tapes. I had a Simple Minds sticker attached to the back of it! I made little girls fall in love by giving away copies of Simple Minds albums. The music accompanied me in everything I did, going to school – and not going! – or going around with friends in the city, out to the sea and travelling by train, always with a big stereo cassette player on my shoulders.

## NICOLA DE CAL

I heard 'Mandela Day' for the first time on the radio and was totally struck by it. I loved that piano intro, the guitar arpeggio and Jim's voice. I was 15 and didn't have much money and couldn't afford the album so every Friday morning I went to my local record shop in search of the *Ballad of the Streets* EP. When I finally managed to buy it, I spent whole days listening to both 'Mandela Day' and the A-side, 'Belfast Child', so much so that I decided to copy it on a cassette so as not to damage the disc. That 45rpm disc is still here next to me, after 31 years. The world has changed in the meantime. Nelson Mandela is sadly gone, but the sense of freedom and struggle of 'Belfast Child' and 'Mandela Day' still resonates every time.

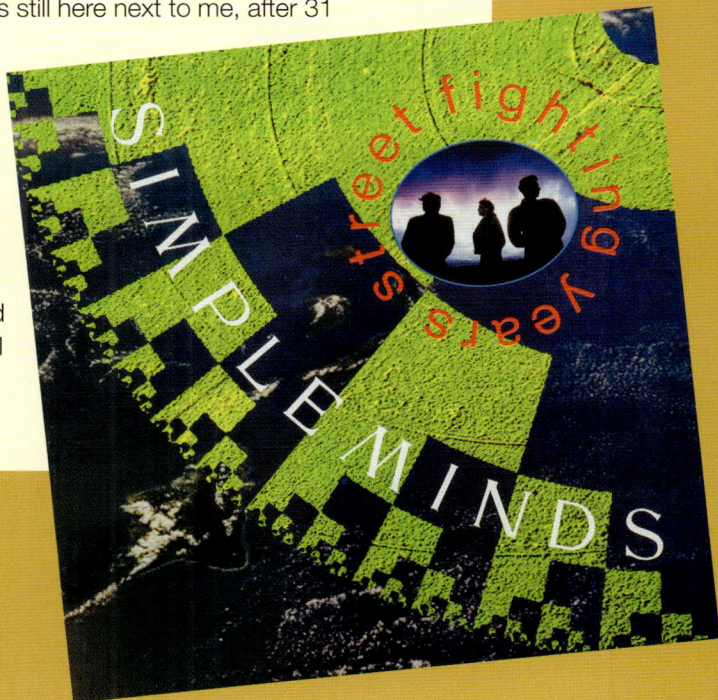

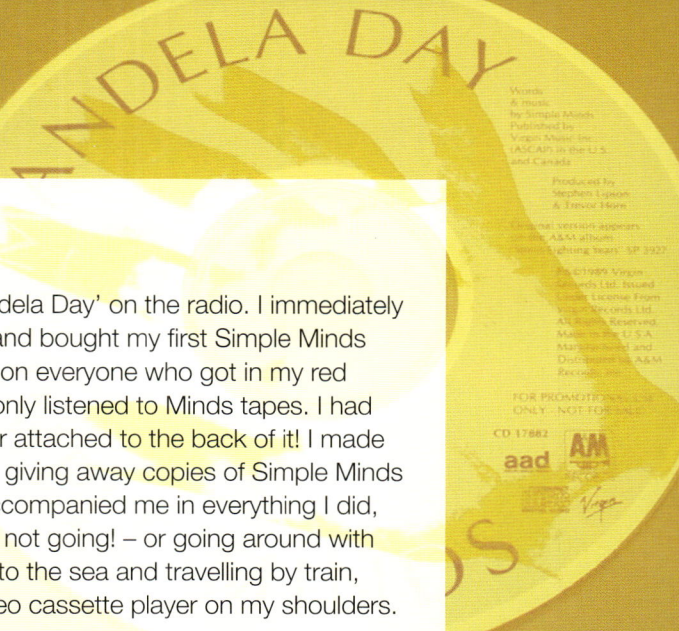

## MICK MACNEIL

On the final world tour at the end of the Eighties, we were actively involved in quite a few political causes, mainly with the African National Congress (ANC) around the release of Nelson Mandela, who was still in prison at that time. There were campaigns around the world exposing what the South African government was doing, incarcerating these political prisoners for years. We started getting quite involved in it. But I was conflicted about whether the people paying ticket money to come see a band were trying to get away from reality. Music is a form of entertainment where you buy a ticket, go see a band, and take yourself away from the difficulties of mundane things in your life. And try and enjoy yourself and (I didn't know) whether you were wanting to be fed political statements about prisoners of war.

Before that point, I would say 1987 or '88, I hadn't a clue who Nelson Mandela was or what the ANC were. I didn't know anything about South Africa, apartheid or anything like that. All I was doing was writing songs and tunes to play to people, to entertain them. So the idea of using the microphone as a political tool was new to me and I found it difficult to understand the importance of it. And how the little that we did was a big step in helping bring attention of the world to this cause. The irony about my reservations about being involved politically with the music is that we wrote this song for Mandela, 'Mandela Day'. I believe it turned into the best song that we had ever written.

## GIANPIERO DI GIACOMO

My favourite record is *Street Fighting Years*. I saw them live two times in Milan and Turin. My heart and my mind still get excited at the sounds of 'Let It All Come Down', 'Dolphins' and 'Sense of Discovery'.

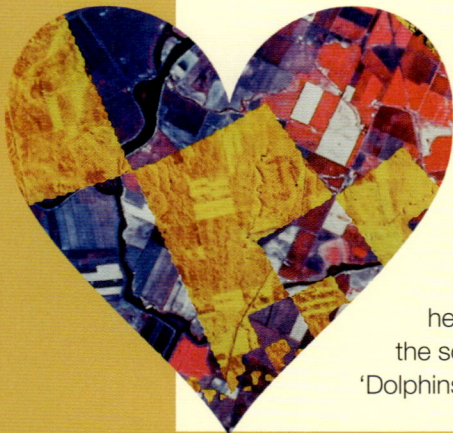

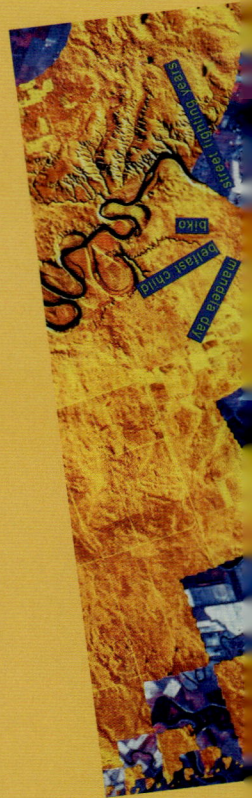

## MONAKO DIBETLE

In the summer of 2014, I was temporarily resident in a small town in Switzerland on a work secondment programme. Bored stiff and lonely in a foreign country, I took musical comfort in a small record bar on the outskirts of town and spent most of my evenings there with the old ponytailed owner from Montreal, whose name I never got to know.

Quixotic Records had a very impressive collection of 1960s American and African jazz. But also Eighties new wave, rock and punk rock – mostly used and old. I loved the vibe of the record bar and the sounds from the old analogue sound system. It reminded me of my township childhood in South Africa.

Rummaging through the used records one evening, I pulled out Simple Minds' *Street Fighting Years* on vinyl and was suddenly overtaken by emotions, as 'Belfast Child' and 'This is Your Land' crowded my mind. Noticing my excitement, Ponytail pulled out a box under his counter and bellowed, 'I am sure you'd like these too,' handing me three more Simple Minds records. In one evening, I found what I had been looking for in so many years. And I found it in a place I thought only sold jazz records, on a decaying sleepy corner of La Tour De Peilz.

Simple Minds is widely regarded as 'the white guy's band playing white guy's music' in South Africa, and not too many people of colour, at least in my circle, appreciate it as I do. Be that as it may, I know for fact, however, what 'Mandela Day' and 'Biko' can do to any South African irrespective of their race - a cry, a smile and a dance.

3" CD (SMX CD3) – CASSETTE (SMXC3) – 12" (SMXT3)

## JOT SHIRLEY

My Simple Minds journey began in 1985. I was 15 and was drawn in after hearing 'Don't You (Forget About Me), 'Alive and Kicking' and 'All the Things She Said' on the radio. I saved my pocket money and one Saturday morning caught a bus to Warwick and purchased *Once Upon a Time* on cassette from Woolworth's. I listened to it constantly the following week. Aside from the two singles from that album I wasn't too fussed by the rest. The following Saturday I returned to Woolworth's to request an exchange for something else. They refused and I was distraught, my pocket money wasted on something I didn't particularly like! I walked to my grandmother's and told her and she walked back with me to the store and shortly after I walked out with The Eurythmics' *Be Yourself Tonight*.

Two close friends, Jim and Guy, also had *Once Upon a Time* and told me I was missing out. A few weeks later I purchased it again and this time it stuck. I took it with me on a football tour to Blankenberge in Belgium and listened to nothing else during the hours of coach travel. That's when my love for the music created by the band was cemented.

I had to wait to see them live, but it was worth it. In 1988 I was working and was able to purchase a ticket to the *Nelson Mandela 70th Birthday Tribute* concert at Wembley. I travelled with Jim. The concert was mind-blowing. This was only my second concert, my first being Frankie Goes to Hollywood at the Odeon, Birmingham. This was on a totally different scale. I went home with fantastic memories of Sting, Stevie Wonder, and Dire Straits among many others, but it was Simple Minds that caused the most excitement for me.

---

## GARY BURNETT, AGE 18

*Loch Lomond, Scotland*

In 1988 you'd often find me at Balloch Marina on the banks of Loch Lomond. One day I had driven up to see my parents. They were out on the water in the cruiser they kept berthed there and I was due to meet them at the pontoon jetty before going to lunch on Inchmurrin, one of the islands.

Walking onto the jetty I couldn't believe my eyes when l saw Jim Kerr with someone I didn't recognise but later found out was his brother, Paul. Being a starstruck teen, what else could I do but go right up to the guy and say, 'Hey Jim, I'm a huge fan. Can I ask what you're doing

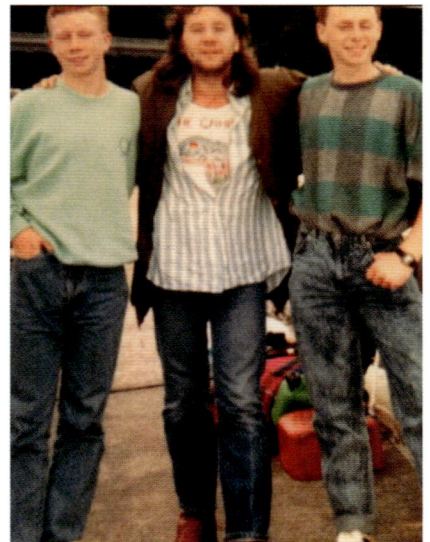

*Jim with Gary Burnett on the Bonny Banks of Loch Lomond*

around here? I've just been listening to you in the car on the journey up and I'm shocked just to be standing talking to the singer in my favourite band!'

They had come to Loch Lomond to investigate buying a boat and asked if I could advise on a few of the boats for sale in the yard. At this point my parents pulled up. Before my parents could ask, I blurted out that I was talking to Jim from Simple Minds and his brother Paul and they should join us for lunch at Inchmurrin in order to get a taste of boating on the loch. The only trouble was I hadn't asked Jim or Paul if they wanted to join us! They just said, 'Are you sure you don't mind?'

We arrived on the island and I had the most fantastic time chatting to Jim and Paul about the thrill of playing huge gigs like *Live Aid* and how much respect he had for Chrissie Hynde and his new relationship with Patsy Kensit. For me it was also a great insight into what it's like to walk into your local pub with someone hugely famous and so well respected. It was such a thrill and an absolute pleasure to take these two gentlemen out. It made me very passionate and patriotic about our mutual love of Scotland and the Bonny Banks.

## NATHAN JAMES VANDEN AVOND

Like many my age, my first exposure to Simple Minds was via *The Breakfast Club*. 'Don't You (Forget About Me)' was especially poignant as, a few weeks after the film's release, I was moving with my parents to a small town from an urban city, leaving all I knew behind. As I settled into new surroundings, I listened on repeat.

Months passed and I watched MTV religiously to feel connected to big city life. One day, I saw the video for 'Alive and Kicking' and felt overwhelming joy. While the song was amazing, it was made even more amazing as I recognised the gorgeous back-up singer as Robin Clark, who waved at me from the stage as she sang with the band Belouis Some, touring the States with Frankie Goes to Hollywood.

I immediately dove further into the world of Simple Minds, acquiring all the music I could at two small record stores in my area. Surprisingly, both stores carried imports, so I was able to find quite a bit. What I discovered was a band engaged in creating music with different styles other than just pop. When *Live in the City of Light* was released, I snatched that up immediately in the hopes that my back-up singer crush would appear on the record. And lo and behold, there she was!

Fast forward many years. When I got married, my friend reached out to several musicians she knew I loved and asked if they would create congratulatory wedding videos for us. She approached Robin, and she and her husband (the amazing Carlos Alomar) and their daughter Lea-Lorien reworked 'All the Things She Said', singing it for us in a surprise video. I'm not one who sheds tears often but broke down at this.

## LENA RETTORI

*Palasport
16 May 1989,
Florence, Italy*

Through the years, Simple Minds have always been a source of stamina and comfort, in both the good and bad moments of my life. Jim's voice is my safe harbour. I first saw the band live in my hometown

*Lena Rettori in the crowd in 2017 - pic Vince Barker*

of Florence at the start of the 1989 tour. I worked in a record shop after school. We got the first batch of tickets to sell so I bought the first ticket. I eventually managed to enter the venue with a pass and my much-treasured ticket was left unused. Ticket number 00001 now hangs proudly on my wall.

## STEPH CAVEGLIA

I was lucky enough to travel a lot in the Western Sahara, just south of the Moroccan coast. We'd drive at night, listening to *New Gold Dream*. What a sublime feeling, to savour 'Big Sleep' or 'Hunter and the Hunted' on the desert slopes in the Saharan night. Even the Moroccan soldiers who accompanied me loved this soaring music. These memories anchor in me a unique sense of happiness. I've followed the band all over the place and met Jim and Charlie several times. My most intense memory is meeting Jim's parents one night at a concert at Kings Tut's, Glasgow.

I don't know if it's a symbol or a miracle, but the name Simple Minds has remained written on a pole in my teenage street since 1985, despite the years, the weather, the storms, the works…. Magical!

# FABRIZIO RISTORI

## *Stadio Alberto Braglia 20 May 1989, Modena, Italy*

I've been following Simple Minds since the early 80s but remember the day I went into a record shop in Trento after school to buy the *Ballad of the Streets* EP as if it was yesterday. My first concert

*Simple Minds live in Florence - photos by Lena Rettori*

was in Modena in May 1989, and then Verona. Me and my friend Andrea are in the *Verona* video with the 'Wall of Sound' banner.

---

# CARLO MARIANI

## *Palatrussardi 22 May 1989, Milan, Italy*

One of my classmates gave me a tape of *Live in the City of Light* and it was love at first listen. I was 16 and had already listened to some of their songs

*Carlo Mariani was in the heart of the crowd in Milan - photo Vince Barker*

on the radio but that recording, those sounds, those live songs, left me breathless. In May '89 I saw them live for the first time on the *Street Fighting Years* tour. I remember excitedly waiting for the day, the Vespa trip to Milan with a friend, the long wait, the incredible atmosphere and, finally the curtain fell and Simple Minds appeared, a roar welcoming them on stage to the sound of 'When Spirits Rise'.

It was an incredible concert and unique emotion. Jim hypnotised the audience with his voice and charm while the rest of the band blew up the Palasport with the music. That night, I had so much adrenaline pumping, I couldn't sleep!

## DOMENICO CAPOBIANCO

*Palazzo dello Sport*
*25 & 26 May 1989, Rome, Italy*

I heard Simple Minds for the first time in 1986, age 12, thanks to my friend and schoolmate Antonio. Living in a small village in southern Italy, we didn't have so many fancy places to go, so spent hours and hours listening to *New Gold Dream*, *Sparkle in the Rain* and *Once Upon a Time* and started to wonder, 'What can we do to be part of this magic? Why don't we try to recreate those sounds and atmosphere?' I started to play keyboards, Antonio tried singing and in a few months we put together a cover band, rehearsing 'Someone Somewhere (in Summertime)' because of its apparently basic structure. Very soon that was followed by 'Don't You', 'Waterfront' and many others.

Three years later, with the release of *Street Fighting Years*, we finally had the chance to see our idols play live. Rome was the closest place they were playing, but it was still 500km away and we were still 15-year-old village boys. How were we going to get there? Our parents finally decided, the day before the gig, to drive us. We arrived in the early afternoon at the Palaeur. There were *Street Fighting Years* tour billboards everywhere!

But - a minor detail - we went without tickets, so our parents started to negotiate with local 'bagarini'. We finally got our precious (and way expensive) tickets and entered the venue. It was then goosebumps all over from the very first bagpipes note of 'When Spirits Rise', the white curtain dropping for Malcolm Foster's entrance with his acoustic bass. It was an emotional storm from start to finish.

## DAVID IAPAOLO

I was listening to the radio when I was struck by a song, 'Up on the Catwalk'. I didn't know who the group was. I still remember that fantastic melody combined with the amazing force of that song to leave an indelible trace on my soul. I planned to see the band in question in Rome in February 1986 but a combination of pneumonia and my parents not giving me permission meant the *Street Fighting Years* tour was the first time I got to see them. In 1998 I met the whole band except for Jim in Pesaro in Italy.

There were no smartphones then so the memory is only captured in my mind. In 2017, during the *Acoustic* tour, I took my daughter Jasmin to Rome when she was only three (the youngest person to attend a Simple Minds concert?). During 'New Gold Dream', Jim and I danced for a few seconds while I held her in my arms.

---

# GERD VAN POUCKE

*Vorst Nationaal*
*4 June 1989, Brussels, Belgium*

When *Street Fighting Years* came out in 1989 I was eager to see Simple Minds for the first time. I went in a group of five; Piet, Tony, Filip, Tim and myself gathering at the venue at 1pm. By 3pm, there were about 20-30 fans outside. We had already done our recon and knew that below the venue there was parking for a supermarket next door, which gave access to the venue itself. Around 3.30pm the tour bus arrived, drove down to that parking lot and the band got out. We were screaming, waving, etc. Security held us back, but suddenly Jim waved us down. For 10 minutes he signed autographs and had some pictures taken (my pictures came out black, so no lasting memory there) and had a chat. For me, a 16-year-old kid, this was amazing. This guy actually talks and is friendly. Next, we sneaked into Vorst Nationaal to listen to a soundcheck. At one point Jim, walking around in the arena, walked straight to the curtains we were hiding behind. It felt as if he looked right at us and was going to expose us, but nothing happened.

The concert itself I still see and hear in my head, from the start with 'Theme for Great Cities' playing. The sound was very loud and later I read they forgot to turn off the heating in the arena. It was so hot. They played 'When Spirits Rise' then the real start with 'Street Fighting Years'. Those first bass notes still send shivers down my spine. Next came 'Wall of Love', 'Mandela Day', 'This is Your Land', 'Soul Crying Out' and then… the place exploded with 'Waterfront'. I had to get out from the front. I was exhausted from all that had happened, so watched the rest of the concert from the side. At the end of this magnificent day I even got myself a setlist, a precious prize.

I have so many memories, including Flanders Expo in Gent in 1991, where we slept in our car next to the venue. We had no clue where Nijmegen – the next gig – was so decided to follow the tour bus the next morning. There was one other car doing the same. I guess the band must have had a funny time watching this car with waving guys behind the bus for two to three hours. On arriving in the city outskirts, I drove through four to five red lights trying to keep up. We went into the band's hotel, sat at a table, drank something and watched some of the band eat together. Then we were clever enough to ask for directions to the stadium.

At Dublin in 1995, I was studying there at the time. For three days in a row we cycled from Blackrock campus to the Point Depot. The first day we listened to a soundcheck. The second day we were allowed inside by Mark Schulman, the drummer at the time. My friend Koen and I sat there for hours. We watched and heard 'Let the Children Speak' 10 to 15 times, 'Room' and so many songs. Patsy Kensit passed by to say 'hi' to Jim. It was amazing to hear the band rehearse over and over to perfection. The concert itself was one of the best ever, with a brilliant setlist and a superb audience.

In 1997 in Antwerp, I did two *Nights of the Proms*. What made this special was that I was one of a handful of fans who got to do a short interview with Jim live on radio. All I really remember is I had to go first and Jim took me aside while a song was playing to ask me about the internet, how I got info about the band, how many times I would look at a website, and so on.

For Brussels in 2002, my friend Koen won another radio interview with Jim and when we came into the studio, Jim saw us and said, 'Oh no, not those two again.' Jim explained to the presenter he'd seen us a few times and would reverse the interview and ask *us* the questions. He started with, 'Which colour of shirt was I wearing last time in Brussels, black or blue?' We both looked baffled and guessed wrong, to which he replied jokingly, 'You call yourself true fans when you don't even know the colour of my shirt?' That was a funny moment.

Also in 2002 in Taormina, the 'white tribe' concert with my wife to-be Katy was a gift from my parents for my 30th birthday - four days in Sicily. One of the best concerts ever, seeing Jim on his small motorbike around the city, sitting in the restaurant where the whole band with friends was eating after the concert, together with 25 other fans simply watching them eat. Creepy and funny! There was a brilliant vibe around the town those days, difficult to describe. The concert ranks in my top three.

Gent in 2005 was also memorable. It was the day my grandfather was buried. I lost my parents the year before. My eldest son Thomas was born a month before. So there I was, dressed in black. It was a weird experience, but felt really good. I only had one ticket as it was invitation or winners only, but Eddy Duffy allowed my wife Katy to come in. The concert basically gave me hope. That's definitely one I will not forget, as it was in my family's hometown.

# HANS PARDON

1989 was my first Minds gig at Forest National in Brussels. I bought the concert ticket in the basement of a famous record store in Antwerp and remember the gig as if it were yesterday. I've lots of memories of gigs, of places I discovered through my Simple Minds travels and friends I've made. There's a special relationship between the band and fans and I hope Simple Minds' musical life can continue for many years to come.

*Hans first saw Simple Minds in Belgium in 1989 and met Jim in a hotel in Zurich in 2016*

# GERALDINE TUCH

I was five in 1985 when 'Don't You (Forget About Me)' came out and my big brother Fabrice and sister-in-law Mylène were teaching me to sing it. In 1989, they took me to my first concert. I was nine. I'll never forget that evening. Being in the stands but quite close to the stage, Jim spotted me very quickly and paid me a lot of attention. He sang while pointing his finger at me. It was magical. At the end I was able to meet the band, get an autograph and have my photo taken with Jim.

Since then I've seen them in Europe and the USA – I think 95 times altogether. I've made new friends and had the privilege of meeting the band, the staff (Jim's bodyguard Kenny nicknamed me 'my crazy' and Ged Malone nicknamed me 'Baby's Simple Minds'). Today, I'm 40 but still look at Jim through the eyes of a little girl.

*Geraldine Tuch aged 5 with Jim*

---

# MARTIN HANLIN

## *Forest National, 6 June 1989, Brussels, Belgium*

Jim invited The Silencers to join the *Street Fighting Years* tour. We'd just released our second album, *A Blues for Buddha*, and it was doing really well in Europe. We were getting lots of good press and the radio play was picking up.

Every night we were winning more fans with a tight 35-minute set of eight or nine songs. Simple Minds were playing sets that last easily two to two-and-a-half hours. As the tour progressed, their songs stretched out and their performance became richer and more developed in the live setting.

We pulled into Brussels for a three-night stint at the Forest National arena.

*Martin Hanlin's AAA pass for the Street Fighting Years tour*

Everything for The Silencers was going from strength to strength. The tour was really stretching us as a live band and watching the Minds play each night inspired us to improve.

The opening night we played really well and even got an encore. The crowd reaction was incredible, and we left the stage happy and exhausted. I quickly got changed so I could get back out to watch the Minds set. I liked to watch their performances to see what I could learn. And of course, first and foremost, I was a big fan of the band.

As usual, the Minds played a great show, the fans so into it that the hall was a cacophony of noise from the first song to the last encore.

After the show Jim found me sitting rather dejectedly on a flight case back stage.

'What's up?' he asked.

'Every night we give our all and the crowd shows their appreciation,' I said. 'Which of course I'm thankful for.'

'So what's your problem, then?' he asked.

'All you need to do is take off your jacket three songs in, and the crowd goes fucking crazy,' I said. 'Where's the justice in that?'

At that moment, I realised that sometimes you just had to accept you're only an opening act.

---

## MATS KALLMYR

*Stockholm Stadion*
*9 June 1989, Stockholm,*
*Sweden*

I went to see Simple Minds in Stockholm in 1989 and stood on the left side. A blonde woman stood next to me. I was tall and she asked if I could take some pictures for her, which I did. I asked if it was possible to send copies if they were good quality. I gave her my address on an old business card and she promised to send them to me. They never arrived.

EMA proudly present
**SIMPLE MINDS**
+ special guests
**STOCKHOLMS STADION**
**Fredag 9 juni 1989 kl 16.00**
Publikinsläpp kl 13.00
Burkar, flaskor, kameror, bandspelare förbjudet att medföra.
Fotografering och bandupptagning förbjudet.
Konserten genomförs oavsett väderlek.
PLANEN ingång   Klocktornet
Pris 180:– + förköpsavgift        Nr   0760

On Facebook, a few months ago, I recognised the exact photos I took at that time. I checked who posted them and realised it was the woman who stood next to me back in 1989. I contacted her and, amazingly, she remembered me … and sent me the photos, 30 years later!

# STEPHAN MEYER

*Alsterdorfer Sportshalle*
*12 June 1989, Hamburg,*
*West Germany*

I had a taped copy of *Once Upon a Time*. I bought *Live in the City of Lights*. With *Street Fighting Years* it was clear. I had to see them live. Tickets were purchased by phone after countless redials. I was in my final year of vocational education and having already bought tickets, we were informed that our final oral examination would be held the following day. Bad luck, but nothing could stop me from attending.

On gig day, my girlfriend (now my wife) and a friend and I drove the 120km to Hamburg. We strolled through the city, passing Radio Hamburg where we spotted barriers at the entrance. Later we learned that Simple Minds had been there to give a live interview. We missed them by minutes.

We managed to get into the venue early and stood in front of the stage. Lights off, music on, curtain down and there we go! Malcolm Foster in front of us and the band on fire. I managed to catch Malcolm's plectrum. What a night!

After the show we drove the 120km back home and by 1am I was asleep. The examination came and I failed and had to go to school for another six months. It was worth it for every minute of that concert.

*Stephan Meyer saw the Minds in Hamburg*

# TOMMY BEHLE

*Waldbühne*
*14 June 1989, Berlin,*
*West Germany*

I still remember the summer of 1985. I was 16 and Simple Minds came to my consciousness with 'Don't You (Forget About Me)' at *Live Aid* from Philadelphia. I was seriously ill in

*Tommy Behle was seriously ill in hospital when he discovered Simple Minds*

hospital then, with blood poisoning caused by a motorbike accident in Mallorca, and doctors couldn't find out what the problem was.

On the positive side, being that ill means that all your wishes are fulfilled and my mother presented me with a copy of *Once Upon a Time* when I could finally leave hospital and return home. I remember being a bit disappointed when I found out 'Don't You' wasn't on the album. But *Once Upon a Time* led me to Simple Minds. I still remember getting goosebumps when I first heard 'Alive and Kicking', 'Ghost Dancing' and 'Sanctify Yourself'.

My personal live highlight with Simple Minds was a sold-out Waldbühne in Berlin with 22,000 spectators in 1989 on the *Street Fighting Years* tour. Jim invited the whole crowd back to the Bristol Hotel Kempinski at Kurfürstendamm. I don't know if anyone accepted his invitation - I was a bit too shy.

---

# OLIVER SCHWEITZER

## *Westfallenhalle*
## *16 June 1989, Dortmund, West Germany*

I first heard Simple Minds with 'Someone Somewhere (in Summertime)' on a German radio station. When I bought *New Gold Dream* and started playing that, my parents were glad to finally hear something different to Diana Ross' 'Upside Down' and Visage's 'Fade to Grey'. I listened to *New Gold Dream* almost every day. I had to enjoy it for a long time because my age didn't allow me to think about going to a concert.

My friends at that time were listening to Spandau Ballet, Duran Duran and various German artists so I had no choice but to listen to Simple Minds at home on my beloved stereo equipment or record the records on cassette then listen to them on my Sony Walkman on the road, which became my true friend.

When *Live Aid* happened, I was going on holiday with my parents to southern Germany on a hot Saturday and the concert was played on the radio for the whole eight-hour drive. My parents had to really love me. When I arrived at the holiday apartment, I immediately turned on the TV so I didn't miss a minute more. That day and the following night I didn't care about southern Germany, the mountains, the forests, the landscape. I absorbed the breathtaking performance of Simple Minds and was in a trance. I was in such a trance that a big spider was moving in my room, which my father removed for me when he brought in my food, because spiders are not my best friends!

It was the highlight of my summer in 1989 to finally see Simple Minds on stage. I was impressed by such talented musicians with so much energy, clearly enjoying playing. It was an unforgettable atmosphere and the Westfallenhalle shook. I'd never seen such a long concert. They gave everything for almost three and a half hours.

My first Simple Minds live experience went by way too fast. I was really pleased that they played additional concerts that summer. For me it was Dortmund (again) and the open-air show at Loreley, with fantastic weather and a great atmosphere on a late summer evening above the Rhine. An unforgettable experience for me and my friends, by now also under the Simple Minds spell.

30 years after the release of *Live in the City of Light*, I got the heart, hand and crown logo tattooed on my right hand.

## PHIL MORRIS

I first saw Simple Minds at Pinkpop in 1983. They were great. But the game-changer was the *Street Fighting Years* tour. Me and my pal Glen, a big Pink Floyd fan, decided to go to Germany as the Minds and the Floyd were there within days of each other. Simple Minds were first. The venue was bouncing, even during the double-intros, giving me time to get to the front. 'Street Fighting Years' kicked in and the place erupted. Simple Minds had arrived. They'd grown as a live unit and sounded fresh and exciting. Two and a half hours went in a blink. Pink Floyd in Cologne was two days later and Glen had to admit that Simple Minds were much more entertaining. So much more in fact that we went again to see them in Cardiff! Nothing has come close to that tour, although *Acoustic* was close.

Freitag, 16. Juni 1989 · 20.00 Uhr
**DORTMUND · WESTFALENHALLE**
MAREK LIEBERBERG PRESENTS
**STREET FIGHTING YEARS**
**SIMPLE MINDS LIVE '89**
**Vorverkauf: DM 35,–**
zzgl. Vorverkaufsgebühr, inkl. 7 % MwSt.
**Abendkasse: DM 40,–**
inkl. 7 % MwSt.
**KEIN SITZPLATZANSPRUCH!**
VA-Nr. 08
15150
**Wichtiger Hinweis siehe Rückseite!**

## MARK FRENDO

I was more interested in the music coming out of London clubs than BBC Radio 1. Until one night at Trax Camden Palace, the DJ faded out one track and faded in some notes that were familiar to me. What sort of DJ fades out like that? If they can't beat match, then they have no business in the booth. I knew those notes, but what was it? It was The Corporation of One's attempt at 'Theme for Great Cities'. If the two tracks were living things, they would share more than 99% of their DNA.

A few weeks later, in the same club the DJ was going through a tried and tested set. The music faded out and in came those familiar notes. Except, this time it was different. 'This is Simple Minds', somebody said. Heads tilted and ears cocked trying to discern the truth, the beat dropped and the lights came on. We were all treated to the sight of 1,000 sweaty bodies in sodden t-shirts, grinning and gurning to their wild-eyed abandonment. One loose bolt and the roof would have disappeared into the night. This was not the Corporation of One, this was Simple Minds, but it *was* 'The Real Life' and we were living it.

Simple Minds were touring Europe at the same time as I was due to be InterRailing. Dortmund's Westfalenhalle was made for me. I called the box office. I was relieved that my call was answered by a fluent English speaker. I couldn't buy a ticket from the UK but a ticket would be left for me at the box office. I should arrive when it opened at 6pm and pay then.

The night before the gig, my InterRailing chums and I decided to spend a night in Amsterdam. When we arrived at our hostel the vibe was not great. I was fearful if I slept in this place if my money, passport and - most importantly - my body would be safe? All it took was a few glances for us to take our leave. We chose to get pissed and pass out in the railway station until our train arrived at 5am. This would have worked well if the police didn't come around at midnight and kick me out of the huge locker I had sheltered in. We were out on the street.

On the cold pavement, the next five hours looked pretty bleak until one of our number offered to stay awake and guard our stuff. When I mention that the person in question was affectionately known as 'Alky Gary' you'll understand my misgivings. But we, our stuff and our bodies made it safely through until 5am and we were on the train to Germany.

At 6pm I was first in line at the box office. The staff member was as fluent in English as I was in German. I wrote my name down, repeatedly said 'ticket', pointed to myself. The lady got impatient, asked me to move aside. I didn't, and she asked the next person to come forward. Short of shouting 'ticket!' all night long, my only option was to formulate a new plan. A tout!

I spied one and asked if he had any standing tickets. He quoted me four times the face value. I scoffed. 'Ah, you'd like the ticket for less money, ja?' 'Less money, yes,' I responded. This haggling lark was easy. 'Go and find von!' He laughed.

Over the next hour I watched as the tickets in his grasp dwindled. It was time. I asked again, fully expecting the price to have risen, but he was true to his original quote. I paid up.

Simple Minds entered the stage to a recorded version of 'Theme for Great Cities'. I can't recall the setlist, but the ticket was worth every extra Deutsche Mark I had paid. I bumped into two Brits. It turned out they had driven to the gig and their route home passed my hotel. I confidently asked for a lift. 'No.' What about all that Brits abroad sticking together stuff I'd heard about? They didn't even try to make an excuse, like they had a two-seater or something.

Post gig I tried to retrace my steps back to the hotel. My path was crossed by a black cat. I'm not superstitious, it just jumped out with a 'meeow!' and I nearly crapped myself. I've never attended a gig abroad since.

# FRÉDÉRIC BOUTIN

*Palais Omnisports de Paris-Bercy*
*19 June 1989, Paris, France*

I was 17 and I went with my cousin. We lived 50km north-east of Paris and went there by train and metro. In 1989 coming by train to Paris, despite the short distance, was a real expedition for provincials like us. We had never come down to Paris by train without our parents. What a great concert, with songs like 'Mandela Day' and 'Belfast Child'. To this day, *Street Fighting Years* remains my favourite album.

---

# LAURENT PRUNIER

I was living in the provinces in France when my parents bought me a Sony hifi system with one of the very first CD players for my 14th birthday. One of my first CDs was *Sparkle in the Rain*. It was a few years before my dream of seeing Simple Minds live finally came true. And the day after the concert I was walking near the Arc de Triomphe and bumped into Jim on the street corner. What a great moment! I got his autograph. I've seen Simple Minds many times since, listening to their music for 35 years, enjoying it as much now as the first time I heard it.

---

# JOT SHIRLEY

Having seen them at the *Nelson Mandela 70th Birthday Tribute* at Wembley, I now had the concert bug and my next venture was on the *Street Fighting Years* tour, again with my Jim. We travelled on an organised trip by coach. The trip was fraught with problems. Our coach broke down on the motorway and we had to wait for another to collect us. We arrived late to our hotel to meet our rep, who would furnish us with the tickets, only to find they'd left for Bercy. We arrived late at the venue but eventually met the rep and got our tickets, but our positions were taken and we found ourselves in the upper tier towards the back. The Silencers had already started their set. Despite the issues the concert was stunning. This was my first full Simple Minds live gig! It flew by in a flash. From the moment 'When Spirits Rise' commenced and the band entered the stage until the closing chords of 'Alive and Kicking' it was truly magical. We returned to the coach and everyone was buzzing, despite being shattered from our journey. The coach driver then reversed the coach in to a wall and smashed the back window. It was a chilly drive back to the hotel!

---

# DARREN WILLIAMS

The first time I was able to go and see them I was 18 in Paris. I went with my best friend from school. It has to rank as one of the best concerts ever.

My first experience of Simple Minds was in 1984 when an older friend gave the 13-year-old me a cassette of 12-inch remixes. Within the first few listens I was hooked.

That Christmas I got *Sparkle in the Rain* on cassette, which I listened to religiously on my Walkman in the car on family trips to London. Soon my bedroom walls were covered in posters. At that age, I was still getting over my dad leaving us and, strange as it seems, I looked up to Jim as a father figure. Their music got me through this tough time. My memories in the next few years are of collecting everything I could,

*Darren Williams got the VIP treatment at London's O2 in November 2015 and met the band in Colchester in 2018*

listening to the first three albums and wondering if it was the same band and getting ribbed at school for wearing t-shirts and hearing 'wonder why they are called that?' But nothing was going to put me off the music that was in me already. And I'd have the last laugh when nearly all these friends ended up going to see my favourite band.

I remember sitting in college with my copy of the *NME* with Jim on the front and the band at number one. I was so happy.

I've been to so many great concerts, have so many amazing memories and have taken so many people to see Simple Minds along the way, including my mum, brother, wife, kids, work friends, etc. I've briefly met Jim and Charlie in the last few years and thanked them for everything and told them they should never stop, which I'm sure they won't. This band have been such a massive part of and soundtrack to my life. Other music has come and gone but Simple Minds music has always excited me, and will forever more. I'm so glad that as a 13-year-old boy getting into music I chose this band to pin to my chest. It's the best decision I ever made.

## WAYNE LEE LEBARON

I'm Simple Minds' biggest fan. Their performances and music has got me and countless others through some tough times. Their heart in hand symbolism is colossal. Thanks for the world-famous soul food music!

## ALEX GROH, AGE 15

*Eisstadion*
*26 June 1989, Mannheim, West Germany*

I became aware of Simple Minds in 1988 through Stephanie, the older sister of my friend Christoph, who I thought was pretty great. When I heard *Live in the City of Light* for the first time, I became completely addicted to the band. I listened to the whole of the back-catalogue. And when *Street Fighting Years* was released, I feverishly awaited the tour. My father drove Christoph and I to Mannheim because my mother was afraid to take us because of the crowds. My father wasn't bothered about going. The concert was incredible. For The Silencers' set, our pants fluttered from the bass and our hearts fluttered with anticipation!

Then the intro, the thunder, the curtain fell and the rest was pure ecstasy. Two hours later we met up again with my father, who insisted I make him a Simple Minds mixtape with 'Biko' on it at least twice. Many concerts have followed - alone, with friends and with my parents. I proposed to my wife with a Claddagh ring. My daughter was born exactly 26 years to the day after the concert in Mannheim.

# SØREN W ESKILDSEN

'Belfast Child' on the radio for the first time. Jim grabbing my hand during the Skanderborg gig in '97. The 'Street Fighting Years' bass line pumping to open the 1989 gigs. The *5x5* tour reinvigorating the band. Meeting Mel G and Eddie D backstage at Denmark's *Green Concert series*. The disappointment when *Our Secrets are the Same*, an overlooked gem, wasn't released. The excitement when *Black &White 050505* hit the shelves, putting SM on track to their current triumphant journey, album-wise and concert-wise. For the last 30 years, Simple Minds have been the most important band in my life. Barrowland stars and more. In dreams and beyond.

---

# THIERRY G

I discovered their music via my brother. We have listened to the 45s, tapes, CDs, so many great moments. We have played their music all over Europe, in our camper van on the road, on the beaches, on the sea and under the sky.

---

# WENDY BROWN

I purchased tickets for me and my friend Heidi. Not particularly good seats but seats all the same. My friend's boyfriend was a roadie and a friend of his was working this event. The friend came over to us while we were waiting patiently in line and handed us two backstage passes. We were beside ourselves with excitement!

As we were ushered into the arena, we sashayed past the thong of waiting fans and took our new seats for the evening, in a box to the side of the stage. It was a fabulous concert – and just when we thought it couldn't get any better, we were invited to the after-show party.

We didn't meet Jim because Patsy Kensit was waiting to whisk him away straight after the show. But we still enjoyed the party. We mingled and enjoyed a drink or two. By the end of the evening we were exhausted and went to freshen up in the toilets. When we came out, the whole place was in darkness – everyone had gone and all doors were locked.

We eventually found a fire exit door which led directly into the arena car park, where the tour coaches and lorries were parked up overnight. We wandered around trying to find a gate, which we did – but it was locked with a huge padlock. Then the (heavy) rain started. My friend started to rock one of the tour coaches gently back and forth, hoping someone would let us in. Eventually someone did, reluctantly, and we slept peacefully until early morning when the arena car park opened and we slipped quietly away from our extended night out, proudly sporting SM t-shirts we had purchased the night before, and subsequently finding that we didn't have enough money for our train fare back to Oxford.

## VAL SAWBRIDGE

*Olympiahalle*
*1 July 1989, Munich, West Germany*

Where do I begin? I've had a love affair with Simple Minds since I can't remember. 'Don't You (Forget About Me)' was the song that truly got me hooked but I have always loved Simple Minds' music. I love how it has evolved and each time has surprised and excited me. The first time I saw them in concert, my husband and I were travelling Europe and couldn't believe it when we discovered they were playing at the Olympic Stadium in Munich. Amazingly, we managed to get tickets. That concert is etched in my memory forever. I remember we caught our train home from the stadium feeling elated and happy, a feeling that lasted for days. Since then I've seen them every time they have come to my fair city of Perth, Western Australia. I really can't get enough of their live performances. Jim Kerr has an amazing voice and I love the way he moves around the stage. I've seen them perform six times, and hope to make it seven very soon. I truly cannot get enough. Their music is like no other and I'll never get tired of listening.

269

## JAN JOCHUMSEN

*Hallenstadion*
*2 July 1989, Zurich, Switzerland*

Bands come and go and music hits you and in time fades away again, but what started with 'Love Song' turned out to be a long-term relationship with a band that's filled my home, my life and my heart with joy, love and songs ever since. My first concert was part of the *Street Fighting Years* tour, and kind of coincidence that Zürich became the first place I experienced Simple Minds live. Two days before the tour was announced, I bought an InterRail ticket and immediately saw I couldn't attend the Danish concert. Fortunately, my sister - working in Switzerland - saved the day when I paid her a visit on my ride through Europe and she bought tickets for the show. I remember them playing 'Gaelic Melody', while 'Let It All Come Down' and 'Belfast Child' before the encores gave me chills.

Since then I've attended a lot of concerts all over Denmark. The *Walk Between Worlds* concert in Vega, Copenhagen on 20 February 2018 still stands as a fantastic, unique experience. Choosing to play a complete album followed by a 'best of' set was a brilliant idea. I remember it as clearly as a summer sky.

## ALBERT MONFORTE

*Velodrom D'horta*
*11 July 1989, Barcelona, Spain*

The concert in Barcelona at the Velòdrom was the first big gig I went to. Simple Minds being my favourite band, it's a special memory. It was so unreal, my favourite band just metres away from me. I still get goosebumps thinking about it. I went with friends, one of whom knew very little about Simple Minds. When The Silencers finished their half-hour set, he thought that was the end of the show, complaining about Simple Minds having come on at a lousy time, offering poor value for money!

## MOISÉS PRENDES

The first time I saw them was at Barcelona in 1989. But that's not my best Simple Minds memory. In 1995, listening to the radio, I learnt they were in Madrid to promote *Good News from the Next World*. At 2am I left Barcelona for Madrid, driving five hours on my own to the hotel I guessed they were staying in. And they were! Very busy with the promotion, Jim and Charlie just had time to chat for 10 minutes and sign album covers. But the Virgin guy said, 'We have no time now but tonight we're having a dinner at this restaurant with all the media. You can come if you want.' I drove five hours home, picked up my girlfriend and drove another five hours back to Madrid. We had the most amazing experience ever, dining with Jim and Charlie. In fact, we ate nothing because of our excitement. After that, we went to a restaurant on our own to celebrate the night, and the next day drove five hours home again, exhausted but SO happy.

## HAROLD ROUMIMPER

*An Amsterdam Restaurant*
*13 July 1989, Amsterdam, The Netherlands*

It was 1989 and I worked in a restaurant in Amsterdam where Simple Minds came a few times for dinner. One evening Charlie was smoking something you can easily buy in Amsterdam. Since management knew I was a big Simple Minds fan they asked me to go up to him and ask him to refrain from smoking this particular kind of cigarette. A bit nervously I went up and said, 'Sir, I'm afraid you can't smoke this here.' Charlie was really nice and apologised a thousand times. He asked my name and wanted to know if I had tickets for the concert on 30 July in Rotterdam. I said, 'I have ring tickets.' Why did I say that? Perhaps he was about to say 'come backstage and watch the concert from there.' Why didn't I say, 'I am your biggest fan ever since 1982'? Instead, I walked off and let them have dinner. At night after finishing work, I was walking in front of the American Hotel to get the bus when suddenly someone called my name. 'Hey, Harold!' It was Charlie, my new friend, and his pals Neil, Jim and Mel. Charlie and I started talking while fans recognised the other lads. Charlie then asked, 'You know any Blues bars around here?' I said, 'Of course I do.' 'Great,' he said, and started to assemble the rest of the guys. I was standing there, thinking, 'Jah man, my heroes. I am going to have a drink with my heroes.' I think it was Neil who then said. 'Nah, guys, I'm gonna go back to the room. Tomorrow is the concert.' Charlie agreed to do the same. We said goodbye and walked off. No backstage concert, no drinks with my heroes. Could have been unforgettable.

## ANITA DIJKMAN

*Feijenoord Stadion*
*14 July 1989, Rotterdam, The Netherlands*

I started listening to Simple Minds after I heard 'Don't You' on the radio, then bought *Once Upon a Time*. My first show was at the Feyenoord Stadium and, a month

*Anita Dijkman met Jim backstage at Loreley*

later, in Ahoy Rotterdam. I've since seen them many times in the Netherlands, Belgium, France, Germany, England and Scotland. Every time I'm at a Simple Minds concert there's always a song or a moment which makes me smile, with so much energy in the crowd and in the band. The longer you go to concerts you eventually know which are the better venues, where the sound is much better, and 2018 at Slessor Gardens, Dundee was a great concert. Going backstage at the Rockpalast at Loreley with a friend was memorable. And I saw Charlie after the Usher Hall concert in Edinburgh in 1995. I've met some great friends through Simple Minds. Through my friends and the band I've discovered beautiful Scotland. In my spare time I love to listen and sing along with so many bands. But Simple Minds is the one with a special place in my heart.

## CHRIS VERHEUS

My first acquaintance with Simple Minds was a copy of *New Gold Dream* on a TDK SA90 cassette. I didn't really like it. I was more a fan of Vangelis and Jean-Michel Jarre. Then I heard 'Themes for Great Cities' at a party and wow, what a song! I listened to that cassette again. Then I was sold. My first concert was July 1989 at the Kuip in Rotterdam. I've now seen them 15 times. Every performance is a surprise, from an evening of rock like the *5x5* tour to a fantastic *Acoustic* performance at Carré in Amsterdam.

I always carry Simple Minds on my shoulder as an angel.

## ADDY DE HOND

As a big fan I'd been in the long line for a ticket. I bought an extra one. At a party I told a friend I had this. He introduced me to a beautiful girl who said she wanted to come along. We exchanged phone numbers and the next day she called to say her friends also had tickets but didn't know how to get there. I didn't hesitate for a moment and rented a van, along with some friends. On the day, we went with nine people to De

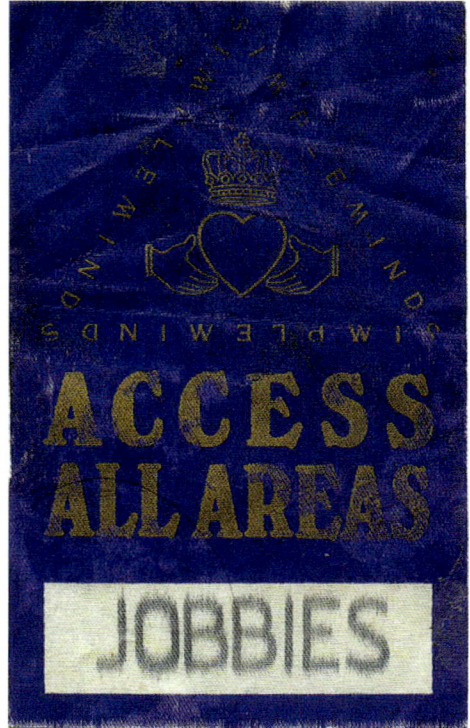

Kuip, got there early and got a place right in front of the stage.

The pretty girl was right in front of me. When 'East at Easter' was played she leaned back with her back to me, took both my hands, put them on her bare belly and held them there. We stood like this for a long time and the world stood still for a moment, the band right in front, the beautiful music, the setting sun. This intimate embrace is my fondest memory from my teenage years.

The song came to an end, and 'Sanctify Yourself' started. Unsure what to do, I let go of her and started dancing. The magical moment was over. The next day we met in a bar but somehow missed each other. I never saw her again. Now, more than 30 years later, I think back every 14th of July and still cherish this moment. I've seen many concerts, but it's never been as beautiful as then.

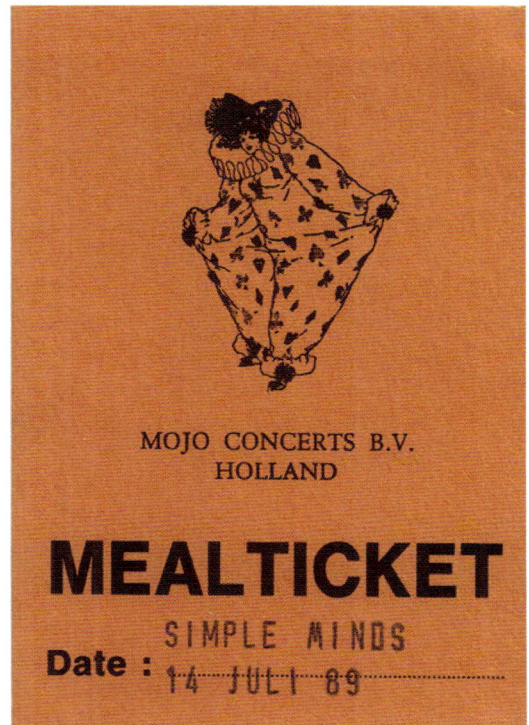

MOJO CONCERTS B.V.
HOLLAND

MEALTICKET

SIMPLE MINDS

Date : 14 JULI 89

## LEO VAN DEN BERG

I was 14 when I became a fan in 1985, with the song 'Don't You'. That echoing guitar of Charlie and Mel's drums did it for me. I became a drummer myself because of that song. I saved up money to buy *Once Upon a Time*, and taped a lot of songs off the radio. All my pocket money went on the singles, 12-inches and albums. In '87, *Live in the City of Light* came out. I had to work on the land to be able to buy that. I treasure it to this day. I saw them on TV at *Live Aid* and the Mandela concert, listening to the radio all day. When they did the *Street Fighting Years* tour in Holland it was my first concert. The show was great but I missed the train and it took me about 10 hours to get home. I travelled with 'Street Fighting Years' in my head.

## MARTIN POTAPPEL

I was 17 when Simple Minds played the Rotterdam Ahoy. Unfortunately, I was on the other side of the world so had to wait until 1989 to see them on the *Street Fighting Years* tour at de Kuip, Feyenoord's football stadium. More gigs followed, 46 so far. I've also collected over 2,300 unique items of memorabilia so far! My concert highlights? Edinburgh Castle in the rain, the Hydro show on DVD, the small Paradiso *5x5* gig – and Jim wearing my scarf at the Bospop Festival. Their music has kept me going in my sunniest and darkest days.

*Martin Potappel saw the band in Rotterdam*

## GODFRIED MENSINK, AGE 17

I was 17 and it was my first gig. My brother, nine years older, thought it was a good idea for us to go together. I'd been listening quite a lot to the *Live in the City of Light* album and couldn't stop looking at the booklet inside the album, thinking, 'Wouldn't it be great to be at a Simple Minds concert'.

That day we went to Rotterdam by train. It was so impressive to hear Jim Kerr and his band in real life. We'd listened to the *Street Fighting Years* album a few times, but hearing it live with all that energy from the band was impressive. From that day on I was officially a fan and have never stopped being one.

31 years later, I invited my brother to a Simple Minds concert again, in Münster. Unfortunately, it was postponed but we'll be there in 2021. I'm sure it will bring back the memory of my first gig, the day I became a real Simple Minds fan.

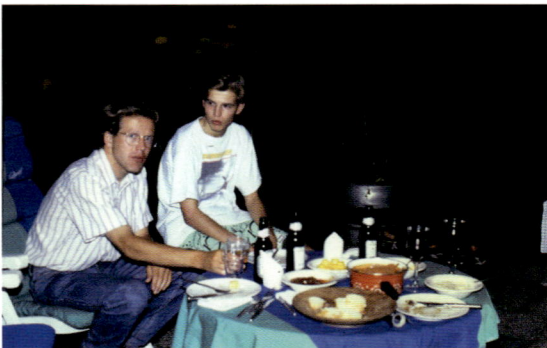

*Godfried Mensink 'officially' became a Simple Minds fan the day he saw them live for the first time*

# PETER JENNINGS

*Arènes De Frejus*
*15 July 1989, Frejus, France*

I became a fan after seeing the video for 'Speed Your Love to Me' on Australian TV one Saturday morning in early 1984. For some reason the song and video hit me instantly. Soon after I bought *Sparkle in the Rain* for my 16th birthday - a life defining moment for sure! I very quickly fell in love with all their music.

My first Minds show should have been in late 1986 at Sydney Entertainment Centre, for which I had close to front row seats. But I couldn't go - my parents insisted I stay home and study the night before one of my biggest final school exams. It was very hard to study knowing I was missing out on seeing my favourite band play my hometown, a show I'd been looking forward to for months.

Apart from a brief set at a concert for Nelson Mandela in London in 1998, my first full Simple Minds show came in June 1989 in Frejus in the south of France. I missed the first few songs, having wildly underestimated how difficult it would be to travel there from nearby St Tropez. But as I finally made my way into a wonderful Roman amphitheatre I knew I was in for a very special concert. In truth I can't remember much about that night, but I was absolutely buzzing by the end.

I ended up seeing five other shows that following week – in Lyon, Toulouse, Bordeaux, Nantes and Brussels. I remember catching trains across incredible French countryside then hitching a lift on the band's coach from Nantes to Brussels. Each night is collectively burnt into my mind, from the opening bass of 'Street Fighting Years' to the soaring guitar of' Let It All Come Down'. A week I will never forget.

---

# CAROLIN GAUSE

*Eilenriedehalle*
*17 July 1989, Hannover,*
*West Germany*

I was one of millions who heard 'Don't You (Forget About Me)' for the very first time on a German radio station. I remember standing in my bedroom, electrified by the voice and powerful drums. While watching them on TV after school one day, I decided I needed to see Simple Minds in concert for myself.

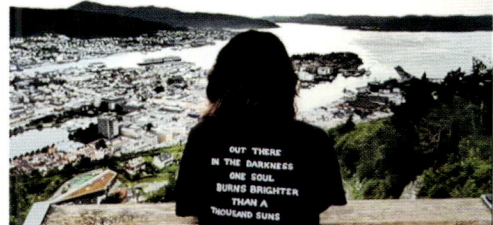

*Carolin Gause saw the Minds in Hanover*

It took a while but finally the day arrived. It was a warm summer's day when I went to the Eilenriedehalle. After The Silencers' fantastic opening act, the venue was already heated up by the crowd. Then Simple Minds entered and all my expectations were exceeded. They were excellent musicians. A rock concert with violin and accordion is rather unusual but it was just terrific. And the more people couldn't stand the heat in front of the stage, the more my mate and I could move closer to it. Maybe another reason for the heat wasn't just the weather but also the charisma and aura of singer Jim Kerr. When he looked into your eyes, you felt energised, suddenly wide awake again. It was an awesome experience I didn't expect. Simple Minds played for three powerful hours and left everyone happy. The next days I spent in a parallel universe – I think it was withdrawal symptoms - dreaming of the concert and listening to *Street Fighting Years* again and again.

---

# IAN HOPKINS

## *Roundhay Park*
## *23 July 1989, Leeds, England*

Growing up, I wasn't aware of much popular music at home, let alone bands such as Simple Minds. My father was a great jazz fan, a passion he passed on to me, while my mother mostly listened to country and western, and a fan of The Seekers. So, wherever I was going to hear modern music, it wouldn't be at home. But in 1980 I started at the local grammar school and my horizons started to broaden. I remember the 1982 release of 'Promised You a Miracle' and loved it but, shocking as it seems today, wasn't then aware of its parent album.

That year I joined the Air Cadets and fell in with a couple of lads, JJ and Doug, who were mad keen on Ultravox, as was I. By 1986 I'd joined the Royal Air Force and, home on leave from technical training at RAF Halton, Doug sat me down and said, 'listen to this'.

The album he played was *Once Upon a Time*. I bought the cassette, played it endlessly (in between Ultravox) on my Sony Walkman, and was consumed with fiery jealousy when two of my coursemates, Tom and Mac, disappeared one summer weekend to the legendary Milton Keynes concert.

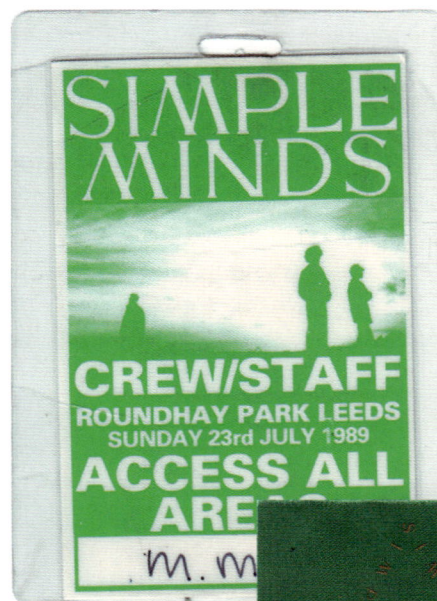

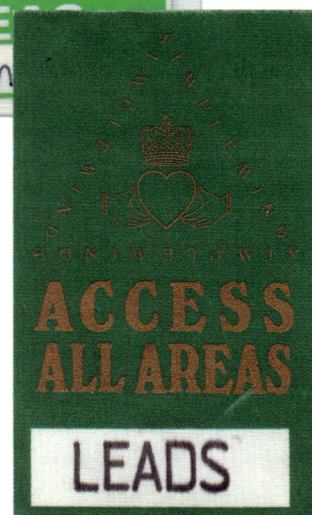

By the time *Live in the City of Light* came out I'd been posted to the Harrier Force at RAF Wittering. I soon found myself owning every Simple Minds album, the band fully displacing Ultravox as my favourite.

1989 saw the release of *Street Fighting Years*. And this was my moment. I sorted out tickets and on Sunday 23 July my RAF mate Tim, my old school pal Doug, his girlfriend Tracey and I piled into Doug's Peugeot 205 for the run to Leeds. And that night, in Roundhay Park, I experienced the most magical evening of my 20-year-old life. The journey had begun.

## PETER KANE

By 1989 I'd been fortunate to see them on a couple of occasions, but when news broke that Simple Minds would be touring *Street Fighting Years* and playing their first gig in the UK in my home city, it blew me away. Roundhay Park in Leeds was an enormous venue; the Rolling Stones, Springsteen and Madonna had all played there. Simple Minds were about to step into the largest arena in Yorkshire. It was a red-hot day. The 20-minute walk from my house seemed to take forever, the crowds swelling as we approached Soldiers' Field. Walking into the concert area the stage was huge. Support act All About Eve really got us all up and ready, then around 8.30pm the 'Theme for Great Cities' started. Jim's opening line about it being great to be back in Yorkshire will forever be etched on my mind. The next three hours were euphoric. They were playing songs old and new and we danced and danced well into the night. A gig I'll never forget.

## AMANDA HORNBY, AGE 16

My Love of Simple Minds started when I heard them through my brother's bedroom door. He had great taste in music, we've liked similar stuff through the years, although I don't think he will take credit for my love of Duran Duran. But that was me, a lifelong fan with Simple Minds emblazoned on all my school books, written in the *Live in the City of Light* album font.

In 1989, me and a couple of friends finally got to see them at Roundhay Park. We travelled from Blackpool bus station in a rickety (it broke down on the way home) and full-to-bursting double-decker bus, full of excited people.

Finally getting there after what seemed like hours, I was astounded on walking in to see the size of the park. We ran to be as near to the front as we could get and got our spot. We started talking to another couple next to us, who'd followed the tour all over the UK. They seemed so old and ancient to 16-year-old me. In reality they were probably only in their 40s.

I don't really remember the support acts apart from All About Eve, but they were all good. When finally Simple Minds came on, the crowd surged towards the stage. I had goosebumps and from then on was in awe, loving every minute, even the four minutes I burnt my finger from holding my lighter aloft while they played 'Biko'.

Sometime during 'Don't You (Forget About Me)' I decided to get on my boyfriend's shoulders and about 10 feet from the front, I had an amazing view. Jim spotted me and sang directly to me, then blew me a kiss. Since then, I've seen them quite a few times. On a couple of occasions I managed to get to the front and I've high-fived Charlie and shaken Mel's hand. I'll just have to settle for a 31-year-old blown kiss from Mr Kerr.

## STEVE BAMBURY

I have two distinct memories. One is the gig at Roundhay Park, Leeds, which ended up with my car being broken into and smashed inside. We spent all night being towed back to Stoke-on-Trent by the AA. The other memory is meeting the band in Zurich Airport's business lounge. I did say hello but was too nervous to start a conversation so just sat by them, in a dream.

## CHRIS COMBE

I was just a lanky, spotty teenager at a Yorkshire boarding school listening to the music of the day on compilations like *Now That's What I Call Music!* Especially volumes 4, 5 and 6. I enjoyed the music of OMD, A-ha, The Thompson Twins, Heaven 17 and Big Country, but two bands really connected with me: U2 and Simple Minds. The release of *Once Upon a Time* really sealed that love affair. The evolution from punk and new wave through to electronic pop then stadium rock was fascinating and enthralling and I knew I had to see them live, especially after seeing the Ahoy Rotterdam gig on Channel 4's *The Tube*.

In summer 1989 I left school, and managed to get a ticket for the *Street Fighting Years* tour at Roundhay Park, Leeds. It was my first proper concert and I was ridiculously excited. That day will live long in my memory. A scorching hot day, a huge crowd and a cracking atmosphere. The Silencers and All About Eve supported ably but finally the main event arrived, the spine-tingling bagpipes of 'When Spirits Rise' started, the Claddagh-adorned curtain was swept aside and there they were. I found myself quite close to the front, right in front of Charlie, and spent the next two-plus hours jumping and singing along to a selection of songs from the new album and greats like 'Waterfront', 'Book of Brilliant Things', 'Alive and Kicking' and 'Don't You'. To this day, knocking on 50, this gig lives in my top three of all time.

It's easy to see how people can get addicted to following Simple Minds and going to gig after gig, even on the same tour, and I wish I could have had the funds to see more, but I've managed to see them over a dozen times, in a variety of venues - from Gateshead Stadium to Manchester Apollo, the O2 in London and Edinburgh's Usher Hall in 2015 on the *Big Music* tour. Every gig has been special in its own way, with the band on great form and sounding fresh and vibrant, always eager to please, bringing in new songs and the odd glittering prize of an old song I hadn't heard live before. I genuinely feel there's a unique bond between the Minds and their fans, and at every gig it feels like we're having a properly good time with great old friends.

## DEAN WOLSTENHOLME

This was my first live concert. A mate bought me tickets for my 18th. I don't know why as I'd never really been that clued up about Simple Minds. But, wow, what a day and how my thoughts changed on this band. The quality of the vocal, the sound of a live band and sheer spectacle of a live performance, albeit mainly in daylight due to local council bullshit rules. Simple Minds became the yardstick by which I measured all other bands – they have to be able to sound as good live as on an album and the Minds surpassed this. Jim's vocals on the day was outstanding. A day that will remain with me forever.

## DARREN FOSTER

Roundhay Park was the first time and I've seen them 15 times since, each time trying to get a better place to view them. The best place has been front row, dead centre, which I've managed twice, just to see Charlie work his magic. How can anyone get a sound out of a guitar like that? I've got loads of favourite songs, but I love to hear and sing along to 'Alive and Kicking' as it brings back so many memories, while 'Mandela Day' reminds me of the story behind the man and what he went through. And the beat of the drum, the penny whistle and guitar on 'Belfast Child' send tingles up the spine.

# GARETH WILLIAMS

Sprawled out exhausted in the back of our school minibus as we headed south after a week-long geography field trip in Cumbria, a mate passed me a double cassette and said, 'Here, play this....' I put it in my Walkman, pressed 'play' and thus dawned a relationship that would be part of my world forever more. The album was *Live in the City of Light* and I was 17. Hungry for more, I went back to the start and bought all the albums from *Life in a Day* onwards. The following year I got to attend my first Simple Minds concert at Roundhay Park, Leeds.

It was a scorching day and anticipation grew as the support acts played. I especially liked The Silencers and Texas, their music also a part of my life to this day. What is it with Scottish bands? I'll never forget the feeling as the curtain finally opened to a thunderous roar and Malcolm Foster got us underway with those first few bass notes. I was so blown away that I went and got tickets for Wembley Stadium the following month!

Ever since, Simple Minds have been with me as I've gone through life, the ups and downs, and of course the travels. Living in Dubai for 20 years, trips back to the UK to catch concerts are always a treat, but my dream came true when Simple Minds played Dubai Tennis Stadium in 2016 – my band playing my town! Being in the crowd during the opening moments of a concert still takes me straight back to Roundhay, only better! I owe my mate big time for passing that cassette on the school bus.

*Gareth Williams has seen the band at Roundhay Park and in Dubai*

# GEOFF MCCORMACK

I first saw Simple Minds at Roundhay Park, Leeds in 1989 with 75,000 other fans. What a day out! I remember driving over from Liverpool with friends, having recently passed my test. It took forever to get out of the car park after, and I only just made it into work the following day, my concert t-shirt still on, visible under a work shirt. I made it through that day on pure adrenaline .

Come the 1990s and I'm living in Cleveland, Ohio. Simple Minds are touring the US with their

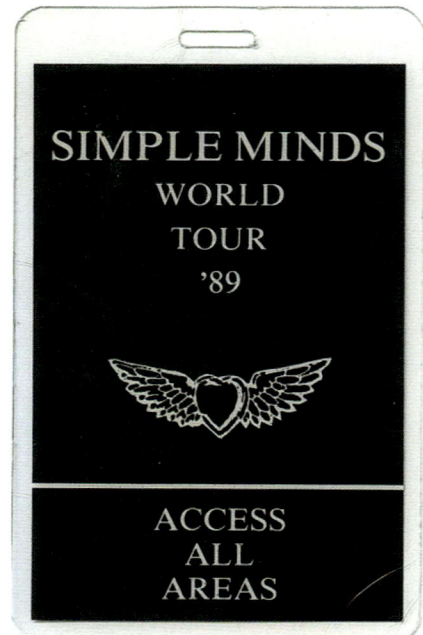

*Geoff McCormack was at Roundhay Park with 75,000 others and at the Agora Ballroom with a few less*

*Good News for the New World* album, playing the Agora Ballroom, holding maybe 800 people. I remember the day the tickets went on sale. My wife worked next to a Ticketmaster booth and I asked her nicely if she'd start queuing a couple of hours before they went on sale. 'It's going to be mental down there…' Long story short, there was no queue out the door (I was astounded) and I bagged a pair of standing tickets to see my favourite band in a small theatre.

I can't describe how amazing it was to lean against the stage with beer in hand, listening to stadium anthems up close and personal. I met Jim and Charlie after and Charlie shared with me that Simple Minds weren't that popular in the States. I couldn't believe it, and still can't. It took another 25 years for them to come back to Cleveland. It was well worth the wait.

## GRAHAM HIRST

Simple Minds announced their Roundhay Park show, it was the day after my forthcoming wedding to Diane. I was disappointed to be missing this concert on my doorstep, but the wedding had been planned well in advance. Our wedding was blessed with beautiful weather. At the end of the evening we retired to our hotel room, at which point I found out Diane had purchased two tickets for the concert!

And so it was that we spent the first day of our honeymoon and married life with 80,000-plus others, stood in a park watching the great Simple Minds. And 31 years later we're still happily married. I don't have any pictures from the concert - but plenty of our wedding!

## ROBERT GRAY

Back in 1986, Christopher Taylor, my best friend and brother from another mother who I've known since the first day of school, asked me to listen to 'Ghostdancing' from this Scottish band he was really enjoying. At the time I was listening to my favourite lady pop star. Madonna was to be my future wife, so nothing else could compare. Anyway, that didn't happen and as a 16-year-old I was devastated so listened anyway. And I couldn't get enough of it! I went out into Liverpool city centre and purchased *Live in the City of Light*. That was it - I couldn't believe what I was hearing. Plans were made to see Simple Minds live, but with both of us working on a YTS scheme we didn't have a lot of cash.

The next opportunity for us to see them live was in 1989, after purchasing the brilliant *Street Fighting Years*. I remember waiting for the tickets to go on sale and queuing for hours to finally get our hands on the golden tickets. We'd done it - got the album and got the tickets. Our dream was almost complete.

On the day in question we set out from Liverpool to Leeds at stupid o'clock as the sun was starting to make an appearance, Simple Minds blasting out on cassette and a flag in the back window. We arrived at Roundhay Park at about 9am, jumped out of the car and joined the queue. At 10am the gates opened and that was it – we were in!

After what felt like a marathon, we made it to the front(ish), the sun really warming up. Chatting and telling stories to all these new friends kept us going all day - scousers never shut up! Come early evening, the support bands came on and blew us away, but we were here for one reason only and that reason was about to happen.

Shivers down my spine time, the lighting stage started to rumble, the curtains came down and there we were. Our dream had come true. Two and a half hours of unbelievable music. I'll never forget that moment. The best day and night of my musical life.

That was the beginning of an amazing 34 years listening to Simple Minds and watching 20-plus gigs together. Christopher unselfishly helped me get a photo with an autograph from Jim after the *Black and White* tour in Manchester in 2006. Jim was about to get on the tour bus after signing autographs when Chris shouted, 'Just one more, Jim!' He heard the shout and let me have a photo and signed the poster we'd found on a lamp-post outside the venue (scousers again).

Hopefully we can carry this on for a long time into the future. If it wasn't for Chris, I'd have probably still been going on about how good Madonna is.

# TONY JEWITT

My association with the band started when I was 17, in the summer of 1988. Every Saturday night I went to a nightclub with a group of friends. One particular night, the DJ played 'Don't You (Forget About Me)'. I'd never heard it before but thought it sounded amazing. That following Monday, I went to my local record shop and bought the 12-inch single. To this day, no song has ever had such an effect. I quite literally wore the grooves out!

The following summer I went to the first of many gigs, at Roundhay Park, Leeds. That was followed by Maine Road, Manchester in 1991. The years went by. More gigs. In the late Noughties I decided to create my own YouTube channel. That, along with other social media, put me in touch with other fans. In late 2014, I answered an ad to supply fan footage for the music video of 'Let the Day Begin'. I got my stepson, Daniel, to film me walking out of my front door. It

*Tony Jewitt was at Roundhay Park and later in a Simple Minds video*

was just three seconds long but included, and you can imagine my reaction when I first saw this. A claim to fame with Simple Minds!

## DAVID JOHNSON

It was a sweltering hot day for the two-hour coach trip from Liverpool to Leeds. It was the first gig for my younger brother and we smuggled in two cans of Fanta! High on the hill we waited and waited until the huge curtain sails fell and we were into 'Street Fighting Years'. I think Simple Minds played all 11 tracks from *Street Fighting Years* and the show was just on three hours long. I have a bootleg double-cassette somewhere.

## MARK LOWE

I'd heard many tracks by Simple Minds on the radio since the name change from Johnny and the Self Abusers to a more acceptable title taken from David Bowie's 'Jean Genie' (we're all very simple minded). I liked that. So in 1989 my then-wife managed to obtain tickets to Roundhay Park. We were both excited and eager to actually see the Minds live. A beautiful summer's day in July, sat on the ridge of a grassy amphitheatre enjoying bands such as All About Eve, Texas and Seal until this wall of sound filled the air as Simple Minds took centre-stage. Wow, this is what it was all about - what I'd been looking for in music.

## PHIL ROGERS, AGE 18

I sometimes rue my age as I missed Milton Keynes in 1986 by a year. I was too young to go and hadn't discovered Simple Minds yet. What a line-up! I still adore Lloyd Cole and the Commotions and The Waterboys. It's probably my dream gig.

That autumn I moved from Spear of Destiny (big in Stoke) and The Cramps and King Kurt to something bigger. It started with *Under a Blood Red Sky* by U2 and by Christmas I had all their albums. But I also chose *Once Upon a Time*. There was something so positive about it and there still is – it's that kid called hope that does it.

The next year we were old enough to see U2 on the *Joshua Tree* tour and waited patiently for Simple Minds, while amassing the back-catalogue. We didn't get the very old stuff to begin with – that would come, and overtake in favour in time. Then came Roundhay on the *Street Fighting Years* tour. Steve and I camped overnight outside Mike Lloyd's Record Shop in Hanley. We were third in the queue and didn't sleep but got our five tickets and coach travel.

The day was white hot, with a massive crowd, and we were shouting for water during 'Don't You (Forget About Me)'. The gig was brilliant. There was no secondary barrier in those days and us 18-year-olds got as far as we could get down the front. We'd gone with Dave's younger brother, Gareth. At the end of the gig we got to the coach park early enough to claim the back seat. One problem – no Gareth. Dave asked who was coming to help him search. We looked in various directions. 'Cheers lads!' Dave got off the coach. Within seconds it slowly set off from Leeds to Stoke, inching its way through the traffic. Five minutes later, Gareth climbed aboard to much mirth from the back seat. We sailed home to Stoke. Meanwhile, Dave was taken in by Leeds' finest, given a cell for the night and put on a train the following morning, with a request for his parents to pay the fare to the police, who'd meet them at Stoke station. Dave's never lived it down. The mere mention of Simple Minds when we're together means this story is recycled, with much merriment at Dave's expense.

My own story took me into venue management. I missed Jim when working at the Point in Dublin when he was apparently in the backstage bar one night – 'Jim Kerr was in here earlier, over in the corner wearing a fur coat.' 'NO WAY!' Bono was easier to spot, in Dublin of course. I walked past Charlie in Dublin too, being too shy to disturb him.

I met Jim post-gig in Manchester, on the Arena tour with OMD and finally got to work a Simple Minds Manchester Apollo gig. I hope they play the Apollo - my venue - again.

## SIMON TATTERSON

What a day! I'll always recall the great weather we had, with wall-to-wall sunshine. A perfect day for an open-air gig, with temperatures well into the 80s, which seemed quite apt as we were well into the 1980s. I remember the Fire and Rescue Service spraying the crowd with cold water, just as well as one of my friends passed out in the heat! This was the fourth time I'd seen Simple Minds and one of the best. Roll on next time….

## WENDY TASKER

The first track I ever heard was 'I Travel' on John Peel whilst studying for O-levels. In my first year at Newcastle Poly, I was unable to get a ticket to see them at Newcastle City Hall in the early 80s so resorted to standing in the foyer, peeking through the doors as the band played 'Someone Somewhere (in Summertime)'. I remember buying the 'Waterfront' EP from Callers record store, Northumberland Street, Newcastle (no longer there) and playing New Gold Dream on my Walkman on the many train journeys back down to Yorkshire as a student.

The first time I saw them live was Roundhay Park in July 1989. It was a beautiful Sunday, sat on the slope of a natural bowl made for gigs and nights like that. I remember the support acts being Martin Stephenson and the Daintees, The Levellers and All About Eve … then Simple Minds. An unforgettable night. The weather was kind and I have memories of 'Let it all Come Down', 'Mandela Day' and 'This is Your Land'.

I still have the ticket stubs for many of the gigs I attended and I have never been disappointed by Simple Minds, except when the 2020 gig at Leeds Arena was cancelled due to coronavirus. Like many fans, I'm looking forward to creating new memories when I see the band again.

---

# MARK LONGBOTTOM

*Mark Longbottom was at Roundhay Park but only got to meet the band years later*

It began in April 1982. I was 12. I remember the synth hook of 'Promised You a Miracle' as it played on Radio 1. The song shone like a blinding light, speaking of hope, golden days and the promise of a future. Yes, we needed a miracle and it came in the form of *New Gold Dream*. A perfect vinyl album where you put the needle down and listened to both sides without pause, shuffle or skipping.

My next stand-out memory was 'Don't You (Forget About Me)'. I'd heard the band were doing a song for the soundtrack of the movie *The Breakfast Club*. I remember listening to Johnnie Walker's American chart show on Radio 1, sitting in my bedroom with a Ferguson cassette player waiting to hit play and record as the track was played for the very first time in the UK. Those first beats of Mel Gaynor pounding the skins were unforgettable. I knew I'd heard the sound of a future classic.

I became obsessed with buying bootleg tapes of concerts at record fairs, listening and imagining what it would be like to see Jim on stage screaming 'let me see your hands'. I swapped bootlegs with other Minds fans across the UK, Europe and the US, sharing my A4 photocopied handwritten list of recordings to swap and waiting for the postman to deliver a jiffy bag of concert tapes from around the globe.

It was 1989 when I saw the band for the first time at Roundhay Park. I'll never forget the opening chords of 'When Spirits Rise', the roar of the crowd, dry ice and the curtain dropping to reveal the band.

I got soaked to the skin at Gateshead on the *Real Life* tour, driving home in just my underwear. I waited in the freezing cold after the Manchester Apollo show but eventually got to meet Jim. He took the time to talk to and greet all the die-hard fans.

He signed the lining of my Armani bomber jacket and kissed my wife on the cheek – the charmer. Sadly I forgot my camera so couldn't capture the moment.

After the show at Birmingham Academy, I got my chance for that great photo opportunity. A fellow fan took my photo of us side by side. To my despair, the flash didn't go off. I was left with a picture of two shadows in total darkness. But a fan meet and greet at the O2 in London was the Glittering Prize. A day I'll never forget, as you can see from my ear to ear grin.

---

# ANDY JORDAN

Our wages were so poor we couldn't afford travel and tickets to gigs, but in 1989 the Minds were playing Roundhay Park in Leeds, literally a bus ride from home. My brother and I were like kids at Christmas. This was our day, a day and memory we captured and re-ran for weeks after. 'When Spirits Rise' echoed around the park, we knew our time was near. The Claddagh curtain fell and we both stood in awe and said, 'Holy shit, this is it!' and Roundhay Park suddenly blew into a rapture of applause as 'Street Fighting Years' rang around my beautiful city and filled the air with Simple Minds magic. The concert reflected what we already knew about the band's magical persona. Being there, experiencing it, feeling the warmth, the love, the magic of the music, everything - it all came alive in front of us.

I still feel that magic to this day. Although my brother's no longer with us, I take him to every concert I go to. The band's music makes me feel as though he's by my side.

---

# JULIANNE REGAN

## All About Eve

At the age of 17, listening to the *John Peel Show* in January 1980, I heard a song with a jangling, nagging guitar part, a juddering synth line and lightly industrial disco beat. It reminded me of a favourite album, *Systems of Romance* by Ultravox!, in that it seemed to draw on a similar sonic palette, largely an astonishing blend of guitar and electronics over which a strange and compelling voice carried intriguing lyrics. That song was 'Changeling'. On the back of that I bought the *Real to Real Cacophony* album, and subsequently *Empires and Dance*. With my best schoolfriend Rachael, I would listen to the albums in my bedroom while drinking sickly, syrupy fruit wine and eating jelly babies.

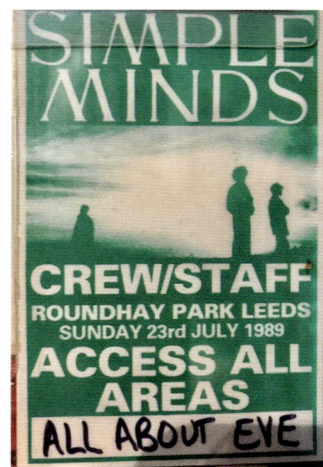

*Julianne was on the bill with Simple Minds - photo Graeme Cooper*

On 24 October 1980, she and I took the train from Coventry to Birmingham, all dolled up in our new romantic clothes, our faces painted creamy white with a Biba make-up shade called Geisha. We were due to see Simple Minds at the Cedar Club, but at the door, a telegram from the band was being waved around; we were given the news that the gig was cancelled but a local band had stepped in at the last minute. They were called Duran Duran. Rachael declined, with a terse 'Simple Minds or nothing!' We walked the 20 minutes back to New Street Station, and on the train home discussed whether or not we'd made the right decision. We spent the money we saved on ice cream.

I continued buying Simple Minds albums and fell particularly in love with the then double-album, *Sons and Fascination/Sister Feelings Call*, with several tracks across the albums being wonderful to dance to in the Birmingham clubs Rachael and I would frequent, such as the Rum Runner and Holy City Zoo.

I eventually managed to see Simple Minds, on 16 May 1984 at Hammersmith Odeon, having moved to London in 1981. Back then, I was something of a conceited snob with crimped black hair, looking down on the gathered audience of 'normals', i.e. supremely decent people I assume worked in banks and offices. Simple Minds weren't cult anymore.

There should have been a second time I saw Simple Minds, and that would have been at Roundhay Park on 23 July 1989, after my band All About Eve supported them. Regrettably, following our set, myself and our guitarist had an almighty altercation, and while the rest of the band had the pleasure of meeting Jim and Charlie, we were fighting it out somewhere. I still feel a little sad about this, not least because I'd have liked to have met them and told them how much their music meant to me, but also because it seems so rude not to have thanked them in person for having invited us to play. I have vivid memories of the gig itself, performed barefoot, with the evening sun glowing amber, the crowd overwhelmingly welcoming, not to mention massive, and for a while, Jim Kerr himself watching us from side of stage.

Simple Minds were one of three bands whose names I'd written on my school bag, the other two were Ultravox! and Japan; I still love all three of those bands. They shaped me as an artist and as a person. I'm grateful to them.

# NIGEL BARTER

*Wembley Arena*
*27 July 1989, London, England*

Simple Minds have evolved as a band and stayed true to themselves, and so has my friendship with fellow Minds gig-goers Martin Perkins, Andy Scott, Adrian Macdermott, Tom Conway and Mark Murphy. I remember being at *Live Aid*, looking up at the Wembley screen and wishing Simple Minds had been in London. It was a wakeup moment for me. But what really captured my attention was 'Belfast Child'. It was epic, beautiful and a No.1 hit back when having a No.1 single really meant something.

At Wembley Arena I still remember the moment they came on stage to 'Street Fighting Years', Charlie's guitar solo slowly building, with a massive silhouette of him on the backstage wall, the band materialising as the song kicked in. The album stayed with me all summer, as did the memories of the concert.

The band's appreciation of the fans seems to grow stronger through the years and every tour has unique memories for me and my friends. Being able to meet the band briefly outside the Cliffs Pavilion, Southend meant the world to me. The band are a great reason for true friends to come back together when life paths have taken us in different directions, to meet up for a beer, catch up with each other and cheer on a band that's given so much to music.

# STEVEN HOLDEN

My introduction to Simple Minds came when a neighbour purchased *Live in the City of Light*. As 'Ghost Dancing' faded in then burst into life, I thought to myself, 'Oh my God, how have I not heard these before?' The hairs were standing on the back of my neck. Before the second verse of the opening track I was a fan, and after 'Waterfront' I was a huge fan! This amazing music just kept filling the room and I sat transfixed, unable to say a word until 'New Gold Dream' faded away, bringing the album to a close. 'Again', I said and sat through the entire album for a second time.

What was very clear to me, even as a young teenager, was that not only did the band consist of excellent individual musicians, but Simple Minds seemed to be greater than the sum of its parts. Their skilled musicianship combined with deliciously-crafted songs would ordinarily be enough to be a good live band, but here there was an extra ingredient which evidently made Simple Minds a great live band and gave *Live in the City of Light* such a considerable dynamic, what I now know to be their enthusiasm and passion for playing to live audiences. I now wanted to be a drummer, just like Mel Gaynor, and be in a band of my own!

The chance to see Simple Minds finally came at Wembley Arena during the *Street Fighting Years* tour. I remember the tear of happiness that rolled down my cheek as 'When Spirits Rise' began blaring out of the sound system. The following two and a half to three hours were an amazing spectacle, from the start of 'Street Fighting Years' to the last note of 'Alive and Kicking'. I'd just witnessed the best rock 'n' roll band in the world at the top of their game. It had been well worth the wait.

## ROB FORD

*National Exhibition Centre*
*1 August 1989, Birmingham, England*

I was so jealous of my older friends when the local coach company sold out a trip to Milton Keynes Bowl in 1986 before I had enough pocket money to join them piling up the motorway to see Simple Minds. By 1989, I was working at a local theatre and we were agents for the coach company, so I wasn't missing out this time. And the NEC was positively intimate compared to Milton Keynes. My friends were jealous of me now.

The set that night was epic and from the intro tape onward I was captivated. The next day I wanted more and borrowed money from my dad to see them again at Wembley Stadium in August, an early Christmas present. Countless miles, gigs and years have followed. Very few bands can connect in the way this band does. Big Country did. Springsteen does. When spirits rise and the band get back on stage, it will feel like the first time all over again.

## JED CAWTHORNE

I've played their songs across 10 years in the Navy, eight stressful years working as a prison officer and throughout my life. I've seen Simple Minds play Glasgow, Milton Keynes, London and Toronto, where I now live.

Although a fan since 'Promised You a Miracle', life in the Navy and in a trade that got a lot of sea time meant I didn't get to see Simple Minds until 1989. I was lucky enough to be on summer leave and grabbed a ticket for a trip down to the NEC. I recall chatting to a few people on the coach. We all had different seats, not together in a block.

*Street Fighting Years* wasn't and isn't one of my favourite albums, yet it was an awesome atmosphere and a brilliant show. It was the first time I heard Jim utter the immortal words 'is everyone alright?' - which I've heard many times since!

The last two gigs in Toronto were stand-outs, with 2018's gig at the Sony Center special as my 16-year-old son Philip asked if he could join me. After the first song, Jim apologised for not visiting Canada for so long and said, to make it up for it, it was going to be a long night, with two sets and an interval. Well, we picked a great night for my son's first rock concert. He absolutely loved it.

## JOHN MURTIE

### Scottish Exhibition and Conference Centre
### 9 August 1989, Glasgow, Scotland

I first went to see them at the SECC Glasgow with my mate Steve, his second time as he'd seen them on the *Once Upon a Time* tour there. We got the train from Motherwell.

The place was buzzing. Everyone was in high spirits, a massive line of people waiting to get in. We poured in. The atmosphere was vibrant. I've been to football matches but this atmosphere was like nothing I'd felt before.

The band were excellent. The light show was spectacular. Great music from the greatest live band in the world.

## VALENTINA DANEO

My friend Federica and I were 23 in 1989, the year we followed Simple Minds on their *Street Fighting Years* tour. A chance to visit wonderful Scotland and go to a Simple Minds concert? How could we resist? We didn't have much money, so travelled by train from Rome to Calais, crossing the English Channel then going to London and finally Edinburgh. I had a beret and was delighted to find the Kerr clan crest badge, which we wore just like Jim did. August 8th arrived and we caught an early bus to Glasgow - at a concert you must be crushed against the barriers or it isn't worth it! At last the SECC opened the gates and we ran like crazy to get in the front row. Then the band appeared and Jim saw the beret with the badge and gave us a sign and smiled. In that micro-second he knew we existed.

*Edimburgo, 6 agosto 1*

*Valentina and Federica travelled from Rome to Scotland*

# ANNETTE STROHMEYER

*Meadowbank Stadium*
*12 August 1989, Edinburgh, Scotland*

I was sweet 17, on holiday in Austria in 1983, and struck like lightning when a very handsome boy from Sheffield (heavens, he looked like David Bowie!) entered the room. He was smitten with Simple Minds, and I with him, and he gave me his beloved *New Gold Dream* cassette. Six years of teenage pen friendship started, and almost four decades of Simple Minds.

In the summer of 1989, I booked a ticket to London and on up to Edinburgh to meet my friend Gitti, who was travelling through Scotland. Going to Scotland by train felt like coming home. I was impressed by the breathtaking beauty. She had a ticket to see Simple Minds and I was lucky and managed to get one too, and we celebrated an amazing open air *Street Fighting Years* concert in Edinburgh. If that wasn't enough, we went up to Lochearnhead in search of the band and stayed there for a few fantastic days, visiting St. Fillans and Balquhidder and buying warm lambswool sweaters in Callander. It was so cold!

---

# PETER CARLIN

*Once Upon a Time* was my first album, played on rotation through a Walkman – I'd be lost in my own world, walking or on buses or trains, and knew each nuance of that album. My mother was battling alcoholism, which was putting a great strain on the family. I suppose Simple Minds became my escape from it all. These songs were songs of hope and love and ethereal in a spiritual sense. They took you to a different place and tugged at the heart-strings while making you feel positive and think of everything good about the world. At 15, it made me feel I could conquer the world and could not wait to embrace it. Nothing was going to stop me.

*Peter Carlin was at Meadowbank*

Having missed Ibrox in '86, I had to wait a further two years for my first gig at Meadowbank Stadium. The excitement began walking through the streets of

Edinburgh, posters of the band everywhere. There was a large line of people snaking around temporary fencing waiting to enter, moving incredibly slowly. There was a sense of tension and excitement as everyone cracked jokes, sang Simple Minds tunes together, and were generally warm and friendly. I felt some envy looking at people with early *New Gold Dream* and *Empires and Dance* t-shirts, clearly the mark of uber-coolness, veterans from the early years.

My immediate emotions on entering the stadium were speechlessness and awe at the sheer size and scale. People sat around in small groups on the ground chatting on black protective sheeting. I could swear Jim Kerr was wandering about with shades on, mingling in the crowd. I looked on in disbelief, quizzing myself, my heart pounding. The support acts were good but it's excruciatingly painful when you're just pining for the main act, almost to the point of exhaustion, like a kid waiting for Christmas Day.

Then it came. Sunset was upon us, the crowd almost instantly seeming much bigger and more boisterous. The tension was unbearable. A large white linen curtain hung from the stage, emblazoned with a black claddagh. The atmosphere became electric as the sounds of the instrumental 'Theme from Great Cities' coursed through those giant stadium speakers, before breaking into the piercing swirl of bagpipes and the beautiful lament of 'When Spirits Rise'. As an opening, this was epic, adrenaline taking over me as a low rumbling cacophony of thundering sound surrounded the stadium.

Simultaneously, the curtain came down while Malcolm Foster pulled the opening bass chords to 'Street Fighting Years', and surprisingly Jim was in the background, next to the drum-riser. As the bass was pulsing, the drums cracked into life, followed by MacNeil's keyboards, then subtle guitar decorations from Burchill. What was instantly impressive was the dynamic size of the music, three-dimensional in scale and scope, a wall of sound so complete you felt you could touch it. Kerr's voice somehow managed to pierce through this and I recall thinking how much I really liked his voice. He hung onto notes and seemed to have so much tonal range.

The setlist was heavy on songs from the new album and it was great to hear the live interpretations. I made my way closer to the front, eager to see the band, while a subdued 'Soul Crying Out' was being played. The crowd obligingly let me snake in until I was almost at the front barrier, meeting some girls who travelled from Newcastle. We had more or less said hello when our insides vibrated to the bassline of 'Waterfront'. The front of the crowd went completely nuts, so much so that both the girls and I were lifted off our feet in the throng. It was a bit scary at first, but wild, and we were beaming big happy smiles as we seemed to be floating in a wavy sea.

I made my way back to a slightly more comfortable area, maybe one third of the

**Just Desserts**

**FOOD PASS**

**SIMPLE MIND**

Tour

way back, and just out of the throng. This was full of people who seemed to be just relaxed and taking it all in. I suddenly realised this area was pin-sharp in terms of acoustics. It's the area I now head to for every gig. Jim has alluded to this in the past, finding the sweet spot and taking it all in. I never understand those that seem to be so intent on the front row. The music just cannot breathe, and this became so apparent to me when my jaw dropped at the opening strains of 'Once Upon a Time'. It sounded alien to me, completely different to the album version, MacNeil's huge synth sounds dominating and the whole thing absolutely epic in scale. For the first time I realised this band came to life live.

At the end I was completely hooked and already calculating how to get to the next gig. If girls from Newcastle could travel to Scotland, why restrict yourself to the band coming to you? That's what it's meant to me - trains, planes and automobiles for over 30 years, meeting some of the nicest fans in the world all over Europe, Australia and beyond.

## SANDY GARDNER

I first started listening to Simple Minds after I heard my sister play *Live in the City of Light*. I got my own copy and ended up getting the back-catalogue from Woolworth's and John Menzies on cassette in pre-CD years. I remember working on the farm and hearing the first play of 'Mandela Day' on Radio 1. Then there was 'Ballad of the Streets' and 'Street Fighting Years' with an exclusive play off the album and an interview on the Gary Davies show. My first concert was at Meadowbank Stadium and I went with my sister and future brother-in-law. It was an amazing day – I ended up losing my voice because of too much singing. I kept up with the albums although I never got to another concert, what with getting married and having kids, until the *Celebrate 30 Years Live* tour at the SECC,

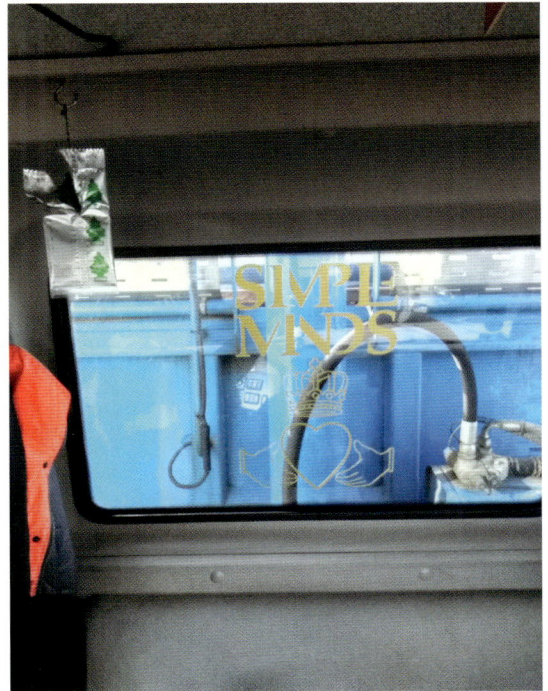

*The window of Sandy Gardner's lorry*

Glasgow. Since then I've been to just about every concert in Scotland and down to England as well. My son comes now, a new generation of fan. The music keeps us all going through good and hard times. Thank you Simple Minds, for the music and 110% performances every time.

## JIM GOW

When we went to see them at Meadowbank we were that excited that we left our tickets on the bus and had to make a mad dash back to the bus station to retrieve them.

## JIM LOVE

At school in Paisley in the early 1980s, there were only three bands that mattered – Simple Minds, U2 and Big Country. When we were 14, a few of my mates dogged (bunked off) school to go to Ibrox Stadium, home of Glasgow Rangers. They got caught and I don't think they got in. The next assembly at school, they were out the front and it was all a bit of a laugh. The year teacher asked one who they'd tried to see and when he said 'Simple Minds', the teacher knocked him on the head a few times as he said, 'Bloody Simple Minds, right enough.'

In 1987 I queued with my mate to buy the gold leaf edition of *Live in the City of Light* from Virgin Records in Glasgow, where the Minds were in attendance and signing copies. The queue was huge and after a long time we gave up. I went back another day and bought the album, but no signed copy! Then I got the bright idea to take this back and swap it for a cassette. I worked in an ice cream van in Pollock, Glasgow and could play it in the van while working. It seemed like a good idea at the time, swapping a limited-edition gold leaf LP for a cassette. I realised the error of my ways about a week later, took the cassette back to exchange for the LP again, but by this time the limited editions were all gone so I ended up with a normal LP. I was even followed by a store detective, who collared me in Central Station and thought I'd nicked it. Luckily I had my receipt!

I actually went to see them at Edinburgh's Meadowbank Stadium in 1989 with a mate. That concert was supposed to be at Murrayfield, but the Minds changed it to Meadowbank because the Scottish RFU were touring South Africa, despite sanctions against the country's apartheid policy. That was an amazing day, with The Silencers and Texas supporting. I loved The Silencers too, and while we were still queuing outside, it started raining a little while still sunny, just as The Silencers started playing 'Scottish Rain'. That day felt more like an all-day festival, with great bands, and when the Minds came on they were obviously amazing. Jim Kerr announced later that there was a good result from the other side of Edinburgh that day, as Celtic had beaten Hearts 3-1 at Tynecastle. A memorable day all-round!

# JOHN MURPHY

My brother was home from leave with the Royal Navy. He had two cassettes, *Real to Real Cacophony* and the new album, *Once Upon a Time*. I loved this album and its iconic songs. I was 18. I then thought I'd listen to the previous albums and was instantly a huge fan. My first wife and I saw them on the *Street Fighting Years* tour, where the show was switched to Meadowbank Stadium from Murrayfield. What a gig! I then saw them on the *Good News from the Next World* tour and all the concerts they've played in Scotland since.

In 2014, Pamela and I went to Taormina to see them. What a concert, what a venue. We fell in love with Taormina and have been every year since. The *5x5* tour was special too, hearing songs I've never seen performed live before. Andy Gillespie brought a whole new sound and creativity to the band, the beat from the amazing Mel Gaynor really powers the music, and Ged Grimes is a brilliant bass player.

---

# DANNY ROARTY

Funny business, big brothers. I get that having an older brother who is significantly older might lead one to regard him as some kind of hero, a benchmark against which to measure all achievements or lack of. Having a brother only slightly older is somewhat different. He's virtually a peer/rival and in that sense nothing he did, said or liked could ever be conceded to be cool. I'm one of five kids – four boys and a girl. The first three boys, of which I was the middle one, arrived with almost indecent haste between November '71 and March '75. There wasn't a huge gulf in age between myself and either brother. Still isn't!

One by-product of our closeness in age was hand-me-down clothes. By the time I got my mitts on them they were just the right amount of months out of fashion to miss the mark, which big bro might have achieved when wearing (not that he would have heard such sentiment from these quarters!). But the one thing I wasn't going to have second-hand was music. I'd be an original, not prisoner to someone else's tastes.

By the time I was 12 Steven, for reasons which to this day remain unclear, was going through a phase of liking the LA hair rock of Mötley Crüe and Ratt. A seemingly-endless production line of Wham! classics George and Andrew were churning out gave me the high ground in every sense.

Then I heard it. From his little box room (by this time he'd graduated from the bunk bed-infested 'boy's room') came beautiful sounds emitting a kind of vastness that was at once both elegant and powerful (chances are 12-year-old me probably wasn't half as wanky about it as that though, and just thought it sounded ace). Steven had, probably by pure fluke, stumbled across *Once Upon a Time*.

I wasted no time in making a copy of his original cassette. As a Sunday night Radio 1 chart enthusiast of at least two years standing, I was vaguely familiar with the band. But as a complete entity, *Once Upon a Time* was the deal-sealer.

I trawled second-hand record shops (vaguely recalling someone stating steadfastly, 'One thing I wasn't going to have second-hand was music') and hungrily looking to find more of what the band had to say. By 1989 and the long-yearned release of the first new music since the onset of my affliction, *Street Fighting Years*, I was ready to consummate my relationship with Jim, Charlie and the gang.

As luck would have it the lads were playing Meadowbank Stadium in Edinburgh. I was going. No two ways about it - assuming briefs and permissions could be arranged. After some carefully-crafted arguments, pleadings and downright begging, both were successfully secured. The latter, however, came burdened with caveats:

*You have to stay at your capital-dwelling Granny and Grandad's house (not a problem - we didn't spend nearly enough time with them since being domiciled in the Granite City)*

*You'll return to grandparents' house straight after (I'm not altogether sure what alternatives were available to a very fresh-faced 16-year-old)*

*You'll attend the gig with your big brother, who's also scored a ticket.*

While my slightly-unhinged bond with the band developed, Steven had continued to enjoy the music of the Minds, albeit in a more rational, less bunny-boiling way. He'd benefitted from never having to dip into his own pockets in order to access a decade's worth of the good stuff, because his daft wee brother had blown paper-round, birthday and Christmas money on every note the lads ever recorded.

As caveats go, however, they were all pretty reasonable, although it wasn't clear what Steven and his pal big Seamus were to get up to post-gig. All I knew was they were staying at Seamus' uncle's flat on Thistle Street and the proximity to a place called Rose Street seemed to excite the chaps.

The gig itself was a triumphant whirl, a set of new and classic tracks powerfully and skilfully performed by an ensemble at the heights of their stadium powers. I scored the latest tour t-shirt, programme and all other tokens you'd expect the obsessive geek to pocket.

After the gig, the big boys went off to perform whatever absolutely non-alcoholic deeds they had lined up, while I dutifully hopped on a bus to my grandparents' house. As ever they were delighted to see me and this capped a damn good day by anyone's reckoning.

There have been many more equally awesome Simple Minds gigs down the years, and although my grandparents are no longer with us and my post-gig curfew has relaxed, I always, without fail, still adhere to caveat number 3. Like I said, funny business, big brothers.

# MARK BYRNE

*RDS Arena*
*19 August 1989, Dublin, Ireland*

My first memory of Simple Minds was 1985 when I was 16 and settling down to a day of music on *Live Aid*. They went from London to Philadelphia and Jim came on stage in a gold-coloured loose shirt and white strides, cool as you like and looking like he owned the gaff. On hearing Charlie strumming the intro to 'Ghostdancing' then Jim singing in his inimitable tones, 'Cities, buildings falling down, satellites come crashing down', I remember thinking to myself, 'Wow!'

My first chance of seeing the Minds live was when my then-girlfriend bought tickets for the show at the RDS Arena in 1989. I remember the atmosphere then sheer feeling of euphoria on hearing the intro music, 'When Spirits Rise', the curtain coming down and hearing 'Street Fighting Years'. It's a memory of my youth I shall never forget and the reason I rate *Street Fighting Years* as the best album among all the gems the Minds have produced.

Among my memories is introducing my 17-year-old guitar-playing nephew to their music at the Olympia, Dublin on the *5x5* tour before he unfortunately passed away, too young. Simple Minds have given me great memories I shall cherish always.

---

# GAIL HARTLEY

*Wembley Stadium*
*26 August 1989,*
*London, England*

I was first introduced to Simple Minds when I happened to record the *Nelson Mandela 70th Birthday Tribute* at Wembley in 1988. At the tender age of 13, my taste in music up until this point had been very pop-orientated. As soon as Simple Minds stepped

on stage, I was mesmerised. I had no idea who the band were but was drawn to the music and energy, the atmosphere and crowd participation. 'Are you ready? Come on then, let's go, everybody!' I was so blown away by the performance that I watched it over and over again until the tape wore out! From that day until now I've been a huge fan and have seen them live over 30 times. Since my first time at Wembley Stadium for the *Street Fighting Years* tour, accompanied by my dad, every concert has been an indelible memory for different reasons. I've seen the band in venues big and small and they never fail to amaze me. Simple Minds is the soundtrack to my life and always will be. I look forward to many more concerts. Let me see your hands!

---

# ADRIAN GREEN

In the summer of 1985, I was 13 when a friend invited me round to his house so we could watch *Live Aid* and a full day of music on TV. I wasn't really into music at the time but my cousin had recently introduced me to Dire Straits and Queen, so I jumped at the chance, particularly as the friend said his mum was getting the snacks in! My friend's sister was a lot older than us and had given us a list of bands she thought we should listen to. On the list were U2 and Simple Minds. As the day went on I was amazed at the joy that music brought me. We spent the entire day in awe as band after band played the main stage.

Simple Minds finally came on in Philadelphia once the broadcast had switched to the States, and I found myself thoroughly engrossed by the performance and 'Don't You (Forget About Me)', which I'd heard on the radio a few days. The next weekend we went shopping and spent a lot of time in HMV, Our Price and Virgin Megastore in Manchester. I bought the 12-inch of 'Someone Somewhere (in Summertime)' and the cassette of *Sons and Fascination*.

A few years later I was thrilled to hear Simple Minds announced to play the Nelson Mandela concert. I was ready at home to record the concert, two radios tuned in with cassette tapes at the ready and my Betamax video primed to record what I'd waited almost three years for - the opportunity to hear what was by now my favourite band live for the first time since *Live Aid*.

Roll on 1989 and *Ballad of the Streets*. I was studying for A-levels and old enough to leave school if I had a free period. The day of the EP release finally came and I walked to Oldham, a mile and a half away, to buy the single in four different formats! I came back to school buzzing with excitement in anticipation of hearing these tunes for the first time.

A few months later the band announced they would be touring arenas and playing Wembley Stadium on the *Street Fighting Years* tour. I saved up as much as I could and bought two tickets. The tickets arrived a few weeks later, then the reality of what I'd done hit me. How the hell was I going to get to London and where the hell was I going to stay? Luckily, it turned out I had an uncle who lived in London, so I stayed in his student digs. The gig was amazing, despite the deluge that persisted all day. At long last, after four years waiting, I was finally seeing my favourite rock 'n' roll band on the biggest stage of their careers. It was absolutely amazing.

# LAWRENCE HAMILTON

It all started aged 14 in 1985 at the CD rack of WH Smith's, buying my very first compact disc. It was a close-run thing between *Once Upon a Time* and Level 42's *World Machine*. The choice was made based on how many songs I knew on each. Pocket money was hard won! I clearly chose right. *Once Upon a Time* remains my most listened to album, every note known like the back of my hand. Still to this day, I yearn to hear 'Come a Long Way' as the finale to a gig – to me, the perfect outro song. And in some ways, a prophetic title as I too have come a long way since that first CD purchase.

What followed was a rapid filling of the back-catalogue – *New Gold Dream*, *Sparkle in the Rain*… then the rest. *Street Fighting Years* hit during that ideal pop culture time of big concerts for big causes. As a confirmed fan, the Mandela concerts and Live Aid were fresh in our minds. Nelson Mandela's birthday concert only served to cement my view that Simple Minds was going to be a life-long favourite band.

My first Simple Minds concert was the *Street Fighting Years* tour at Wembley Stadium. I was 17. It was my first stadium gig. Excitement stoked by *Live in the City of Light*, the day ranks as one of my best ever. The warm-up bands were amazing alone – Gun, Texas, maybe even The Silencers. Simple Minds elicited an energy in me like no other band live. They still do. They have always been my happy place.

I made Edinburgh Castle, front row at Guildford, twice in a week for *Real Life* and a very small club in London for the *Black and White* tour. There have been countless others. They have never disappointed. Now I have sons, even they get it. I've a poor singing voice and 'Don't You (Forget About Me)' is the only thing I try at karaoke. Even I can get a crowd going with it.

Last request? Don't. Ever. Stop. The anticipation of the next tour or album is a 30-year habit.

# DAVID MOON

I booked three tickets to see them at Wembley Stadium on the *Street Fighting Years* tour - one for me, one for my mate, one for my mum. I was still only 15. She liked them anyway and had bought 'All the Things She Said' when it came out three years previously. I got the tickets by calling the box office, getting the number from the ITV Teletext service, which had pages listing acts on tour. Tickets were £16.50 each.

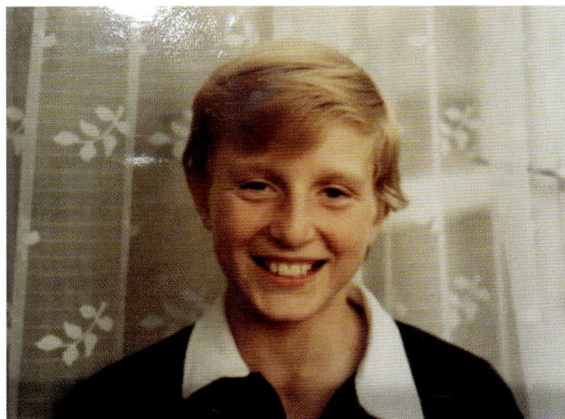

*David Moon was at Wembley*

My dad drove us to the stadium from my nan's place in south east London through Saturday afternoon traffic. He was going to pick us up at the end. The weather was awful; it rained pretty much all day. The crowd were having fun though, sliding belly first through big puddles on the pitch. I remember there being a human pyramid at one point. The guy who made it to the top pulled his pants down, which got a big cheer.

I didn't pay too much attention to the support bands, spending most of the day stood on the terraces at the back of the stadium keeping dry. At some point a tannoy announcement stated they would take to the stage at 7.30pm. As that time got nearer we made our way onto the pitch, ending up next to the scaffold tower in the middle. The big white curtain with the claddagh icon was pulled across the stage.

A video played on the big screens about what was going on in South Africa and the atmosphere started to build as the intro started. I made sure I could see clearly and was just about ready to wet myself with excitement as 'When Spirits Rise' boomed out of the PA. I was surprised at the volume - it was deafening, and the ground was shaking. At the moment the big curtain was pulled back to reveal the stage and band, I understood why people screamed uncontrollably at The Beatles. I didn't scream uncontrollably, I'm just saying I get it.

I was mesmerised for the next three hours. I've since seen Simple Minds live over 35 times but that day will always be my fondest memory. I've read that Jim said that the sound that day was the worst on the whole tour. What a shame, because for all these years since, I've been holding on to the hope that footage from the gig will be released.

---

## MICHELLE SMITH, AGE 17

*Michelle Smith on her way to Wembley*

The first time I saw Simple Minds play was at the age of 17 at Wembley Stadium. It was my first actual concert and it's still one of the best I've been to. The atmosphere was electric, even with the downpour partway through the afternoon between support bands Gun and The Silencers, which soaked everyone on the pitch. When Simple Minds came

*Michelle Smith was at a wet Wembley and remembers an amazing day*

on, the crowd went wild but you could still hear everyone holding their breath in the quiet moments. I've still never experienced anything like the closing rendition of 'Alive and Kicking'. What an incredible, uplifting experience. And what an amazing day!

## AMANDA WILES

At 15 I was mad about music (still am) and was wandering around Camden Town on a Saturday afternoon when I went into Rhythm Records and bought *Once Upon a Time*. After taking this home and playing on my old record player, I couldn't stop listening to it. Over and over I would play it.

Fast forward to 1989 and aged 16 I was lucky enough to see them play the old Wembley Stadium. Prior to the concert Simple Minds played a short film about prisoners of conscience, detailing the plight of Brian Keenan, John McCarthy and others. I was so moved by this, a subject I knew nothing about.

From that concert I then read *Cry Freedom* by Donald Woods and it shocked me how people were treated so violently just because of their race. This opened up to me an interest in supporting the release of prisoners of conscience

*Amanda Wiles went to Wembley twice*

and abolition of the apartheid movement. I was lucky enough to go to the concert given for Nelson Mandela when he was released. The fact a band could play such an important part in the release of Mandela and the ultimate breakdown of the apartheid regime is incredible. That short film influenced my life to this day.

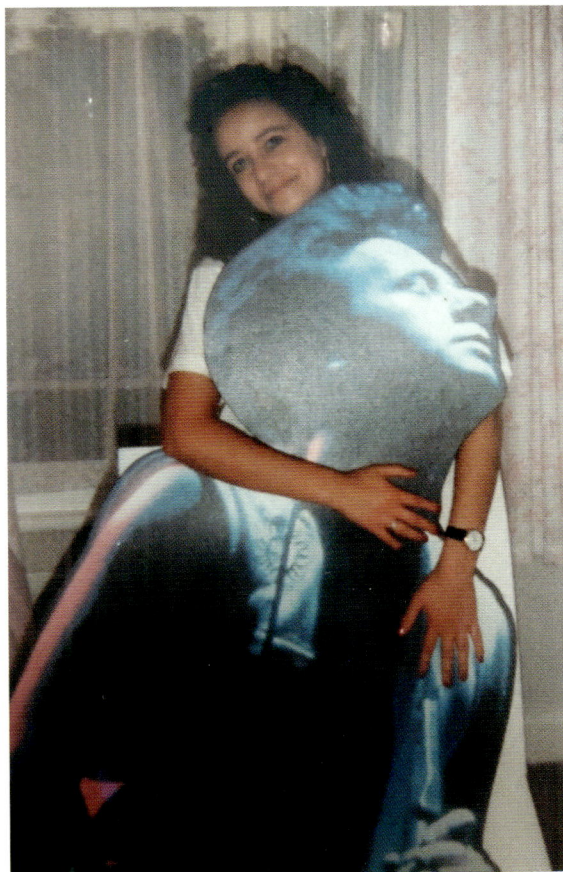

## DARREN WEBB

Never mind the 'Book of Brilliant Things', I wrote the book of brilliant excuses at work to get time off to go to a series of stadium and arena gigs on the *Street Fighting Years* tour. God bless my old boss, and I'm so glad my mother let me off the rent too – 'Don't tell your father!' It brings a tear to my eye just thinking about it.

The last one was Wembley Stadium. My cousin Nick and I were getting a coach from Bath and we'd just got on the M4 to London when I said 'something is burning'. The driver pulled over and said, 'Sorry, we have a problem.' No fucking shit, driver - the Minds are on tonight!

After a couple of hours, a new coach pulled up and we were back the road. By the time we parked up at Wembley and got inside, Gun were on. I said to Nick, 'I can't believe it. Look, the stadium's packed to the rafters.' We pushed our way to the front. I remember Jim saying, 'It's every band's dream to play Wembley Stadium. Are you ready? Let me see your hands!'

## NICK HELFRICH, AGE 17

I discovered the back-catalogue after watching *Live Aid* and spent all the money I could get my hands on buying everything on vinyl and cassette. The experience of Wembley Stadium in 1989 blew me away and I've since seen the band 20 or more times.

I never thought I'd get tickets for *5x5* at the Barras but found myself driving up from Oxfordshire. It was worth every mile. I was offered a lot of money for the tickets outside the gig but didn't mention that to my wife! After a Liverpool gig I went straight to bed at my hotel only to hear next morning that Charlie and others were in the bar I'd walked past after talking myself out of another pint.

Sicily with my wife in 2014 was outstanding. We flew from Luton on the Wednesday and bumped into Andy, Ged and Mel that night, but I was too full of gin to make any sense or even take a photo. After a fabulous gig on Thursday it was back to Luton on Friday and on to pick the kids up from my parents. On the Sunday we moved house - to the Western Isles. We also drove from Oxford to Brussels in an old Mazda Bongo for the Forest National gig in November 2013. We found a cracking walled campsite near the centre of town. I love Belgium and this night was the best the band have ever been - everything just clicked!

# MIKE OSBORNE

The first time I remember hearing Simple Minds and thinking, 'Wow, this is something special' was when I got the compilation album *Raiders of the Pop Charts Parts 1 & 2* for my birthday in January 1983. I was 15. On the final side of this double-LP was 'Someone Somewhere (in Summertime)'. When I listened to it, I instantly fell in love. It was so uplifting and had a lovely melody. Out of 30 songs on this LP, that was without doubt the song I played most.

I started buying *Smash Hits* and remember the issue with Jim Kerr on the front cover, looking resplendent in blue suit. This was December 1983, and I found out Simple Minds were releasing an album in February 1984. I really couldn't wait. But I had to wait five more years to see them live.

On 26 August 1989 I travelled to Wembley Stadium with six friends. My first stadium concert; my first Simple Minds gig. Boy was I excited!

I'd been to Wembley before to watch football, lucky enough to see my team, West Ham United, win the FA Cup in 1980. The crowd seemed big then, but for the gig, with people standing on the pitch, the crowd seemed huge.

It was a gorgeous day (it may have rained but I wouldn't have noticed). As soon as 'Theme for Great Cities' started, I knew I was in for a treat. It was a fantastic concert. The songs I knew and loved sounded great live, and I sang along, punched the air, jumped up and down and danced the whole time. I sweated so much that my shirt was drenched by the time it was over. But I didn't care about that. My favourite band had delivered an amazing performance, I'd loved the experience, and wanted to experience it all over again.

---

# JAN SCHMITZ

*MECC*
*28 August 1989,*
*Maastricht,*
*The Netherlands*

Pink Floyd's *Dark Side of the Moon* changed my musical mindset in 1974, but Gustav Mahler's *Symphony No 2 (Resurrection)* changed my sense of music in 1970, when I was 10. The early Simple

Minds albums were interesting but hearing the first song off *New Gold Dream* made me buy the album the same day. It was a game-changer.

I'm a percussion conductor. I conducted a band in Maastricht, most of whose members were Simple Minds fans. The percussion band were aiming to become Dutch national champions. I wrote a percussion score based on 'Alive and Kicking' and 'Book of Brilliant Things' and we won the Dutch championship in Amsterdam in April 1988, playing 'A Brilliant Book Alive', based on these two songs. The only songs we played during the two-hour drive back to Maastricht were Simple Minds songs. Where Mel Gaynor plays his short drum solo at the end of 'Alive and Kicking', all the percussion players played the solo with him.

# JEROEN TER BRAKE

My first concert was on the *Street Fighting Years* tour. Jim jumped off the stage and broke his elbow and the concert was stopped for a moment. Then he continued with a broken elbow!

# BERNIE SMEETS

The Maastricht Corps of the Red Cross was present at the MECC. I had my Red Cross diploma with me, because you never know. It was just after a break by the band when suddenly the lights went out again. 'Another break?' I heard someone calling. Jim Kerr had fallen from the stage. They sprayed the fans with water to cool them down (the newspaper called us 'heated stoves'), splashes of water hit the stage and Jim slipped and fell off the stage. The lights went back on after a few minutes and Jan Smeets, the boss of Pinkpop, walked off the stage with him. Smeets came back on stage

*Bernie Smeets saw Simple Minds at the MECC in Maastricht*

alone and told the crowd what had happened and said Jim had gone to first aid. 10 minutes later, he came back on stage like a fresh frog, with a bandage over his left eye, and they played for another hour. The first aid people had told him to quit and go to the hospital. But Jim kept performing, giving us another great show.

# STEVE VERSCHAEREN

*Vorst Nationaal*
*29 August 1989, Brussels, Belgium*

I'd just turned 13. My parents owned a pub and there was always music going around. All day long, a local radio station played through the loudspeakers. They played a lot of Flemish songs, Sinatra, disco, etc. But in the evenings there was space for younger DJs to play more modern music. When they were on air, I always went to my room and turned on my radio cassette player. One evening came the song that changed my world, my youth, my lifestyle: 'Promised You a Miracle'. It sounded like a miracle to me, a revelation. My ears and my mind were instantly into it.

Tom, the DJ who played 'Promised You a Miracle' that night, would drink in my parents' pub. The next time he came for a drink I asked him about Simple Minds. He said he'd put the *New Gold Dream* album on a cassette tape for me. A few days later he brought me the cassette and my dad rewarded him with a few free beers. I went directly to my room and played the tape. I played it so many times that the tape broke.

In August 1989 I'd just finished my first holiday job and went to a record store in Antwerp with my pay. The basement was the rock and new wave department. I was buying the 'Kick It In' single, maxi-single and CD. When I arrived at the counter to pay, I saw a poster advertising tickets for Simple Minds at the Forest National. I had just enough money to buy the records, CD and a ticket.

I enjoyed every second of the show. I sang all the songs from start to finish, bought my first Simple Minds t-shirt and also a poster and the tour programme. This day and night will be forever in my memories.

This page contains a ticket image for a Simple Minds concert.

## ANDRE HOF

*Ijsstadion Thialf
2 September 1989,
Heerenveen,
The Netherlands*

*Andre Hof saw Simple Minds at Ijsstadion Thialf*

I was 15 and lived in a small village in Friesland in February 1989. Before going to school one day I heard a song on Radio 3 and recognised the voice. But the music was completely different. The DJ said, 'You have to get used to it, but what a good song from Simple Minds, 'Belfast Child'.' It became the Alarm Disk that Friday and the song was played every hour.

I had a lovely surprise in August 1989 when I discovered my parents had bought tickets for a Simple Minds concert. We went to the concert with my brother, sister and friends that Saturday 2 September. The moment the curtain fell, I got goosebumps. Jim Kerr said, 'This is the last time in Holland, let's make it a special one. This is Your Friesland.' What a great concert! Simple Minds were forever in my heart.

## JEAN-PIERRE BENZ

*Patinoire de Malley
6 September 1989, Lausanne, Switzerland*

My first Simple Minds concert was in Lausanne, where I lived at that time, in the Patinoire de Malley. It was a great experience. I was with friends and my sister and her friends. The show was great, the music very good. I will never forget feeling the bass in my stomach. It was loud but we loved it. Some bands are disappointing in concert but this was not the case with Simple Minds. It was the other way around – in concert we discovered an even better band.

I moved then to Zürich, where I saw them at the Hallenstadion, Volkshaus and at Komplex 457, where I enjoyed being very close to the stage. The *5x5* gig was very good. I recorded some videos with my little photo camera. I remember Jim saying, 'Be sure that your batteries are charged, because mine are!'

# ANDREAS HUSSING

*Lorelei Freilichtbühne*
*9 September 1989, Loreley, West Germany*

In 1982, I'd listen to the German radio broadcaster WDR, where one of the deejays liked to play Simple Minds. When *Sparkle in the Rain* was released I and my friend Thomas bought it. At the time I had no hi-fi system, just a ghetto-blaster my parents gave me for Christmas. I used it to record the current pop, rock, reggae and disco music on cassettes. I was always up to date with my music and recommended music to my friends. But I preferred Simple Minds, earning me the nickname Simple Jupp (Josef).

The following year I bought the back-catalogue and played them on my brother Stefan's stereo. It's a miracle the needle didn't wear through to the other side of *New Gold Dream*.

In 1989 I went with my friends to Lorelei by the Rhine to experience a Simple Minds concert. We found a place up a big tree so had a great view of the stage. I sang along with almost all the songs, and it was a wonderful feeling to be there. At the end there were fireworks. It was a great atmosphere. As they left the concert, fans were still singing the songs.

---

# NICOLA CATINO

*Stadio Lamberti*
*12 September 1989, Cava De Terreni, Italy*

When I was a young boy, I felt excluded and different from others, but then I put *New Gold Dream* on and dreamt about becoming a musician and getting noticed. I felt different when I was listening to that warm vinyl record, less shy and more ready to conquer everyone's friendship and respect when playing drums like Mel or singing á la Jim, jumping here and there on a stage.... Dreaming was the sweetest thing and Simple Minds helped me with that.

My father drove me, 16, and my brother, 18, to see Simple Minds at Cava dei Tirreni, dropping us at 7am as he had to drive back to Barletta for work. We were the only ones there as a lot of people started to arrive from 10am. Then, finally inside, we were right in the front line, under the stage! Jim was looking at us one by one, no one excluded, his deep and good eyes and a hypnotising look, conveying one single but clear message: music will never let us down and will always be there - cathartic, incomparable. At the intro to 'Waterfront', I turned back to look and saw a human wall jumping behind me. I looked up to the sky and thought, 'This is the best day of my life.'

After that, I didn't see them live for many years. I was too busy studying, working and playing. I graduated in 1998 and, leaving the university building, heard the sound of bagpipes pulsing in my head. The intro from Cava was coming back with such persistence and remained there for many days. It was a sign of my destiny!

In 2002, I was very much into hotels and the accommodation industry and a friend suggested I apply for a job at a hotel in Sicily. The logo of this hotel is now tattooed on my skin.

Everything is possible in the game of life! An excellent down-to-earth person, Jim himself was there during the interview. He was staring at my drum-necklace, my talisman ever since, and at the end of the interview he played on it with his finger, and I replied with a percussive sound of my mouth. I will never forget that interview in English, finished like we were good old friends!

I just wanted an autograph, and ending up working for Jim in Taormina for the opening of Villa Angela in 2004 was a dream come true and such an honour!

---

## ADRIANA MUSSOLIN

*Arena Di Verona*
*15 September 1989, Verona, Italy*

I saw the *Street Fighting Years* tour in Milan in 1989 (I fainted and they took me away from the front row after five songs), in the Arena of Verona (where I lost my little bag and the ticket) and in my hometown of Turin (where I crashed my dad's car close to

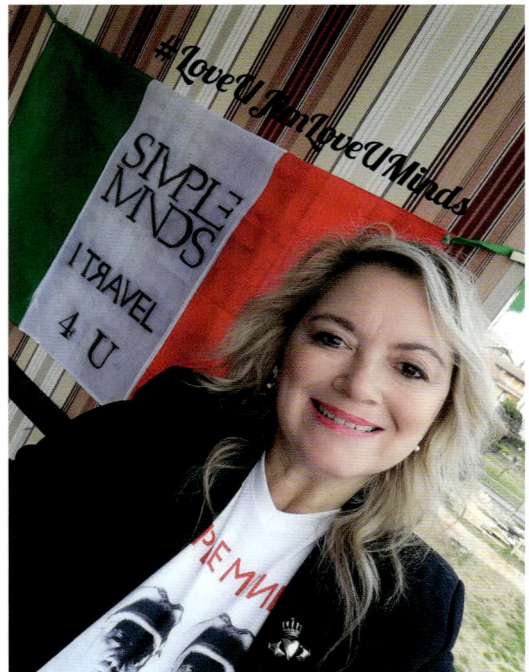

*Adriana Mussolin fainted at the Verona show*

the Pellerina Park on the morning of the gig). So I was quite sad as I queued for the concert in the sun. But the concert that night was great and I got some precious and cool photos that I keep safe like jewels.

---

## ANDREW WATT

My schoolmate Adam in Leeds gave me a proud demonstration of his bedroom drum kit (he had a big bedroom). 'I want to be Mel Gaynor' he said. He'd tap out drumbeats next to me in French lessons. He drove me nuts with that, but helped me straight into the sound of Simple Minds. Oh jungleland…

---

## HEMINDER AHLUWALIA

My brother and I are big fans of Simple Minds. We heard Simple Minds first in the mid-Eighties when our father returned from a work-related UK trip. We had asked him to bring some nice music on the way back home to Mumbai, India, as those were the days, when we were in our late teens, when we could look forward to gifts from foreign trips. Our dad had visited the largest music store in London and the person working there suggested Simple Minds' *Once Upon a Time*. We listened to all the songs on the cassette for months and months - and so our interest in Simple Minds started. All the songs on that cassette were great, and an era one can still enjoy today.

---

## DYLAN HARPER

*National Exhibition Centre*
*22 – 24 September 1989, Birmingham, England*

My first experience of Simple Minds was hearing their latest album, *Once Upon a Time*, as a teenager in the back of a friend's old Ford Fiesta in 1986. I was instantly drawn to their music and began collecting their back-catalogue on cassette and vinyl. *Live in the City of Light* and their involvement in the following year's Mandela concert really drew me to their live performances. In 1989 I first saw them play at the NEC in Birmingham on the *Street Fighting Years* tour. I was blown away by their performances. I still am. I didn't know then how influential their music would be on my life.

Through their website and Facebook pages in recent years, there's a more personal connection between the band and their fans from all over the world. After 31 years and 11 concerts all around the UK, I still have the same if not more interest and passion for their music. It's formed the soundtrack of my life. In 2021, I am looking forward to celebrating my 50th birthday with my wife Mandy and a trip to Taormina to see them play in the great Teatro Antico amphitheatre. I can't wait!

## ROB HOLLEY

My journey started as a 15-year-old growing up in the West Midlands. You could say I was late to the party. It was late 1986 or early 1987 when my best mate at school started banging on about this band and loaned me a VHS recording of the *Alive in Rotterdam* Ahoy Stadium gig. He was that taken with the band he even had the iconic *Once Upon a Time* LP font replicated on his luminous yellow paper round bag in black marker pen. This became a favourite past time of ours, repeating this font all over our schoolbooks.

This introduction to the band had me hooked and I started exploring the back-catalogue. I remember having a dodgy copy of *Sons and Fascination/Sister Feelings Call* on a TDK D90 cassette which I played to death on my Sony Walkman. Whenever I listen to that album today (I now have a remastered version) it takes me back to a happy time and place.

By 1989 and the *Street Fighting Years* tour announcement, my excitement levels were through the roof. This was going to be my first proper gig. I remember queuing for tickets for hours in the rain at the Birmingham NEC Arena box office.

The gig itself is still vivid in my memory. I can't quite believe how many years have passed. My lasting recollection is getting carried around in a wave of people standing at the front. I was about 30 feet from the stage at one point. The next thing I knew I was crushed at the front looking up at the band. It is a lot calmer at gigs these days.

I haven't missed a tour since that first gig in 1989. And I could never have envisaged that this lad from the West Midlands would spend the last 18 years living near the hometown of his favourite band. I'm now married to a Scottish lass, live near Glasgow, with the Barrowland Ballroom my local venue.

## MATTHEW BURTON

My girlfriend Sarah (now my wife) and I went to our first gig together at the NEC in Birmingham, and it was the most amazing experience. When the Claddagh curtain dropped and 'Street Fighting Years' began we knew we'd want to see them again and again and again. The first gigs both my son Cory (at Birmingham) and daughter Darcey (at Southampton) went to see were the Minds.

## LEE MORGAN

I was 11 when I first became aware of their music, in 1982. I heard 'Promised You a Miracle' on the radio and at the end of the next year, 'Waterfront' on the first *Now That's What I Call Music!* album. I loved them both but really became a fan a couple of years later when I first heard 'Alive and Kicking' then the whole of *Once Upon a Time*. It was around that time that I saw *The Breakfast Club* and first heard 'Don't You (Forget About Me)'. The film is one of my all-time favourites, and the song *is* my all-time favourite! My friends back then all loved their music and we came to see them at the NEC, Birmingham in 1989 on the *Street Fighting Years* tour and again in 1991 on the *Real Life* tour, both phenomenal shows. I went to Wolverhampton Civic Hall in 2013 too, and that was the icing on the cake for me … so far!

## IAN BOURNE

I got into Simple Minds as a 14-year-old thanks to my brother's cassette of *Sparkle in the Rain*. I'd simply never heard a song like 'Waterfront'. *Live in the City of Light* is my favourite album of all time. I was desperate to see the band live and watched the Mandela concert at Wembley, having heard 'Mandela Day' on Radio 1 a few days before. The band were incredible that day, I was so proud of them.

    With the release of *Street Fighting Years* and accompanying tour announced, I was desperate to get a ticket despite my meagre YTS income. Living in the Midlands, the NEC dates were the best bet. So I went to the NEC to take my place in the queue at 2am ahead of a release time of midday. I stood there for hours in February but didn't care one bit. I just wanted my ticket. Eventually the site opened and someone had the great idea to play Simple Minds songs over the tannoy, including 'Saturday Girl'. I duly got my ticket about an hour later. I saw them twice more on that tour, and many, many times since. But I'll never forget that Sunday, queueing with fellow devotees.

## MARK CROASDALE

Being from Lancashire most of my mates were heavily into Joy Division, New Oder and The Smiths. But Simple Minds were my group. At 14, it was cool and the music was great. I was ecstatic and in love with their music around 1985, but also loved their earlier stuff. And I tried to grow a mullet like Jim.

    My friend Ruben and I first watched Simple Minds at the old NEC in Birmingham. It was my first live gig and we pushed right to the front. About halfway through, Ruben said, 'Get on my shoulders', so I did. Jim saw me. I was about five people deep by then and Jim tried so hard to reach me and at least touch my hand. He kept trying and trying and I was trying to reach him, but I was too far away and he had to back off.

Teenagers try to make a difference and find their direction and Simple Minds fulfilled that emotion and direction for me. The day Nelson Mandela was released from prison I played 'Mandela Day' very loudly in my bedroom to celebrate.

They are a great live band and I loved their arrogance in comparing themselves to The Who, The Doors and Led Zep playing live. I later took my wife to see them at the NEC. That was her first live gig.

---

## ANDY HOWARTH

*King's Hall*
*26 September 1989, Belfast, Northern Ireland*

Having just started my first job after school, getting paid what I thought was a massive £40 a week, walking past a record store in Belfast I saw a poster for Simple Minds' *Street Fighting Years* tour in the King's Hall. I'd only heard *Live in the City of Light* plus the odd bit on the radio but thought, 'Why not?' I think I paid the princely sum of around £15 for the privilege. From the start to the finish of the show I was hooked. I'm so proud to say I was there the first time Simple Minds played 'Belfast Child' live in Belfast. What a reaction it got too.

---

## KRISTIN ERICSON

*Scandinavium*
*30 September 1989, Gothenburg, Sweden*

My friend from school owned both *Sparkle in the Rain* and *Once Upon a Time*. I really liked the covers and asked her to play *Sparkle*. Wow! A couple of months later I saw the 1985 Ahoy show on TV. Great songs but I wasn't really sure about the singer to be honest…. Fast forward to the release of *Live in the City of Light*. That's where my love and, dare I say it, my obsession really took off. The songs, the atmosphere, the audience and the singer! Since then I've never really looked back. Now my collection consists of everything from guitar picks and used drumsticks, setlists, tour posters and programmes to rare and not so rare pressings and tons of live recordings. I really love the collector side and the great people I've met through the years sharing a passion for Simple Minds.

First time I saw them live was September 1989 on the *Street Fighting Years* tour in Gothenburg, Sweden. Standing close to the stage and almost three hours of music magic! I seem to remember Mel wearing a wig when playing a few songs with support act Gun as well.

I've seen the band on numerous occasions, with the best show by far in Copenhagen, Denmark during the *5x5* tour in 2012. What a great concept! I was too young to have been able to see the band in the late 70s and early 80s, so that night sure made up for it. 'Changeling', 'This Fear of Gods', 'Chelsea Girl', and my all-time favourite, 'Room'! My biggest regret is not buying tickets for Berlin the day before.

A special mention has to go to the show at Växjö rock festival on 30 May 2009. It was freezing cold but the band and audience enjoyed it and we got to hear the little gem that is 'This is It'. And I'll never get tired of 'New Gold Dream'. Great memories!

The last show I attended was at Partille Arena, close to Gothenburg, in March 2020 before the great lockdown, on the *40 Years of Hits* tour. Who knows when we'll be able to see them next.

---

## MVH ÅKE

In 1989 Simple Minds played Stockholm, but it was a disappointment. The concert started early in the evening and all the effects and light were erased. I remember Jim was unhappy with the show so they came back to Gothenburg that autumn. The Scandinavium Arena was filled and the tension sparkled in the air. All of us wanted so much to support them and to play and feel this was the best gig ever. And 20 minutes before, the crowd exploded and applauded and shouted. I've never seen and heard a more excited crowd. It was a roar and I think the band heard that. That concert was a mind-blower and a memory for life. Everything was perfect that night.

---

## ROBERT NILSSON

I got into Simple Minds through an older neighbour who let me borrow *New Gold Dream*. It was followed by the albums before and after, until I was old enough and had the money to buy my own. Eventually, I saw them live. I'd listened to live bootlegs over the years, so thought I knew what to expect, but it was a lot better. A friend came with me to the last show of the *Street Fighting Years* tour, which remains one of the best concerts I've been to. It was so good that unfortunately none of the Simple Minds shows I saw after came close.

I remember Jim coming back on stage after the show, jumping down in the front of the crowd and starting to walk around, greeting the fans. I remember being approached by street vendors outside assuring us their t-shirts were the real deal since they made them. I also remember stopping at the side of the road on the way home, running laps around the car to try and stay awake.

These are memories forever etched into my mind, but it's the music itself that makes you hang on to a band or artist. The various different phases of Simple Minds give you something for each occasion or period in life. I used to favour the mid-period stuff, the songs I knew first. In later years I've gone back to the earliest stuff, but also some of the later records. I'm not sure if it's the 'bleak Scottishness' that connects well with us Scandinavians, but they always seemed popular over here. It could just be the great songs.

---

## EVA THORDSTEIN

I've been a fan since 1981 and I'm still very much a fan. The first Simple Minds song I heard was 'I Travel'. I thought it had something unique. I was gifted the single for my 14th birthday and have been hooked ever since – for life it seems.

I wrote to Jim years ago to tell him about when I saw them in 1989 in Gothenburg and met him after the show. I told him I've always imagined I'd get paralysed and nervous but I didn't. In fact I've never been so calm. And he was calm. I took some photos and we talked about the gig in Copenhagen in June. We agreed it was special. He said, 'You should have seen us in Copenhagen,' and I answered, 'I did!' and he had the cutest, funniest smile on his face. I thought about things to ask him but suddenly it didn't matter. All that mattered was that he was there, a few metres from me. I could have touched him, but didn't. At that moment I realised how he must feel every time a fan approaches. All these people every night, in every city, all the same. In his place I wouldn't have gone out to talk to them. I would have been too tired and all too fed up. I realise how precious Jim and the band were and I was proud of him. I don't think any other band of the size of Simple Minds would go out to meet their fans in this way.

---

## ROBERT GRZEGORZEK

*Flinders Park*
*22 November 1989, Melbourne, Australia*

It was a choice, and I chose *Live in the City of Light*. I had a Walkman and the tapes were played over and over and over. It was the most awesome thing I ever heard. I got to see Simple Minds a few months later in Melbourne. The ticket cost $22. I'm still owed 22 bucks by some random chick, but that's beside the point. I so remember the very first song, 'Street Fighting Years'. And Jim sounded so much like Aussie singer James Reyne, from Australian Crawl. I couldn't understand a single word he was singing. He had chewing gum in his mouth. But heck, it didn't matter. It was Jim! And CHARLIE! And Mel! And I got to see Mick! Woo-hoo!

## PETER BOLLAND

*Entertainment Centre*
*24 November 1989, Sydney, Australia*

My first experience with Simple Minds was in '82, when my mate played *New Gold Dream* in his caravan and 'Someone Somewhere (in Summertime)' came on. I was hooked. My first concert didn't come until 1989 in Sydney, on the *Street Fighting Years* tour. My love for them is stronger than ever. I only wish they still had the original band together. Simple Minds forever.

## GRACE WARD

*Entertainment Centre*
*28 November 1989, Brisbane, Australia*

Scattered thoughts: a reel-to-reel player in the living room, a recording off the radio obtained by my elder brother, bedazzled by 'Love Song', my 10-year-old mindset thinking 'they sound French' and 'wow, that pulsating opening synth - never heard anything like it.' 'Love Song' certainly paved its way big time here in Australia in 1981.

Sitting on the backstairs landing, looking out towards the motorway and inner city madness, a hot golden sunset creating a golden haze whilst enjoying the pure magic of *Live in the City of Light* in the summer of '87.

A crazy time camping out late into the night and early morning trying to secure excellent tickets for my first concert, the *Street Fighting Years* tour. Great memories, great friends. It's amazing to catch up with older friends who you don't see often in your life and yet run into after many years, sometimes in different Australian cities, purely because Simple Minds are touring.

The excitement that lies ahead. With any tour or new record release it's always a buzz, and with Simple Minds the pulse always seems to remain.

# TERRY INGLIS

I heard an amazing song on the radio called 'Promised You a Miracle' when I was a little boy and thought, 'Who is this great band?' It wasn't until my older brother bought the album *Once Upon a Time* that I realised what a great band they are. But what stunned me was hearing *New Gold Dream 81, 82, 83, 84* - my No.1 album of all time.

The first international band concert I saw was Simple Minds on the *Street Fighting Years* tour at Brisbane in 1989. It was amazing and, let's face it, you don't forget your first time. Since then I've always seen their magic concerts when they're touring Australia. The last show I saw was at Newcastle at the end of 2018 where I was lucky to get hold of one of Cherrise's drumsticks - with lots of cracks in it!

Keep the dream and magic going.

---

# BRUCE FINDLAY

From *New Gold Dream* onwards, it became more bombastic, more dry and large. And of course, the larger venues, as soon as it became bigger, production became bigger. We were going on tour with 40 trucks. It became ridiculous. We became a stadium act. So, we're doing stadia. And the whole production, the whole organisation became so big. We were planning a year, two years ahead.

It was not comfortable for me. I never saw myself as a big time, heavyweight manager. I was delighted with the success, but at the same time the dream for me was to manage the best band in the world, not the biggest. I wasn't Paul McGuinness. Paul's ambition was to make U2 the biggest band in the world and he very nearly achieved it. But every band is unique and I wanted us to have our place in history. One of the most famous bands in the world is the Velvet Underground and they never sold any records.

There are bands that have become huge and retained some kind of integrity. But success can be a poisoned chalice. The band began to squabble a little. Derek Forbes got kicked out of the band just after 'Don't You (Forget About Me)'. By the end of '89 we were so big, and tired. The band could have done with a break. And Jim was about to turn 30. Cracks began to show.

We'd already had several major hits in the UK and Europe, and there were so many bootlegs coming out of Simple Minds live concerts, it really began to piss us off. So we decided to make a live album, a double-live album which also went to No.1 and sold millions of copies in Britain and Europe. But we insisted the Americans release it. They said, 'You're only a baby band, you've only just broken through here'. We said, 'Yeah, but we've been around almost a decade in Europe and we've built a massive following and are on our seventh or eighth album. We're selling out stadia all over Europe and the rest of the world. It's time.'

This was my big mistake. In many ways I wish we'd taken a year out from America and said, 'Don't release it', but they wanted a follow-up album. So we followed *Once Upon a Time* with *Street Fighting Years*. The live album completely stiffed in America.

*Street Fighting Years* was a very serious and political album, the Nelson Mandela period, and the Americans didn't get the seriousness. The whole thing was too dark for America. And, again, it stiffed and the band refused to tour America.

Our agent organised a massive tour, but it was coming down from the arenas. We were taking a step back. He said, 'Look, the best thing to do now would be to go back into the big halls, play to big crowds. It will be great.' Essentially, eat a bit of humble pie. And the band disagreed. So they didn't do the American tour for that album.

The American record company were quite happy because they hated the album. *Street Fighting Years* was a smash hit in Britain and Europe – they were doing Wembley Stadium and all the rest of it - but it was a very awkward year for all of us. I left the band at the beginning of January 1990, and so did Mick, the keyboard player.

From then on Simple Minds had to regroup. They had to rethink things over the next decade, which they did.

I decided I didn't like the way it was going. The whole magnitude of the thing was uncomfortable for me. And I'm sure it's wonderful making money, you know, big money stuff, but otherwise not comfortable. We're still good friends. I see Jim and Charlie quite a lot.

## street fighting years
# DAVID PRICE

I was a marine engineer in the Royal Navy and spent a lot of time at sea. On naval ships there is a control centre called HQ1. It is a hub for monitoring a lot of the systems on ships. During my first set of rounds during a Middle Watch (Midnight to 4AM) I walked into HQ1 to talk to my mate, 'Titch' Ince. He had a very Eighties sound system with him and as I walked into the compartment all I could hear was this amazingly rich, anthemic sound. I didn't recognise the track or the artist so I asked Titch who it was. 'Have you never heard of Simple Minds?' he said. 'No,' I replied, 'but I am an instant fan.' We played it and rewound the cassette numerous times. The track he was playing was 'Someone Somewhere (In Summertime)'.

# CHARLIE ROCKWELL

I had been hoping and waiting for Simple Minds to come to the US. But the last time they came through I was in the hospital having a leg amputated. While doing my rehab I would listen to songs like 'Waterfront' to help keep my mind focused on the long journey ahead and help me through the toughest of times.

---

# CARINA SCHMIDT

*Radrennbahn Weissensee*
*26 August 1990, Berlin, Germany*

My older brother had his room next to my room. Our rooms were connected by a door and he was lucky enough to have a radio recorder. He had a terrible taste in music - hard guitar sounds, loud drums and terrible screams, which he liked to call singing. I jumped out of bed to open the door and ask him to listen to his AC/DC a little more quietly, when I heard the first sounds of *New Gold Dream*. My anger at the previous screams was gone and my fascination began. Everything matched - the voice, the guitar, the keyboard, the drums, the rhythm, then this '81-82-83-84'. I beamed all over my face when I carefully opened the door and politely asked my brother who was singing. He just shrugged his shoulders, said something about 'minze'. I wanted to know if he already knew the song and the group he was listening to on the radio. He said no, shrugged his shoulders again and like big brothers sometimes do, he immediately sent me back to my room and said I shouldn't bother him again that evening. I fell asleep and the next morning I woke up, humming '81-82-83-84'.

Then came the fall of the Berlin Wall in 1989. I was studying at a technical school for economics in Voigtland (Saxony), not far from Bavaria. 10 days after the Wall fell, I went to the town of Hof with a friend. Instead of going to boarding school on Sunday evening and sitting in the school the next morning, we met in Zwickau and took the completely overcrowded night train. It was a great journey for us, between a new world and an old world. There was overcrowding, bullying, the smell of beer, cold cigarette smoke and all kinds of human exhalation. We arrived in Hof, completely tired, at 5am. It was cold, it was wet, the train station was as crowded with people as the train, and that bad smell crept into my nose. However, I had a clear goal in mind. I finally wanted to buy the record with the song that I loved so much. I wanted to hold this treasure in my hands. I wanted a copy of *New Gold Dream*. It was getting light and we went downtown. I didn't find the city particularly beautiful. Unlike West Berlin (I had been there the weekend before), I found Hof bleak and smelly. It was probably the smell of the many people on the train I remembered. A feeling so difficult to describe.

On one hand, I felt infinite euphoria that the Wall had finally fallen, the world was open and I could finally do what I wanted. On the other, I felt uncertainty at this time - nobody really knew how these days would go on. What I knew was that it was going to be better than what was behind us.

We squeezed through the much too small inner city of Hof with many other thousands of people when I discovered a second-hand record store on a corner. I was going to buy my first Simple Minds record. I didn't care which record it was. But I couldn't find a Simple Minds record. The disappointment was clearly written on my face as the shop assistant came from behind his counter and asked what I was looking for. 'I'm looking for *New Gold Dream*,' I said. He looked at me and said, 'For your age and coming from the East, you have a damn good taste in music.' He no longer had *New Gold Dream* but *Sparkle in the Rain* was still in stock. He trudged off to get it. 'Would you like to listen?' He put the headphones on me and I listened to 'Waterfront'. I was enchanted and beamed at that moment.

I beamed even more on a brilliant Sunday evening in August 1990, in the second row at my first Simple Minds concert in Berlin.

---

# RENÉ SPOIDA

As a kid living in the former German Democratic Republic it was never easy to get access to good music in 1984. Fortunately we lived close to the border of Berlin, so music played by the radio stations of West Berlin filled our cassette tapes. And sometimes somebody knew somebody who had a grandma who was allowed to visit West Berlin and she would smuggle records or fanzines across the border, so we could make copies. One of my best friends was a die-hard Simple Minds fan. Thanks to my friend's continuous advertising - he also played some old stuff to me - I started listening to the catalogue of Simple Minds, and I was overwhelmed.

When my friends and I went to the disco, we'd create a wish-list of songs like Simple Minds' 'Love Song' or Kraftwerk's 'Trans-Europe Express'. We had to lend the DJs our tapes but they were mostly nice enough and brave enough to play our choice of music, even though it emptied the dancefloor! It sounded so cool and we danced mystically, like there was no tomorrow. We were so avant-garde with our black-dyed clothes and fancy haircuts.

In the summer of 1988, I was able to watch the Mandela concert live on TV. I remember how proud I was of my band making a political statement. It wasn't pompous pop. Those times were so important and so full of change and hope. The first thing I did after the Berlin Wall came down in 1989 was go into a West Berlin record store and buy *Real to Real Cacophony*.

My first Simple Minds concert was a white-hot day in August 1990 in Berlin. They shared the bill with Tina Turner, Gary Moore and Die Toten Hosen. I'd just finished a late shift at work, jumped into my car and drove straight to Berlin-Weißensee. I was running late, the show had already started and I could hear 'Waterfront'. I ran into the arena, saw my band playing and was the happiest 21-year-old on earth. I was watching from a distance but felt closer than I'd ever felt before.

---

## MICK LANG

*Flugplatz*
*1 September 1990, Lüneburg, Germany*

It was the spring of 1989 when I heard 'Belfast Child' the first time. This wasn't rock music like I'd heard before. A few days later, after pestering my mother for the money, I went out and bought *Street Fighting Years*. As a 15-year-old, I didn't hear the political side of the album until maybe a month or two later. I was just captivated by this huge orchestral sound. But soon I wanted to educate myself about the names I was hearing about - Mandela, Jara, The Troubles, the poll tax. These names and subjects made me want to know more about the world – what was really happening and what had already happened.

By the end of the summer, I'd got myself a wee job so I could fund buying everything Simple Minds had done. I also bought artists I knew had influenced them.

First time I ever got to see them live was at a festival in Lüneburg. I was just 16 and managed to persuade a friend of mine who had a car that it would be amazing to go, so off we went with my girlfriend. It rained the whole time we were there, and we overnighted in a tent by the side of the road.

They shared the bill with Tina Turner and Gary Moore. There were two stages, side by side, but we got there early so we could be at the front of the correct stage. I remember the excitement building during Gary Moore's set that finally I'd get to see my heroes. From the first bassline of 'Waterfront', I don't really remember much about the gig, except Jim jumping off the stage and grabbing hands in the front row. I was just an inch or two away. The rest is a blur.

## ULF HUNTE

In the summer of 89, age 16, I went with my good friend Christian on a bike trip through Northern Germany. We took a small

*Ulf Hunte saw Simple Minds in Lüneburg*

cassette recorder with us and only two tapes (for whatever reason). One was *Street Fighting Years*. I remember sitting on a very small sailing boat, our shelter back then, looking out over a big sea listening to 'This is Your Land' and all the other tracks on the album.

I wanted to see Simple Minds live as soon as possible as I'd missed the *Street Fighting Years* tour. Luckily, they returned to Germany in 1990 to play a few summer gigs. My friend and I took our bikes and jumped on a train to witness the sheer power of Simple Minds at an airfield in Lüneburg. It was unbelievable. I'd never experienced something like that before.

---

## PETER-JOHN VETTESE

*Pianist, Simple Minds 1990-91 and appears on Big Music & Walk Between Worlds*

One abiding memory of my time in Simple Minds was when I joined them to play keyboards on the *Real Life* album. One moment in particular sticks in my mind. After a pretty gruelling day recording (starting at 10.30am each day and consisting of selecting a song, figuring out parts, discussing direction, etc. and playing it as a band), I remember being very tired but satisfied the song we were focusing on was now in good shape and I was ready to turn in. But then Charlie suggested we start another song. It was now around two the following morning. I could barely believe they were serious. However, pie and beans all round revived our senses and we started work on what would be the title track, 'Real Life'. As I sat programming sounds and practicing parts, I remember looking at Jim and Charlie, thinking, 'You guys deserve every bit of your success.' Their commitment to the work was phenomenal. Of course though, the ensuing uncontrolled farting generated by the beans caused a temporary cessation in music-related activity. I'll never forget how the fun and laughter that accompanied those long hours and hard work made real life such a beautiful experience of *Real Life*.

THE CONCERT COMPANY
MAMA CONCERTS & RAU

NDR2 OPEN AIR
ROCK OVER GERMANY

29844

Sa., 25. Aug., und So., 26. Aug. '90
2 TAG OPEN AIR
LÜNEBURG · FLUGPLATZ
AN DER B4
Vorverkauf: DM 73,–
zzgl. VVK-Gebühr

Wichtiger Hinweis siehe Rückseite!
Das Verlassen des Geländes ist nur mit Auslaßkarte möglich

# BERNIE SMEETS

As an artist Simple Minds gave me the inspiration to paint. I made this little oil painting back in 1989. I was listening to the *Street Fighting Years* album, where this chapel was shown on the inside cover with Jim sat in the grass with the chapel behind him. At first I thought the chapel was in Scotland, so in the beginning my painting was named 'Little Scottish chapel'. I later learned that the chapel was actually in Ireland so I changed the name.

I love the threatening sky and the colours it brings when the sun tries to shine through the dark clouds.

I had some very positive comments about my painting when I posted it online as a way to show the world my art.

# THOMAS HAACK

Simple Minds are not just a band for me, they are an inspiration, and a feeling I find difficult to describe. Their music is like magic. I'm just in a different world when I listen to the music. Nervous like a little kid, I always get goosebumps when they

*Photo - Bernie Smeets' oil painting*

enter the stage. In Münster, between Bob Geldof and Simple Minds, the Dalai Lama entered the stage and spoke to us. Wow! Through the Simple Minds official fan club I got to know my wife, who is from Thailand. I have visited Taormina and spent nice days in the Villa Angela. To my great happiness I also met you, dear Jim, in person. No planned meet and greet. Two normal guys who met along the way and had a bit of a chat. Wonderful....

## REAL LIFE
## 'AFRICAN SKIES'

*Alfred Bos, author of*
*The Race is the Prize*

*Alfred Bos centre played on African Skies - left*
*producer Pete Walsh and right Charlie Burchill*

February 1990. 1989's *Street Fighting Years* stadium tour is history. Mick MacNeil has left the band. Jim is on the phone. 'Charlie and I are at Wisseloord.' It is the studio where they recorded 'The Amsterdam' EP (with 'Sign O' The Times'), the band's final release with Mick. 'We are writing new songs and we'd like you to listen to some tracks.'

In the basement of Wisseloord, Jim, Charlie and engineer Heff Moraes have set up a recording studio. They play me some tracks, or sketches of tracks, that will be released on 1991's *Real Life album*. 'Woman' is atmospheric, intimate, cinematic. It is Simple Minds without Mick and still sounds like Simple Minds. I am pleasantly surprised.

The playback session is over and I am hanging around in the basement. Jim and the engineer are hovering over the mixing console and Charlie fools around with his guitar and a wah-wah pedal.

Charlie unshoulders his guitar and sits behind the piano. He ad-libs a tune. 'Feel free,' he says to me and points at his guitar. I haven't fingered an axe for ages, yet I am intrigued by the wah-wah pedal. I strap on the guitar and look for a pick.

'I've got an idea for a song, 'African Skies',' Jim suddenly says. 'Charlie, play again that melody you were fiddling with.' He instructs the engineer on the rhythm track. 'Okay, let's go.' Charlie plays the piano. Jim sings. I'm standing strapped in Charlie's guitar, my foot on a wah-wah pedal.

African skies? In my mind's eye I see a savannah, vibrating with heat. I hear the buzz and hum of insects. An idea pops: the wah-wah pedal will help to create crickets. We do it twice. When I leave for home, they hand me a cassette.

It's August and Jim calls: 'The album is finished and 'African Skies' is included. We've kept your guitar part.' Take two, it appears later.

Some songs are not written, they drop from the sky. In dim-lit cellars that imagination transforms into a steaming savannah. That afternoon at Wisseloord is my favourite Simple Minds recollection.

## SHAWN WILSON

*Massey Hall*
*4 June 1991, Toronto, Canada*

I remember seeing them in the early '90s at Massey Hall, Toronto. It was during the *See the Lights* tour and the show was amazing. Even more special was Jim coming out the back door afterwards to sign autographs. All I had was a white shirt and my girlfriend's lipstick, but Jim smiled and signed the shirt in ruby red.

U2 had their apex in the 80s and 90s. Simple Minds have weathered the years by focusing on creating new music and challenging themselves. It really is incredible to listen to 'The American', then 'Someone Somewhere (in Summertime)' to 'Oh Jungleland' to 'Real Life', all the way to 'Blood Type O' and 'Walk Between Worlds'. The musical creativity is astonishingly authentic and honest.

## SCOTT MORRIS

*The Warfield*
*15 June 1991, San Francisco,*
*California*

There was no barrier between the stage and the fans. The Warfield gives the band the choice and they had chosen to waive security and did not create a gap. I was front centre, right against the stage, two feet from Jim's shoes for much of the night.

Halfway through, I felt a tremendous weight on my right shoulder. Some guy was leaping on top of people, trying to get on stage. I turned my head to see what was happening and when I turned back, the guy had grabbed hold of the back of Jim's foot, trying to use it to pull himself up on stage. When the guy pulled, Jim fell over and his right foot hit me squarely in my forehead. The guy got pushed

*Scott Morris still bears the scar from seeing Simple Minds at the Warfield*

back and didn't make it up on stage. During the instrumental part of the song, Jim looked down at me, got on one knee, placed his hand on my forehead, turned his hand around to show me blood - which I didn't know was there - and looked at me confused, like, 'What happened?'

I pointed behind me, pointed at his foot, made a pulling motion, pointed back at his foot, then pointed to my forehead. He immediately got my made-up sign language, nodded his head, looking disappointed and upset. Then, 15 minutes later, the guy trying to get on stage did the same again, on the right side. He had better momentum this time and actually got a leg on the stage. Jim saw what was happening and - not missing a beat - casually walked over, reared back and kicked this guy in the face like he was clearing a football from the penalty area, the guy flying back.

Jim completed the song like nothing happened, then said, 'San Francisco! You guys are a great audience. But it's assholes like you …' - pointing the guy out, now with a bloody face off to the side of the venue – 'Yeah you! You want to be on stage? Get your own fucking band!' The crowd went wild. Vigilante justice had been served.

Jim's accidental kick to my forehead left me with a small scar I have to this day. I can only speculate that the solitary reason he reacted so forcefully is because one of his fans had been injured by someone else's careless behaviour. It was his opportunity to administer some payback. No regrets. I love the character scar I have - and it's an opportunity to tell a great story.

Last time Simple Minds came through the Bay area I thought about getting the meet and greet ticket to tell Jim the story in person, and see if he remembered it, but I figured it would be much like other meet and greets, where the band has time for a picture and five seconds of talking then move on. Much to my surprise, the people who did the Simple Minds meet and greet came out talking about getting a chance to talk to Jim for a couple of minutes each. I was kicking myself for missing the opportunity.

---

## GREGG SIMON

*Universal Amphitheater*
*19 June 1991, Los Angeles, California*

The *Real Life* tour. My friend convinced me to take magic mushrooms for the first time beforehand. Not many shows have matched the magic I felt at that amazing concert, celebrating that fantastic album. Was it the mushrooms? I don't think so! They just enhanced the show and made Charlie Burchill's guitar wash over me. The following day I was having lunch on Sunset Plaza and Jim Kerr walked by my table. I thought it was a drug flashback and couldn't be real. I told him how much I enjoyed the show. He couldn't have been nicer. I haven't missed a Simple Minds show since. In 2018 I was in Washington DC to protest the Brett Cavanaugh Supreme Court hearings and shamefully was worried about being arrested because I didn't want to miss the Simple

Minds show that night at the 9:30 club. That concert and the sheer joy you could feel sweeping across a sweaty, swaying adoring audience made my anger and disgust of the Kavanaugh hearing melt away. The power of music.

---

# ANDREW FAIRWEATHER

## *Palais Omnisports de Paris-Bercy*
## *2 July 1991, Paris, France*

It was a mixture of my cousin's mix-tape in his car and the school jukebox that converted me to Simple Minds. It was a few years before I first saw them at

*Andrew Fairweather got to chat briefly to Jim*

Wembley for the Nelson Mandela 70th Birthday tribute concert. I sat there all day listening to great artists, then they were introduced and the stadium erupted. I jumped to my feet and the man beside me turned to say, 'I guess that's what you've been waiting for!'

After waiting what seemed like a lifetime, I decided I had to see them live in the city of lights at the Bercy, Paris. A small bus picked some people up in Colchester, me in Ipswich and some others in Norwich - 10 in all. We made our way to Cambridge to join the main coach, but it wasn't there. It had left without us.

We clubbed together and two coaches, an overnight ferry crossing and the hiring of two taxis from Calais to Paris later, we arrived at the hotel just as the others in our original party were about to go on a city tour. Two of us managed the tour. I was the only one to stay awake!

We freshened up, got back on the bus, and headed to the venue to see Transvision Vamp and Simple Minds, returned to the hotel, slept, got up and headed home. Was it worth all the hassle? Of course it was, every moment!

I always wanted to see them in Glasgow and to meet them. I paid for a VIP evening at the Hydro on 28 November 2015. We got a soundcheck ('Love Song' and 'Hunter and the Hunted'), a Q&A and a photo-shoot. We were told, 'Just go up, stand there, smile, have your picture taken and walk away.' No interaction due to timing. I was fourth in line.

When I stood next to Jim the cameraman decided to change the equipment round. I shook Jim's, Charlie's and Mel's hands and had a chat with Jim before the photographer was ready to take my photograph.

# JONATHAN LLOYD

As a 16-year-old in 1988, I remember hearing their music coming out of my friend's brother's window whilst we were playing football in the garden. I had no idea who was making this music, only that I really liked it. Possibly I didn't know who was producing this fantastic music due to being in a road traffic accident and a coma in the year before. Since then there has been no turning back.

The first time was Wembley and the Street Fighting Years tour. The last time was the *Walk Between Worlds* tour at the Albert Hall in Manchester. I invited a friend, but he said he was already going with a group of friends so I joined them. What a night!

I have so many memories linked to hearing their music whether at concerts, on my Walkman in the back of my Aunty Lesley's car in Australia or on wireless ear buds as I walked across Sydney Harbour Bridge. They have been with me through thick and thin, hard times and happy times. I hope that they realise how much a part of people's lives they have been. It hasn't just been the music and their words, but everything they are linked with through what is going on around us whilst listening.

# GRAHAM MONKS

I remember going to the Nelson Mandela birthday concert at Wembley because Simple Minds were playing. There were security guards dancing and it was a great atmosphere. And I remember queuing overnight at the NEC in Birmingham for the *Street Fighting Years* tour tickets, one of the best concerts I have ever seen.

# DAVID DOWNING

I remember seeing Simple Minds for the first time in 1991 in Paris. It was an amazing set. The people next to me were clearly smoking some interesting stuff and offered me some to get 'into it'. As I was on my feet the whole time and they were sitting down the whole time I felt I was 'into it' enough! Nothing else needed - just live Simple Minds!

# MATTHEW ASHTON

Following Simple Minds is such an education. I once had drinks with people I didn't know, one being a brain surgeon and the other a hooker from Germany. I think I've seen them in 23 different countries.

I got ill when I was 23. My thyroid died. I spent 20-plus years walking around the planet quite ill, and probably annoyed some band members because of my angry communication. But music kept me alive. I'm cured now but having thyroid deficiency means a lack of memory. All I remember are my Simple Minds adventures. The doctors are puzzled!

I come from Shropshire in the Midlands. My dad wasn't really into music, my mother had a few Beach Boys and Beatles records but I got off listening to 'Popcorn' by Hot Butter, loved Kraftwerk and music from the '70s. But my tastes were varied. Every Saturday I woke up early, put on headphones and searched up and down the dial on our FM stereo. I picked up Radio Leicester, Radio Liverpool, Birmingham Radio, even Radio Sheffield sometimes. I felt I had a tracking station and worked for NASA! It felt so wonderful listening to radio from other cities. Then my life changed. To this day, I've no idea what station it was on but I heard a song. I adored the repetitiveness. Loved the bass. The words seemed different to ABBA or BA Robertson. Then it ended, the DJ playing 'Black Water' by The Doobie Brothers. Even at 10 I knew 'Black Water' but was so annoyed at the DJ not telling his audience what he'd just played.

Later that morning, I went to a record shop and said to the guy behind the counter, 'I want the song that goes 'love song'.' 'Who's it by?' he asked. 'I don't know, the radio DJ never said. It just goes 'Love Song' - kind of synth, but guitars too....'

'Son, as you grow up, you'll realise most men and women write about love. It could be anything. I don't know...' I left without a record. For years I wondered what the song was.

A few years later the teachers were on strike. We were let out of school at 11.30 and myself and three girls went into town. We got to Boot's, which had a wonderful record department. At first, the manager thought I was there to steal records as I got out heaps of Madonna albums and showed them to one of the girls – 'Do you have this?' 'I have them all,' said Amanda. I was gutted. I had such a huge crush on Amanda and wanted to buy her a Madonna record. The manager said, 'Who do you like?' I said, 'Simple Minds.' 'How much money have you got?' I did a very profitable paper-round and had £35 on me. He went to the back and returned with two carrier bags full of 12-inches, singles and albums. 'Here you go - £30,' he said, before explaining he needed to get rid of all the records as the record department was shutting down. I also got *True Blue* by Madonna for myself and gave him £35. That man at Boot's was a guardian angel.

For the next 10 months, I played and played *Celebrate, Empires and Fascination* and the 12-inch version of 'The American'. I always listened to records on repeat, never straight through. Sometimes months would pass before I heard every song. One day I put on *Sister Feelings Call* and played the B-side for the first time. 'Love Song' came on.

The song I heard when I was 10. 'Love Song' was my anthem. My life was complete.

My mother didn't let me go to Birmingham for the *Once Upon a Time* tour. I didn't get *Record Collector* or the *NME*. There was no internet. I stumbled on an ad for *Street Fighting Years* at Wembley. That was my first and up until then the only time I'd seen them live.

In April 1991 I was looking at Teletext. Up came an ad to see Simple Minds in Paris at the Bercy. Shortening a very long story I went alone and met people who are now lifelong friends. I had never been to France before, but we were there for a reason.

## CHRIS MUTCH

Starting college in 1989, three strangers spotted each other in tour gear from the *Street Fighting Years* tour - me, Stuart Hobrow and Gordon Mather. Between us, we'd seen incredible gigs from Wembley to Glasgow. I was jealous of their Cardiff and Leeds stories, particularly Stuart seeing a Cologne gig where he recalled Jim talking about Elvis knocking on his hotel room to join the band, and him replying that he didn't need Elvis – he had Charlie Burchill! Our bedrooms were plastered with concert tickets. I had piles of bootleg tapes, and a poster of Jim Kerr competing with Betty Blue for wall space.

The three of us went to the Paris gig and we became 'The Bercy Boys'. I had an aunt in Paris who bought tickets for us. They arrived in the post like tickets for Willy Wonka's chocolate factory. We were blown away just looking at them, imagining the gig, and on the night we weren't disappointed. The band played 'Hunter and the Hunted' and 'Woman', which we didn't hear the rest of tour. Later, Loreley in Germany was the most beautiful venue I've been to, in forests above the Rhine. Stuart likes to reminds me of my dodgy dancing to support act OMD.

We met again for the '95 tour. Stuart and I were at the first night in Dublin at The Point. 'Room' was the first track played and worth the trip in itself. We met Charlie in the car park that morning, which was great although he probably wondered, 'Who are these strange lads when there's not a gig for nine hours?' It seemed important though.

## JANNIKA PHILIPP

'Don't You (Forget About Me)' was played at a birthday party and it drew my father and me to the dancefloor. It has become our special song. Whenever it is played, I instantly think of my father and all the great memories we share. Whenever we're at a party together, one of us requests that song from the DJ and pulls the other one up to dance as soon as it begins.

# DAN MILLARD

The *Real Life* tour provided a defining moment in my passion for this band and their high-octane, adrenaline-pumping, masterclass gigs. This was the first time I travelled overseas to see them. I recall the first time I heard *Real Life* when it was released. Jim and Charlie delivered a stroke of genius by engineering a set of tracks just written to be played live. Some have become classics in their own right, but also some of my favourite live tracks, that still the case today – 'See the Lights', 'Stand by Love', 'Let There be Love'.

*Dan Millard (centre) in Paris in 1991*

*Real Life* also provides my favourite guitar solo from Charlie – haunting and beautiful, the spine-tingling 'Banging on the Door'. Man, I love this even more live.

Having persuaded my dad to drop me in Stockport at 3am to catch a bus to Paris, I endured the most convoluted, indirect route to Dover, doing multiple picks-up of Minds fans en route. It seemed to take forever. We stopped in Wolverhampton and a guy got on who was also travelling on his own. We sat together and Matthew and I started comparing notes about our favourite band and anticipation of the forthcoming gig.

We arrived in Paris the night before the show and took in a meal with fellow fans we got to know on the bus. For the first time I felt part of a community, the first of many gatherings which would become a constant over coming years at gigs close to home and many miles away.

Gig day came and we trotted around the streets of Paris, getting soaked in the rain along the way. We took shelter in a bar, drank wine and ate cheese before we met the bus at our rendezvous point to take us to the Palais Omnisports de Paris-Bercy.

We asked the driver to get us there extra early so we could ensure a place at the front of the queue. This we achieved and when the gates opened, we ran for all we were worth to get that prized position, pressed to the barrier in front of Charlie's monitors.

Transvision Vamp supported, Wendy James cavorting like someone possessed. By the time they finished, the adrenaline was off the scale, waiting for the lights to dim and the main event.

And boy did it ever. The lights went down and the intro to 'Real Life' intro fired up, Jim introducing the band one by one and welcoming Mark Taylor to the band. Then off we went and, wow, it was deafening. When Mel came in the sound from him and Malcolm Foster's bass were like being kicked in the ribs. But it felt so good.

Then 'Love Song', the place turning into a mosh-pit. Gosh, it was mental. There was a huge surge from the back. I was trying to bounce along with the rest but was pinned against the barrier. I couldn't move. Next thing I knew, I felt myself lifted up as security pulled me and a few around me out to stop us getting crushed.

I was pissed off initially. Having had such a build-up, a long journey and having such a great position, we were herded to the side of the stage then along a walkway to be dispersed about halfway back at the side of the crowd. But once I dusted myself down, whilst I wasn't so close as before I realised I could actually see the light show. Breathtaking. The sound was even better and even louder – so crisp and sharp. The set was spot on - fast, furious and faultless.

I was wet through with sweat. It was like somebody tipped a bucket of water over me. We left the arena to board the bus back home. We travelled directly back through the night, catching the ferry to Dover in the early hours. We were knackered but buzzing with euphoria. As we got close to Wolverhampton, Matthew prepared to get off. I faced several more hours on the bus, heading home via Chester and other places that weren't on the way. Matt said if I wanted to get off the coach at Wolverhampton he'd drive me home to save me time. What a gent!

When I finally arrived home about 15 hours after the gig finishing, the clothes I'd worn the night before were still soaked. I walked up the drive dazed, still buzzing, wishing I could rewind 24 hours.

---

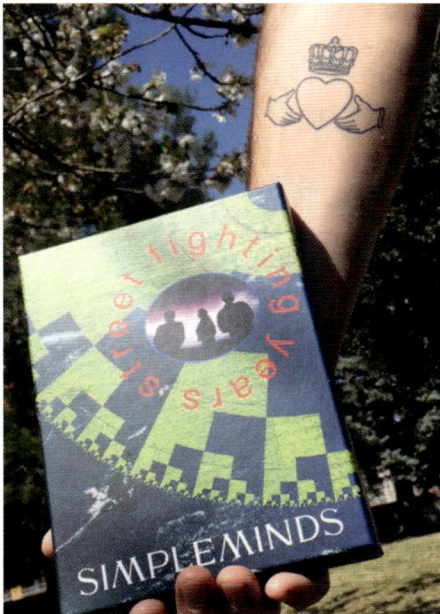

*Robert Marchegiania was at the Modena gig*

# ROBERT MARCHEGIANI

## *Stadio Alberto Braglia*
## *8 July 1991, Modena, Italy*

A fan since I was 15, Brianteo Stadium in Modena in 1991 was my first time seeing my favourite group. I was so excited I only remember a few blurred images - Jim in the hat, the full stadium. They were almost unreachable. Fortunately, over the years there have been many opportunities to see them and I've been to more than 20 concerts. I particularly remember Roseto Degli Abruzzi in August 2010, Charlie playing seated because he injured his leg, and the tennis stadium in Rome in July 1997 which started late and where after the first song, 'War Babies', I ran away in tears because I was going to miss my train.I just want to say thank you to Simple Minds. Without you, my life would have certainly been different, and less bright.

---

# DIRK MOUS

*Vorst Nationaal*
*10 July 1991, Brussels, Belgium*

In the early '80s I was at a party when the DJ played 'Promised You a Miracle'. It was the first time I heard it. I had no idea who it was and had to ask the DJ. From that moment on I became interested in Simple Minds. My first live gig was at Vorst National. I was blown away and have seen them over 40 times now.

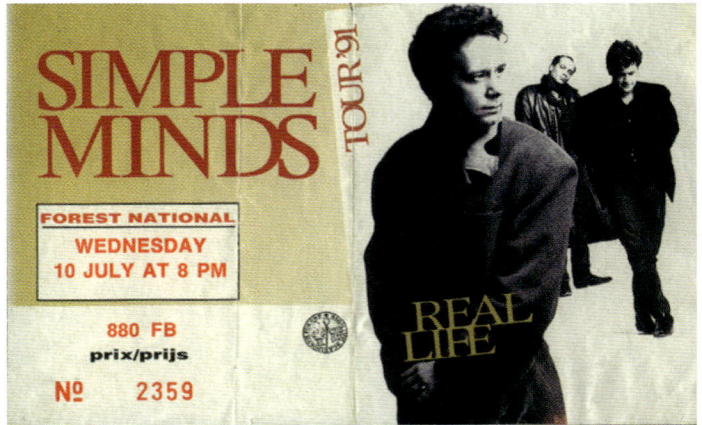

# JESSICA HAASE

*Muengersdorferstadion*
*14 July 1991, Cologne, Germany*

First time I saw them was in the football stadium in Cologne, in summertime. It was an overwhelming atmosphere; so many people who wanted to hear and see the same band. The same year in October we went to see them in an ice rink, where we were much closer to the stage. That was cool - the band a few metres away on stage. You could see how everything was prepared by the technicians and what the musicians did in the short breaks between songs too.

During the *Good News from the Next World* tour we followed them through the whole German Republic, but also Belgium and Luxembourg, and I managed to get Jim's autograph.

Getting tickets in the days before the internet wasn't easy. I recall listening to an interview with Jim by chance on radio to promote an upcoming tour. You had to be attentive and write down the relevant dates to buy the tickets in the next big city. But it was absolutely worth it. It still is. When the music starts it feels like, 'Let's move to the music and fly….'

We've seen so many other musicians, celebrities and cities with the band: Debbie Harry carrying her little dog on stage at *Nokia Night*, Sheryl Crow standing next to me to take photos of Neneh Cherry while she was performing in Loreley. One summer festival the Dalai Lama spoke to the crowd. And Simple Minds' version of 'Neon Lights' by Kraftwerk encouraged us to get tickets for Kraftwerk!

# SONJA RAUSCHEN

I bought 'Don't You (Forget About Me)' as a single and played it every day. For my birthday I got the LP, *Sparkle in the Rain*. I then got all the others. Most of my friends liked Depeche Mode or U2, but I was always Simple Minds. I saw them for the first time on stage in Cologne on the *Real Life* tour and it was so wonderful.

My three children have grown up with their music. My son wrote in his friendship book in answer to the question about his favourite music, 'Mama's music', because he couldn't remember their name. He still listens to them.

In 2003 I drove to the E-Werk in Cologne to see them. The support band said hello to the crowd with a loud 'welcome to Munich!' Oh dear. But it was a great concert. In 2017 I took in part of the *Acoustic* tour in Essen. That was great. in 2019, I saw tribute band MIND2MODE play songs by Simple Minds. Really good, but nothing compared to the originals.

# KONRAD KUBICZEK

## *Praterstadion*
## *18 July 1991, Vienna, Austria*

It was the summer of 1985 when I spent my holidays in south London that I got to know Simple Minds. 'Don't You (Forget About Me)' was such a powerful song. When I started listening to them, I moved the Stones albums aside. I put the Simple Minds lettering in black letters on the bonnet of my first car, a yellow Volvo 144. It looked great! In Vienna in 1991, there was a great opening act, Transvision Vamp, then Simple Minds came on. I was in the first row. Jim started singing 'Real Life', came to me and shook my hand. The band played a fantastic concert. I'm disappointed they never got that popular in Austria. The *Graffiti Soul* tour might have been the last tour there. But it gives me a good reason to travel abroad to see them, and the *5x5* concert at London's Roundhouse was phenomenal.

*Konrad Kubiczek was in Vienna for his first Minds show*

## JOSÉ BARROS

*Estádio José de Alvalade*
*31 July 1991, Lisbon, Portugal*

I traded my copy of a Dire Straits album with a friend and got *New Gold Dream.* I wanted it because it had 'Someone Somewhere (in Summertime)' and 'Glittering Prize' on it, which I heard at a disco. I've seen them 11 times, first in July 1991 at the Alvalade Stadium, Lisbon. I had tickets for two shows in 2020 so I'll be seeing them twice in 2021!

*José Barros first saw the Minds in Lisbon in 1991*

## ANTONIO NARVAEZ RODRIGUEZ

*Estadio Municipal*
*2 August 1991, Marbella, Spain*

I was 15 in the summer of 1987. I became interested in music the previous year. My friends listened to The Communards, The Smiths, The Cure, Depeche Mode and U2, but none had heard of Simple Minds. At home there wasn't much money to buy records so I listened to the radio for the songs I liked most, recording hours and hours on cassettes. One day I heard 'Someone Somewhere (in Summertime)' live. It was a direct bullet to the heart. Which group had written the most romantic song I'd ever heard? I ran to the record store, Electro-Radio, and asked for Simple Minds.

At Christmas 1987 I got a turntable. I started my collection with the LP *Sparkle in the Rain* then *Life in a Day*, *Empires and Dance* and *Real to Real*. My friends met in my house to listen to the vinyl

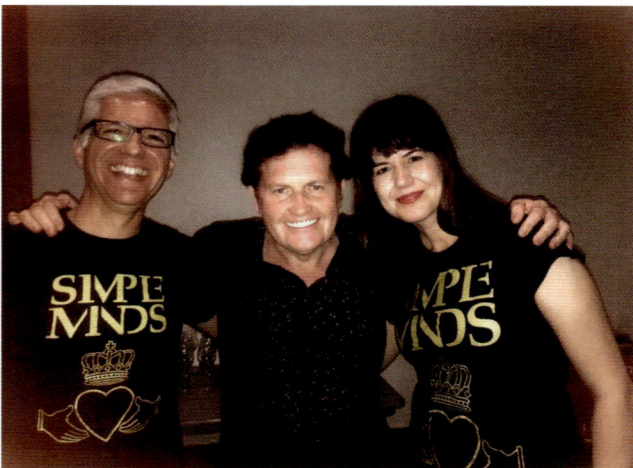

*Antonio Rodriguez and friend with Charlie and (opposite) a live shot taken by Antonio*

and we commented with great interest the stylistic changes, the lyrics, the guitar, keyboards, and covers. I remember the shock of listening to *Empires and Dance*. I hadn't heard anything like it. I had chosen my group, or rather it had chosen me.

It was August 1991 before I could finally see them live. I couldn't believe it, my band coming to play Marbella. I put on my black *Live in the City of Light* t-shirt, previously kept immaculate. I was stunned and impressed. That night still rings in my head. Since I have been able to travel to Madrid, Barcelona, Valencia, Burgos, Granada, London, Gibraltar, Glasgow and Venice to see them. Piazza San Marco was something magical. My love and respect for the music of Simple Minds continues until this day.

# ENRICO MALVANO

*Stadio Comunale Valerio Bacigalupo*
*5 August 1991, Savona, Italy*

I bought my first ticket to see the band in September 1989 at the Pellerina Park, Turin, but hadn't checked the train times. I couldn't get home after, so didn't go. I should have slept at the station!

I had the opportunity again two years later in Savona. It was a splendid, warm summer evening. I'll never forget those hours waiting in the sun, hearing the soundcheck and 'Stand By Love'. I was shivering with excitement! That evening the band sounded great and Jim Kerr was in great shape! It was really incredible to see them in front of me. I positioned myself under Malcolm Foster and couldn't believe my eyes. I was in front of one of the biggest bands around!

# DAVID HILLIAM

*Maine Road Football Stadium*
*10 August 1991, Manchester,*
*England*

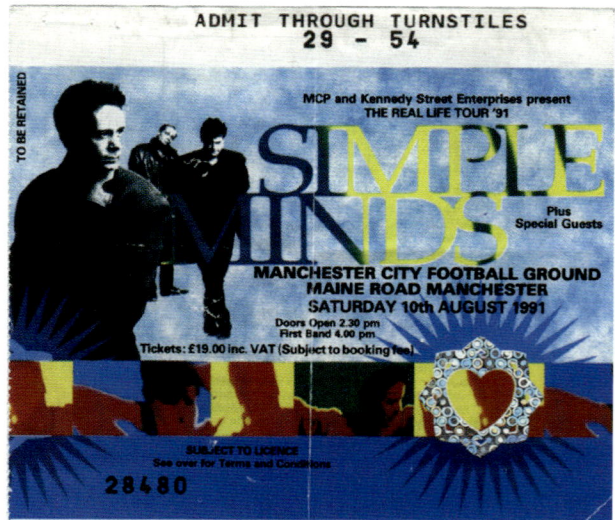

I borrowed a cassette back in 1988, aged 15, of *Once Upon a Time*. I knew the big hits, but instantly fell in love with the entire album and pretty much played it to death. I never gave it back. I saw them live at Maine Road in 1991. The coach broke down on the way and we arrived just as Voice of the Beehive were playing their last song! My sister was gutted. She loved them and never got to see them live again.

In 2013, I met my wife and her best friend's husband, now my best friend. He's also a massive fan and was also at Maine Road. We could have easily passed each other. Little did we know years later we'd be bessie mates!

## TONY KEGGIN

August 1991 - my second Simple Minds outdoor gig, after the wonderful Leeds show two years earlier. Here I was, 21 years old, hungover, just a ticket and no transportation to and from Manchester. Ah, the vigour of youth. I got to Liverpool Lime Street and bought a ticket for Manchester Oxford Road, guessing that could be the closest station to Maine Road. Lucky guess number one. Very lucky guess number two was seeing a lad on the train with a *Real Life* t-shirt on. I got talking to him and found he was meeting mates at the gig who were going to give him a lift home. He gave me his Barnes Travel coach ticket for the journey back to Liverpool. What a stroke of luck! Rain wasn't going to dampen this day.

The show was wonderful, with support from Voice of the Beehive, OMD and a Hugh Cornwell-less Stranglers, who were great despite some hardcore Hugh fans not being happy (Paul Roberts did very well). There were some strange things in the pre-match warm-up, including bananas, a Manchester thing at that time. But who brings a blow-up doll to a gig? There was lots of laughter in the Kippax!

## STEVEN HOLMES

Simple Minds are the soundtrack to my life. Through highs and lows, their music resonates through me and has always been there. Where friends moved on, Simple Minds were and remain constant. My first gig was at Maine Road, Manchester and I remember being in the madness at the front as the cloud of sweat hovered above. My gig companions spanned three generations, including my dad and my son (my six-year-old is already a fan). I still argue with my dad as to who introduced who to the band. I struggle to find another who have spanned 40 years and are still producing and touring fantastic, original music that comes close. Long may it continue.

## LEON JACKSON AND DAZ

Simple Minds played Maine Road, Manchester along with OMD, The Stranglers and Voice of the Beehive on a typically rainy British summer's day. That day, lives changed forever - not only was I lucky enough to see the band that inspired me since I was a boy for the first time, I also met the guy who would become my best friend and would go on to be my best man, godfather to my daughter and true confidante. The Minds brought us together and we've remained fans of the band and each other ever since.

## MARK LOWE

Manchester's Maine Road Stadium in 1991 was a brilliant day, with singing and chanting from the crowd. We were near the front, in the rain. The music echoed in my ears for what seemed like days later.

---

## ANDY NICKELS

I was just nine and very influenced by my 18-year-old brother, who listened to various types of music. One band he played really stood out to me... Simple Minds - their music, lyrics and sound. When I was in secondary school everyone was into The Stone Roses, Happy Mondays, The Charlatans, etc. as the Madchester scene emerged. But I was still hooked on Simple Minds.

It wasn't until 1991 that I got to see them live, at Maine Road during the *Real Life* tour, but I've been to every tour since, sometimes more than once. On a few occasions my brother and I have been on the front row. And regardless of where we are in the crowd, for those two and a half hours I lose myself in the music, along with all the other fans. Some 35 years on I'm still as mad about them.

*Andy Nickels caught up with Jim ahead of the Acoustic show in Liverpool in May 2017*

---

## CRAIG PEGGIE

*SECC*
*13 August 1991, Glasgow, Scotland*

I've seen them dozens of times. First time was August 1991 at the SECC. They blew my mind, and since then I've been at pretty much every Scottish gig they've done. My favourite was Edinburgh Castle, despite torrential rain, which is standard for

Simple Minds outdoor Scottish gigs! I have too many memories to list them but they've never let me down for a single second at any gig.

## ALLY HUTCHISON

### Exhibition Centre
### 15 August 1991, Aberdeen, Scotland

I discovered Simple Minds at the age of 13 in the mid-'80s and was immediately encapsulated. My dad, from Maryhill, joined the Army in the late '60s to get out of Glasgow and see the world. With postings around Germany and the UK, Simple Minds travelled with me and

*Ally Hutchison (far left) left Glasgow but 'New Gold Dream' takes him home every time*

reminded me of a place deep in my heart which I looked forward to returning to every year. Dad would play 'New Gold Dream' on the car stereo as we headed home, Mum navigating our way around the AA Atlas and my brother and I belting out the lyrics, pretending to be JK!

I've seen Simple Minds live more times than I care to remember and enjoy each as if it were the first. At every gig, I reminisce about the good old days, my old boy and Glasgow!

Bizarrely, the *Real Life* tour was the first time I saw them. I was 17. We moved to the north east of Scotland in 1990 and my dad drove a friend and I to the Exhibition Centre, Aberdeen. An Emotional Fish were supporting and did not go down too well! I'm sure JK and the guys will remember that gig well. I saw the band the next time they played at the AECC some years later, and Jim apologised to fans on stage about the previous gig!

## ROBERT KELLY

### Gateshead International Stadium
### 17 August 1991, Gateshead, England

I became aware of Simple Minds during the *Once Upon a Time* period, when the songs and Claddagh logo on somebody's *Live in the City of Light* t-shirt caught my attention. Like many 15-year-olds in 1989 I was searching through fashion, music and interests for an identity I could call my own when 'Belfast Child' hit the airwaves. I fell in love. In my opinion it's the most incredible adaptation of a folk song ever. It was that song that led me to a band that captured an intoxicating blend of musical power, energy and optimism.

After buying the *Street Fighting Years* album I made frequent visits to a little independent record shop called Pink Panther in my hometown of Carlisle to buy the back-catalogue. Eventually I had the albums, posters and boxsets. The *Verona* video led me to plead with my parents to buy a video recorder and each and every day I would listen to or watch Simple Minds.

I didn't get to see them live until 1991, when I joined some friends at Gateshead's International Stadium. We had an incredible day out, the band supported by Roachford, OMD and The Stranglers. The headline act left us all mesmerised.

For the past 31 years the music of Simple Minds has accompanied my life, and despite different phases of the band's music and lineup, I've never lost the love or loyalty for their music or deepest respect and admiration for the band. In 2013 they visited my hometown and showed that, even in a pretty forgettable sports hall, they could create an unforgettable night. My favourite gig however has to be the *5x5* concert at the Barrowland. Watching them perform sent shivers down my spine.

---

# MICK LANG

Living with my parents in Inverness, Scotland, I wanted to go to as many dates on this tour as I could but at 17 it wasn't possible financially. So I picked Aberdeen on 14 August and Gateshead three days later. Thinking back, it was quite a journey, Inverness - Aberdeen - Inverness - Gateshead and home again by bus in the days without mobile phones, social media and the like. My mother was obviously concerned, but knew there'd be no stopping me. This was also my first big journey all on my own.

Aberdeen wasn't a concern, but Gateshead was. Nevertheless, off I went. I arrived in Newcastle and just followed the others wearing SM tour t-shirts in the hope I'd be going in the right direction. It was a lovely day and the stadium was full, so I found a place around halfway and sat down to enjoy support

acts An Emotional Fish (whatever happened to them?) OMD and The Stranglers. Simple Minds played as fantastically as I'd expected. It was colder in the evening and towards the end my mind started to drift to my journey home, including an overnight stay in an open Newcastle Bus Station waiting for a 7.30am bus back to Inverness. A scary place for a smalltown boy. But all worth it.

## LUKE MOORE

*Milton Keynes Bowl*
*24 August 1991, Milton Keynes,*
*England*

The journey began on my 11th birthday in 1985 when I received the album *Once Upon a Time.* I listened with my best friend from school and for life, Dean Whiteside, at the energy and vibrant sound. It was like nothing which had hit us before.

Years later, on a hot August night at Milton Keynes Bowl, we waited for Jim Kerr to appear in the darkness above us on the vast stage. His words summed up the feelings of all when he said, 'I can just tell it's going to be one of those nights by the size of the moon up there!'. He kicked into 'Real Life' and the greatest night of our 17-year-old lives had begun....

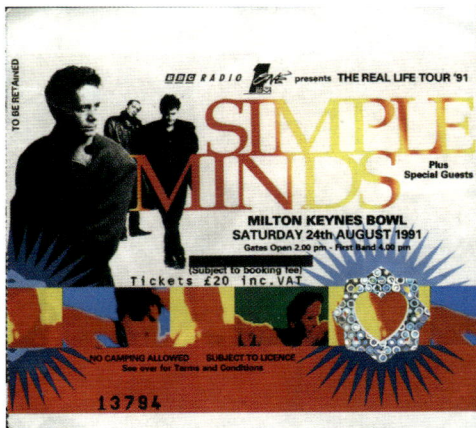

## DOMINIC ALATI

From the moment I first heard 'Love Song', Simple Minds had a new fan. Such power, such amazing guitar work and such unusual lyrics – 'Love Song' sounds like anything but a love song. The first time I saw them live was at Sydney's Coogee Bay Hotel, and it was the first concert I ever went to. They had recently released 'Waterfront'. After doing a second encore, the crowd urged them to come back for a third. They had run out of songs, so they did 'Waterfront' again.

# NYCKI DAY

It all began with an envelope from my auntie Ann. She ran a pub in deepest, darkest North Wales and would occasionally buy records from the jukebox man and send them down to me. This particular package consisted of six records and included 'Rebel Yell' by Billy Idol and 'Alive and Kicking' by Simple Minds. I played both non-stop for a week until I got fed up with 'Rebel Yell' (sorry Billy!), but my passion for 'Alive and Kicking' didn't wane. I immediately went and bought *Once Upon a Time*. I'd search a local indie shop for memorabilia, pin badges and the like. I needed to listen to the back-catalogue, my Saturday job money duly spent buying whatever I could afford.

In 1989 I went on a school exchange to Moscow and my trusty *Live in the City of Light* t-shirt came too, with *Street Fighting Years* played non-stop on my Walkman.

When we first got dial-up internet in our house, the very first thing I did was join a Simple Minds fan forum. I loved it. It was email-based and I'd never been so happy to connect with like-minded souls.

Fast forward a 'few' years and Simple Minds have been there for me during good and bad times. I even had a compilation of songs playing in the background whilst having my boys in hospital.

I've been lucky enough to see them a few times. First time was on the *Real Life* tour in Milton Keynes, live on Radio 1 - my dad was charged with recording it so I could listen to it over and over again. The most recent time was down in Colchester, where the weather was biblical! My passion for their music has never dipped. I'm proud to say I'm a Simple Minds fan through and through.

# VIRANJANI YOGAKUMAR

I was in England spending the summer with my aunt, uncle and cousins before starting university back home in California. One of my cousins had a summer job somewhere and managed to get two tickets to the show. He wasn't interested in going, but I sure was! My radio back in Los Angeles was always tuned into KROQ. Simple Minds were playing with OMD and The Stranglers and it was the most amazing show. I'd never been to a festival-style performance like this. I was blown away. The people, the energy, the music were all something else.

In April 1997, travelling back to England to spend time with my fiancé (now my husband), I pulled an all-nighter for some unknown reason and listened to *Glittering Prize 81/92* on repeat the entire night. I couldn't get enough of it. Now, every single time I hear 'Someone Somewhere (in Summertime)', I think about that night and how excited I was.

You can't imagine how overjoyed I was to see they were coming to Los Angeles again in 2018 after so long. I bought two tickets immediately. I took a friend who wasn't a huge fan - or didn't realise she was! We sat there, amazed how good the band sounded and by Jim Kerr's energy, and I chuckled each time my friend said, 'Oh! I know this song. I didn't know this was Simple Minds!'

# ALEXANDER GERHARDS

*Loreley*
*1 September 1991, Loreley, Germany*

The very first time I saw Jim Kerr and Charlie Burchill live was on the *Real Life* tour in Loreley, Germany. The weather and the environment were perfect. Since then, every time Simple Minds have been in my region I've tried to see them.

One of the things I'm most proud of is my 'Dolphins' video project, the idea for which was born one early spring morning on my way to work, driving through a forested area close to Frankfurt airport. The sun was still very low and there was fog on the ground in a glade where deer were grazing. I was playing 'Dolphins' on my car stereo and had some pictures in my mind. It took me months to finish but just a few days after I uploaded it to my fan-site Simple Minds featured it on their official website.

---

# RICCARDO MASSETTI

*Palaeur*
*7 September 1991, Rome, Italy*

I first encountered Simple Minds when I was a kid. My older girlfriend said to me, 'This track drives me crazy!' It was 'Glittering Prize'. From that moment on I started the journey into their albums. I used their sound to write my degree thesis, my first book of poems, my first novel, some television programmes. They remind me of my girlfriend, lost friends, and 40 exciting years. I saw them in concert 20 times, all in Italy, the first time when they recorded *Live in the City of Light* in France. The concert I will never forget was in Rome for the *Real Life* tour; it was great, immense, poetic. Then the dream comes true: working in Milan for television, I interviewed Jim at the Feltrinelli bookstore on the occasion of the launch of *Black and White*. He told me about his beloved Sicily, where he had put down roots, cultivated olive trees and set up a hotel. As for me, I moved to New York and opened Cremini's

*Expect to hear Simple Minds if you eat at Cremini's in Brooklyn*

restaurant in Brooklyn, and guess what's on my playlist? When I hear 'New Gold Dream' I blow up the audio speakers in the restaurant and people look at me amazed and amused!

---

## PAUL VAN HAEFF

*Arena di Verona*
*12 September 1991, Verona, Italy*

After hearing a live recording was going to be made of the Verona show, I took the train there to try and buy a ticket. I had no money to sleep in a hotel so took a sleeping bag, which I put in a locker at the railway station. In the afternoon I saw Charlie, Lisa and Mick perform in the square. I attended the concert, which was epic and fantastic, then went back to the railway station to sleep on a bench until it was time to take the train back to Holland the next day.

I've lots of other concert memories but the most important was May 2002 at the Vredenburg, Utrecht. That April I almost lost my life and had to stay in intensive care for a few days. My best friend told me whatever happened we were going to see Simple Minds, even if he had to take me there in a wheelchair. That gave me such a boost, and I was completely recovered by the time of the show. The most beautiful moment was when they played 'Belfast Child'. It made me cry, that song reminding me that no matter what happens or how bad things are, it always turns around and better times will come because life goes on.

---

## KEITH LARKWORTHY

*Wembley Arena*
*21 September 1991, London, England*

At secondary school I was into synth music and Depeche Mode in particular. Nothing else mattered. Friends were into Simple Minds and *Once Upon a Time*, the current album, but it wasn't my bag. But by the time of the release of 'Belfast Child' my musical tastes had broadened and I loved the song. My friend Lee lent me a cassette of *Street Fighting Years*. I've loved them ever since.

My first gig was Wembley Arena, a pre-paid coach trip. I went with my mate Tom. Another friend was a massive football fan and he gave up his ticket to watch Swindon Town instead!

---

## LORNA SCHMID-ROTA

*Patinoire De Malley*
*27 September 1991, Lausanne, Switzerland*

In the summer of 1987, aged 14, on my way back home from Italy to Switzerland with my brother in his car, a cassette was playing in an endless loop. I loved the songs and at some stage asked my brother who was singing. He replied Simple Minds. All the way back, we listened to *Live in the City of Light*. In 1989, when *Street Fighting Years* was released, this album was a revelation. The band's greatest fan had just been born, and I've never stopped being that since! In 1991, I was so glad to be able to attend my first Simple Minds concert in Lausanne, Switzerland. Almost 30 years have passed since and every time I listen to those songs, time stops and I feel transported back in time - more powerfully than using a DeLorean time machine! In January 2020, I got my first tattoo ever, the Claddagh symbol on my right forearm. Simple Minds one day, Simple Minds forever. Thanks guys for everything you've given to me so far with all your wonderful songs and gigs.

---

## GARY QUINEY

*National Exhibition Centre*
*29 September 1991, Birmingham, England*

Working in a law firm in 1991, I happened to bump into a new employee, Jon, at the coffee machine. He had not easily made friends. Unfortunately, having undergone various treatments and kidney and liver transplants, he looked different and jaundiced. Some considered he was weird and had attitude. Let's just say, he did not fit in. Jon constantly wore headphones. I happened to ask what he was listening to. He muttered, 'Genesis'. I started to ramble on about Phil Collins and Jon stopped me in my tracks - he was listening to the *real* Genesis, with Peter Gabriel. Our conversation flowered as I described the influence Peter had with my favourite band, Simple Minds. He had no clue who Simple Minds were aside from 'Don't You (Forget About Me)'. Over the days and weeks, we began to talk more and share stories of bands and concerts, always concluding with Gabriel and Simple Minds.

It wasn't long before the *Real Life* tour. I'd already secured tickets for Birmingham for myself and two friends. A few hours before the gig, one of my friends became ill and we were left with a spare. En route, we drove past the law firm where I worked and lo and behold Jon was walking home, finished for the day. I swerved the car over to the side of the road and Jon peered in, wondering what on earth was going on. I explained we had a spare ticket and he should come with us. After some reluctance - he hadn't eaten - Jon jumped into the back seat. The promise of a burger at the venue seemed to be more attractive than seeing the band!

The *Real Life* concert was amazing, especially having bagged front row seats. I think Jon was drawn in as soon as the curtains opened. I could faintly hear him mutter 'Korg' as the riffs to 'Real Life' powered from the overhead speakers. We didn't talk much during the show, how could we? There was too much singing and dancing and just being absolutely hypnotised by the band, Jim reaching out to us from only a few feet away and the constant Burchill grin and lip-synching. The curtain closed at the end and we headed back to the car, more than slightly deaf, when Jon piped up, 'Gary, that was amazing, better than I could ever have imagined. Thank you for introducing me to Simple Minds!'

I sit here watery-eyed as I type this, as it was not long after this that Jon sadly passed away. I was so glad I took the time to speak with him that one day at the coffee machine. A complete stranger at the time but we quickly became friends through interests in music and bands. It was a pleasure, Jon, to introduce you to Simple Minds.

# MATTHEW ASHTON

## *Hallenstadion*
## *11 October 1991, Zurich, Switzerland*

After going to Paris to see them on the *Real Life* tour, I was looking at the dates on the t-shirt I'd bought. I'd just been paid. It was a Thursday. I went to a travel agent and asked for a ticket to Zurich that next afternoon. The time of the flight fitted in perfectly with my schedule. After much tapping away on a computer screen, the girl told me there was one ticket left but it was business class and £753! I thought, 'What the hell?' and got it. Next day, the flight took off after a delay. The air stewardess could see my anxiety and asked if I was scared of flying. I said I was anxious about missing the gig. When the plane landed the captain apologised for the delay over the loudspeaker, wishing the Simple Minds fan a happy concert!

I ran out of the airport and got a cab. I said 'Simple Minds' to the taxi driver and he started playing a cassette of *Live in the City of Light*. 'Ghostdancing' was playing.

I couldn't speak a word of German but eventually was able to make him understand why I was in Zurich and he took me to the Hallenstadion. I paid him and ran into the venue. 'East at Easter' had just finished. I saw five songs and slept at the airport before going home, still getting into work next day for 9am. One of the guys in my office was enthused, as that Friday night he had pulled a girl who later became his wife. After listening to him for half an hour, he said, 'What did you do last night?' Still wearing the same clothes, I pulled from my pocket one of the many tickets I'd picked up off the concert hall floor and showed it to him. I said, 'I went to see Simple Minds.' He looked at me and uttered the words, 'You are so weird!'

## ROBBIE PATTERSON

*Wembley Arena*
*23 October 1991, London, England*

They say everyone remembers their first. Well, Simple Minds were the first band I ever saw live, they made the first cassette album I bought and they were responsible for the first and only CD I ever pinched – from Woolworth's in 1992. I still feel a bit guilty about it.

I actually wanted *Street Fighting Years* that Christmas, but my dad decided the cassette to debut with my new Walkman would be *New Gold Dream* instead. I quickly discovered why. It was years before I discovered it wasn't a *best of* compilation from '81, '82, '83 and '84! The music was so good I assumed the year part of the cover marked everything on it as a single. It ended up becoming more than just an album to me. The cover art literally changed my life. Malcolm Garrett was the main inspiration in my decision to follow graphic design as a profession, and it all started with *New Gold Dream*. Nothing was the same again.

# GLITTERING PRIZE

## JUSTINE HANSBERRY

I first discovered Simple Minds in 1982 as a 10-year-old, when my younger brother received a compilation tape called *The Winners 1982*. It included John Cougar Mellancamp's 'Jack and Diane', Dexy's Midnight Runners' 'Come On Eileen' and 'Glittering Prize' by Simple Minds. The music would ring from our portable tape player. I fell in love with the song and remember dancing to it in my room. I only recently saw the video for the first time and what an absolutely dashing group of lads - all dressed in black, with eyeliner and shiny boots. I fell in love again!

## ALEX MC

I fell in love with a girl at the end of the summer of 1991 in Spain. After meeting her and having my first kiss, I had to fly back to the UK and boarding school the next day. We spent the next three months sending each other letters and I would save up my pocket money to go into town and make the long distance call from a phone booth every two weeks. It was typical teenage emotional suffering, but now I look back on it as the moment I felt most alive in my life.

It was her birthday in November and I wanted to send her something special. We spoke about music when we were together, and she mentioned some groups I had never got into - U2, UB40, Simple Minds. I went down to the local record shop in Colwyn Bay. They had almost no inventory but a massive catalogue you could order albums from. I chose a Simple Minds multi-CD collection, thinking to impress her by my sophistication in ordering a CD and not a cassette. CDs were quite new and I had only just got a CD player. After a long wait it arrived and I sent it off.

When her birthday came, I asked her if she liked the present. She said yes but had not listened to the CDs yet as she didn't have a CD player. Curious as to what she was listening to, I bought myself *Glittering Prize 81/92*. And when I went to see her for the last time in Granada, where she lived, I played these tracks on the eight hour bus ride and whenever I could. Listening to Simple Minds whilst in teenage love, walking round the Alhambra Palace with majestic views over Granada, drinking red wine in side street tapas bars and sipping mint tea in Moorish tea houses with a beautiful girl; at 17 years of age, I thought I was James Bond!

### IAIN DARREN

From the start I could quote all their lyrics perfectly because I listened to them so much. From seeing them for the first time in 1981 in Glasgow to the midsummer concert at Milton Keynes Bowl in 1986 and now, 35 concerts later, they still give me the same warmth and smiles with all their music. I'm looking forward to another 35 concerts and singing away till I'm hoarse – perfection! 'Glittering Prize' is mine and my wife's song, so much so that we have the lyrics framed and as both our ringtones.

### JANE GRAINGER

On a sunny evening in 1993 he took me out. We talked and laughed and at the end of the night he loaned me his *Glittering Prize* tape from his car. I was already a Simple Minds fan but from then on 'Let There Be Love' became our song. However, he was in the merchant navy at the time so 'See the Lights' grew to be my personal favourite. The words resonated for me during the long periods we were apart and reminded me that, no matter where in the world he was, we were still connected. 27 years later we still listen to your music. We have three amazing kids and a mad dog. Would our love and family have happened if that tape hadn't existed? He would say that our story would surely be different.

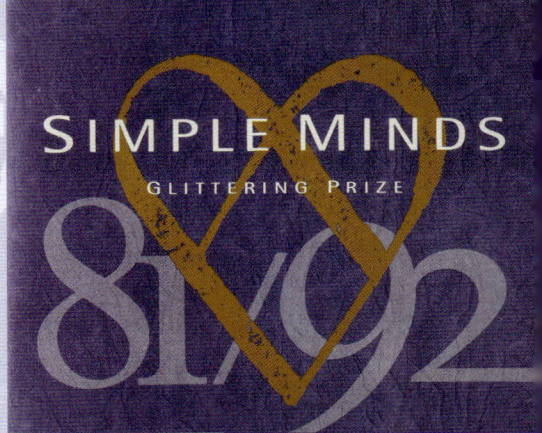

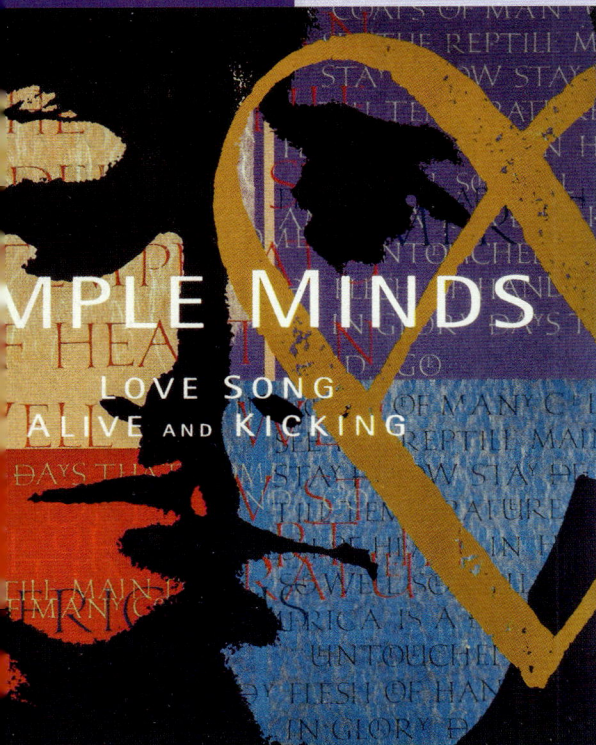

### ANGELIQUE VAN FESSEM

I met Bert back in the Eighties on a railway station platform. He was 18 and I 16. We immediately clicked. We both loved Simple Minds – *Sparkle in the Rain* and *New Gold Dream* – and playing our records. After a while we lost contact. 35 years later, we bumped into each other again. Immediately we were best friends again. That sparkle between people? We still had it. Even better now, because we felt in love with each other. We're still huge fans of Simple Minds and our most beloved song is 'Hunter and the Hunted', which is the song we listened to most in the Eighties when we didn't realise, back then, that we were already in love.

### FLORA FARGES

I'm pretty sure I was already dancing in my mother's womb when I 'saw' them live for the first time, in 1995 at the Paris Olympia. My parents were already very much addicted. When I was a little girl, the songs echoed in the different houses we lived in. My dad's favourite song is 'Dolphins', my mom's is 'Someone Somewhere (in Summertime)' and mine's 'Hunter and the Hunted'. We have so many memories of the band, of their love of performing and creating beautiful concerts. One thing I also share with them is my admiration for the Glasgow Celtic. I used to wear my Celtic t-shirt to the shows I went to.

### MICHAEL MCLAUGHLIN

October 1981. I had just started my first part time job and music was everything to me. *Top of the Pops* on a Thursday night, *Smash Hits* and *The Face* magazines and the UK chart show on a Sunday evening with Tony Blackburn and Tommy Vance was all that mattered to my 16 year old self, being fully consumed by the music that was dominating the charts and the fashion industry at the time. *Modern Dance*, the compilation album of the top new wave/synthpop artists of 1981, was purchased after seeing the promo adverts in the magazines and started my lifelong love affair with Simple Minds, the songs 'Sweat in Bullet' and 'Love Song' included on a tracklist alongside hits from Visage, Gary Numan, Japan and the Human League. 1982 saw the release of one of the greatest albums of all time, *New Gold Dream*, which includes my favourite Simple Minds song ever, 'Hunter and the Hunted'.

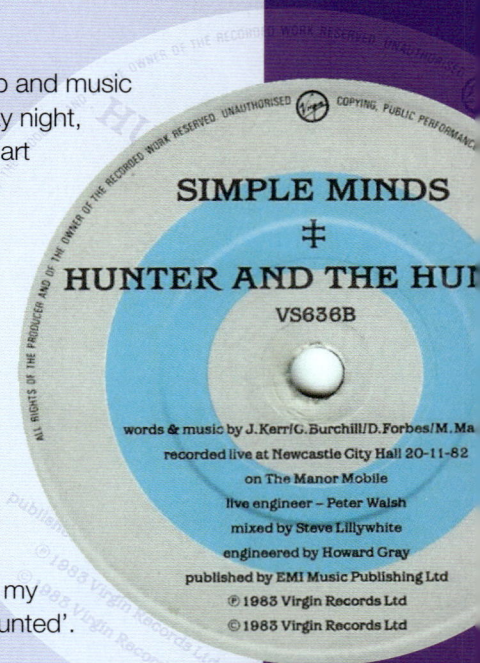

SIMPLE MINDS
‡
HUNTER AND THE HU[N]
VS636B

words & music by J. Kerr/G. Burchill/D. Forbes/M. Ma[
recorded live at Newcastle City Hall 20-11-82
on The Manor Mobile
live engineer – Peter Walsh
mixed by Steve Lillywhite
engineered by Howard Gray
published by EMI Music Publishing Ltd
℗ 1983 Virgin Records Ltd
© 1983 Virgin Records Ltd

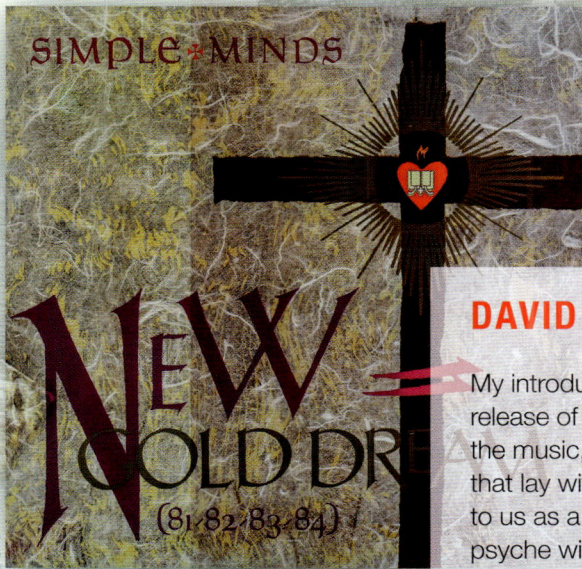

SIMPLE MINDS

NEW GOLD DREAM
(81-82-83-84)

## DAVID TADMAN

My introduction to Simple Minds was the release of *New Gold Dream*. The scale of the music, the depth, the grandiose beauty that lay within that album not only spoke to us as a generation but also defined our psyche within the 1980s. Each song on the album was a feature film in itself, and each of those songs had its place and time best to be heard. For example, 'Hunter and the Hunted' on a rainy day thinking of a lost loved defined who I was at that time. Simple Minds gave us the music to the stories of our lives. For that I am truly grateful - Simple Minds gave us meaningful and long lasting connections.

Words & music: Simple Minds

SOMEONE SOMEWHERE
(IN SUMMERTIME)

GLITTERING PRIZE

PROMISED YOU A MIRACLE ✦ SIMPLE MINDS

1
SOMEONE SOMEWHERE IN SUMMERTIME
COLOURS FLY AND CATHERINE WHEEL
PROMISED YOU A MIRACLE
BIG SLEEP
SOMEBODY UP THERE LIKES YOU

2
NEW GOLD DREAM (81-82-83-84)
GLITTERING PRIZE
HUNTER AND THE HUNTED
KING IS WHITE AND IN THE CROWD

OTHER THAN A HANDFUL OF AMERICAN SHOWS IN DECEMBER 1994, SIMPLE MINDS WERE OFF THE ROAD FOR THREE AND A HALF YEARS

## ANTHONY ROYBAL

*Mayan Theatre*
*13 February 1995, Los Angeles, California*

My first experience listening to Simple Minds was through radio station KROQ in Los Angeles in 1984. Their sound was sublime yet still spoke to the human experience. They had depth and substance and just sounded amazing. I really wanted to get into the cool kids' groups in school and at social gatherings. They looked like the kids in John Hughes films! I got one to be my friend and he had *Sparkle in the Rain* on cassette. I took it on vacation with me, listening to it whilst watching the changing landscape of the desert between California and New Mexico. Needless to say I was blown away.

   Since then I've been a fan. One of the things that bugs me about many bands is that they put out good songs but not so much good albums. Simple Minds have always struck me as an albums band. The first concert was on the *Good News from the Next World* tour. I was struck by their performance, the best concert I'd been to at the time. Simple Minds have been the soundtrack to my life. One time I had to go to hospital for an operation. I was in a lot of pain. I remember *Street Fighting Years* playing over and over in my head, and thought, 'This is good music to die to, this music is me.'

## DEANNA O'MARA

*Ogden Theatre*
*16 February 1995, Denver, Colorado*

Having been a massive Simple Minds fan for well over a decade, I was at work looking forward to their show in Denver that night. Just before lunch, I heard an ad on the radio saying Jim and Charlie would be doing a radio interview in about an hour - at a radio station right across the parking lot from where I worked! I told my boss (who had a camera) and ran down to my car and grabbed the CDs I had with me. We spent a chilly lunch hour waiting

*Deanna with Jim in 1995*

for them to arrive. When they did, Jim and Charlie could not have been more friendly, gracious and kind. They spent several minutes chatting with me, signed my CDs and posed for a picture. I still haven't forgiven my boss for only taking one photo and that not turning out well. I remember thanking them and telling them I was really looking forward to the show. Jim replied, 'It will be a great show!' I ran back to the office to listen to and tape the interview on the radio. I recently listened to the interview again – it's a great snippet from that time of their history.

The show was amazing! I was second row and they played an energetic set. I made notes in my journal the next day that they played a good mix of new and old songs. I was excited that they played so many songs from the new album. I also noted that the encore was 'Someone Somewhere (in Summertime)' and 'Waterfront'. A highlight for me was that Jim dedicated a song to 'all the people we met today'. I was blown away.

---

## PATRICK MCDOWELL

*First Avenue*
*18 February 1995,*
*Minneapolis, Minnesota*

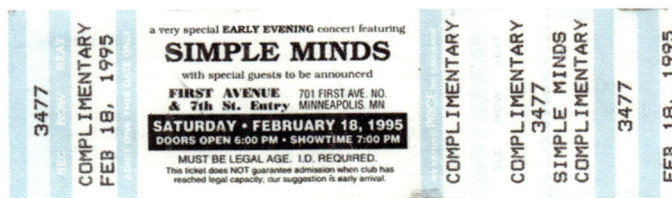

*Once Upon a Time* was the first cassette I owned. I was 15 and I listened to it non-stop. I remember my mom yelling at me to turn down the stereo because I was blaring 'Pleasantly Disturbed' on her stereo in the basement. But later I got her hooked on 'Waterfront'!

I saw the *Good News from the Next World* tour. Jim shook my hand during the show and Charlie threw me a pick. My adult son came with me recently in Milwaukee. What great experiences!

I watched a TV show about the band in the '90s in which a super-fan had an SM tattoo on his arm. I remember thinking I'd get one too when I was old enough. I now have a cool-looking fleur-de-lis tattoo on my arm, inspired by their album cover artwork.

---

## CRAIG LEONARD

*Agora Theater*
*22 February 1995, Cleveland, Ohio*

Back in 1986, my sister Ann and I got tickets to see Simple Minds on the *Once Upon a Time* tour at the Richfield Coliseum. A week before the show, she was in a serious car crash that left her in intensive care. She told me to go to the show, even though I didn't want to go. Even though it was one of the most exciting shows I'd ever seen, my thoughts were with her throughout.

Fast forward to 1995 and the band returned to Cleveland to play the Agora Theater. I was writing for a local newspaper and talked my editor into letting me review the show. The band's management sent me two tickets and a photo pass. I called my sister with the exciting news that she was finally going to see the band.

After another great show, I used my photo pass to talk my way backstage. I'd brought my programme from the 1986 show and wanted it autographed. I found myself face to face with Jim. He politely signed my programme as I told him my sister's story. 'Where is she?' he asked. When I said she was out in the theatre he headed out the backstage door.

When we found her, he introduced himself then spent the next 20 minutes talking to her about the show she missed in '86 and the show she just saw. He flipped through the programme with her and told her about different photo shoots. Finally, his manager found him, said they had to get going. He gave her a hug and was gone.

I interacted with a lot of performers when writing. Some good. Some bad. Some awful. Jim Kerr was the most human of them all.

## TIM SULLIVAN

*Avalon Ballroom*
*25 February 1995, Boston,*
*Massachusetts*

I was raving about the band after a friend suggested I check out music produced by Steve Lillywhite. I listened to *Sparkle in the Rain*. My now-wife and I had only been dating a short time when she showed up at my job and handed me two tickets for the *Once Upon a Time* tour. I'd been talking non-stop about wanting to see them - and she couldn't go with me! I fell hard for this band on seeing them live that first time, and then and there decided I had to marry this amazing generous woman.

Life became busy with starting a family and it wasn't until the *Good News from the Next World* tour in 1995 that I got to see them again. It was a special show for me. Thanks to WBCN I was given tickets and back stage passes. The show was intimate and amazing and the band was incredibly gracious.

## SIMON CORNWELL

'I hope they play something from *Sparkle in the Rain*,' said the hyped-up fan to my left, slightly younger than me, jittery with nervous energy. 'My favourite track's 'Up on the Catwalk',' he said. We chatted, pinned on the front barrier, nervously awaiting the start.

I'd moved to Boston for a year, my work requiring a relocation to America. I jumped at the chance to spend a year in Massachusetts, experiencing life in America, soaking up the East Coast charm. As luck would have it, I arrived in Boston a week before Simple Minds did. A fellow colleague bought tickets and I couldn't believe my luck when I entered the Avalon Ballroom – it was more of a small club than the echoing arenas and huge bowls I'd previously experienced. Here was a chance to be front row. I grabbed it.

The lights dimmed and the opening chords of 'Great Leap Forward' blasted out, announcing the band. This was the closest I'd been to the group in my life and I was expecting the surge and some elbowing so clung on to the front bars. But this American crowd were much cooler than the frenzied UK audiences I'd experienced before, so there were no problems.

It was a concert firmly rooted in *Good News from the Next World*, *Real Life* and *Once Upon a Time*. I'd been slightly disappointed by the *Real Life* tour, feeling the songs had reverted back to their album guises. But I loved that they were now playing around with the music again. The keyboard arpeggios of 'See the Lights' still remain a favourite whilst I loved the new acoustic take of 'White Light/White Heat', most of the band appearing on stage with acoustic guitars. It would take them decades to fully embrace the acoustic format, but the seeds were sown during this tour.

Because I clearly knew the words, mouthing them during the show, I had the microphone thrust towards me for the chorus of 'Stand by Love'. I listened to a bootleg sometime later and was partially relieved that my lyrical contribution couldn't be heard. But it was great to be recognised.

And they did play 'Up on the Catwalk'. My fellow fan, as the distinctive keyboard opening trilled out, completely lost it and went bat-shit crazy. Brilliant.

---

## MARK JONES

### National Exhibition Centre Arena
### 24 March 1995, Birmingham, England

For me, the beginning of my journey through life, along with Simple Minds, came about due to my auntie and uncle. Both were massive music fans and had an expansive collection I envy to this day. I was

*Mark Jones with his Auntie Sheila, who introduced him to Simple Minds*

given the chance to listen to anything I wished, had a look and picked a black-covered album with gold writing embossed upon it. The vinyl was placed on the turntable, the first few sounds of Charlie's guitar on 'Ghostdancing' into my sonic view. I was hooked instantly.

*Mark Jones worked 38 Simple Minds song titles into his wedding day speech*

## KAMRAN UMAR

I was 10 years old, on holiday with my family in Valletta, Malta. It was really hot but the clearest memory of that holiday is finding a record shop and discovering a CD called *Sons and Fascination*. Instantly I was drawn to its cool artwork. The shop had a stack system with over the ear headphones and I recall to this day the feeling of hearing those first few notes of 'In Trance as Mission'. That day in that little shop I listened to the first six tracks. The next day I dragged my family back again and listened to the remaining seven tracks. In a daze, I spent all my pocket money and bought my very own first album.

But my Simple Minds story starts with my dad. When I was growing up he would play lots of the music he grew up with - Uriah Heep, Supertramp, Crosby Stills Nash and Young, to name a few. In the early '90s one of the most worn cassettes in our car was a homemade copy of *Live in the City of Light*. I grew up listening to 'Waterfront', 'Book of Brilliant Things' and 'New Gold Dream'. I remember coming home from school in 1995 and my dad saying the new Simple Minds song had been on the radio. We tuned in to Northants FM and on came 'She's a River'. Wow, what energy!

That year I saw Simple Minds live for the first time at Birmingham NEC. In a flash the gig was over and only a few days later did the whole event sink in. Simple Minds are still a big part of my life, as I dance in the kitchen with three-year-old daughter Thea to 'Up on the Catwalk' or bounce three-month-old daughter Aurelia to sleep listening to 'Somebody Up There Likes You'.

## RICHARD GWYN

*Docklands Arena*
*26 March 1995, London, England*

My first gig was on the *Good News from the Next World* tour. I was a student in Swansea, so travelled by train on the new Docklands Light Railway. I ended up sleeping on a station bench with my schoolmate Tony Rahman, as we missed the last train home.

---

## PAUL TWYMAN

The first song that got me into Simple Minds was 'Love Song'. I played it over and over again. I just loved everything about their sound and their songwriting. I loved Jim's look, and used to copy it and wear what he was wearing to the local nightclubs. I'd ask the DJ to play Simple Minds and six of us would take over the dancefloor. My favourite song is 'See the Lights'. Simple Minds and that song helped me get through a very emotional and dark time in my life, for which I'm eternally grateful. My best concert was the *Good News from the Next World* tour. Me and my mate Andy arrived at London's Docklands Arena eight hours before the doors opened and heard the soundcheck and everything. When the concert finished, we ran up to the stage while the band were still on. I was lucky enough to get a pair of Mel Gaynor's drumsticks (which I still have today, in our front room cabinet) and Andy got one of Charlie's plectrums. This band is just so inspirational in everything they do, and one of the best you will ever see live. Thanks for giving me so many happy memories - and many more to come.

---

## FLORENCE CHALVIN

*Wembley Arena*
*28 March 1995, London, England*

As a teenager I had no idea who these boys were. But Nottingham University had a library, from which I borrowed *New Gold Dream* and *Sparkle in the Rain*. When I recognised the gems I'd heard years before, it was like seeing the light. I taped the records and listened on my Walkman on the long coach ride home to the French Alps. I'd wonder who on earth were the boys who had created such genius, powerful, mesmerising music.

  When I first saw the boys on *Top of the Pops*, I was struck by Jim's deep mystical blue eyes, and Charlie was very handsome. But I never got girlie back then, finding out they were married. The first gig I ever went to was in '95 at Wembley. I remember dancing the whole way through and being totally entranced. Living in Wembley and knowing where the backstage area was, I rushed back after the gig. Some roadies were chatting me up when Charlie came out. He was as lovely, sweet and helpful as he is today. He protectively told me there was no party back at the hotel, despite what the roadies had tried to lure me into! As for Jim, Charlie said he'd already left, but I still went in, never saying no to a glass of champagne.

It wasn't until June 2018 that I got to meet Jim, with Charlie in Paris. He was beyond what I imagined - a prince, a king, a King of Hearts as I've called him since. Meeting them was magic. Simple Minds are in my heart to stay!

# CHRISTOPHE DURON

## Le Zenith
## 31 March 1995, Paris, France

I was living in Cognac, France, in the early '80s and listening to Bernard Lenoir, a kind of French John Peel, and his *Feedback* show on France Inter, when I heard 'I Travel'. It went through me like a musical tornado. On this day, Simple Minds started to be part of my life.

I saw a memorable gig at the Zenith Arena, Paris in 1995, after which I met Jim Kerr and Charlie Burchill in a private club. It was an exciting moment. Working for advertising agencies and due to my relationships with a lot of record company people, I got to shoot lots of bands on stage, with Simple Minds the first. From 2002 to 2018, I hung out at all the Parisian venues to take pics of Simple Minds everywhere – the Olympia, Zenith Arena, Casino de Paris, Salle Pleyel, Le Réservoir….

Jim kindly wrote words of support for my exhibition of paintings at the Museum of Art in Cognac in 2018, 'Christophe's creativity shines through in his paintings. Much as it does in his remarkable photography.' Thank you, Jim.

*Jim at Wembley - photo Trevor Benbrook*

# GIUSEPPE GILIBERTI

*Casalecchio di Reno Palasport*
*19 April 1995, Bologna, Italy*

I was 15 and I'll never forget the role Simple Minds played in my political evolution with *Street Fighting Years*. But an angry three-hour long live show with 'Belfast Child', 'Sun City' and 'Biko' used to end with 'Alive and Kicking', an anthem of a generation of desperate romantics. And I'll never forget the role they played in my romantic evolution as well. In 1995, on a spring morning in Bologna just outside the Casalecchio di Reno Palasport before the *Good News from the Next World* tour, the embrace between me and Daniela, and the smile on Claudia's face, showed a passion for something not physical, but ethereal – the music of Simple Minds.

---

# SUSANA GARRIDO

*Palau Vall D'hebron*
*22 April 1995, Barcelona, Spain*

When I was 16, my high school organised a 15-day trip to Edinburgh to learn English. It was my first contact with Scotland and it changed my life. I went back in 1990 for a few months living and working in Edinburgh, then again in 2001, although this time I ended up spending eight years there, meeting my future husband. Now I'm back in Catalonia but go to Edinburgh at least two to three times a year. Scotland will always be my home away from home.

Back when I was 16, studying English at a school down the Royal Mile and living with a family in Corstorphine, one day they said to me they had

*Susana Garrido has seen Simple Minds more than 30 times*

a family house down in Moffat and were going there overnight if I wanted to join them. I was doing a dissertation on Robert Burns so I jumped at the chance. At dinner time, the lady's brother joined us and asked me to choose the music. He gave me two cassettes to choose from, Simple Minds or Deacon Blue. I didn't hesitate and for the first time I paid real attention to the music and fell in love hook, line and sinker with *Street Fighting Years*.

Back home, I bought all the cassettes and one day met a friendly chap at an English class in my hometown who turned out not only my best friend but also a big Simple Minds fan. A bond formed.

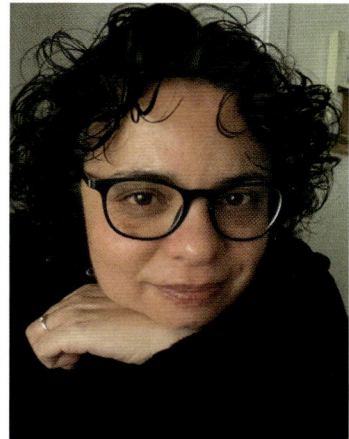

I went to my first concert in Barcelona in 1995 for the *Good News* tour. I'll never forget it. Since then, we've attended more than 30 concerts and never miss them if they come to Barcelona or somewhere we can easily reach. Don't ever retire!

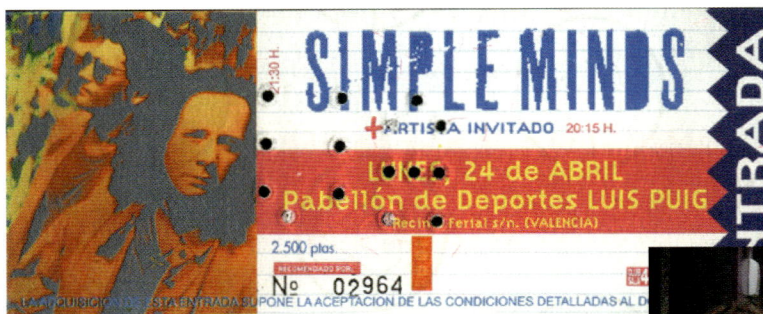

## DAVID ALOS

*Palacio Velódromo Luis Puig*
*24 April 1995, Valencia, Spain*

I started listening to Simple Minds when I was 14. My brother had an album and when I heard it I loved it. The first song I fell in love with was 'Up on the Catwalk'. I've seen them live in Valencia, Madrid, Barcelona, Estepona, London and Edinburgh, for the launch of *Graffiti Soul*. Thanks for putting a soundtrack to my life. Always Simple Minds.

*David Alos with Jim....*

*... and Charlie*

## SILVIA SCHLICKEISER, AGE 17

*Deutschlandhalle*
*4 July 1995, Berlin, Germany*

I first came across Simple Minds sat in front of the TV one Saturday afternoon in 1989 watching German music show *Formel Eins*. The song 'Belfast Child' was introduced, and Jim was interviewed. I don't remember much from the interview but remember the song pretty well as it was powerful and epic and has stuck in my head ever since. I had no idea what it was about as I hadn't learned a single word of English yet and had never heard of The Troubles either. After all, I was 11 and growing up behind the Berlin Wall, in the GDR. There was no chance I would be able to get hold of the single. I kind of forgot about the band.

Until 1991, when Simple Minds performed 'Let There be Love' on a German game show called *Wetten, dass…?* By that time the Wall had come down and I was able to buy the album. And I did, on 8 July 1991, somewhere in the south of Bavaria while on holiday with my parents. I didn't stop listening to *Real Life* during the whole of the holiday and to this day it's one of my favourite albums.

From that point on I looked for every album in every shop possible, but it took me until July 1995 to see the Minds. The ticket was about 50 DM. I was 17 and not allowed to go on my own but managed to be right in front of the stage and was able to enjoy every minute of the *Good News from the Next World* tour. Since then I've seen Simple Minds a few times in Germany and the UK and enjoyed every concert immensely.

---

# GEIR JONE JESS

## *Sentrum Schene*
## *7 July 1995, Oslo, Norway*

*Geir with Charlie*

I grew up in a town called Ålesund in the north-western part of Norway. We had only one TV channel. I moved to a small place called Ski, just outside Oslo in 1984. At our new place we got many TV channels. I really loved the music programmes on Sky and watched them every day after school. The first time I heard about Simple Minds was when they released 'Alive and Kicking'.

I remember buying the 7-inch single of 'Alive and Kicking'. Me and a schoolmate cycled 6km each way to get to the record store. I got *Once Upon a Time* for Christmas from my parents. I became a huge fan and bought more and more Simple Minds albums.

In 1995, 10 years on, I saw them live for the first time in Oslo. It was an amazing gig. In 2009 I was supposed to see them a third time, but got sick. I had to go to the hospital. That was very depressing. But I've seen the band in their hometown of Glasgow and had a great time. I also met a few guys from England I'd met before at a Simple Minds gig at the O2 Arena, London. The gig in Glasgow was great. I was supposed to see them in Dublin the day after, but my flight was cancelled. I couldn't go until the day after.

In 2014 I saw Charlie Burchill walking towards me in a street in Bergen. I stopped him and we talked for a few minutes. I got an autograph and a picture with him. A very nice guy. He'd been to a pub to watch football and was going back to Bergenhus Fortress, where the concert was that evening.

I saw both the Oslo gigs in 2020 before the coronavirus pandemic meant they couldn't tour any more.

---

# DIANA MUELLER

## Staussi Ferienpark
## 26 August 1995, Erfurt, Germany

I was 15 when my mum and dad said I could go and see Simple Minds in my hometown at the Hohenfelden reservoir. My friends and I decided to make a banner.

How could I forget my first concert, with Jim's hair and red shirt fluttering in the wind? If I wasn't hypnotised at the show I was after, when we were waiting for my friend's dad to pick us up and bring us back home. The band's bus couldn't move until the trucks had been moved so we stood in front of the bus with our banner. The driver was waving to us to come around to the door. I was the only one brave enough to do so. After I asked for autographs Jim, sitting on the right side above the door, asked me with that lovely Scottish accent, 'How do you do?' That's when I was finally hypnotised.

*Diana and her friend Nadja were after a date*

---

# NEIL CARR

## Usher Hall
## 3 – 5 September 1995, Edinburgh, Scotland

I was going through a phase at secondary school of liking A-ha, styling myself on Morten Harket, then Bros. I was also going through a hip-hop phase with the likes of NWA and Public Enemy. It wasn't until '91 when I heard 'Stand by Love' on the radio that I was blown away by Simple Minds. My friend worked in Bandparts record shop, Edinburgh and gave me a live cassette single from Glasgow Barrowland. I heard 'Someone Somewhere (in Summertime)' and 'Banging on the Door' live and was hooked. By the time I purchased *Live in the City of Light* I was Simple Minds daft.

My first gig was at the Usher Hall on the *Good News* tour. They played three nights and I attended two. My mum bought me the tickets and I went with different friends each night. I was in awe. Since then I haven't missed a gig in either Edinburgh or Glasgow. The furthest I travelled is north to Inverness Northern Meeting Park, where I got soaked. I didn't give a toss.

## DAVE MOORE

*Capitol Theatre*
*7 September 1995, Aberdeen, Scotland*

After purchasing tickets a few months earlier for myself and my then new girlfriend, I travelled from Forfar to Perth to pick her up then head off back up the road to Aberdeen. I at least was full of excitement about the upcoming gig.

It poured with rain from the minute we left Perth. We finally got to the Capitol 30 minutes before the gig started. I was in a slight panic that we might miss the start. And I like to watch the support act. The fact that we could not get parked near the theatre didn't help.

We finally found a space in a street a few blocks away from the venue, so parked up and began the long walk/run to the gig, running through streets, dodging cars and getting soaked in the rain. 'There it is, over there,' I said to my now fed up-looking girl.

We crossed another street, then another. My girlfriend waited as an old Jaguar came towards us. 'Ah,' I thought, 'this car is close.' It stopped just a couple of yards before me. I looked up and behind the wheel, wearing a sort of beret, was Jim Kerr. I looked and waved and as he drove off, waved again, this time a sort of 'Shit, sorry about that Jim' wave. He waved back with a wry smile.

I'm still alive and kicking. And the girlfriend? Now my ex-girlfriend.

## ROB WASMUTH

*Royal Concert Hall*
*10 September 1995, Glasgow, Scotland*

In 1988 I had heard of Simple Minds but hadn't heard Simple Minds. That all changed whilst sat in my bedroom as a moody 16-year-old watching *The Breakfast Club*. The

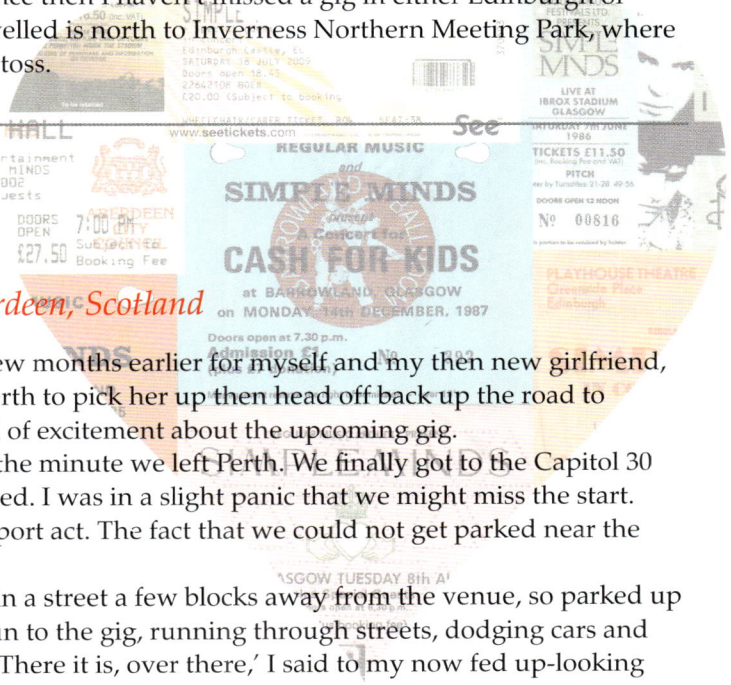

film and soundtrack were a revelation. I had become a fan. My education was an intense affair. *Live in the City of Light* was the first album, a Christmas present that was followed by the rest of the back catalogue over 1989. What a year that was, including my first gig in July. As clichéd as it sounds, Simple Minds have been the backdrop to a host of wonderful life experiences. The night before I got married in 2002, I went to the Royal Albert Hall gig. And I was there in Glasgow in 1995, the show broadcast live on Radio 1. I've still got the plectrum, Charlie!

## IAN MILNE

*Royal Concert Hall*
*13 September 1995, Glasgow,*
*Scotland*

I was brought up in the punk era and liked Johnny and the Self Abusers. I got into Simple Minds around the early '80s, seeing them on *Top of the Pops* and other music shows. I was a teenager, but it didn't stop me sneaking away to Glasgow on a Saturday to go and see them at the Barrowland. I can't remember anything about it now, but just wanted to see them play live! I liked that they were Scottish, like me.

I've seen them many, many times, mostly in Scotland - Edinburgh Castle, Caird Hall and last time at Slessor Gardens, Dundee, are a few highlights. I was part of a fan club set up by another fan and very soon made lots of contacts and new friends who were also big Simple Minds fans.

When they played at the Royal Concert Hall, Glasgow in the '90s, my German friend managed to get us backstage passes and we got to meet the whole band, who were very down to earth.

I've also met Jim Kerr at the recording studios at Loch Earn. The band were there and Jim came to the gate and spoke to us, making a comment about 'Dundee pehs'. I remember that. Oh, to still be young and naïve enough to do such things....

They know how to engage with the crowd, no matter big or small, and always put on a good show. What other band or artist can live up to that? Not many.

# LEANDRO AFRICANO

*Stadio Obras Sanitarias*
*17 September 1995, Buenos Aires, Argentina*

I had to wait 10 years from discovering Simple Minds on the radio, when I was 14, until I got to see them live in Argentina. I bought a ticket but never used it. I was working on a newspaper in Buenos Aires and asked the show's organisers for a pre-concert phone interview with Jim. I believe I was the first journalist from Argentina to interview Jim Kerr.

I also asked for - and got - accreditation to attend the concert. I was also taking my first steps in photography so could do the work of two people, taking pictures and writing a review. The interview was never published due to lack of space, but my review was.

When, 10 years later, Simple Minds returned to Argentina to play a festival, I went with my wife, just a few days after our daughter was born. We were paying attention to the cell-phone in case something happened to her and we had to leave quickly. But we saw the whole show. I think it's the only time she slept the whole night through.

SIMPLE MINDS

RIVER
CATWALK
SEE THE LIGHTS
THE AMERICAN
BIG SLEEP
GREAT LEAP FORWARD
SOMEONE SOMEWHERE
HYPNOTISE
LET THERE BE LOVE
BELFAST
WATER FRONT
LOVE SONG
ALIVE & KICKING

THE BAND
DON'T YOU
SANCTIFY

*Leandro Africano bought a ticket for the Buenos Aires show but never used it because he got in as a journalist*

# MARIANO POLACK

It was probably 1986, I was 14, and the American Top 40 was on (and dubbed in Spanish) every Sunday evening in Argentina. That's where I heard 'Sanctify Yourself' the first time, which sounded like a train was going through the home! This was at a time when getting new releases in Argentina was not easy, and it would've been poorly-pressed vinyl or a cassette with a poor 'photocopy' of the artwork.

*Mariano Polack had to wait nearly 10 years to see Simple Minds in Buenos Aires*

My parents went on a trip to the US shortly after and brought my very first CD (impossible to get in Argentina at the time). I remember staring at the cover for hours. What a cool logo! I loved the fonts connecting together. And what were those pieces that looked like a jigsaw puzzle? And where could I find the other half of the faces of these performers?

After that, my best friend Hernan Kraviez and I became huge fans. We played in a band together as teenagers and idolised SM. Unfortunately, international acts were not that common in Argentina during the late '80s. Finally, the band came to Buenos Aires in 1995 with *Good News from the Next World.* Two shows and we got tickets for both.

The first night, in the standing room section, we were very close to the stage. With not many English-speaking people in the audience, my friend and I sang every song. The second night, as the bass for 'Waterfront' was thumping, Jim looked at us, pointed at us, making a 'v' with his index and middle finger, and said 'twice'. We were jumping up and down and screaming so hard we lost our voice.

At the end of the show someone we knew said he had a backstage pass. He didn't care for Simple Minds, but wouldn't give us the pass, even though he knew how much it meant to us, dreaming of having a picture taken with Jim and Charlie. He later told us of his conversation with Jim, making us really mad.

Fast forward to 2002, living in the US and Simple Minds touring for *Cry.* The same friend came from Argentina and we went to a one-night only concert at the 9:30 Club, Washington, DC. Afterwards we begged and begged - and begged! - the security guy to let us backstage. He did. We met Charlie and had a picture with him, which was great! Jim, unfortunately, had gone to the bus early. We waited outside the bus but he didn't come out.

Fast forward to 2004, my best friend now in London. I flew there and we went to see them two nights in a row. The first night we waited outside to see if we could finally get a picture with Jim. He came out and we gave our camera to a guy next to us to take it. But he only got my friend in the photo with Jim. I had to Photoshop myself in!

Then in 2013, Simple Minds came again to the US. This time I waited for Jim and got a picture taken with him. I was very happy, but almost 20 years later, still no picture of Jim, Charlie, Herman and I in the same shot.

But in 2018 I got VIP tickets for a concert in Toronto, including a meet and greet. Herman was living in Spain. He flew over and we got together in Toronto, went to the concert, met the whole band and got our picture taken with Charlie and Jim, as well as the band - after trying for 23 years!

Jim is so charismatic on stage, and unlike other performers, he makes a point of making eye contact with individuals in the audience. What more could a fan ask for? Well, maybe a photo after 23 years.

---

## ADRIAN FABIO DEL VALLE

I went to the band's concert on the *Good News from the Next World* tour with three friends. We were late going in and didn't want to miss our train. We went through a half-fallen fence and my shoulder got caught in the wire. We no longer had time to change my shirt so I decided to go with my injury. When we arrived at the gate, my shoulder was leaking blood and security officials thought I'd been shot and would not let me in. It took a lot of talking to persuade them it wasn't that serious. Eventually they let me in. After the concert I had three stitches. I didn't care. My dream was fulfilled.

---

## DAVOR JAKOLIC

*Hala Tivoli*
*19 October 1995, Ljubijana,*
*Slovenia*

My first gig was in the Republic of
Slovenia in October 1995 at Tivoli Arena,
only two hours from where I lived. I
remember that Mel wasn't on drums.
It was a crowd of 5,000 people and I
remember Charlie's performance and
Jim's longer hair.

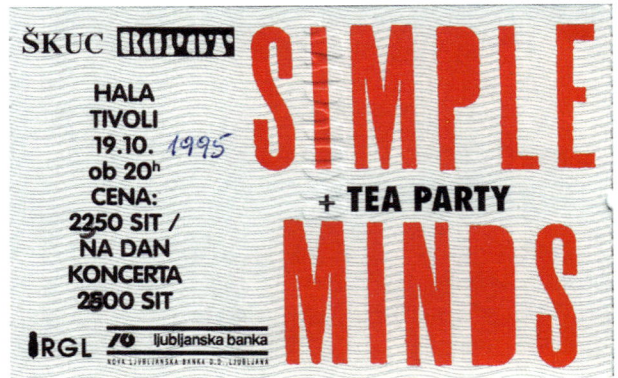

   I've seen them several times since, including in Zagreb with my brother and sister-
in-law, which was a brilliant atmosphere and where we got to speak to Charlie after
the gig.

## DENIS DUBOIS

*Parc Expositions*
*28 October 1995, Le Mans, France*

I went with my best friend, Fred, and my little sister, Stéphanie. A great concert, but
after the concert was even more memorable for my sister. We were at the store when
the salesperson put backstage tickets on the counter. I looked at Stéphanie and said
'take it!' She got to spend a good half-hour with Jim and Charlie. I had given her the
concert programme, telling her, 'If it's not signed, you can walk home!' She got it
signed!

## NADINE SCHACHT

*Rockpalast Festival*
*21 June 1997, Loreley, St Goarshausen,*
*Germany*

I liked football and the credits of a football
programme were accompanied by a tune
that fascinated me. It was quite a puzzle
to find out what song this was. Finally I

*Nadine Schacht discovered Simple Minds in 1995,*
*when she was 21*

discovered it was 'Hypnotised' by Simple Minds, who I confused with Simply Red. My older brother said, 'Simple Minds – do they still do music?' The summer holidays were about to start and I bought *Good News from the Next World* and *Jump Back*, a Rolling Stones hits compilation. What can I say? In those six weeks I listened to *Good News* over and over again and left the commendable Stones quite orphaned.

I 'friendly forced' my then best girlfriend to accompany me to the Rockpalast Festival. The whole trip was fantastic, travelling there by train and sleeping in the youth hostel next to the venue on top of that romantic mountain, overlooking the river Rhine. A great memory. And the festival, broadcast on German television, was superb too. I really liked The Levellers and INXS were amazing. Michael Hutchence was impressive. He promised to return soon but, sadly enough, wouldn't keep his word.

I was pretty excited and at the same time a little afraid to see Simple Minds live. Would they sound almost as good as on tape? You know the answer: Simple Minds were a blast.

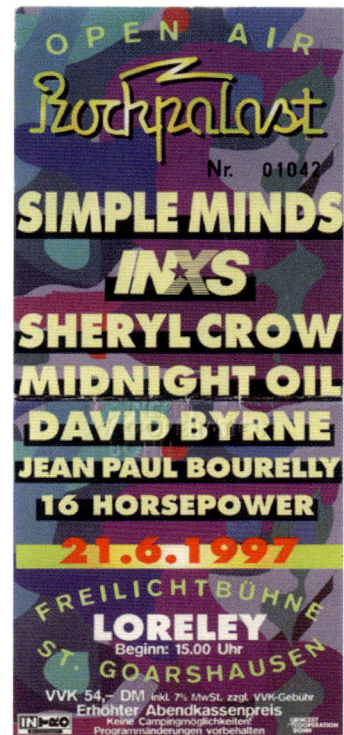

---

# SIMON CORNWELL

## *Stadtpark*
## *22 June 1997, Hamburg, Germany*

I distinctly remember a terse, yet friendly, email in 1996 from a 'Jim Kerr'. Concise, to the point, with a title 'Simple Minds 1996', it read 'Hallo Spaceboys, Hi to you and Shaun. If you ask then maybe I can help. JK.' I didn't know what to make of it.

A year later, chasing across Germany to get to Hamburg for the second Simple Minds gig in two days, we followed the advice of the German fans, did not loiter and pushed on hard. There was barely enough time to find the hotel before jumping back in the car, finding the venue, then the ticket office. Our names were on the guestlist and they were about to usher us in when Dave, our travel companion, stopped. 'No,' he said, 'We need something?' It was met with blank looks. 'A pass. We're not just guests. Is there an aftershow? There has to be a pass or something?' After a brief back and forth, we were given blue wristbands with a single black flower on it. It seemed odd – I just assumed we'd be asked our names at the end of the show – but Dave was insistent.

The venue was a small circular grassed area enclosed by bushes and trees. There was barely time to get a drink before the cheers started, the lights pierced the overcast gloom, and the band came on to the opening synth rhythm of 'War Babies'. We'd listened to a cassette bootleg of the Loreley show whilst tearing down the Autobahn, so were already familiar with the song, judging it to be classic Simple Minds. The jury was still out on 'Glitterball' though.

The set was the same as Loreley and we were well versed in the *Néapolis* restyling of the classic Simple Minds songs, thanks to the endless playing of the bootleg cassette. We played it twice before Anne rightfully complained - its appalling sound giving her a headache. But that was enough for Dave and I to excruciatingly dissect every new melodic and lyrical change. One change which really impressed me was a new arrangement of 'Belfast Child' – the backing synth chimes based on those used for a rare outing of 'She Moved Through the Fair' on French TV show *Taratata* back in 1995.

The smaller, almost-intimate venue also allowed a more thorough appreciation of the band. Jim dominated the proceedings, but I spent most of the gig watching Derek, a far more dominant bass player than either John Giblin or Malcolm Foster. He almost made the bass the most important instrument on the stage that night. And it dawned on me that I was almost watching the 'classic' Simple Minds line-up; far closer to the glory days of *New Gold Dream* and *Sparkle in the Rain* than the *Good News* lineup I'd seen in Boston.

At the end of the show, we met Dave and tried to get backstage. Again it was chaotic. Fans who also had their names on the guestlist were denied access by stern-faced security. Turned out that Dave was absolutely right to stand his ground and insist on some form of pass. That simple little black flower wristband got us backstage.

There was no aftershow. It turned out the venue was too small to host a razzmatazz marquee like Loreley, and it was Derek's birthday so everyone was off somewhere else to celebrate. Yet everyone was asked to stand in a line, as if to greet a visiting dignitary. And duly Jim appeared, working his way down the line, shaking hands, signing items, speaking to everyone in turn.

I offered him a Stylorogue proof of the album's artwork to sign. He took it and signed it, a brief flourish with a gold pen, as if he was given Simple Minds proofs to sign every day. 'Hi Jim. My name's Simon Cornwell and...' Jim paused, then looked at me. 'You're Simon Cornwell?' He then followed with a phrase which haunts me to this day: 'I sent you an email last year and you never replied.'

Hallo Spaceboys indeed.

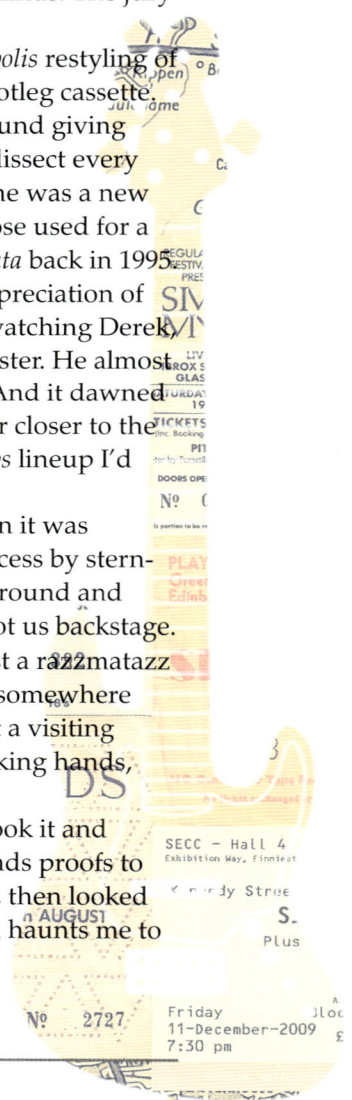

## DAVE DUBIN

I was in high school and college in the Eighties, playing soccer and listening to music including Simple Minds. After developing cancer at 29, then once again at 40, my wife Robin Beth and I started the foundation AliveAndKickn. Regardless of how many obstacles we faced, we always knew there was something more keeping it together. If my story of hereditary cancer, Lynch Syndrome, could make a difference in others' lives, we felt compelled to share it. My playing days are over, but I've coached each of my sons, one of which has inherited my mutation. We are Alive and Kicking. www.AliveAndKickn.org

## JEAN-MARC DUGAS

I discovered Simple Minds when I was at college. I was drumming a bit at the time and was immediately attracted by the dominant playing of Mel Gaynor. I have been a fan of Simple Minds since. The atmosphere in which Simple Minds music immerses me seems to reconnect me with my Scottish and Celtic ancestors and origins (on my mother's side). I hope you will carry on like the Rolling Stones. Please keep playing!

## LUKE WHITBURN

Profound effect on a generation. First kisses, heartbreaks, first concert with anticipation and electricity in the air. The glow of the lighters....

## MIKE TAMBLING

Simple Minds and Jim's dancing have been part of my life. I discovered them at college when I was 16 and any time I was on the dance floor at Bowleaze Cove nightclub in Weymouth or at Brockenhurst College, I would dance like Jim, with my arms out and legs low on the floor, thinking it was so cool. I would want people to think, 'Wow, he dances like Jim! He's good…' Oh dear.

371

## MARC HEESBEEN

*Bonnie Wee Studio*
*25 July 1995, Loch Earn, Scotland*

*Marc Heesbeen and family at Loch Earn with Jim*

My first encounter with Simple Minds was at Pinkpop in 1983. A few years later, after the *Street Fighting Years* concert at Ahoy Rotterdam on 30 August 1989, the band signed our programme. Simple Minds fever had hit! On Dutch television I saw an interview with Jim Kerr about the *Street Fighting Years* project, the interview filmed in Jim's Range Rover as he drove to the village of Killin. The Falls of Dochart provided the background, then there was footage along Loch Earn and inside their recording studio, Bonnie Wee. How we would like to take a look there!

Those images gave me an idea as to where the studio could be, and on a summer's day in late July 1995 we drove to Loch Earn. Soon we saw the striking shapes of the studio. I remember the text Simple Winds above the directions on the weather vane on the roof of the studio. I parked the car by the open gate. My wife, daughter and son stayed inside as I walked to the small jetty on the lake shore. I secretly hoped to see a familiar face, but didn't recognise anyone among the people who were there. Disappointed, I walked back to the car, where I was surprised to find three excited faces.

When I walked to the lake, Jim had passed the car from the house opposite the studio. He'd already had a chat with my wife and children. Back at the lake, he took time to chat with us and answer our questions. We also met Jim's father, who took our picture with him.

My son got a set of Mel's drumsticks from Jim. How proud he was and what impression that made on him. Now, 25 years later, he also has two children… their names? Djim and Charly. Coincidence?

## PIET HILLEWAERT

*Axion Beach Festival*
*19 July 1997, Zeebrugge, Belgium*

I asked a bakery to make a loaf that was 39 inches long, made a hole in it, put

salad inside and hid my flagpole inside. I took it to Zeebrugge, said to security, 'I'm hungry', and got in. I was the only person at the festival with a Simple Minds flag.

## JOZEF JASPERS

*Sportpaleis*
*13 November 1997, Merksem, Belgium*

My first acquaintance with Simple Minds was on the *Night of the Proms* in Antwerp many years ago. When they played 'Belfast Child' I really got goose-bumps. I decided it was my favourite song. I started looking up the lyrics and the history behind the song. When the group next comes to Antwerp, I hope they play it.

## ANJA JANSEN

*Ahoy Rotterdam*
*25 November 1997, Rotterdam, The Netherlands*

First time I saw Simple Minds, it was only Jim and Charlie, at the *Night of the Proms* in November 1997. After a few artists performed, the orchestra started playing and they got on stage. Charlie sounded great on guitar and Jim's voice was so beautiful. They played 'Alive and Kicking', one of my favourites, 'Belfast Child', and finally 'Don't You (Forget About Me)'. Jim stepped onto a platform, hovering over the crowd and over me. It was great. I tried to sing along with all three beautiful songs. Luckily, I wasn't alone. Then, unfortunately it was over. It was an evening to never forget, and from that great night on I've been a huge fan.

## JEAN-YVES LAURIER

*Cyber Theatre*
*25 February 1998, Brussels, Belgium*

The *Once Upon a Time* tour was my first live encounter with the band. I had tickets for both shows and was devastated I couldn't leave school to attend the shooting of the 'Sanctify Yourself' video in Forest National in the afternoon. I still remember lip-synching in front of my mirror, all dressed up with my sister's black panties, Dad's white and oversized shirt and a beret with one of my mum's brooches pinned on it. Jim, do you realise what you did to 15-year-old boys back then?

My fandom gained a new high in 1987. Playing hide and seek with friends, me and a girl climbed into a paper-only waste container. A first kiss was on its way until I found an old *RifRaf* music magazine with what appeared to be a young Jim Kerr on the cover. I couldn't believe my eyes. In the middle of all these cardboard boxes and newspapers there were literally hundreds of old music magazines, running from the early '80s until the end of that decade. Clearly someone had cleaned up his room or attic and left me at least about 20 books with interviews or gig reviews of Scotland's finest. This was pre Google/YouTube/Facebook, so the information and pics I got from it were priceless. So much that I forgot about the girl and left her broken-hearted in the container, carrying home my new treasures.

I've seen the Minds many times live but there's one gig that stands out - Brussels Cyber Theatre, in a very small club with only a very select crowd (you had to be a fan club member). This must have been one of the very first live gigs to be streamed over the internet, hence the location. Nowadays that's a walk in the park but imagine what a hassle it must have been then.

This was my first gig with Derek back on bass and his influence was immediately notable. A lot of the old stuff - my favourite era - was back on the playlist. More so, I was able to meet Jim and Derek during the after-party and got Derek's plectrum, the night completely magical.

I moved on musically. Madchester, Britpop and Acid Jazz came along. I discovered old funk and soul, but still added every new release to my collection. Simple Minds have now become that old girlfriend you'll never forget and are always happy to bump into.

---

# SIMON CORNWELL

Unofficial fanzines come and go – it's the nature of the beast. They're either tentative dipping of toes into a fan-based world before burning out or giving up; or they're launching pads to greater and better things. Lone fanzine writers can buckle under the enormity of it all; collectives can squabble and fall apart. Some last one or two issues, others manage to get to double figures, quality can improve or wane. It's a tough undertaking.

Knowing these pitfalls, I decided to have a go myself. What was there to lose? It was 1994 and news about Simple Minds had been extremely sparse. The band had an information service coupled with colourful publication *Shadowlands*. Output during this lean period, where typically the band were tight-lipped about what they were doing, was sporadic. I felt I could at least write something bigger, more informative and more frequent.

I decided to take the plunge, and working on various pieces for the debut issue, then unimaginatively called *Good News from the Next World*, whilst living in America in

1995, fellow fan Shaun Tranter, avid live collector, regular auctioneer in *Record Collector* and co-conspirator and supporter of the fanzine, was anxious to let the band know about it. I mailed him a collection of articles, all neatly printed on A4, as proof that something was happening. He set off to Paris to hawk it around and generally blag his way into all manner of interesting band-based scenarios.

Firstly, he managed to crash a meeting between Jim and a company putting a Simple Minds orientated CD-ROM together. The proposal was rather dull, and didn't amount to anything in the end, but it allowed Shaun to talk to Jim about the forthcoming fanzine.

'What's it called?' '*Good News from the Next World.*' 'That's crap. I'll think of something better.'

Next was a meeting with a TV company filming the gig at L'Olympia that night. Shaun ended up helping with the opening shot, a walk through with a steady-cam, parting the crowds at the venue. For someone who was supposed to be simply plugging a forthcoming fanzine, he'd done rather well.

True to his word, Jim contacted Shaun later with two potential titles: *Who's Doing the Dreaming Now?* and *Dream Giver*. I loved the first title, so the fanzine was duly christened. The first issue was finished that year and I immediately had the problem of how to mass produce it. The inkjet printer I was using was too slow, and the ink too pricy, so that was not an option. But by printing a text-only version, photocopying hundreds of sheets, then filling in the blank areas with colour pictures from the inkjet printer did work. It was hard work, with thousands of photocopies, loads of error-prone printing, hand-folding and stapling, but it was worth it. By issue five, I'd discovered digital printing, the whole process automated from then on.

The highlight was an exclusive interview with Jim after a VH1 gig in 1998. The biggest disappointment was not publishing a massive Bruce Findlay interview. It started with one question, 'How did you get involved with Simple Minds, Bruce?' then he talked for six hours straight.

The demise of *Who's Doing the Dreaming Now?* wasn't one of those examples I've given. I was just devoting more and more time to my Simple Minds website, realising that more of my readership were online, and I could do away with the sheer hassle of preparing, writing, formatting, designing, printing and posting a physical product. I thought when the band slowed down a bit, I'd have time to fill in the gaps and get something out. But the band never slowed down.

*Who's Doing the Dreaming Now?* lasted ten issues, and some fans call it the best unofficial fanzine produced for the band. Very generous, but I was up against great titles like *Le Menti* and *Endless River*. In the end it stayed true to two principles formed when I first put pen to paper: keep it to Simple Minds and keep personal opinions out. I believe that kept it in the right place.

# CRISTINA CANCIANI

*head of the Italian fan club*, Le Menti, *1996 – 2000*

I am in Firenze, Italy in August 1996. All alone I wander in an empty city. I go into the music department of a book shop where I discover a book, *Simple Minds: the Jim Kerr Saga*. Loving *Street Fighting Years* I buy the book. It's very, very good. I buy another book, containing all the lyrics of their songs. I listen again to *Street Fighting Years*. My interest in the band grows dramatically. By now I am their prey. I'm looking for their fan club. It's in Bologna but is now closed. I enquire and find that the next fan club in Florence has also closed down. By now the fire consumes me: I have to re-establish their fan club!

Slowly I met various fans - Italian and foreign – but also professionals who helped me in my fan club activity. I collected other books, other biographies and photos, articles and merchandising. It wasn't easy to re-establish the fan club and find new fans because the internet was not widespread. I wrote a fanzine using a typewriter and was always on the phone.

I couldn't have done the fan club without Michele Garofalo, one of the very first members of the club, Giancarlo Passarella, the founder of Ululati dall'Underground which brings together all the Italian fan clubs, or Simon Cornwell and Shaun Tranter.

I love Simple Minds' music and we share the same political ideas. I appreciate their seriousness and their moral sense. They are not rock stars but friends who live on my own continent: Europe.

# JEANET VAN BOMMEL

As a 16-year-old girl I went with friends to Fuse in Bakel in the Netherlands. I liked to dance all night long, eyes closed and moving with the music. No one was 'normal' and it was wonderfully liberating because you could empty your head and fill it with music, words, feeling, crying, laughing and dancing, dancing, dancing. I fell in love with an English boy who introduced me to Simple Minds and explained their lyrics. When I hear Simple Minds now, I am immediately taken back to those days and am once again that girl from the country who meets a boy who opens up a whole different world to her - a world of love, sex, excitement and discovery. The love didn't last. But when I hear the music and the lyrics of Simple Minds I am that young girl again.

# GUIDO HIDBER

I was sitting in the back of an Opel Rekord in 1983 when my colleague put a new cassette in the car radio. Back then we still had amplifiers, an equalizer and four kilometres of cables installed in the car. That Simple Minds cassette accompanied me throughout my time in the Swiss Army.

My first concert was at Rock am Ring. It rained buckets and water got into the power supply but they still played!

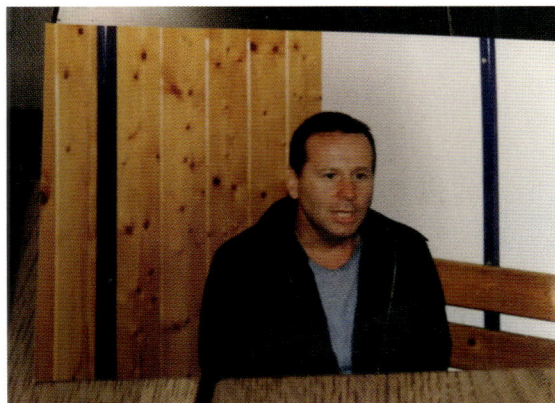

*Guido Hidber got to interview Jim*

I've seen them all over and seen every concert they've played in Switzerland. The highlight of my life took place on a Swiss football field when I got to interview Jim before a Simple Minds concert at Stadion Schnabelholz. I asked Jim why he would play such a small stadium. He said, 'It doesn't matter whether 300 or 50,000 spectators are present. The main thing is that you go home with a smile and happy.'

# KIM THONGER

I once shared an elevator with Jim Kerr in the Principe Di Savoia, Milan. We didn't talk to each other. That would have been gauche, obviously.

# FINN FREDERIKSEN

I've always thought they were better live than in the studio. I'd love to hear and see a *Street Fighting Years* tour CD or DVD. In fact, I'd like a big box of live recordings from 1985 until now!

# DAVIDE BACCOLINI

This is a short story about a great love. Together with U2, Simple Minds are the soundtrack of my life. My first concert was in Modena on the *Real Life* tour. I was 17 and still have the t-shirt 30 years later. Thank you Simple Minds - love you!

# SHAUN TRANTER

Having helped Simon Cornwell launch the *Who's Doing the Dreaming Now?* Fanzine, we'd struck up a great friendship, at times involving me driving to Cambridge to see how things were progressing with the *Dream Giver* website and the fanzine. Simon's site had been the bible of Simple Minds - if you wanted to know anything about the band you would go there.

With Simon being a computer genius and me only having minimal knowledge or use of a PC at work, seeing him do things was amazing. He invited me down to Cambridge to listen to the broadcast over the internet of Simple Minds live from the Cyber Theatre, Brussels. He explained that we may not get to hear the full show due to 'the amount of traffic heading to Brussels.' Me not being IT-savvy, I asked, 'Why will the amount of traffic in Brussels affect the broadcast? Will they squash the cables?' I was soon put right.

Simple Minds have always been a band at the front of tech stuff (look at the keyboards Mick MacNeil had over the years and how 'I Travel' was ahead of its time) so I think they were one of the first to broadcast a gig over the internet. The broadcast was also to coincide with the launch of the official website and the gig invite only.

We settled down to listen, cups of tea drunk slowly to make them last as long as possible so we didn't miss any of the broadcast. Yeah, there were a few drop-outs but we were treated to a decent set. There was then a short question and answer session. Totally out of the blue, Jim came out with, 'I would like to give special thanks to Simon Cornwell for publishing his fanzine *Who's Doing the Dreaming Now?* but more importantly for his website, called Dream Giver. Basically, if you want to know what Simple Minds have done over the years check it out – there's stuff on there even we can't remember doing. But we have also launched our official website tonight, hence why we have played this gig over the internet. But keep up the good work, Simon.'

After Jim said that over the internet, I don't think I've ever seen anyone with a smile as big as Simon had. To get recognition from your hero for stuff you've done about your hero. No words were said as Simon took a last drink of his by then lukewarm cuppa.

We headed to the kitchen, where Simon's mum and dad were. They asked about the gig. Simon told them what Jim said. He wasn't on Cloud 9. He was on Cloud 999.

## MAURO BARELLA

*Piazza San Giovanni*
*1 May 1998, Rome, Italy*

I remember when I went to Festa Primo Maggio in 1998 in Rome just to listen to the band play 'War Babies' and 'Glitterball'. And I remember Milan, when I touched Jim's hand – fantastic. Ciao Jim, ciao Charlie. You are my life.

---

## ANDREA SIVIERO

I began listening to Simple Minds music before I was born, with my parents listening to *Once Upon a Time* during the summer of 1988. The second album I fell in love with was *Street Fighting Years*. I listened to it in my parents' Fiat Uno or on their stereo, over and over. It was a white cassette and still sounds great!

I remember the first time I saw Simple Minds live like it was yesterday. It was the Concerto del Primo Maggio and I took the first VHS cassette available and pressed 'record'. It was the first time I heard 'Don't You (Forget About Me)'. Wow! The 100,000 crowd were jumping up and down and singing along.

A few days after that, I started my personal collection of cassettes, VHS tapes and CDs. The first album I bought was *New Gold Dream*. In 2002, I wanted to see Simple Minds live and in particular the Milan gig in late May. Unfortunately I was sick. But thanks to my parents, we went to see Simple Minds in Fano in July 2002 and were on the front row. It was my first concert, and it was magic. All Simple Minds concerts are magic. Then in 2009, I saw them with my partner, Lara. But that's another story, and she will continue it.

---

## ANNELORE BRANTEGEM

*Festival Park*
*20 & 21 June 1998, Werchter, Belgium*

Saturday 20 June 1998, and despite the fact I'm still in the middle of exams, my mum and I are boarding a coach to Werchter. A few months earlier, she decided it was time her 14-year-old daughter got to experience a proper legendary band live, so we're off to see the Rolling Stones. I can't pretend I remember every detail of that day – for a historian, I have the shoddiest memory – and yet it's no exaggeration to say it was a life-altering experience.

*Annelore Brantegem saw the Minds supporting the Stones*

We spent the late afternoon chilling on the grass and watching the World Cup. Despite the Red Devils drawing after an early 2-0 lead to Mexico, there was a lovely relaxed atmosphere when the support act came on: Simple Minds. Of course, their hits are engrained in the Belgian collective memory, but it was the energy and engagement with the crowd that blew me away. Even at the back of that huge field, I was completely transfixed, and while the Stones put on a great show, it was the Simple Minds gig that became the standard of a proper live show for me. Two days later, I spent all my pocket money on Minds albums - *Néapolis* (the most recent), *Once Upon a Time* (which I thought had songs on it I recognised) and *Real to Real Cacophony* (the only one I could still afford). My journey of Simple Minds discovery began in earnest.

Fast forward eight years, and after a frantic week participating in a radio contest, impersonating my mother (long story) in order to win, we visited the Radio Donna studios where Jim is being interviewed, promoting *Black and White 060606*. Asked on air to explain how 'a young person like me' got into Simple Minds, I talked about that magical day at Werchter and how their show completely mesmerised me, and Jim burst out laughing. While my first thought might have been, 'Prick, can't you see how nervous and earnest I am, least you can do is not make fun of me,' he quickly recovers and explains why that story strikes him. Turns out he wore a new pair of trousers for the occasion, but all that enthusiastic running around stage and engaging with the crowd, took its toll in the first song of the set and the trousers split at the back. Inconvenient for someone who's taken to wearing no underwear on stage and now finds himself hobbling around trying to hide the damage, which Derek Forbes later described as 'watching a Black Forest gateau trying to escape' (I didn't know what to make of that, but it put me off that cake for life).

Two completely different points of view of the same day. Jim had been convinced they didn't put on the best show possible due to his wardrobe malfunction, but that gig blew me away and made me a steadfast fan. It made my life so much richer by shaping friendships with people from all around the world whom I'll always cherish, encouraging me to travel even more and discover new places. It led to so much laughter and shared exhilaration, gave comfort in truly dark days and while I'm sometimes led astray by other bands, a Simple Minds gig always feels like coming home. For that and the band's generosity and kindness over the years, I will always remain indebted and grateful.

# EDMUND MURRAY

*Sala Kongresowa*
*1 July 1998, Warsaw, Poland*

Back in 1998 I saw the first ever Minds gig in Warsaw (and the first in Poland) during the *Néapolis* tour. In my excitement a few songs in, I threw my friend's Saltire onto the stage, much to the annoyance of both Jim and my friend. After the gig I promised my friend I would not only get them a new one, but one signed by the band.

Fast forward to the 2002 *Floating World* tour at the Armadillo (Clyde Auditorium) and I still hadn't replaced my friend's flag. I got one out a shop and after the gig hung about by the stage door with a few other hardcore fans in the hope of getting the band to

sign it. We had a great time, singing Minds songs among ourselves, the one young lady there, Marichal (I think) not only utterly gorgeous but obviously with great taste in music.

Eventually the guys kindly signed my flag and it was time to find my way home in the wee small hours. It turned out my new crush was also heading back to the southside so she offered to give me a lift part of the way. Unfortunately, stage fright got the better of me on the drive to Battlefield - I was too shy to ask for her number before we went our separate ways. I'm not really one for regrets but if only I'd had the courage that evening….

## OTTO JUNG

*Beach House*
*2 July 1998, Siofok, Hungary*

I became a fan in 1998 when they were in one of the deepest points in their career. After the communist era in Hungary, more and more international artists came to perform, more and more record stores opened and great new music magazines were published, the world literally opening to us. I went to the record stores once or twice a week to check new releases. As a university student

*Otto Jung has Derek's special Rangers tour pass*

I didn't have much money to spend on records so usually checked the second-hand record stores to see if there are anything interesting for a good price. It was like a drug - I couldn't get in without buying something.

In 1997 there was a new music mag, *Z Magazine* (Z for zene, which means music in Hungarian), and in one issue I saw a half-page ad for a new album by a band I'd never heard of. The ad was nothing special, just four men sat in a railway station, but I liked the simple design and pure font type. It said, 'The new album by the legendary Scottish band.' It was an ad for *Néapolis*.

Next time I went to the record store I discovered there were two versions of the album, one in a jewel case featuring the same artwork as in the ad and the other (limited edition) in a tin case with the band name embossed into the tin. It looked fabulous! But I was out of money so began searching elsewhere. And one day a third version appeared in the shop window of one second-hand store, in a 10-inch diameter round tin box, a very limited version containing the promo album, promo interview

CD, *Glitterball* VHS cassette, three colour photos, a band biog and interview transcript. It was pretty expensive compared with the price of the regular album, but way cheaper than its real value. I just couldn't afford to buy it!

I started saving, going to the shop once a week to see if they still had it. Days passed to weeks and after two months I finally had the money. I went there to buy it, and it had gone from the shop window! But it turned out it had just been moved inside. I bought it, took it home and loved it from the first moment. I still remember the day, 1 July 1998.

Next day I saw Simple Minds live for the first time, their first (and unfortunately only) performance in Hungary. They'd become my favourite band.

Over the years following them, I've been very lucky to meet incredible people all over Europe and can proudly say I have true friends worldwide. Simple Minds connect people. One day my mother called me to say a package had been delivered from France. I went to my parents' house to collect it and found it contained the limited edition version of the newly released *Graffiti Soul*, signed by the band to me. A collector friend in France I had only met virtually via a fan website had travelled to Glasgow for the album signing, bought 30 copies of the album which he asked the band to sign for various fans he knew from the internet, somehow got their addresses and posted the CDs, spending time and money travelling thousands of miles, buying the CDs and posting them to people he'd never met in person!

With Jim and Charlie great supporters of Celtic FC, who in 1997-1998 won a Scottish League Championship and League Cup double, the tour passes used by the band and crew during the *Néapolis* tour were in Celtic green, with a photo of head coach Wim Jansen on the other. Derek Forbes, the original bassist, back in the band at the time, supports Celtic's rivals Rangers. But they made a special blue tour pass for him, with a photo of Rangers player Paul Gascoigne on it. I've got that in my collection too.

# DAVID CRAIG

*Olympia Theatre*
*6 & 7 July 1998, Dublin, Ireland*

I first became a fan in 1992 after hearing Sky Sports use 'Alive and Kicking' as the Premier League theme song. I loved it. I went down to my local record store and bought double A-side single 'Alive and Kicking'/'Love Song' on cassette, which was in the reduced section for 50p! It turned out I loved 'Love Song' too. I asked my parents for the *Glittering Prize 81/92* compilation for Christmas. I was surprised to recognise a lot of songs on there. That was it! I was a Simple Minds fan for life.

I'll never forget the feeling and experience of seeing my favourite band walk out on stage before me for the first time, the first of many unforgettable nights. Every Simple

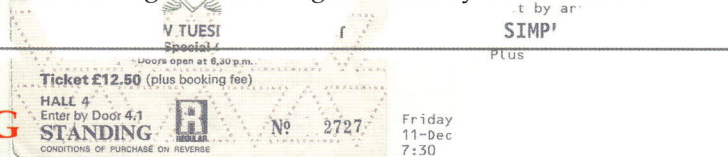

Minds gig is special but two places were extra special for me - my home city of Belfast ('Belfast Child' live in Belfast is indescribable) and their home city, Glasgow. I've always found the band members so friendly and willing to have a chat, which speaks volumes for the type of people they are. Of course, I was starstruck!

## DAVE KELLY

I was drawn in by the band's energy at *Live Aid*, despite the BBC only showing half of 'Ghostdancing' and a fantastic version of 'Don't You (Forget About Me)' before the satellites packed in. I was further sold on the band when I got a bootleg of the Sydney Musicians' Club 1981 gig with a brilliant version of 'Room'. Hearing *Once Upon a Time* sealed the deal.

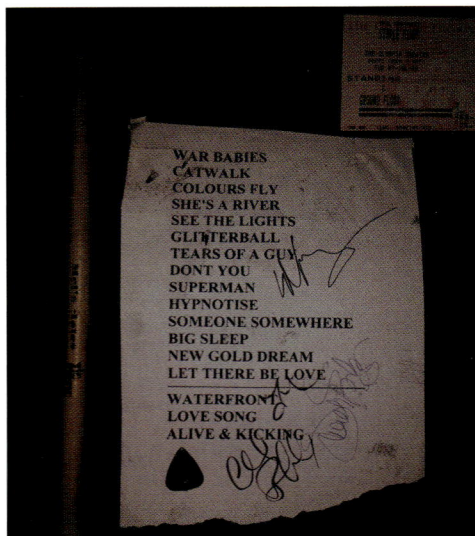

My first gigs were the following year at Milton Keynes Bowl, a reward for finishing our O-level exams. A few friends went both nights and we had a great time - my first lost weekend. After that, I was pretty much going to their gigs as a lone wolf, not knowing any other fans.

That all changed in the late '90s. I got a modem, and my first websearch took me to the *Dream Giver* site. This became a daily visit for news of the band, with so much to catch up on. When the *Néapolis* tour was announced I thought this would be the first tour since 1986 I'd miss, even more so after their only UK gig got cancelled.

After seeing fantastic shows at Loreley and Karlsruhe on satellite TV, the thought of missing out was unthinkable. On a Simple Minds forum someone posted that they had spare tickets for two nights in Dublin, I snapped them up without thinking. It was completely out of my comfort zone, I'm not good at meeting new people - shyness has always got the better of me.

Not knowing who I was meeting, I made my way to Liverpool's Seacat to meet three fellow fans. I was

*Dave Kelly saw the band at Dublin's Olympia*

pretty nervous greeting Adrian, Craig and the now-infamous Steve Robinson. But at 7am, we hit the ferry bar, all my nerves gone as we shared our Simple Minds stories.

The two nights in Dublin's Olympia Theatre were more than brilliant. It was a proper back to basics tour and the atmosphere was as expected for a Dublin crowd in a small venue. The shows kicked off with the brilliant 'War Babies', complete with Johnson Somerset's intro, 'Up on the Catwalk' sounded as good as ever and 'Colours Fly' was a surprise addition. We were watching a band in form, and the songs flew past.

The highlight was 'New Gold Dream', the first time I'd seen it played live since Milton Keynes '86. It was worth the wait. There was only one difference between the sets, 'Love Song' replacing 'Tears of a Guy' on the second night. We had a fantastic time in Dublin, partied hard, having a great laugh with new friends and other fans that made the trip over. I've been to many gigs before and since, but Dublin was the first time I felt part of the gig and got to properly meet so many fellow Minds fans. An absolute blast, the start of something special.

## ALESSANDRO TONON

I'm from Verona. I was on holiday with friends in Taormina in Sicily and one evening, returning from the beach, we saw a man who'd left his boat at the port and was sat on the steps of a small church to look at the view and think. It was Jim!

*Jim off duty in Taormina*

## LINDSAY AMANDA LOWCOCK

*Manchester Apollo*
*24 April 2002, Manchester, England*

I was too young to be into the band from the early years but in my adolescence nothing my peers were listening to interested me. I was, however, an avid viewer of MTV and VH1 and recorded any videos I liked, discovering everything I'd seen by Simple Minds I loved! In 1998, I managed to inveigle the princely sum of £10 from my dad and went into HMV, Manchester with the specific intention of purchasing something by the band. For reasons known only to God and

*Lindsay Amanda Lowcock saw the Minds at the Apollo in Manchester*

the shop itself, *Empires and Dance* was the only release on the shelves. Buying it for £5.99 - halcyon days indeed - I made my way back through Manchester's legendary rain to a very soggy 163 bus, whose drenched floor and condensation-covered windows created a dank atmosphere that dovetailed nicely with the sounds emanating from my Discman, appropriately starting with 'I Travel'.

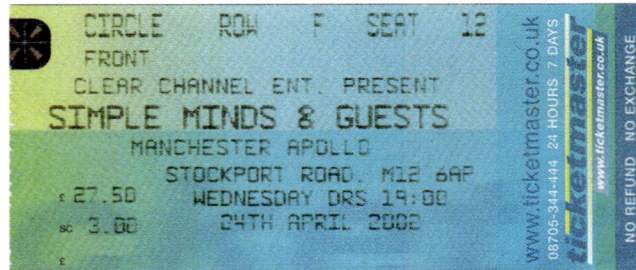

So enraptured by the powerful music and transcendent voice about unstable world affairs was I that the sounds embedded their way into my brain and never left. By the time 'Room' came on, that was it. Simple Minds had me for life. In a few months I had everything they'd released. I couldn't wait to see them live, achieving my wish on 2002's *Floating World* tour, lucky enough to meet them outside Manchester Apollo, my ticket signed by Jim.

It's truly difficult for me to convey the level of emotional attachment I have for Simple Minds. In every point of my life - extreme lows and rare highs - their music has supported me, giving me a soundtrack for every emotion. I've suffered great loss in my life and at certain points suffered from suicidal ideation. It seems their music has powers beyond sound, covering me in a weighted blanket and instilling me with a feeling of acceptance, following the band all over, attending gigs on every tour since 2002. I guess it's the Simple Minds Effect.

# JAN GIELES

*Vredenburg Muziekcentrum*
*5 May 2002, Utrecht, The Netherlands*

After years performing in the biggest stadia all over the world, experiencing all the madness show business and stardom brings, Simple Minds had landed back on their feet in Utrecht on a very small stage floor. Jim Kerr was well aware of it. He was so down to earth, so humble when he thanked the audience for being there, that we still believed in him and Simple Minds and we were so kind to make the effort and come to the concert after all those years. The pleasure was ours as well, of course, but it was an emotional moment we won't forget easily.

For my wife Jeltje it was even possible to shake hands with Jim. A great time and sweet memory for a lifetime.

# SANDRA SABORROSCH

## Stadtpark
## 14 May 2002, Hamburg, Germany

I was a U2 fan chatting with another U2 fan who mentioned Simple Minds. I was like, 'Who?' 'Don't You' and 'Alive and Kicking' were the only songs I knew. A couple of weeks later I bought the *Glittering Prize* album from a flea market, about the time *Cry* was released. They were coming to Germany for a couple of gigs, so I bought that. I loved it from the first listen. The two songs I listened to on repeat, probably driving my parents crazy, were 'One Step Closer' and 'Disconnected'.

*Sandra Saborrosch ended up on the second row in Hamburg in 2002*

I remember speaking to my friend Tina about how much I liked it. I told her about the advert I saw in a magazine about the *Floating World* tour. She said, 'Oh, I'd like to see them live.' We got our tickets! How little did I know about the band and their music apart from a few old and new songs? But that evening was magical and never had I thought a band and their music could have such an effect on me. Surprisingly we ended up somewhere in the second row. It wasn't a very warm day and it had been raining, but when the first few notes of 'New Gold Dream' started, the sun came out. It was just perfect!

All too soon the last song was played, the concert over. We were on such a high and could only think about when and where we could see the band again. Next day we looked at the dates. There wasn't a gig anywhere close. Thinking back now it really makes me laugh that we considered driving 300km for a gig was crazy when I've been to Paris, Glasgow, Lisbon, Madrid, Dublin, London, Aberdeen, Rome, Taormina, Ljubljana, Vienna, Stockholm, Riga, Prague, New York and more since.

I can't really pick a certain song or anything in particular that made that Hamburg concert so memorable. The music, the band, the atmosphere... but something happened on that evening that was indeed truly magical and changed my life. Thinking about it makes me want to turn back time and experience it all again.

## DAVID JOHNSON

*Patinoire Du Littoral*
*23 May 2002, Neuchâtel, Switzerland*

In 2002 I was working in Switzerland, had a role with UEFA and managed to squeeze in this gig a full 14 years after my first one! It was a more intimate venue, but the band were on top form. It was a brilliant gig and I remember the audience were quite young – well, compared to 32-year-old me.

I was working on the Champions League Final in Glasgow that year. Being a massive Minds fan, I suggested having the final opened by a live rock band from the host city. UEFA and TEAM Marketing ran with the idea and I was delighted Simple Minds would be involved. Then the head of ceremonies came back, thanked me for the great idea and announced that The Proclaimers had been signed up!

## JAVIER OTADUY

*La Riviera*
*29 May 2002, Madrid, Spain*

I was living in Mexico City. In 1981, my sister's Dutch boyfriend brought over tapes of groups he liked, mainly new wave groups like The Cure and Simple Minds. He gave me a tape with the song 'Life in a Day' on it. I liked it a lot. I bought the LP *New Gold Dream 81, 82, 83, 84* and loved the new sound, the music, the atmosphere. 'New Gold Dream' is my favourite song of all time. I never get tired of it.

I went to see them when I lived in Madrid in 2002. I was lucky - it wasn't too big a place, around 2,000 people. Jim's voice live was amazing!

## GABRIEL SATORRE

A friend left me a recording of *Once Upon a Time* and, listening to it, I knew it would be with me all my life. From that day on, I started buying all the old and new discography until my collection was completed. I'd also search for information about the band. It wasn't like it is now, where with a click on the Internet you have everything. You had to really look!

Because of that, I missed many concerts but finally saw them live in 2002 at the Riviera. We were able to go backstage. It was Mel Gaynor's birthday, and he gave us a huge hug and invited us to eat some cake while Jim asked what we thought about the sound. What an incredible experience, and great to see how grateful and accessible the band are to their fans.

Walking to the *Night of the Proms* in Benidorm, I found Charlie on the way. He seemed a little disoriented. After agreeing to have his photo taken, he asked where the concert was. I showed him. Thank goodness I found him - there might have been no concert!

---

## RON GRISBROOK

*Molson Amphitheatre*
*4 June 2002, Toronto, Canada*

It was a really nice outdoor venue, about 3,500 seats and lawn seating on a warm night. My attire for a show is a no-brainer, the hoops of Celtic proudly on display. I am not alone. There are 50 to 100 Celtic jerseys among the crowd. The fifth song in, 'See the Lights', and Simple Minds are rocking out. I'm in heaven, dancing and singing along as always. Jim approaches the front of the stage, looks out and points right at me. He gives his shirt a little tug where the Celtic crest would be. I don't know why, but I grab the crest of my jersey and give it a little kiss. Jim smiles and, still looking directly at me, gives a thumbs-up. That moment, we had a communication that was just the two of us. And all along he is still singing, entertaining the thousands. That moment is forever locked away as a concert highlight.

---

## EDDIE DUFFY

*Simple Minds bass guitarist, 2002 - 2010*
*Reno Hilton*
*15 June 2002, Reno, Nevada*

The weirdest tour for me was the US, 2002. So many incredible stories in the truest sense. To start with, we had a full-on cowboy bus driver (I still have his hat) who had large, framed photos of spaghetti western-era Clint Eastwood all over the bus. You know things can only get weirder after that. I woke up in my bunk one morning to a large bang, followed by him swearing repeatedly outside, kicking the bus. He'd crashed on the motorway. I think he got the sack after that....

Or the time we played in Konocti. It was a 'chicken in a basket' gig. I'm almost positive there was a parrot right beside me the entire gig, but I may have dreamt that bit. Anyway, a guy and his date were sitting at a table right in front of me, eating dinner. A female Simple Minds fan comes running down in front of me and sits on the aforementioned girl's dinner. They end up in a full fight, pulling each other's hair. For a long time after, Jim called us 'The Konocti Vets'. The feeling was, if we survived that, we could survive anything.

Or the revolving stage gig. I can't remember where it was, but the strippers from next door came in en masse, climbed onto the stage and began lap dancing with each member of the band. My dancer managed to stand on my cable and pull it out of my amp. I don't think anybody noticed or cared. I certainly didn't. If we weren't dizzy enough with the revolving stage....

But my favourite has to be the Reno Hilton gig. There was an Elvis impersonator gathering at the hotel for some reason. I think I was pretty stoned coming off the bus and couldn't really get my head around it. But I nearly collapsed when I was going up in the elevator to my room and it stopped at a floor and a midget (sorry, 'little person') came in on a tricycle. Did that really happen or was I smoking some serious shit? Decide for yourself, but that's not my favourite bit. Behind the stage is something else. Frank Sinatra still had his own dressing room there and there were various props for a magic show, including a large model of a jumbo jet.

Before the encore, I managed to find a rickshaw and told Mel if he jumped in the passenger seat I'd drive him to the side of the stage. He did, but I didn't stop at the side - I cycled onto the stage and rode around with Mel on the back for several minutes. The audience clapped politely. I think they thought it was part of the show.

Oh, and I met my wife on that tour. She came to a gig in Anaheim. She'd never even heard of Simple Minds before. How weird is that?

---

# THOM MESSENGER

*Celebrity Theatre*
*17 June 2002, Phoenix,*
*Arizona*

The music of Simple Minds was an escape from and a glimpse into a world seemingly far away from the small border town of Douglas, Arizona. During the late '70s and early '80s, late at night when conditions were just right, you could pick up KFI

*Thom Messenger's ticket from Phoenix*

out of Los Angeles on AM radio. Through the crack and pop of static came music from The B-52's, Roxy Music, Gary Numan and Simple Minds. MTV came a little later and I was finally able to see what the band looked like. In the mid- to late-'80s I continued to listen to Simple Minds while attending the University of Arizona in Tucson.

After graduating from college in 1988, I got a job in Phoenix and moved there. In 2002 I finally got to see Simple Minds in concert at the Celebrity Theatre, an intimate venue with a revolving stage. The band sounded awesome and put on a great show. After all those years I couldn't believe I was hearing them live!

Many years later, I came close to seeing them again while on vacation in Venice, Italy in 2009, my wife and I walking in St Mark's Square and seeing a banner announcing they were going to be in concert that next month. Unfortunately, we couldn't stay that long. Looking back, it seems crazy how a kid from a small desert town can be writing about one of his favourite bands and just missing them in Venice. I know it's taken faith, hard work and much luck to make it in life. Music has been a constant in my life, allowing me to dream, laugh and cry, and carry on one more day. To all the members of Simple Minds, past and present - thank you.

## JOE GALLEN

### Jones Beach Theater
### 27 June 2002, Wantagh, New York

I've always wanted to see Simple Minds in America. Me, my brother Kevin and our cousin Daniel booked tickets to see the band outdoors at the Wantagh Amphitheater in Long Island, New York. We decided we'd visit a mate in Pittsburgh, PA then, on the day of the gig, drive from Pennsylvania to New York. We gave ourselves 10 hours to get there. Between getting lost about five times, a storm with epic thunder and lightning that seemed to follow us for five hours, horrendous rush-hour traffic in Manhattan and Brooklyn and various beer stops, we were late arriving. As we parked up we heard the band on stage

Thursday June 27th, 88.3FM The Sting presents

**simple minds**

**Some Sweet Day 2002**

**18 Hours of Simple Minds music**

Including the hits, live tracks, B-sides, remixes, and rare recordings you won't hear anywhere else.

Exclusive interviews with members of the band, and updates from the *FLOATING WORLD* tour, their first US dates in seven years.

Plus giveaways of the new albums *Neon Lights* and *Cry* .

**Thursday, June 27th**
**7am - 1am**
Hosted by Todd Richards and friends

for more information www.wbwc.com
**Request Line:**
**(440) 826.2187**

www.wbwc.com
Part of the *2002 Summer Marathon Series* including:
Steely Dan July 18th, The Beach Boys Aug.1st, The Beatles Aug.8th, Genesis August 22nd

in the distance. We ran to the venue, handed in our tickets and - feeling pleased with ourselves - took our seats, 10 rows from the front. We'd finally got there!

The first words out of Jim's mouth were, 'You've been an incredible audience, thank you. Goodnight!'

Fucking nightmare.

# SEAN KOEPENICK

*9:30 Club*
*29 June 2002, Washington DC*

In the fall of 1985 I was an aspiring bass player and high school student in suburban Maryland. I'd just started a band with two close friends. We couldn't stop listening to *Once Upon a Time*. We had no keyboard player so covering a song off this record wasn't possible. But many weekend nights were spent driving around in a scrappy grey Ford Escort, listening to songs like 'Oh Jungleland' over and over again on a beat-up cassette. But in a blink of an eye, the 1980s were gone.

I was still aware of the band after that. I loved *Street Fighting Years*, especially 'Take a Step Back'. I recall seeing the band on *David Letterman* play 'She's a River' a few years later. But I'd still never seen them live. I became a bit more focused on the band's recent output, having really enjoyed the *Cry* album. When they announced a show at the 9:30 Club, Washington DC, I was on it. I was excited to see them in a club setting and they certainly did not disappoint. Powerful, energetic and thrilling. Everyone was playing with full force and on all cylinders. Highlights included 'See the Lights' and 'Ghost Dancing'. Then the show finished with two more songs from *Once Upon a Time* - it really was a concert that left me amazed! I've since made it a point to catch the band live at every opportunity. Although 2013 and 2018 allowed me chances to see the band live again in Boston, the first show in DC will always remain an incredible memory. Thank you Simple Minds!

# R TODD RICHARDS

*Freedom Hill Amphitheater*
*3 July 2002, Detroit, Michigan*

I host Simple Minds Marathons on a college radio station. But I'm just a fan. I grew up in smalltown Pennsylvania. I played my chrome-oxide tape of the A&M release of *Once Upon a Time* endlessly on my Walkman. Over the years I found myself fascinated by all the material from the band I'd never heard, wondering how they'd evolved. My college radio station has a summer tradition of featuring one band or artist each Thursday for the entire day, so plenty of time to dig into a catalogue for the most amazing music. *Néapolis* wasn't yet released in the USA. A trip to the import section of the best record store in town found me reaching for it, only to have it snatched away by another fan who previously hosted the first Simple Minds Marathon. Aaron Burke was the first of a long line of wonderful people I'd meet through travels to see and hear Simple Minds.

*R Todd Richards with Simple Minds*

The following year, thanks to the relatively new internet, I started reaching out into the fan community hoping to contact the band. Eventually a plan was made. Jim would be on the second Simple Minds Marathon I did in 1998. He called and I managed to forge a conversation and weave in some great music. No one said anything about Jim being on a cell phone, or in his car. If you hear the tape, you can hear the hazard lights flashing.

Over the next 18 years, I was always ready to be on the air and play the Minds, able to share the stories of many band alumni - including Robin Clark, Eddie Duffy, Derek Forbes, Michael MacNeil and Mark Schulman. We've also gone deeper into the production process with Bruce Findlay and engineers Ronald Print and Peter Walsh. And Jim Kerr has been so generous with his time.

I'd never seen the band live until the tour to support *Cry* and *Neon Lights* at the Freedom Hill Amphitheatre. It was more like a giant bowl of seats in a hillside in front of a loading dock with a stage. It was also the hottest day of the year, on 4th of July weekend, the band playing in the blazing sun.

Simple Minds and a reformed INXS switched opening and closing slots each day and today Simple Minds opened amid the heat, everyone drinking to stay cool, and drinking a lot! But the band won everyone over quickly - and won the evening. After the show, my first time meeting the band really felt like catching up after the great phone interviews we'd had over the previous five years. The entire band and crew were very gracious and welcoming. Before we knew it, Aaron and I were on our way to Toronto for the next night's show and another guest overheard my conversation with Aaron and yelled out, 'You're the guy from the marathon!'

# SERA BISHOP

## Teatro Greco
## 26 July 2002, Taormina, Italy

Trevor and I were members of the original SimpleMinds.com community in 2000. Our friendship grew as we found we had lots in common, specifically being fans of the band since 1982, albeit on different continents - Trevor in the UK, me in Australia. We finally met in person in November 2002 when he flew to Brisbane to watch the Ashes. Our friendship grew and in February 2003, I moved to the UK to live with him in South Wales. 10 months later we moved to Brisbane, Australia. We were married in March 2008, with friends we met through our love of Simple Minds coming from all over the world to celebrate our big day.

*Sera and Trevor met through a mutual love of Simple Minds*

We lived in Brisbane for 14 years but have now moved back to England and the Cotswolds. Over the years we've seen Simple Minds in many different countries - Germany, Italy, France, Scotland, Wales, England, Belgium plus Brisbane, Sydney and Melbourne in Australia. Trevor always wore his Birmingham City shirt to gigs and Jim would often spy him in the front row.

We both have specific shows that were personal highlights. Trevor still talks about travelling to Taormina in 2002 with many of our 'community' friends for an epic Teatro Greco gig. I think that particular gig is probably a highlight for everyone lucky enough to attend.

I loved the shows in my hometown, Brisbane as it felt so special to have Simple Minds play there. I was always front and centre! The shows we have attended together these past 17 years have been fantastic, not only to see our favourite performing but sharing the experience with so many like-minded people from different countries, making lifelong friends through our love of the band, keeping in contact with many of them via social media. These experiences and friendships all form a tapestry of a much-enjoyed life following Simple Minds, and we've lots of memories we will always treasure.

# CLYNT HISCOE

Being a Minds fan for 35-plus years has been an incredible journey. Being a part of so many great gigs, meet-ups and conversations has resulted in friendships forged for life. The Taormina 2002 venture is something to hold close to the heart, knowing a gathering of this scale from all over the world will probably never be seen again. This for me was the start of the rollercoaster ride that being a Minds fan brings. A real pleasure and privilege to be a part of the 'white-shirted tribe'. It was here that the friends I hold the closest met and to this day we are still on this grand tour, forever having banter on the music and our lives as a whole. I've been fortunate and lucky to have been a small piece of the jigsaw to the history of Simple Minds.

# LAWRENCE ROWE

The first day I was up and running with internet access I decided to look up info on the band and discovered Dream Giver, which was ridiculously comprehensive and provided a fantastic backlog of band information. The discussion boards were pretty intense and I was often out of my depth in conversation but enjoyed having a back seat in reading other fans' thoughts. From here I learnt about SimpleMinds.com and its community.

The Simple Minds community was a page set up by the then very new official fansite to enable fans to chat about experiences and future of the band and its old, new, and ever-changing fan base. I probably scared off a number of posters more used to level-headed chat, but was so excited to have a chance to talk about the band I'd adored for so many years that I just posted constantly. Gradually a number of other fans emerged from the darkness and started to private message their thoughts and how they shared mine and loved the opportunity to chat without the worry of being laughed at for their enthusiasm. I realised I was just one of many fans who grew up influenced by Simple Minds.

I may not be good at many things, but I've always been willing to organise events and have never been shy about a quick pint, so we started to organise meet-ups. The first was suggested by a French fan who wanted to come to London to meet other fans, so I arranged a meeting at The Hole in the Wall pub just outside Waterloo station. I expected three or four people to turn up and brought along a portable stereo and some rare Simple Minds music. After a few minutes we had a private room and 20/30 fans who started to open up and party like teenagers again. This was just the start. Suddenly organising pre-gig meet-ups was easy.

One I particularly want to mention is Taormina in 2002. Over 50 fans organised to meet up, staying in Taormina before and after the gig for a long weekend. It was the most incredible concert in the most beautiful venue, with such memories as handing out specially-made tour t-shirts and seeing Mel Gaynor in one after the gig, sat with Jim outside a restaurant with my mate Trevor and being unable to say anything to him (I never am), having a round of drinks bought for us in a restaurant by the band, gatecrashing the band's after-party celebrations and seeing the locals feel so proud of the town's superstar. Even the Mayor mentioned to Jim that he loved seeing the white-shirted fans in his town.

But the best memory was sitting with people I'd only spoken to on a computer and chatting for hours as if we had been friends for years. Then, at the concert, encouraging the locals who would normally just sit and watch a show to get up and dance with us!

# PAOLA MAROCCO

Some people say it's just a concert, but people like me who have attended Simple Minds concerts for 30 years know that's not the case. Simple Minds have been able to generate new emotions and new ideas, celebrating a glorious past but never being nostalgic. I've attended 129 concerts but that's just a number - it doesn't explain anything about this long journey – the music, the life lived, the emotions, friendships, travel, places visited, disappointment at flights not departing, lost concerts, small misunderstandings - all lived with heart in hand, with the magic that makes you be there.

I've followed them in Italy, all over Europe and around the world: New York, Toronto, Montreal, Dubai, Miami. Each stage of this journey is a gem embedded in my heart, each stop has brought me to meet new friends, to see old friends, discover new places and return to places again. In my personal book of brilliant things, there are a thousand memories and unforgettable emotions and many images I captured at concerts.

I've many images from those concerts and places. It's very difficult to choose the ones that most testify to this long journey, but perhaps it's the first photo with Jim and Charlie in Taormina in 2002, a memorable concert that brought together fans from all over the world.

# CLARE KNOX

Taormina gigs have gone down in Simple Minds folklore as something rather special. Sicily is a special place for the band too, Jim putting down some roots there and opening the Villa Angela Hotel. When the band announced a gig there in summer 2002 as part of the *Floating World* tour, we were intrigued… in particular by the incredible setting of a Greco-Roman amphitheatre overlooking the Mediterranean.

Fast forward to the end of July and a tribe of fans from across Europe descended on Taormina, a beautiful town whose streets tumble down the hillside to the sea. Thanks to some fabulous pre-gig organisation, the Tribe were kitted out in personalised 'We Travel' t-shirts – with a lovely New Gold Dream cross on the front and our names and a meaningful number (football kit style) on the back. The organisers even printed navy-blue shirts for the band. The garden of the Time Out Bar was promptly colonised, gig stories were swapped and new friendships made. I remember a huge Simple Minds tour banner being held up outside the pub, and a real sense of community between fans from several countries. On a personal note, I took a huge leap of faith travelling to this gig – I flew solo and knew no-one! But this is the great thing with Simple Minds fans – it's a family; and pretty quickly I was 'adopted', not least because I knew how to order a pint in Italian!

The gig was Friday night, and by mid-afternoon there were worried faces due to a fierce thunderstorm and a lot of rain. Was it going to be cancelled, after we travelled all that way? But after a few quick Hail Marys, the clouds cleared, and on a balmy evening we pushed through the hordes to get into the theatre – only to see Mel Gaynor try to get through the crowds too! A delayed flight made it very tight for him to get there on time.

The theatre's ancient walls were lit up by a stunning light display as we climbed up the old stone steps, marvelling at how many people would have done likewise over the thousands of years since it was built. Through a gap in the wall we could see streetlights lining the beachfront, and Mount Etna silhouetted against the evening sky – magical. As soon as the insistent drum beat of 'New Gold Dream' took hold, we were on our feet! But the Italians behind us were fuming and gestured at us to sit down – no way! We've travelled and we're going to sing and dance! I'd been out since 4am to get to this gig - no way was I going to sit down like some old grandma.

It was an evening of sheer joy and exuberance – one of those gigs where it just clicked – a band very happy to play there, and a crowd welcoming them with open arms. We were high on adrenaline, and went to bed late, very late. But our weekend of merrymaking was not over by a long shot. We found the local internet café and feverishly updated the simpleminds.com forum about the gig, then it was time for the Cup of Brilliant Things on a local football pitch. A feverish afternoon of five-a-side football with English, Scots, Belgians, Dutch, Italian, French and Irish fans fighting it out to win the glittering prize! But then, a dramatic injury during play after a particularly energetic tackle, and a race to Taormina hospital, me interpreting for our injured player to sort out an X-ray and splint. Ah, the battle scars we endure.

After some medicinal pints at Timeout, it was dinner at the famous La Botte, run by Jim's friends the Chemi family. La Botte had a tree-covered terrace, fairy lights, gentle conversations, waiters bringing out steaming plates of fresh pasta and local swordfish. We chatted, ate, drank, and bumped into some of the band, having dinner inside.

A lazy Sunday rolled round, and a group of us were staying for another night. We explored the town, chilled out on the beach, and before we knew it, a 'Last Supper' for the Taormina Tribe. The La Botte team found us a long table inside, so we swapped a few last photos and reminisced about the concert. As I stood up to take a last group photo, I suddenly heard an abrupt voice behind me – 'hey, ye've nicked our fuckin' table!' I turned around open-mouthed to see Jim Kerr cheekily beaming from ear to ear. The band, some of the crew, and Jim's parents were there for a last supper too before moving on to a gig in Rome the next day. Mel was wearing our Simple Minds 'We Travel' t-shirt and chatted away with a couple of us, whilst Jim kindly agreed to a few photos outside. An incredible end to an extraordinary weekend.

I met some amazing people during that weekend and am so pleased to still be in touch with them. And in 2009 I travelled to Taormina again for a concert, where I met yet more amazing fans. Our worlds collided in music for a few hours, and it's always such a pleasure to travel and meet for concerts across Europe. Thanks for the music and friendship, Simple Minds.

## GED MALONE

We'd just finished a run of six festival dates in Denmark as part of the *Green Festival*. The last was 21 July 2002 at Valby Parken, Copenhagen. The next date was the Greek Amphitheatre, Taormina, Sicily. Just another date on the tour, you probably ask. Not that simple. Jim had been building a new hotel on the island and this gig was part of a bigger picture. Not only as a thank you to the local politicians who helped with his venture but, more importantly, a big thank you to the people of Taormina.

After the gig in Copenhagen we had four days off before the Taormina gig. Most band crew decided to continue to Sicily and have their days off there. After all, it was summer and the weather was going to be beautiful. However, Mel Gaynor decided he wanted to go home to Nuremberg and would fly back to Sicily the day before the gig, which at the time I didn't see a problem with. How wrong was I?

Things started to unravel when I got a call from Mel saying he'd missed his flight and there wasn't another flight to Catania (the closest airport) until the next day, the day of the show. Not ideal, but the flight would still get him in to Taormina in plenty of time.

The day arrived and I got another call from Mel: 'You won't believe this but the flight has gone technical and they don't have another plane to replace it.' When I told Jim I thought he was going to kill me. After all, it's my job to make sure the band are where they need to be at any given time. Also, given the importance of this show, it only amplified the horrible situation I/we found ourselves in. I immediately got to work. The closest airport I could get Mel to was Rome, nearly 800km away. I stuck him on that flight then started working on how I was going to get him from Rome to Taormina. As there were no scheduled flights I started to look at private planes, then realised we were running out of time. Catania Airport is over an hour from Taormina, so that wouldn't work.

Someone mentioned there was a helicopter pad close to the Greek Amphitheatre, used for emergencies. So, after many phone calls, we managed to find a pilot who happened to have a twin-engine helicopter, which was needed for such a long flight. We weren't out of the woods yet though.

The helicopter would have to make one refuelling stop, adding precious time to the journey. I was also told that he would have to arrive before sunset or he couldn't land - there were no lights. By this time the narrow streets were teeming with people going the gig. I went down to the landing zone and waited and waited. Then, out of the fading light, we spotted the helicopter. We lit up our phones to help guide the pilot in safely. We had less than 10 minutes before it was completely dark.

The time was 8.30pm. Stage time was 9pm. We had to fight our way through the crowds and narrow streets but Mel made it just in time. Never again.

---

# SANJA GRGURIĆ

## *Sportski Centar*
## *4 August 2002, Krk, Croatia*

The magical love between Simple Minds and me has been going on for almost 35 years. I was 14 when I first listened to *Sons and Fascination*. I've been attending Simple Minds concerts for more than 25 years and have seen them in Croatia, Slovenia and Italy.

When I found out Simple Minds would be staying at a famous hotel

*Sanja and her friend Josie with Jim*

399

in my hometown, Rijeka, I told myself it was now or never. A unique opportunity to meet my idol, the one and only Mr Jim Kerr. I took the *Glittering Prize* book and waited patiently in front of the hotel. It was Saturday morning and everything was quiet. Not even in my wildest dreams did I expect what would happen.

I saw Jim coming out of the hotel. I shyly approached him with the book, telling him I was a big fan and asking for an autograph. Not only did he give me an autograph but also invited me for coffee. We sat on the terrace for over 40 minutes, talking music, history, food, Glasgow, The Cult, U2, Annie Lennox, etc., in a relaxed way. At first I was tense, but Jim's a very kind, open man.

I asked if he would walk with me to Dallas, the small music store where my friend Josie works. He agreed immediately. My friend almost fainted when she saw us. We wanted to take a photo and the camera didn't work. Jim set out to fix it, then asked which Simple Minds CD I was missing - he wanted to buy it for me. I had to tell him I have them all! When other customers recognised him he patiently gave autographs to everyone.

It's a day I will remember all my life. At almost every concert I attend now, when I am stood in the front row Jim waves to me and my friend Josie.

## CHARLIE PARKER

*Festival de la Foire aux Vins d'Alsace 2002*
*Théâtre de Plein Air*
*9 August 2002, Colmar, France*

Perhaps like others, my first introduction to a live Simple Minds performance and to the band was through *Live in the City of Light*. The sheer energy of the performance was unlike anything I'd heard before - the strength of Jim's voice, Charlie's shimmering guitars, the power of Mel on drums and depth Mick gave on keyboards. That's not to take anything away from John Giblin or Robin Clark, all critical contributors. Whilst there was such strength and power to each performance, each element was allowed to breathe and contribute to the greater sound rather than competing with each other, creating beautiful sonic tension, emotion, strength and delicacy all at the same time. Who could forget the link between 'Oh Jungleland' and 'Alive and Kicking' or the version of 'New Gold Dream'? In my opinion, the greatest live recording of all time.

One show that stands out is from the summer of 2002 when I dragged my best mate out of bed at 4am in the morning to jump on an EasyJet flight to Colmar to watch the band play. Colmar is a beautiful medieval town in France, on the German border, a place I knew nothing about. We arrived late morning with time to discover the town before seeing the band play a slightly incongruous venue - a mix between a farmers' market and a wine/beer expo. But it was a memorable venue and one that embraced Simple Minds to the core!

---

# IGNASI CALVO

## *City Festival Concert*
## *17 August 2002, Bilbao, Spain*

You could only pick five CDs to borrow from my local public library and I remember going every two days to pick five to listen at home, after school. This is how I discovered Simple Minds. I remember putting *New Gold Dream* in the CD player, listening through my headphones to that sound, those melodies, that production. I just could not stop listening. 'Glittering Prize' filled my soul completely, to the point that, 25 years later, I still remember how I felt sitting in my room at night, before going to sleep, listening to that one song on a loop for 30 minutes. One gets to remember these special moments in life, like the happiness of swimming in the sea with your sister and grandfather in a Spanish summer, that very first love with that countryside girl, that day you kiss your bride on your wedding, or that day when you and your best friend just look at each other and understood the glittering prize of a lifetime friendship was discovered.

My friendship with the band took off that day. Years later, with my driving licence, newly 18, I drove 500km to Bilbao to my first Simple Minds gig. The first of many.

---

# JAN VEREECKE

## *Sportpaleis*
## *17 November 2002, Antwerp, Belgium*

I can tell many stories about the relationship between *Night of the Proms* and Simple Minds. How Jim and Charlie bypassed their agent to hear in person what our show was about and decided within half an hour to participate, resulting in some unforgettable moments during our 1997 shows. I could mention the work ethic they told me about on their way to the stage: 'If we don't perform at our very best level, this could be our last show. We could be forced back to our jobs in construction.'

I could mention their readiness to help us out in 2002, when Marie Frederiksson fell ill and Roxette had to cancel less than three months before the start of the tour. The news that Jim and Charlie would appear again boosted ticket sales to an all-time record!

I could tell how a duet of Sinéad O'Connor with Jim and Charlie on 'Belfast Child' sent goosebumps through our venues in 2008. Or how, in 2016, Charlie compared performing at *Night of the Proms* to being a member of the Mafia: 'Once you get in, you never get out....'

But my favourite story is related to the darkest moment in our 35-year history in 2002, when Jim and Charlie graciously replaced Roxette at the last minute. Gert, a member of our crew, made a fatal fall during the last load-out in Antwerp, right before the start of the tour in Holland and Germany. Needless to say, we were all devastated and, together with his employer, we decided to set up a fund for his two young children. As soon as Jim and Charlie heard about the fund, they insisted on contributing their fee for the next show, making them the largest donor to that fund.

## CHRISTOPHE REYMOND

*Stade des Gorguettes*
*7 July 2003, Cassis, France*

In 2002, the city of Cassis, where I live, asked me to organise a concert. I contacted Virgin, who gave me contact details of Alain Lahana, Simple Minds' French agent. Soon, a dream became a reality - Simple Minds in Cassis in a stadium of 5,000 people. It was crazy! I was very privileged as a fan to organise a concert and get to meet Jim, Charlie, Mel, Andy and Eddy. We talked about football, music and gastronomy. Extraordinary memories, difficult to recount. My next goal? Another Simple Minds concert in Cassis!

## SILKE & OLIVER GEHRMANN-BECKER

*Museumplatz*
*19 July 2003, Bonn, Germany*

In the summer of 2001, I was happily vacuuming my flat whilst wearing headphones. Music always gives me a special boost of energy so I was listening to 'Alive and Kicking'. Singing too loud, I was disturbed by a knock on the door. My neighbour

*Silke and Oliver are alive and kicking*

Christopher from the floor below looked at me, totally freaked out. 'I have never, never ever in my life known someone besides my younger brother who listens to the horrible, boring, out of fashion music of Simple Minds!' Then he started to laugh.

The only thought I had was 'damn'. Since we had first met, my neighbours were always telling me stories of their younger brother Oliver, wanting to pair us off. I was absolutely not interested. I quite definitely did not want to meet him. That changed after his outburst. I definitely wanted to meet this man who liked Simple Minds.

We met at a party held by Iris and Christopher. We talked a lot. On Oliver's birthday, I decided to put all my eggs in one basket. I made a chocolate cake, got hold of two tickets for an *Alive and Kicking* tour in Bonn and drove the autobahn from Cologne to Wiesbaden. I rang his doorbell at midnight and…. the *Alive and Kicking* tour was our first Simple Minds concert together.

Simple Minds are the reason we met and fell in love. After Oliver popped the question on top of Schiehallion in 2011 we got married. Simple Minds have brought us energy and love – and a son. We are alive and kicking.

---

# IAN JOHN

## King's Dock Arena
## 22 July 2003, Liverpool, England

I was more into football than music. I'd tune into games and *Football Focus* on the TV each week, taping the bits of action I could find and wonderful montage sequences put to music. It was on one of these sequences that I first heard an

Chas Cole for CMP in association with Liverpool City Council presents

2003 LIVERPOOL SUMMER POPS, Kings Dock
SIMPLE MINDS
+ Support

TUE 22 JUL 03 Doors 7.00pm Start 8.00pm
LL SEAT 8

AREA N      £39.50 plus booking fee

iconic guitar kick in. For once, the football on screen didn't matter so much. 'What the hell was that music?' At school on Monday, I sought out my friend Jonathan, far more musically minded. All I had was a terrible recording from my video to listen to. Within two seconds he said, 'Oh, that's 'Ghostdancing' by Simple Minds.' Not being flush with cash a trip to our record library was in order, where I found *Once Upon a Time*. I listened for two weeks, went back to the library and rented it back out again immediately. But something wasn't quite right. The version I heard had no vocals. I wanted to hear the instrumental. A trip to Jonathan once again proved fruitful. 'You need the 12-inch version.'

The library didn't hold 12-inch versions of songs so it was a case of saving up a few weeks' pocket money until I could head down to Woolworth's to purchase the record. By then, I was hooked. Simple Minds became the soundtrack to my formative years. When I learned they were going to play the Big Tent in the King's Dock in May 2003, I had to go.

I was not disappointed. From the moment the first track, 'One Step Closer', kicked in I was lost, once again a teenager. Hit after hit followed and we sang along until about 45 minutes in. 'Love Song' had just ended, when Charlie kicked in with the guitar intro, Jim joined in and I lost it.

'Cities buildings falling down...'

However, this was no ordinary 'Ghostdancing'. This was a 15-minute 'Ghostdancing Deluxe', Jim chatting with the crowd, Van Morrison's 'Gloria' then heading back to the incredible 'Ghostdancing' finale. I felt like they knew I was there, waiting for this moment almost 20 years, deciding to give the song a memorable flourish.

I've seen them several times since. Every show has produced a memorable snippet for the memory bank, from Cherisse's wonderful introduction to 'New Gold Dream' on the *Acoustic* tour to the fabulous instrumental version of 'Book of Brilliant Things' featuring Andy Gillespie and Charlie, Jim leading the crowd in a spot of community singing at various points of the evening.

And the reason Simple Minds endure to this day, why they've been my friend and why they will be until the bitter end.

# LAURA DOCHERTY

When my neighbour let me borrow *Once Upon a Time*, I played it over and over and never stopped. My bed became the stage, my hairbrush my mic and I was a backing singer for Simple Minds! Aww, those were the days when my dreams were possible...

I was buzzing like a bee on amphetamines as we made our way down the motorway from Glasgow to Liverpool for my first Simple Minds concert in 2003. As we entered the grounds of the King's Dock it was like going to the circus as a kid, with the big top in situ. My heart was pounding like a shamanic drum and my head evolved into a psychedelic spinning top!

I...me...wee Laura fae Bute Terrace (as my neighbours called me), the 'Simple Minds Bedroom Backing Singer', was in the same building as Jim Kerr and his musical geniuses. Holy Balls, this was happening! I was lucky enough to be seated near the front, on the middle right of the stage. The lights went down... the music began... 'One Step Closer' - quite literally! As the recorded voices played, it was cutting edge, very Pink Floyd-esque (another of my favourite bands). My night just got better. Artists like Beyonce use video voiceovers at live concerts, but Simple Minds were waaaay ahead of her. The build-up was indescribable, my heart was thumping, and then – boom! Out he came, classic shirt and trouser combo, with his sultry tones. I remember gasping and thinking, 'That's Jim Kerr!' It's like time froze, my lungs seized. I've no idea how long it took to regain my composure or kick-start my lung function. It's a feeling I'll never forget to the day I die.

When they performed 'Alive and Kicking', the temptation to run forward to the mic and fill in for the absent female backing singer was incredible, but I was too damn scared. Instead I stood watching other audience members scream with delight into Jim's mic. It's one of my biggest regrets in life that I didn't seize the moment.

I grew up in a household fuelled by alcoholism and domestic abuse, I ended up in two long-term relationships which saw me endure a further 24 years of abuse, but I wasn't watching on helplessly this time, it was happening to me. That's why I could never attend concerts the way I'd have liked. That's why my dreams of becoming a backing singer never happened. However, on a positive I'm now safe and happy, have lovely kids and have done a couple of Stevie Nicks tribute shows. I even got to meet Gordy (Goudie) on the set of a music video (I was the choreographer) - one of the nicest people you can ever cross paths with. So it's not all been bad.

I still blast Simple Minds music in my car. My kids love it and I'm ensuring another generation learn to appreciate the talent you bestow! Thanks for getting me through the really tough times with 'Belfast Child'. Thanks for giving me backing singer dreams (I may not have achieved them, but they felt good to have!). Thank you for your amazing music and talent. You're appreciated and absolutely amazing. Thanks for the journey.

---

## SOPHIE PAYNOT

*Le Zénith*
*4 November 2003,*
*Paris, France*

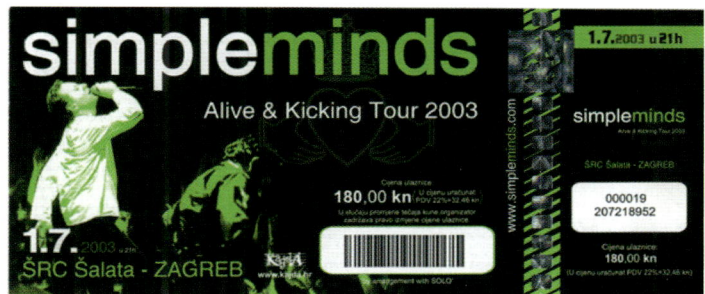

Loving Simple Minds is a family story. My father, Christophe, has listened to their music since he was 17. He saw the band first in August 1986 at the Zénith, Paris when they recorded the *City of Lights* live album. My little brother Sven and I were raised on and rocked by the music of Simple Minds. My mother, Betty's a fan too.

I attended my first show at age 10. It was in 2003 for the *Alive and Kicking* tour and I remember it like it was yesterday. We were right in front of the stage and my father carried me on his shoulders. When Jim Kerr saw me, he sat on the stage in front of us, sang 'Hypnotised' and held out his hand to me. It was amazing!
My father is a huge fan and did everything to meet them. One day in Paris, he waited all day near the Olympia's artist entrance. He met Mel Gaynor with his wife and baby, Andy Gillespie, Charlie Burchill and his idol, Jim Kerr. My father offered Jim a bottle of French wine. Jim said Charlie would like that a lot!

In December 2008, my parents, aunt and I decided to go to Glasgow for three days. We wanted to see our favourite band in their own country. We visited the famous

Celtic Park and then had our day with the band at the SECC. My father tattooed the Simple Minds symbol on his chest and 'Alive and Kicking' on his arm.

We haven't missed a Simple Minds tour in Paris since 1986. We go as a family and my father always wears a Celtic t-shirt as a nod to the band. Every time, we're right in front of the stage, reaching out to Jim. We'll be there next time they play France.

'Let me see your hands!'

# CLIVE UPTON

*Apollo Theatre*
*13 December 2003,*
*Manchester, England*

In the 1980s with a young family, I wasn't able to go to concerts but enjoyed the music of Simple Minds and was really impressed by 'Alive and Kicking'. With family grown I went to my first concert when they appeared at Manchester Apollo in 2003. I didn't know all their music then, but was impressed and amazed everyone was standing for the whole concert, by the feeling of energy produced by the band and the link between band and audience.

I've seen the group several times in Liverpool, including twice at summer concerts in a circus top by the River Mersey. Again, the atmosphere created was electric and Jim's desire to involve the audience meant the concerts were most enjoyable. More were enjoyed at the Manchester Evening News Arena, where post-gig I drove the stranger sat next to me back to where his car had broken down on the way, at Birmingham with my young niece (also a fan) and at Leeds. I also enjoyed watching – and filming – the Alnwick Castle show in 2014 in the rain.

For 2020 I had five shows planned, all postponed, but I look forward to seeing them in 2021 instead, especially as the concert in Birmingham is planned for my 70th birthday! And for two of the concerts I've bought VIP tickets, so I can thank the members of Simple Minds for the enjoyment and happiness they've given me.

# NEIL ADAMS

*Music Hall*
*20 December 2003, Aberdeen, Scotland*

A cold, dreich winter night. A few songs in, the fire alarm went off. We all had to troop out into the drizzle and were not allowed to collect out coats. Turns out the artificial smoke had tripped the alarm.

---

# JEAN-PIERRE DE MOL

It's 1984 and my older brother brings home a new LP he's just borrowed. The sleeve immediately catches my eye: a vision of purple and gold. Then I hear the music, a jangling guitar, a vocal that somehow manages to mix passion with melancholy, thundering bass and keyboards producing a fierce, breathtaking sound. This album speaks to me in a way I can't explain. The band is Simple Minds, the album is *New Gold Dream* and it's the start of a lasting attachment to this band.

In December 1985, Simple Minds are playing the Brielpoort in Deinze, near my hometown, Ghent. I desperately want to go, but I'm only 15, which my parents think is way too young. The disappointment is crushing, it seems so unfair. There are six of us at home, which means choices have to be made, something I understand better now than I did then.

The first time I finally manage to see 'my' band is May 1995, when they play Flanders Expo, Ghent on the *Good News from the Next World* tour. My first time, but definitely not my last. Over the years I made up for lost time, attending concerts whenever I could: Belgium, Netherlands, France, Germany, Italy, England, Scotland. I travel! But the date that forever occupies a special place in my heart was 20 December 2003 at Aberdeen Music Hall.

Together with friends I'd been doing a mini-tour, following the band around the UK for a few days in December for the final gigs of 2003's *Alive and Kicking* tour. Halfway through a set in Aberdeen, a rogue smoke machine set off a fire alarm during 'Don't You (Forget About Me)', at which point a reluctant crowd was herded out into

Jean Pierre's ticket for the show where he met his 'umbrella girl'

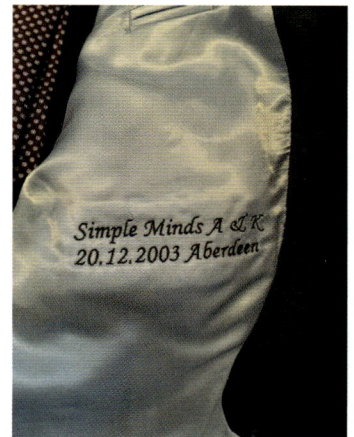

the freezing rain. None of us wanted to leave, not least because we knew it meant relinquishing hard-earned front-row places. Huddling together outside, we agreed it must be a 'Don't You' jinx - the song is a staple in the set, well liked by casual fans but less so by some of the more hardcore fanbase who tend to prefer earlier, less commercial songs.

On a brighter note, this unexpected intermezzo gave me a chance to get closer to the girl who'd queued behind me before the gig, under the pretext of sheltering under her umbrella. As the gig resumed, the umbrella girl was standing next to me.

A year later, she moved from the UK to Belgium....

---

## MAAIKE JACOBS

*Maaike Jacobs and Jean-Pierre with Charlie*

I was 16 and my local annual music festival, PinkPop, was held in the town of Geleen. The lineup featured a band called Simple Minds but top billing was reserved for a Dutch band at the peak of their popularity. 'New Gold Dream' had been getting airplay on the big Dutch radio stations and I loved the song, so I spent a hot day at the festival, more than a little curious to see what this band actually looked like. I was not disappointed. Being of a new wave persuasion, I instantly related not only to the sound but also the look of the band, in particular the singer and guitar player. On that stage they looked like the coolest guys on the planet. The following Monday I ran to the record store to buy *New Gold Dream*, listened to little else for weeks, finally progressing to their back-catalogue (which, money being a bit tight, I borrowed from the local library).

By December 2003, I'd been living in the UK for nearly 20 years. On a whim, I decided to fly from London to Aberdeen, where Simple Minds were due to play their final gig of the year. The mood was Christmassy, fans from all over the world congregated outside Aberdeen's Music Hall. In the queue in front was a guy speaking Dutch. I don't know him, but we had a chat. He had a gorgeous smile and made me laugh. He said he'd travelled all the way from Belgium. Halfway through the concert, the smoke machine used on stage caused the fire alarm to go off. Reluctantly, we were all herded out into the sleet and snow outside. I had an umbrella. Mr Belgium asked if

*Maaike Jacobs saw Simple Minds at PinkPop*

he could shelter under it with me....

Fast forward nine years... 31 August 2012. I've been living in Belgium since 2004. Today is my wedding day: Mr Belgium asked me to marry him. Our wedding reception includes a table filled with fellow Simple Minds fans who have become great friends over the years. We will spend our honeymoon in Taormina, staying in Villa Angela for the first time. That evening, many people dance to Simple Minds songs played at our wedding reception. Life is good.

## DAVID JOHNSON

*Summer Pops*
*Liverpool Docks*
*24 July 2004, Liverpool, England*

Still the best gig I've been to! For some reason the local council had to put up tents miles from the original venue, near to the old docks in Liverpool. All very trendy now but back then not the best area to walk around with a pregnant wife! The band played all the hits and a few oldies to keep me and other hardcore fans happy. Maybe it's because of the heat or the tent but the vibe inside that night has never been repeated. Superb.

# MARCO CASAROLA

*Arena Di Verona*
*12 September 2005, Verona, Italy*

Simple Minds have always been the soundtrack of my life. I was 15 when I first saw them, on my own and despite my mother's ban, in Milan. My first concert.

As a teenager I had two idols, Michel Platini (the Juventus football player) and Simple Minds. You can imagine the joy and emotion I felt when they came to stay in my hotel on Lake Garda in 2002, as they played a gig near Verona. Sometimes dreams come true.

From that dream, a friendship was born with Jim, Charlie and Mel. Since then, I've discovered that the idols of my youth are real, kind, sensitive people, and friends. With Jim I talk more than about music. We talk about hotels, my world. We talk of tourism, travel, the wonderful Sicily, where he too owns a hotel. Of relationships between people and cultures. We are both careful observers.

I'm sorry that we often talk about SM music and so little about the lyrics which Jim writes. In those words, there is their story and personal life, the moments of light as of darkness. Of suffering and joy.

An anecdote I keep is when I accompanied them to the Festivalbar finale in the Arena of Verona, extremely popular in Italy. We were all together in the van bringing us backstage from the hotel. My rock star moment!

Simple Minds not only accompanied me in many beautiful and some difficult moments of my life. Their songs convey the energy I need before an important meeting or decision. And to date the decisions have always been the right ones. When 'the mind is simple', when it listens to the right vibrations, the answers that come can only be those that make you reach your goals. Thanks for your friendship, Jim, Charlie and Simple Minds, and for always making me feel part of your family. Promise me that before writing the last page of your 'book of brilliant things', many more will be added.

---

# CLAUDIA DEUS

*Personal Fest 05*
*2 December 2005, Buenos Aires, Argentina*

I'll never forget when I first saw the video for 'Don't You (Forget About Me)' on Argentine TV; that boy in a

*In Buenos Aires - photo Claudia Deus*

*Jim in Buenos Aires - photo Claudia Deus*

suit, singing and walking between television sets. I had definitely fallen in love.

I was able to see the Minds live on their second visit to Buenos Aires in 2005. After decades of watching them on video, that night at the Personal Fest 05 I was going to have that boy and his band sing in front of me. And so it was. When the chords of 'Hypnotised' sounded, a song I adore, my emotion turned to tears and caught the attention of Jim, who approached the edge of the stage to sing it. I will never forget that night.

After the show, as a teenager desperately searching for her idol, I went with other fans to the Hotel Madero to wait for the band. Luckily, Jim came to chat, sign CD covers and have photographs taken. I keep the photo of me next to him as my most precious treasure. Unfortunately it was the first and last show I saw of them in my country. Although there are many fans in Latin America, it's not easy to bring the band to play Buenos Aires. And although I stopped being a 15-year-old girl in love with the boy who sang among television sets, my love for the band is eternal.

## PAOLA PIETRIBONI

I'm from Argentina and a Simple Minds fan since I was 13, when I first heard Jim sing 'Hypnotised'. From then until now they have been my favourite band. I saw them in December 2005 in Puerto Madero, a dream come true. Thanks for being, thank you for each letter, each song for us. All your albums are special. It is a joy for me to know Simple Minds. I dream of seeing them again.

# LUCIANO CONTI

*Villa Angela*
*December 2005, Taormina, Italy*

In 2005 I had the pleasure of meeting Jim Kerr at Villa Angela, Taormina. He was very kind and we talked about music and Taormina. It was a simple meeting between artist and fans. That Christmas, helped by my friend who is a sculptor, I decided to give Jim a gift. When we met him again we gave him a unique piece created especially for him, the Simple Minds logo.

---

# JENNIFER GOULD

*Waterfront Hall*
*31 January 2006, Belfast,*
*Northern Ireland*

I was born and raised in Northern Ireland, a child from The Troubles. From a very early age I listened to radio for my music to escape the news of what was happening around me.

In June 1987 I was struck really bad with tonsillitis. Confined to bed with painkillers that knocked me out from one four-hour period to the next, I kept the radio beside me playing continuously. I heard all the favourites of the day on Radio 1 and there was music I hadn't heard before or even hated. There was one song constantly played day after day and as soon as I heard it starting I would groan, turn over and think to myself this is awful. By day three I'm assuming the antibiotics had kicked in and I was on the road to recovery and this song I dreaded soon became 'ooh this isn't too bad' and then 'ooh I really like this' and 'ooh i need to buy this song!' The song in question was the live version of 'Promised You a Miracle' from *Live in the City of Light*.

At 13 I couldn't afford to buy the double-album and no way were my parents going to buy me something that would do their heads in! Luckily the local record shop stocked other Simple Minds albums. I soon discovered this song I now loved to hear was on *New Gold Dream*. I hid the album cassette in the country section of the shop to stop anyone else buying it until I could return with the money. My 14th birthday came in August and I had birthday money at my disposal. The *New Gold Dream* was my present to me. I still have the original cassette, it's always moved house with me. The other albums were then purchased with money earned from Saturday jobs. My goal was always to get them all.

Due to the country's situation, I never saw Simple Minds live in Belfast anytime they came. I was never allowed to go by my parents. I remember begging to go to the *Street Fighting Years* tour and must have talked about it a lot in school because I remember a lad who sat in front of me in history turned to me one day and said, 'That group you like? Yeah, I'm going to see them tonight with my brother. I'd never heard of them until you talked about them.' I could have cried!

As life went on Simple Minds almost felt like a childhood memory. But 2006 saw the *Black and White* tour and I was there at the Waterfront Hall in Belfast. My first live encounter. I went with a girlfriend and she endured me wanting to be there in the afternoon just in case I could catch a glimpse of the group. While we didn't see anyone, we did hear the soundcheck. The concert was great, everything I ever wanted, totally euphoric. When I knew it was finishing soon, I felt a real sense of sadness. What if this was my first and last SM gig? What if they never tour again? What if they never come back to Belfast again?

I feel so grateful and fortunate that this group have constantly worked hard and still continue to tour. I've now seen them seven times. With the introduction of social media, first Twitter and then Facebook, the interaction between Jim and the fan-base has always been great. I've made a lot of new friends through these outlets. I just want to thank the band for their obvious hard work. I admire their determination to keep making new music and tour. Long may it last!

---

# PAUL JAMESON

*Academy*
*6 February 2006, Newcastle, England*

Simple Minds first came to my attention around 1978, as a Dundee University student. A flatmate from Edinburgh told me about a new Glasgow band due to appear on *The Old Grey Whistle Test*, so I watched them for the first time on TV. I wasn't really into electronic music, so that first experience of Simple Minds did not energise me to seek out more of their music.

On to the '80s, hearing 'Don't You (Forget About Me)', the catalyst which led to my purchase of *Once Upon a Time*. *Street Fighting Years* was next, followed by *Good News…* but I then lost a bit of interest, something that puzzles me now, seeing as that album is probably my most played. There are some brilliant tracks on there that I would love them to play live - but they never do!

My first Simple Minds gig was at Newcastle Academy, a small venue that used to be an old music hall. 'Alive and Kicking' nearly took the roof off!

*Black & White 050505* renewed my enthusiasm. I've bought every release since, as well as going to a lot of gigs. I recall driving through snow from Newcastle to Glasgow SECC, several gigs at Newcastle City Hall, Edinburgh Castle in a downpour (how fitting that they started with 'Waterfront') and most recently Durham Cricket Ground on the *Walk Between Worlds* tour.

If anyone asks about my music, I reply that Simple Minds are 'my band' and I always look forward to the next gig. I've seen a lot of bands over the years, but Simple Minds live are always special.

## JON AANENSEN

### *Rockefeller*
### *19 February 2006, Oslo, Norway*

My life with Simple Minds started in the mid-'80s when I heard songs from *Once Upon a Time* on the radio in Norway as a 10-year old. Then, in the late-'80s I received a tape of *Street Fighting Years* as a gift from my sister, who had been in Asia. *Real Life* and *Good News from the Next World* followed, both of great importance to me. I also remember the thrill of hearing SM would work with Planet Funk on the *Cry* album in 2002. The years went by. Me and my friends even made our own amateur horror movie with 'Shake Off the Ghosts' as the end-credits song...

But the big question remained: would I ever get to see Simple Minds in concert? They had played Oslo in 1995, but for some reason I wasn't there. But in 2006 I finally saw them at the Rockefeller club in Oslo. I remember it felt quite unreal to see the band enter the stage and see them in real life (no pun intended) during a set that leaned heavily on old and new material, not so much the years in between. That changed in 2010 though, when I saw them play outdoors at the Stavern Festival in Norway, with a fine selection of songs from their whole career, including my favourite 'One Step Closer', written with the aforementioned Planet Funk. And in 2015 it was time for SM concert number three in Stavanger, Norway, with several tracks from the great *Big Music* album. And I don't think it's over yet.

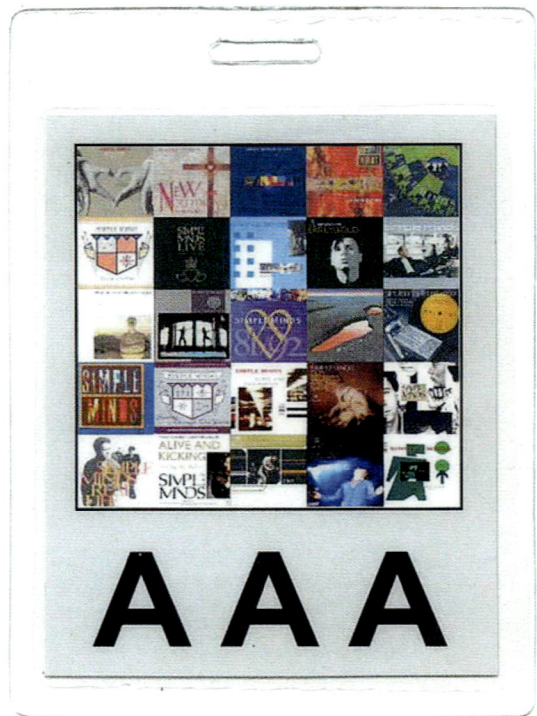

# MILAN BOJOVIĆ

*Sava Center*
*7 March 2006, Belgrade, Serbia*

I bought *Sons and Fascination* in the old Jugoton store in Nušićeva Street in Belgrade. With equal fervour I awaited releases like 'Someone Somewhere (in Summertime)', *Sparkle in the Rain*, until the last acoustic album and *Walk Between Worlds*. And the live stadium performances are forever emblazoned in my memory.

When my country, Yugoslavia, was demolished in a brutal, bloody war, during the 90s, it was a dark period in our lives, so I'd raise my energy and spirit by listening to Simple Minds. I strongly related to politically-engaged hits 'Belfast Child' and 'Mandela Day'. I remember how excited I was in the mid-'90s when word got out that they'd be coming to Belgrade for a first time, having cancelled a concert in Northern Italy. I booked my tickets immediately. Alas, the concert never took place, and I had to wait until 2006 for my first live SM concert, in front of 6,000 Serbian fans. It was simply spectacular. I was all the more ecstatic as they were promoting an extraordinary album, *050505*.

I went to their subsequent performances in Belgrade at the Arena in 2009 and the Beer Fest in 2011. I'm very sorry that due to the COVID-19 pandemic their concert tour was cancelled. I'd been hoping the concert in Zagreb would erase my bad memories and the horrors of the civil war in Croatia and former Yugoslavia. I honestly couldn't think of a better remedy than having Serbs and Croatians at a Simple Minds concert together. Hopefully someday, we'll have an opportunity.

---

# ELLEN VAN OTTERLO

*Heineken Music Hall*
*28 March 2006, Amsterdam,*
*The Netherlands*

In 1985 I heard 'Don't You' on the radio. That moment I was in love with Simple Minds. My first concert was in 2006. Too late! Oh, if I could go back to 1985 to see the gig in Rotterdam. But in 2006 I saw them at the Heineken Music Hall. It was after my breast cancer. 'Dolphins' was a very emotional song for me and I cried.

In 2016 I visited Jim's hotel in Taormina. It was only one day, but it's a great hotel with very nice people. I hope to be back one day. Let the music play. Let There Be Love.

*Ellen visited Jim's hotel in Sicily*

# DONATAS SKIRKEVIČIUS

*Siemens Arena*
*5 April 2006, Vilnius, Lithuania*

I was at the concert in Vilnius. It was a little different from seeing them in Scotland, where the audience understands them better. The sound, music and lyrics are fantastic. They are very creative and I think they are one of the best bands in the world.

---

# ADI BICAKCIC

*Zetra Arena*
*10 April 2006, Zetra, Sarajevo, Bosnia & Herzegovina*

Simple Minds = first love. The music that went to my heart and will never leave. Their words and notes have created an unbreakable bond. We've grown up together, changed, become better, more mature but always remained unique. I could hardly wait for Spring 1991 and my departure from Sarajevo for their concert in Zagreb. But the damn war - it tried to stop everything beautiful. The concert was postponed. But my hope for better times and enjoying live gigs never disappeared.

The music of Simple Minds I listened to during the war in Sarajevo gave me the psychic strength to overcome difficult situations. I knew that my beautiful city would rise from the ashes and it would be visited by Simple Minds one day. It was International Women's Day in March 2006 when I read the headline in the newspaper, 'Simple Minds coming to Sarajevo on April 10'. It was the most beautiful gift I could receive on that day. The concert that followed was unforgettable.

*Simple Minds played Sarajevo in 2006 - photo Adi Bicakcic*

# MARIO BUDIMIR

I fell in love with Simple Minds as a boy. I worked as a DJ and for half of the evening show I played them. All my crew became fans. When the war started in Bosnia and I became a refugee in Montenegro, all I took with me was my childhood photos and my Simple Minds LPs. I dreamed of seeing them in concert and was supposed to see the *Néapolis* tour in Belgrade in 2002. I went by train, even though I was sick and had a temperature - but the concert was cancelled. But I got to see them in Sarajevo in 2006. My heart was full and I cried.

After that, they came to Podgorica 2019. The concert was great and I got a baton from Cherisse (Osei), but I was looking all over town to get an autograph from them, only to find out afterwards they were staying in the hotel next to my building. Oh, the irony.

---

# CHRISTOPOULOU PARASKEVI

*Principal Club Theater 16 April 2006, Thessaloniki, Greece*

September 1996 and I'd just moved to my new apartment, a small attic in the central square of Xanthi. My first year at university and first time ever living alone. It was the only apartment in the building and on my new CD player I'd play 'She's a River' so loud you could hear it all over the square every night. So many

*Jim in action - photo Christopoulou Paraskevi*

memories, tough and good times, but their CDs were with me at home, in the car, everywhere!

Thessaloniki 2006, 10 years later and a dream come true. I'm in the front watching my all-time favourite band and Jim Kerr is singing a few metres in front of me, the crowd singing with him, including me! The best concert of my life. We are few but we are the luckiest people on earth. I can't believe it's almost 15 years ago already.

---

# LEIGH WILSON

I first became aware of Simple Minds in the summer of 2004. I chanced upon *Simple Minds: Best of 81/92* in the family music collection. The CD was enthralling for two reasons: the cover for its beautiful design, bold colours and transcendental imagery, and the fact that the band had fallen so far off my family's musical radar. I skipped into my bedroom to hear what delights had thus far eluded me. The first track on the album, 'Waterfront', pounded out of my speakers – the pulsating bass crashing into my mind – and I knew from that point on that undoubtedly 'this was my band'.

I remember purchasing *Street Fighting Years*, much against the wishes of some family members, for whom it was a step too far for them. It was a seminal moment because although I had never heard rock music recorded so majestically, it also helped anchor my political views to the flag of social justice – something which has remained important to me ever since. I can't recall ever listening to an album which, on closing my eyes, assisted my mind to such an extent in developing a procession of images and moving pictures, perfectly complementing the hue of sound whirling around my ears, transporting me to other countries – South Africa, for example – and colouring the landscape with hope for a better future and anger at the unjust present.

I spent hours perusing music stores across the country to find hidden gems – the wonderful Dundee Fopp regularly had an extensive offering and One Up in Aberdeen assisted in procuring some of the more elusive earlier albums. Store managers helpfully ordered stock in, directed me to alternative shops and generally played a significant part in the whole operation.

I was 11 when I first got to see Simple Minds play live; I harried my father for weeks to get tickets for their forthcoming gig at the Music Hall in Aberdeen, a date included as part of the 2005 *Black and White* tour.

Being a youthful fan brought disadvantages. Jim announced a small tour of UK club venues to a select group of fervent fans to promote *Lostboy* but at 16 I was too young to enter the club. Consigned to missing the concert and consumed in a sulky trance, I decided to write to Jim on his then Facebook account detailing the depths of my morosity. A chance, unlike any other, to see him perform in such an intimate setting – alas, the vagaries of age stymied my ambitions. My eyes, now seemingly glittering in that downcast way, darted to a message which had appeared on my computer screen. 'Don't you worry, you're coming backstage for the night and your job is to tell us how we sound.'

I remember the night of the concert itself vividly. A number of fans were congregating in the side street before the doors opened. I, a gawkish school-boy, probably looked like I'd taken the wrong turning to the library. My instructions were to make my way to the exit door and introduce myself. I spoke to some of the roadies and, in the most ridiculous deep voice imaginable, informed them that, 'I'm looking for Jim. He invited me.' A lanyard was slung around my neck before I was shuttled into the club for the soundcheck. Jim arrived – the earliest he had been late, he would later admit – and greeted me with the most genuine, welcoming embrace imaginable.

Having bought the album a matter of weeks before, he asserted that I perhaps knew more of the words than him. That was maybe so, but he could certainly perform them.

The soundcheck was a thrilling experience – in essence a private performance – and as the crew asked me my thoughts, I attempted to exude an air of sagacity by suggesting that the vocals were too low in the mix, drowning Jim out. Much nodding of heads followed as the mixing deck was adjusted to greatly improved results; who knew that my true calling was as a sound technician?

The band, consisting of people who had been loosely connected to Simple Minds over the years, sounded excellent – but interestingly it also introduced Ged Grimes to Simple Minds, before his arrival as bass player a few years later. As I sat listening to the band, it struck me there was an interesting confluence between the Lostboy project and my own experience. Lostboy was established as a vehicle for Jim to return to his childhood, reflect on the aforementioned artists who had inspired him and write songs through the prism of an impressionable boy; here I was, a teenager – a lost boy, even – watching from the wings the artist who had inspired me more than any other. The Sorcerer's Apprentice indeed.

That night in a small Aberdeen club demonstrated to me why Jim Kerr is undeniably one of rock's great frontmen: he can lift the ambience in a club to that of a stadium, but he can also perform in stadiums and make it feel as if it's the most intimate performance of all.

That's the magic of Jim Kerr. That's the magic of Simple Minds.

---

# PRITHAM RAJ

I lived in Washington DC but was travelling between Frankfurt and Paris with my family on vacation. I boarded a Lufthansa DC-10 aircraft for the short flight. As we were getting seated, I saw someone with a Simple Minds jacket move past me down the aisle. I didn't think twice about it until later in the flight when I happened to look over at my dad who was sat across the aisle. I had to do a double take. Seated by the window next to him was Jim Kerr! I was giddy with excitement the whole flight. But the real challenge was how to engage my heroes without coming off like some lunatic.

When the plane landed, I was too nervous to approach the band so grabbed a postcard from the seatback pocket and waited. On the moving walkway at Charles de Gaulle, I mustered up the courage when Jim was about to pass by. 'Um, Mr Kerr, could I possibly get your autograph?' I stammered. He kindly signed the postcard and smiled. Charlie followed suit and gave this then 16-year-old the thrill of a lifetime by asking me where I was going, where I was from, etc. 'Ah, Washington DC – very pretty city' he said. Beyond all of the SM concerts I have attended since, that signed postcard and encounter has given me much musical and emotional inspiration over the years.

# ALEXANDER TATE

*Brisbane Convention Center*
*9 May 2006, Brisbane, Australia*

August 1987. I was 13, my eldest cousin and his family visiting during the school holidays. We went into town and he bought *Live in the City of Light* on vinyl from Bayes Recordium, an independent store, for A$6.99.

He played it. I taped it. I was mesmerised. With the '1-2, 1-2-3-4' of 'Waterfront' I felt at home. This is what I want to be listening to. Too young to buy the back-catalogue. That came in 1989 with a paper-round. Upon the release of 'Belfast Child' - I clearly recall hearing on the chart rundown it debut at No.2 - is where I moved into obsession. Earlier albums and 12-inch purchases took up my Saturdays and my money.

Posters, songbooks, tour books, t-shirts, cowboy boots and a voluminous white shirt filled my room. I took on influences - Bowie, Roxy, Lou Reed, The Doors - which opened up even more great music. I learned about Amnesty, Greenpeace and Mandela through Simple Minds, a wider education than just great music.

The only time this waned was around *Néapolis*, but on hearing 'Home' for the first time I knew the band were creating music I could fall in love with again. And it hasn't let up. Seeing the band play Brisbane on the *Black and White* tour after so many years missing out as I travelled the world was such a wonderful experience.

At Melbourne in 2010, sharing the weekend with many other fans was euphoric. The air crackled with electricity, but after 'Moscow Underground' even hardcore fans looked at each other, blown away by the performance. Hearing 'This Fear of Gods' in Brisbane in 2012 was another unforgettable live moment.

I can't pinpoint why Simple Minds, but the past 10 years have seen my life turned upside down, and I also suffer with various chronic illnesses. It's hearing *New Gold Dream* in my hospital bed which brings most comfort, still knowing each note, hand clap and word to *Live in the City of Light*.

---

# CRAIG DENT

*Palais Theatre*
*12 May 2006, Melbourne, Australia*

I grew up in the rural area of Thurgoona, New South Wales, 10km from Albury on the Victoria border in Australia. The only access we had to new music was through the Australian Broadcasting Commission's show *Countdown*. In 1980 we had an AM band station, 2AY, which only really played classic hits, and new FM station 2REM FM, located in an old farmhouse. It was there that I discovered a show called *The British*

*Sound*. The first encounter was 'Love Song' and then my mate out at Lake Hume played me *Sons and Fascination*.

Simple Minds came to Albury to support Icehouse but I was too young. It wasn't until they played the Palais with INXS and Arrested Development that I got to see them.

My brother and I are looking forward to the next Melbourne show. We love *Walk Between Worlds*, especially the line 'the heart starts beating now'. The Simple Minds' 'New Gold Dream' reborn...21, 22, 23, 24!

---

## LENA PEDERSÉN

*Götaplatsen*
*10 August 2006, Gothenburg, Sweden*

Simple Minds have been No.1 for me when it comes to music for over 35 years. My first show was in the '80s in Gothenburg during my teens, but I've so many memories: a fantastic outdoor concert at Götaplatsen 2006, with so many people and Jim saying he arrived just an hour before the concert; the 2015 concert in Gothenburg to which I brought my son, Magnus, now also one of their biggest fans; the *Acoustic* concert in London in 2017, to which I brought all my family; and March 2020, when I went to the Gothenburg and Stockholm concerts, hearing all the old and new hits! Many thanks to Simple Minds for this musical trip so far.

---

## LAURETTA MORTON

My first experience of Simple Minds was aged 16 while getting my weekly *Countdown* music TV show fix. Molly Meldrum introduced the band and to me they looked like none of the Australian bands that I followed – all dressed in black, with Charlie's flash of red and Jim wearing dark sunglasses and a leather satchel across his body. They performed 'Love Song'. As a young art student with dyed blue-black punk hair, this was the seminal moment that triggered my 40-year long devotion to Simple Minds. I have been fortunate enough to see the band every time they have been Down Under. I was there in 2017 during the hottest day on record in the Hunter Valley (48.5 degrees). There was genuine concern that the concert would be shut down. With a water-soaked towel on my head I watched Jim saunter across the stage in a jacket and scarf, declaring (as only he can): 'We are Simple Minds and we have never cancelled a gig in our life. Now let me see your hands!'

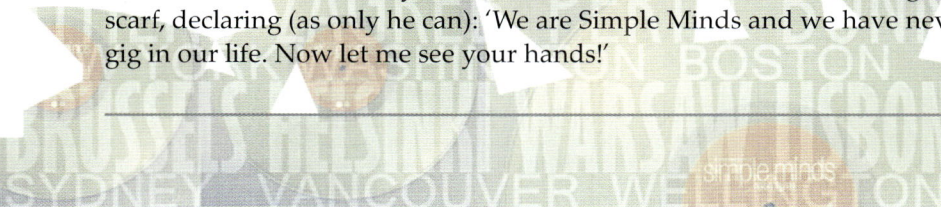

# JAN FAZAKERLEY

*Plaza De Toros*
*17 August 2006, Estepona, Malaga, Spain*

I booked tickets to see Simple Minds in Malaga. They were playing the Bullring. That evening, myself and my then boyfriend jumped into our car and made our way from Nueva Andalusia across to the city of Malaga, around an hour's drive. We had an animated journey, excited about the concert and blaring our favourite SM tunes in the car. We arrived, parked the car and made our way to the Bullring. As we approached, we could distinctly hear the sound of a roaring crowd and the words 'olé' being shouted. Confused, thinking we must be either early or there was some mistake, my boyfriend called his brother back in England, asking him to double-check the details. About ten minutes later he called to say the concert was actually at the Bullring in Estepona, Malaga! The concert was due to start and we were still an hour away.

Unlike the first journey, this was a silent but speedy drive back to Estapona (20 minutes away from our point of origin) with a very sullen driver. Not me, I might add. Eventually we arrived in rainy Estapona and again were surprised that there didn't seem to be many people around. The bullring was almost empty; strange given that we should have been at least an hour in.

One of the concert staff approached us asking if we were looking for the concert. He explained that because of the rain the venue had changed at the last minute, with the concert delayed. Reenergised with this news, we jumped back into our car and made our way to the new venue. The concert had yet to start and we were able to walk to very near the front of the stage area and enjoy a fantastic view of an eagerly-anticipated concert. The concert did not disappoint. The perfect end to what could have been a complete disaster!

---

# LOURDES FERNÁNDEZ BARO

*Plaza De Toros*
*17 August 2006, Estepona, Malaga, Spain*

I saw Simple Minds for the very first time on Spanish TV and discovered a different sound: wonderful guitar and bass, and a singer who moved

*Jim in Malaga - photo Lourdes Baro*

*Lourdes Fernández Baro with Charlie*

like a panther, his socks over his trousers. I fell in love. My first gig was in Madrid in 1989 but I was far from the front and my dream was to be in the first row. Los Alcazares in 1997 was the first of many, many first rows. I travelled around Spain and other European countries. It´s my favourite hobby: musical tourism. I used to travel alone. But it's an opportunity to meet other fans and now I have real friends I've known for more than 20 years!

Estepona in 2006 is my favourite gig. It was a small place and incredibly hot. I don't know what it was that made that gig so magical, maybe the fans' hearts beating together. But I can´t choose just one gig. All of them are in my memories.

Another special moment was Madrid in 2009, with 10 or 12 fans out walking and Jim seeing us and coming over so we could take photos and shake his hand. For me Jim and Charlie are old friends who I need to see to live happily. They're a part of my family, a part of me.

---

# CRAIG BURGESS

## *Entertainment Centre*
## *30 March 2007, Sydney, Australia*

My dad passed away in 2005. Music was my escape and comfort during this sad time. Losing Dad made me more determined to not take life for granted. Seeing Simple Minds perform was on my bucket list, as was a trip to Australia. In 2007 a friend in Sydney invited me to visit and I booked a holiday around their tour. Having secured flights and a ticket, I had something I could look forward to for the first time since my dad had passed.

Arriving in Australia, I met some other friends and discovered they also had tickets. One knew Jim's mum and dad from back home. I said I'd look for my friend during the interval. My tickets were just two rows back and I was able to introduce myself to Jim's mum and dad, who were so nice. Finding out how big a fan I was, they said, 'Please come backstage and meet Jim.'

Every time I listen to Simple Minds I'm transported to Sydney and the best trip of my life.

---

## NIGEL HOBDEN

As a young lad in a sea scout troop from Sydney, I went on a fabulous 30-day journey from Brisbane to Cairns in the summer of 1981/82. I'd never really heard rock 'n' roll music when the older kids pulled out their tapes to play in the VW Kombi tape deck. One happened to be a compilation album, *1981… The Sound* which I thought was pretty cool. On returning home I purchased the newly-released *The Winners 1982*. 'Glittering Prize' was the tenth track, and what a beauty. As a young teenager, I travelled into the city of Sydney, pounding the pavement barefoot and walking from one second-hand record store to the next on the hunt for Simple Minds vinyl, which I still have to this day.

Too young to go to Narara, I had to wait years for my first live gig, when they supported INXS, long after the death of Michael Hutchence. I've seen them four times so far, including at the Horden Pavilion, Sydney and A Day on the Green venues. I can't wait for the fifth.

## MATT DOBB

*Westpac Trust Arena*
*4 April 2007, Christchurch, New Zealand*

I am an '80s child from the UK and now reside in New Zealand, but my story with Simple Minds didn't begin until I was 15, in 1991, hearing the *Real Life* album. 'Let There Be Love' was the track that caught my attention. I instantly connected with the music and, along with a handful of schoolmates, got stuck into listening to all the previous Simple Minds records. The music captured both myself and my twin brother. We'd listen for hours in our bedroom. *New Gold Dream* was mind-blowing and tunes like 'Hunter and the Hunted', along with so much of Simple Minds music, send me to a happy place.

I've seen Simple Minds live 10 times, mostly back in the UK. I was absolutely gutted that I didn't see them last year performing in my hometown, Newark-on-Trent. I did manage to catch them here in NZ in 2007 when they supported INXS. If Jim remembers a bra landing at his feet during this one, that was my missus. It was her favourite Marks & Spencer bra!

## SIMONE JACOB

I live in Brazil. I was a teenager, talking with a boy in a café, when 'Don't You (Forget About Me)' started playing. We looked at each other, and started dancing. My first kiss happened listening to this song.

# RAFFAELLA MAGGIULLI

*Gran Teatro Geox*
*8 November 2008, Padua, Italy*

I've loved Simple Minds since I was 14 or 15. I have all the music on CD or vinyl. I've been to the Italian concerts over the years and I'm looking forward to the next gigs. My favourite song? 'This is Your Land'.

---

# JOT SHIRLEY

*LG Arena*
*28 November 2008, Birmingham, England*

I saw two gigs on the *Real Life* tour, one in Birmingham, the other at Manchester City's Maine Road stadium, with Simple Minds supported by OMD and The Stranglers. What a gig. By now I'd amassed a decent collection of their back-catalogue, along with many CD singles and picture discs, key rings, badges and T-shirts.

Then, Simple Minds drifted out of my life. This didn't change until 2008. We went to see them in Birmingham and that gig hooked me straight back in. I began listening to the back-catalogue, buying the albums from *Good News from the Next World* onwards and finding the music I'd missed out on, in particular the brilliant *Black and White 050505*. I was back on board and the music of Simple Minds was ever present at home and in the car.

I entered a competition on the band's website prior to the launch of *Graffiti Soul* in 2009. The competition was to create your own design for the album cover using images and text provided on the website. I received a signed copy of the album in the post. My first piece of signed merchandise.

I was exceptionally lucky to get a ticket to a gig for Jim's solo adventure. *The Lostboy AKA* album promo tour in London in May 2010. The Borderline in London was a small and cramped venue and I think the sell-out crowd numbered about 300. I was so close to the band. The gig was phenomenal.

Then, 2012 took me back to Birmingham for the *5X5* tour, the venue the smallest I'd seen Simple Minds at, used to seeing them in stadia and arenas. Now they were playing to around 3,000. Prior to this gig I created my own setlist of what I'd love to hear them play, songs I never thought I'd get to hear live, but this gig provided me with that opportunity. Another gig that raced by, up there with my favourite Minds gigs.

# YASMIN KERR

There is nothing like a live music event: the surging fans, the anticipation, the electricity in the air as you wait for the performers to grace the stage and take the audience off into another place entirely. And there is no band I can think of that can do this quite as well as Simple Minds. A time I remember with particular fondness is when I joined the band in Germany for the weekend circa 2008. I have a hazy recollection of harbouring some heartache over a silly boy and wanted to be around family for a couple of days, so Dad invited me to come and stay with the band on the tour bus for a few nights. The gig that first night in Berlin was fantastic. The crowd went bananas, especially at my favourite part, which as always is the pounding bassline intro to 'Waterfront'. I defy the most reserved audience member not to jump up and punch the air at that moment… But it was the impromptu after-party on the tour bus that made the weekend extra special.

Dad had been in an impish mood that night and, after playing this epic gig to thousands of hardcore fans, he decided on a whim, as part of the encore, to put on Cornershop and Norman Cook's 'Brimful of Asha'. And I don't mean Simple Minds playing a cover of the song. He just got the production team to blast it out of the area speakers. He then proceeded to shimmy along to it and encourage the audience to dance and sing along. It was hilarious, watching all these confused German fans, still soaked with sweat, ending their deferential homage to Simple Minds by being goaded into a collective karaoke to a short-lived smash hit from almost a decade previous. But he can be eccentric like that and I knew it was going to be a fun night.

Dad is a bit of a health freak and stays off the booze (except for the odd glass of whisky here and there) but the rest of the band, I'm sure they won't mind me saying, are always game for a party. Just the sound of Charlie Burchill's rasping chortle lets you know you're in for a good night. After the gig, we changed into pyjamas (like I said, game for a party) and everyone piled onto the bus, setting off for the next city. The mood was jolly, thanks to a great gig just gone and a well-stocked on-bus bar.

I don't remember how the tour bus disco came about, but as Dad had just jettisoned the last song on the concert setlist for one he fancied dancing to instead, he was in the mood to be iPod (it was 2008 remember) DJ on the bus that night. The 'set' was typically eclectic including Bowie, James Brown and Kraftwerk. I think it was at 'Love is a Stranger' by Eurythmics that the supernaturally talented and gorgeous Sarah Brown and I, resplendent in our nightgowns, took to the bus gangway, which for that night became our Studio 54.

Dad is pretty strict on quality control when it comes to music, but by shouting our requests loud enough, he had to concede to our Seventies disco playlist, which was evident the next day when I found bruises from flinging my limbs into bus bunks whilst exerting my most energetic Gloria Gaynor impression. By that point in the evening, and after a few additional proseccos, Sarah and I had sensibly decided you need to wear stilettoes to really bust shapes, and so swivelling like a pig in an ice rink,

I managed to knock over eight opened bottles of beer onto Charlie's lap as the bus roared along the autobahn. He assured me it didn't matter – and tried to convince me they hadn't all been his!

And so after what seemed like hours of this ersatz raving, the playlist fizzled into Eddy Duffy's slightly less dance-friendly Joy Division odyssey and the evening ended in the best way possible: by taking a tube of Pringles to my bunk and being lulled to sleep by the motion of the bus, and the sound of the band playing cards and joking well into the wee hours - relieved no doubt, that our caterwauling and 'vogueing' had finally run its course.

In the morning when the bus rolled into the next venue, I woke up with a sore head but a happy heart, and despite a few raised eyebrows from the band – doubtless concerning my attempt to out-sing Sarah during an Aretha Franklin marathon the previous night and the Pringle shards indented on my puffy face - I was glad to be part of the circus for at least another day.

## ALISON WILKINSON

Simple Minds are the very air that I breathe, the blood pumping through my veins often giving me the strength to carry on. When all around seems chaotic and crumbling, they give me hope. Hearing their music transports me to another planet, somewhere magical, mysterious, and exciting, enveloped in pure pleasure. I am oblivious to all around me whilst on my Simple Minds planet, and submerged in the special memories that are evoked from each song! The anticipation, excitement, adrenaline… feelings cannot be put into words strong enough for me to explain the emotions they make me feel. Totally alive, they are life itself.

A fan since 1982, and over 60 shows spanning Newcastle to New York and of course Sicily, it's impossible for me to choose a favourite gig or venue. They're all very special in their own way but what they all have in common is that they ignite a spark and arouse a passion which is truly addictive. I can't get enough of them. That gig when Jim *really* did look at me and wave! You never forget those moments and feelings, they're priceless. And not forgetting the wonderful people met along the way, people on your wavelength who also feel the passion and excitement, people who become true friends for life because of Simple Minds. Thank you.

I've been lucky enough to meet the band a few times in its varying line-ups. They're always friendly and polite, never making you feel like you're 'just another fan' but instead making you feel special and unique.

I feel so truly blessed to have discovered this very special band and I feel so sorry for anyone who has never been touched and experienced this euphoric feeling. I cannot think of life without Simple Minds. They make it complete!

# ANDY INNISS

In my student days at Bournemouth University I would be working at gigs as a wannabe roadie for visiting bands in return for free chips and beer. I'd ask various artists how they produced their music even though the costs were beyond me. Advice and encouragement was always free and an afternoon playing keepie uppie with Norman Cook weeks before he morphed into Fat Boy Slim left me thinking that one day I would reimagine some Simple Minds songs. And in 2008 I built a small home studio and finally executed some of the ideas in my head.

At the Simple Minds 30th anniversary weekend event at Rotherham I found myself driving Derek Forbes to our shared hotel so he could have a pre-gig meal with Mick MacNeil. I also met Billy Short, a fan who was dabbling with his own music production, and at the Edinburgh Castle gig we shared ideas.

A year later we met up again in Glasgow with the same crowd of Simple Minds fans. I had a version of 'Room' on my iPod. Billy Short loved it but so did others, with Jane Crawford demanding I share it. Around that period, I had made several trips from Devon to Glasgow to see 4GM/XSM. XSM then played a gig in Cheltenham and I made the two hour drive from Devon to see them. When they heard how long my drive home was, Derek Forbes and Brian McGee insisted I join them afterwards for supper before I left. Singing with XSM was George Porter. When George heard my take on 'Room' he called me suggesting we could take it further. Working with Gordy Goudie we produced a reinterpretation that we called 'Another Room'. We intended to share our creation by placing a video on YouTube. Martin Poschinger, another Simple Minds fan who had grabbed our attention with his Sweet Invader Movies productions, agreed to help us. We released our track under the name Empires That Dance.

When Jim Kerr shared our video on Simple Minds' social media we had requests for digital downloads from across the globe. A free video on YouTube was one thing but selling music was something completely different. I started speaking with various music publishers to obtain legal clearance and agree contracts whilst arranging digital distribution and artwork. It felt incredible to see 'Another Room' on iTunes.

Billy Short and I went to see Simple Minds in Glasgow. When I told George Porter and Gordy Goudie I had been working on a version of 'Changeling', George wanted to make a video featuring us and Martin wanted to fly from Germany to Glasgow to film it. We got into trouble with Glasgow Underground Police for filming on the underground. While Provyn (aka Johnny B Good) from Belgium enthusiastically confessed everything, George and I feigned innocence despite us carrying camera equipment with us. Fortunately Brian McGee was able to appease the authorities, who took no further action.

A highlight of the 'Changeling' video was filming in Gordy Goudie's kitchen knowing he and Jim Kerr had written some Simple Minds tracks in there. I was just a Simple Minds fan from Devon… this was not something I imagined would happen years previously. Pictures with Bruce Findlay became part of the project. Bruce happily modelled t-shirts we had designed based on Zoom Records whilst surrounded by the most amazing memorabilia of his time managing Simple Minds.

George Porter had often mentioned 'Boys from Brazil' as a song that he loved and inevitably we managed to get some ideas together as file sharing was so easy. Gordy Goudie took our ideas and produced a version with a real Georgio Moroder feel to it.

George had managed to acquire the use of a refurbished studio that needed a run through with dummy clients before *T2 Trainspotting* was filmed there a week later. Gordy was finishing off the *Acoustic* album that week and I half expected him to be staying in Glasgow with Simple Minds as they made full use of their studio time. But to his credit he travelled to Livingston to meet up, dress up and film 'Boys from Brazil' with us. I was elated when, carrying Gordy's guitar out whilst getting some fresh air, Gordy grabbed his guitar and played an impromptu acoustic version of 'Waterfront'.

When we released 'Boys from Brazil' we thought about remixes by other Simple Minds fans. Michael 'Baggers' Lees was doing great stuff on social media and stepped up with a remix, as did John Provyn.

I had written a track called 'Star Gazing' and had some lyrics. George also had lyrics he had written years before that fitted perfectly. Gordy Goudie was once again available to produce it and added the most beautiful slide guitar.

I had been messing about with 'New Gold Dream' and had an acid version of Derek Forbes' original bass line set at 160BPM. George loved it but it was way too fast as a vocal track. But despite the distances separating us we soon created 'New Gold Dream'.

George and Gordon were organising *White Hot Day*, a Simple Minds fan convention supporting Children's Hospices Across Scotland. Mick MacNeil offered his 'Once Upon a Time' presentation gold disc for auction and when George and Gordon went to collect it, Mick heard our working version of 'New Gold Dream' and agreed to add accordion.

I've composed original music for promotional videos for *White Hot Day*, a walk on track for George's tribute band Simple Minded and helped George release his solo singles 'Futureproof' and 'Life's Too Short'.

Playing *Once Upon a Time* constantly on my Sony Walkman in the Eighties, I could never have imagined I'd one day meet Simple Minds. To have done so and worked with so many ex and current members on my own music and videos has been incredible. But as George Porter said to me. 'If your dreams don't scare you, Andy, they are not big enough.'

# GIULI PRELLWITZ

It was a late summer afternoon more than 30 years ago, between the end of school and the rush of people coming from work. Two hitchhikers were busking. There they were in the pedestrian zone, in front of the local cinema, belting out 'come on baby, light my fire'. The singer was accompanied by the guitar player, they were remarkably good. After they had finished, we started chatting. Pointing to their tiny baggage, consisting mainly of sleeping bags, and the meagre earnings, they explained that they were hitchhiking. I wanted to know where they were staying for the night. They said they still had to find that out. All I could offer was some space on the floor of a shared room, with a shower and free meals. They accepted and we went on our way. The buskers had introduced themselves as Jim and Charlie. Charlie didn't speak much, maybe because he found out I couldn't understand him.

They said they were in a band and had an album out. They told us the name of their band, but Magali and I couldn't remember it afterwards. At some point we exchanged details of favourite bands and three names were dropped: Lou Reed, Velvet Underground and David Bowie. My bands at that time were the Doobie Brothers, Genesis and Led Zeppelin. Next day I left home early and the hitchhikers went on their way….

When Jim mentioned on social media those three names again - Lou Reed, Velvet Underground and Bowie, It got me thinking. For the first time in decades, I recalled the two hitchhikers from 30 something years ago that were called Jim and Charlie….

---

# JÜRGEN GRENZ

Travelling on business I got into the habit of listening to 'Big Sleep' just before leaving the house. And again when I returned home, after taking my jacket off and switching on the hi fi. The circle was closed and I felt at home again. Playing the instrumental version of 'Big Sleep' at my funeral is one of my last wishes. The circle will then be closed once more. Hopefully that's a while off yet!

---

# EDMUND KELLY

It was 1981 and I had been tipped off in school about this Scottish band whose Tiffany's gig would be featured on Billy Sloan's Radio Clyde show. That show existed on the nocturnal hinterland. I was only 16 and not allowed up that late. I really only heard tapes of the show at my pal's house, where we would gather to play poker. I must have been very keen to hear the band, but equally keen to retain my paper round earnings because I recorded it myself on my brother's radio cassette player. After pressing 'record', I turned the volume to silent and went to bed. After school next day I remember plugging in the headphones to listen to what I'd caught on acetate.

I still have the Memorex C90 cassette, a memento of an evening when I went on what felt like a Bilbo Baggins adventure. It was one song in particular that hypnotised me. 'It's the last song,' Jim announced. 'Give me an echo Gallagher…' and 'This Fear of Gods' began. At the risk of sounding all trippy, it was like being lifted and swept into some great cathedral of hope, one in which thoughts could soar as if borne in the hands of angels. Dreams were vivified, aspirations clarified, possibilities magnified. Great cities and landscapes came into view, and resolutions were made to go.

When the tape suddenly ended I was still in Kansas, still in Cardonald, and still had my homework to do. That it was the Minds that first transported me to that place, gave them a unique place in my heart which I have reserved for them ever since.

While the music has been a gift to me, the greatest beneficiary I hope will have been someone unknown. The band introduced me to Amnesty International and, 34 years later, I am still mailing letters. If any letter ever helped release just one person from unjust captivity, then the Minds' legacy will have been rich indeed.

## LAMBERTO BELLANI

It was autumn '83. After the show in Milan I was wandering backstage and found myself in front of a strange room. It was empty and dark with only a dim light coming from a small half-closed window. I went in anyway, opened the window and looked out … Jim Kerr was just passing by! Without thinking about it I just shouted: 'Mr Kerr!' His gaze towards me at that precise moment resembled that of a cat when he is caught off guard. It was a funny and somewhat absurd situation. Reaching out from my unlikely position I said, 'Give me your hand!' Without saying a word, Mr Kerr retraced his steps and came under my window to shake hands. And from the way he looked at me in that moment, I have always imagined that for him it was the moment of entry into Italy.

## CHRISTIAN OSSANNA

Music is a very powerful glue that's invisible but leaves indelible traces. With humility and without ever invading their ground, over the years I got to know many members of the band personally, composing for them a video made public on the simpleminds.com website. My friendship with Elisa Darù and the friendship that binds us for years with Ada Cifali. The sounds drove us to Sicily and even to the island of Barra, in Scotland. There was a before, a during and there will always be a tomorrow for Simple Minds' music.

# DARRYL FARLAM

*Wembley Arena*
*29 November 2008, London, England*

My first encounter with Simple Minds was at the age of 10 when I heard 'Waterfront' on a compilation LP my late brother Roland bought. My passion for music began from the age of seven and I was very much drawn to music that had guts. I then spotted a 'Don't You (Forget About Me)' 7-inch in his collection and, after playing it constantly, just had to find out more about this band. Weeks of pocket money was then spent buying the back-catalogue. I was amazed to find

*Darryl Farlam met Jim backstage at Wembley*

they'd had a six-year career before I discovered them.

My brother sadly passed away exactly two weeks before the release of 'Let There be Love' in 1991. I was 17. In the weeks and months ahead, I found such comfort in *Street Fighting Years*. Whenever I listen to the Minds I think of him. I went on to see Simple Minds live all over the UK and Europe and in 2008 met Jim backstage at Wembley. I don't often get star-struck but did that night.

---

# OLIVIER DIDIER

I was part of the Sparkle Belgian Simple Minds fan club which has brought together so many people from different corners of Belgium and the world. Encouragement and support were incredible. As a result, many friendships have been formed. It's always great to see fans who have travelled to see the band in famous venues. So many people have helped other foreign fans discover their cultures.

In November 2008 I did eight gigs in 10 days across the UK – Manchester, Birmingham, London, Sheffield, Cardiff, Newcastle, Glasgow, Belfast and back to

Glasgow. What a trip, with Sylvie, Stephanie Z, Arthur and Henri, their boys, and my best friend Christophe V. And 200 Belgian fans made the Wembley Arena trip. One of the best experiences I've had. Another great memory was *Night of the Proms* in Rotterdam in 2008. Jim put my white and green Celtic scarf on his shoulder and around his neck during 'Sanctify Yourself'.

It's only Simple Minds (but I like it!).

---

## JOHNEY D'HALLA

*SECC*
*4 December 2008,*
*Glasgow, Scotland*

I first saw Minds in Sydney in May 2006. The show was so good I went back and saw them again the following weekend. In Sydney again, March 2007, with INXS and Arrested Development, they absolutely stole the show, although I remember there was no memorabilia for sale.

Minds shows are distinct: there's a sense of magic encompassing and filling the theatre, giving a real sense of meaning to

WATERFRONT
SPEED YOUR LOVE
MANDELA DAY
LOVE SONG
AMERICAN
SEE THE LIGHTS
CHELSEA
HYPNOTISE
SOMEONE SOMEWHERE
COLOURS
PROMISED YOU A MIRACLE
BIG SLEEP
SOMEBODY UP THERE LIKES YOU
NEW GOLD DREAM
HUNTER + HUNTED
GLITTERING PRIZE
KING IS WHITE
CATWALK
DON'T YOU FORGET
BELFAST
+++++++++++++++++++++++++++++
RIVER
SANCTIFY
ALIVE AND KICKING

WEMBLEY ARENA. - 29ᵗʰ NOVEMBER 08

*Jim at the SECC - photo Johney D'Halla*

433

*The Minds on stage in Glasgow at the SECC - photo Johney D'Halla*

being there. It's like you're exactly where you're meant to be – right here, right now. Nothing else matters. Not because of the spectacular special effects or anything else, but because of the music, the magic. That takes real talent, to give a sense of meaning to a concert without gimmicky gadgets like a giant million dollar LED screen (like a certain Irish band's concert, where I didn't enjoy myself nearly as much). You feel like you're at the centre of the universe, which stimulates you and makes you believe that nothing's impossible, there's always hope for success in any field of endeavour. They leave you with a huge smile on your face and a rejuvenated sense of soul in your being.

The best show was easily when I crossed the world to see them perform in their hometown on the 30th Anniversary tour. I loved hearing several pre-*New Gold Dream* songs – the experimental, edgy, tight, raw, unnerving, bass-driven early Minds. Eddie Duffy shone on these tracks and did Forbes great justice. *'Chelsea Girl'* being sung by Mel was indescribably brilliant. That alone was worth the trip, satisfaction sweeter for knowing any average Minds fan walking in right then would have no idea what songs we were all singing!

During 'Ghostdancing', Jim told the audience a young journalist had interviewed him and suggested Minds fans 'must be getting quite old by now'. He asked if they were still coming to shows in as big numbers as in the '80s. Jim's reply was, 'Well, you can come and see tonight if you'd like… if you can find a ticket.'

## SIMON CORNWELL

The first rule of the 'tame expert' is that you never talk about being the tame expert. The second rule of the tame expert is that you keep your big mouth shut.

Val Jennings, label manager at Demon Records, first used this phrase when introducing himself: 'Glad to meet the tame expert.' Val had been using *Dream Giver* to form an initial pass for the *Rejuvenation* boxset track-listing, and the time had come to finalise plans and start to formalise artwork with Stuart Crouch. I liked the term.

I'd worked in the same capacity with Steve Hammonds at Universal: compiling releases, sorting out artwork and occasionally writing sleevenotes. I learned on the job with Steve, so was able to help Val out far better, being far more proactive.

It all started back in February 2009. An email arrived from Martin Hanlin, then managing the band, 'Can you take a quick look at these? It needs to go to the printers tomorrow.' It was all the artwork for *Graffiti Soul*: the CD, Jake CD, and gatefold vinyl. It all turned up completely unannounced. I guess he was happy with the work I'd done the previous year on the *30 Years Live* tour programme and needed another pair of eyes.

He completely distracted me by sending me the entire album as MP3s. Therefore, instead of watching TV as planned, I spent the evening correcting grammatical errors and typos whilst listening to the new album. It was useful for double-checking the lyrics, but then, printed lyrics and their musical counterparts rarely match.

In addition, I had learned the hard way whilst running *Dream Giver*: do not leak anything, do not tell anyone, keep your big mouth shut… don't whatever you do, put this on your website with a big 'tada!' exclusive. I was not that stupid anymore.

Quietus took on managerial responsibilities in 2011 and I met with Ian Grenfell and Elaine Gwyther. Coming from a background managing Simply Red, they'd been using *Dream Giver* to bring them up to date. Could I help out on projects? Of course I could. I was introduced to their favourite designer, Stuart Crouch at Peacock. We were off. The first project, a compilation album, didn't make it, but I worked closely with Stuart on *5X5*, ensuring the artwork was correct. It was the start of a working relationship which continues to this day. I can't thank Martin, Ian, Elaine, Stuart, Steve and Val enough for placing their trust in me.

Did I ever screw up? Of course – I published a bit of a work-in-progress to a Simple Minds Facebook art group. It was from the forthcoming and unannounced *New Gold Dream Super Deluxe*. The group posted some great stuff over the years and I wanted to give something back. Give them a hint as to what was happening. After all, it was a closed group of about 200 people. What could possibility go wrong?

That group was leakier than a colander and my image spread everywhere. I had my fingers rapped for that. No one's fault but mine. I put it in the public domain after all.

Despite my numerous indiscretions, I've learned. And I believe I've gradually grown to earn the title of tame expert. If *Dream Giver* ever goes quiet, you know I'm working on something. But….

See rule two. Then see rule one. Which I've just broken.

---

## LARA CATALDO

*Milano Jazzin' Festival*
*Arena Civica*
*3 July 2009, Milan, Italy*

In 2008 I discovered Simple Minds thanks to my boyfriend Andrea, who shared with me a *Best Of* compilation and told me the Simple Minds story from the beginning. He said they were releasing a new album, *Graffiti Soul*, which contains my favourite song, 'Stars Will Lead the Way'.

The first time I saw them live was my first concert, during Milano Jazzin Festival, 3 July 2009. Jim took the stage with a 'Buonasera Milano! Come stai? Tutto a posto?' During 'Don't You' he indicated us (my partner and I) and told us 'Per i giovani (For the young people).'

*Lara Cataldo was at the Milano Jazzin' Festival*

Since that concert, we've gone all over Italy, from north to south and east to west to see them, but also London to see the fantastic gig at the Roundhouse for the *Walk Between Worlds* tour. I can't wait to see them again.

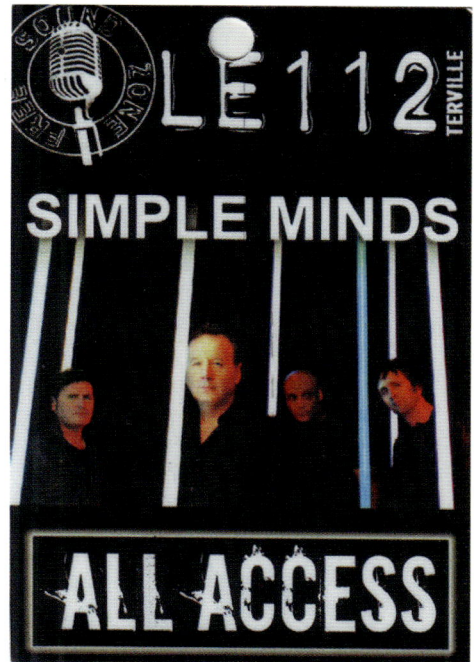

# DANNY LABRANA

## Olympia
## 8 July 2009, Paris, France

I listened to 'Alive and Kicking' on a loop for weeks when *Once Upon a Time* was released, but it was with *Live in the City of Light* that the passion really started. I had it on vinyl but also on tape so could listen on my Walkman. That's the double-album version, with a box twice as long as the others and two orange cassettes.

It's the central element of this album that makes my relationship with Simple Minds so special: the stage. Every time I go to a concert at Le Zénith I can't help but think this is where it was recorded. It makes me so proud, as a Parisian, to think such a beautiful album, listened to by so many people on our planet, has been recorded in my hometown.

I like their energy and that a Simple Minds concert is a kind of 'greatest hits live' and not just a promotional tour for the latest album with the addition of two or three 'good old songs'. I liked the emotional tribute Jim paid just a few days later to the victims of the terrorist attacks in Paris on 13 November 2015.

But above all, how could I forget that Jim spoke directly to me between songs at Paris Olympia during the *Graffiti Soul* tour. I was jumping all over the place, right after the 'I Travel'/'Waterfront' combo, my hair all wet on my forehead and my t-shirt soaked. In short, I was dripping with sweat. I was in the front row and by pure chance, Jim turned around to me and dropped into the mic, in perfect French, 'Il fait chaud, hein?' ('It's hot here, eh?').

---

# MARC AUBANEL

## Le Palio Arena
## 11 July 2009, Les Nuits D'Istres, France

I've seen them in concert nine times. My only regret is that it's not enough. I remember those two unforgettable days in July 2009 when I went to Argelès sur Mer and waited for them in front of the stage from five in the afternoon until midnight, when they played until 2am and where, the next evening, I returned to see them play the arena at Les Nuits D'Istres. After the concert I was able to talk briefly to Charlie. Seeing him in the flesh almost brought me to tears.

---

# DAVID ASHTON

## Edinburgh Castle
## 18 July 2009, Edinburgh, Scotland

I've never seen such rain. It was torrential. There were wooden pallets floating down a river of water, it was relentless. My sister-in-law contracted pneumonia. But to be fair to the band, when it eventually subsided a little, they came on rather than cancel and disappoint. Guess what they opened with? 'Waterfront'. Brilliant!

My best memory was after a Bournemouth gig. We happened to be in the same hotel as the band were staying in and I got to spend a little time with Jim. We didn't talk about music, but about football for 20 minutes. That sums up Simple Minds. Fantastic musicians who have no egos and really care about their fans and what their music means to them. Roll on another 40 years.

---

# HILDE VAN DEN EYNDE

I was born and raised in a small village close to Werchter, Belgium. I'm sure the name rings a bell. As soon as I was allowed to go out on Saturdays, I went to a new wave disco in Mechelen where I got to know Simple Minds music. In 1983, I went to Rock Werchter for the first time. My socks were blown off: the smell of alcohol and sweat, the amazing atmosphere and an absolutely fabulous concert by Simple Minds!

In 1989, I was working as an HR business partner in a Swedish company when Paul, an interim worker, started talking to me at the coffee machine. He had big brown eyes and a BMW motorbike. It turned out we both had tickets for a Simple Minds concert in Vorst Nationaal that evening. I suggested we go together. It was absolutely magic. This common interest brought us together; throughout the years we've been to many more.

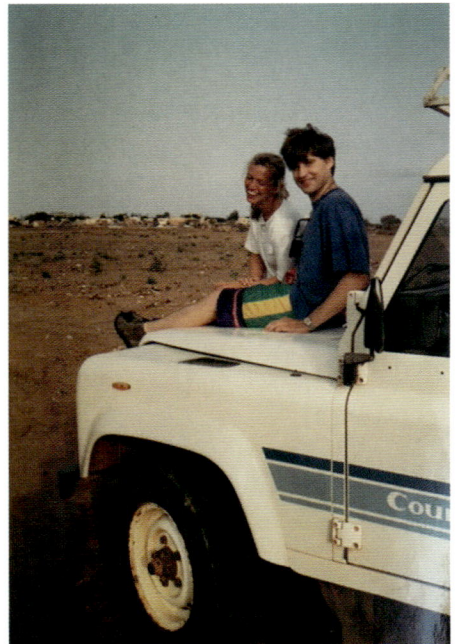

*Hilde and Paul with the big brown eyes*

When Paul turned 40 in 2009, I organised a surprise city trip to the lovely Edinburgh. I managed to buy tickets for the concert at Edinburgh Castle, later described in the press as 'a thorough drenching'. Indeed 'rain keeps falling, rain keeps falling, down, down, down'. But that couldn't spoil the fun! The location was so exceptional, we didn't mind getting wet to the bone.

In 2020, I was supposed to celebrate my 60th birthday with a wild party and Simple Minds performing at Lotto Arena, Antwerp. Unfortunately, coronavirus decided differently. I spent the day video-conferencing my kids, family and friends, not exactly the party I had in mind.

## DIETER HÜLSMANN

A friend of mine told me about Simple Minds and their music so I listened to the radio station SWR3, which played Simple Minds songs the whole day long. *Street Fighting Years* and the 1989 tour was the kick to become a fan. For my 50th birthday and the *30 Years Live* tour, I went to the Edinburgh Castle show. The atmosphere at this concert was unbelievable. It was raining cats and dogs during the concert. The sun had been shining the whole day.

## DAVID JOHNSON

We treated ourselves as a wedding anniversary and took a chance with the weather. Boy, did we get that wrong! Deluge doesn't do it justice. But even with the rain, the band were tight and up for it. Great outdoor gig.

## GRAHAM MCDONALD

I first heard 'Promised You a Miracle' on the radio in Scotland in 1982 while playing with friends in my back garden. I've been a big fan since, seing them six times in total in Glasgow, London, Edinburgh, Lisbon (twice) and most recently Oslo, my wife Carolina and I lucky enough to meet the band and listen to the soundcheck.

A less pleasant memory was Edinburgh Castle in 2009. There was a huge black cloud overhead before the concert started and we got absolutely soaked. Our clothes were still dripping wet when we got home and were actually drier when they came out of the washing machine than before they went in. It took days for my boots to dry out.

My favourite live performance is the version of 'Book of Brilliant Things' from the *Sparkle in The Rain* tour in 1984. Charlie and Mick produced a truly wonderful instrumental sound in the latter part of the song.

*Graham and wife Carolina enjoyed the Oslo show, where they met the band, more than the Edinburgh one – where they got soaked through!*

## DANIELA PLUESS

I've been a fan since the '80s. I love the melodies, the storytelling in every song and the CD covers! I met Charlie Burchill in Locarno's Moon and Stars, the whole band backstage at Frauenfeld open-air festival and Charlie again at Edinburgh Airport after the soaking wet concert at the castle, which we travelled to beautiful Scotland for especially. Unforgettable moments, and their music deeply touches my heart and soul.

## CRAIG WATSON

I was at high school when I bought *Once Upon a Time*. I was at Ibrox in 1986, helping stewards out around the stadium. In 1987, when the *Live in the City of Light* album came out. I bought it with a gift token I was awarded at school. I loved the album so much I bought the vinyl album a second time after my brother scratched it, then again when it came out on CD. I didn't pay much attention to what Simple Minds were doing in the late '80s and early '90s until I saw them at the Royal Concert Hall, Glasgow promoting *Good News from the Next World*. Since then I've bought just about every album and been to just about every concert performed in Glasgow and Edinburgh, including the night I got drenched at Edinburgh Castle. It cost me a new phone - the one I had got ruined. It was worth it though.

## PETER MINNEBO & HANS PARDON

*Amphitheatre*
*27 July 2009,*
*Taormina, Italy*

We had the holiday of our life! The *Graffiti Soul* tour brought Simple Minds to Taormina. With our VIP package, the organisation only booked us into the same hotel as our heroes. In the afternoon we were swimming in the pool with Charlie Burchill, Mel Gaynor and their family and crew. We didn't use our cameras or speak to them because we respected their privacy. But we missed Jim Kerr. Maybe he was rehearsing 'In Your Room'. And we had a little holiday chat with Charlie's girlfriend. The morning after, we realised 'Swimming Towards the Sun' wasn't only a song or dream, but real life, with Simple Minds in the breakfast room.

*Peter Minnebo and Hans Pardon shared a swimming pool with Charlie*

---

## LELE MERLINI

*Arena*
*3 November 2009, Vienna, Austria*

After years of insane passion for the band, attending 60 concerts across Europe, identifying a single highlight is almost impossible. But what often comes to mind is Jim reading my lips during a festival in Cap Roig, Spain in 2012, when I was singing 'Celebrate' among an audience of non 'loyalists' and he decided to show me his appreciation several times from the stage. I also remember a concert at the Palaeur, Rome in 1991 when he realised I had a cast on my arm, making a sign.

But the anecdote that perfectly represents Simple Minds' dedication to their audience was in November 2009. I was in Bratislava for business as the *Graffiti Soul* tour started in Vienna. It wasn't coincidence. I was going to Vienna Arena. I arrived too early, 4.30pm, all the doors were open, but with nobody around. I sneaked in and within seconds found myself in front of an empty stage. Someone from the staff asked who I was. As a typical Italian man living in the south, I said I was one of Charlie Burchill's friends, so I was allowed to stay. Soon after, Eddie Duffy appeared and started to tune his bass, ignoring my presence. Charlie also joined after a very short time. He noticed me. He called somebody from the staff and made my lie completely collapse.

Here was the twist. While I was asked to leave, Jim joined the stage and I asked for his help rather pathetically. I raised my arm and told him in Italian I was a long-time fan from southern Italy. I made him laugh and he gave me the opportunity to stay. This is how I crowned the dream of joining an entire Simple Minds soundcheck quite unexpectedly. But this is not all. At the end of the soundcheck, a little teasingly, Jim looked at me and asked 'Everything OK? Can we play tonight?' I still feel ashamed, but I raised my thumb for approval.

# KATHYRYN RICHARDS

*SECC*
*11 December 2009, Glasgow, Scotland*

Simple Minds never fail to please the crowd. They clearly love their fans. That's what I love about Jim, Charlie, and co.

It started back in the late '80s. My mum and older brother are fans and I was introduced at an early age to albums such as *Sparkle in the Rain, Empires and Dance* and *New Gold Dream*. 'Speed Your Love to Me' and 'Up on the Catwalk' are tracks which evoke those earliest memories. 'Shake Off the Ghosts' is particularly stirring - when I hear that rousing music it encourages me to do just that. 'Colours Fly' and 'Catherine Wheel' are other favourites, the latter just because it has my name in it!

I've got a few great memories of seeing them live. In Glasgow on the *Graffiti Soul* tour in 2009, they handled the technical difficulties with such flair. 'Just talk among yourselves.' I was next to a couple of local lads. One reappeared from a toilet break, asked what was going on and his mate replied, 'Ah, they knew you'd gone for a piss so said they'd hold on a few minutes.'

# CHRIS CONNOR

*Wembley Arena*
*7 December 2009, London, England*

I've been a fan since 1982 when I first heard 'Promised You a Miracle', then bought *New Gold Dream* on cassette, playing it incessantly for six months. It's still in my top-five albums of all time.

For years I was too busy with work to go to concerts, but kept listening to the band on CD. Then in 2008 I saw a good review for the *Black & White* album, downloading it into my iTunes collection. It had a massive impact on me and brought me straight back into the fold.

In 2009 I got to see the band for the first time. I had always known they had an unbelievable reputation for live performance, but that show just knocked me out. I've been to see them on every UK tour since. In 2014, my wife and I travelled to Taormina to see the band play the Greek Theatre. What a trip! We met Mel Gaynor, Ged Grimes and Andy Gillespie on the plane and got the chance to congratulate them on the Kew concert we'd seen the week before. After the show, they saw us at a bar down the hill from the venue and said we should go back to their hotel to meet Jim. I was too embarrassed though, and said no – which I now regret. The band were superb and the venue sensational. We watched the sun set over the Mediterranean, Mount Etna erupting gently in the background.

In 2017, I visited a close friend and his family in Perth, Australia. Unbelievably, Simple Minds were performing in King's Park and a whole group of us went along. I was the only die-hard fan, but everyone was knocked out by the quality of sound and by how current the performance and music were. I got to see the *Acoustic* show at the Palladium with my brother and a friend. We had a great time, made all the better when Jim came down into the auditorium and clapped hands with my brother. He and three other friends in their late 50s and early 60s are now devoted SM fans.

## COLIN COWAN

*Scottish Exhibition
& Conference Centre
11 December 2009,
Glasgow, Scotland*

I was too young to experience the glam or punk eras, my interest in music fired up during the new romantic days. I'd lap up anything that had an element of that sound. Hearing 'Love Song' for the first time opened my ears to Simple Minds and then *New Gold Dream* came along and I was hooked. It became a family affair as my mother was, and is, a massive fan. Teaching myself to play drums by ear was enhanced by the amazing Mel Gaynor's work on the extended versions of 'Waterfront' and 'Don't You (Forget About Me)', showing how powerful a sound could be made from a tight piece of skin. It was a long time before I managed to see Simple Minds live on the *Graffiti Soul* tour in Glasgow.

## DIRK COOLS

*FNAC
29 May 2010, Brussels, Belgium*

I guess I've seen every concert in Belgium. I particularly remember the concert in de Vooruit, Gent, in December 1985, supported by The Waterboys; shows at Vorst Nationaal in Brussels; and a great day at Torhout/ Werchter with Simply Red, Talk Talk, the Robert Cray Band, Lloyd Cole and Elvis Costello. But my highlights are the intimate concert in May 2005 for the launch of *Black & White 050505*, where I met the band (apart from Jim, who had already left for Amsterdam, where they would perform the day after) and a signing session in May 2010 at the FNAC, Brussels for the launch of the *Lostboy* album, when I met Jim.

# GED GRIMES

*Simple Minds bass guitarist, 2010 - present*
*Fête De L'humanité*
*11 September 2010, Paris, France*

First time I met Jim and Charlie was in the late 1980s when my band Danny Wilson were on the same record label, Virgin Records. We met again in 2008 when I was with Deacon Blue, supporting Simple Minds on several UK dates that year.

After getting involved in Jim's *Lostboy* project, he called to see if I'd be interested in some recording in London. I arrived at the studio to be met by Charlie and it dawned on me - this recording was for a Simple Minds album!

Things went well and as I was packing up and saying my farewells at the end of a productive few days, Charlie enquired if I'd be keen to play a show with the band at the weekend in Paris. Obviously I said 'yes!' but since it was already Wednesday, my thoughts turned to how the hell were we going to rehearse for this show? 'Och, it will all be fine,' says Charlie. 'We can send you some links and recordings to recent live shows and we will see you Saturday in Paris.'

On the flight back to Scotland, the reality of what I had agreed to began to set in. I spent the next two days immersed in the live set recordings and consoled myself with the thought that the show must be a low-key affair, maybe a small venue, an 'under the radar' show.

Saturday - show day - I arrive in Paris and whilst travelling to the venue with Jim he just happens to say, 'Oh I forgot to mention - the show is going out live in France and is being streamed worldwide, but no worry, we are going to have a great night. I can feel it….'

The car pulls up. Given the scale of the backstage area and some distant crowd noise, I'm suddenly acutely aware this is no 'under the radar' show. As the clock ticks down to the show, in order to steady my nerves I decide to take a quick look at the audience out front from the side of the stage. My stomach hits the floor - 80,000 people. It's one of France's biggest music festivals, the Fête de l'Humanité, and Simple Minds are the headline act.

'Five minutes to showtime,' utters the tour manager - and the rest is a glorious blur of sound, adrenaline and the power of music.

As a band, Simple Minds have always been willing to take musical risks and follow their own path and instincts. My 'baptism of fire' that night in Paris was testament to the faith Jim and Charlie placed in me, and 10 years on it remains one of the best nights of my life.

# SHARON GODWIN

*Bedgebury Pinetum*
*& Forest*
*10 June 2011,*
*Bedgebury, England*

*Sharon Godwin (left) and her mum and sister went to Bedgebury*

I've been a fan of Simple Minds since I was five, when I first heard 'Up on the Catwalk'. I loved Jim's voice and the sound and energy of the band, and have remained a fan since, because they continue to make great music. Although band members have changed over the years the heart is still there, beating strong, and they are a band that touch many people's hearts.

I first saw them at Bedgebury Forest with my mum Christine and sister Karen. It was amazing. I loved the *5x5* tour as they played early songs I never thought I would ever hear live. I especially loved watching and listening to Charlie play violin on 'Pleasantly Disturbed', as the violin is one of my favourite instruments. But the highlight for me has to be when they played Margate, where I was born. We got to see them twice at the Winter Gardens. It was quite emotional, plus at the end of the gig their setlist landed on my head! I now have it framed on the wall.

# ALISON LINDOE

*Simple Minds Shop*
*Hampton Court Palace*
*16 June 2011, East Molesey, England*

I first met the band at the start of their *Forest* tour in 2011, a series of dates set in spectacular woodland locations. We were building an online shop and thought it would be an opportunity to get a feel for the fanbase before we opened, so I took on the job of manning the merchandise stall during the UK leg of the tour.

I was a bit nervous meeting the band for the first time, but they were so welcoming and friendly. I soon felt at ease. The work was hard, but so enjoyable; being held at outdoor venues I got to see and hear the whole show. Once or twice I even managed to get to the after-show get-together, before we all headed off. There was one gig at Hampton Court in the middle of the tour; it was bizarre rolling my flight case through the cobbled pavement of the palace grounds ready to set up stall.

It wasn't the best night, as all the stalls were placed far from the crowd and stage, the weather was dreadful and hardly anybody ventured out to find me. I didn't sell anything and couldn't even hear the show. I remember packing up and going to the after-party a little dejected; Ged found me rather cold and wet and made me a cup of tea, which, although not very rock 'n' roll, was much more welcome than anything alcoholic!

The gigs in the forests were so much better from my point of view; when the gates opened there was always a frantic rush of fans to get to the front of the stage, but also a big crowd around the merch stall. The end of each night was always the busiest; I'd have a rush of people wanting to buy on their way out, then there would be a quick stock take before packing up and getting the flight case back over to the trucks before the crew had finished loading up ready to go. The fans were also very friendly and passionate about their band. I started to recognise some of the hardcore fans that went to several shows; they didn't hold back in telling me what they wanted to buy and what they loved about the band. I realised how appropriate the Simple Minds logo was – the Claddagh is the symbol of love, loyalty and friendship, and I saw that in abundance on this tour.

*Alison Lindoe remembers a very wet gig at Hampton Court Palace - pic Alison Lindoe*

## ANGELA HILL

*Westonbirt Arboretum*
*17 June 2011, Tetbury, England*

I first became aware of Simple Minds at *Live Aid* in 1985. I was disappointed by a brief loss of transmission during 'Promised You a Miracle'. I decided to find out more about the band and have followed the music ever since. I love Jim's soaring vocals and Charlie's wibble-jingly guitar. The most memorable concert was a slightly rainy Westonbirt Arboretum in June 2011. I got there really early and determined to nestle myself in at the front of the stage and was thrilled when, as the band appeared, I waved at Jim and actually got a kind 'hello' and a smile back. Thanks for that acknowledgement, and for all the rousing songs over the years.

## STEVE HARGREAVES

*Sherwood Pines Forest*
*18 June 2011, Edwinstowe, England*

Friends come and go, girlfriends come and go, jobs come and go. But one thing remains – Simple Minds. I've had the pleasure of seeing Simple Minds three times over the years - Sheffield Arena in the early '90s and more recently Leeds O2 Academy and Sherwood Forest Pines. The years have passed but their passion to entertain is still unbelievable. When I saw them all bound on stage at Sherwood Forest it sent shivers down my spine. 'Let me see your hands please.'

*Steve Hargreaves saw Simple Minds at Sherwood Forest and Leeds O2 Academy - photo Steve Hargreaves*

## ROBERT WILLIAMS

*Dalby Forest*
*24 June 2011, Pickering, England*

My first Simple Minds gig was at Tiffany's, Glasgow in 1982. People ask, 'What's your favourite song?' and expect a well-known hit. But it's 'In Trance as Mission'. The bassline live at Tiffany's never left me. It was mind-blowing, the start of a lifelong affair with the band. I haven't missed a Glasgow gig since. My wife and daughter now share my passion, having a fantastic time at all the Scottish gigs and overnight stays down south. Every gig is fantastic. Dalby Forest in 2011 was a great combination - fabulous music and a brilliant atmosphere in a perfect setting. I loved the *5x5* tour too. I never thought I'd hear all those amazing songs the same night!

---

# ROY ASHMAN

*Cannock Chase Forest*
*25 June 2011, Staffordshire, England*

My Simple Minds journey started on a sunny day on the canals of our not quite capital city, Birmingham. I decided to cycle to Cannock to see my beloved band in a forest. Feeling fit, I climbed on my bike in search of the glittering prize!

It wasn't a great start when I came off the canal in Wolverhampton. It seemed like an honest town but then it went all wrong. I asked, 'Which way to the forest?' and was told it was a long way. 'How far?' I said. 'Oh, ages that way, as the light travels.' Off I went, realising I'd maybe bitten off more than I could chew. I was struggling. I had drunk all my drink and eaten all my food and was well off the pace to get to the gig!

As I slowly worked my way to the forest, in a trance and on a mission, I realised time was against me so I sped up to 30 frames a second. But alas there were no signposts, nothing to tell me where to go. I saw a police car and asked them the way. One of them said, 'Are you in the band?' 'Yes, I play the drums', I said, hoping to either get a lift or be asked for an autograph. 'Well, you'd better hurry up,' they said and pointed the way. 'It's over there, past the waterfront.'

As the evening turned to shadows and light I finally arrived, battered and bruised. Now sparkling in the rain, it had gone from warm and me sweating in bullets to thunderstorms. I could see the crowd, the stage, but…

As the concert started, I was told I couldn't take my bike in, so I watched the gig from over the fence. Magic as usual, I was totally hypnotised. Concert over and cold, wet and hungry, with nothing but stars to lead the way, I slowly got life from my tired legs. Someone somewhere, lost in summertime.

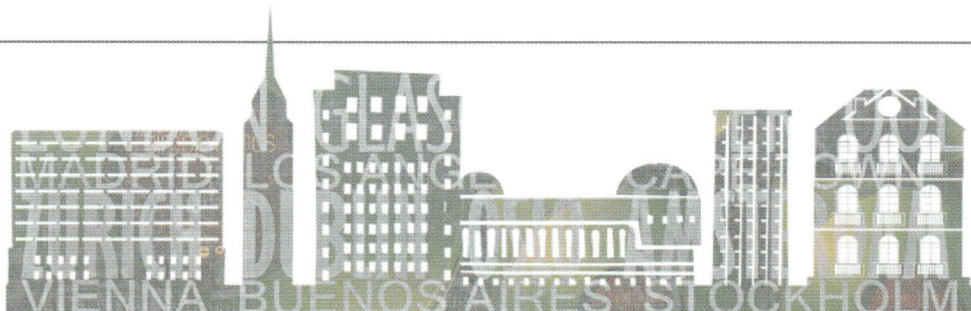

# CARL STANTON

*Cannock Chase Forest*
*25 June 2011, Rugeley, England*

I first saw Simple Minds on 1985's *Sparkle in the Rain* tour. This has since been one of the joys of my life and I've seen them at Birmingham NEC, Milton Keynes, Wembley, the National Indoor Arena, Wolverhampton Civic, Birmingham Academy, and Cannock Chase.

Several couples we've been friends with for over 40 years are all big fans. We are Carl (Stana) and Shaz, Dawke and Shell, Gibbo and Alison, Shawy and Julie, Westy and Sara. Whenever the dates are out, I'm the one who usually books to ensure no one misses out.

Simple Minds are our band. I feel like I know Jim and Charlie. They've been a big part of our lives and every gig we go to, sometimes years apart, our friends regroup and it's always a pleasant reunion. We look forward to hearing Jim ask us once more, 'Let me see your hands!' God bless 'em!

# IAN SHEEN

*Delamere Forest*
*3 July 2011, Delamere, England*

I started seeing Simple Minds in the late '70s at Eric's in Liverpool. Since then I've had some of my best nights out at their gigs. The highlight was a balmy hot night in Delamere Forest in 2011. The band just gelled with the fans that night and the fans responded with amazing gusto to turn it into a night to remember forever. Jim tweeted the next day to say it was in the top-five concerts he'd played.

# MICHELE CAMPAGNI

*Hard Rock Café*
*4 July 2011, Florence, Italy*

I grew up with Simple Minds. They were the soundtrack of every trip I took with my father, and it's thanks to him that I love them. But there's also another reason they're very important to me: I'm a photographer, and nine years ago was called to document the inauguration of the Hard Rock Café in Florence. It was my first job after

*Michele Campagni was there when Simple Minds inaugurated Florence's Hard Rock*

a long period not working and an emotional crisis for me. While I was photographing their concert, Jim squeezed my hand while singing, and you cannot understand the emotional strength that simple gesture gave me.

*Yolanda saw Simple Minds in Madrid. Photo Yolanda Candelario Flores*

## YOLANDA CANDELARIO FLORES

*La Riviera
15 February 2012,
Madrid, Spain*

I've been a Simple Minds fan as far back as I can remember. Unfortunately, I've not had many chances to attend concerts. In 1991 a show in

Las Ventas, Madrid was cancelled the day before, one of the greatest disappointments of my life. After that, every time they came to Madrid I'd be out of town. So my first Simple Minds concert was not until February 2012 in La Riviera for the *5x5* tour. I was so nervous and excited I couldn't even take a picture. I was too busy singing and dancing.

## LIDA VAN STRAATEN

*Paradiso*
*18 February 2012, Amsterdam,*
*The Netherlands*

My love for Simple Minds started around 1981 with *Sons and Fascination*, one of my favourite albums. My sister is also a big fan, but she's a bit shy. I knew she wanted to get her picture taken with the band after a concert. When we got tickets for the *5x5* concert in Amsterdam at the Paradiso, it was

*Lida's sister Anita van Straaten with Jim outside the Paradiso*

the same day as my sister's birthday, so I made it my goal to get that picture.

Afterwards, we stood outside and waited and waited. Suddenly Jim Kerr came out of the backstage door and a lot of fans wanted a picture or autograph, but Jim went straight to his van with chauffeur. I asked him, 'Please, can you manage one picture? It's my sister's birthday - you will make her so happy.' He did, and she was.

## MARC MIDDENDORP

I was 17 in 1987, at a party with friends, someone playing *Live in the City of Light*. I asked a girl which band this was and she gave me the album to look at. From that point on I became a fan, and also found I knew more songs that I thought.

*Street Fighting Years* is one of my favourite albums. It came out while I was in a turbulent period in my life. My mother had died and I still had to work this out. The song 'Street Fighting Years' helped me get my life back on the road and pick up again.

I've been to 14 concerts, from the big stadium show in the Kuip, Rotterdam to one of Jim's *Lostboys* tour in Utrecht. I love all the concerts they give, whether in a small or big venue. One of the best was *5x5* at the Paradiso, Amsterdam. It was an amazing performance and the best vibe ever. Jim, Charlie and the rest were absolutely in high spirits that night.

---

# MONIQUE ATWOOD

*Admiralspalast*
*19 February 2012, Berlin, Germany*

Growing up in New Delhi, India in the 1980s, the youngest child of a CARE director and his shrewish wife (my mom), I was incredibly shy and withdrawn, living a cloistered, inhibited life because of my mom's appalling parenting skills. At 15, I'd retreat to my friend Nicole's house every weekend, relieved to be out of my mother's diagnostic, disapproving gaze. Nicole was the daughter of a diplomat at the Australian High Commission, Delhi, and had access to an amazing collection of records/cassettes imported from Canberra – Depeche Mode, Spandau Ballet, Adam Ant, U2. But it was the Simple Minds records that invaded my repressed soul and helped bring me to life.

My lifelong love affair with them began in my teens and still burns bright. Now an American diplomat, having been assigned to a dozen countries overseas, I've managed to see Simple Minds in concert five or six times. In January 2012, I ruptured my Achilles tendon playing tennis in Frankfurt, Germany, but still managed to fly to Berlin the following month to catch the show at the Admiralspalast. I had to repurchase a balcony ticket because I was on crutches and had to inject clot-busting agents into my abdomen so I wouldn't develop DVT while my foot was in a cast. But I could tap my other foot as Jim belted out 'Up on the Catwalk' and 'Someone Somewhere'. Bliss.

The following year, my foot finally healed, I remember feeling utter, unfiltered joy while dancing to 'New Gold Dream' and the entire oeuvre at NYC's Roseland Ballroom in October 2013.

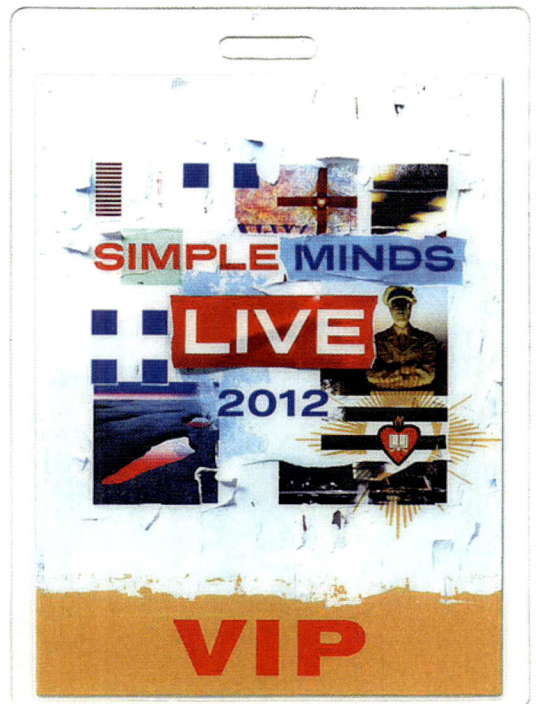

It's truly incredible that a band and its songs can colour the tapestry of your life; they can remind you of some of the most beautiful, poignant moments of your existence, and continue to make every synapse, cell and nerve-ending inside your body hum with energy and vigour. In 30 years, as I enjoy retirement in Sedona, Arizona, I will leap out of my rocking chair at the faintest strains of 'Alive and Kicking', look up at the infinite heavens and feel blessed that Simple Minds' songs sustained me my entire life and brought me incalculable happiness.

## ROB MCCANN

*Birmingham Academy*
*24 February 2012, Birmingham, England*

In 1984 my parents bought a new stereo for the sitting room and said I could have the old one for my bedroom. I was 13, just getting into music but without anything to play on it. A schoolfriend badgered me for a while to listen to a cassette he seemed to carry around with him everywhere he went. The band? Simple Minds. The album? *New Gold Dream*. It took one play before I decided I had to buy it so, armed with my pocket money, I headed to the record shop at the bottom of Leamington Spa to buy it. They didn't have it in stock, but had the 12-inch singles of 'Glittering Prize' and 'Someone Somewhere' along with a plain navy blue-sleeved LP, *Real to Real Cacophony*. I bought all three.

Because I knew the *New Gold Dream* singles, I put *Real to Real* on first. My initial reaction was that it was very different and maybe they'd given me the wrong record. I was at that point unaware of their soon-to-be-bought back-catalogue (purchased from a hifi shop in Warwick) and their changing musical styles.

There have been many live highlights but the *5x5* show at Birmingham Academy is at the top. I never dreamt I would get to hear tracks like 'Scar', 'Changeling' and '70 Cities as Love Brings the Fall' in a live setting. I'm never happier than when driving along shouting out the Italian cities with Jim whilst listening to '70 Cities' from the live boxset for *5x5* released after the tour.

# RON HUTCHISON

*Barrowland*
*25 February 2012, Glasgow,*
*Scotland*

It was Tony Blackburn's fault really. And Adam Ant. It was 1982, and I needed a new band to listen to. Adam had split up his Ants, leaving 11-year-old me distraught. I looked for somebody else to fill that void, and the wall space vacated by the torn-down Ant posters.

I found them on Radio 1, and Tony Blackburn's show. 'Promised You A Miracle' was the song. I'll be honest and say it didn't really grab me first listen, but the fact Simple Minds were Scottish sealed the deal for me. A Scottish band? I'd never heard the like. So began the journey that continues to this day. The old albums were snapped up and pored over, and by the time of *Live in the City*

*Ron Hutchison has Tony Blackburn to thank for introducing him to Simple Minds*

*of Light* in 1987, I was taking Mondays off work on the day of Simple Minds album releases, so I could have the whole day with my shiny new records.

As good as the albums were, seeing them live was where it was at. It started with a gig here, a gig there, then two in a row, then three. I think you can guess the rest. The meet-ups soon followed, and over the years I've met some wonderful people I'm now very proud to call friends, always available for a pint or two, and a chat about the latest tour or album.

Highlights? If I had to narrow it down, I'd say the Barrowland in 2012, when they had the marvellous idea to tour the first five albums. To hear old classics like 'Pleasantly Disturbed', 'Wasteland', 'Chelsea Girl' and 'Room' in what you could call the spiritual home of Simple Minds was a night that will stay with me forever.

And 2002, Aberdeen. I guess you could say it was the comeback tour. I hadn't seen them live in seven years, and to be honest, I didn't know what to expect. Had they still got it? I left the venue two hours later knowing I shouldn't have worried. Looking and sounding totally fresh, they gave a performance in my hometown I don't think they've bettered since.

I'm very grateful I tuned into Radio 1 that day almost 40 years ago. I'm even more grateful I chose Simple Minds to be 'my' band. Not only have they given me wonderful music and gigs over the years, they've introduced me to some marvellous cities on my travels seeing them, and I've met fantastic friends along the way.

'Some say we'll be together for a very long time,
Some say that our first impressions never will lie.'

I think that sums it up very well. Thank you, Tony Blackburn.

## MARC NJIST

My buddy Jan and I are travelling to Glasgow to see the band perform as part of the *5x5* tour. It's my 29th Simple Minds gig in 25 years and I'm as excited as ever. Whilst flying Jan tells me about an article in his computer magazine. A new program enables users to retrieve deleted pictures from their SD card. This information will later prove to be of utmost importance....

The band rock everyone's world. A trip down memory lane to my youth and experiences with several

*Marc and Jim in the photo security tried to delete - photo Marc Njist*

old songs. The performances have only become better throughout the years. At the end the band receives a thunderous applause.

The next day we're walking through security at the airport. Jan forgets to take off his belt. Whilst waiting on him, I see Jim Kerr waiting for his trolley. I'm not sure whether to approach him or not. I finally gather the courage to ask if he's willing to take pictures with us. He turns out to be really friendly and down-to-earth. He warns me of possible problems with security because of the background of our picture, which I ignore.

After having pictures taken with us and a chat about the concert and venue, Jim leaves for his flight. An airport security guard approaches me, wants to check the pictures. Jan's picture with Jim is okay - the background is neutral, but he tells me to erase my picture with Jim - you're not allowed to take pictures with security equipment in view. With a heavy heart I delete it.

Back home I recall the article Jan mentioned. A Google search finds the program I need. I feel my heartbeat racing. I see all kinds of deleted pictures reappearing on my computer screen, when I finally notice the one I'm looking for. The sensation I'm experiencing almost parallels the one at the concert. I'm so unbelievably happy I got that picture back. It's an unerasable collector's item for my 'Book of Brilliant Things'.

# MEGAN GUY

It wasn't until my final year at university in Belfast that I stumbled upon a welcome distraction to my exams: Simple Minds' back-catalogue. I watched all their videos on YouTube and listened to all their albums on Spotify. I just loved the sounds and atmospheres created, a complete escape from the pressures of final year. I played those albums non-stop, finding any excuse to play them at house parties and trying to convince the DJs at the Queen's Student Union to play Simple Minds during the busiest student nights. I even bought a t-shirt with the *Empires and Dance* cover on it.

I learned that Simple Minds hailed from Glasgow. At the time I'd never been there, despite it being fairly close to home, but the more I listened to Simple Minds, the more I was keen to visit.

I graduated. Jobs were scarce post-credit crunch. I was starting to give up hope but noticed a three-month engineering job in Glasgow, right on the waterfront, so naturally that was my go-to song when I was gearing myself for interview. I found myself moving to Glasgow in September 2011. I knew no one but within a day felt completely at home walking around the city with my iPod, listening to Simple Minds. Their music was a guided tour of the city.

A few months later I learned Simple Minds were playing Barrowland, performing their first five albums. It felt like the show was put on just for me! I went along: my first Glasgow show and my first seeing Simple Minds. It was simply magical. I knew every song and was jumping up and down in my *Empires and Dance* t-shirt, much to the amusement of others.

I immediately bought tickets for Manchester the next weekend, convincing my brother to come along. Again, I jumped up and down in my *Empires and Dance* t-shirt, and brought a banner with me reading 'Simple Minds love Simple Minds', the love a Claddagh of course. After the show my brother and I hung around outside the venue for an hour or so and managed to strike up a conversation with Charlie as he was leaving. He asked about my accent - Armagh - and was pleasantly surprised to find I'd been at Barrowland the week before. We got a picture taken with him holding the banner, which he insisted be turned inside out to look more like the Cyrillic typeface on *Empires and Dance*. I haven't come across a stronger Weegie accent than Charlie's!

I've now seen Simple Minds five times and introduced friends and family to their music and shows. If it wasn't for Simple Minds, would I have ever gone to Glasgow and got myself a job I really enjoy, met a ton of amazing folk and met my other half, a native Southsider? Who would have thought music could have that impact?

# SIMON HAYWARD

'I know you, don't tell me… I'll get it,' said the taxi driver, looking at Jim in the rear view mirror. 'Simply Tony?'

Following my induction of being 'Burchilled' (which involves a four day recovery programme), I found myself playing keyboards with the Simple Minds 'Electroset'. This was a stripped-down format which enabled promotional show performances that historically had been impractical to do.

Having enthusiastically followed the band for 30 years, in 2012 our parallel existence finally converged. For a fan, this was a dream and the ultimate ticket. Never meet your heroes? My expectations could not have been more exceeded.

*Simon Hayward and the kitchen tsunami incident*

Despite having an encyclopaedic knowledge of all things Simple Minds, my first discovery was I knew but the tip of the iceberg. The behind the scenes anecdotes were endless and usually hysterical. On our numerous adventures together, Simply Tony (as we would fondly dub the Electroset) would add to that legacy with an array of situations.

These briefly include:

'Oh no, the dog is dead'.

'It's spitting' – 'Tsunami' – 'Run!'

Half of the stage is now missing.

'The keyboards are underwater – does this matter?'

Standing ankle deep in water as lightning strikes all around.

Jim climbs a ladder to help a kitchen girl fix an imploding roof.

4x4 off-road evacuation is not complementary to a sound engineer's spinal surgery recovery.

Finding two broken acoustic guitars and making them into one so the show can go on.

Charlie heroically (and appropriately) can perform 'Riders on the Storm' solo with two broken strings.

The strangest after-show party involves debating that the length of an Olympic swimming pool is not to the kitchen and back.

And this was just one show! Amidst the chaos, my defining memory is of Elaine, our canine-bereaved tour manager, calmly announcing, 'I've ordered more hummus… and alcohol.' Fixes everything.

It's been a privilege to have a small part in Simple Minds continuing story. I visited the top of the mountain… and it was good. Burning gold memories indeed.

Until Simply Tony ride again…

# ALEXANDER CALDEIRA

My history with the band started in the Nineties, when I started going out with friends at night to enjoy parties. The band marked so many good moments in my life, good and bad moments, that I adopted them as the soundtrack of my life. I got married to the sound of Simple Minds - the songs I entered the church to were two songs from the band!

---

# ELIZABETH PARKER

A gleaming white (okay, there was rust), Mini Cooper blazes past me. The driver - a bronzed boy, unaware that he is my current obsession - has the windows down, shades on, and 'Sanctify Yourself' is blaring. He glances my way, that nanosecond of attention confirming that he must share my epic teenage passion. Hmmm, nope! And hindsight tells me that if the universe had any hand in that romance, it would have picked 'Ghostdancing' for the backing track.

The boy has faded to a charming memory but the music has never left my side. If a movie were made of my life, think *Bridget Jones* meets *Silence of the Lambs*. The soundtrack would be almost exclusively Simple Minds. From the mid-Eighties on, I have devoured every track, every lyric, and any and all media. I'm the shy type of stalker. I take any opportunity to promote and share the minutiae of the band's existence, but would squirm with mortification to learn they'd ever been aware of it before now.

I should confess that I nearly ran Jim over once. Lost after the Hyde Park Mandela Rally, I was high-fiving my navigator for finally reading the map round the right way when Jim wandered into the road right in front of us. One weirdly perfect emergency stop later I slunk as low as I could, beetroot embarrassed, and peered through my fingers, as Mr 'Oblivious To His Near Death Experience' vaguely acknowledged us with a wave and sauntered off.

Their music and lyrics have been solace and inspiration for decades. They have helped deter a suicide attempt, they've played matchmaker, been my crutch through grief, helped bring me out of a coma and played at the birth of my youngest child, They've been the epic theme and the gentle incidental music behind so many moments. I am simply, deeply thankful.

# BERT PEETERS

*Rock Werchter 2012*
*30 June 2012, Werchter, Belgium*

The *5x5* show I saw at Werchter was amazing, and I convinced some of my friends to come along. It was magic, playing Werchter in the afternoon. After the show, I went to Holland and Bospop at Weert just across the border to see them again.

# ALISON ANDERSON

*O2 Academy*
*8 July 2012, Newcastle, England*

I've been a fan of live music since my brother took me to see Adam and the Ants when I was 12. He followed this by taking me to *Live Aid* at Wembley when I was 17. It's pretty easy to see how I got hooked. It would be fair to say live music became my joy, my love and my solace.

In 2011 I was diagnosed with multiple sclerosis. I played badminton on the Monday night and by Sunday was in a wheelchair. I was 42 and being taught to walk again. I had five severe relapses, in and out of a wheelchair, within the year. I retired from an amazing career as a psychiatric nurse that spanned 26 years. My life as I knew it was over. I thought my days of live music and gigs were over as well.

Simple Minds' music had seen me though some great times and some very difficult ones. The music has given me great joy, education (where I first heard of Nelson Mandela) and comfort. I decided to make the trip to Newcastle to see them at the 02 Academy on the *5x5* tour the following year. I wasn't sure how or if I would manage. I also, stubbornly, wanted to stand.

I had the most amazing night, remembering why I love live music so much and the importance of living your life. The words simply hit home more. I realised live music would always be a major part of my life. I can't express enough the great joy Simple Minds and that night brought me. Music is in my veins, their music runs freely in my heart, and I was so grateful for the confidence that I had 'got my life back' that I dropped an email to them. I wanted to express my gratitude for all they had brought to my life and for giving me a reason to 'carry on'. I truly felt that gig gave me not just hope but my life back.

I was delighted to be invited to meet the band during the next tour. That 10 minutes of their time was a delight for me and will stay with me always. Thank you, Jim and Charlie, for the joy you've brought. You should be very proud of how you've touched the lives of others through your music. It means so much to many than you'll ever know. And I hope there's so much more to come.

# STUART HOLLAND

My live adventure with the band ended on 8th July 2012 at Newcastle due to ill health. But if I could have made up in my head a way to end my live adventures with a band who have nearly always been a part of my life, I would never have seen it end this way. It all started with me getting a backstage pass after me telling my story to Elaine at Simple Minds Management. On that day I felt that bad I'd decided not to go. That was until Elaine phoned me that morning at home asking if I'd like to come down earlier and watch the band rehearse. Wow! I couldn't turn that down, no matter how I felt. When I arrived they'd already started. To stand in the middle of a concert hall watching the band play, it felt like my own personal Simple Minds concert.... It blew me away.

Then to hear the band do an instrumental and watch Jim Kerr walk towards me, I could feel my legs shaking. I was that nervous, meeting my idol. After about 20 minutes chatting, Jim said he needed to go and get something to eat before the show, shook my hand and thanked me for coming. I thought that was it, but Elaine told me she's never known during the history of Simple Minds for Jim to ever do what he did next.

After walking away to get his dinner he stopped and shouted at me, asking if I'd like to join him for a bite to eat. For the next hour or so I sat at the same table as Jim, Charlie and Ged with Andy and Mel at the next table. We talked about everything, Jim gave me a handful of souvenirs and it was like some big blur - I think I was in shock the whole way through.

That was the first and last time I saw the best band in the world live. And I couldn't have wished for a better way for it to end. So thank you to everyone that helped make a dream come true.

---

# BILL BARCLAY

*Simple Minds tour manager 2010 - 2015*
*Dalhalla*
*13 July 2012, Rättvik, Sweden*

We played an incredibly-unique venue in northern Sweden called Dalhalla, an amphitheatre built at the bottom of a huge abandoned quarry. I believe that thousands of years ago a large meteor had hit the location. The night before, we stayed at a small family hostel called Villa Langbergs in Tallberg. The views from the hotel were amazing. We arrived at Dalhalla in the late afternoon for the soundcheck. The amphitheatre stage was encircled by a moat with fish in it. After the soundcheck, Jim decided to go for a swim. Nobody else took up the challenge but out popped Jim and plunged straight into the moat. In the buff! Skinny-dipping at his own show! I believe Charlie has photos….

I also remember a one-off at the V8 Supercars weekend on the Gold Coast in Australia. It was quite a long haul for one show, but a beautiful location. We stayed at the Palazzo Versace Gold Coast, the hotel used by *I'm a Celebrity… Get Me Out of Here!* It's a great place, surrounded by a marina and nice restaurants. Jim, Charlie, Andy, Jim's dad, Charlie's partner and I went whale-watching off the Gold Coast and were lucky enough to see a few whales (I think Jim got a photo of a whale onboard the boat, but that's another story).

On our day off, myself, Charlie, Ged and Andy went to see Steely Dan and Steve Winwood at a local vineyard. It was a fantastic show and the Minds returned two years later to play the same vineyard tour, with Devo supporting. We also visited Blondie at their show in Sydney, where she had The Stranglers supporting.

On the way home, Jim, his dad, Charlie, Andy and myself stopped over in Hong Kong for a few days and did the tourist sightseeing thing, sailing around the harbour,

*Facilities-Dalhalla-Stage and aerial shot. Photos by Bill Barclay*

the mountain viewpoint, Kowloon, etc.

Another nice moment was playing the Rolling Stones show at Rock Werchter, Belgium in 2014. Minds had a great show to a huge crowd, plus a close-up view of the Stones camp!

In Tromsø, Norway for a show inside the Arctic Circle, Charlie, Ged, Andy and I went to a great seafood restaurant for dinner the evening before. After nice food and a few glasses of wine, we headed back to the hotel to find some of our loyal crew getting in a minibus to go up the mountain, hoping to see the Northern Lights. We decided to jump in too. We parked the vehicle then had a 45-minute hike through deep snow to a small round shed up on the mountain. There was a lovely blazing fire inside, and refreshments. Within five minutes of arriving - Eureka! - there in front of us was the full display of the Northern Lights. The sky was so clear you could also see satellites passing overhead. I'll remember that the rest of my life. We were so lucky - it had been overcast in Tromso for three weeks prior to us playing there.

A few days later we were invited to the F15 airbase in Bodo, Norway. Not only were we allowed to sit in a fully- operational F15 fighter jet, but Mel went up in a trainer aircraft with a pilot instructor. The hospitality was fantastic and we were able to reciprocate, inviting the base commander and a few pilots to the show in Bodo.

---

# ROBERTO COPELLO

*Piazza Grande*
*26 July 2012, Modena, Italy*

When in my life I have the wind in my stern and the energy that emanates from all my pores, I look for Simple Minds and listen to Simple Minds to seal my state of pure spiritual and intellectual power. And in this state, my emotions come out like a river in flood, and my mind begins to dream. Simple Minds are the power that mixes with melody, with mystery.

*Roberto saw the Minds in Modena. Photo by Roberto Copello*

# CAMILLO CORSETTI ANTONINI

*Ippodromo Delle Capannelle*
*27 July 2012, Rome, Italy*

Simple Minds are back in Rome, at Capannelle, an immense arena set in an hippodrome on the southern outskirts of Rome, a 40-minute drive from home. I ride my motorcycle to meet friends there. Halfway, I have an accident and my leg is stuck under the bike. I manage to stand up, apparently with no major damage. It looks like I am okay. I ride to the gig. It's towards the end, the band playing 'New Gold Dream', that my left foot begins to hurt. And swells. I manage to make it back home, carefully picking a route without many junctions, so I won't need to use the foot to change gear. Next day I'm in ER and the left malleolus (my ankle) is in pieces. Yes, 40 days in a cast. But what a gig!

# KENT GRATION

*A Day on the Green, Sirromet Wines*
*9 December 2012, Mount Cotton, Brisbane, Australia*

My fascination with Simple Minds started when I was 14, when I borrowed (and kept!) my brother's cassette of *Once Upon a Time*. I'd play it over and over and realised this was the same band that did 'Don't You (Forget About Me)'. What a revelation! With posters on my wall of Jim, Charlie, Mick, John and Mel, I'd wonder at the chemistry and magic these maestros created, especially when listening to *Live in the City of Light*, which came with a live Australian recording of 'Someone Somewhere (in Summertime)'. This showed their true connection to time and place, and how valid their music was, wherever it was played in the world.

I missed out on the Simple Minds tour of 1989, but bought the tour t-shirt anyway, along with a paisley vest similar to Jim's onstage wardrobe style at the time, to emulate his style and take on a Jimmy-like persona.

In the summer of 2012, after all those years following the band, my dream came true and I got to see these guys at Sirromet, Brisbane during their *Glasgow* tour. With The Church and Devo as support, this was surely going to be a night to remember, and I bought the tour t-shirt to relive it beyond that night. With Mel on drums, Charlie with a busted hand on guitar, and Jim ever the showman owning the night and the crowd, my voice was hoarse from belting out their back-catalogue. I drove home that night thinking it was well worth waiting 25 years to experience these magicians.

## GARETH BUTLER

*Waterfront Hall*
*28 March 2013, Belfast, Northern Ireland*

My story begins with 'Promised You a Miracle' from the days of school discos but my true love for the band stems originally from the *Live in the City of Light* album and in particular the 'Promised You...' version from that. It was a complete rework and a much more bombastic arena-sounding Simple Minds. I followed them intently from there, but what made me (and many others) feel my band connection was 'Belfast Child'. Aside from me being a Belfast boy all my living years, they shot the video in the Castlereagh Hills, off The Rocky Road to be exact, and I live less than a mile from there, up in those hills. So the connection us fans occasionally feel was a personal one for me.

I saw them in Belfast at the Waterfront Hall (fitting, eh?) six or so years ago and it served only as a reminder of why I did and still do hold them and their music as a talisman in the journey of my life.

Never sway from what you do best, lads. You certainly do it best! Thanks for the music and the journey.

## RICHARD GILDER

*Civic Hall*
*6 April 2013, Wolverhampton, England*

I guess it all began when I was working at Webster Mouldings with a great bunch of lads - Bucko, Barney, Daz, Wadders and Rob - five lads who, like me, loved music. We'd borrow each other's records and recommend bands to listen to. We all loved

Simple Minds. Most of the lads had seen them before but I hadn't until the *Street Fighting Years* tour, when I saw them play Birmingham, Cardiff, Wembley Stadium and then three more nights in Birmingham.

I've now seen them 37 times. My favourite gig has to be when they played Cannock Chase in 2011. It was so close to my home area, it was like having them play in my back garden. Another gig that stands out was the *Acoustic* tour at Birmingham Symphony Hall in 2017, with the opening track of 'New Gold Dream'. Jim came into the crowd and started shaking hands with fans. I was sitting in the balcony and missed the chance.

The lads all went their different ways - got married, had kids, moved away to different places. But in 2013 we started to get in touch again. Simple Minds announced a gig in Wolverhampton and we arranged a reunion, a night out and a chance for us all to go together to see Simple Minds again. That night, we talked about gigs we'd each been to in the intervening years and realised we'd attended the same ones, not knowing. But we'd heard each other's favourite songs being played and when we did, we'd think of those days together.

## GISELA JACKSON

*Plymouth Pavilions*
*9 April 2013, Plymouth, England*

It was 1989. I was 16. I heard 'Belfast Child' for the first time on the radio. I fell in love. The words and the instruments played created this moving and beautiful piece about something so tragic happening in Northern Ireland. That was it for me. I went to the local record store in Plymouth, bought the tape of *Street Fighting Years* and played it endlessly in my bedroom. Each song represented sad and difficult times. I went to my record store again to find previous albums and one by one bought these over the course of several months. I can honestly say I've never heard a bad album. Each one different, yet unmistakably Simple Minds. When I got the chance to see them in April 2013 at Plymouth Pavilions I was thrilled. They did not disappoint. I was up in the stalls giving it welly, singing and dancing.

## CHERYL WESLEY

We have travelled the length and breadth of the country by car, motorbike, train and even plane to see them. We were also lucky enough to be able to stay in Jim's hotel in Taormina for my husband Paul' 40th birthday present. Whilst we were there we got married and had the pleasure of meeting Jim on our wedding day. Amazing memories

# GRAEME TRUDGHILL

*Winter Gardens*
*16 April 2013, Margate, England*

Simple Minds mean so much to me, my sister Marian and my best friend Crispin. We have seen them so many times at every opportunity possible. It's that one day a year when we all spend the day together, travelling and anticipating the setlist - without looking online first! Always one to try to capture the moment, I try to take few pics of the band performing, which didn't end well at the Astoria when they confiscated my camera. But as I was marched down the stairs by security during 'All the Things She Said' I managed to rewind and remove the film. At Record Store Day many years later, I got to meet Jim and Charlie, who signed the images and complimented me on them.

   We often start queuing around lunchtime to ensure we can get in the front row, on the left where Charlie plays, and my sister was delighted to catch his plectrum at *Rock the Dock* at the Excel Centre. We are so grateful for such golden memories. A top one is 1991 and the *Real Life* tour, when Jim appeared at the start under a single spotlight in a white shirt, saying 'Let me see your hands', as the wall of sound began.

---

# MICHAEL C GRASSO

I was living with my mother on the top floor of a building in Candida, a small Italian hill town near Avellino, when a Hare Krishna monk came to our door, I invited him in and we had a long conversation on spiritual matters. Before leaving he gave me the *Bhagavad Gita* to read. Being out of work I ended up reading and meditating on it, including its commentaries, for several weeks. I played *New Gold Dream* while I read it. I tried changing the music to other bands I loved such as Pink Floyd and Genesis. None created the atmosphere of four or five songs from *New Gold Dream*.

   A year later, I had returned home from work and was passing by the living room when I heard one of those songs from *New Gold Dream* on the TV. It was a documentary on the *Bhagavad Gita* and all the songs used in the documentary were the same four or five songs I had listened a year earlier. That's when I remembered the strange encounter with the Hare Krishna monk. I asked my mother and others if they'd ever seen a Hare Krishna monk in our town before or since but no one ever had.

---

# YVONNE BIRD

*Colston Hall*
*29 April 2013, Bristol, England*

One day I saw an advert for Simple Minds' *Celebrate* tour. I booked a ticket immediately for a 2013 gig at Colston Hall. No one I knew wanted to see them so I went on my own. I was curious as to how they looked and sounded after so many years. I was up in the balcony, well away from the stage. Jim wore just a white shirt and jeans, when I had it in my head he would be wearing something quite unusual, having remembered how he looked in the 'Promised You a Miracle' video and how he dressed at *Live Aid*. During the first half of their gig, I didn't know many of their songs, but

*Yvonne Bird didn't like 'Promised You a Miracle'. It was 30 years later that she saw the band*

it didn't matter. The music was wonderful and had a great beat! During the interval, I got a bottle of water but the barman kept the top ('Bottle tops off by order of the band!') and just as the music started after the interval the bottle tipped over under my seat and my new unread tour brochure was ruined. After the gig I had to buy another and didn't look at it until I got home, whereupon I opened it to the first page and there was this lovely welcome message from Jim to fans past and present. My first thought was, 'Wonderful words, Jim'. And that was it! My lightbulb moment!

I've been extremely fortunate to have attended 33 Simple Minds gigs since, my favourites being Taormina Teatro Antico in 2014, the most beautiful ancient venue I have ever been in, the wonderful Laeiszhalle in Hamburg during the *Acoustic* tour in 2017, and the Wentworth BMW golfing event gig in 2019. Luckily most of the fans in attendance were right at the front, and with great lighting and positioning, I managed to take some amazingly clear photos.

# JOHN COLQUHOUN

*Count Basie Theatre*
*12 July 2013, Red Bank, New Jersey*

My wife and I flew from Florida to New Jersey to see Simple Minds for

*John and his wife flew in from Florida. Photo - Vince Barker*

the first time. I have the ALAN tattoo and my wife is next to me in the photo. This is definitely my favourite concert ever.

---

## PETE BELL

### *Radio 2 Live in Hyde Park*
### *8 September 2013, London, England*

After hearing *New Gold Dream* and seeing Simple Minds at Earl's Court, I tried to see them on every tour. In 1991, we visited our folks back up north and I got tickets for Gateshead Stadium. My wife was dropping me off. Just as we pulled up, the heavens opened up and torrential rain came down for 15 minutes. OMD were playing. When the rain stopped, I went into the stadium. Everyone was soaked. Simple Minds came on, did another magical set, including 'Let There Be Love' and a superb version of 'Belfast Child', Jim's voice haunting. Halfway through, the wind picked up and kids started falling over with hypothermia, being wrapped in aluminised blankets and carted off. In August!

In 2013, I got a ticket to the special enclosure for *Radio 2 Live in Hyde Park*. When I arrived I could hear Simple Minds performing and by the time I got through the gate they'd finished their set. Bollocks! I watched a couple of other bands then went to the special enclosure, where I got a burger and coke for lunch. I was sat at a table and two women joined me, so we nattered. I told them I had got there late and missed Simple Minds. One of the women said, 'Isn't that the bloke from Simple Minds?'

We were sat just where the performers went between the stage and dressing rooms. I rushed over. It was Jim Kerr! I shook his hand, told him I was a long-time fan and I'd got there late. In his soft Scottish accent he said, 'Aye, we were on a wee bit early.' I chatted to him for a couple of minutes and told him he had a fantastic voice.

Five minutes later I looked over and shouted 'Charlie Burchill!' I rushed over to shake Charlie's hand, told him I was a long-time fan, loved the band and his playing. What started out as a disappointing day turned out to be a fantastic one. You couldn't meet nicer blokes. The only mistake I made was that I asked a bloke 'is that Jim Kerr?' and he said yes. I think it was Mel Gaynor, one of the finest drummers that ever hit the skins. Sorry Mel.

---

## ANNA KARINA MAGALHAES

*Auditório Oi Araújo Vianna*
*5 October 2013, Porto Alegre, Brazil*

I was a child when I heard 'Don't You (Forget About Me)' in Rio de Janeiro in 1988. I was sat on the sofa at our beach house and remember thinking, 'Wow! This song is incredible.' That night I fell in love with Simple Minds.

When I knew the *Celebrate* tour was to pass through Brazil, I didn't think twice! I bought a ticket for the first row and travelled six hours by plane to see Simple Minds for the first time in Porto Alegre. My heart almost exploded when I saw my favourite band on stage, singing all the hits that have marked my entire life. Jim commented on the photo I posted on Facebook, saying 'great pic'. He is adorable!

---

## JON JASKOLKA

*9:30 Club*
*18 October 2013, Washington DC*

Until 'Don't You (Forget About Me)' was being played seemingly everywhere in America in 1985, none of their music had come across the airwaves to the small rural town in which I grew up. And the nearest proper record store was 40 miles away. Does that tell you anything about the scene - or lack of - surrounding my teen years in the 1980s?

My wife and I drove almost 700 miles to attend the show at the 9:30 Club in DC after securing tickets via the internet. It's my kind of concert hall, with its small stage and standing room only arrangement. Seeing the band live for the first time and hearing so many iconic songs from across the years was a lot to take in. I knew them all, but the live performance was so amazing that I quickly realised one show was not going to be enough.

When the band announced that they would be returning to the USA for an extensive tour for the *Walk Between Worlds* album, I started making plans to attend several shows and went to 10 gigs in total. Aside from taking the train from Atlanta to the show in Washington DC, the rest of my travel was by car - 6,320 miles all told. My wife and I attended the Nashville show together, as that's our home city, and my brother and his wife joined me in Atlanta. All of the rest I attended solo.

I've numerous memories - the soundcheck sessions, asking a question during the Q&A in Bethlehem, receiving various stage souvenirs (setlists, drumsticks, guitar picks), a meet and greet in New Orleans, and all of the fans I met at the different shows. I could have asked Jim and Charlie so many questions regarding their music but spent almost the whole time answering questions they asked me! I walked away from that with the impression of how genuine they seemed to be as people, and how gracious they are to their fans.

They bring an enormous amount of energy to the stage, as if they're still trying to prove themselves, even after 40 years. I pretty well had the setlist down after the first three or four shows, generally knew what was coming each night, but not for one second thought, 'OK then, I've had enough.' If anything, I enjoyed the next show even more than the last. Their performances are among the best I've seen in 35 years attending concerts.

# BENJAMIN HATCHER

*Metropolis*
*21 October 2013, Montreal, Canada*

It was 1981 and I was 12, playing billiards in a coffee shop with my dad in hometown, Quebec City, Canada. Over the loudspeaker came pulsating drums and bass, followed by screaming guitar, then a singer sounding just so cool, so sure of himself, like he understood it all. The chorus, 'Love song... love song... love song', accompanied by its assuring keyboard counterpart, penetrated my psyche and emotional interior.

I took a bus to the record store and found a tape of *Sons and Fascination*. I was a very sensitive kid and music affected me greatly; it was my refuge. I was instantly grabbed by the atmospheric world of that album; it headed right to my core. The songs were haunting, edgy, raw, futuristic... I hadn't heard anything like it. I played that tape constantly on my Walkman until it breathed its last breath and gave its life to that great audio cassette heaven in the sky.

As a teenager of the '80s, I became very involved in social causes: nuclear disarmament, the environment, anti-apartheid. I admired artists putting their money where their mouths were - denouncing, promoting, organising concerts for noble pursuits. It was a great time to be alive... and kicking. By the end of the decade, with *Street Fighting Years* on my Walkman, Mandela walking free and me marrying my beautiful wife, anything seemed possible.

I can't remember why I didn't see the band in Montreal in 1986 where I was studying, but better late than never. When I told Jim Kerr in 2013 after the Montreal show that Simple Minds were the soundtrack to my life, I meant it. Thank you for the music.

# MARTIN GIROUX

Simple Minds at the Montreal Forum in 1986 was a show I did not want to miss. My older brother, Ben, saw them a few months earlier at the Maurice Richard Arena. Now it was my turn. Montreal was an hour east of Granby in Eastern Townships, where I lived with my parents. But the end of my high school semester was approaching and I had to study for exams. And although it was beautiful Spring outside, I was anxious because Chernobyl happened a month before.

The timing was not good. An exam was scheduled at school on the morning of the show. Clearly, I couldn't go to Montreal. My consolation was Les Canadiens winning ice hockey's Stanley Cup that year! I was delighted when the band released *Live in the City of Light* though, giving me an idea of what I'd missed the year before.

I finally saw Simple Minds in October 2013 at the Metropolis. After work I changed into my Levi's and my favourite *New Gold Dream* t-shirt and got to the second row. Jim Kerr saw me as the show was about to start, smiled and said, 'Nice t-shirt'. The best show of my life!

---

# JULIE FOURNEL

*Massey Hall*
*22 October 2013, Toronto, Canada*

I was 10, going on 11, in the fall of 1983. I used to religiously watch the TV show *Radio Vidéo* produced in Montreal. That night, host Claude Rajotte introduced he video for the newly-released 'Waterfront'. I've been under the band's spell since.

I purchased a tape of *Once Upon a Time* in 1985. I'd recorded 'Don't You (Forget About Me)' from the radio). A high school classmate recommended *New Gold Dream*, which, in her opinion, was even better. I was happy I followed her advice. I listened to it daily, sometimes many times each day, for at least a full year. It gave me the strength to go through a difficult period of my teenage years.

*Julie Fournel was at Massey Hall*

Being a francophone, my English was not very good, but I would read the lyrics and try to translate them with my French-English dictionary. I remember not being able to understand the meaning of 'Catherine Wheels', being quite frustrated. I certainly

learned a good deal of English vocabulary trying to make sense of their lyrics.

I remember vividly Simple Minds' performance during *Live Aid* and thinking, 'What a great band! They're as good live as in the studio.' That was another milestone.

I was about to start college and had just started working part-time. I was asking myself many questions about the meaning of life and my future. *Street Fighting Years* accompanied me through those soul-searching years. 'This is Your Land' was very special for me. I probably didn't understand it for what it was. For me, it meant 'this is your life, follow your dreams'.

I saw *Simple Minds Live in Verona* on Much Music, the Canadian version of MTV, and recorded it on a VHS cassette, which I watched an incredible amount of times. I knew every one of Jim's moves by heart. And my hope was to be able to see them live one day.

Suddenly they disappeared from the North American market. It was difficult to get information about the band, and even more difficult to get albums. But I kept listening to my Simple Minds collection.

In 2005, I saw them perform on a show called *Taratata* on TV5, the international French-language television channel, playing a song from the album *Black &White 050505*. I was in love again!

The most meaningful year of my life is 2013: my sweetie and I got married, and we saw Simple Minds live for the first time in Toronto a couple of weeks after our wedding. It was the best wedding gift I could hope for and a full circle moment. I felt like my soul had left my body for a few hours. I was in heaven.

We got to see them live again in Toronto in 2018. We had pretty good tickets. I never thought I could see them so close up. I even considered going to the stage to shake hands, but shyness made me refrain from it.

They are close to my heart and always will be. Thank you for the great music, the beautiful lyrics and the special moments.

---

## MATT NELSON

*Roseland Ballroom*
*24 October 2013, New York, New York*

As an American, I was late to the party. I knew in the mid-'80s '(Don't You) Forget About Me' was something special. It went on a mix-tape and I moved on with life, never buying a Simple Minds album but instead torturing my ears with the loud and obnoxious sounds of glam bands. In 1996, I discovered *Glittering Prize* in my girlfriend's CD collection. It changed my life. I began to gobble up everything I could find in record stores and married the girl with the good taste in music.

In 2002, I received *Cry* and fell in love with an underrated album. 'New Sunshine Morning', 'Spaceface' and 'Sleeping Girl' are candidates for the famous Simple Minds

Matt Nelson saw Simple Minds at New York's Roseland

live treatment, like 'Book of Brilliant Things' and more recently 'Dolphins'. In 2004, I received *The Silver Box* for Christmas. All five discs are now completely worn out and the box itself has seen better days.

Finally came my chance to see Simple Minds live, in NYC in 2013. I think I sang every word of every song. I loved 'Let the Day Begin' and 'Broken Glass Park'.

Then came the 2018 North America tour with a VIP meet and greet. I got to hear 'Book of Brilliant Things' live, featuring Sarah Brown, as well as new favourites (new to me) 'Hunter and the Hunted' and 'Signal and the Noise'. 'Dolphins' got a nice overhaul for the tour, and everyone raved about that.

I love how Simple Minds can take the recorded version of a regular tune and turn it into a live, epic experience. I have a small list of songs they could revisit. Many of them I sing while I'm out walking.

# SHARON FLORENÇA

### *Carnival City*
### *1 & 2 November 2013, Johannesburg,*
### *South Africa*

Growing up as teenagers in South Africa in the turbulent '80s, my brother and I were avid music lovers. He saved up his pocket money or used money from his part-time job to buy various LPs, including Simple Minds. That's when I became hooked. Their music has supported me through good and bad times, through being a shy teenager at high school, years of studying, an emotionally-draining divorce, long road trips - and just because I love their music. I often play them driving home, and my now teenage daughters know and enjoy their music too.

*Sharon discovered Simple Minds whilst growing up in Johannesburg*

When they played Johannesburg's Carnival City in November 2013, I booked tickets for myself, my hubby, brother and sister-in-law. We kept my brother in the dark - he had no clue where we were driving to and only clicked when we entered the foyer outside the arena and saw the poster on the wall. I'll never forget the pure joy on his face. An amazing, unforgettable night. We lived in the moment and felt like teenagers again.

Their special and instantly recognisable sound makes me feel young, easing away the tension at the end of a long day in my job as a high school teacher. Last year, a class asked what type of music I listened to. They didn't recognise Simple Minds. Oh my, they don't know what they've been missing!

## DEREK FOLEY

*Koko*
*7 November 2013, London, England*

I've seen the band in its many formats at Wembley Stadium, Milton Keynes Bowl and other big venues. At Wembley, 12 of us travelled up. I was on the pitch but right at the back for the support. Just before the Minds came on I began to move to the very front row, where it was absolutely manic, the crowd moving 30ft each way just trying to remain still. I was young, strong and much fitter and managed to last about 30 minutes until my laces came undone, forcing me back.

I remember taking my daughter with me to Koko and a show marking the 40th anniversary of Virgin Records. What a great night and a totally different experience, but memorable nevertheless. Having probably seen them 25 times I thought I was the biggest fan. But one year I bumped into a female travelling alone who'd seen every UK gig that year, then a friend of a friend who'd seen them at least 75 times.

## ALAN BURNS

*Hydro*
*27 November 2013, Glasgow, Scotland*

I've been a fan since I heard 'Love Song' and 'I Travel' at discos. DJ'ing for years in Cumbernauld at Reflections and Sax. 'Promised You a Miracle', 'I Travel', 'Love Song' and my personal favourite 'Don't You (Forget About Me)' were guaranteed floor-fillers. The drums in that are top drawer. I wanted to see them at their peak but tickets were like hen's teeth. But I did see them at the Hydro, with Ultravox as support. Jim's a great showman, and a good Hoops man!

# CHRISTINE MURDOCH

When it comes to Simple Minds - being a lady of a certain age - I was something of a late starter. I didn't go to my first Simple Minds gig until November 2013, when I saw them play the Hydro in Glasgow. I attended as a VIP guest with Jimmy Kerr Sr. His son Jim very kindly sent a car to take us straight to the venue. On arrival, we were met by a nice guy – I'll call him big Mel – who escorted us backstage and offered us refreshments. Did I get a surprise later - when the concert kicked off - to discover big Mel was the drummer!

Jimmy and I had great seats in the front circle. When they took the stage, the whole venue erupted, fans jumping up and down, cheering and singing. I don't mind admitting, but my first thought was, what a load of nutcases! But it seems that's perfectly normal behaviour at any Simple Minds gig.

To be honest, I didn't really know any of the songs apart from 'Don't You (Forget About Me)', so sat in my seat very strait-laced. But I did enjoy myself. I thought they were fantastic and decided, there and then, to find out more. Now I've got many of their records on CD. Every time I'm doing the ironing, on goes a Simple Minds album so I can work AND sing along.

Since that first gig in 2013, I've been to several at venues such as the Usher Hall in Edinburgh and the Opera House, Blackpool, plus hometown shows at the Royal Concert Hall, Barrowland and again at the Hydro. The atmosphere at every one was amazing. It was hard to beat! I also now know many more songs and, if asked to choose a favourite, it has to be 'Belfast Child'.

When we get clear of the current Covid-19 crisis, I hope to see Simple Minds play live again in 2021. But, sadly, without my sunshine, big Jimmy Kerr. It's thanks to him I'm now a real Simple Minds fan. They are simply the best.

---

# GERRY GARDNER

I discovered Simple Minds through Charlie's uncle, the janitor at the Drumchapel Youth Centre in the late '70s. I've followed them ever since and been to loads of concerts - I got soaked at Edinburgh Castle then again at Linlithgow Palace. Also saw them at the Glasgow Hydro when Jim welcomed us to his 'new hoose'.

---

# STEVIE SMITH

As part of my marriage separation, I got two concert tickets for the *Celebrate* tour. Not wishing to profit I decided on an 'all-office' email, offering the spare ticket free to the first colleague who replied, the only proviso a charitable donation of their choice.

Minutes later Angela, who joined the organisation a few weeks earlier, replied. A few days before, I gave her the ticket and - here's the kicker – her friend John had done sound engineer work for Jim and Charlie in the early days and could get us backstage. 'Yeah, that will be right,' I thought, but went along with it.

The concert was absolutely sensational and, post-encore, Angela took me to the backstage door to meet John. I was still sceptical but went along with it. Result! John appears with backstage wristbands. Off we trot to a large room at the back, drinks flowing. As a lifelong fan I'm thinking, 'Does it get any better than this?' It did. A few free beers down and John announces we have to follow him upstairs. We head to Charlie's dressing room! Anyone there that night will remember Jim announcing it was Charlie's birthday.

A short walk and I'm standing with Charlie and his family singing 'Happy Birthday' as he cuts his cake. To top it all I'm introduced and have a selfie with him. Before I left I popped into the toilet and spent a few minutes texting my mates to tell them I'm at Charlie's party. I strolled out of the Hydro and sauntered along the Broomielaw, wondering, 'Did that actually just happen?'

## DAVID JOHNSON

*Phones4U Arena*
*28 November 2013, Manchester, England*

I think that was the night after the Hydro date was filmed. Jim mentioned the band were a little 'tweaked'. Possibly Charlie's birthday too? Stand out was the new lighting rig and a pulsating 'Fear of Gods'. Superb.

## DAVID JAMES WHALE

*O2 Arena*
*30 November 2013, London, England*

Muriel Gray pretty much summed it up when Simple Minds appeared on *The Tube* in 1982: 'Here are the best band in the entire universe – Simple Minds!'

I never got to see them in their heyday but my dream came true in 2013 when they played the O2 Arena. I then saw them at Hampton Court Palace and got soaked in the rain. Another great gig was seeing them perform *New Gold Dream* in its entirety. It took me back to my teens – wonderful memories – those soaring songs I never tire of hearing. Their music, old and new, always resonates.

# PIP PIERREPOINT

My first experience of Simple Minds was at Leicester's De Montford Hall on the *New Gold Dream* tour. I went with a mate to keep him company and I'm so glad I did! Over the years, I mainly attended gigs with workmates here and there and members of my family. It wasn't really until the internet came along that a circle of friends was born for me, mainly consisting of close friend Michael Bagger Lees.

As time went by, I met a lovely lady on a dating site. One of my first questions was, 'Do you like music? Do you like Simple Minds?' Her

*Pip and Deborah got engaged backstage at the O2 and Deborah got to meet Jim*

answer was yes but she said she'd never seen them. 'Well, I can change that,' I replied.

Our first gig together was also at De Montfort Hall. I got in touch with Andy Gillespie to ask a favour. I wanted to propose to Deborah and I asked if he could announce and witness my proposal for her hand in marriage. Andy was very helpful and was going to meet us in the gardens of De Montfort Hall. Sadly it didn't happen - we went down with flu.

My next opportunity to propose would be at London's O2 Arena. This was a different ball game. It was an end of tour gig and there was massive security but Andy – with Jim's blessing - pulled it off. After an amazing show, we were escorted to the after-show party in the green room, where an array of superstars included Ultravox. I was so nervous but Andy put me at ease and the ceremony took place in the presence of band members and Jim's late father Jimmy, such a lovely man. Mine and Deborah's relationship was signed, sealed and cemented. What more could I ever wish for? The greatest band and the finest woman.

# DEBORAH PIERREPOINT

Pip got down on one knee and asked me to marry him. Of course, I said 'yes'. It was the happiest day for me and emotional too. I was so nervous but overcame when Jim put his arm round me for a photo.

# STUART CROUCH

*Simple Minds designer 2011 – present*

I was contacted by their management to do a poster for the *5X5 Live* tour. Then there was a boxset, an audio version of the live shows, and at the same time Virgin wanted to release the first five albums on CD. So I had those two jobs on. I think the next thing was *Celebrate: The Greatest Hits* album.

I've been to every tour since I started working with them. I can't say I was an avid fan before I worked for them but was certainly aware of them and had some of the records. But when you start working with a band you start immersing yourself in their music. I've done a lot of swotting up since.

There were kids at school who liked Simple Minds and U2. I remember at the school dance you'd have Simple Minds come on and a group of moody kids would start dancing. I was very much a Duran Duran fan. I wasn't in that club, but always bought *Smash Hits* and *NME* and everything, so was very aware of the album artwork - that's what I was into. I was a big fan of Malcolm Garrett and sometimes I'd buy albums just for his artwork. So when Simple Minds came along I knew their visual history.

I always try and sneak little references to the past in there. The first studio album I did for them was *Big Music.* The cover's got sort of a giant speaker ball in the sky on the front, but on the deluxe edition is a flat graphic. If you look at it from a certain angle it makes up the Celtic cross on the *New Gold Dream* album. Little subtle references like that. I did a re-issue of *New Gold Dream* a few years back and had to

# SIMPLE MINDS CELEBRATE

contact Malcolm. I was a bit worried about ringing him. I thought, am I taking on his work? I didn't know how he'd react, but he was very helpful and very nice.

Jim and Charlie are very much involved, nothing goes past them. It all has to go under their nose to make sure they're happy. Particularly Jim will come back with faults and sometimes he'll make suggestions or thinks we need to start again, or likes it but wants to develop it another way. There's always input from the band. When we've done various photoshoots with them or gone backstage after a gig with them, we'll often talk about whatever work is going on for a particular album or single and we'll discuss it.

First time I saw them was at the O2 on the *Celebrate* tour, the greatest hits. I thought they were phenomenal, the way they owned the stage and the layers of sound. I was blown away. I think that converted me really. I had friends who were Simple Minds fans but I'd not really paid them much attention. Seeing them cemented it for me. We had really good seats as well, because I'd worked on the stuff. I was looking forward to seeing them on this tour in particular because they were going to have big screens around them. That was quite something, to see all my artwork up on screen.

---

## NEIL HORNE

*Stonehaven Hogmanay Festival*
*31 December 2013, Stonehaven, Scotland*

History was made in a small Aberdeenshire town when Jim Kerr declared, 'Tonight, Stonehaven is the rock capital of the world.' He was speaking as the band starred at Open Air in the Square, one of the biggest Hogmanay music festivals in Scotland and an incredible event pulled off by a dedicated group of local volunteers. A fantastic scoop that only came about through outright cheek and sheer persistence. Before the event Jim took part in an amazing press conference on the clifftops at historic Dunnottar Castle, which made worldwide headlines with pictures of him being greeted by a pipe band and one of the town's famous fireball swingers. On the night more than 5,000 fans, some from as far afield as Australia and the USA, packed the seaside town's Market Square for a blistering live performance and to hear Jim declare, 'The doubters said it wouldnae happen... that it was going to rain... that there would be a plague of locusts... that there was going to be a tsunami. But we are Simple Minds and we deal with that stuff. Thanks for inviting us to your party. We won't forget this - ever!

---

# SIMON CORNWELL

*Facebook*
*7 November 2014, London, England*

Elaine from the band's management contacted me and asked if I wanted to see the band at Facebook. I ended up in Facebook's cavernous London canteen watching a stripped-down version of Simple Minds. It was part of a short acoustic tour - a line-up of Jim, Charlie and Mark Kerr - who'd been appearing on various radio stations and TV shows across Europe. The Facebook event tied in with the social network, so it included an online Q&A with Jim and Charlie after the show.

I turned up to find a small group of fans, including Simon Hayward, who'd been playing with Simple Minds as part of their stripped-down, corporate showcase, electro line-up. Overflowing with enthusiasm, he related several lengthy tales of corporate shenanigans and adventures, none of which I could or would ever repeat, but were hugely entertaining. We unwisely decided to sit at the front.

The concert was broadcast across the internet so there were the usual cameras to avoid. The rest of the canteen was filled with Facebook employees, a younger generation who probably Googled the band's name before coming, to figure out if they knew any of their songs.

Then Jim uttered the dreaded line, 'Get up on your feet and dance.' Simon groaned and in an unlikely combination of unhurried cool and total panic managed to bolt from the front row whilst trying to look distinctly unhurried.

Post-gig the trio moved on, so we hit the canteen to sample the company's food. A couple of female employees, dressed for a night out, complete with dresses with plunging necklines and noticeably fresh make-up, came over. 'We really loved the show,' they told me. 'Oh cool, glad you enjoyed it.' 'Yes, we really like what you do.'

Huh? Crossed wires. The conversation continued awkwardly and it became apparent that neither of us was making much sense. They gave up and moved off.

'Simon,' Elaine leaned over and whispered, 'they think you're in the band.'

That's the only time I was ever mistaken for Charlie Burchill.

---

# SANDRA ROSE GUNN

*Alcatraz*
*25 February 2014, Milan, Italy*

Growing up in Glasgow in the '70s and '80s, Simple Minds was the band you heard playing from someone's kitchenette while playing in the streets. The performance I'll never forget as I stayed up all night as a kid watching *Live Aid*. Simple Minds was the first cassette I played endlessly on my Walkman wherever I would go, and the band I secretly jumped on a bus to see play a free summer concert on Glasgow Green when I was 15. When I moved to Milan to make music at 21, Simple Minds was playing on my CD player, accompanying me on and off metros and trams through the city as I went back and forth to work.

In Milan in 2014 I had the chance to see them live again after many years and loved being out there in the crowd and dancing, having that wave of sound and energy flow through me from yet another amazing and flawless performance.

Through the painful years of losing my best friend and only brother to cancer, Simple Minds were right there with me, playing on my MP3, an escape and font of strength. The first song my then three-year-old son Kyle would sing over and over in the car was, 'Don't You (Forget About Me)'. He too feels the magic and I know it will stay with him throughout his life too.

Their music takes me straight back to Glasgow in a beat, to my people, my roots, a reminder of home with every note and every word of 'Waterfront'. No matter where I go, Simple Minds is a lifeline.

# BICE SACCÒ

*Alcatraz*
*25 February 2014,*
*Milan, Italy*

I'm on the autistic spectrum. For this reason my love for Simple Minds is unique.

My story as a young fan began seven years ago, when I was 13, as I found and listened to their *Live in the City of Light* album and fell in love with it. The song which introduced me to their world was 'Alive and Kicking'. When I listened to the original version on *YouTube* I adored it. Once, with my dad, I wrote an e-mail to Jim Kerr attaching a drawing I did for him and he answered, thanking me for the drawing and the compliments I

*Bice Sacco saw Simple Minds in Milan and, two years later, in Cremona*

had written. I was so happy to receive an answer that I printed it together with my e-mail and framed them both on my bedroom wall.

I've seen Simple Minds perform live four times with my parents, who bought the tickets. First time I was about 14 and went to see them at the Alcatraz discotheque in Milan. I was so excited and happy and we were in the first rows. For me, one of the highlights was the last song played, a magical version of 'Alive and Kicking'.

The fourth and last concert I saw with my parents and special needs teacher was in Cremona, near Lodi, the city I come from, in July 2018. It was two days before I got my high school diploma and this was the best way to celebrate. It was boiling hot and someone asked Jim to take off his blue velvet jacket (who could be able to wear it in July but our Jim?) but he replied 'no'. But after that, he did change the jacket for a white t-shirt just to play 'Don't You (Forget About Me)' and then the encore. A week after, I arrived home and Mummy handed me over an envelope containing Jim and Charlie's autographs, that the kind mayor of Cremona obtained for me. I couldn't contain my joy when I saw it. That too now hangs on my bedroom wall.

---

## VÍTEK KLOZ

*Incheba Arena*
*28 February 2014, Prague, Czech Republic*

It was maybe 1990 when I visited a friend who lived on the Czechoslovakian-Polish border. He listened to Polish Radio Three, which broadcast Western music even during the Communist era. At his house I saw a Sony 90-minute music cassette. On the A-side he'd taped U2's *The Joshua Tree* album and on the B-side, *Street Fighting Years*. It was my introduction to Simple Minds. During my university studies I discovered the older albums and was fascinated by *New Gold Dream*, *Sparkle in the Rain*, *Once Upon a Time* and the incredible live concert from Verona in 1987.

When I saw Simple Minds in Prague in 2014 they didn't play all the tracks from my favourite album, *Street Fighting Years*, but they're one of the best performing live bands I have ever heard. The wall of sound and colours produced is simply great.

---

## PAUL ROBINSON

*Delapre Park*
*18 April 2014, Northampton, England*

Every Saturday, and sometimes weekdays if I cycled into town with my vinyl wish-list, I would frequent HMV, Andy's Records and the music department in WH Smith,

*Paul Robinson saw the Minds at Delapre Park in Northampton - photo Paul Robinson*

where Limahl from Kajagoogoo did an in-store signing and nobody turned up! I took great pleasure in standing next to him and buying the 12-inch of 'Hot Water' by Level 42. Over the counter in HMV was a promo photo of a really strange looking fellow sporting heavy eye make-up. I couldn't get my head around it. What a weirdo! Turns out that was this bloke called Jim Kerr from Simple Minds.

Jump forward to my sister meeting Nigel. He'd bang on about a brilliant album called *New Gold Dream*. There was that name Simple Minds again! I decided to give it a try - it was all killer and no filler! Avant-garde, beautiful, atmospheric, bombastic and delicate all at the same time. My life would never be the same again.

Then *Sparkle in the Rain* happened. I was now a super fan. *Sparkle* just edged *New Gold Dream* for me. A more straightforward but shimmering rock album. Simple Minds were changing and I was along for the ride. I've seen them live, home and away, 15 times and keep coming back for more.

# EMMA CLARKSON

*Royal Botanic Gardens*
*19 July 2014, Kew, England*

In 2004 as a 22-year-old, disillusioned graduate, my life consisted of a dreary job and predictable weekends watching TV and trying not to comfort eat myself into oblivion. There wasn't even anything good on the radio – new metal was never my thing. But then, puncturing the dishwater dullness, came a musical firework. One Saturday afternoon, idly flicking through the Sky channels, my boyfriend happened upon a football game. Don't ask me who was playing – all I remember was the guitar solo that boomed, unapologetically dramatic and backed by irresistible gravelly vocals, swelling the sporting action into a splendid crescendo. I grabbed the remote control so he wouldn't change channel, staring wide-eyed at the screen, seeing nothing, hearing everything.

'What's this song?' I demanded, goose-bumps all over. My boyfriend, who abhorred all things '80s, squirmed. 'You know, don't you?' I pleaded. He sighed, realising I wouldn't shut up until he vended this now vital piece of information. 'It's 'Belfast Child' by Simple Minds,' he sneered, as if I should have known that, despite the barriers he continually created between me and '80s music.

Full of renewed life-purpose, I shrugged on my coat. 'Where are you going?' he asked. 'I need to buy the CD right now. I may have only heard the guitar solo, but I already know this is the best song I've ever heard, *ever*.' He groaned, deciding to come with me, presumably to ensure I didn't purchase the entire back-catalogue.

Our relationship folded a year later, but my love for Simple Minds burns on, stronger and brighter than ever. A few years after discovering 'Belfast Child', I met my now husband. It was this song that brought us closer together. Gone were the mixtapes of the Eighties, replaced by mix CDs. In the first, heady throes of romance, my husband and I were rampant 'mixdisc' makers, lacing our recordable CDs with our favourite songs, hoping to connect with each other via the medium of melody. 'Belfast Child' featured on my first. My husband said when he heard I'd picked that song, he knew I was the one. We married less than two years later.

My musical romance with Simple Minds had been alive and kicking for 10 years when hubby and I signed up for a 'picnic ticket' for their July concert in London's posh Kew Gardens. Hailing from Huddersfield, and blagging a bed for the weekend at my aunt's house in Surrey, we careened down the M1 to the soundtrack of Simple Minds, debating whether they'd open with 'Waterfront' and if they'd treat us to 'New Gold Dream', 'Belfast Child' and 'Real Life'.

On the day, we dressed appropriately or so we thought, ripped jeans and trainers, ready to rock out. However, our peers had gone for summer garden party - rather than rock - chic, dressing smartly in skirts, sandals and linen suits and carrying picnic hampers, blankets and plastic champagne glasses. Undeterred, we pressed through

485

the crowd, hoping security wouldn't separate us from our ill-disguised, cheap booze in paper bags. We probably looked like a couple of hobos! Grass-imprinted knees forgotten – why hadn't we thought to bring blankets? – we got to our feet as the stage lit up and Jim Kerr and Charlie Burchill appeared, opening with 'Waterfront', as we'd decided they would. It's hard to describe the latent teenage hormones frolicking through me at the sight of my favourite band ever, right there in front of me. I wanted to squeal and gush, to insanely shake both my arms and hubby. It's sad that I'd reached my 30s without having had this hallowed experience, yet it was all the more poignant for the long wait.

I managed to spend what was arguably the pinnacle of the concert – 'Big Music' – in a portaloo (the consumed booze had to go somewhere). Then, on my way back to the stage, I was interrogated by a man judging me as being 'too young' to enjoy Simple Minds. What does he know? That concert was one of the most magical nights of my life!

## DAVIDE DI COSIMO

### Cavea Auditorium
### 27 July 2014, Rome, Italy

The passion for Simple Minds in my home is a tradition passed from father to son. My father heard a lot of international and rock music and Simple Minds were his favourites. Years ago, sifting through an old collection of records, I came across *Street Fighting Years* and from that moment began a great imaginary friendship relationship with Jim Kerr.

So, 25 years later, my father and I are at the Cavea Auditorium to see Simple Minds. The atmosphere is very Nordic. In Rome, the rain falls all afternoon. Vincenzo Nibali wins the Tour de France with great humility and remembers the last Italian champion of France, Marco Pantani. Everything foreshadows a date that will remain in history and even the weather is a gentleman at dusk and the clouds go away. The auditorium is full when the group enters and sings the first songs. We all stand up. Before it was a concert for my grandmother, everyone sitting down!

In the second half everyone is standing and dancing like in a disco. I turn to people and see the fun and nostalgia of an era never forgotten and not so far away. By looking at the hearts in the shining eyes of the older fans, you understand certain groups are not just groups, certain songs are not just songs, certain emotions and certain sensations will always move you, both at 20 and 50. That's the power unleashed by Simple Minds' music.

# HRVOJE MAVRA

## *Arena Alpe Adria*
## *29 July 2014, Lignano Sabbiadoro, Croatia*

Radio Zagreb, today called Croatia Radio, had a show called *By Your Choice* and every day at noon it featured a new album. It was September 1982 when they featured *New Gold Dream (81,82,83,84)*. I was immediately hypnotised. 'Someone Somewhere (in Summertime)' became one of my favourite songs.

The first Simple Minds concert in Croatia was announced in the summer of 1991 during the *Real Life* tour and I was ready to go but it was postponed due to the beginning of the war in Croatia. The second time Simple Minds were announced to play in Croatia was in 1998 as guests of the Rolling Stones during the *Néapolis* tour but was postponed after Stones guitarist Keith Richards fell and broke his ribs. So it was third time lucky for me and other Croatian fans when they played Krk island.

One other gig remains in my memory, Lignano Sabbiadoro in 2014. What heavy rain. I've loved travelling to and meeting fans from Germany, Italy and Hungary. Long live the best live band in the history of music.

*Hrvoje Mavra met Charlie*

# OLIVIER GERARD

*Simple Minds sound engineer*
*Arena Alpe Adria*
*29 July 2014, Lignano Sabbiadoro,*
*Italy*

It was the *Greatest Hits* summer tour. We were in Italy for outdoors festivals. In Italy, as everyone knows, it never rains. That day in Lignano, all the concert facilities were basically there but nothing was really prepared for rain. Our crew arrived in the morning. It was raining, and it would rain the whole day. We couldn't set up the gear and prepare for the gig because the stage wasn't waterproof. The whole day the production was hesitating as to whether to cancel. It was hopeless. But Jim and Charlie never cancel. That's how they do it. We did shows where Jim was very ill and nearly couldn't sing…. also in Italy; or when Charlie played a whole week with a broken hand. Cancelling is never an option. They don't want to let the fans down.

At the very last moment, when the rain stopped, we were able to set up and prepare. The weather forecast was telling us the night would be dry. At 9.30pm, it was showtime. No rain. Fingers crossed. We started. The band got on stage and after a few songs, the skies opened and it started to pour cats and dogs. After the song, Jim said, 'They told us it was going to rain… so we are here waiting… This is no rain! We know everything about rain. We are Scotsmen - and we are Simple Minds!'

And we started 'Waterfront'….

*Simple Minds know about rain - photos by Vince Barker*

# MICHAEL AND ELLI BAUGH

*Alnwick Castle*
*16 August 2014, Alnwick,*
*England*

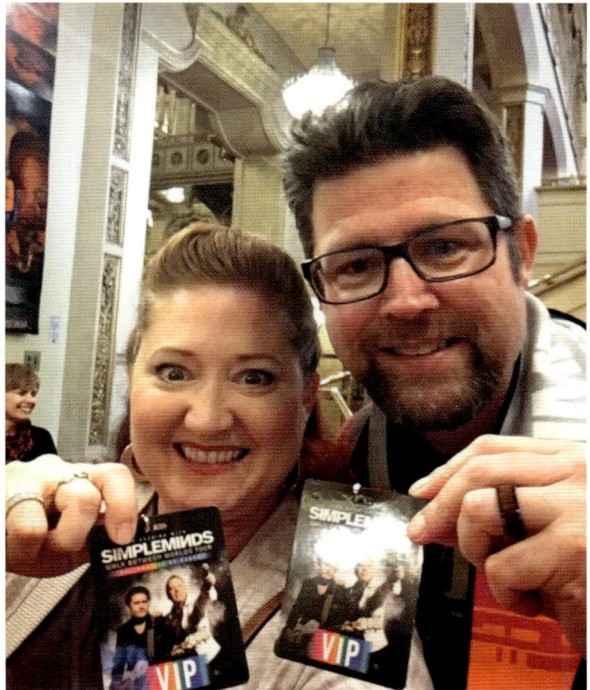
*Michael and Ellie Baugh at Alnwick Castle*

On our first date in 2003, we discovered two things: travelling to Scotland was on both our bucket-lists and Simple Minds was one of our favourite bands. Being '80s MTV kids, we grew up listening to them on KROQ. We wanted a chance to see Simple Minds together. A few years later, Michael proposed and we revisited our first date bucket-list. Honeymoon in Scotland? Yes! Simple Minds? Sadly, not then. We were married in 2008, and as we turned to friends and family after our vows, 'Alive and Kicking' was our first song as Mr. and Mrs. This golden song not only represents an influential time in our lives, but the soulful lyrics carried the emotional weight of a wedding promise.

The band returned to the US in 2013 and we scored tickets to the LA Orpheum Theater. The live set was so intimate and full of energy, and the experience was exactly what we'd hoped it would be - a celebration of our collective love of Simple Minds. At last in 2014, we left for our summer 'honeymoon' in Scotland with tickets to see them across the border at Alnwick Castle. The show fell on our sixth wedding anniversary. We couldn't imagine a better coincidence. That night felt like it had been lifetimes in the making. Beautiful skies, a magical backdrop, friendly crowd, mates passing round cider in celebration, and when the cold rain came, our smiles got bigger and our singing got louder. We danced in the mud and cheered on as sheets of rain spilled over the top of the stage, bending the spotlights into rainbow patterns during a powerful rendition of 'Love Song'. After the encores, the skies cleared and the fireworks over the castle ended the best day, the best concert and most romantic anniversary ever.

# JAMES KERR

*Video technician &
videographer for the Big
Music tour*

The very nature of a videographer is to focus entirely on the artists. Elevated in front of the masses, up on a steel deck, catwalk like stage. We're a vital part of making those engulfing arenas feel more comforting. Even those perched in the highest of rows or camped around the overflowing bars should feel like they can see the whites of their heroes' eyes. From experience, the desired outcome

*James Kerr, filming, Brussels 2015. Photo Vincent Barker*

doesn't always materialise. However, with the Minds' panache this is an impossible case.

I've had a very fortunate opportunity to get into the events industry via SM. Transitioning from high street retail to slinging t-shirts on the band's merch stall. Witnessing the ecstatic faces of fans all over the world. I wouldn't be where I am today shooting various artists, big and small if I had not been thrust onto a front of house camera due to a grumpy truck driver refusing to work two separate jobs a day on the 2015 *Big Music* tour. Luckily for me, he turned it down and I found myself a position to call my own in the production crew.

My joys of working with the band (who I call family and so can you!) are centred around the connected energy they hold with their audience every single concert. Sound checks too! Young or old, whether it's the first or the hundredth time seeing the band live, I can guarantee the fans will be left serenading choruses into the night, questioning, 'How do Jim and Charlie manage to keep prowling around that stage at their age?' Simple - the buzz the fans bring from the minute the auditorium doors swing open to the last crashing beat of Cherisse's drum. That buzz will keep the show rolling on for years to come.

# JULIE SIMPSON

My late husband Ian was a massive fan. We went to Villa Angela initially purely because of the connection with Jim. We both fell in love with the hotel, the people, Taormina and Sicily. The first time we visited we met Jimmy. It was his first year there since his wife had died. We just had so much fun with him. Also, Sam and James were there. About five years later we were there when Jim was and Ian was so excited at meeting one of his true idols, one of the highlights of his life. Jim was so friendly and had a photo with Ian which I have in my kitchen. I often look at it and remember the day so well. Sadly, Ian died in 2017 but I have been back to my friends at Villa Angela. It was a place Ian loved so much. Simple Minds were the soundtrack of his youth. Thank you for your music and for giving so much joy.

## LORA ANGUS

Around 30 years ago a beautiful lady walked into my hair salon. Her name was Irene Kerr, and our friendship began.... I always was a fan of Simple Minds but to do 'Jim's mum's hair' was exciting! She was full of so many interesting and funny stories, one being in the early days after every gig played at the Doune Castle in Shawlands. She had to wait up for Jim to come home so she could sew his black leather trousers as he only had one pair and because of his moves they ripped right up the backside! Not only did Irene introduce me to her family, I then discovered Taormina, Sicily and Hotel Villa Angela! Jim even took us out for dinner to celebrate my 50th birthday there. I was so grateful but he said 'if I didn't my ma would kill me!' We are a family of Simple Minds fans. Our kids were brought up listening to them and every gig is a new experience, pure magic!

## NICOLA DEL BONO

Being a guitarist myself I was probably whistling one of Charlie's riffs whilst browsing the shops on Rome's main shopping avenue. I used to jam with my best friends from high school and was there to buy a new electric guitar for our first gig with an audience, even though I knew we were all moving in different professional directions (I was planning to move to Amsterdam to finish my political science studies). This gig, and the next ones, could well be the peak of our short music career, and we had to be ready.

   Once inside the music shop, I had to rub my eyes in awe. I had literally bumped into Charlie Burchill, on holiday in Rome! He was very kind and gentle. We spoke in English as well as Italian regarding music, our lives and also our common love for Holland, where Simple Minds had just done some recording sessions. Charlie helped me choose my next guitar. Having switched to Italian language, he was not recognised by the shop clerks, who almost kicked us out of the shop after having touched and tried so many guitars. They probably mistook us for two indecisive local timewasters.

# CARLOS PASCUAL GARCIA

*Teatro Nuevo Apolo*
*9 February 2015, Madrid, Spain*

On Saturday August 23, 1986 at the La Nit de Xàtiva nightclub I got a lifelong crush when at 9.30pm the DJ played 'Don't You (Forget About Me)'. That 'la-la-la-la' was enough for me to fall in love with a group, a love which 34 years later has not ended. Since then I've dedicated myself exclusively to Simple Minds, buying their records and going to what concerts I could. And, today, collaborating with Moises and Javi in organising the annual Simple Minds Spanish fans' meetings in my city, Xàtiva, we attend from all over Spain and spend a weekend totally dedicated to the band.

*Carlos was at the 2015 show in Madrid*

Many people love Simple Minds along with other groups. I don't, I just like some songs from other groups who might be influenced by Simple Minds. In Xàtiva people call me Simple Minds, because I'm so devoted. My best moment was meeting Jim in the dressing room of the Apolo theatre in Madrid in 2015, given a chance in a draw by M80 Radio to be able to speak with him and the rest of the band. It was magical.

Their songs have served to cheer me up and accompany me in great and sad moments. I can only say two words I'd repeat a thousand times more – thank you!

---

# FRANCISCO JAVIER TSAO SANTÍN

One night, Spanish public TV channel TVE aired *The Breakfast Club*. Next day at high school, I talked with my mates about the movie and its fantastic main song, that sounded like David Bowie words splashed on the screen. Carlos answered, 'Yeah, it's a Simple Minds song, I've some of their stuff at home.' He lent me *Live in the City of Light* and it became one of my favourite albums.

Living in a little town in Galicia in north west Spain, very similar to Scotland, we had no music stores, so I'd use Discoplay, a popular mail order music store that disappeared some years ago. I received their catalogue each month via post then sent letters with my order and after a couple of weeks finally collected my purchase from the post office. That's the way I acquired my first Simple Minds LP, *Real Life*. I also bought the amazing *Verona* VHS around then, and when it arrived, I ran with it to the library to watch it as my video player was broken!

That was my best Simple Minds live experience until the magical night of 9 February 2015 at the Nuevo Apolo Theatre. My wife Tania and I were living in Madrid. I was counting each day from the year before, when we bought the tickets after the *Big Music Tour* was announced. I couldn't believe it when Jim Kerr appeared on the stage with the first chords of 'Let the Day Begin', 25 years after listening for first time to 'Don't You (Forget About Me)'.

## ALESSIO GENOVESE

*Volkshaus*
*14 February 2015, Zurich, Switzerland*

Thanks to my father, a big Simple Minds fan, I've followed them and their music since I was seven. I'm now 15, and my first gig was in Zürich for the *Big Music* tour. It was fantastic. I remember the whole day, from the journey there to waiting

*Alessio Genovese was introduced to Simple Minds by his father Gianluca*

by the doors before they opened, meeting many other fans who were friends of my father. I was so excited.

And I met my idols in Macerata in Italy. We were on summer holiday and had tickets for their show. My father told me 'we will meet Jim and Charlie' and we did! I'll always remember that moment in the afternoon before the gig, when we saw Jim coming out of a back door. My father called, 'Jim, Jim… please!' I was breathless, my heart spinning like the wheels of a fast train, when Jim said, 'Oh yeah, conosco… ciao come stai?', which means, 'Oh yeah, I know you, how are you?' You can imagine how I felt - in heaven!

# ANJA SOLDAT

*Capitol*
*18 February 2015,*
*Hannover, Germany*

I've had a passion for '80s music since I was 13, although I should have been listening to '90s music, having been born in 1983. I've been to see Depeche Mode, U2, ABC, Duran Duran, A-ha and many more. I wanted to see them all. In 2015, my

*Anja Soldat's love for Simple Minds started in 2015 with the Hannover show*

husband bought me tickets for Simple Minds in Hannover on their *Big Music* tour. I only knew a couple of songs but thought, 'Why not?'

On 18 February 2015 everything changed. Jim and the band came on stage and after the first few songs – bam! - a lightning bolt struck me (but in a good way). The way Jim acts on stage with the audience and the songs I'd never heard before. It was amazing. I'd never seen a singer perform with such passion and in such a personal way.

After the gig I was angry with myself. Why? Because I didn't know anything about their music. Everybody else did. But then I wiped the thought away, because this special evening was the beginning of my journey with Simple Minds.

# FOLKERT & JOSKA DUIPMANS

*Emsland Arena*
*21 February 2015, Lingen, Germany*

My father is 77 and a big fan of Simple Minds. I remember when I was a kid he'd listen to 'Don't You' and 'Alive and Kicking'. When 'Belfast Child' came out a couple of years later that instantly became his favourite song, and still is!

His biggest dream was always to go to a concert and in 2015 that dream came true. He'd been sick for a couple of years but when I heard Simple Minds were giving a concert in Lingen, an hour's drive from our hometown, I ordered two tickets. Fortunately he felt well enough on the day and we travelled to see them perform and hear all the songs he loved. This made it one of the best days of his life.

We wanted to go again in 2018 in Germany but unfortunately he was too ill. When I heard there would be another tour and concert in Germany in March 2020 I again ordered tickets. Too bad Covid-19 led to that being cancelled, but we'll be there in March 2021. Thank you for giving my father so much strength through your music. It has helped him overcome difficult times.

---

# MAGNUS PEDERSÉN

*Lisebergshallen*
*16 March 2015, Gothenburg, Sweden*

When I was 14, my sister was playing a bunch of albums from the family collection over a few weeks. One day, I heard two songs that would change my life. I asked what record she was playing and she answered, '*The Best of Simple Minds*.' I managed to find the songs I'd heard and added Simple Minds to my playlist. 'Theme for Great Cities' and 'The American' have remained close to my heart since.

I went to see them with family and friends for the first time in the spring of 2015, in my hometown of Göteborg. That night ignited a fire in me. High on the energy, I started to delve deeper into their catalogue. I bought CDs and vinyls and hung them on my wall. I started to wear Simple Minds t-shirts. I constantly listened to their music. I'd found the greatest band there was.

In 2017, me and my family went to London to see the *Acoustic* tour. I had prepared diligently and memorised just about every word to every song I thought they might play. I was nervous. Could they really match my sky-high expectations? The show was everything I hoped for. From 'Stand by Love' to 'Sanctify Yourself', I truly was lost in music, singing and dancing the night away.

---

# LAURA JAMES

*Grimsby Auditorium*
*27 March 2015, Grimsby, England*

Before I met my husband Daryl over 11 years ago, the only song I knew was 'Don't You (Forget About Me)'. Daryl had been attending their gigs for years and brought me along to Grimsby. Well, what can I say? The music, the fans, the atmosphere were simply electric. I'm proud to say I'm almost word perfect on a lot of Simple Minds songs. We even had Simple Minded (a tribute band) play our wedding.

---

# JUDITH CARGILL

*Usher Hall*
*7 April 2015, Edinburgh, Scotland*

My very first Simple Minds memory is hearing 'I Travel' being played at a Student Union disco on a Friday night during my first year at Heriot Watt University in 1984. I absolutely loved dancing to this track and asked the DJ who the band were. I've been a fan since, and 'I Travel' remains my favourite dance track to this day. I rushed out and bought a 12-inch version of the track, which I still have. The DJ regularly played 'The American' and 'Love Song' too, which still remind me of my student days.

My first concert was at Meadowbank. The *Big Music* concert at the Usher Hall in Edinburgh is a favourite because the concert was non-stop, with all my favourite hits. And this was the first time I ever heard 'I Travel' live. My most memorable journey to a concert was a train ride from Glasgow to Inverness, where Simple Minds music was played the entire journey - everyone in the carriage singing along. Magical!

# JOSEPHINE BARRON

*Plymouth Pavilions*
*17 April 2015, Plymouth, England*

When I was 16 I heard 'Belfast Child' on the radio, the first piece of music to make me stop and listen. It struck deep to my Irish heritage, the haunting melody from 'She Moves Through the Fair' and poignant lyrics sung by a gorgeous voice. I was smitten with Jim by 'This is Your Land', the positivity of 'Mandela Day', Jim's candid views on political issues and Charlie's guitar, that got under your skin and carried you through every song. The fan club was joined, the posters went up on the bedroom wall and I listened to everything Simple Minded when I should have been revising for GCSEs!

I got *New Gold Dream* on tape and played it on my Walkman as I worked in one of our fields that summer. I travelled to Paris for my first Minds gig. At Milton Keynes Bowl, I remember an already-squashed crowd surging forward several feet when the band came on, terrifying and exhilarating. I couldn't see a thing and was bruised and battered from being pushed and jumped on, but loved it.

I went to Paris again and the music helped me through the angst and confusion of those late teenage years. I saw them in Plymouth and got to meet a lovely couple. I think their names were Doug and Lorraine. He went to school with Jim. They had backstage passes and very generously let me sneak along. I was like a kid, so starstruck - I couldn't string two words together. Jim and Charlie posed with me for pics and were so normal, friendly and kind, but I couldn't speak. It makes me cringe thinking about it. I lost touch with Doug, probably as I couldn't remember his name!

I was three rows from the front at the next Plymouth gig and saw Facebook friend Andy Inniss in the front row. We got chatting and as the lights went down, I noticed that the seat next to him was empty. I scooted forward and had the best concert of my life. Right there in the very front. A couple of people commented after that Jim had been singing just for me. I was back to being 16 again, 30 years later!

I tried but didn't get backstage that time. I would still have struggled to speak but would have loved the opportunity to say 'thank you' to the band. I'll always regret not taking that first opportunity to thank Jim and Charlie. I'm disabled now and don't know if I will get to see Simple Minds live again, but have incredible memories and my own New Gold Dream!

## RITA MATTERS

### Motorpoint Arena 18 April 2015, Cardiff, Wales

My boyfriend, now husband of 30-plus years, and I started going out in 1985. He was into U2, his appreciation fuelled partly by his Irish ancestry. This naturally morphed into following Simple Minds and I quickly followed suit. I remember walking into HMV and seeing a wall of *Live in the City of Light* albums.

I whiled away lonely hours whilst he was at university listening to Minds, especially on Tuesday evenings when my parents were out dancing; I had the Ferguson Music Centre jumping to 'Promised You a Miracle'! The years moved on and we lost touch with Simple Minds, apart from picking up the *Glittering Prize 81-92* album, which has my favourite of all their work, 'Let There Be Love'.

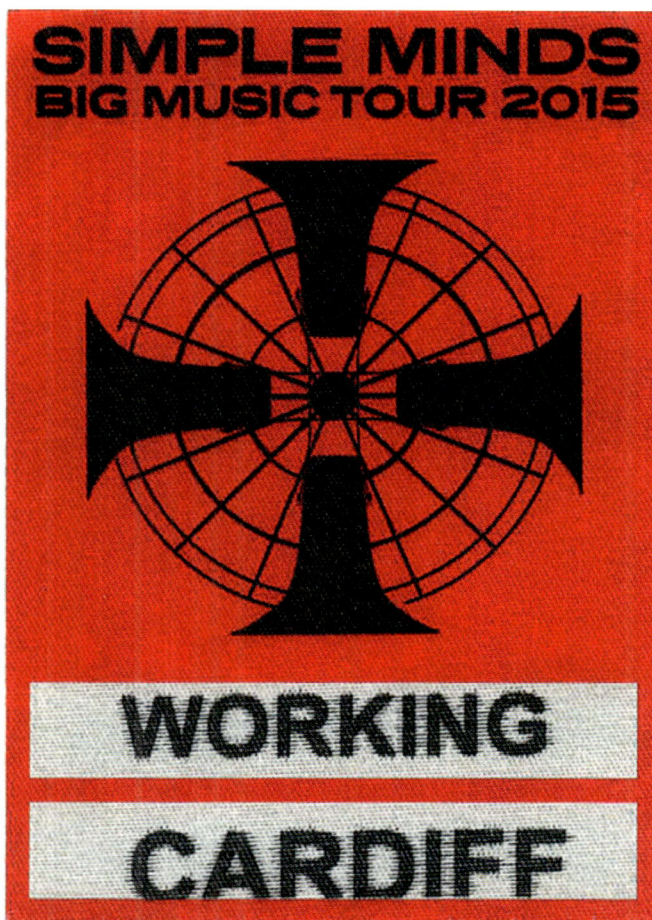

In 2014, I was waiting on a red light when I turned the radio on. I had no idea who the song playing was by, only that it had a hint of Bryan Ferry. I liked it. As I moved off I heard it was Simple Minds and 'Honest Town'! I bought *Big Music* and gig tickets for the old man for Christmas. After all these years he was delighted to be finally seeing the band he calls 'The Simps'.

We hadn't expected such an early start but made it into the Motorpoint just as 'Let the Day Begin' began. Jim was resplendent in red tartan, Charlie in trademark black. My old man was delighted to see Mel. He didn't know Ged but was impressed!

2017 saw the *Acoustic* tour. Arriving at the Cardiff date, we were making our way up the escalator when the old man said, 'There's Charlie! Shall we say hello?' For the next few minutes I was struck completely dumb as I began to realise it was Charlie and myself in the picture. But I'm also struck by his accent and warm personality.

Image: 161202SMacousticUK-latestCMP

Our next stop was Barrowland, early 2018. We flew in to Glasgow the day before. The old man was struck down with flu but well enough to attend, coming to life when they played 'I Travel'. A smile crept across his face as he watched Jim. 'I listened to them at university and they're still up there.' 'They've brought it all back,' I say. 'You've brought it all back,' he answers.

The final part of the story - so far - was Grandslam 2018 in Merthyr Tydfil. We got VIP tickets and were determined to be in the front row. We were escorted to our area, right in front of the stage, having been given a complimentary drink and gift bag en route. What we didn't expect was to meet Gordy. 'There's Gordy,' I said. The old man was determined to meet his hero. Gordy stepped back from the food van and was happy to have a chat and his photo taken with the old man.

So we've met Charlie and Gordy. We're coming for you next time, Jim!

---

# JOHN ARCHBELL

*Corn Exchange*
*21 April 2015, Cambridge, England*

My most treasured, distant, burning gold memory of Simple Minds was listening to the first song I ever heard by them. 'Someone Somewhere (in Summertime)' came just as I was beginning to find my way into style and music as a brash, unapologetic 14-year-old schoolboy in 1981. I found the song so powerful and moving. I really felt it was about me. I remember the intro best, with its sweeping structure and layers. The

*John Archbell and his wife Sharon were at the Corn Exchange gig in 2015*

arrangement was beautiful and its chord changes breathtaking. To this day I love how it transcends, Jim launching into the first verse. It became my soundtrack and a stepping stone to the broad musical taste I've adopted over the years. Brilliant!

My greatest concert memory was at Cambridge Corn Exchange as part of the *Big Music* tour with my wife Sharon. So many songs played over two sets. It was incredible value for money. I recall the band breaking into the magical intro to 'Don't You (Forget About Me)', and just as Jim's cue came to sing, he'd forgotten his first line! He asked the band to stop playing and explained, 'That's what happens when you think about the football results!'

---

# NIC NORRIS

## *New Theatre*
## *26 April 2015, Oxford, England*

My last year of school. Music was my life. We had Music Market in Oxford, the hub of everything cool. I remember 'I Travel' being played and I took *Empires and Dance* home without realising how much effect it would have on my life.

'The American' was released as I left school, a celebration of summer. An energy about that got me, and then 'Love Song' - wow! How could anything be better? *Sons and Fascination/Sister Feelings Call* proved it would be.

David Jensen played a session on Radio 1, including 'Promised you a Miracle', weeks after I heard from one of the guys at Music Market and friends in the village that Simple Minds were at the Manor. We ventured over to Shipton and sat on the wall by the boating lake, to be greeted by some of the band on a boat! Apparently, Charlie wouldn't come out of the studio. New Gold Dream was perfection, gigs at Aylesbury Friars and Oxford before Christmas.

It seemed an eternity to hear new music, David Jensen had a session with the first play of 'Waterfront'. The Lyceum gig was iconic, masses of dry ice and the curtain going up to reveal Jim on a tall stand. *Sparkle in the Rain* started a brilliant year, with five nights in succession at Hammersmith Odeon. Every night was special - atmosphere, power. I went to Rock Torhout, the band headlining with Lou Reed. Somehow, I managed to sit on the stage with a massive flag. I'll never forget the view looking back across the crowd, a sea of flags.

I celebrated my 50th birthday at Oxford on the *Big Music Tour*, a present from my amazing wife. They played for ever, polished as ever.

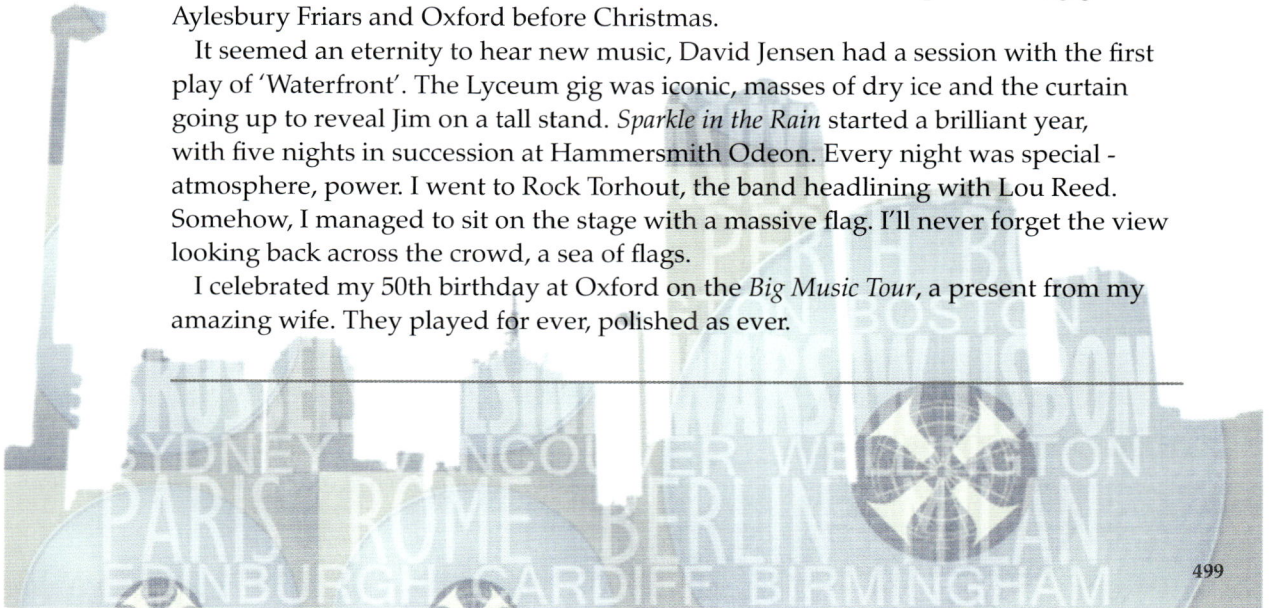

---

## GRANT FULLER

*G Live*
*28 April 2015,*
*Guildford, England*

I've been a big fan of Simple Minds since the '80, and a highlight was seeing them perform at my local theatre, G Live Guildford. The light show, the intimacy of the gig, Jim shouting those words, 'Let me see those hands', and hearing 'Waterfront' performed live, the fans going wild. A memory that will stay with me forever. To be that close to my idols was amazing.

*Grant Fuller photographed Charlie at G Live in Guildford*

## MARK BAKER

*Hexagon Theatre*
*30 April 2015, Reading,*
*England*

The first time I experienced them was the Mandela concert at the old Wembley Stadium. My first tour was *Street Fighting Years,* including a concert in Paris. I haven't missed a tour since. I attended six shows on the 2003 tour. Some people said I was mad and stalking the band! But it's experiencing a concert in different venues and visiting different parts of the country, and of course different setlists.

Both my parents saw them live and one experience stands out at the Hexagon, Reading, during the *Big Music* tour. My father, Frank, 83 years old, and I had an idea. I wrote 'Frank 83 My Old Man'' on an A4 piece of paper. We stood at the front near Charlie, and during the intro to 'New Gold Dream' I held up the sheet of paper. My father wasn't aware. Charlie was amused

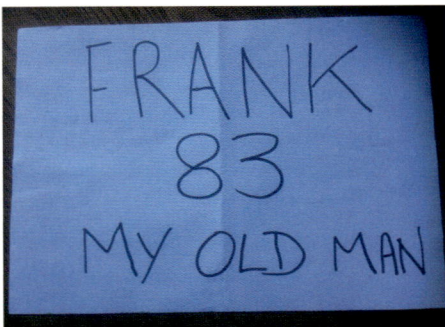

*Mark Baker's sign that had Charlie in stitches*

and other members of the audience also found it funny. Jim, on the other side, made his way to our side of the stage and, during the lyrics, said, 'Let's go, Frank!' Charlie was in stitches - but didn't miss a beat. It made my day and my father, now 88, still talks about it today.

## PETER MÜLLER

*Heitere Open Air*
*5 August 2015, Zofingen, Switzerland*

In 1985, attending the Officers' School in the Swiss Army, days started early and were very tough and long, our nights short. When we returned to our rooms at the barracks late at night, tired and exhausted, one of my roommates played 'Don't You (Forget About Me)' over and over on his cassette recorder. It helped us get back on our feet, get a smile back on our faces and mentally regenerate. And we all survived and finally graduated after many months and listening to the great songs of Simple Minds. I am 35 years older but Simple Minds still accompany me wherever I go. And whenever they play Switzerland, I go along, most recently the open-air concerts at Zofingen Heitere in 2015 - a wonderful night! - and *Rock the Ring* in 2018. I'm always at the very front of the stage, as close as possible to see those guys and their smiling faces and passion and satisfaction when playing that wonderful music.

## SARAH LUDLOW

*The Late Late Show*
*6 November 2015, Dublin, Ireland*

I know a girl who works at *The Late Late Show*, a staple of Friday night Irish telly for nearly 60 years. When she heard Simple Minds were performing on the show, she immediately called and offered me tickets. The presenter Ryan Tubridy said, 'We are going to take a commercial break, and when we return, we'll have some music by Simple Minds', then cut to an ad break. I could see the band set up in the corner of the studio. I thought, 'I've seen these guys about 15 times, but have never been quite as close.' That realisation led to adrenaline.

I'm not a brave person. I'm the kind of person that encounters situations daily where I wish I'd said or done something instead of nothing. Nevertheless, I found myself slinking out of my seat and walking down the stairs to the set floor.

I remember the look of sheer panic in my husband-to-be's eyes, as if to say, 'Oh no Sarah, what are you doing?' In truth, I didn't really know what I was doing. 'Well, I have to tell them how much they mean to me, how their music makes my life better and makes me happy. Will I show Jim or Charlie my Simple Minds tattoo? Will I tell them I'll be walking down the aisle to 'Shake Off the Ghosts'? Will I tell Mel my brother Tosh, living in China, idolises him as a drummer and he got me into the band?'

My bravery seemed to stop once I'd made the trip to the stage. I just hopped on, gave Jim a squeeze and kiss on the cheek and went back to my seat. The host made a show of me when we were back on air, but I didn't care. It was brilliant. After being sent the clip, my brother texted that he was never so proud of me and it was the coolest thing I had ever done. And it was.

---

# TONI MASSON

*Vorest Nationaal*
*14 November 2015, Brussels,*
*Belgium*

I am the only person in the universe that made Jim Kerr change some lyrics.

I fell in love with Simple Minds and *New Gold Dream*. As a gay teenager in the '80s, stuck with myself and in love with my best (straight) friend, I saw no future. One evening Jim was on television, serpent-man, half-human, half-god, on stage in Newcastle City Hall. I was completely hypnotised by the music, the movements, the lyrics. *New Gold Dream*, its five star production and lyrics (every songtext is a damn perfect poem), made me believe in enlightenment and the concept of hope. It was a life-changer and finally I had a compass.

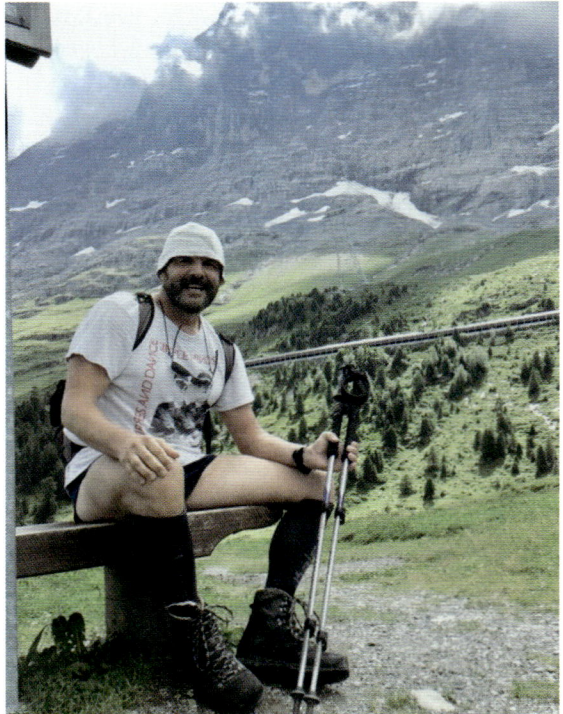

*Toni Masson lobbied Jim to change the lyrics of 'Banging on the Door'*

In 1991, I finished university and after 13 months in the Belgian Army, started a career as an engineer in the 'real life'. I bought *Real Life* and was blown away by the power of the title track but also the brilliance of 'Banging on the Door'. Realising I should not build up the idea of a life with my beloved best friend, the lyrics of 'Banging' just hit me in the face, at that time banging on doors 'that were closed forever'. I felt almost physically sick at Jim's words 'some dreams grow old, and then they just die'. I often fell into despair.

It was a difficult period for me. But I realised I should never give up dreaming and became rather succesful in my career, my social life and in love. I married my German husband in November 2013 and our wedding party was the Simple Minds gig that evening in Brussels.

How happy I was in November 2015 when Jim announced on Facebook that they'd play 'Banging on the Door' on the forthcoming *Big Music* arena tour. But damn! Would Jim really sing those sad words, 'some dreams grow old, and then they just die'? I suggested he should sing 'some dreams grow old, but they just NEVER die'. He answered with a joke.

But, on a particularly emotional evening in Brussels, a day after the Paris massacre at the Bataclan, he really was singing the changed lyrics. I just could not believe my ears. He did it the following nights too. It's all there on *YouTube*, the waving with the fingers on 'never' is quite explicit.

With almost 50 Minds concerts, I'm not the biggest fan in the world, but surely the only person that made Jim change his lyrics. To this day I'm so proud… and yes, dreams are there forever, they never die.

## CHRISTOPHER FLYNN

I grew up in small farm town during the second British Invasion of American music. I was part of the *Breakfast Club* society and was introduced to Simple Minds via 'Don't You (Forget About Me)'. In seeking more from this 'new' band, Simple Minds, I came across *Once Upon a Time*. While most of my schoolmates were engaged in big hair bands and glam rock. At the time, foreign bands were not big through small farming communities, let alone this specific Scottish band.

When *Live in the City of Light* was released, I had to special order it from my local record store. Come the time I graduated high school, *Street Fighting Years* was released and was widely available across the States. What a beautifully conceived album. It gave me faith that Simple Minds were not a one hit wonder or a soon to be forgotten European band as most of the second British wave introduced. To this day, *Once Upon a Time* remains one of my 'go to' albums, while *Street Fighting Years* is top of my 'can't survive without it' list.

## PAUL GALLACHER

I heard 'I Travel' so wanted to go out and buy it but didn't know the song title. I headed into Glasgow and went to HMV on Union Street.

The only thing I could tell the store worker was, 'When there is a break in the song we (the people in pub) all sing 2,3,4'. He knew exactly what record it was!

## ANNE TAVOLIERI

*Lotto Arena*
*15 November 2015, Antwerp, Belgium*

I'm a fan thanks to my three older brothers, who often listened to 'Up on the Catwalk', 'Glittering Prize' and 'All the Things She Said'. I loved those songs and synth melodies. The years passed and I still loved Simple Minds' music. But I had to wait until 2015 before seeing them live with my oldest brother. It was also his first.

It was two days after the Paris attacks and the atmosphere was sad at first. I remember the minute of silence that came before. It was very affecting. After a few songs, I completely forgot the outside world and was able to fully enjoy the concert. What an energy they had, especially Jim, and what a joy to hear all these songs I love. I also made two great discoveries at this gig: Sarah Brown and Catherine Anne Davies, two talented women.

I should have attended Lokerse Feesten in 2018 but was diagnosed with breast cancer and began chemo so had to cancel. I'm in remission today and plan to make the most of it.

## LUDOVIC PAGÈS

*Le Zenith*
*20 November 2015,*
*Paris, France*

I discovered Simple Minds at a nightclub in the French Alps. I heard 'Someone Somewhere (in Summertime)' and it was a real intense moment on the dancefloor. It was the version from *Live in the City of Light*.

*At Le Zenith. Photo by Ludovic Pagès*

My first and so far only Simple Minds concert will forever be etched in my memory. It was played just a week after the dramatic attacks that hit Paris. When we thought the concert would be cancelled, Jim Kerr and his band gave us a show worthy of the moment, starting with a tribute to our victims. An unforgettable moment.

## HENNIE ROBBEN

I was 16 when I got very ill and was in hospital for eight weeks. Simple Minds helped me through it. Then I got into a nasty divorce and couldn't listen to them - it just hurt too much. But 10 years ago I had a stroke and they helped me recover. In 2015, I got to see them for the first time in 12 years - and cried! Me, who almost never shed a tear in all those years.

---

## KARSTEN KAMBACH

*SSE Hydro*
*28 November 2015, Glasgow, Scotland*

*Simple Minds at the Hydro. Photo by Vince Barker*

A friend and I loved to listen to BFBS for new ideas as to what rock music could be, a contrast to the typical chart broadcastings in Germany. On a Thursday evening in 1981, listening to *John Peel's Music*, one song stuck out among all the others. The electronic sound was special, as was the voice. It was 'Sweat in Bullet' from newly-released *Sons and Fascination*. Half an hour later, John played another track from that album, a song which changed my life: '70 Cities as Love Brings the Fall'. The intriguing guitars and synths sounding like a foghorn and complicated but catchy choruses caught me immediately. I bought the album the next day.

It got six stars in German magazine *Musickexpress*. What a surprise to read a year later *New Gold Dream* getting only four. For me, *New Gold Dream* was - and is - a timeless masterpiece.

I've followed Simple Minds over the years. I've had minor disappointments with *Néapolis* and *Cry* but admire most of their songs for their many layers and facets. The best era for me was *Sons and Fascination* to *Street Fighting Years*. They were a rock band and played different and long versions of their songs in concerts, such as 'East at Easter' or 'Book of Brilliant Things'. And the *5x5* live album - what a blast!

A personal highlight was my 50th birthday, playing the Hydro in their hometown. I bought 'Behind the Scenes' tickets for my wife and myself and we flew to Glasgow, went for the soundcheck - including a photo with the band - and what a fantastic gig.

## JOHN DEGG

*AECC GE Oil & Gas Arena*
*1 December 2015, Aberdeen, Scotland*

I remember the warm summer that 'Glittering Prize' was released. I connected immediately with the music, the vocals and driving, complex basslines. My first show was Milton Keynes Bowl and the *Once Upon a Time* tour. The night before I played *Sparkle in the Rain* over and over, revving myself up. Arriving at the Bowl, I made my way to the front. It was a tight squeeze. The afternoon could not come quick enough, but when it did – 'Waterfront'! I'd spent the day fighting my way to the front. Then the call came from JK. 'Let me see your hands!' Nope, sorry Jim. I can't get my hands in the air - it's rammed! Early into the anthem I ended up no longer centre-stage but towards the right side, and it just kept bouncing all night.

My most memorable

*John Degg meets the band*

concert was the *Big Music* tour, being down the front in Aberdeen with long-suffering fellow Minds fan, Ian Jewkes. We arrived early, the gates just opened and ran to where the front barrier was free. Crazy behaviour for 40-somethings. The banter with JK made it all the better: 'Control yourself, love is all you need!'

More recently, the outdoor concert in Eccles was an absolute ball. Jim recalled playing in Philadelphia in front of thousands of fans and stating backstage to Charlie that one day they would reach their peak and play Eccles.

I've totted up 96 concerts to date. Will I make it to 100? I very much hope so. Thank you for the music and live nights where I've stood at the back, sides and down the front!

## JOT SHIRLEY

*Hackney Empire*
*10 November 2016, London, England*

When the idea of Simple Minds venturing into an acoustic sound was released I was sceptical. To me, they'd largely been big and bold. Crashing beats and fantasy, to pinch a line from 'New Gold Dream'. Having heard the first release, 'Promised You a Miracle' with the stunning KT Tunstall, I could see this was going to be an interesting venture. I managed to get a ticket to the first *Acoustic* gig at London's Hackney Empire on my birthday in 2016. The show was live on BBC Radio 2. Any fears I had as to whether Simple Minds could pull off an acoustic gig were instantly dismissed. I loved it and then caught a show in June 2017 from the *Acoustic* tour at the Theatre Royal, Drury Lane, where KT Tunstall made an appearance.

My favourite gig was at the Barrowland Ballroom in Glasgow for the first night of the *Walk Between Worlds* tour. The album was played in full, Billy Sloane interviewing Jim and Charlie. That famous venue I'd heard Jim talk about with such passion for years and there I was - to see my favourite band.

## PETER MCFADYEN

*A Day on the Green*
*Kings Park*
*2 February 2017, Perth, Australia*

Aged 11 in 1979, I heard Generation X's 'Valley of the Dolls' and played it non-stop for a year. With other bands coming and going, I needed a direction for my musical taste. My brother, a mad Iron Maiden fan, brought me a tape of *New Gold Dream*. He said, 'Kid, you gotta hear this album! It's amazing'. And boom!

I began dressing like Jim, black-dyed hair and all sorts of different styles. In '84 I went to the Barras gig, then dragged my best mate to Dortmund. By this time everyone I knew, knew I was Simple Minds daft. I had pictures on the walls and was drawing on the ceiling in my bedroom. I was also driving my mum crazy, *Sparkle in the Rain* thumping out of my speakers. I sold my car to go to Ahoy! Robin Clark was just superb. I felt that night went on forever.

There have been countless gigs over the years, even taking my wee disabled friend Frankie from Castlemilk to the amazing Princess Street gig under Edinburgh Castle. I've now moved to Perth in Australia, where I saw the Day on the Green with The B-52's - absolutely brilliant.

Thanks for the great music and memories. I remember Jim chatting to my then girlfriend in the Horseshoe Bar, Glasgow in 1995. It was our first date. Her dad apparently drove Simple Minds to gigs.

*Peter McFadyen remembers several Scottish shows by the Minds*

*Jim at the Hordern Pavilion. Photo by Julia Kershaw*

## JULIA KERSHAW

*Hordern Pavilion
9 February 2017, Sydney,
Australia*

My journey with Simple Minds began in 1981 with 'The American' and 'Love Song' getting my attention. Their sound just got me. My first concert was Kraftwerk in 1977 and I loved electronica. Simple Minds satisfied that love with their mix of keyboards and solid beats. Jim's fabulous feeling in his voice made the magic that is Simple Minds.

During dark times in my life, the death of my father in 1986 then my mother in 2013, I relied on Simple Minds music to somehow soothe the pain.

I've seen them five times. My favourite show would be 2017 at the Hordern Pavilion. We were at the very front and could see everyone, every instrument, every expression, every smile. I think it made us forget our age. My husband mentioned that Jim looked so relaxed and happy and it showed in the show. I agree. Such a polished band. Such a connection with the audience. Such a great experience.

# DEBBIE GRAVES

## A Day on the Green, Sirromet Wines
## 12 February 2017, Brisbane, Australia

I first fell in love with Simple Minds when I got the compilation album *Modern Dance* for Christmas in 1981, with 'Love Song' and 'Sweat in Bullet' on it, still two of my favourite songs. I never got the chance to see them live back in the day but adored their music and often played their albums (loudly).

In 2014, I got together with David, someone I used to know in Birmingham back in the good old days, when he wore more make-up than me! We love the same music and are both big Simple Minds fans, David seeing them several times. I was still living there, but he'd moved to Townsville, Queensland, Australia. I'd never been on a plane, but he flew to the UK to meet my family, then I flew back with him to live in Australia.

The highlight of my time in Australia so far was flying to Brisbane to see Simple Minds play the Sirromet Winery, The B-52's supporting. The setting was simply stunning and the memory of that incredibly hot day will stay in my heart always.

We're getting married in 2021. 'New Gold Dream' will be the song we walk out from the ceremony to.

# ROBERTO PANATTONI

## Teatro Degli Arcimboldi
## 27 April 2017, Milan, Italy

I started to follow Simple Minds in 1985. I went to all the concerts I could. I met the band after a concert in Milan, in front of the Pierre Hotel. What an experience! I also saw onet in Bologna where I met Jim in front of the hotel. It was his birthday – and mine! I remember him coming back from the shop with the cake.

The last time I was really close to the band was for the *Acoustic* tour in Milan. I'd love to meet Jim and the band again.

*Roberto Panattoni with Jim*

## DAVID GOLA

*Patinoire de Meriadeck
8 May 2017, Bordeaux,
France*

I discovered the band at the age of 13 in early 1986 with the *Once Upon a Time* album. When I listened to *Live in the City of Light* in 1987 I was bewitched! Every album is a slice of my life. I estimate I've listened to the *Real Life* album around 2,000 times since 1991. But I didn't see Simple Minds live until 2017. Shame on me!

I'm a wine producer in the south of France near Bergerac in the Dordogne and in 2017, as an homage, I named a white wine cuvée, 'Simple Minds'.

*David Gola produced a white wine in homage to Simple Minds*

## LAURENT CHABRUN

*Cité des Congrès
9 May 2017, Nantes, France*

I've seen Simple Minds on stage more than 15 times. The last time was in Nantes for the *Acoustic* tour. At the beginning the audience was quiet and people were staying in their seats. My wife decided to go to the stage and dance. Jim saw she was dancing alone and just in front of her started to dance. Since then I think she's a little bit in love with him!

# JADE TUCH

*Palais des Beaux-Arts*
*15 May 2017, Brussels, Belgium*

The music of Simple Minds has followed me since I was born. For as long as I can remember, I've always heard Simple Minds at home and in the car. My parents and my godmother being big fans, I could only have the same genes.

I first saw them live on 23 February 2012 during the *5X5* tour. I was eight and at the barrier. I'll always remember that after the concert my godmother and her friend took me backstage to meet them. I remember running into Jim, who said 'hello'. Then we went upstairs and I was able to take pictures with Charlie, Andy, Ged and Mel. After this first concert, my love for the band was unwavering and my parents took me with them to every concert in Belgium for the *Celebrate* tour, 2013, and *Big Music*, 2015.

One of my best memories was from 2017's *Acoustic* tour at the Palais des Beaux-Arts, Brussels. They started with 'New Gold Dream'. Jim walking around the hall when he took my godmother and me to dance with him in the middle of the room. It was magical! To finish a perfect evening we saw Jim at the exit of the room, where I had my first photo with him.

In 2018, we went to Glasgow with my parents, and to the venue the day before the concert for the soundcheck. As we were about to leave the band went out, took pictures and then we were able to chat and have a picture with Jim in front of the Barrowland. I was amazed! At the Ancienne Belgique a few days after Glasgow, Jim made me dance with him on 'Sanctify Yourself'. Another magical moment for me.

---

# DAVEY VEITCH

*Sage*
*19 May 2017, Gateshead, England*

I was in the RAF in High Wycombe when the first video jukebox came along. It was £1 for three goes. Much to the annoyance of the other squaddies in the NAAFI bar, I played 'Glittering Prize' over and again, Jim dancing around dripping in gold and Charlie playing a beautiful electric guitar. It was the track that introduced me to Simple Minds and my Desert Island Disc, *New Gold Dream*.

Time - and I – moved on. In Belgium I saw the band supported by The Waterboys, a fantastic gig where the backdrop was an assortment of blinds being moved to great effect. I saw them three times that year and have seen more than 40 shows to date, each ingrained in my head, still whistling in my ears.

The last gig was at the Sage. I took a great friend who had been through a difficult time. But for over an hour all that faded into the ether as we danced and sang along to classic tracks. A new band with a lady percussionist. No Mel to be seen.

Now in my 50s, I remember each gig as if it was yesterday. I treasure the posters, artwork and albums. *New Gold Dream* is played every week and transports me to a time when beer was £1 a pint and I shared a Triumph Dolomite Sprint with three others. It was bright yellow, but not as bright as Jim's suit on that video.

---

## DAVID JOHNSON

*Philharmonic Hall*
*22 May 2017, Liverpool, England*

We got second-row seats, which were great apart from being stuck behind the superfans with their range of hats! It was great to see Jim appear from the back of the Philharmonic whilst belting out 'New Gold Dream'. There was some banter with a rowdy scouser followed by some great reworkings. Sadly, we got in that night to hear about the horrors of a bomb going off in Manchester Arena, killing dozens at an Ariana Grande gig.

---

## GUILLERMO FEDERICO GALLEGOS

*Bridgewater Hall*
*23 May 2017, Manchester, England*

Living in Mexico, I first heard Simple Minds in the mid-'80s, probably riding the wave of *The Breakfast Club* hype. I lost sight of them until the early '90s release of the *Glittering Prize* compilation. I was hooked on their music from then on and they remain one of my top three bands, 'Alive and Kicking' an important part of my personal soundtrack.

Despite being an avid concertgoer, for several reasons I wasn't able to see them live. So I didn't hesitate to align a business trip to the UK to allow me to be in Manchester in May 2017 when they were at Bridgewater Hall. However, the night before, we watched in horror the brutal Manchester Arena bombing. The obvious choice would have been to postpone all concerts the following day, but there was the conscious decision from all artists to carry on, performing the best way to honour the victims. As news about the concerts was released, I checked with my colleagues if it was prudent to go. They unanimously motivated me to be there.

I arrived at Bridgewater Hall about an hour before. Besides additional security measures that in Mexico would seem extremely normal, the feeling was similar to any other concert I've seen, the audience wanting a good time and perhaps to forget for a few hours what had happened the night before. The concert started with a poignant 'Banging on the Door' in honour of the victims, followed by a very good performance by The Anchoress.

Simple Minds' performance was mind-blowing, the energy spectacular and connection with the audience intensely felt. Highpoints were 'See the Lights', 'Stand by Love' and 'Alive and Kicking'. After the concert, as I walked to my hotel, I stopped at a candlelit memorial to the victims in front of Manchester Town Hall and thought about the decision to carry on with the gigs. It really felt right. I saw Simple Minds again in Mexico City the year after, but this was a night I will never forget.

## MARK STEWART

As a 16-year-old I fell in love with Simple Minds after seeing them play 'Chelsea Girl' on *The Old Grey Whistle Test* in March 1979. I couldn't wait to see them at Ayr Pavilion, home of the then-famous Tom Jones Powerhouse disco that May. It was very atmospheric.

Many other gigs later the highlight was Ibrox Park. Who'd have thought a bunch of Celtic fans could bring so much joy to thousands of adoring fans at the home of Glasgow Rangers? I also had the opportunity to celebrate my wife's 50 birthday at Llandudno in March 2015.

However, the most moving Simple Minds concert I ever witnessed was the *Acoustic* gig in Manchester at the Bridgewater Hall. It was so poignant, given what happened the night before at Manchester Arena. Jim said the band thought long and hard as to whether the show should go on, deciding that terrorism shouldn't and wouldn't win.

My other lasting memory of that night was, after the fourth song, not knowing the setlist, me shouting at the top of my voice from the front row, 'Go on Jimmy, gee us 'Chelsea Girl'!' to which Jim replied to the audience, 'There's always one!' then launching into the song. Great concert!

## SIMON W SMITH

In 1984, I was sharing a study at boarding school with Martin, a self-confessed new romantic who had Duran Duran's *Rio* on tape and played it all the time. He even dyed his hair with peroxide, such was his devotion. I begged him to play something – anything - else. One day he came back with *Sparkle in the Rain* and after one listen it was goodbye Duran Duran!

Milton Keynes Bowl was my first stadium gig. I was on a hotel and catering BTEC placement near Glasgow and travelled via Halifax, West Yorkshire to meet Martin and on to Milton Keynes by bus. It's a good job I was young and energetic. I had to travel back the next day with no voice after singing my heart out. I was a bit isolated in Glasgow, not knowing anyone and with the placement not long enough for me to settle into any friendships, but the memory of that concert and listening to *Once Upon a Time* helped me.

I've seen Simple Minds play live all over the UK, including in torrential rain at Edinburgh Castle in 2009, when I enticed Martin and his wife to join me dancing in our wellies. I took a lady on a first date to see Simple Minds in Dalby Forest in 2011 and a year later we married and danced to 'New Gold Dream' on our wedding night.

With 2017 at Bridgewater Hall the day after the Manchester Arena bomb, I was in two minds whether to go. Hearing the band were determined to play and not give in to terrorism, I decided to attend. I remember a minute's standing of togetherness and the hush of the audience as we paid our respects to the victims. I had front-row seats and danced briefly with Jim to an acoustic 'New Gold Dream' when he came into the audience. It was a gig that was both poignant and joyous, with a real sense of unity.

Simple Minds will play me out when I shuffle off this mortal coil into my 'Big Sleep'. I'm going to have 'Don't You (Forget About Me)' played at my funeral.

## ANDREW FINCH

*Royal Concert Hall*
*26 May 2017, Nottingham, England*

My wife bought me VIP tickets for my birthday. I was amazed to learn we were on the front row, left of centre, where I thought Charlie might be. Support was provided by The Anchoress, who was brilliant (I already had her deluxe album). At the end of her set she told the audience she'd be in the foyer at the break. As her crew were clearing the stage, I asked a crew member for a setlist and quickly went to the foyer. Catherine was surprised I had the setlist but signed a lovely autograph on it. It was already a great night and the main event was yet to start!

Simple Minds opened with an awesome acoustic version of 'New Gold', during which I reached to give Jim a high-five and to my surprise he grabbed my hand and sincerely shook it! It felt like a really appreciative handshake, a 'thanks for coming'. As always, Jim and the band were brilliant with the audience. When the gig ended, I got to shake hands with nearly everyone! When Ged shook my hand, he gave me his plectrum! I couldn't believe my luck and stuffed I I into my trouser pocket for safe keeping. I also got a Simple Minds setlist.

When we got home, I was looking through my programme and souvenirs but couldn't find the plectrum anywhere. No matter where I searched - in the bag, my pockets, my wallet, outside with a torch in the car. It dawned on me that it may have fallen out of my pocket when I got my car keys out at the car park. My wife said, 'You're going to have to go back and look.' It was well past midnight as I started to drive seven miles back into Nottingham. I got into the car park and managed to park near where I had before. I walked over to where I would have got my keys out, and there it was. Whatever I had to pay to re-enter the car park again was worth every penny.

---

## DALE NOTTINGHAM

I was vaguely aware of Simple Minds through 'Promised You a Miracle' and 'Alive and Kicking'. I liked them and my brother was a fan. I saw the cover of *Live in the City of Light* while shopping and was intrigued, although I hardly knew any of the songs. Then, aged 15 and seriously into music, 'Belfast Child' came out, which I loved. This band I seemed to have a connection with was back.

I bunked off school on a Monday morning to hear an interview and songs off the *Street Fighting Years* album on Radio One, but what sealed the deal was listening to the fantastic documentary, *Street Fighting Years*, on the radio. I listened to that and loved every song they played from the band's past. I then went on my first vinyl shopping spree, buying *Sister Feelings Call*. I liked every song. I was away!

My first show was a 2017 *Acoustic* tour gig at the Royal Concert Hall. I took my sister and brother-in-law and they loved it. I've seen about 34 gigs these last three years and that acoustic concert was by far and away the best I've been to. What a band!

---

## STEPHEN GREENSTREET

*London Palladium*
*27 May 2017, London, England*

I've been fortunate to see Simple Minds many times, from Margate to numerous London venues, including the Palladium show on the *Acoustic* tour, a unique evening and performance. I was fortunate to meet the band backstage and have Jim and Charlie sign a Celtic shirt, even though Charlie signed it upside down!

# EDWIN COUGHTRIE

My Simple Minds journey started in my home city, Glasgow in 1980 at the age of 15 when I bought *Empires and Dance* after hearing 'I Travel' on the radio. From then on it was the Glasgow Apollo every time the Minds played.

Fast forward to the early '90s, living in Glasgow's Merchant City, I regularly saw Jim in our local dry cleaner's in Candleriggs. I couldn't believe it! My next-door neighbour was Mick MacNeil and I got to know him so well he invited me to his house in Glasgow's South Side for a Hogmanay party in which during the evening he played 'Belfast Child' on the accordion. There was silence in the whole house while he played. Magical!

I last saw the boys at the London Palladium in May 2017 and was completely blown away by their *Acoustic* set. As I was now living in Covent Garden I was back seeing them a week later at the Theatre Royal, Drury Lane, a gig I could walk to in five minutes. That was absolute heaven. Another great night of music.

# JUSTIN GREENWOOD

*Waterfront Hall*
*6 June 2017, Belfast, Northern Ireland*

My introduction to Simple Minds came through watching *The Breakfast Club*. I heard 'Don't You (Forget About Me)' but didn't know who sang it. A mate asked if I wanted to see Simple Minds at Milton Keynes Bowl, my first live concert, and I said yes. Only when they played 'Don't You (Forget About Me)' did I make the connection. I loved it. I had my mate on my shoulders. He was small and everyone kept throwing things at him! I then went and bought most of their music.

I moved to Northern Ireland a few years back and started to get a taste for going to events again. When they played Belfast Waterfront in 2017, I jumped at the chance. I was wondering whether they would still have the same power, and they did. It was awesome. I came home buzzing. I also wondered if it might have been the last time.

In 2020 I saw a post saying Simple Minds were playing Dublin so asked a friend along. They said yes, we booked, then I saw the Customs House, Belfast advertising, so got two more tickets. Then the virus thing started to kick off, both shows postponed. When we get to see these shows, Simple Minds will be the group I have seen live the most. They're an awesome group that still hold the same energy as they did in the '80s. Something about their music just brightens my day. I hope they keep going. I'd love to see them a fifth time!

## EVELINE DELVAUX

*Olympia Theatre*
*7 June 2017, Dublin, Ireland*

It must have been the early 1980s when 'I Travel' was vibrating loudly through the family kitchen, my teenage brother dancing his heart out. I was still quite young, legs dangling away somewhere around the kitchen sink. I very much enjoyed taking in the waves of music, letting them filtrate through my whole being.

Over the years, I've been lucky enough to attend quite a few live performances. I'm a Belgian who's resided in New Zealand for 23 years. Whether I find myself at Vorest Nationaal, Brussels or Villa Maria Vineyard in Auckland, once the drumsticks start creating Simple Minds sounds, my feet follow the beat. Jim, Charlie and the band create a special connection with the audience. There's a surge of energy in the air, empowering you to immerse in the music, dancing away until the last note is played. You find yourself on a musical high for days.

In 2017 I flew across the world to Belgium around the same time the *Acoustic* tour was finishing. I landed in continental Europe and basically took off straight away for Dublin, just in time to attend the very last concert at the Olympia Theatre. One seat with an unobstructed view was left. Mine! It proved to be an exceptional concert and I was able to observe the band in close proximity in a unique historical setting. I was there on my own and the Irish fans made me feel so welcome. It really doesn't matter where you're from, or if you've ever met before. When you're chatting away about decades worth of Simple Minds gigs and music, you relate automatically. But what a surprise when I bumped into friends I managed to lose contact with about 20 years ago. The enthusiasm of the night was brought to yet another level.

I've got so many fantastic memories and experiences in my life thanks to brilliant Simple Minds music. I truly hope there's much more to come. I am forever grateful.

## ZAHID ISMAIL

*Barrowland Ballroom*
*13 February 2018, Glasgow, Scotland*

It's a confusing story of when Simple Minds first came to my attention. Whilst, musically, it was 'Promised You a Miracle' on the radio in 1982 that captured my imagination, I'd gone to school with a Jim lookalike from 1980. Perhaps, subconsciously, I was already aware of them. Anyway, there was a Scots spirit mixed with European cool in the music that appealed.

This is not the story of what should have been my first Simple Minds show in February 1986, nor my actual first concert at Ibrox in June 1986, but my first Barrowlands gig in 2018, where I was a human shield, taking a hit for Charlie!

After finally securing a precious ticket, the wait in the freezing cold hastened my steps indoors and to one of the few remaining spaces at stage right, in front of Charlie's station. Notwithstanding that Charlie's economy of bipedal locomotion blocked my sight of Catherine on keyboards, it was a decent enough vantage point. There was excitement when 'I Travel' kicked things off and puzzlement at why the band and Jim were momentarily out of sync (filmed for posterity). Then, when the *Walk Between Worlds* songs were premiered, I felt a hand running up and down my left thigh. Someone was trying to notch up the excitement, a lass behind me no less. Bemusement then amusement then irritation as hands-on appreciation continued for some 20 minutes, punctuated by exuberant cries of ardour towards Charlie and pelvic pressing (by the lass both times, just to be clear).

With my eyes, I signalled the security guy to look downwards, where he could see the third hand in action. Despite my polite request to stop, the frisking resumed a short while later. I eyeballed security again, this time with some annoyance, and he leaned across the barrier to tell the lass to cool it. Thankfully, this did the trick, and I could try to focus on the rest of the gig without hand-on-leg action/distraction. Charlie was oblivious to all that played out, but you're welcome, pal!

# BARBARA MCNALLY

*Albert Hall*
*14 February 2018, Manchester, England*

My journey with Simple Minds began aged 13, listening to 'I Travel' on 12-inch and *Sister Feelings Call* on my bedroom record player. I remember how the music and lyrics gave me a feeling of spiritual freedom in mind, body and soul. To listen to them was exciting, uplifting. I used to get - still do - butterflies in my stomach as soon as the music played. I knew intrinsically Simple Minds would be the backdrop to my journey through life - they were there to lift me every time I felt low or needed a boost of vibrant energy. 'Book of Brilliant Things' brings tears to my eyes when I listen to it.

A white hot day still gives me butterflies now, reminding me of teenage years sat in the hot sun and feeling freedom and love.

It was a pleasure for me to meet Jim and give him a thank you card and red rose in Manchester in 2018, a small token of appreciation for his life-enhancing music. The feelings at Simple Minds gigs are of oneness and a spiritual connectedness to everyone in the room. What a joy we were all on this earth at the same time.

---

# ANITA CARROLL

*Roundhouse*
*15 February 2018, London, England*

The music of Simple Minds has been a part of my life since my teenage years, but they never toured to the ends of the Canadian Prairie and Calgary. Had they done so I would have lined up at the Saddledome to get tickets. My uber-fan husband Kevin had also never seen them live. Every few years, when they toured nearby, or even Australia (not at all nearby), he'd muse about making a special trip. But it was never the right time.

Then Bowie died without us ever having seen him live. And we decided it is always the right time if you make it the right time. So instead of waiting for Simple Minds to come to us, we flew from our prairie home without the three kids (finally old enough to take care of themselves and the dog for the weekend) on a three-day whirlwind London adventure, Simple Minds playing the Roundhouse.

What a venue. What a stage set-up. What a band. They were interviewed every three songs about their new album, so it was an evening of song and stories we will never forget, more than worth the trans-continental journey and 30 hours without sleep (it's a good thing I'm never too tired to dance). On the way out, as the jet-lag started to set in, I bought a t-shirt.

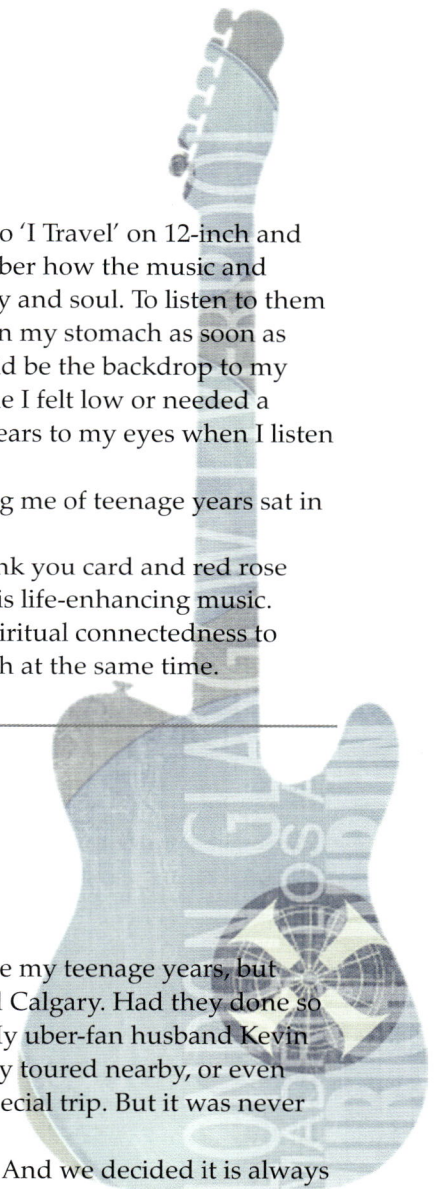

Flash forward several months and they announced a show in Vancouver, so much closer to home. We decide to go again, because it's always the right time and the kids didn't burn the house down on the London weekend so we figured they'd be okay. Again, it was a magical venue, although a scaled-down stage-set and limited merch table, which resulted in the one and only time in my life I have ever felt cool. During intermission, standing in the lobby wearing my *Walk Between Worlds* t-shirt, two ladies approached to find out where I got it. I smiled, saying, 'Earlier on the tour.'

Thank you, Simple Minds, for the music and the experiences my husband and I have had while enjoying your music, live and recorded. It's always the right time, it's always a good time and will always be something special Kevin and I share (besides the kids, obviously).

## DAVID ARCHWAMETY

I heard 'She's a River' in 1995 as a 12-year-old in Nebraska on Hits 106. It was unlike any other song. In the mid-2000s, living in the San Francisco Bay area, I kept hoping Simple Minds would announce an American tour. In 2013 they did, but only one West Coast date (Los Angeles) and I didn't go, wrongly assuming they'd announce a Bay date. LA date came and went and I was filled with regret at not being there. If I wanted to see my favourite band I knew I'd have to take more drastic measures. I saved up the money to cross the pond and see their February 2018 show at the Roundhouse. Two months later, they announced a 24-date North American tour, their biggest in over 30 years. I went to see them five more times. In Denver I got front-row seats. During the last song, Jim Kerr shook my hand. My New Gold Dream had come true.

## MAGNUS GUSTAVSSON

*Store Vega*
*20 February 2018, Copenhagen, Denmark*

I can't remember the first Simple Minds song I heard but bought *New Gold Dream*. I was listening to Depeche Mode, Fad Gadget, Classix Nouveaux, Duran Duran and Ultravox, but hearing Simple Minds was like a bomb exploding.

I missed the gig in Stockholm in January 1984 because I was so young and couldn't afford to travel. But I got a cassette of it via the friend of a friend and listened to it over and over again.

In February 2018 I saw the gig in Copenhagen. It was a beautiful venue to see

Simple Minds in. Before, there was dark and dimmed lighting. They played Gary Numan's 'Cars' and Kraftwerk's 'The Model'. It was like being in a Simple Minds music video!

---

## CHERISSE OFOSU-OSEI

*Simple Minds drummer, 2016 to present*
*Plaža Žnjan*
*5 May 2018, Split, Croatia*

The most surreal show of all, a show that really stood out for me, was when we played Croatia in the middle of an electric storm. The mayor of Split had invited us personally to do a show in his town and invited all the local dignitaries. So with much pomp and ceremony the stage was prepared, then half an hour before we were due to go on an electric storm developed over the mountains. Amid forks of lightning

*Cherisse at the Count Basie Center, Red Bank, New Jersey. Photo Vincent Barker*

and crackling storm clouds, the shout was 'the show's off!', 'the show's on!', 'the show's off!', 'the show's on!' and then the rain started and the shout was 'the show's definitely off!' We all went back to the dressing rooms thinking, 'Oh well what a shame, the show is off.' Before we could even sit down we heard 'the show's on, get on stage now!'

We all hurried onto the stage amid torrential rain and thunderclaps. I nearly slipped and fell getting to my drum kit! The front stage was awash with rainwater and the crew were going backwards and forwards with brooms trying to sweep it off. The set started, then my nightmare began! All the moths and bugs in the area came towards me and my kit. I was batting off giant moths with my sticks whilst others landed and buried themselves in my hair. It was one of the most creepy gigs of my drumming career and thank goodness my screaming was drowned out by the loudness of the crowd! That was a wild show! The crowd kept me going through the plague of insects. The stage is meant to be for the band not for creepy-crawlies! I hope I never have to see another on stage again!

## CATHERINE ANNE DAVIES (AKA THE ANCHORESS)

*Simple Minds keyboard player, 2014 – 2018*

It was May 2018 and the first show of a long summer run in support of the *Walk Between Worlds* album. I'd flown straight from playing a show with Manic Street Preachers at Wembley Arena and we landed in sunny Split in Croatia to glorious weather and serene surroundings. Nothing could have led us to believe that a few hours later the heavens would open and a storm so savage would be raging, thunder and lightning so dangerous that it looked as though the show would have to be cancelled. It was the first show of a long summer of dates across Europe and we couldn't believe we might have to stop before we'd even started.

We sheltered backstage in our dressing rooms listening to torrential rain pour down and thinking of all the waiting fans getting drenched as they stood in anticipation. Now the one thing you should know about Simple Minds is that the show must always go on! This isn't only down to the work ethic and ethos of the band but to the magnificent crew of men and women that work tirelessly behind the scenes to build and set the stages and make sure everything is running smoothly. We waited patiently, primped and dressed and ready to go as Vince, GG, Daniel, Del, Jeff and many more worked quickly to waterproof all the instruments and electrics, conjuring up makeshift raincoats for the synths with gaffer tape and plastic clingfilm, like an episode of *Blue Peter* gone very, very wrong.

And I'm thinking, 'Hell, am I wearing high heels tonight on that stage?' as it more and more resembled a water slide than a stage floor.

The lightning flashes kept on coming but soon we got word that the health and safety guys had cleared the show to start. We all breathed a sigh of relief and played all the harder for each person in the audience singing their hearts out that night, despite getting an outdoor shower!

---

# JESÚS MAS CALERO

*Festival Jardins de Pedralbes*
*11 June 2018, Barcelona, Spain*

I remember hearing a concert in Marbella on the *Real Life* tour being broadcast on the radio. I was able to record it on cassette and listened back a thousand times afterwards. Then I fell in love with the CDs of *Real to Real Cacophony* and *New Gold Dream (81,82,83,84)*, background music for many study evenings.

Simple Minds came to Barcelona on their *5x5* tour and I saw them then and have not missed a tour since 2012. On the *Walk Between Worlds* tour, I saw them in the same week in Barcelona and Nimes and together with my wife (also now a fan) met Charlie after as he was getting into the van. But possibly the best moment was in Barcelona in 2018. Sat the front row while Sarah Brown sang 'Let the Day Begin', she approached the area where I was and encouraged me with her arm to get up and sing with her, 'Here's to you, my little loves, with blessings from above. Now let the day begin, let the day begin.'

When I remember it, my hair stands on end and I feel chills.

---

# LINDA MCGHEE

*Piazza Castello*
*5 July 2018, Marostica, Italy*

Setting out from the Gorbals every day, past Oatlands, up Polmadie and over Malls Mire to reach Toryglen, the shows blasting out great music when they were in town and hanging about with my pals, treading well-worn territory of the *Grande Gruppo*, Simple Minds.

Moving to England, where fate led me into the arms one of the group's biggest fans, who regaled me with stories of the concert in Roundhay Park, Leeds, where we'd end up living. Setting off from Leeds to Glasgow together every Friday night after work and listening to Simple Minds for the entire trip. We declared that we didn't just have our song ('Someone Somewhere (in Summertime)'), we had our group.

My first visit to Hillsborough to see his other passion, Sheffield Wednesday, and the build-up of excitement so magnificently expressed by those big opening bars of 'Waterfront', reeling me in and gaining the club another supporter, after Celtic of course!

Fast forward to realising a long-held dream of working and living in Italy, buying a flat there and visiting Taormina. A myriad of concerts, locations, crowds and venues that can only be described as pure, dead brilliant, culminating in the last comical scenario in my adopted Italian town of Marostica, where the mayor left the concert in full swing to get the carabinieri to stop people getting out of their seats or approaching the stage – something that could only in happen in Veneto!

## KEITH AND CAROLINE MCDONALD

### Piazza Castello
### 10 July 2018, Udine, Italy

There have been so many memories since it all kicked off in 1977. We had not met at that time but were both fans and went to various concerts across Scotland. The best memory is Udine in 2018. We travelled up from Bologna, blagging executive class seats on the train to find Udine was a really lovely place with a cracking castle venue. The weather was smiling on us, but little did we know what was ahead.

The castle was the natural 'go to' place in the town, even if there wasn't a concert on. We headed there for lunch. It was quiet so we chatted to the sound guys and Derek frae Bellshill, the drum maestro, had a lovely slow lunch and then chatted away to Ged and Charlie as they got back to business after their lunch break. After a wee while it was back to the B&B for a quick change.

Keith and Caroline McDonald went to Udine and then Taormino

We arrived at the concert near the front and were puzzled to see so many Italians with waterproofs on when it was beach weather. Having been at the Edinburgh Castle concert we should have been prepared. Just as the concert got going it started to rain heavier and heavier. It goes with the territory at a Simple Minds outdoor concert

based on past experience but we were dressed totally inappropriately. Is it the lyrics? Only four songs that night had no mention or reference to water. Thank goodness for the merchandising tent. Spare polythene got us back to the digs.

After drying off, it was off to Villa Angela via Venice, where we met some great people and remain friends to this day. The staff are as good as the band. All told, Udine - via Bologna, Venice and Taormina - is the best one. So far.

## LUIS ALMODÓVAR PACIOS

*Festival de Carcassonne, Théâtre de la Cite*
*20 July 2018, Carcassonne, France*

In 1987 I was in compulsory military service and a colleague had a cassette tape of *Live in the City of Light*. After hearing it I immediately bought the double-vinyl. It remains my favourite, although *Live in the City of Angels* provides it with competition. I finally saw them in Carcassonne in 2018. It was impressive, exciting, unforgettable - and raining. They transmit so much on stage and make those of us who follow them feel like they are part of us.

## ELLIE DUNN

*Kent Event Centre*
*4 August 2018, Maidstone, England*

I started listening to Simple Minds around 35 years ago. My boyfriend at the time had most of their albums. I had a bit of a break and then, a few years ago, Simple Minds launched their *Acoustic* album and did a live Radio 2 concert. Chris Evans played 'Promised You a Miracle' on his breakfast show and I was instantly hooked. I sat mesmerised and watched the whole concert on the Radio 2 webpage, sang every word and vowed to see Simple Minds every year. I did London Palladium and then Detling Showground (Margate), coupled with Chrissie Hynde. She too was showstopping. I couldn't take my eyes off her.

Sadly, this year is cancelled but I have my ticket, tour t-shirt, tour CD and of course tote bag! I am a totally devoted fan and will keep on coming if they keep playing! Jim Kerr, you are a legend.

## JULIA ROGERS

Since the much talked about gig at Milton Keynes Bowl in 1986 I've been an avid fan, lucky enough to see them play across the UK. But my favourite memory is something I never thought would ever happen. They played Detling Showground in my hometown of Maidstone, Kent, having been to gigs almost every year since '86. Over the years I built up a collection of memorabilia, of which most I have, but sadly due to a burglary all bar one CD and DVD I had were stolen. Heartbreaking! Slowly, I'm trying to rebuild this now. I love to see them live. Thanks for the music and long may I continue to be able to enjoy Simple Minds.

## SIMON DAVIES

*Grandslam 18, Cyfarthfa Park*
*5 August 2018, Merthyr Tydfil, Wales*

I hadn't seen Simple Minds live, despite following them since *Life in a Day,* when I got the chance to see them in Merthyr Tydfil. Let's just say the excitement got to me. I don't remember much about the gig, apart from support acts The Pretenders and KT Tunstall being immense. So I've booked to see them again. Sorry Jim, I'll behave this time.

## NIGEL WILLIAMS

I first knew I'd heard something different and something special when I saw *The Tube* special on TV of the *Once Upon a Time* tour at the Ahoy, Rotterdam. I was mesmerised at the opening bassline of 'Waterfront' and watching JK waiting in anticipation to run up the steps and enter that massive arena. What was going through his mind? It must have been a massive adrenaline rush as the waiting audience finally got a glimpse of the lead singer entering the lion's den. What an awesome performance, one that will forever be ingrained on my memory banks. From that day on, this 15-year-old wet-behind-the-ears boy from the Valleys saved up pocket money and Saturday wages to spend on the entire back-catalogue.

*Nigel Williams was at the GRANDSLAM 18 show at Cyfarthfa Castle*

My first live experience was at Wembley Arena for the *Street Fighting Years* tour. It was absolutely awesome and I felt as though my association with the band was now complete. And 35 years later, having bought every album since and attended many concerts, I'm still enjoying the music and experiences. At Merthyr Tydfil's Cyfarthfa Castle, I finally got to meet the band in person, which was fantastic. I've seen many bands live in my time but not one has come close to the Simple Minds experience.

---

## MARK HAMILTON

*AJ Bell Stadium*
*10 August 2018, Salford, England*

Me and my wife Gill have memories from the *New Gold Dream* days. The first time we saw them was at Roundhay Park. The sound was fantastic on 'When Spirits Rise'. Our three children grew up with Simple Minds. Our younger son Jed was born when they released 'Alive and Kicking' and our daughter Amber was born when they released 'Let there be Love'. It was played as I walked her down the aisle at her wedding in a church in Cheshire. I wasn't expecting that and was both surprised and emotional. Zach, our eldest son, keeps threatening to take us to Taormina.

The last time we saw them was at the AJ Bell Stadium. We'd only got off the plane from Greece an hour before and managed to get down the front. We loved Jim's comment to Charlie about Eccles.

---

## SARAH MCFARLANE

*Butts Park Arena*
*18 August 2018, Coventry, England*

A school friend's older sister introduced me to their music. The raw sound of 'Chelsea Girl' and 'Love Song' spoke to me. At 15, I had the obligatory poster of Jim on my bedroom wall. And 37 years on I'm still a fan.

The sound has changed but my love for the band has continued, with numerous gigs all over the UK. They are always full of energy, as though the band was just starting out, not nearly 40 years old. My most memorable gig was Coventry in 2018. My long-suffering husband said the meet and greet option was a step too far. I sulked through breakfast that morning, saying I'd understand if it was any other band but this was Simple Minds!

He gave in. We got to meet the band just prior to them going on stage. What do they say about meeting your idols? The whole band was so friendly, especially Charlie. Jim, the heart throb on my teenage bedroom wall, was just a regular guy. I was acting cool until I heard my husband say, 'She watches you guys all the time on YouTube while doing the ironing' - very rock 'n' roll!

Meeting the band can now be crossed off my bucket-list. Simple Minds have accompanied me on my life journey: finding love, getting married and having children. They've been a part of the family, my hubby totally accepting of Jim as the other man in my life. On relaying my perfect day to my mum, she said, 'I thought you would have grown out of them by now.'

---

## JOSEPH LOVERIDGE

*Colchester Castle Park*
*26 August 2018, Colchester, England*

I was at the meet and greet at Colchester. There was a lady there, and it was her first Simple Minds gig. But, hey, that's cool because that's what it's all about. I met her later that night and she loved it. That's Simple Minds, still mesmerising fans 40 years on.

---

## JOLLY TAYLOR

*Lydiard Park*
*31 August 2018, Swindon, England*

My first gig was Glasgow Barrowland in 1983 or '84. I remember the floor bouncing and me jumping with no effort. The last time was Swindon 2018. I'm still jumping even though I'm in my 50s. With a lot more bounce and a lot less jump.

---

## COLIN WEARN

*South of England Event Centre*
*1 September 2018, Chichester, England*

I didn't get to see them live until 1986 at Milton Keynes Bowl. I remember The Bangles and recall The Cult being much better than I expected. And The Waterboys too. But

Simple Minds blew me away. 'Let me see your hands,' said Jim. I'm still showing him my hands to this very day.

I've lost count now how many times I've seen them. Early gigs were stadia and large arenas. Great gigs with vast crowds. Cardiff Arms Park in the late '80s was terrific. The anticipation from the crowd matched by the performance from the band. Jim singing on his knees and his back. A wall of love from us all, watching and bouncing as one.

I've enjoyed every single one of them. But one show stands out for me. Chichester Beer Festival. Two tents. One full of beer. The other full of Simple Mind fans. Jim came on and said, rather sarcastically, 'It doesn't get any better than this. A tent in the Sussex countryside.' The atmosphere was electric. The crowd were wild from start to finish. We jumped and danced and sweated and sang through the whole gig. Sanctify Yourself. Sanctify Me. Sanctify Simple Minds fans.

## JAMES WAKEHAM

*Taunton Racecourse*
*2 September 2018, Taunton, England*

I live near St Austell in Cornwall and after hearing *Once Upon a Time* realised my older brother owned the *Life in a Day* LP and had *New Gold Dream* on cassette. These soon moved from his bedroom to mine. I've seen Simple Minds a number of times over the years in London, Plymouth and most recently Taunton Racecourse and they sound as awesome as ever. The visuals and energy put into the show by the band and production are also awesome. Hopefully one day they might play the Eden Project Sessions, right on my doorstep.

## VIBEKE MIDLANDER

*Slessor Gardens*
*9 September 2018, Dundee, Scotland*

I've been listening to Simple Minds since the age of 10. Having a rough childhood, their music brought me through the worst of it. I remember a concert in Gentofte stadium in 1989 where me and a friend climbed a fence and watched the whole show from there because we hadn't the money to get in and our parents wouldn't let us go. I remember saying out loud, 'Jim Kerr is the best singer in the world and I have to tell him that!'

*Vibeke Midlander was at the Slessor Gardens gig in Dundee*

The years passed by and suddenly I'm 42! This year was a real crappy one - I lost one of my very dearest friends to cancer and taking care of him until his last breath made me realise you shouldn't postpone what you've always wanted to do in life. Then I wanted to catch up on everything like I was going to die tomorrow.

I invited my best friend to go with me, all the way to Dundee for a three-day stay to see Simple Minds at Slessor Gardens, with a meet and greet. It was the best concert I've been to in my life. I got to tell Jim what I've wanted to say all that time.

'Hello, I have to tell you, you are the best singer in the world.'

Jim answered, pointing at the band, 'Yeah, I keep telling them this!'

## RODRIGO GH ZAUNBOS

*Pepsi Centre WTC*
*20 September 2018, Mexico City, Mexico*

Simple Minds in Mexico City – wow! My dream came true after 40 years listening on LP, cassette and CD. Being able to see them live was the best thing I experienced. Thank you, Jim Kerr and Charlie Burchill, for so many years of excellent music and passion. I've shared each stage of my life with your music and you are the best.

---

## MARK T SCHWENKSVILLE PA

*Sands Bethlehem Event Center*
*24 September 2018, Bethlehem, Pennsylvania*

I've been a fan since the days of 'Alive and Kicking' and 'Don't You (Forget About Me)'. I'd try to keep up with things when I could, but somehow life seemed to get in the way. Then along came 'She's a River' and I was hooked again. I was checking every few days to see if and when Simple Minds were coming to the States. In 2018 I couldn't really believe the band were coming to the Sands. As a surprise, my daughter bought tickets and took me as a birthday gift. We rocked out with the band for the entire show. It was such an awesome experience that I went to a second show at the Tower Theater, Philadelphia a couple of weeks later.

Here's to continued success and not taking another 20 years to revisit.

---

## GUY BOISVERT

*M-Telus*
*28 September 2018, Montreal, Canada*

I started college in 1983 in Trois-Rivières, Québec. I was living with my parents in a little village about 40km away so rented an apartment with friends. The first night in Trois-Rivières, we went to a bar called Le Gosier near one of the college buildings. When we entered The Eurythmics' 'Sweet Dreams' was playing, followed by David Bowie's 'Let's Dance' and Simple Minds' 'New Gold Dreams'. That was really something, musically new for me, coming from high school. I bought *New Gold Dream* on cassette the following day.

I played my cassettes until they died and bought the vinyl when I at last had money to buy a decent sound system with a turntable. I played my records until they died and then bought CDs. Finally, I turned all my CDs into FLAC files and now have a network music player with all my music at my fingertips, a Raspberry Pi plus Volumio hooked up to my NFS server.

Simple Minds came to Montréal in 2013 but I missed them. I didn't know about it. I was so disappointed. But at M-Telus in 2018 in Montréal I at last saw the band live. I was not disappointed - very good visuals, great sound, unbelievable music very well played and the singer in great shape! All the hits and more. Unfortunately, we arrived late and I couldn't get the goodies that came with my 'premium' tickets. But this was one of the best shows of my life. Long live Simple Minds.

## THE CANADIAN LOVEBIRDS

*Budweiser Gardens*
*29 September 2018, London, Canada*

Where do I begin? I fell in love with Simple Minds in university around 1983/84 and saw them in concert at Maple Leaf Gardens in Toronto around that time. My first concert! Being an arts student, I was in love with the vibe and style of Simple Minds. I met my husband a few years later when 'Alive and Kicking' was big. It's still our theme song. We saw the band in our hometown, London, Ontario. It's the only group my husband will dance to with me, cranking the volume whenever they're on air.

## ELAINE GIRARD

I was at a local record shop and they played *New Gold Dream*. I stood there, mesmerised, until it was done. The clerk played 'Chelsea Girl' for me (his favourite) and it became my nickname for years. Before I left I had two albums in my bag and had been put on the wait list for anything new - picture discs and books alike. I've happily followed their musical progression, finding at least one gem in every release.

Due to work and school schedules I was unable to see them live until September 2018. I was set to see them in Toronto in 2013 but a presentation at school was pushed up - ironically, it was Music Appreciation class, with Simple Minds my subject matter! I love the complexity of the music and various tones of Jim's voice, especially when the accent comes through! They're always my go-to music selection.

# JEFF MORRISON

## Orpheum
## 3 October 2018, Boston, Massachusetts

I went solo on a school night to the legendary Orpheum in Boston. Because I had to drop my son off at basketball practice in the suburbs, I wasn't going to be able to get into the city, find parking and make the gig by 8pm. I was tired from a tough day at work and did consider bagging the show.

*Jeff Morrison nearly missed out on second row seats at the Orpheum - photo William Zahoruiko*

Fortunately, cooler heads prevailed and I got there by 8.15ish, just three songs in. I showed my ticket to the usher, and to my huge surprise, was led all the way up to the second row! Are you kidding me? I hadn't looked closely at my seat number and wasn't familiar with the venue.

Needless to say, the gig was fantastic and I'm a huge fan of *Walk Between Worlds* so enjoyed those tunes as much as the hits. Hopefully not the last time I catch Simple Minds, but it'll be hard to top my seat!

# JIM LAVERTY

The big music and the spiritual themes in Jim Kerr's lyrics on *New Gold Dream* drew me in. I joined the fan club (I still have pins from the *Sparkle in the Rain* era), bought every album and many singles and drove hours with my girlfriend to see them open for The Pretenders in Rhode Island. I still have a programme from that show carrying the band's autographs.

In 2018, I got to see Simple Minds perform again and walked away with a memento I will treasure, a guitar pick Charlie Burchill handed me when he greeted us after the encore. What I appreciate most about Simple Minds is their child-like belief that spreads hope in a world that desperately needs something to hope in. I remember a quote from Jim: 'When I was in school, if you said someone was a dreamer, it was like he was a fool or he didn't get anything done. I don't believe that.'

---

# STEVE ROBINSON

November 1985. Walking to school, ghetto-blaster on shoulder, full belt. The band? Simple Minds. The album? *Once Upon a Time*. So many great bands at that time, but only one has the same impact on me today that they did that autumn. I've always felt I've played a role in the Minds' success over the years. To this day the local Woolworths store manager must wonder why a Simple Minds album would always be showing in the No.1 album spot after I left the shop!

*Steve Robinson and pals in DC on the way to Boston*

Many fans I meet say Roundhay Park was one of the best days of their lives. It certainly was mine. Taormina is another fan favourite, while everything came together in their performance at Delamere Forest in 2011. Taking my daughter Charlotte to the Bridgewater Hall the day after the awful bombing at Manchester Arena was also incredibly emotional.

Simple Minds have brought Andrew, Neil, Bob, Drew, Clynt and I together over the last few decades. No matter where we are in the world we've thrown ourselves passionately into every tour. We have one rule – the obligatory city bus tour so we can go home and say we saw a little of a new city and didn't spend the entire weekend inside a bar.

In 2018 we got together for consecutive gigs in New York, Philadelphia, Boston and Washington DC. Travelling in from the UK and Australia, it was a challenging tour itinerary. We very much appreciated the kind invite from Jim to meet backstage in Boston. The band and its crew are great people to be around.

## WILLIAM ZAHORUIKO

When my wife Theresa and I set out to the Orpheum Theater to see Simple Minds on the *Walk Between Worlds* tour, anticipation was high based on the fantastic sound of the new album and a rare chance to see them in the USA again. We settled into stage-right seats, next to the speakers with a slightly obscured view. That didn't matter - Jim visited often and was particularly engaging with Theresa as she danced to her favourite song, 'Hypnotised'. He was also pleased to see the Scotland cap I frantically waved.

*William Zahoruiko's wife Theresa with Jim*

Due to the abundant love and camaraderie in the venue, some new friends invited us down to the front of the stage to enjoy the show even more. They had noticed our enthusiasm and felt they had to get us closer. As a veteran of 400-plus shows, this did not disappoint and rates as an all-time favourite. Jim and company were spot on.

Blown away by the spectacle, we unwound over a pint at a bar. We said, 'Hey, let's see if the band's still around,' not really expecting to have any more luck on what had already been a legendary evening. Waiting with a handful of others, we saw Jim emerge, and he was genuine and courteous, signing autographs and taking pictures. He even looked at Theresa and said, 'Now, you had a good time.' It melted our hearts that he remembered folks from the show. This was as unforgettable as every one of the seven Minds shows I've been lucky enough to attend.

# HERSHEY BELL

*9:30 Club*
*6 October 2018, Washington DC*

I grew up in Toronto listening to CFNY, where I first heard 'Love Song' - thus began a lifelong love affair with the music of Simple Minds. In the fall of 1983, I was driving home from visiting my fiancée (now my wife of 36 years) in Connecticut. As I approached Rochester, New York along Interstate 90, I tuned into CFNY and for the first – and only – time in my life had to pull off the highway to stop and listen to a song. It was 'Waterfront'. I'd never heard anything like it. Soon as I got back to Toronto, I drove straight to Sam the Record Man and purchased the 12-inch.

My first live experience was at the 9:30 Club during the *Walk Between Worlds* tour. My son and I purchased VIP tickets. The soundcheck was

*Hershey Bell treated himself to a copy of the guitar used by Charlie*

amazing, but that was nothing compared to the show we watched from the front row. Of course I wanted to hear 'Waterfront' and didn't have to wait long – it was second in the set.

We positioned ourselves on the left of the stage so I could be as close as possible to my guitar hero, Charlie Burchill. While he played a wide selection of guitars that night, the one I waited for was his famed Gretsch White Falcon, which appeared in the tour poster. Coming full circle from first hearing 'Love Song' on CFNY, this year for my 63rd birthday I purchased my very own Gretsch White Falcon. I name all my electrics and there was only one choice for this incredible work of art – Charlie!

---

# SCOTT STREIBICH

In October 2011 my cover band, The New Romance, had a fantastic show at the 9:30 Club in Washington DC, and set-closer 'Don't You (Forget About Me)' had the house singing along, waving hands throughout. It was an electric moment I was lucky enough to share with my wife Erina and my sister Romy. Fast forward to October 2018 and Simple Minds are playing the 9:30 Club. My wife and sister are with me, wedged up against the stage barrier. Close to the end Derek is standing in the same spot on the 9:30 Club stage where I stood playing that song. With the same amazing bassline and energy pumping through the bass-bins, Jim, Charlie and the entire band had the room feeling like we were intimate friends sharing the same party, together as one.

Two magical moments in my life I will always treasure. One stage, one band, one song: Simple Minds' 'Don't You (Forget About Me)'.

## PAUL WETHERHILL

I was at Roundhay Park at 16 with my best friend James. We pretended we were at each other's houses but camped out overnight and got to the front. An amazing day. The 'Street Fighting Years' intro in front of 50,000 people and the way the white sheet dropped at the beginning of the show was amazing!

I met Jim in Washington DC on the *Walk Between Worlds* tour. I told him me and James had been at Roundhay Park and my mum didn't know. Jim said, 'So was I - and my mum neither!'

*Paul Wetherhill met JK in DC*

## KENDALL KEELING

*Tabernacle*
*8 October 2018, Atlanta, Georgia*

I worked in a record store called Turtles. *New Gold Dream* had just been released and was getting airplay on college radio station, WRAS. I adored it, went back and bought the previous albums immediately. I've loved everything they produced.

I saw them for the first time in 1986. I was working in a different record store by then. Since they'd had top-40 hits in the US, the audience wasn't nearly as full of true fans as I hoped, but the show was great.

I finally saw them again in 2018. This time I was ready! I bought VIP meet and greet tickets and front-row centre seats. I'd been sharing their music with my husband over the years and he was very excited. They didn't play anything from my favourite album, *Life in a Day*, but the setlist was fantastic. The energy of the band, especially Jim, was astonishing. It truly was one of those experiences where the band was feeding off of the energy of an audience full of hardcore fans. It was an absolute delight. Jim had his father with him at this show. They were all so lovely and gracious backstage. It's in my top-three shows of all time.

## LORI K LODEN

I've loved Simple Minds since 1982. 'Promised You a Miracle' was rotating on the newest craze called MTV. I bought *New Gold Dream (81~82~83~84)* on gold vinyl and then on cassette so I could play it in my car. I was already into the British Invasion of the early '80s and this Scottish band was becoming a favourite.

My crush for Simple Minds has endured such that my children also love the band. My daughter and I watched a DirecTV presentation of a 1995 concert at the Olympia in Paris several years ago. That's when she fell in love with the band.

They hadn't been to Atlanta, Georgia in over 20 years. I never got to see the Minds live before so was totally ecstatic when I heard they were coming for a 2018 tour. I wasn't going to miss them this time. My husband, son and I saw them at the Tabernacle and were not disappointed. Just seeing their name on the marquee before we got inside was exciting. This extensive tour consisted of two full sets spanning most of their career, which shows how much they truly care about their fans. My only regret is not paying extra for VIP tickets. Given a chance to experience Simple Minds again we will be going all out!

## IAN WILLERS

*Tabernacle*
*8 October 2018, Atlanta, Georgia*

Hearing 'Don't You (Forget About Me)' for me was how it would have been for a teenager hearing The Beatles for the first time in 1964. The song instantly demanded attention - the razor guitar that cut right to your soul, the pounding drums and soaring vocals that just begged to be sung along to. I immediately rushed out with

*Ian Willers saw the band at the Tabernacle*

*In action at the Tabernacle - photo Ian Willers*

Mom on her next shopping trip to the mall to raid the record store for any Simple Minds album I could find. This was middle America - Kansas to be exact - and they were just starting to get on the radio, so the local music shop only had one cassette. But one was enough for a proper introduction and I couldn't wait to hear their music. That day I came home with *Sparkle in the Rain*.

A few months later *Once Upon a Time* dropped. Over that next year Simple Minds ruled American radio. Finding out they were coming to my hometown of Kansas City was as thrilling as it was heartbreaking. I was too young to attend by myself and didn't think any of my friends even knew who they were. How wrong I was when the girl I had a huge crush on came into school wearing a tour t-shirt the next day.

I'm not sure exactly why but Simple Minds dropped off my radar for many years, until 2009 with *Graffiti Soul*. I don't recall how I came across it but like a long-lost friend they came back into my life with a vengeance and prompted me to go back and catch up with what I'd missed.

Finally, in 2018 I was close enough to see them on their huge but long overdue North American tour. It was a four-hour long car trip to Atlanta but nothing was going to stop me. As a drummer, hearing the news of Mel Gaynor not joining on the tour was frankly disappointing. Who and how could anyone possibly begin to fill those shoes? Hearing an unknown woman was taking over was both fascinating and scary, almost like I was nervous for her. I think it took about 30 seconds of hearing and watching Cherisse Osei play before I was thinking 'Mel who?'

The one thing that will stick with me is the enthusiasm between Charlie and Jim. They play each and every song like they just came out of the studio and can't wait to share it. That they can do that with songs they have been playing their entire lives and not simply go through the motions makes them one of the most exciting live acts around. They truly look like they're having a blast and that makes the audience go even more nuts. I sure did.

---

## ELAINE GWYTHER

### Ryman Auditorium
### 9 October 2018, Nashville, Tennessee

I've worked with Simple Minds for over 10 years and it's been an amazing experience. Jim and Charlie work so hard and are two of the kindest people I know. I love to travel and explore new places and they've taken me with them to countries and cities I never expected to see. When Jim asked if I would like to come out to join the 2018

*Jimmy Kerr in the Ernest Tubb Record Shop in Nashville - photo Elaine Gwyther*

American tour for a few days and bring his dad Jimmy, I jumped at the chance. Jimmy was a country music fan and had always wanted to go to Nashville.

Luckily Simple Minds were playing the Ryman Auditorium, Nashville, so I worked our plans around that. We flew into Atlanta first, saw the show there then travelled on the band tour bus down to Nashville the next day. The trip wasn't without incident. Jimmy's suitcase arrived a day later than us, having missed the connection in London, but it turned up before we left Atlanta. Jimmy took everything in his stride. He could tell a story like no other, I loved listening to him and could tell he was loving this new adventure/story, even the bit about the missing luggage and how I offered him some of my clean underwear - which he politely declined!

In Nashville there was so much to see and I couldn't have wished for a better travelling companion. Before the soundcheck we walked up and down Broadway looking in all the shops and bars, including the Ernest Tubb Record Shop which Jimmy knew all about. He explained the history of the place to me. There was a day off after the show so I arranged a visit for Charlie and the rest of the band to the Gibson Custom warehouse, on the outskirts of Nashville, to see beautiful guitars being handmade. Jim spent the day with Jimmy instead, exploring more of Nashville, and then (too soon) it was time for us to leave.

It was a wonderful trip, one of many with Simple Minds that I will treasure forever.

## GARY JENKINS

Simple Minds brings back special memories from the '80s and memories of a musical love affair. Seeing them at the historic Ryman Auditorium in 2018 just added to the excitement! My favourite moments were 'Don't You (Forget About Me)', 'Alive and Kicking' and the beautiful 'Belfast Child'. A stunning show from start to finish, and a bucket-list item for me.

## JEFF REEP

I have an older brother, John, seven years older than me and a very talented artist. Through the years, I always looked up to him and tried to follow in his footsteps. I thought he was the best! As he entered his college years, he was exposed to lots of music and exposed me to it too. At 11 I was listening to bands like Yellow Magic Orchestra, Kraftwerk, Visage and Ultravox. Always listening, the two of us would

*Jeff Reep reaches out to Jim - photo Jeff Reep*

swap headphones in the hallway of our parents' house to hear what each other was listening to. Whenever we were mad, scared or sad we could always escape into music. It was our lifeline.

The first song I ever heard by Simple Minds was 'Promised You a Miracle'. I thought, 'Wow, what a great song!' I came home and told my brother. He'd already heard the song from a dubbed cassette tape from one of his art school friends. He played it for me again and I was hooked!

We always went to shows together, and he stood or sat to my right for whatever reason. Sadly, in 2009 John lost his life due to a long battle with mental illness. He was my best friend. Now, when I'm at a show, I always imagine him there with me, smiling, to my right.

I promised John I'd keep our love for music alive, live it for the both of us. He'd have loved that I finally got a chance to see them live in Nashville, at the Ryman Theatre in 2018. If he were here today and had a chance to speak with the band, he would tell them, 'Thank you so much for your music and talent. You are an inspiration.'

---

## JULIE FINLEY

*Hard Rocksino*
*11 October 2018, Cleveland, Ohio*

Simple Minds tours of North America have been few and far between. Last time they were in Ohio was 1995, an absence of 23 years. Jim remarked. 'We thought you may have forgotten about us.' How could we? By the attendance, we clearly abided by Kerr's crooning when he sang '(Don't You) Forget About Me'. We didn't forget.

They started promptly at 7.45pm. It's rare for performers to acknowledge and respect that their audience probably has to go to work the next day. The early start time also helped accommodate a two-hour plus performance. They performed two full live sets and did the smart thing, with a 15-minute intermission. I think they realise they've got older, and so have their audience. Plus, if they're playing for over two hours, we're clearly getting our money's worth. Quality and quantity.

They were touring their latest, rather excellent album, *Walk Between Worlds*, but knew they had to give the audience what they'd been longing for. They kept the songs off the new album to a minimum, but Jim Kerr is very talkative and comical onstage and builds a great rapport with his audience. He's self-deprecating and amusing. When they were gearing up to do a new song, he'd ask, 'Can we please do a new one? It's really good, I promise!' They opened with a new one, 'The Signal and the Noise', and also performed the title track and 'Sense of Discovery'.

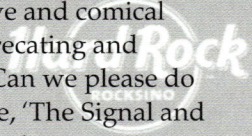

The bulk of the material was from my favourite album, *New Gold Dream (81-82-83-84)*, and they graced us with a funny anecdote from Kerr about how on the plane over, a woman recognised him, said, 'Hey, you're that guy from that band… Simply Red, right?' She claimed to like 'Glittering Prize' so he dedicated that to her.

I also recall 'Promised You a Miracle', 'Hunter and the Hunted', the exquisite 'Someone Somewhere (in Summertime)' and before their encore - yes, on top of two setlists, there was 'New Gold Dream' and a real highlight for me, 'Love Song', the song I'd truly been hoping to see live. They delivered - such a kick-ass tune!

They also performed 'The American' and when they came back for a second set, led into it with the instrumental 'Theme for Great Cities', a moment that truly gave band members time to shine, and Charlie Burchill's a vastly underrated guitarist!

They performed 'Alive and Kicking' during the encore, but also other essentials from the *Once Upon a Time* record, like 'All the Things She Said'. The vocals originally provided by the incredible Robin Clark were handled equally superbly by Sarah Brown. They also did the classic 'Sanctify Yourself' during the encore.

Photo Julie Finley

Jim joked about knowing a 'local girl' by the name of Chrissie Hynde. He said she sent her regards then continued to jest a bit with quips like, 'I think she misses me a little bit… she still says I'm the best kisser!'.

I also remember 'Up on the Catwalk' and 'Waterfront' from 1984's *Sparkle in the Rain* and various others like 'See the Lights' from *Real Life*, 'She's a River' from *Good News from the Next World*, 'Dolphins' from *Black and White* and a cover of Ewan MacColl's 'Dirty Old Town'.

Oh, and how can I forget? They performed the quintessential classic '(Don't You) Forget About Me', which everyone went wild for. Even some of the elderly ushers at the venue were dancing around, the first time I've seen that!

# KEVIN G YOHO

I'm originally from West Virginia, a very Scotch-Irish place in America. I first became aware of Simple Minds when 'Promised You a Miracle' was a single. The first album I purchased was *Once Upon a Time* on cassette. As a keyboardist, I really appreciated their synth arrangements and quickly scooped up the back-catalogue, following them from there. I first saw them in 2018 outside Cleveland, Ohio. We had front row seats, and I fell in love with Cherisse.

# KENT WIEN

Before the doors of the train had closed, I knew I was in for the adventure of a lifetime. It was 1986 and I was leaving Paris and heading to the west coast of France to begin a summer high school exchange programme. As I looked around the train I saw a girl who was absolutely stunning. Since I had only been in France for a few hours I was excited to try out my language skills. I used the excuse of temporarily exchanging cassettes in our Sony Walkmans to sit next to her. I gave her my Cars *Greatest Hits* cassette and she handed over her Simple Minds tape.

We didn't end up listening to the music; instead we started a conversation, partly in French and partly in English. Her name was Valerie. She had medium length blonde hair and I was amazed that we could converse so easily. She then invited me, a 16-year-old kid, to go to the bar car. I hadn't realised that was legal.

At some point she discovered our train would be skipping her stop, but that was nearly four hours down the line, so plenty of time for her to figure out how to get to her place. After a few hours of laughter and joking, the conductor told her that the train she wanted was there at the station we were stopped in. Suddenly she jumped up, gathered her stuff and kissed me on each cheek. 'Do you have a phone number?' I asked. 'Yes!' She responded as she was stepping off the train. The doors closed and she was gone.

I sat down in my seat. I still had her cassette. I pressed play. The song that began was 'Someone Somewhere (in Summertime)'. It couldn't have been more fitting. I smiled and fell in love - with the band known as Simple Minds.

# ROBB DUFTY

I was 13 when my mate said, 'You have got to listen to this.' The song was 'Themes for Great Cities'. I was blown away.

It is the song I go to for a lift if I'm feeling down.

# BRIDGET YOUNG

Living in Western Pennsylvania, working in local government, I'm a second generation Simple Minds fan. My dad taped the Ahoy Rotterdam 1985 concert off the radio for my mom when they were dating. They'd play the tape often when I was a child, and I believe Simple Minds became a part of my subconsciousness.

In my early 20s I decided to purchase the *Live in the City of Light* CD set for my parents. When they played the album, I fell in love with Simple Minds. I began to purchase one CD after another until I'd collected every album. As an artist, I like to play Simple Minds when I'm drawing or painting because the music puts me into a creative mindset. I think I enjoy their music so much because it's

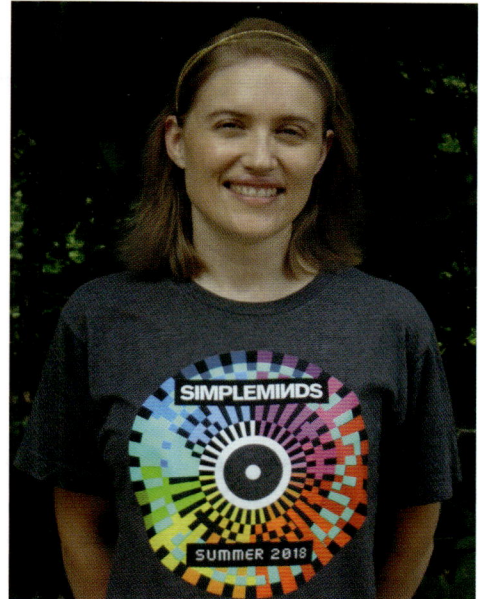

*Bridget Young saw Simple Minds in Ohio*

well-written, catchy and hard-rocking! I also like that Simple Minds music makes me feel something in my soul, and really appreciate the spiritual/Christian content of the lyrics.

I was so excited in 2018 when I heard they were going to tour the United States. I was able to purchase tickets for me and my parents for the concert at the Hard Rocksino and we had the time of our lives. It was the first time any of us had seen Simple Minds live. We all agreed it was one of the best concerts we had attended.

My favourite part was how Charlie and Jim interacted with the crowd. I could tell that Simple Minds truly appreciates all of their fans.

---

# ALFRED HARTEMINK

*Pabst Theater*
*13 October 2018, Milwaukee, Wisconsin*

Music is like family; you don't pick them, and they stay with you for the rest of your life. Like family members, there's music you grow up with, learn to live with, and eventually it becomes an intrinsic part of the fabric of your being.

I was 18 when *New Gold Dream* came out and the band was on tour in the Netherlands. As a poor student I couldn't attend, but I saved money, bought the album, and played it frequently. That bothered some of my friends at the time.

Was the world once divided between followers of the Rolling Stones and The

Beatles? In the 1980s my world was divided by those that admired U2 or like myself enjoyed the music of Simple Minds. As adolescents we had fruitless discussions about what was good and bad music. Some of that was indeed about the music but much of it was about the image that went with it. Several of my friends did not like Simple Minds for the cross on the album. It jarred with their atheist world view. Another issue was the obscure symbolism and their haircuts. I couldn't be bothered with any of that. They'd become a part of me. Discussions withered when the cross was replaced by the heart. Love always wins, and family never leaves.

Almost 40 years after *New Gold Dream* appeared, I finally saw them in concert in Milwaukee, an hour's drive from where I live in the USA. Although Derek Forbes and Mel Gaynor had left the family, the music felt like a reunification of ageless feelings and fresh sensations. There were new cousins and nieces and Charlie played the guitar like a six-stringed Stradivarius, radiating divine chords and solos across a jubilant crowd. There was happiness in the air and lots of people of my age were equally mesmerised by the music and liveliness of the band. Somewhere along all the songs, I had to think 'Simple Minds think alike'.

## MICHAEL BRANSCH

*The Fillmore Detroit*
*14 October 2018, Detroit, Michigan*

Living in metro Detroit we would get Canadian TV back when MTV was launching. Canadians across the border would play a lot from *New Gold Dreams*. I remember having to drive across to get the cassette in Windsor, and the same for *Sparkle in the Rain*. I fell in love with their music and style. I've acquired every release they've had and been to several concerts in metro Detroit, the most recent 'An evening with Simple Minds' in the fall of 2018. It was a brilliant double set. Thanks for being part of the soundtrack throughout my life.

## ALAN KOVAN

It started when I bought the UK import of 'Promised You a Miracle' in 1982. I used to read the *NME* and *Melody Maker* religiously then. Then I read a review of *New Gold Dream*. The next landmark was being invited to the Michigan vs UCLA football game in 1982. Being a Michigan State graduate, I was less than enthusiastic but realised Schoolkids Records may have the UK import of *New Gold Dream*. I reluctantly said 'yes' and made it to Ann Arbor early enough to go to Schoolkids and, lo and behold, there was a fresh copy in the front of the import section. I bought the LP and just wanted to go home and listen to this record. Unfortunately, I still had a game to attend. Well, I rooted loudly for UCLA and they won 31-27. I made zero friends in the Michigan student section where I was seated.

I went home, listened to *New Gold Dream*. It wasn't immediate, but those next few months I grew to love this record. Most of my all-time favourites happened like this, like the Rolling Stones' *Exile on Main St* and Spiritualized's *Lazer Guided Melodies*.

My fandom continued with an ill-fated drive from Detroit to London, Ontario in 1982. Amid a torrential downpour we hydroplaned for two hours to the University of Western Ontario student venue, only to find out the show was cancelled. There followed another two hours hydroplaning home.

Finally, Simple Minds were playing Detroit in 1983 at St Andrew's Hall on the *New Gold Dream* tour. I had a friend handpaint the Japanese obi strip from *New Gold Dream* on a sweatshirt which got me invited on the tour bus by their manager Bruce Findlay. From then on, I was treated incredibly well by the band.

I've been all over seeing them, and never once having to put my hand in my pocket for tickets. This includes two shows at Edinburgh Playhouse, several Toronto shows - including four at Massey Hall and sold-out Maple Leaf Gardens shows – and the Beacon Theater, NYC, the Tower Theater in Philadelphia and even a few days in Poughkeepsie, New York watching the band rehearse for then open the *Once Upon a Time* tour, as well as several Detroit and Ann Arbor shows.

There are so many memorable moments. Jim shouting my name from the stage at the Michigan Theater in 1984 and giving me a dozen after-show passes at the Hill Auditorium in 1985 so he could meet many of the most ardent Simple Minds fans who shopped at my store. My brother and I also drove Jim 45 minutes to my shop after the Hill Auditorium show. Waiting there were some good customers and my parents. They wanted to meet one of the band responsible for my fandom. It was so nice watching Jim take such an interest in my parents.

In 1995 I saw them at Royal Oak Theater. It had been 10 years since I'd seen them. It was nice to catch up. Then, 23 years later, Simple Minds were playing the Fillmore in Detroit on their 2018 tour. At this point I'd totally lost touch with Jim, the management or anyone to do with Simple Minds. I posted a note on their Facebook page asking if it was possible for an old friend to come and say hello. I was immediately messaged asking for my email address. I sent it and Jim emailed, inviting me to their meet and greet prior to the show. I'd never been to one of these so had no idea what to expect. When the band walked out and lined up to take photos with the fans who bought this package, Jim said, 'Ok, Where is Alan?' I got a great big bear hug and we caught up. It was so nice, one of my highlights of 2018.

## MOKHTARI MANU

I've been a fan since the magnificent *Black & White 050505*. I was having a difficult time, a separation, and this album was a revelation, a hope for better times and above all a moment of support during the doubts. The following years, thanks to a fan friend, I was able to attend concerts on the *Graffiti Soul* tour. I admired this sweet friendship between Minds fans, this love for the group since the beginning of some fans, this magic bond between Jim and his audience... incredible! Thank you for this musical happiness that is part of our lives.

## ALLAN MCKENZIE

I hadn't had the opportunity to see SM until 2005, when the *Black and White* tour reached Australian shores. Fortunately, getting a seat close to the stage, I sat there for almost three hours totally enthralled. Two more shows, both at Sirromet Winery near Brisbane, were to come in 2012 and 2017. The 2012 show was my two nephews' first show and both loved it. Discovering Simple Minds on Facebook was brilliant and I've had the pleasure of interacting with Jim a few times and in January 2018 was honoured to be personally acknowledged by Jim himself for helping to encourage him to record 'Sense of Discovery', now my favourite song of all time.

**SIMPLE MINDS**
BLACK & WHITE
050505

## JULIAN BURROWS

Out of the blue, my wife was diagnosed with advanced breast cancer at the end of November 2017. Despite the need to be seen to be outwardly strong, and to rise to this life or death challenge, in private I feared for the future and had my world rocked by the very real prospect of losing a wonderful wife, mother and best friend. To my delight and surprise, she bought me *Walk Between Worlds* on Valentine's Day 2018. As far as I was aware, she had no idea that Simple Minds have been embedded in my heart and soul for the best part of 40 years. I played the CD at full volume every day on every commute to work for months to keep me going through the toughest times of my life. The music took me to another level spiritually.

The soft, poignant, emotional introduction followed by the most meaningful words of 'Sense of Discovery' superseded my love and passion for all other Simple Minds songs. It still brings a tear to my eye. My wife pulled through. A woman of great courage and bravery. A band of monumental influence. Thank you from my heart.

SIDE ONE: STAY VISIBLE. HOME. STRANGER. DIFFERENT WORLD (TAORMINA.ME). UNDERNEATH THE ICE.
SIDE TWO: THE JEWELLER PART 2. A LIFE SHOT IN BLACK & WHITE. KISS THE GROUND. DOLPHINS. TOO MUCH TELEVISION.

## LAURIE LOWE

'Spaceface'. It's not a big hit, it's hardly ever played live and has never been mastered live either. It just totally turns me on. It could have been a pretty boring track in all honesty, but then it opens, like so many classic Simple Minds tracks, and pulls at the heart. It has the vulnerable voice of Jim mixed in with the strong. It has the melody, but also the inspiration. Just listen to that drum and hear that rhythm just before Jim whispers 'close your eyes'. From that point he drags me into heaven - but then he continues with - 'tell me what you see, I'll be there if you wait for me'. His voice in these moments is totally full of passion and vulnerability. My imagination just goes into its own in these moments, thinking of a cold wet night at a concert, my shirt half-buttoned, hair wet and dripping, rosy cheeked, hugging friends. Just living the dream. Oh, to be a Simple Minds fan.

## KRISTOFFER GAIR

While I was taking my father for drives during his years suffering from Alzheimer's, I brought the *Graffiti Soul* CD, a gift from my mother, to play for him during one such occasion. The song 'Stars Will Lead the Way' played and I kept repeating the track. The music and lyrics stayed with me. I started writing my sixth novel two years after Dad passed with a scene in which the main character's father strings Christmas lights across the bedroom ceiling, explaining that whenever he feels lost 'stars will lead the way.' That comes true in the novel when the character remembers his father's words about the stars. And me? I remember the song, who gave me the album, the group who sang it, and the inspiration it gave me.

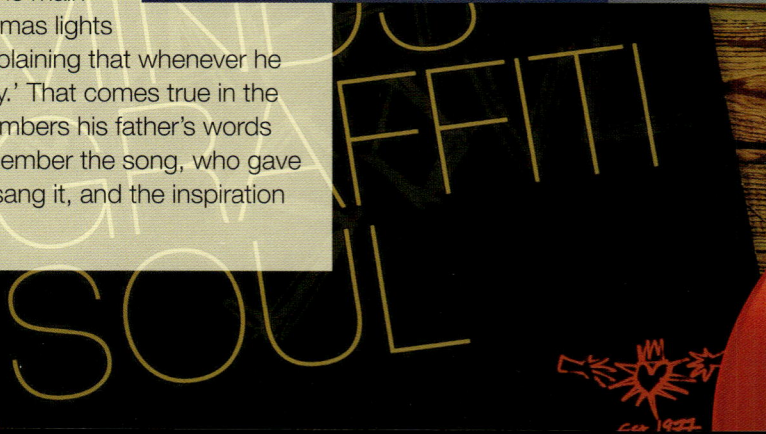

## CHRIS WOLTER

I always seemed to be more interested in other bands. When *Walk Between Worlds* was released, I was forced to rethink my opinion. There's just something special about a band who can sing an overdone phrase like 'I believe in magic...' and make it sound like just that – magic. A band like Simple Minds deserves my undivided attention. I feel bad it took so long to realise it.

## DANIELE TIGNINO

It was a dream come true and I experienced it, first meeting Jim casually in a soccer match thanks to our mutual friend, Antonio Chemi, and then as if by magic finding myself in my small studio in Taormina, with the leader of the band of which I was a big fan.

I then met Charlie, a wonderful person and super fine guitarist and we spent afternoons working together on ideas for new songs and even making me sing on the chorus of 'Beautiful Stranger'!

I will never stop thanking them for giving me a dream and the highlight of my entire career as a producer and DJ. I will never forget our days in the studio and, between making music, the wonderful panorama of Taormina, tea with Amaretto at 5pm and dinners with mega salads with the rest of the band.

Jim told me, how our enthusiasm had awakened in him and the band the desire to start again and to continue doing important things in the music scene. Thanks forever to Simple Minds for giving me this great dream and these emotions.

I will always feel lucky and proud to have been part of their musical journey in some way.

## SUSAN DIPACE

My first exposure to the Simple Minds phenomenon was around 1981. I recall sitting in the balcony of the old State Theatre in Detroit (now the Fillmore) with a good friend who wanted to go to the show. I didn't know how things would translate from record to stage but was transfixed and quite wonderfully transported by the energy I saw and heard up on the stage. The feeling was similar to what I experienced in the Grande Ballroom days, when the house band was the MC5. This same energy, this power that reverberated into my interior, was setting me up for a long internship of listening to and appreciating Simple Minds.

Over the years the dates become more hazy, but I remember a tour with INXS (without Michael Hutchence) at Freedom Hill Amphitheater on a steaming hot summer night in the Detroit suburbs. Simple Minds took the stage and played an incredible set. The sight of poor Jim, soaking wet in a navy blue shirt, is etched forever inside my cranium. The friend I brought with me was blown away by the sheer force of energy in the set of great offerings.

At Toronto's Massey Hall, my husband and I saw an incredible concert, topping off a memorable visit to the city that coincided with a double exhibit at the museum of David Bowie and Ai Weiwei.

Detroit Fillmore in 2018 saw another kickass set. I was so happy to see them again. I never tire of this fabulous group that brings the goods with every live performance. In his blog, Jim said he grew up in Glasgow listening to the MC5 and Stooges and wanted to attain that level of intensity. To my mind, it's a goal he and Charlie and the rest have attained.

## ALTON BOYCHUK

*Chicago Theatre*
*15 October 2018, Chicago, Illinois*

Growing up in the prairies of Saskatchewan, Canada in the '80s, everything seemed distant. How does a band from Glasgow navigate oceans away right into the cassette deck of a vehicle sitting on a hill, or by a lake? Trunk open, music playing, numerous kids from all over standing by a bonfire, dancing, socialising. A hit song to a soundtrack became a gateway for me to a vast list of songs that opened my ears and mind to how diverse music really is. It came full circle for me in 2018 when I had the opportunity see them live in Chicago. Surreal and in awe, I was back at the lake, in the hills, among friends, socialising, dancing.

# NEESHA CRAWFORD

I've been a fan since I was an early teenager growing up in London. Simple Minds were such a huge influence on me that I did a school project on Nelson Mandela and apartheid in South Africa. It was not only the music; it was the band's views, dress and actions that moulded me at such a fragile age. I moved with my family to the US, missing England dearly and faced a difficult time adjusting. Simple Minds kept me strong. I never dreamed I would see them sing live again.

I was blessed with the opportunity to do a meet and greet with Jim, Charlie and the rest of the band in Chicago in 2018. I never felt so many emotions beforehand. I memorised what I wanted to say. Well, the evening came and I nervously introduced myself to Jim and Charlie and shook their hand but… lo and behold, I was too starstruck to say anything. So this is my chance to say, 'Thank you for always being there with me and keeping me young.'

# SHARYN K BALENTINE

*Grand Sierra Resort 20 October 2018, Reno, Nevada*

My love and passion for Simple Minds began in 1982 when I discovered *New Gold Dream*. It was truly magical and I immersed myself in the entire album. 'Someone Somewhere (in Summertime)' became a lifetime, very special song.

I grew up in Clairemont, a modest community of San Diego, California. At 17, my friends and I thrived with the post-punk rock scene. We discovered new and exciting bands from local radio station, 91X, a great record store named Licorice Pizza and MTV. It was all about good friends, great music and our early glory days!

I lived and breathed the early albums and continued to love and grow with each that followed. In 1995,

Sharyn Balentine's daughters loved the Reno show

Ian and I began our relationship and found a wonderful connection with the band, raising our daughters Kylie and Amanda with their music.

Dreams came true at the Grand Sierra when we drove from northern California to Reno to celebrate our 20th wedding anniversary with our daughters to see them. It all came full circle the moment they walked out on stage. I felt all the love and connection between the band and fans. 'Dolphins' was extremely powerful and brought me to tears. Watching my husband and daughters singing and dancing with expressions full of excitement made this my all-time favourite concert and one of the best times of my life!

---

# DEBBIE CAMERON

*The Pearl, Palms Casino Resort*
*21 October 2018, Las Vegas, Nevada*

I didn't have the best start with Simple Minds. My older sister got *Once Upon a Time* for Christmas and kept me awake playing it on a school night. So 30 years on you could say I'm a fan through marriage. My husband and I have very different tastes in music, but Simple Minds we agree on!

Initially we would see one date when they toured the UK – two at a push. Through discussions with an old boss I discovered that her husband was also a hardcore fan so he and my husband now go to some concerts together, including three in one week. From Inverness to London and from Glasgow to Thetford Forest we've pretty much covered all the UK.

In 2015 we went continental with a trip to Paris with friends who are also fans - they don't live near us so it was perfect for a meet-up. Imagine our shock when the week before the concert the Paris attacks took place. Do we go or not? The concert went ahead, so did we. Sadly we were in a similar situation following London's Borough Market attack and the Manchester bombing, but again we went.

In the year of my husband's 50th birthday, we went to a concert in Las Vegas, a smaller venue to what we were used to, with a much more reserved audience. Before coronavirus struck in 2020 my husband was due to see them six times - two in Europe, four in the UK (it was a modest five for me) and it's a joke among our friends that the band have a restraining order against him!

My friends joke that we've seen Simple Minds so many times we could be on stage with them. I can certainly time to the second when Jim will say, 'Let me see your hands.'

---

# CASEY STEINMILLER

*Simple Minds road crew*

I work for CID Entertainment. We handle VIP coordination for bands and run meet and greets, Q&As and on the road services for events bands host. I did a lot of work in Kansas and that area, but the company asked me to do a bus tour. I said, 'Well, who is it?' They told me Simple Minds. I was 24 so there was a bit of a generational gap between the Minds fans and myself. I had to look up who that actually was!

Going off on tour was pretty exciting. It was my first bus tour, and I hadn't worked with a lot of international artists before. It was a little intimidating to find out I was one of only two Americans working on the crew, everyone talking with all these crazy accents! It took me a minute to catch on. I had to keep asking, 'Sorry, what do you mean by that?' They'd be like, 'Oh, I'm just taking the piss' and I'd say, 'You what?'

But they were all really welcoming and hospitable, with everyone on the tour super nice, so that was amazing. Running VIP and merch every day was a pretty easy gig so I had some extra time and after a while I started taking photos during shows to pass some time. The band were so easy to photograph, super energetic on stage.

My main line of work is photo/video work for musicians. I enjoy this more than the VIP co-ordination - it's a little bit more creative. I had my camera on me on the off-chance I could take photos, even if it was just of cities whilst on the road. I asked the band if they minded, and they were like, 'Oh yeah, sure'. I had such a fun time doing it and they loved the photos, so I kept doing it every night.

Schedules vary with each show when it comes to setting up the VIP programme. I'll have a couple of local staff members help me prep and check in all the guests, and from there we'll do meet and greets with the band. They were always entertaining to watch - the fans have crazy stories about how many times they've met the band and seen them live. After the meet and greet we'd get everyone into the main hall and do a Q&A soundcheck. Typically it'd be a song and I'd have the mic and take a couple of questions from the crowd back and forth a bit until we were done.

Being a VIP meant fans got early access, so if there was standing room they could be right out front. But typically they'd reserved seats. Simple Minds' VIP programme is one of the better ones out there - you get a lot of value and get to ask the band some of those personal questions, especially if you do the meet and greet. It's not just a quick 'hi' and handshake. I've heard artists call it 'grip and go' as it's 'get in, get out and you're done', but Jim and everybody were so genuine and nice to everyone, took their time and really made connections with fans. They definitely care.

A lot of the shows on the tour blended together, but Vegas was really fun. Our bus actually lost power after the show and we had to sit on the kerb, wait for it to come back on. So the crew had a little picnic after the show, which was kinda nice.

# ERIC DEYERL

*Orpheum Theatre
24 October 2018, Los
Angeles, California*

As a Minds fan since the mid-
'80s, I was thrilled when they
returned to tour the US in 2013
for the first time in 11 years. After
being blown away by that concert
and lucky enough to see Mel
still solidly banging away on the
skins, I vowed to see them the
next time they were to tour here,
which turned out to be 2018. By
then, Mel's position behind the
drum kit had been filled by the
uber-talented, award-winning
Cherisse and the band seemed as
fresh and energetic as ever.

Having purchased the VIP
experience I was dumbfounded
to learn the experience included
a three-song mini-concert
performed just for our VIP group.

*Simple Minds, Paramount Theatre, Denver Colorado 2018. Photo by David Archwamety*

If this wasn't enough to warrant the 'best concert experience ever' tag, imagine my
delight when I learned this concert was later turned into the fabulous *Live in the City
of Angels* album. If I listen hard enough, I'm convinced I can hear my singing and
screaming!

# GORDON ANTELL

My wife and I had fourth row seats in the orchestra. When the Minds took the stage, I
was getting drinks so I missed opening song, 'Signal and the Noise'. My wife was just
enamoured with Sarah and Cherisse. So was I for the rest of the night. The cherry on
top was the show being released on CD.

# LESLEY O'TOOLE

In 1984 three words likely changed my life: 'Yes, Sunday 2pm.' Handwritten. No signature. In a self-addressed envelope. My 20-year-old Bristol University law student self was ecstatic. A bold ask had secured my first professional journalistic commission and days later, I pitched up at London's famed Columbia Hotel, beloved of Scottish bands, including this one. I was there to interview Jim Kerr. We'd met more than once before, on the *New Gold Dream* tour.

It was everything I hoped it would be, my piece duly published - and I was paid! Legal profession be damned, I could become a music journalist and earn money interviewing my favourite bands. It sounded too good to be true. But it wasn't. 'Do what you love,' say the career advisers. So I did.

It gave me days like these I'll never forget. 6 June 1986: Simple Minds, Lloyd Cole and the Commotions and Hipsway at Ibrox, Glasgow. 28 June, 1986 (my birthday): Simple Minds and Lloyd Cole and the Commotions, Croke Park, Dublin. I'm half-Irish, Dad's from Dublin. As I write, I'm wearing a Claddagh ring I was given that day.

*Lesley O'Toole with Jim in 1982 and 2018 and (below) with Ged in 2018*

By an accident of immigration, I arrived in Los Angeles for 'three months' in 1993. I saw the band on and off over the years but then, for an extended period, Simple Minds didn't tour America. Their return to LA in October 2013 at art deco gem the Orpheum Theatre was a showstopper, the performance as sublime as the venue. Even better, Ged Grimes, from another Scottish band I adored personally and professionally, Danny Wilson, had joined the band.

Five years later, Simple Minds were back at the Orpheum. I never dreamed it could be better. I was front row stage right, perfectly happy. Then JK was climbing

some steps in front of me, standing directly above me, and wait - whaaat? He was singing my favourite Simple Minds song right in my face. 'Someone Somewhere (in Summertime)'. We madly pointed at each other, I sang less well.

What synchronicity I thought, commonplace in my life. Then I thought again. Years ago I told Ged my favourite song. Could he have spotted me in the crowd and told Jim? Eventually he 'fessed up. It's my favourite song by my favourite band. Still. And I'm forever in their debt.

---

# BOBBY & CAROLINE WOOD

My wife Caroline and I had the privilege of seeing the legendary Simple Minds not once but twice in a few days when they toured Southern California in 2018. It's rare they tour here. We were so excited, the shows were amazing! First up an outdoor theatre in San Diego and it was pure magic. The band playing with Jim and Charlie were top notch, especially the amazing Sarah Brown. That night I felt I made a connection with Jim Kerr. He is so into the crowd. I felt he saw me and acknowledged me.

A few nights later we saw the band in Los Angeles and did the meet and greet. I met my childhood music idols, Jim and Charlie, and the rest of the amazing Simple Minds band. I told Jim how much I loved new album *Walk Between Worlds* and it had such a good vibe. He liked that. And what knocked me out was he remembered seeing me in the crowd at the San Diego show. I was amazed! Simple Minds are the real deal. How awesome is it that the Jim Kerr - a legendary front man - could connect so well with a fan? Long live the Minds!

---

# JOSEPH MICHAEL R

*Masonic Auditorium*
*25 October 2018, San Francisco, California*

My mom passed away from a heart attack in 1984. I was 17. It was a tough time. I took a job when I turned 18. This very cool person who'd just started at the same company was sat in the cubicle next to mine carrying a black briefcase. It caught my attention because it had Simple Minds stickers all over it and I'd never heard of them until that day. This guy was so excited to talk about it and shared everything he knew about Simple Minds. Being a young musician, my ears were wide open. He said Simple Minds changed his life and the music was like nothing else he'd ever heard before. He told me to go and buy *Once Upon a Time*. Nothing else has captivated me like that album. Every song on it has a meaning to me.

I will cherish forever the last concert Simple Minds did in San Francisco. I went with my wife and, when I saw Jim come out, I was like a little kid. He forgot one part of the lyrics of 'Once Upon a Time'. I looked at him and sang the line 'love was a white dove' and he looked at me and thanked me. I responded with, 'I love you brother.'

## SIMPLE MINDS REJUVENATION

## JAMES MATHAN

My introduction to Simple Minds came via import, a record from Sweden called *Modern Dance*, which a friend gave to me. It included 'Theme for Great Cities', which stood out because it was the only instrumental. There was just something about the chord changes and keyboards that really touched me. It gave me a sense of ambition and hope. Falling in love with a girl at the time also elevated the song to a whole new level. Next thing I knew, I had to listen to more and more Simple Minds.

There have been so many great shows over the years. The last one I saw at San Francisco's Masonic Auditorium in 2018 was no different. But it was the first time I ever saw them perform 'Theme for Great Cities' live. It took me right back to when I first heard that song and I couldn't help but wonder what happened to the girl I was in love with then. But 'I've got a new gold dream, I'm moving on!'

## KIRSTEN SCHROEDER

I was an '80s music dancing fiend and *New Gold Dream* was my ultimate album at college. I played it religiously. I never got the chance to see a live Simple Minds concert back in the day so when they booked an October 2018 San Francisco gig I jumped to buy tickets. I wasn't quick enough to get VIP tickets but was elated me and my sister were finally getting to see my all-time favourite '80s group.

My mom, suffering from Alzheimer's for nine years, collapsed a week before and was rushed to ER. I got the news while at work and dashed to the hospital. Starting the car, 'Don't You (Forget About Me)' came on the radio on SiriusXM. My sense of panic and heavy heart were eased by hearing this song. 'Promised You a Miracle' was the first song on the radio after I left the hospital that day. My sister and I decided to attend the concert, even with our mom still in the ICU. We felt a strong connection to the music and knew she would approve and encourage us to attend if she could speak. Getting to see Simple Minds perform helped to lessen the pain of seeing her suffer. We danced the night away gleefully.

Our mom sadly passed a few weeks later. While driving by her resting site, I will sometimes hear either 'Promised You a Miracle' or 'Don't You (Forget About Me)' on the Eighties channel. I know my mom is sending love from above. Music heals and soothes and I thank Simple Minds for their beautiful gift which touches my heart.

# LISA HAFF

*The Moore Theatre*
*28 October 2018, Seattle, Washington*

The day I discovered the wonderful Simple Minds was a good one. 'Up on the Catwalk' and 'Don't You (Forget About Me)' were the first songs I heard on KJET in Seattle. That station played all the new cutting-edge tunes in the early '80s. The tight instrumentals, good songwriting and great vocals put a bounce in my step and made me smile. In 2018 my hubby and I wasted no time buying VIP tickets for Seattle.

The best concert I've ever seen, the energy the band brings to the stage and music and lyrics are better than ever. The band keep getting better as the years roll by. It was three hours non-stop playing. I was in heaven. My feet never stopped moving. The messages the band bring to their music have always resonated with me. They are one of the reasons why, at 61, I feel younger than I did at 25 - alive and kicking!

# KENNETH MILLER

*Orpheum Theatre*
*29 October 2018, Vancouver, Canada*

My journey began not long after the release of *Once Upon a Time*. At the time, we lived in a small town close to Calgary, Alberta and I dreamt about the album cover as I slept. Next morning I asked my dad to pick up the cassette on his morning commute. I remember loving the energy and positivity. I was just discovering music then, and also discovering I was a drummer at heart. Mel Gaynor's pounding rhythms hooked me right away. The music has such great messages and there's a wonderful sense of joy I feel when listening to songs such as 'Summer'.

By 2018 I had a wife, young daughter and a life in a different city. Simple Minds had announced a worldwide tour. They rarely played in Canada and money had been an issue when they did come. When they announced a Vancouver show I decided, 'Money and debt be damned – I'm going!' This was my last best chance to see them.

I got seats in the fifth row, close to the middle, and access to the soundcheck. I went with my best friend from Calgary, who was not really a huge fan. It's a short flight to Vancouver. We landed, got to our hotel, and did a bit of sightseeing and then went to the hall, got our swag bags and waited for the soundcheck. We chatted with many other Minds fans and found we're all a part of a wonderful community. I remember looking down a hallway and seeing Jim, Cherisse, Charlie and the band walk past, heading to a meet and greet. I was like a little kid. I started jumping up and down. 'There they are - OMG!' Cherisse and Charlie saw me waving and waved back.

In the arena for the soundcheck, I was amazed how low the stage was, and that I could walk right up to it. I found a spot and when Jim and the band walked out, I can't describe the joy and excitement. It makes me teary-eyed remembering it. Jim has wonderful banter with the crowd. I remember him telling us to take all the photos we wanted, and dance as much as we wanted, and (jokingly) dance around naked if we wanted. I quipped to Jim that it wasn't 1985 anymore, and he and Charlie laughed out loud. Not all of us had aged well, and most would not have looked very good dancing with no clothes on, myself included.

They played 'Summer' during the soundcheck and it was fantastic to hear it live. I was very happy. Some of the band came along to shake our hands and I was able to high-five Jim and shake hands with Charlie as I thanked him for the music. As the soundcheck ended, I knew I had one chance only to get a drumstick.

As the band was getting ready to head backstage, I summoned up all my courage and caught Cherisse's attention. I motioned playing the drums, then pointed at her. She knew what I was asking and put a finger up as if to tell me to wait a minute. She went back to her kit. Some grumpy git – maybe a stage manager for the band? - was shooing us away. As I told him 'I think I'm getting a drumstick' Cherisse walked over. Before she could say anything, this cheeky sod said to her he needed to clear the stage. She handed me the stick, shook my hand and said, 'Hello, nice to meet you.' She'd given me a broken stick she had signed - and it had some of her hair in it as well! If there's a cloud higher than cloud nine, I was on it.

Simply incredible, the best show I've been to; the positive energy from their music was much more powerful in concert. They all have wonderful auras and give off such a fantastic vibe. I sang my little heart out to the 'la-la-la-la' refrain in 'Alive and Kicking'. At the end, we were chatting close to the stage with a couple we met and all of a sudden, a drumstick came flying across the stage and hit us, landing at our feet. I was the quickest to step on it, giving me my second drumstick of the evening. What a night! The energy from that experience took days to wear off.

Later, there was a caption contest on the website for a photo of the band, to win a pair of new drumsticks signed by Cherisse. Guess who won?

---

# IAN FORRESTER

My wife Renee and I have been Simple Minds fans since we started dating in 1987. It took us 31 years to finally see the band live. I first heard them when I was playing in a beach volleyball tournament in my hometown, Vancouver. A nearby ghetto-blaster was playing some cool tunes I found unique and inspiring and after the match I found out I'd been listening to *Once Upon a Time*. I immediately had to share this information with my new girlfriend, Renee. She was equally enamoured. In my rocking 1981 Toyota Tercel we always had a Simple Minds album playing. They became an important part of our relationship as we shared many memories together.

I joined the fan club and kept waiting for a North American tour announcement which never came. It seemed the only way to see the band live was to travel to Europe. This required some saving and planning until we could afford such a luxury. In 2001 I decided we would travel to see Simple Minds in Brighton the following year and impulsively bought two tickets to commit us. But we simply couldn't afford to go. I ended up with two unused tickets.

In 2004 we were finally going to do it. I would be working as a tour guide for an international sports tour company and assisting in taking a group from Canada to attend the Euro 2004 Soccer Championships in Portugal. I was ecstatic to see the band was playing in Valencia around the time of what would be our 10th wedding anniversary. This would be a trip of a lifetime - we'd see Portugal and Spain, enjoy the Euros and cap it off with finally seeing Simple Minds live in a beautiful Spanish city. Unfortunately, things were not to be. Even after 16 years I still have some issues discussing the events that transpired but in summary my wife was the victim of a kidnapping and we never made it to Valencia. Strange but true story.

In the following years, I religiously checked the upcoming tour schedule and could never match up a concert with a trip. After 30-plus years, time was surely running out. How long would the band continue? Would they ever come to North America? In early 2018 Renee called me from work in an excited state exclaiming, 'You won't believe this - Simple Minds are actually coming to Vancouver!' They were not only coming to North America. They were coming to our town.

Needless to say we huddled by our computers the morning tickets went on sale, praying we wouldn't miss out. We didn't! We snapped up VIP soundcheck tickets and when the date finally arrived we were beside ourselves. The private soundcheck experience was amazing. The best thing about it was how personable and down to earth the band were. Too often you hear people have bad experiences when they meet people they've admired for so long and from afar. Charlie and Jim were just as great in person. We were even prouder to be Simple Minds devotees.

The concert itself did not disappoint and the crowd stood throughout, danced and sang. It was surreal to be in a crowd of 5,000 people as enthralled with the band as we were. Simple Minds almost seemed to be our little secret for so long. In reality we were part of a large fanbase, and in our hometown no less. It was great sharing the experience. Finally, after 31 years as fans and as a couple, we got to see our favourite band play live. It will always be a life highlight.

## MARC MARSE

When I read they would perform in Vancouver and you could meet them I thought, 'Why not fly over there just for a gig?' At the airport in Brussels I passed the chocolate store and decided to buy two big boxes for Jim, Charlie and the band just to see how they'd react. I was a little intimidated to meet them but to my surprise when I gave them the chocolates they were really happy and surprised. I thought they'd be like rock stars, used to everything, but they were so human and humble.

I don't know if that action triggered them to give more energy that night for the gig but I was blessed, along with 3,000 other fans, with a three-hour performance I'll never forget and carry with me for the rest of my life. A performance of a lifetime, and when Jim passed by on my side I got a high-five now and then. Wow!

*Jim in action at Vancouver's Orpheum Theatre - photo Paul Yanko*

## PAUL YANKO

I'd graduated high school, started university and was still pining for my 'one that got away'. 'Don't You (Forget About Me)' pushed all the right buttons for me and every time I heard it I thought about my high school crush, a gal named Heather.

Life intervenes, and by 2009 I'd married and had three beautiful children. My spouse was working on a master's degree through a university in Sweden, and as luck would have it I got to travel along during one of her visits. While my wife attended class, I explored the university town and Sweden in general, including an overnight trip to Stockholm to catch my favourite band in concert in Solna.

The concert lived up to every expectation I'd built up during nearly 25 years being a fan. 'Don't You (Forget About Me)' performed live was absolutely sublime.

Fast forward a few more years and I find myself divorced, and through the magic of social media reconnected with Heather, my high school love - the one that got away! Turns out she's also a fan, with 'Don't You (Forget About Me)' as the ringtone on her phone. So you can imagine my delight when she bought us tickets for the concert at the Orpheum Theatre, Vancouver in October 2018. That night they provided yet another absolutely magical concert, with 'Don't You (Forget About Me)' the highlight.

In the most beautiful instance I've yet to find of life imitating art, it seems Heather had not forgotten about me either. Needless to say, that song has become our song.

## DARA SOSA

*Moody Theater*
*2 November 2018, Austin, Texas*

Simple Minds became a part of my life after my mom introduced the band to me 14 years ago. I never looked back. The music and lyrics are nothing short of an art that speaks to you. I had the honour of attending a concert in November 2018. What a great experience! Jim Kerr was kind enough to say hi to my mom, Maggie at soundcheck and Ged Grimes pointed me out right before playing the end bass solo of 'See the Lights' during the concert. I enjoyed the show and got to meet cool fans.

*Dara Sosa and her mom got to meet the Minds in Austin*

## LAURA SAMFORD

*Toyota Music Factory*
*3 November 2018, Dallas, Texas*

In 1995 my parents invited me to meet them in Athens, Greece for vacation. I purchased a CD player so I could listen to music during the flights and bought a couple of CDs, one of which was *Good News from the Next World*. This was my first big flight alone to another country and I felt excited but a little scared being by myself. I was soon distracted by hearing Charlie's amazing guitar playing and Jim singing 'She's a River'.

I spent a lot of time working, going to college and not listening to music much.

Then, in 2014 I thought of bands I used to enjoy and Simple Minds came to mind. I started following them on Facebook. Jim's posts were humorous and gracious.

One day he posted a link to 'Street Fighting Years'. I hadn't heard it before and couldn't believe what a beautiful song it was. I saved it as my wake-up alarm clock song on my iPhone. At the time I was waking up in a hotel on the beach in San Juan, Puerto Rico for a long-term project. Falling asleep to the sounds of waves on the beach and waking up to 'Street Fighting Years' was very nice.

*Laura Samford went to the Dallas meet and greet*

When they came to Dallas, I purchased the meet and greet package. It was a true joy to meet the entire band. Such wonderful and talented people. What a concert. Great energy, great music.

## JOE HEBERT

*Revention Center*
*4 November 2018, Houston, Texas*

When I saw Simple Minds were coming to Houston, I knew the time had come to right a wrong. I'd never seen Simple Minds play live in spite of having been a fan since the early 1980s and despite knowing they had a sterling reputation as a live band. I was in, but let's face it, music is best as a shared experience. I reached out to best friend Sabrina to see if she might be interested, her first time too.

When the day arrived, we were so ready. The band hit the stage and they weren't there to rest on their massive past success. They were there to claim their present and chase their future. They were tight, they were present in the moment, and hungry to earn the respect of each and every person present.

We walked out after the show with our souls filled with the fire Jim and the band had distributed. Like the firemen in the classic novel *Fahrenheit 451*, the music had ignited us. Transforming that feeling into words was virtually impossible. We placed high hopes on this being a great show, and Simple Minds greatly exceeded our collective hopes. And it feels amazing to erase a regret.

# HEATHER JONES

*No.1 Sports Oval
24 November 2018,
Newcastle, Australia*

This gig was memorable for so many reasons, the first being that it was a complete surprise that the band were coming until a week before it happened. Scrolling through the website I found they were playing at the car races and, after checking the listing a

*Heather Jones saw Simple Minds in Newcastle, New South Wales*

few times to make sure I hadn't got it wrong, I booked tickets pronto, wondering how to avoid the racing whilst maximising band time!

The second thing that made it memorable was that my partner and I ended up almost on the front row. I'd never been able to get near the front of a gig for years and there we were, a few feet from the great JK himself! It felt like he was there for us alone. The first song was 'Signal and the Noise' and, on hearing the opening bars and seeing the band all walk on, it felt like Christmas had come early!

The third reason was that we made a friend. We got talking to a girl who made the brave decision to come on her own to see her idols. She approached us, seeking company away from some increasingly boozed-up, amorous petrol-heads. We sang along to all the songs together and she invited us for a drink after. She became a firm fan after meeting the band in a hotel lobby in Germany many years ago and said they were so nice - she was in from then on!

It was in that Newcastle pub after the gig that we put together the bones of Simple Minds tribute band Thirty Frames a Second. Just over a year on we've played a number of gigs in and around Sydney and slowly balanced out cover versions with our own tunes, including a tribute to Simple Minds, 'In Dreams We Travel'.

Their music has seen me through good and bad times as long as I can remember. Keep on dreaming and inspiring.

## MALIN RYDELIUS

*Partille Arena*
*4 March 2020,*
*Gothenburg,*
*Sweden*

I first heard 'Someone Somewhere (in Summertime)' on the radio in 1982. It was magic. I was only 10 and my interest

*Malin Rydelius saw the Minds in March 2020*

in music became really intense from that day. Jim's powerful voice and the electric, magical sound were mindblowing.

I've seen them numerous times in Stockholm, Dalhalla, Solna and Örebro. In 2020 I got to meet them backstage in Partille, Gothenburg and had a photo taken. It was a dream come true. I really got a huge Simple Minds dose that week - three concerts, a photograph, autographs, a pick from Charlie and drumsticks from Cherisse.

My mom didn't quite approve of my stereo playing at maximum volume when I was 10, but I still like to play their music loud and feel the power in every song. And they've been in my heart ever since.

## LASSE DAVIDSSON

*Annexet*
*6 March 2020, Stockholm, Sweden*

In 1981 'Love Song' was played on the radio and I was blown away. Weeks later I heard a really cool tune at a disco, asked the disc jockey what it was and

*Lasse Davidson saw Simple Minds in early 2020*

# SIMPLEMINDS
## 40: THE BEST OF 1979-2019

he replied, 'It's 'I Travel' by Simple Minds.' There it was, two great tunes in a short period that have been with me for a long time now and still blow me away!

Live goodies: I could never forget the *Street Fighting Years* gig in Gothenburg in '89. Brilliant. And the 30th anniversary gig at Wembley when they played the whole *New Gold Dream* album live. How great is that? Unbelievable. And for the *40 Years* gig in Stockholm in March 2020, not long before the coronavirus struck, the band were on fire. So this is my Simple Minds story… so far!

## SCOTT GIBSON

Four times previously I'd almost got to see Simple Minds but – ah, circumstances. The first time was in 1995. I had tickets for Edinburgh Playhouse and the day before had a family emergency. But in 2020, I finally got to see them, in Stockholm.

I grew up in South Queensferry and lived there the same time as Jim. Going to the Hawes Inn, just beside Jim's flat, I'd put 'Waterfront' on the jukebox, that song always reminding me of the ferry and the shores of the river Forth. Sometimes, I'd see Jim with his long leather jacket and sunglasses. It was so cool to have a rock star living in our wee town! But that's not all. One evening, circa 1988, me and a couple of friends thought, 'Hey, why don't we try and meet Jim?' We went to Bridge House, pressed the button on the intercom that said 'Kerr' on the intercom, and to our surprise, Jim answered. I asked if we could meet him - yea,

*Scott Gibson and his wife Arina saw Simple Minds in Stockholm in 2020*

as if - and we got the appropriate response. 'Get lost!' Well, what else did we expect? Anyway, we hung around near the house contemplating our naivety. Next thing, Jim came down to meet us. We had a 10-minute chat and got some autographs. We were ecstatic.

After I left school, I was a window-cleaner in Queensferry. One of my jobs was for the couple who bought Jim's flat. It's stunning and has the most amazing views of the Forth Bridge. I wonder if it was the inspiration of any Simple Minds songs.

In 2019 I was living in Latvia. My wife, now a fan, is fed up with hearing me describing every time I haven't seen Simple Minds. The new tour was announced. We got tickets for the nearest show, in Stockholm, and booked our flight from Riga for the Friday, flying back on Sunday.

I finally saw Simple Minds, 32 years after meeting Jim outside his house and 25 years after having tickets to a concert I never saw. And what a concert. The setlist was amazing, Jim and the band rocking, me and my wife enjoying one of the best concerts we've been to. One week later, concerts were starting to get cancelled because of the coronavirus. I waited a long time, but in the end saw them just in the nick of time.

---

## STEPHEN SINNETT

My father hated Simple Minds, probably because we played them often - and loud. He'd call them 'that bloody racket!' I'd often hear 'turn than bloody racket down - even better, turn it off!' Until one night. 'Belfast Child' premiered on *Top of the Pops*. The intro to the video, the two kids running in the grass, and the haunting, powerful, pulsating drum. Then Jim's intro vocal, the song taking you on a journey about troubled times. At the crescendo, I turned to my dad. He had tears streaming down both cheeks. 'That will go straight to No.1. Who's singing it?' I replied, 'That bloody racket, Simple Minds.'

I saw them several times after that, getting to shake Jim's hand during 'Waterfront' at the *Night of the Proms* in Stockholm in 2016. On the *40 Years of Hits* tour I stood in the crowd, watching them perform 'Belfast Child' live, haunting, powerful, pulsating drums from Cherisse leaving me with tears down my cheeks. I think Jim even gave an acknowledging wink to the wee guy in the crowd from Airdrie, with his Airdrie top on witnessing the best live act in the world, still on top of their game after 40 years.

Unless they do an orchestral *Street Fighting Years*, family commitments mean our paths may never meet again. If so thanks for the memories and, in the words of a famous Swedish band, thank you for the music.

---

## BETINA RYE PETERSEN

*Store Vega*
*10 March 2020, Copenhagen, Denmark*

Simple Minds mean love, kisses, parties, chilling time, lovely people and great times.

When they performed at Roskilde Festivalen in 1993, I didn't have the courage to go. There were way too many people for my taste, a decision I later regretted. But a dear friend took the greatest pictures, enlarged and framed them, and gave them to me as a surprise. These pictures followed me for many years until suffering water damage.

Every visit to Denmark by the band since I've been unable to go and as the years have gone by, I thought it would probably never happen. I didn't know they were playing in 2020 but – lucky me – a friend bought tickets.

Because of Covid I thought it might not happen. But it did, and what a show! The atmosphere, the music, how the band's enjoyment at being there shone through. 'Belfast Child' almost made me cry. I've never been so emotional as I was then and wasn't alone in that feeling. I didn't know this, but about 10 classmates and friends also attended. We all agreed it was the best trip down memory lane ever.

I only have one thing more to say. Please come back!

# OTTO JUNG

When the band released their compilation album *40 - The Best of Simple Minds* to celebrate their 40th anniversary, for the cover artwork Stuart Crouch created 235 virtual badges forming a heart. When I first saw it I thought what a great idea it would be to make it with actual real badges. So I individually re-designed those badge artworks during the past months, and got them manufactured at a badge company. Because there are two non-round badges in the artwork from 1991, I had to make the badges to that size, so this final piece of artwork is about 30" by 30".

*Otto Jung with his badge artwork*

# EDDIE CAIRNS

From the start they were one of the hardest working groups I've known. If it wasn't touring it was writing, rehearsals, more writing and even more rehearsals and touring. Being able to sit and watch masterpieces forming from nowhere out of the brains of the tightest band I've worked with is something that will live with me forever.

Going into a rehearsal room and Brian and Dan starting off a rhythm, Mick's keys soaring and filling the room with the drums and bass throbbing, Charlie using his guitar as a magic wand – fills, solos, etc. Jim listening to what was being created in front of him, trance-like, then putting words to what was fast becoming a song. Looking at the notes he continually took when travelling for inspiration – magical!

# RONNIE GURR

A couple of years ago, I was asked to help curate an exhibition at the National Museum of Scotland, *Rip It Up*, on the history of Scottish rock and pop. I wanted the guitar that was on the front of the Acoustic album they gave me and the little guitar they had on stage at the acoustic tour. That was basically remembering Charlie's mum, who bought him his first guitar. They presented Charlie with this little acoustic that was the same as his first guitar, but it was covered in Embassy coupons. So we got that, and got a poster for the Grafton Bar, which I think was the band's third or fourth gig, the first time I saw them.

Johnny and the Self Abusers was the earliest ticket I've got. I think it was their third gig. I couldn't remember the name, but remember the gig clearly because it was essentially two rooms in the basement of a pub and the band were in one room – they literally filled that one room - and then there was a gap in the wall which was only big enough for Jim to fill and there was one light above him. If you were right at the front of the other room, you could see everything, but if you were second row you couldn't see anything. That poster was designed by Jaine Henderson, who did the band's lights, and her brother did the sound. She designed it and saw it on eBay, got in touch with the seller and said, 'I really want that because I designed it'. The guy found it folded in half. He'd moved into a flat in Aberdeen and was taking the carpets up and it was under the carpets. He said, 'If you designed it, you don't have to pay.'

Over the years I think I've probably seen Simple Minds more than any band ever. I saw them in Hollywood when I was still working for Virgin. I've seen them all around the world now, so I'm delighted to be friends with them and still a fan.

# RICHARD JOBSON

There was just non-stop laughter. Jim was a bit of a stand-up comedian, a very funny guy. He had something to say about everything. It was great fun. I got on well with Dan the bass player as well. We were all Celtic fans and he was a Rangers fan. That was problematic. But they were all my friends, you know? I still speak to Mick, the original keyboard player.

I was a massive fan of everything. I loved the music. I loved the words. I loved the way they looked. I thought they were super cool and loved their friendship. Charlie and Jim reminded me of me and Stewart at the beginning. They were really great. Charlie's one of the nicest men I've met in my life. He's the most charming, sweet guy. A lot of people don't know Jim Kerr is one of the funniest guys, but we'd laugh about so many different things. They were a very tight-knit bunch of guys, which I really admired about them.

Jim had a sense of where this band was headed. With Charlie as his aide, he was going to get them there. They were the crux of the band, the energy force and where all the musical and lyrical ideas came from. I was very close to them. I still regard them as friends and still admire them greatly. I've nothing but respect for them.

---

# BILLY SLOAN

They've never decided to sit and count their money for 10 years. They were gigging constantly. They haven't cancelled even five gigs in their entire career. They always turned up, always play. It was great watching them play places like the Art School in Glasgow then move up to Barrowland and then venues like the SECC and eventually to stadia. They get it in the neck a lot - people dismissing them as stadium rockers. But they're only stadium rockers because, instead of 5,000 people wanting to go and see them, 50,000 people wanted to. They could have made the decision to keep playing these small theatres. But if 50,000 people want to see you, you'd be churlish not to give them the opportunity.

They have the distinction of being the first Scottish band to play an outdoor gig in their own right, playing not one but two nights at Ibrox in 1986, to 60,000 people per day. That had never been done before. And when you're playing big stadia you've got to write big songs, but Simple Minds songs work in small clubs with 500 people and work in big stadiums with 50,000 people. It didn't dilute the music for me in any way, shape or form. If anything, it made the music bigger, better and stronger.

I've probably seen Simple Minds more than any other single band. I've been on tour with them. Sitting in the Royal Box at Wembley Stadium and watching our pals on stage was pretty special. I went to Brazil with them for two weeks in 1988, a week in Rio de Janeiro and then in São Paolo. We met Ronnie Biggs, still on the run from Scotland Yard. He ran a nightclub. We went there after the gig and spent two hours talking to him about the Great Train Robbery.

I've seen them in America, and all over Europe and toured with them in 2018 when they brought out *Walk Between Worlds*. They played the whole album in its entirety but didn't want to just play eight tracks one after the other that people didn't know. So I'd go on stage, interview Jim and Charlie and ask about the making of the album. Then they'd play side one and I'd interview them again for another 10 minutes and then they'd play side two. We went to Glasgow, Manchester, the Roundhouse in London, Paris, Stockholm and Amsterdam.

I've been all round the world with them and seen them in lots of different venues - from the tiniest to the biggest, and they've never disappointed. I don't think in all the years I've seen them I've ever come away thinking, 'They weren't that great'. They always deliver, they've a great work ethic and every night is like the first time you've ever seen them. They always try to make it special.

I've done loads of stuff, probably more than anybody else over the years, in terms of interviews, radio, TV and newspapers. What's difficult for me now is to make the distinction between Jim Kerr, friend, and Jim Kerr, singer of Simple Minds. I've got to flip the switch in my mind to get into broadcast or journalism mode, because one minute I'm sat talking to a guy who's one of my five best friends in the world, then I've got to put the professional mask on and talk to the singer in the band.

Even though I know more about them than probably any other journalist in Scotland, if I'm going to interview Simple Minds tomorrow I'll be sat up until two in the morning doing all my notes and research and getting all my names, places and figures so I have everything at my fingertips, in the same way I would if I was interviewing Mick Jagger, Paul McCartney, Bruce Springsteen, Elton John or Rod Stewart.

So that's a bit of a weird feeling, to try and go into work mode. Having said that, they make it easy because they've always got a lot to say and they're engaging company when you're interviewing them.

It's been great to see them come from third on the bill to a reggae band in January 1978 to hitting the heights and achieving all the stuff they've done these last 40 years. Looking back to when I would play Simple Minds on my radio show and write about them in the paper, I'd get people going 'never heard of them'. I'd say, 'This band are from Glasgow and they're going to be the next big thing' and people would say 'Ah, they'll never do anything.'

When they got in the charts and started having a bit of success, it would have been nice if all the people who dismissed them and who said I was talking a lot of rubbish had come back and said, 'Fair play to you, you were right, we were wrong.' But they never did. So I was every bit as thrilled as the band when 'Promised You a Miracle' went up the charts and they were on *Top of the Pops* that first time, because that vindicated it. I could write about them in the paper, I could play the records on the radio. But until you go on *Top of the Pops*, you hadn't really made it.

I'm sure it was thrilling for the band to see themselves tick these boxes one by one over the years. And it's been very gratifying for me too, because I remember seeing them at that first gig, thinking, 'You know, this band are really going to do something.'

# THANK YOU

Simple Minds would like to thank the hundreds of fans that sent in their stories and memories of seeing the band. The publishers would like to say a special thanks to Kev McCabe for the introduction, Otto Jung for making his Simple Minds collection available to use throughout this book and Simon Cornwell for his help and advice.
https://sm-tours.com/
http://www.simpleminds.org/

---

# ACKNOWLEDGEMENTS

Richard Houghton would like to thank:

Jim Kerr and Charlie Burchill, Ian Grenfell, Elaine Gwyther and Kim Horton at Quietus Management, Malcolm Wyatt and Emily Powter-Robinson, Neil Cossar and Liz Sanchez at This Day in Music Books, Stuart Crouch, Malcolm Garrett, Ronnie Gurr, Bruce Findlay, Casey Steinmiller, Billy Sloan, Richard Jobson, Peter Barton, Simon Cornwell, Vincent Barker, Ross Stapleton, Gordon Machray, Jonty Young, Nigel Proktor, Howard Devoto, Bruce Foxton, Oonagh O'Neill, Bill Houghton and Sidney Sullivan-Houghton.
And Kate Sullivan for her endless patience.

Album/singles images, additional artwork & photography by Ian T Cossar, except where noted:

Pages 26-29, 36 - *sleeve artwork/band photos by Carole Moss*

Page 33 - *sleeve artwork by Thomas Rathmell*

Page 43 - *sleeve artwork by Mary Ruth Craig*

Page 54 - *photo by Michael Ruetz, sleeve artwork by The Artifex Studio*

Page 63 - *band photo by 'Coward'*

Pages 66, 72, 74, 81, 85-95, 98, 118, 132-135, 150-153, 240-243, 248-251, 287, 350-351 - *photos/artwork by Malcolm Garrett/Assorted Images*

Page 83 - *band photo - unknown*

Pages 164-169, 240-243, 178, 234 - *sleeve artwork by Mick Haggerty, photos of band by Anton Corbijn*

Pages 240-243, 248-251 - *photos by Guido Harari, original 'Claddagh' drawing by William F Ryan*

Page 320 - *photo by Simon Fowler*

Pages 320, 323, 327, 348-349, 355, 371 - *sleeve artwork by Stylorouge*

Page 374 - *band photo by Andy Earl*

Pages 388, 397, 400 - *band photos by Martin Hunter/Toorkwaz Design/Mick Hutson*

Pages 388, 413, 431 - *design/photos by Fabrique*

Pages 427, 435 - *sleeve artwork by Curious*

Page 480 - *design by Daniel Reed/Ruth Rowland*

Pages 485, 503, 552 - *sleeve artwork/design by Peacock/Daniel Reed*

Page 486 - *band photo by Paul Cox*

Pages 507, 517, 532, 546, 568, 571-572 - *design/photos by Stuart Crouch Creative/Heitor Magno/Dean Chalkley*

Pages 559, 562 - *sleeve artwork & design by Anthony Dry/Stuart Crouch Creative*

Pages 388, 413, 418, 427, 435, 439, 485, 503, 548-552, 559, 562, 575 - *Copyright Demon Music Group Ltd.*

# SPECIAL THANKS TO:

ALFONSO SORIANO COLIN ANDRE HUY ANDREW LEASK ANDY ROBERTSON ANDY BATTYE

ANNALISA QUARONI ANTONIO VIRGOLINI CHRISTIE PRIODE CHRISTOPHER TAYLOR

CHRISTOPHER PLATTS CRAIG PATERSON DAMIEN LETANG DANIEL SUTTON DANIEL ASHPLANT

DANIELE BERNADINI DARIN KIRWAN DAVE MAC DOROTHEA CONRATH ELAINE BUIST

FRANCESCA FROESCH FRASER COWAN FRIEDRICH GRIEPENTROG GARY DAVISON

GERARD LECKEY IAN GATENBY INGRID VAN CORTENBERG JESSE GIBBS JIM DONATO

JOHN DINGWALL JON ROUND JULIE BERESFORD JUSTINE WELLER KAYLOTTERMOSER KENNA WARE

KRIM BOUZOUAOUI LUCA LEONE MARGARET PULLAR MARK TIPPING MARK HERITAGE MARK D

MARTIN HARKIN MAX MICHAEL KELLY MICHÈLE VANDENDORPE MICHELE HANCE

OLIVER MENSING PAT O'BRIEN PATRICK VAN DER VEKEN PAUL GALLACHER POL DELANGE

RICK C KORDTS ROB CHRISTIE ROBB DUFTY ROBERT C SCEATS RON MCKINNON SHAWN BRYANT

STAVROS DAMIANIDIS STEFANO DAGOSTEVE RUSSEY STUART HUSKISSON STUART LOGAN

TONY WEYTENS VENESSA GIUNTA WILLIAM HARRINGTON WOJCIECH WRONA